Handbook *of* Strategic Alliances

Handbook *of* Strategic Alliances

EDITORS

Oded Shenkar
The Ohio State University

Jeffrey J. Reuer
University of North Carolina at Chapel Hill

For information:

Sage Publications, Inc.
2455 Teller Road
Thousand Oaks, California 91320
E-mail: order@sagepub.com

Sage Publications Ltd.
1 Oliver's Yard
55 City Road
London EC1Y 1SP
United Kingdom

Sage Publications India Pvt. Ltd.
B-42, Panchsheel Enclave
Post Box 4109
New Delhi 110 017 India

Printed in the United States of America

Library of Congress Cataloging-in-Publication Data

Handbook of strategic alliances / edited by Oded Shenkar, Jeffery J. Reuer.
p. cm.
Includes bibliographical references and index.
ISBN 0-7619-8863-7 (cloth)
1. Strategic alliances (Business)—Handbooks, manuals, etc. I. Shenkar, Oded.
II. Reuer, J. J. (Jeffrey J.)
HD69.S8.H35 2006
658′.044—dc22 2005006696

This book is printed on acid-free paper.

05 06 07 08 09 8 7 6 5 4 3 2 1

Acquisitions Editor: Al Bruckner
Editorial Assistant: MaryAnn Vail
Production Editor: Diane S. Foster
Copy Editor: Gill Kent, Print Matters, Inc.
Typesetter: C&M Digitals (P) Ltd.
Proofreader: Kevin Gleasm
Indexer: Will Ragsdale
Cover Designer: Glenn Vogel

Contents

PART I

Introduction to Strategic Alliances

1

The Alliance Puzzle

Known Terrain, Black Boxes, and the Road Ahead

Oded Shenkar

Jeffrey J. Reuer

Strategic alliances have been a focus of attention among management scholars for more than two decades, coming on the heels of earlier work in economics, sociology, and law, among other areas. Interest in the formation, operation, and performance of alliances has not abated but rather seems to be growing stronger by the day. In academic conferences such as those of the Academy of Management, the Strategic Management Society and the Academy of International Business, strategic alliances now capture a substantial, sometimes dominant, share of papers, symposia, and panels. Management journals as well as their counterparts in economics, sociology, marketing, and international business publish a large number of alliance-related papers, and many have devoted special issues to the topic. Alliances have been the subject of numerous scholarly and trade books, research reports, policy papers, and "how to" guides produced by scholars, practitioners, consultancies, law firms, government agencies, and nongovernmental organizations (e.g., the Conference Board). Business schools offer alliance courses and training programs, whereas corporations, some with newly established units dedicated to alliances, have developed best practices. Associations of alliance professionals permit them to share experiences and develop remedies for the problems that often plague these hybrid forms of cooperation.

Past research has greatly enhanced our knowledge of alliances. It has produced deeper understanding of the workings of alliances, from initiation and formation to operation and termination, and has yielded important insights into their shortcomings and vulnerabilities. This research has also shown, however, the confines of the current theoretical frameworks and the limitations of prevailing methodologies, which have produced often-inconsistent findings and numerous "black boxes." A vast, untapped terrain appears to lie beneath the revealed patterns of alliance diffusion and performance, which past scholarship has shown little inclination to explore.

The aim of the *Handbook of Strategic Alliances* is not to replicate existing research, though the summary of the current knowledge base is an indispensable foundation of the book. Contributors have been asked to summarize and draw conclusions from past research as a way of deciphering and crystallizing the existing knowledge base, yet the ultimate goal of the *Handbook* is the paving of directions for future alliance research. Outlines of what we know are hence accompanied by mapping what we do not know but should, if we are to further advance alliance knowledge, and by suggestions of how those advancements can be achieved in a meaningful and rigorous fashion. The introduction of theory interfaces, empirical challenges, unconventional methodologies, and "black box" phenomena are all parts of this thrust.

All in all, we view the intersection of multiple environmental and organizational systems in alliances as providing a fertile ground for theory development that can be leveraged and eventually applied to other organizational forms, for which it will become increasingly relevant. The complexity, ambiguity, and permeable boundaries that characterize alliances are typical of the future business environment and, as such, have to support theory development while simultaneously enhancing relevance. The emergence of frameworks in which an alliance is viewed not merely as a hybrid, transitional form but as a viable strategic and organizational course may in turn challenge, develop, and offer substitutes for the theories that have spun those views.

In This Book

The *Handbook* begins by laying out the principal theoretical foundations for alliance research. In this part, Part II, we cover the plurality of theoretical approaches that have been utilized to study strategic alliances, their disciplinary roots, topical correlates, and the empirical evidence pertaining to their explanatory power. Also discussed in this part are key theoretical constructs, major debates, the challenges and opportunities associated with each theoretical approach, and the interfaces and cross-fertilization opportunities across the main theory streams.

Although a considerable amount is known about alliance formation, governance forms, and performance antecedents, surprisingly little is understood about actual implementation—the specific managerial challenges involved in establishing and operating alliances from their initial setup and throughout their life cycle. Part III is intended to fill this gap by looking inside some of the "black boxes" that have been acknowledged in the alliance literature but seldom opened. Chapters in this part seek to expand the boundaries and depth of traditional alliance topics such as structuring and trust formation; they are also set to develop the behavioral and human resource perspectives that have been given scant attention in the literature to date but whose importance extends well beyond their respective functional domains.

The next two parts are focused on the diversity of alliance forms and the repercussions of diversity, from theory intersections to questions of universality. Part IV starts with a set of chapters on cross-border collaboration, a setting in which much of the early work on joint ventures has been conducted and which continues to pose some unique challenges to alliance theoreticians and practitioners. Chapters in this part examine alliances within the context of the theory of the multinational enterprise and other international business theories, the problems and opportunities posed by cultural and other differences across the environments in which parents and alliances are anchored, and the special challenges related to the launch and operation of alliances in emerging economies.

Part V takes up alliances that might be considered nontraditional inasmuch as they represent relatively recent phenomena or have not been given much attention in prior scholarly work. As with their cross-border counterparts, these alliances raise questions regarding the applicability of current theories and methodologies but at the same time accord unique opportunities to develop insights unavailable from more traditional alliances. Chapters in this part are devoted to alliances in the new economy, the networks of alliances initiated by entrepreneurial firms, and alliances that bring together for-profit and not-for-profit entities.

The final part, Part VI, is devoted to methodological issues. Chapters in this part are focused on the challenges of devising and performing alliances research, from the intricacies of interdisciplinary scholarship to issues of research design, measurement, and instrumentation. This part critically reviews existing methodologies, but much of the emphasis is put on describing unconventional research and its promise for further advancement in the field. We see methodological progress as fundamental to theory development, without which alliance research will likely remain confined to a narrow range of problems and perspectives and fail to reach the level of rigor that will enable it not only to draw from current theories but also to enrich and refine them.

Part II: Theoretical Foundations

In the first chapter in this part, Mark Casson and Michael Mol ("Strategic Alliances: A Survey of Issues From an Entrepreneurial Perspective") trace the alliance literature's theoretical beginnings to industrial organization economics, broadly defined. This is not surprising, given that alliance research took off on the back of advancements in transaction cost analysis and the rising popularity of the structure-conduct-performance paradigm in economics and strategy. That interest in the way in which alliances impact rivalry and ultimately consumer welfare has been rekindled is evident from the draft antitrust guidelines on alliances recently issued by the United States Department of Justice and the Federal Trade Commission. Following an overarching historical overview of the theories that have dominated alliance research and their topical correlates, Casson and Mol recommend that theoretical discourse be redirected toward a view of alliances as entrepreneurial endeavors undertaken with a specific project in mind rather than as organizations with operational domains. The chapter sketches out the contours of an entrepreneurial theory of alliances and outlines the ramifications of a departure from the theoretical routes previously undertaken.

The second chapter in this part ("How Alliances Reshape Competition," by Benjamin Gomes-Casseres) also returns to industrial organizational economics as a key root of alliance research, but is focused on the competitive repercussions of alliances, a question that has served as a launching point for both scholarly and public-policy interest in the phenomenon. Linking the past, present, and future of alliance research, this chapter considers how industry-level constellations of partners align with oligopoly theory and how alliances reshape competitive, interfirm dynamics. In so doing, the chapter offers the promise of resuscitating the mostly severed link between the macroenvironment and the firm level of analysis.

In the latter part of the twentieth century, industrial organization economics has spawned multiple new theories that might be grouped under headings such as organizational economics or neo-institutional economics; however, the theory that arguably has had the greatest impact on alliance research is transaction cost economics. Incorporating behavioral elements into industrial organization economics, the transaction costs approach focused on firm boundaries, asking, for instance, when a firm should partner with another and when it should go it alone or acquire another; and, when opting for alliances, what the circumstances are under which various alliance forms should be used. Because alliances often operate in a context in which property rights are ill specified and bargaining power and inputs are unevenly distributed, many of the hazards that are central to alliance management can be cast in transaction cost economics terms. The chapter by Yadong Luo ("Opportunism in Cooperative Alliances: Conditions and Solutions") highlights the role of opportunism—a transaction cost construct that underlies various alliance hazards—as a key obstacle in crafting and managing alliances. Luo shows how opportunism is affected by industry characteristics and how it can be mitigated during both the ex ante and ex post phases of alliance formation and management.

Another branch of organizational economics, one that is oriented toward production efficiencies rather than transactional efficiencies from exchanges across or within organizations and that is free of assumptions regarding opportunism, is evolutionary economics. As research attention shifted away from explaining why firms entered into alliances over alternative arrangements and shifted toward alliance capability-building and partnering processes, the evolutionary perspective has taken on new importance. The chapter by Prashant Kale and Maurizio Zollo ("Understanding Partnering Processes and Outcomes: The Contribution of Evolutionary Theory") identifies ways in which evolutionary theory brings distinctive strengths and offers a fresh approach to alliance research at the dyadic, organizational, and network levels. The chapter also suggests the use of evolutionary economics to revisit investment choice and alliance management issues that have been the grist for other theoretical mills in the alliance literature's past. The approach opens up the possibility of using evolutionary frameworks to complement existing theoretical bases when considering topics such as governance choice, partnering, relationship dynamics, and performance sources, among others.

A second theory that has attracted increased attention in recent years is real options. Anju Seth and Tailan Chi ("What Does a Real Options Perspective Add to the Understanding of Strategic Alliances") illustrate the use of option-related concepts, imported from financial economics, in explaining certain features of alliances viewed as organizational investments. Real options theory is distinct from transaction cost theory and evolutionary economics in that it combines the concepts of uncertainty and managerial discretion in a dynamic view of firms' investment decisions. Like financial calls and puts, alliances can be attractive investment vehicles with which to test the water in a new technological domain or market, allowing firms to limit their downside risk while investing sequentially as they receive new information about the merits of a technology or product. Some scholars see promise in real options as a normative theory that can bridge corporate strategy and finance by injecting strategic reality into capital budgeting models, all the while bringing the discipline of financial markets into strategic thinking; others see this promise mitigated by important differences between financial and strategic investments.

The final chapter in the "Theoretical Foundations" part is by Gordon Walker ("Networks of Strategic Alliances"), who injects a sociological thrust into a theoretical landscape dominated by economic scholarship. Network analyses of alliances can be traced to the 1980s, if not earlier; however, recent developments in theory and method have triggered a resurgence of interest in alliances as a form of intraindustry links among firms. Although network analyses are often treated at a methodological rather than at a theoretical level, they are firmly connected to sociological theories focusing on interorganizational ties. For instance, Walker's earlier work considered whether patterns of collaboration in biotechnology could be explained by firms repeating their alliances in very familiar domains to preserve stability and individuals' social capital or to broker opportunities to span more distant actors in the network. The chapter reviews the development in this area over the last decade and presents the robust results from these efforts, which challenge existing models and conclusions. The chapter also shows how the network approach might complement and contribute to current thrusts in alliance research.

As alliance research moves forward, economic and sociological approaches may move closer, offering opportunities for cross-fertilization across such areas as competition and interlocking directorship and management. Future research may also see the introduction of fresh disciplinary inputs from seemingly unlikely areas such as biology (where cooperation and competition underlie the life of species) to political science (where nation-state alliances have been studied for a much longer period). These new approaches will not only bring new lenses with which to see strategic alliances but will also present more evidence pertaining to current theoretical frameworks. For instance, game theory, only sporadically applied to business alliances, has been widely applied in political science research on nation-state alliances. Future alliance research may also be associated with a revival of system theory–type attempts to synthesize and synergize multidisciplinary efforts. Already an intriguing application ground, strategic alliance research thus holds the promise of becoming a locus of theory development that will yield insights into the broader phenomena of cooperation and competition among agents. The final chapter of the *Handbook* takes on interdisciplinary challenges such as these.

Part III: Alliance Management: Opening the "Black Boxes"

With scholars and practitioners shifting some attention to implementation issues, the next set of chapters considers alliance management, examining on-the-ground collaboration issues across the life cycle and functional spectrum. Implementation, broadly defined as the setup and execution of an alliance governance, management, and control structure, is not only important in its own right; it is also intricately tied to the fundamental logic and predictive power of the theories discussed in the earlier part. For instance, some of the opportunism hazards discussed in transaction cost economics can be mitigated by effective management, the deployment of human resources in a way that would permit better monitoring, for example. Hence the opening of the managerial "black boxes" also offers new insights on transactional and strategic issues, from initial investment to termination.

The first chapter in this part, by Stephen Tallman and Anupama Phene ("Structuring and Restructuring Alliances: A Theory-Based Process Model"), lays out the process of alliance management and considers the key decisions that firms make at the crucial stages of the alliance life cycle, including alliance choice, partner search and selection, negotiation, operations, and termination/renegotiation. For theoreticians, this chapter indicates how certain theories might map over to particular alliance stages and decisions more or less effectively than others. For practitioners, the chapter illustrates how design and management, although intricately related, require different lenses and approaches to devise effective solutions.

The starting point of the second chapter in Part III, by Africa Ariño and Jeffrey Reuer ("Alliance Contractual Design"), is that most research on alliance design compares equity and nonequity alliances or uses similar broad-brush distinctions. As a result, the literature offers only limited guidance and few specifics on how firms should design their collaborative agreements. To address the degrees of freedom that managers have, this chapter views alliance design through the keyhole of the alliance contract and considers the various contractual provisions that alliance partners use. The authors suggest how we can go beyond prior research on alliance contracts to examine particular dimensions of contractual complexity and their strategic and managerial correlates.

Although crafting a sound alliance contract is an important initial step in thinking through potential contingencies that affect an alliance, in devising alliance processes, in articulating the business plan, and in getting an alliance off on the right foot, the role of informal governance and the interaction between the formal and informal aspects of alliance management are critical. The third chapter in Part III, by Akbar Zaheer and Jared Harris ("Interorganizational Trust"), addresses the topic of trust among partners, which has been the subject of a great amount of research in the last decade and yet remains mired in much confusion and inconsistency. The chapter helps to synthesize and consolidate the scholarship on trust in alliances into four central questions: (a) What is interorganizational trust? (b) How is it created? (c) How does it work? and (d) What does it lead to? This categorization scheme helps in taking stock of prior work while outlining areas where future studies might contribute to understanding the importance of trust, its boundary conditions, and how it relates to other inputs and consequences of alliance management.

Whereas trust has received significant attention from alliance scholars, issues surrounding group dynamics and, more broadly, organizational behavior have been given surprisingly short shrift. The fourth chapter in Part III, by Kwok Leung and Steven White ("Exploring Dark Corners: An Agenda for Organizational Behavior Research in Alliance Contexts"), takes up this challenge. Their chapter shows how organizational behavior scholarship could contribute to the alliance research agenda by highlighting the group dynamics that are fundamental to the successful establishment and operation of alliances. Thus, organization behavior can shed light on critical implementation issues as well as economic considerations. For instance, partner relations can serve as a substitute for certain contract provisions, especially in environments that prioritize relationships (e.g., East Asia), and their importance can outlive a focal alliance; for instance, by creating a positive experience, partner relations may serve as a basis for subsequent cooperation. Finally, although holding the promise of contributing to alliance research, organization behavior can also be informed by the unique setting of alliances in which mixed teams are subjected to multiple authority structures and their attendant behavioral correlates, such as conflict, ambiguity, and diverse loci of control.

Just as alliance research can inform as well as be informed by organization behavior, so can a second vital, yet neglected, facet of alliance management and research, namely human resource management. The fifth chapter in Part III, by Randall Schuler and Ibraiz Tarique ("Alliance Forms and Human Resources Issues, Implications, and Significance"), focuses on the promise and challenge of building new links between this field and the alliance literature. Specifically, this chapter lays out the human resource concerns and issues that emerge at various life cycle stages of an alliance; indeed, even at the formation stage, human resources play an important role, as many alliance contracts contain provisions regarding senior management assignment. The authors note that the limited previous research on human resources in alliances has been exclusively devoted to joint ventures while neglecting nonequity alliances, thus missing out on important insights regarding the establishment, operation, and performance of purely contractual agreements and the actual mechanisms that facilitate cooperation in such alliances that are so widespread in use. Alliances also pose challenges regarding issues such as career paths and rotation decisions that must mesh among two or more firms. At the same time, alliances can be viewed as a form characteristic of an increasingly unstable human resource environment in which outsourcing and multiple affiliations play an ever-growing role and hence are a harbinger of things to come in this area.

The final chapter in this part is by Marjorie Lyles and Siegfried Gudergan ("Learning and Knowledge Development in Alliances"). This chapter helps to open another black box that assumes many alliances are motivated by a learning desire without empirically demonstrating how such learning actually takes place. Opening this box is particularly important because learning has become a popular area of alliance research, with some studies considering knowledge transfer and learning within the dyad or partnership itself, whereas others are concerned with learning about how to manage alliances at the organizational level. This chapter presents ideas on how to connect the two levels, considers learning under routine versus more novel conditions, and examines cognitive as well as social dimensions of the learning processes. It also offers normative guidelines for executives charged with managing alliances.

Part IV: Cross-Border Collaborations

Although much of what is discussed in previous chapters applies to alliances in general, this part is the first of two focused on the research challenges and opportunities that are special to particular types of collaborations. Cross-border alliances have been an important part of alliance research over the past quarter of a century and in many ways have colored the general approach toward the phenomenon to such a point that it is not always clear to what extent their features are a product of multiple environments or of shared ownership and governance. International alliances offer opportunities to draw from the theory base of international business as well as to inform this body of knowledge in which the establishment and operation of cross-border alliances are viewed as key capabilities of the multinational enterprise and part and parcel of global business.

First in this part, Andrew Delios examines alliance research in relation to research in international business ("Alliances and International Business Theory"), two literature streams that were practically inseparable at the onset of alliance research. This chapter specifically takes up the links between alliance research on the one hand and internalization theory, or the theory of the multinational corporation, on the other hand. The author also covers internationalization theories and the role played by strategic alliances in that process. Recent work anchored in institutional economics and institutional theory is showcased as a way of suggesting future research directions in the resource-based treatment of international business and in the area of international social networks.

Next, Piero Morosini ("Nurturing Successful Alliances Across Boundaries") takes a grounded theory approach, using the Renault-Nissan alliance as a case study with which to illustrate the limitations of existing theories and approaches that would not have predicted the success of this alliance. The author suggests that previous research may have overemphasized interpartner competition at the expense of cooperation and the social capabilities that promote cooperation, and he proposes new ways of thinking about social processes in alliances from negotiation and setup to the operational phase.

Jaideep Anand and Prashant Kale then direct attention to alliances in transition economies ("International Joint Ventures in Emerging Economies: Past Drivers and Emerging Trends"), the setting for many of the early studies on alliance formation, structuring, and outcomes. The authors revisit some of the early work on firms' partnering motives, specifically the desire for multinationals to secure local market access on a stand-alone basis coupled with host governments' regulations preventing full foreign ownership. Under the circumstances prevailing at that time, taking on a local partner was the price of admission to a potentially lucrative market. With rapid liberalization of foreign investment rules in many of the emerging markets, the question arises whether alliances will continue to be as popular in these countries, and if so, what alliance forms will take hold in those settings. The authors argue that the experiences gained by multinationals might further diminish the need for local partners in emerging economies, and they delineate the implications of these potential trends for the international joint venture literature. At the same time, they discuss the theory-relevant lessons that could be drawn from the research on emerging market alliances both then and now.

Part V: Nontraditional Strategic Alliances

We next present three chapters on so-called nontraditional strategic alliances, that is, alliances that have not been widespread in the past and have not been considered, let alone studied, in terms of their potentially unique features. Lalit Manral and Kathryn Harrigan ("Alliances in the New Economy") focus on alliances in the new economy. Compared to many of the alliances Harrigan studied in the 1980s in commodity industries, these alliances among Internet firms display many different dynamics and features, offering new insights regarding firms' boundaries and alliance strategies. After detailing the ramifications of the Internet for firm strategy, the authors highlight opportunism and promiscuity as the central features of these alliances, which are often formed and brought to a close in rapid succession, particularly in the early stages of industry evolution. This chapter flags a number of new motives for entering alliances, including the search for legitimacy and the promotion of technological standards, motives that did not figure in the literature even ten years ago.

Just as with the alliances that have flourished in the high-tech sector, the emergence of alliances in entrepreneurial settings raises questions regarding the universality of the alliance phenomenon. Duane Ireland, Michael Hitt, and Justin Webb draw attention to the alliances and networks established by entrepreneurial firms ("Entrepreneurial Alliances and Networks") and propose that entrepreneurship scholarship can open new frontiers in alliance research. The authors specifically outline opportunities for integration and cross-fertilization between the strategic management and entrepreneurship fields as a way to develop alliance-relevant theory. They highlight the different requirements imposed by alliances to explore new domains versus alliances that are more exploitative in nature, considering how key alliance variables such as governance structure, trust, and resources have very different implications for partner selection and deal structuring for these exploratory and exploitative collaborations. Broadly speaking, their call coincides with that of Casson and Mol (see Part II), who suggest we view alliances as entrepreneurial endeavors.

Finally, Ted London, Dennis Rondinelli, and Hugh O'Neill examine a new type of alliance: those between public-sector and private-sector organizations ("Strange Bedfellows: Alliances Between Corporations and Nonprofits"). The authors indicate a flourishing of such alliances but note that the gulf between the partners' values, missions, and structures complicates the process of building and managing collaboration. They suggest that key differences exist across reactive public-private alliances and proactive partnerships; the former are induced by the threat of regulation, and the latter are driven by opportunities to work with key stakeholders. Although some of their recommendations are also applicable to interfirm alliances, the chapter represents a call for better understanding of new types of alliances, the extent to which they can be accommodated by current theoretical frameworks, and the theory development work that needs to take place as a result of the challenges these new hybrids pose.

Part VI: Alliance Research Methodologies

Although the prior chapters cover a broad spectrum of issues relating to the theory of collaboration and the practical challenges that firms face regarding different alliance life-cycle stages, functional requirements, and investment contexts, we believe that it is important to give methodological considerations their due in order to appraise the field's current state of the art as well as provide guidance for future studies. In the final part of the *Handbook,* Part VI, Arvind Parkhe reviews and summarizes the methodologies and research approaches undertaken in recent alliance literature ("Research Methods in Alliances"). His conclusion is that progress is being made on a number of fronts but the field has yet to grapple adequately with some of the core behavioral variables that explain alliance processes and outcomes. The author also suggests that qualitative methods continue to receive inadequate attention despite their considerable promise in capturing topics and facets that are not considered or properly covered due to the limitations of prevailing quantitative research.

Jane Salk and Davina Vora discuss how research methodologies used outside the core of alliance research might be used to make progress in a number of alliance research areas ("Research Outside the 'Core': Opportunities in Alternative Approaches and Methods for Studying Cooperative Alliances"). The authors review methods and theories that might be applied to the alliance setting to better understand social phenomena and processes (e.g., social identification and social capital) in order to address the cross-level dynamics that are at the heart of many alliance phenomena.

One of the arguably thorniest methodological problems in the alliance literature has been the measurement of alliance performance, an issue that obviously carries significant theoretical and practical implications. This problem arises because of the heterogeneous motives that two or more partners bring to an alliance, the gap between alliance-level and parent-level outcomes, the lack of performance metrics, practical issues such as firms' transfer pricing policies and the presence of contracts auxiliary to the focal agreement, and various challenges associated with data collection. Paul Olk takes up these and other issues in his chapter, entitled "Modeling and Measuring the Performance of Alliances." This chapter catalogs the various ways in which alliance performance has been measured and then draws links across nine different performance indicators. The chapter provides a number of suggestions for the field to take steps toward better evaluation of alliance performance.

The final chapter of the handbook, by Mark de Rond and Sonja Marjanovic, takes on the challenge of conducting interdisciplinary research in the alliance domain ("The Legitimacy of Messiness: Interdisciplinary Research, Systems of Innovation, and Strategic Alliances"). The authors discuss the promise of interdisciplinary research and how it might be conducted so as to advance a "systems of innovation" approach as a framework that might guide future alliance research. They then focus on particular questions that are amenable to interdisciplinary research and that would be worth revisiting with such an approach. Beyond making the case for an interdisciplinary approach, they identify a few of the pitfalls and risks that such a research agenda might entail.

Where Do We Go From Here?

The progress we have made in alliance research so far is impressive in scope and reach. We have a reasonably good knowledge of formation motives, performance predictors, and organizational governance. We also have a developing understanding of alliance evolution and alliance networks. We have nascent knowledge of the human role in alliances, in particular human resource management; however, we know very little about what motivates employees who work in alliances, what the leadership qualities are that may be required to be an effective alliance manager, or how we can train individuals to be more effective in alliances. Although we keep reminding readers of the complexity and risks of running alliances, we as yet have effectively no knowledge of the training and development that could potentially alleviate the problems associated with this increased complexity and enhance performance at the individual, team, and organizational levels.

We also have only limited knowledge of process issues, from negotiation through formation and termination. Without due attention to process, we may be attributing too much to static performance antecedents such as preformation attributes of participants or the design of an alliance without addressing process factors that may be key factors behind success or failure. Much of the problem rests with alliance research being conducted via large data sets that are not amenable to longitudinal, let alone process, research. Case-study methodology, among other methods described in this book, can be useful as a complementary vehicle here.

Despite the enormous amount of research done on international joint ventures, we also do not truly know if cross-border alliances are fundamentally different from domestic alliances. International business scholars will probably say yes, as political and social systems and the clash of cultures weigh on the formation, operation, and performance of those alliances. The dearth of studies comparing domestic and cross-border alliances weighs down on our ability to answer this question definitively, as does the dearth of studies comparing domestic alliances in different locations. In a similar fashion, evidence is needed on the similarities and differences between entrepreneurial and nonentrepreneurial alliances, between alliances spanning corporations and those linking for-profit and not-for-profit organizations, and between those on the Internet versus more conventional domains. These alliances might be studied in their own right and for obvious practical reasons, but a deeper question arises as to how such studies might advance theory development in broader fields such as strategy, international business, technology management, marketing, organizational behavior, and so forth.

We have also made progress, albeit limited, on the theory front. Some theories, such as resource dependence, were used early in the field's development and are less influential today, yet there has also been a renaissance of sociological perspectives on alliances in the last few years. There is considerably more theoretical pluralism today than ten years ago, and these theories have connected well with many alliance phenomena and problems. Individual studies of alliances also routinely draw on more than one theoretical perspective, either to establish a horse race among theoretical perspectives that can address a key phenomenon or to exploit areas of conceptual convergence. These theories also speak to different levels of analysis that meet in the alliance context—country, industry, network, firm, dyad, and so forth—and debates exist about the relative influence of these different levels and the importance of accounting for relationships across these levels. For instance, network theorists argue the importance of indirect ties for many alliance phenomena, raising the question of when it is crucial to account for network-level features in studies geared to explaining dyad-level attributes or outcomes.

Many of the theories in currency are drawn from different theoretical traditions within economics, and in many cases the theoretical treatments of alliances amount to a "patching up" of existing theories to accommodate the rise of alliances of various sorts. For instance, in transaction cost theory, alliances are hybrid organizational forms that blend the features of organizations and markets. In agency theory, alliances are an amalgam of sort of principals and agents. In evolutionary economics, routines can develop at the interorganizational level. Hence, although much progress has been made in modifying theories to apply them to alliances, three key questions emerge: First, can additional theories be used and also accommodate strategic alliances to yield new insights? We have mentioned human resource management, organizational behavior, and entrepreneurship as three fields where such progress might be possible and would be fruitful. Such questions might also be posed of the root disciplines. For instance, initial models in the property-rights approach did not allow for ownership sharing in equilibria that had Party A owning Party B completely, or vice versa. Yet the property-rights approach has recently been helpful in less mathematically formal studies that examine the details of which party is given which control rights and how these allocations might change over time.

Second, is adequate feedback being given to the fields, theories, and disciplines rather than simply using alliances as an empirical testing ground? The alliance literature might be characterized as undergoing an important transition in recent years, as the focus has shifted from applications geared to understanding alliances per se to an examination of larger theoretical questions and the use of alliances as the crucible for the validation of a theory. In this latter case, the alliance context either uniquely lends itself to theory application or provides some important source of variance that can be exploited to examine an unexplored theoretical facet.

Third, rather than accommodating alliances in existing theories by treating them as "mixed forms" or other hybrid arrangements, is there a need to develop theories specifically for alliances as the key phenomenon of interest? Clearly, the merits and promise of all three issues need to be debated, and one might also ask whether it is important to diversify our theoretical bases still further and be ready to import new insights from far-flung areas such as biology and political science, to name just two.

Studies We Would Like to See

Our selection of chapters and discussion of them above convey where the field is at as well as signals fruitful research agendas on alliances, but we can conclude with a few thoughts on methodology and the relevance of the collective research agenda in the alliance literature. Longitudinal research, although seemingly endorsed in universal terms, remains something most researchers push to the back of their papers under the "Suggestions for Further Research" title, much like the need to examine both sides of the alliance dyad rather than adopting a "focal firm" for analysis due to data limitations when conducting survey research and even in studies using secondary data. Yet research needs to be performed—and can be performed—by obtaining measures at the time of alliance formation (or better yet, at the time of strategic intent) and again some time into the venture's life. For instance, measuring culture at these two points in time will enable us to see whether and how interaction has changed the culture of the participating organizations and their members rather than treating it as a static variable measured at the onset only.

As a second example, despite the plurality of theoretical approaches used, researchers commonly impose a formation motive on alliance participants, even if implicitly. For instance, studies examine alliances as learning races and do not accommodate other motives, such as transactional efficiencies, standard setting or entry deterrence, and so forth. Other studies examine joint ventures as real options but do not determine whether firms actually had any intention of investing sequentially or, rather, established an alliance as an equilibrium arrangement. The mix of motives likely varies across investment contexts and firms, and firms may not adhere to a single motive and hang onto it during the course of collaboration. Examining both parties' multiplicity of motives and how these motives change over time would therefore enhance the descriptive value of theories in use.

The last few years have seen several case studies on alliances that have been instrumental in identifying processes, dynamics, and evolution. Yet the number of scholarly case studies on alliances remains limited and their scope narrow. In particular, cases studies of alliance termination and failure remain rare, despite the substantial learning promise such studies entail. Multicase study designs also remain a rarity despite their potential contribution. Yet for many of the research needs this volume has flagged, such studies offer considerable progress in advancing the alliance literature. For many of these questions, studies that adopt multimethod designs might also enrich our understanding of collaborative strategy and alliance management.

Finally, as in other management areas, the question of relevance haunts the strategic alliance area. Although alliances are a topic of great interest to firms and their executives, this does not necessarily translate into use of scholarly work in that area. Are we producing work that is relevant and applicable to the world of practitioners? Are we making appropriate use of the wealth of studies on the topic put out by consulting firms (e.g., Deloitte; Booz Allen, etc.), nongovernmental organizations (e.g., the Conference Board), or related sources? At what rate, and how, is practice advancing and how is scholarship tracking by comparison? Although there is no available evidence on this topic, it is plausible that scholarship is ahead of practice in many areas (e.g., criteria for adopting alliances over acquisitions, contracting arrangements, etc.) and behind in others (e.g., alliance structuring, human resource management, metrics, etc.). Because much alliance research is conducted by using large data sets, we may be forfeiting an opportunity to learn from people who are directly engaged in the formation and operation of such arrangements.

Conclusion

In the chapters appearing in this volume, readers will see the considerable progress that has been made in many areas of the alliance literature. Although the volume is far from exhaustive, it highlights the impressive contributions that have been made in a relatively short span of time in which this work has been conducted. We are also optimistic about future prospects for this literature: The theoretical foundations are strong and getting stronger and more diversified, the scientific rigor of studies has increased greatly in the last few years, and a vibrant research community exists of young and established scholars from a number of different disciplines and methodological traditions. At special conferences and other gatherings of these scholars, we are always impressed by the many unanswered questions on alliances relative to what is known with certainty, the possibilities of contributing to broader fields and theories, and the enthusiasm surrounding a phenomenon that has had such an enormous impact on organizations and society in the past twenty years. By their very nature, alliances challenge thinking about organization and markets, levels of action and analysis, and traditional business principles. Although a volume such as this cannot cover all of the theories, contributions, and perspectives on this important topic, we hope that readers will find it both a helpful reference and overview of an interesting literature as well as a guide for future work on collaborative strategy and alliance management.

PART II

Theoretical Foundations

2

Strategic Alliances

A Survey of Issues From an Entrepreneurial Perspective

Mark Casson

Michael J. Mol

The Alliance Phenomenon

It has often been noted in recent years that strategic alliances have become increasingly important vehicles for business activity (Doz & Hamel, 1998). It might even be suggested that strategic alliances have come to be seen as the main means to improve the output of the firm, with an underlying reasoning that by focusing on a smaller set of activities while obtaining inputs from many specialized outside suppliers, firms can get the best of both worlds (Quinn, 1999). The academic literature on the topic appears to have been equally abundant. Nevertheless, a number of reasons for confusion remain. There is no agreed definition of alliances and no standard classification of the different types.

This chapter examines current literature on alliances from a broad theoretical perspective. It outlines the key decision-making stages in strategic alliances and, building upon this analysis, categorizes the articles on strategic alliances from six top management journals. This establishes the main dimensions along which previous studies of alliances have varied. The chapter then considers, in the light of the literature, how alliances are most usefully defined for the purpose of analysis. It considers whether there are general principles that apply to all alliances or whether "alliance" is merely a label that covers a range of fundamentally different modes of organization, each of which requires its own analysis.

It is argued that an integrated theoretical analysis of alliances must recognize explicitly the entrepreneurial dimension of business behavior. It is suggested that alliances are principally employed not to coordinate activities but to coordinate projects. Routine activities, which can be expected to carry on continually in a steady state, will normally be coordinated by the classic modes: either arm's length market transactions between independent firms or managerial control within a single firm. Projects, on the other hand, require a reallocation of resources when they start, in order to get them going, a reallocation of resources at the end, when they close down, and further reallocations of resources when they are in progress, because of the uncertainties that they face. Neither market nor hierarchy is well adapted to locking independent parties into flexible arrangements; the market discourages lock-in, whereas the hierarchy discourages flexibility. It is therefore in this context that alliances come to the fore in the role of temporal bridging mechanisms.

Historical Perspective on Theory Development

Until the development of internalization theory, there was no systematic discussion of contractual alternatives to the fully integrated multinational enterprise for the coordination of international business activities. There had been studies of individual modes, such as technology licensing, but no formal comparison of alternative institutional arrangements for technology transfer. In an aptly named book, *Alternatives to the Multinational Enterprise,* Casson (1979) examined a range of contractual alternatives—in particular, licensing, subcontracting, and management contracts—and argued that they would become increasingly widely used. This echoed the prediction by Buckley and Casson (1976, p. 113) that,

> firms will tend to rely more on licensing and less on foreign direct investments as a means of exploiting their knowledge. . . . Joint ventures will become more prevalent as a means of harmonizing the profit-maximizing objectives of foreign investors with the social policies of host governments.

These alternative modes were sometimes referred to as "non-equity foreign investments" (Oman, 1980)—a rather misleading name that served only to highlight the disproportionate emphasis traditionally placed on equity-based foreign involvement. In an effort to bring order to an increasingly chaotic field, Buckley (1985) provided a typology of ten different modes of "international industrial co-operation," which included, in addition to the usual modes, turnkey contracts, fade-out agreements, and minority foreign-equity holdings. At the same time, Casson (1985) drew attention to the historical significance of international cartels—often underpinned by cross-licensing agreements—as an alternative to the multinational enterprise.

It was generally agreed at this time that the theory of transaction costs as embodied in internalization theory provided an adequate account of the factors influencing the choice of contractual mode. Many authors continued to believe that the fully integrated multinational enterprise was the most efficient mechanism for globalizing the exploitation of new proprietary technology and that licensing and joint ventures were mainly appropriate as a response to political constraints. In economic terms, multinationality was "first best" and other forms were "second best"; other forms were used to overcome obstacles to market access, it was believed.

By the mid-1980s, however, there was increasing evidence that joint ventures were being used more widely and more creatively and that this phenomenon could not be explained simply by a growth of government intervention. Indeed, it seemed as though it was the liberalization of trade and investment, rather than government controls, that was responsible. Some large firms, it seemed, now regarded international joint ventures as a first-best solution.

The 50:50 joint venture was a very common form, but because of the ambiguity over managerial control that is created, it seemed particularly difficult to explain why this form would be used (Contractor & Lorange, 1988). Some idealists claimed to have identified a new spirit of cooperation in the world of business that was going to supplant the spirit of competition, whereas others claimed that a new synthetic business principle of "co-opetition" was emerging (Brandenburger & Nalebuff, 1996). On the other side of the debate, cynics (such as Porter, 1980) argued that—in essence—cooperation was for wimps. No firm that dominated its market niche would ever cooperate with a potential rival, it was said, for that would threaten its lead; cooperation was for "number two" firms who realized that they could take on the dominant firm only if they joined forces.

In the 1990s the debate over alliances was partially subsumed into the debate over globalization. The spread of Western democracy was demolishing traditional political barriers to market access in many countries, and opening up new areas to foreign business involvement. These changes created a large amount of volatility in the international business environment. Highly integrated global markets had emerged for many products, which meant that even new products had to be sold at very competitive prices. At the same time, new low-cost locations had become available. Innovation was speeded up as firms raced to the market with their new products, and logistics were improved as just-in-time production lines were increasingly sourced from distant locations. Few long-established firms had sufficient accumulated expertise to effect the transition entirely on their own. At the same time, they were reluctant to sell off their expertise to others, and so the idea of sharing expertise with carefully selected partners came to the fore. This was further strengthened by the blurring of industry boundaries—for example, supermarkets starting to act as banks—that led to new and unexpected entries into industries. Alliance partners no longer needed to be existing competitors but could come from other industries too. Strategic alliances seemed to be the ideal mechanism for adjusting to these new realities of global competition.

This line of argument, which relates the growth in the number of alliances to the globalization of markets, suggests that the study of alliances has finally begun to deliver some useful results. At the same time, however, a review of recent literature on alliances in management journals suggests some less-welcome developments. Although the early literature on alliances was characterized by a rather fragmented focus on individual types of alliance, the most recent literature seems to be characterized by the opposite problem. Much current work on alliances does not properly distinguish between the different types involved and hence does not provide a basis for comparing them. In particular, the distinction between equity and nonequity arrangements is played down, whereas the specific issues relating to joint ventures are often ignored altogether.

As the study of alliances has proliferated, so the intellectual division of labor within the subject has been refined. For example, it is now quite usual for scholars to examine specific stages in the alliance process—such as policy formulation, partner selection, project implementation, and so on—rather than focus on the alliance as a whole. The results of such specialized studies are sometimes difficult to interpret within a broader framework. For example, internal management processes in joint ventures are often analyzed as though they were divorced from any profit imperative that may have motivated the establishment of the alliance in the first place. Because a unifying framework is missing, this fragmentation appears to hinder knowledge accumulation in this area.

A Framework for Analyzing the Literature on Strategic Alliances

The literature on strategic alliances can best be categorized in terms of four main characteristics (see also Barringer & Harrison, 2000):

1. the stage of alliance decision making;
2. the type of alliance;
3. the objective of the alliance; and
4. the functional area in which the alliance is rooted.

In addition, we consider the conceptual framework employed by the authors for the study of alliances. In contrast to the early literature, which was heavily influenced by transaction costs, many different theories and frameworks have recently been brought to bear upon the alliance phenomenon (Barringer & Harrison, 2000; Osborn & Hagedoorn, 1997).

Although the exact number of *stages* in an alliance is debatable, there is always a preformation stage, a formation stage, and a postformation stage. These three stages can be further resolved into six key phases of an alliance:

1. initial conditions;
2. opportunity recognition;
3. setting of objectives;
4. design and specification of project;
5. implementation;
6. delivery and performance.

The *initial conditions* consist of a range of economic, political, social, and technological factors in the firms' environment prior to the formation of the alliance. We visualize the firms as being embedded in a spatial system with a complex division of labor. Plants at different locations are linked by transport networks and coordinated using communications networks. The messages that flow through the communications network comprise internal orders and requisitions made by multinational firms as well as the ordinary price and quantity information required in arm's length market trade. Each firm has its own network of relationships with customers, suppliers, governments, research establishments, and so on.

When contemplating these initial conditions, an entrepreneur working for one of these firms may be able to spot a potential disequilibrium—for example, an unsatisfied demand that can be met using underutilized resources elsewhere in the system. This is an example of *opportunity recognition.* In a simple case, the entrepreneur may be able to exploit the opportunity directly by matching supply to demand through a process of arbitrage, as suggested by Kirzner (1973). Other cases are more complex, though. For example, an entrepreneur may recognize that recent scientific research indicates it is feasible to develop a new technology that, if combined with existing technologies, would make possible the development of a new product; this product might be an alternative to some other product that is becoming very scarce because of the depletion of natural resources. The new product is therefore a potential substitute for an existing product, even though consumers of the existing product do not yet realize it. Although there are no price signals or direct evidence of frustrated demand, nevertheless the opportunity is there. The difficulty is that a large number of steps are involved in bringing the product to market, and a wide variety of resources must be brought to bear on this task, including scarce specialized skills. A single firm cannot hope to supply all the resources from its own internal resources. An opportunity for an alliance is thereby created.

If an alliance is believed to be the appropriate response to an opportunity, the *objectives* must be set and the alliance's scope determined. In this context, the usual distinction in the literature is between exploration and exploitation alliances (following March, 1991), although other categorizations exist too. In the former, the chief aim of the alliance is to create new assets, including intangible assets such as technology, whereas the aim of the latter is to make better use of an existing asset; for example, by exploiting a technology across countries through a network of international joint ventures (Shenkar & Jiatao, 1999).

Alliance *design,* traditionally the stage on which many studies focus (e.g., Gulati, 1995), is concerned with a number of issues, including the choice of mode, as discussed above, equity shares, management structures, and decision-making procedures.

The *implementation* phase includes taking decisions, monitoring outcomes, and reporting back to the stakeholders. Conflict-resolution

Table 2.1 Raw Findings of Articles on Alliances in 6 Top Management Journals

	Prior to 1990	*1990–1994*	*1995–1999*	*2000–2004*	*Totals*
AMJ	0	5	13	10	28
AMR	3	1	4	4	12
ASQ	2	0	5	4	11
JM	0	0	1	17	18
OS	0	2	18	12	32
SMJ	5	11	20	35	71
Totals	10	19	61	82	172

mechanisms play an important role in the smooth running of the alliance.

Finally, the *performance* of the alliance must be measured. Measured performance will be compared to targets to assess whether the alliance is a success. A successful alliance may well be extended, whereas an unsuccessful one may be terminated before the planned finishing date.

Search Methodology

To execute a limited yet useful search of the literature, we ran the keyword "alliance(s)" in the six journals that are presented as the most important strategic management outlets by the Business Policy and Strategy Division of the Academy of Management. These journals are *Academy of Management Journal (AMJ), Academy of Management Review (AMR), Administrative Science Quarterly (ASQ), Journal of Management (JM), Organization Science (OS),* and *Strategic Management Journal (SMJ)*. Of course, any selection of journals and other sources is arguable, but we believe these are generally thought to be very good journals, and they regularly include articles on alliances. Furthermore we acknowledge that the product of this search method will include some pretty poor papers and will at the same time leave out good and interesting work that has appeared in books and other journals.

We split the articles we found into four distinct time periods: prior to 1990, 1990 to 1994, 1995 to 1999, and 2000 to 2004. The timing of the search was September 2004, so any work appearing in 2004 but after that cutoff point will have gone unnoticed. Our search generated numbers of hits ranked by journal and 5-year time period, as shown in Table 2.1.

The list produced initially contained 25 hits that were not useful for our purpose. They included editorials, calls for papers, comments on other articles, book reviews, and articles that used the term *alliance* in a different sense (for instance interpersonal alliances, as in "who is your ally inside this organization"). Thus, we were left with the numbers of regular articles on strategic alliances shown in Table 2.2.

Some straightforward conclusions can be drawn from these findings. Perhaps unexpectedly, alliances have been studied much more over the past 10 years than before, with this period accounting for 83% of hits. Prior to 1990, there was not much mention of alliances. This trend can supposedly be linked to the increasing use of alliances in practice (Barringer & Harrison, 2000), but some of it might also be attributable to increased use of the term *alliance* where more specific terms, such as *joint venture,* would previously have been used. The primary outlet for research on strategic alliances has clearly been *SMJ,* which accounts for 39% of all studies in

Table 2.2 Cleaned Findings of Articles on Alliances in Six Top Management Journals

	Prior to 1990	*1990–1994*	*1995–1999*	*2000–2004*	*Totals*
AMJ	0	4	13	10	27
AMR	3	1	3	4	11
ASQ	1	0	5	1	7
JM	0	0	1	13	14
OS	0	2	17	11	30
SMJ	4	10	16	28	58
Totals	8	17	55	67	147

these six journals. We suspect there are two primary reasons to explain this. First *SMJ* publishes more issues a year than any of the other journals included in the search and consequently publishes a large number of articles. Second *SMJ*, with *Strategic Organization*, is the only specialized high-quality outlet for strategic management research. Hence, the likelihood of finding work related to strategic alliances is higher in this journal. In all other journals investigated here, strategy-related work has to compete with work from other branches of management and organization studies.

In *ASQ* there is a particularly low number of hits. *ASQ* does not publish as many articles a year as some of the other journals and is perhaps less focused on issues of performance. It is also worth noting that a fairly high proportion of articles on strategic alliances have been published through special issues rather than through regular channels, a further recognition of the increasing academic status of the phenomenon.

Analysis of Abstracts

Our basis for further analysis was the abstract provided with the papers. Although it would have been preferable to read the entire set of 147 papers, this was not possible due to time constraints. Abstracts generally provide a very good picture of the overall direction of the paper, especially in journals of good standing where fairly standardized procedures are in place. Below we will tackle one by one all the different categories we sketched above. Where categorizations are not immediately obvious, they will be created bottom-up by employing the same terms in use in the articles we analyze. The frequency of occurrence of a certain stage, type, and so on will be presented, as well as the frequency of nonoccurrence of an entire category (e.g., where no distinguishable alliance stage was mentioned). In all there were 12 articles that discussed alliances but from which not a single categorization could be obtained. Some of these articles, for instance, described the growth of the alliance phenomenon without providing any clear focus on any stage or conceptualization. The fact that these 12 articles amount to only 8% of the articles initially discovered, meaning that 92% did produce some information, provides further evidence that abstracts are a meaningful way of finding the data for which we are looking.

Stages

Table 2.3 summarizes the stages that were described in the articles. Most articles seemed to describe clearly one or multiple stages of the alliance decision-making process. For instance,

Table 2.3 The alliance literature by stage of the alliance decision-making process

Stage	*Number of hits*
1. Initial conditions	21
2. Opportunity recognition	5
3. Alliance objective	9
4. Alliance design	54
5. Alliance implementation	38
6. Alliance performance & consequences	56
Article not describing any clear stage	22

there were quite a few articles that discussed initial conditions (stage 1; Steensma, Marino, Weaver, & Dickson, 2000), and many that discussed the impact of alliance design (stage 4; Saxton, 1997). Implementation (stage 5; Zollo, Reuer, & Singh, 2002), and performance (stage 6) were also strongly represented. Few articles dealt with either opportunity recognition (stage 2) or setting of objectives (stage 3). Several possible explanations come to mind. Perhaps stages 2 and 3 are so straightforward that they merit little research. Perhaps opportunity recognition leads directly to setting of objectives, so there is just one stage rather than two. Perhaps the design is so crucial that it attracts attention away from other issues. We would like to suggest another explanation, though; namely, that opportunity recognition and setting of objectives are crucial aspects of the entrepreneurial process, and that research on alliances has not yet made proper use of this area of theory.

Type of Alliance

The term *alliance* includes a variety of arrangements between firms (Barringer & Harrison, 2000; Nooteboom, 1999). Whereas it initially referred mostly to joint ventures, it now also includes nonequity arrangements such as buyer-supplier agreements. In Table 2.4 we have specified the types of alliances we encountered during the literature search. The joint venture, as might be expected, is still the dominant alliance form, and mention of other forms is a fairly marginal phenomenon. What is more interesting, though, is that most authors do not seem to specify what type of alliance they are discussing. Rather, alliance seems to be an all-encompassing term. It is potentially worrying to see such a large literature discuss alliances in general terms while the underlying measurement unit may differ from one paper to another. This raises the question of how efficiently research knowledge is being accumulated in this area.

Objectives

As noted above, most of the literature does not seem to discuss objective setting as a separate stage. Where objectives are discussed, this is usually in terms of exploration versus exploitation of resources, a distinction first popularized

Table 2.4 The alliance literature by type of alliance

Type	*Number of hits*
Syndicate	2
Horizontal	3
Vertical	3
Buyer-supplier	1
Joint venture	16
Interlocking directorates	1
Consortia	1
Strategic groups	3
Venture capital partnership	1
Articles not describing any clear type	117

Table 2.5 The alliance literature by alliance purpose

Objective	*Number of hits*
Resource exploration	12
Resource exploitation	8
Link	2
Scale	2
Articles not describing any clear purpose	132

Table 2.6 The alliance literature by functional field

Functional field	*Number of hits*
Financial	2
Technological, R&D	15
Marketing	2
New product development	5
Articles not describing any functional field	126

by March (1991). Discussion of exploration tends to emphasize the recombination of resources, whereas discussion of exploitation emphasizes better use of existing skill sets in organizations. Most of this literature has learning in alliances as the central concern (see Table 2.5). There were also two articles that discussed alliances in terms of scale versus link alliances. Although there are similarities between this distinction and the distinction between exploration and exploitation, there is also a crucial difference. *Scale* refers to the alliance partners bringing together very similar resources, whereas *link* refers to combining essentially different skills. Theoretically, the scale-versus-link approach seems to be based on the resource-based view rather than the learning perspective.

Functional Area

A further classification of alliances is according to the functional area in which they are employed. Again the largest category is that of articles that do not describe any functional field (see Table 2.6). As we discussed earlier, more than anything this may be taken to indicate that authors do not think it matters much whether an alliance is in marketing or production. The main exception is the work on research and development (R&D) alliances (Hagedoorn & Schakenraad, 1994); studies of R&D tend to adopt a "resource exploration" stance by discussing the creation of innovations as a form of recombination of the technological skills of the alliance partners.

Theoretical Perspective

Our final category is the theoretical perspective. Unlike the earlier categories, we find quite a wide range of approaches in use (see Table 2.7). Although some 78 articles did not explicitly put forward any perspective, there were 21 different perspectives altogether. Arguably some of these might be combined, but even so, this is a fairly rich range of explanations for the alliance phenomenon. Overall, however, there appear to be three dominant perspectives—namely, transaction costs, network and embeddedness, and organizational learning—which together account for 51 hits. The large number of articles for which no theoretical perspective was found can probably be explained largely by the limitations of the method we used. Many authors simply do not state their theoretical perspective in the abstract, as we learned from inspection of a small number of articles.

There is a fairly strong link between the theoretical perspective chosen and the alliance stage or stages an article discusses. The transaction costs perspective appears mostly in the alliance design stage, where a governance structure is chosen, and sometimes extends into performance issues (Reuer & Ariño, 2002) under the header of "alignment," the premise being that misalignment causes a loss of performance. The network and embeddedness perspective is often concerned more with initial conditions and alliance design and discusses primarily how partner choice is affected by the existing social structures in which the firm operates (Gulati & Westphal, 1999; Uzzi, 1997). The organizational learning perspective, on the other hand, typically focuses on the objective-setting and implementation stages. Such articles often discuss the distinction between exploitation and exploration alliances and how interorganizational learning takes place within alliances (Barkema, Shenkar, Vermeulen, & Bell, 1997; Beckman, Haunschild, & Phillips, 2004). Both the learning and the network and embeddedness perspectives occasionally discuss performance implications. However, relatively few performance-oriented articles put forward a clear theoretical perspective.

There is also a link between the theoretical perspective chosen and the journal in which an article is published. Comparisons reveal that *SMJ* is a primary outlet for articles involving transaction costs and resource-based explanations. *ASQ* has published many articles on networks and embeddedness and, as such, demonstrates a greater concern with social structure. Articles using the organizational learning perspective are more widely dispersed but have appeared regularly in *OS*. The trust and familiarity theme (ranked 4th in Table 2.7) is also somewhat spread out, although a few of these articles have appeared in *AMJ* (Gulati, 1995). Tentatively, therefore, we can suggest that the disciplinary base of a journal influences the type of articles on alliances found in that journal. Because the core research question of strategic management is what influences competitive advantages, *SMJ* alliance articles draw substantially from theories that explain competitive advantage, such as the resource-based view, and from theories that explain the economic efficiency of decisions, such as transaction costs. *ASQ* articles, on the other hand, tend to display an interest in social structure, because *ASQ*'s early roots are in sociology. *OS*, being a core organization theory journal, features individual and organizational-level bridging concepts, such as learning.

Table 2.7 The alliance literature by theoretical perspective

Theoretical perspective	*Number of hits*
Inertia	1
Trust, familiarity	7
Ecological	1
Economic	1
Institutional	2
Transaction costs	18
Network, embeddedness	14
Resource dependence	3
Resource-based view	6
Organizational learning	19
Multiple or many	5
Game theory	1
Social dilemma	1
Social exchange	2
Control	1
Strategic choice	1
Stakeholder theory	1
Dialectics	1
Evolutionary economics	1
Structuration theory	1
Public goods	1
Articles not describing any theoretical perspective	78

More generally, it seems that the various literature streams are not well connected or, to put it more bluntly, largely ignore each other. We recognize that a full cross-citation analysis would be needed to assess whether this actually holds true. But this kind of unconnectedness, if it exists, can seriously harm the accumulation of knowledge across the field. Because our previous analysis suggested that the different theoretical perspectives deal on the whole with different stages of alliance decision making and are therefore more complementary than competitive, this unconnectedness is also an unnecessary source of harm. In fact, we would like to suggest it is possible to combine at least some of the theoretical perspectives into a single model. Our purpose will be to provide some stepping stones for such a model.

Implications for Theory

The preceding review suggests that the study of alliances has lost rather than gained cohesion since the survey edited by Contractor and Lorange (1988). In particular, the sharp distinction previously drawn between joint ventures, on the one hand, and nonequity alliances such as licensing and subcontracting, on the other, has become blurred. The main justification for blurring such a distinction would be that a general theory had emerged that showed that at some deep conceptual level these different forms of alliance were all fundamentally the same. But no such principles have come to light. Although general theoretical approaches, such as transactions costs, the resource-based view, and organizational learning, all explain why alliances in general can be beneficial, they do not establish that they are all fundamentally the same.

In searching for general principles, the first step is to define the boundaries of the field. In order to encompass all of the articles reviewed above, a very broad definition of alliance must be used. A suitable example would be,

> A strategic alliance is a long-term agreement between two or more firms relating to the use of their resources. It does not consist merely of a spot market transaction, and neither does it involve the complete merger of the firms.

It is evident that this is a very nebulous definition: it is clear about what an alliance is *not,* but not about what it actually is. It captures Hennart's (1993) notion of a "swollen middle": a long spectrum of intermediate contractual arrangements laid out between two well-understood limiting cases. From this perspective, "alliance" is little more than a label to disguise our ignorance about the economic rationale for the intermediate forms—a terminological fig leaf designed to preserve professional modesty.

To achieve a more workable definition of "alliance," we believe it is important to introduce two distinctions. The first is between *activity-based alliances and project-based alliances.* Although this distinction is not new (Hickson & Pugh, 1995), it has not been systematically applied to the study of alliances. An *activity* is something that can be repeated indefinitely; although it has a start time, it does not necessarily have a finishing time. Many activities have been in progress for a long time, and their operations are therefore well understood. Although they may be exposed to volatility, there is plenty of experience available to optimize responses. These responses are embedded in routines. Despite volatility, therefore, many routine activities spend much of their time operating in a steady state.

By contrast, a *project* is an activity that is limited in time; it has a start date and a finishing date. Projects generally involve investments. The first part of the project involves a commitment of resources, which is costly; the revenues are generated later, once the setup phase is complete. The timing gap between costs and revenues creates a need for finance.

Projects can be very risky. Setup costs are normally sunk; they cannot be recovered if the project fails. Even if a project fails, however, it does not mean that it should never have been undertaken in the first place. Given what was known at the time it was undertaken, it might have been a reasonable prospect, and a firm that undertook many such projects might, on average, turn out to be very profitable.

Most projects are "one-offs." Because they differ from previous projects, their risks are more difficult to manage. Although lessons learned on previous projects may be relevant, judgment is required to apply them because the circumstances are different in every case. Shocks of an unprecedented type are more likely with projects than with activities. They therefore require greater powers of improvisation to manage them successfully.

A focus on projects helps to explain why many alliances are relatively short-lived. It is in the nature of a project to be short-lived. This accords with the view that the termination of an alliance is not necessarily a sign of failure; a short-lived project may simply be a project that—unusually—was completed on time. Of course, in many instances projects eventually become activities when they are better understood and more routinized.

The contrast should not be exaggerated, however. Some activities may be regarded as a sequence of projects. Nevertheless, an activity that is comprised of a sequence of projects will differ qualitatively from an activity that is not. R&D activity, for example, is comprised of a succession of research projects, but because every project is different, R&D differs fundamentally from mass production, in which every successive item of output is the same.

On the upside, successful projects can generate significant spillovers. Because every project is different, each project adds to the variety of experience accumulated by the firm. Learning may suggest new opportunities and therefore lead to spin-off projects. Thus, projects have "option value" (Reuer, 2000). The breadth of learning acquired from a succession of novel projects is fundamentally different from the narrow learning derived from the continuous repetition of a single activity, as discussed earlier in reference to the exploration-exploitation distinction.

The principles of managing routine activities have been extensively studied in mainstream management and economics literatures, and we believe that the study of alliances is unlikely to contribute much that is new to such a mature field. We therefore suggest that a theory of alliances should focus on project-based alliances rather than activity-based alliances, because it is project-based alliances that are most difficult to analyze using traditional techniques.

The second distinction important to our definition is between *contractual* and *cooperative* alliances. In this context, a *contractual alliance* is based on a legally binding agreement to provide a measurable supply of resources to a partner according to a specified time schedule in return for specified payment (in either cash or kind). A pure licensing agreement exemplifies a contractual alliance. It is little more than a pure sale; the licensor leases the right to use a technology it has patented to a licensee in return for a fixed schedule of fees related to observable outputs. It is no different from a tenancy on a building, except for the facts that the asset is intangible and that the tenant pays according to how much it uses the building. Similarly, a franchise, such as a car dealership, is little more than a long-term distribution contract with a small amount of training provided.

A *cooperative alliance*, by contrast, involves a reciprocal commitment to make available resources whose benefits can be shared between the partners. The quantity of resources may be difficult to measure, and the assessment of benefits may be inherently subjective. As a result, the agreement, even if it takes a legal form, will be difficult to enforce in law. The legal sanction is really just a threat that each party holds to make life difficult for the other party if it thinks it has been cheated.

Unlike the contractual alliance, it is difficult to know when a cooperative alliance has been completed. A cooperative alliance is usually open-ended; it remains in force as long as both parties believe that they will continue to benefit from it. If one party loses confidence in the alliance, that party can effectively kill off the alliance by reducing the quality (if not the quantity) of the resources it contributes, therefore making the alliance of no further value to the other party either.

It is fairly clear that a contractual alliance may well be adequate to coordinate an activity, but that a cooperative alliance is likely to be required to coordinate a project. This leads to the hypothesis that *project-based alliances will be coordinated by cooperative modes, whereas activity-based alliances will be coordinated by contractual modes.*

Because activities are better understood than projects and contracts are better understood than cooperation, we suggest that future research on alliances should concentrate on the coordination of project-based activities using cooperative modes. As with the distinction between projects and activities, we understand that contractual and cooperative alliances are ideal types and that actual alliances can switch between these types. A buyer-supplier relation that is initially strictly contractual in nature, for instance, can at a later stage encompass joint development activities for the next product generation that are not governed by a well-specified contract. At the start of production the alliance could again revert to a more contractual mode. Contracts and cooperation act as complements, and the choice between them is sometimes based on availability of one or the other (Rosenkopf, Metiu, & George, 2001).

Although many contractual alliances take a nonequity form, and many cooperative alliances are equity-based, the contractual/cooperative categorization is distinct from the nonequity/equity categorization. A firm that takes a minority equity stake in another firm for purely speculative purposes and with no attempt to intervene in management is essentially pursuing a contractual approach even though equity is involved, whereas a firm that relies on informal, open-ended procurement contracts is pursuing a cooperative approach even though no equity is involved.

An Entrepreneurial Theory of Cooperative Strategic Alliances

We conclude this chapter by outlining an entrepreneurial theory of cooperative strategic alliances. We claim that although it is impossible to generalize effectively about alliances as broadly defined, it is possible to generalize about them when they are defined in a specific way. For this purpose, we define a cooperative strategic alliance as *an open-ended agreement between two or more independent firms to make complementary investments in a project or set of projects and to share the benefits.* We are particularly interested in the question of how the equity contributions of the two partners are determined in such alliances (Tokuda, 2004).

To avoid any possible ambiguities, we examine in detail the meaning of the key terms used in this definition:

- The *strategic* element of the alliance resides in the fact that a project is being undertaken, *investments* are made, and sunk costs are incurred.

- The investments are *complementary*—the value of any single investment is increased by the fact that the other investment is also carried out. This is because each investment generates positive *spillovers* that increase the productivity of the other. The firms do not sell these benefits to each other. They determine at the time of making their agreement how much each should contribute, but thereafter they *share* the benefits with each other.

- The agreement is *open-ended* in the sense that it does not simply involve one party delivering a fully specified product to the other in return for some fully specified payment to be completed by a specified date. In other words, the agreement is not simply a spot or forward contract. It continues for as long as both parties consider that it is in their interests to sustain it.

- The firms are *independent* in the sense that participation in the alliance does not remove all their own freedom of action; it is not a complete merger of the firms. Although the firms may consult and cooperate on issues relating to the alliance, they may act independently in other spheres. Indeed, it is quite possible that although they cooperate through the alliance, they may compete in other areas.

• The success of an alliance depends on both parties honoring their obligations. In some cases, however, it may pay one party to seek short-term advantage by not investing as planned and thereby placing the other party in a difficult situation. This indicates that *trust* is an important issue in strategic alliances.

• Trust can be managed in several ways: by selecting the right partner, by embedding the alliance in a wider network of mutual obligation, and by establishing a monitoring system to ensure that compliance takes place. This shows that *partner selection, social embedding,* and *monitoring systems* are all important determinants of alliance performance. Our review of journals confirmed that these are recurring themes in the literature on alliances.

• The open-ended nature of an alliance means that the implementation of the alliance is likely to involve *continuous communication* between the two parties, a necessary prerequisite to maintaining trust (Young-Ybarra & Wiersema, 1999). This creates an incentive to establish a management structure specialized for the alliance. Each partner may appoint a liaison person, or project manager, to oversee the project jointly. This may be formalized into a *management board.* In some cases the project may also have a ring-fenced budget to which both parties contribute. This may be formalized by turning the project into a *joint venture* with its own corporate identity.

Entrepreneurial Projects

Opportunities for new projects are typically recognized by entrepreneurs. An entrepreneur has been defined as someone who specializes in taking judgmental decisions (Casson, 1982). A key feature of judgmental decisions is that different people placed in the same situation would take different decisions. This applies particularly to complex decisions that need to be taken quickly in an unprecedented situation. Senior managers in large firms qualify as entrepreneurs because they are responsible for deciding about large investments made in volatile and competitive conditions. They are specialists because they take decisions on behalf of other people; they are delegated by shareholders to invest their funds in the best possible way.

It is obvious that the quality of entrepreneurship required to identify new projects in international business is very high. The entrepreneurial manager has to synthesize information from sources distributed around the world. The quality of entrepreneurship is much higher than that needed by a small-firm founder to spot an opportunity for self-employment in his or her local economy. Given that the quality required is high, the talent is very scarce. Managers with entrepreneurial qualities who work for multinational enterprises therefore command high salaries because their skills are much in demand by rival firms.

A firm that employs expensive entrepreneurial managers to identify new international business opportunities needs to appropriate profit from these opportunities. In a market economy, ownership is the device most commonly used to appropriate profit from entrepreneurial skills. To implement a project, the entrepreneur must acquire control of the resources that are needed to implement the project. He or she increases the value of these resources by putting them to a better use than before.

In some cases an entrepreneur may discover that the firm that employs him already owns all the resources needed to exploit the project opportunity. In this case there is no need for an alliance. The project is implemented by an internal reallocation of resources; mature or unprofitable projects are closed down, and the resources are transferred to the new project by placing them under the entrepreneur's control.

In other cases the entrepreneur may discover that although his firm does not have all the resources that it needs, the missing resources can be acquired readily in spot markets. Provided that the firm requires only a small proportion of the total resources available in the market, the entrepreneur's procurement effort is unlikely to force the price up to a prohibitive level. Once again, therefore, there is no need for an alliance.

In other cases, however, the entrepreneur may find that there is an obstacle to buying up the resources through a spot market. For example, the supply of the resources may be monopolized, and the monopolist, when approached, may correctly infer the use to which the resources are to be put. He may then offer to supply the resources to a joint venture but refuse to sell them outright; the joint venture becomes the mechanism by which the monopolist attempts to extract a significant share of the rent for himself. As the firm becomes active in more and in more complicated markets, as multinational enterprises inherently tend to do, the number of instances in which such joint ventures are needed will increase exponentially.

Another possibility is that the firm does not know where the resources it requires are to be found. It needs a broker or middleman to access them. The broker, recognizing the entrepreneur's dependence on his expertise, may stipulate that he will retain a share of the ownership of the resources that he has supplied. Once again, therefore, a partner with market power may stipulate a share of ownership.

In other cases the firm may realize right away that it is not the only firm to have recognized the opportunity. Smart entrepreneurs are working for other firms as well, and as a result, another firm may have discovered the same opportunity. If the two firms compete, they will dissipate the rents. Competition to procure inputs will force up input prices (if supplies are price-inelastic), whereas competition for customers will force down output prices (if demand is price-inelastic). As a result, the profit margin will be squeezed. The rents will accrue to suppliers in terms of higher supply prices and to customers in terms of lower product prices, instead of to the firms themselves.

An obvious solution is for the firms to join forces. They need to collude—to establish an informal cartel through which they agree not to compete in either input and output markets. Collusive arrangements are notoriously unstable, however; each party has a major incentive to cheat in order to take market share away from the other firm. Collusive agreements cannot be enforced through the courts because they are usually illegal, because they contravene competition policy or antitrust policy. A merger of the two firms is a possible solution, but, for reasons already discussed, to merge two entire firms for the sole purpose of colluding on a single project is normally prohibitively costly. A joint venture is, therefore, a suitable solution.

Equity Shares

An entrepreneurial approach, therefore, suggests that most cooperative alliances will take the form of joint ventures. Some of the literature that we have reviewed implicitly assumes that this is the case. But the evidence suggests that not all cooperative alliances involve joint ventures. Another feature of the evidence is that a disproportionate number of alliances involve 50:50 equity shares. This suggests that a crucial test of a theory of alliances is whether it can explain equity shares. In this context, a nonequity alliance can be interpreted simply as an alliance in which one party takes all the equity—that is, it involves asymmetric 100:0 equity shares. An entrepreneurial theory is, in fact, well adapted to address this issue.

The Initial Distribution of Information. If one entrepreneur has discovered the opportunity before anyone else, then he or she is more likely to hold a dominant equity share. Because the entrepreneur believes that the resources have greater value than that perceived by other people, he or she therefore wishes to own as high a proportion of these resources as possible. Conversely, if two entrepreneurs have discovered the same opportunity at the same time, then each will wish to hold majority ownership, but each will also understand that the other party has the same aim. Recognizing that their requirements are incompatible, they must compromise. Compromises often converge on 50:50 as a "focal point." Hence, exclusive discovery favors a nonequity alliance in which the discoverer retains all the equity for him- or herself, whereas simultaneous discovery favors the 50:50 joint venture instead.

Secrecy. An entrepreneur who is the first to discover an opportunity has a limited time in which to make agreements before others recognize the same opportunities. Some opportunities are easy to disguise from other entrepreneurs, but others are not. For example, an entrepreneur who is looking for a distributor for a new product may not need to fully disclose the nature of the product in order to explain the distribution requirements, whereas an entrepreneur who wishes to commission R&D will have to disclose much more. The more difficult it is to find a partner without significant disclosure, the easier it is to for the entrepreneur who has discovered the opportunity to retain 100% ownership. Conversely, the harder it is to prevent disclosure, the more likely is the outcome to be a 50:50 joint venture instead.

Relative Optimism. Although two entrepreneurs may have discovered the same opportunity, one may be very much more optimistic than the other. It pays the more optimistic entrepreneur to buy the other out. Conversely, it pays the more pessimistic entrepreneur to accept insurance from the other. Hence, the most optimistic entrepreneur will stipulate for equity, whereas the pessimistic entrepreneur will prefer to supply services for cash, and hence the more divergent the expectations of the parties, the more unequal the equity stakes are likely to be.

Size and Liquidity of Firm. Projects are risky, as already noted, and large projects therefore involve large risks. In addition, some types, such as R&D projects, are inherently more risky than others. Some projects have particularly large downside risks—for example, environmentally sensitive resource-based projects, where firms could face huge compensation claims. The failure of a large project could therefore bring down a participating firm; there is a potential negative externality between projects within the firm, because one failure could bankrupt the entire business. Taking a share of a big project may pose more of a threat to a small firm than to a large one, because the project would represent a higher share of the total asset base. Similarly, a firm that is illiquid because of financial commitments to other projects is in greater danger than a firm whose other projects are "cash cows." Hence, larger or more liquid firms are likely to take a larger share of the equity than smaller or less liquid firms. Conversely, if the two firms are of roughly equal size and liquidity, they are likely to share the risks equally because this is the best possible way of spreading the risks between them.

Reputation. Large multinationals trade very much on their reputation; this is important not just for developing the brand but for retaining investor confidence too. We noted earlier the view that "alliances are for wimps." If a firm believes that its participation in an alliance could be construed as an admission of its weakness because of its need to find a partner to supply a missing resource, then it will be keen not to exaggerate this negative perception by being seen to be a minority partner. This is particularly true if investors believe in the theoretical principles set out above, which suggest that the most entrepreneurial firms with the deepest pockets tend to take the largest equity shares. In this case, the equity share becomes a "signal" of the hidden capabilities of the firm. Firms with large reputations are therefore most likely to take large shares. In dealings between large firms of comparable size, the 50:50 solution is likely to prevail because neither partner feels that it can afford to be seen taking the smaller share. The main exception relates to firms that feel no pressure to defend their reputation. One such class of firm is the family-owned firm, where investor confidence is not such a major issue. Another case is where the logic of the alliance does not involve an admission of a weakness—for example, where a large firm is acquiring a long-term "growth option" in a small high-technology firm.

Table 2.8 List of factors influencing relative equity stakes

Factor	*50:50 Joint venture*	*Nonequity alliance*
Simultaneity of discovery	Simultaneous (no firm has temporary monopoly)	Sequential discovery (one firm has temporary monopoly)
Secrecy	Difficult to exclude partner from secret	Easy to exclude partner from secret
Differential optimism	No differential	Equity owner is much more optimistic
Differential size of firm	No differential	Equity owner is larger
Differential liquidity	No differential	Equity owner is more liquid
Differential in value of firm's reputation	No differential	Equity owner is more reputable
Ease of valuation of resources offered: knowledge-intensity	Equal knowledge-intensity	Equity owner is more knowledge-intensive
Ease of valuation of resources offered: tacitness of knowledge	Equal tacitness	Equity owner contributes more tacit knowledge
Differential management expertise	No differential	Equity owner is more expert and takes responsibility for project management
Defective property rights	No differential	Equity owner is most exposed to risk from defective property rights

Valuation of Resources. Some resources are easier to value than others. Hence, a warehouse building is easier to value than a brand, whereas a brand is easier to value than a new technology still under development. If entrepreneur A can more easily value his partner B's contribution than B can value A's, then A is likely to take the dominant equity stake. This is because B requires insurance from A regarding the value of A's contribution, whereas A is willing to comply by paying in advance for B's contribution. Hence, if the two partners are contributing different types of resources, it is likely that the equity stakes will be different. If one of the resources is much less tangible than the others, for example, and the intangible resource is more difficult to value, then the supplier of the intangible resource is likely to acquire the dominant equity stake. Knowledge is, of course, a significant intangible resource where alliances are concerned, and it is often difficult to value, as indicated above. The theory therefore suggests that the partner who makes the most knowledge-intensive contribution is likely to acquire the largest equity stake. The resource-based view emphasizes the tacit nature of information. Other things being equal, the more tacit the information, the more difficult it is for others to value it. The value of a relational network allowing access into markets closed to outsiders, for instance, is very hard to determine. Where both partners supply knowledge, therefore, it is likely to be the partner who supplies the most tacit knowledge who takes the largest stake. Some entrepreneurs appear to be better at valuing resources than others. They specialize in acquiring ownership of undervalued resources and selling them off later at a profit; an entrepreneur who believes that he has a special skill in valuing resources is likely to take a dominant equity stake.

Management Expertise. This leads to the possibility that the partner firms differ in their management expertise. If the project on which they are collaborating is complex and sophisticated, then it is likely to benefit from expert project management. One of the partners may be better equipped to supply the project management than the other, perhaps because it is more experienced in the field. But this firm then needs to be "incentivized" to select its best manager and supervise this manager well. The greater its equity stake, the more "high-powered" this incentive becomes. Hence, the firm with the best managers is likely to supply the manager for the project and take the largest equity stake. In some cases this may be the older firm. In the case where one partner is already well established in the field whereas the other is a recent entrant diversifying into the field, the established firm, being the most experienced, is likely to take on the management of the joint venture and hold the larger equity stake.

Imperfect Property Rights. In classic internalization theory, the weakness of property rights in technology and other firm-specific assets encourages firms to transfer their technology using 100% equity control. A natural generalization of this result is that where two firms contribute resources to an alliance, the firm whose property rights are least secure will take a majority equity stake because this gives it greater power to protect its asset. We mention this factor last because it is already well known and derives from the theory of transaction costs rather than from the theory of entrepreneurship.

The results of this analysis are summarized in Table 2.8. The first column lists the factors that influence relative equity stake. The second column identifies the conditions that favor a 50:50 joint venture, and the final column identifies the conditions that favor a nonequity alliance in which one of the partners takes 100% control of the project.

Project Characteristics

The factors identified in Table 2.8 are mainly (though not exclusively) firm-specific. Other factors also influence equity stakes, two of which merit particular attention. They are both concerned with the nature of the project.

The first concerns whether the project involves investment in *stand-alone new capacity.* For example, an R&D alliance could involve the establishment of a new research facility with the most modern equipment or collaboration between existing facilities. Similarly, an arrangement for the distribution of a product in a foreign market could involve the construction of a new warehouse or the use of an existing warehouse owned by a local partner firm. It is obvious that a joint venture is a more natural mode where a new facility is created than where existing facilities are used. Assuming that existing facilities are initially wholly owned, the establishment of a joint venture requires that one of the partners must sell out a share to the other; in other words, a partial divestment is involved. In the case of market entry, the local firm must sell a share of its warehouse to the foreign investor. In the case of R&D collaboration, each firm will typically acquire a stake in the other's facility; simultaneous cross-investment and cross-divestment will occur, with the second being used to finance the first. The transaction costs incurred in such divestments may be quite high. This suggests that equity alliances will be most common where investment in stand-alone new capacity is involved. Conversely, nonequity alliances will be most common where no new stand-alone investment occurs.

The second project characteristic is whether a *horizontal* or *vertical* linkage is involved. Theory

Table 2.9 Principal motives for either creating new capacity or rationalizing existing capacity in order to facilitate horizontal or vertical linkages, with their implications for equity stakes

	Horizontal	*Vertical*
New capacity	Exploit economies of scale: share fixed costs of new facility *50:50 joint venture likely*	Enter new market or industry from an adjacent stage in the supply chain *Minority equity stake likely*
Existing capacity	Specialization agreement to improve use of capacity, or Collusion to increase market power, or Share public good (e.g. knowledge) or Implement benchmarking *Nonequity alliance likely*	Improve coordination between stages in existing supply chain *Non-equity alliance likely*

suggests that a horizontal linkage is more likely to lead to a 50:50 equity joint venture, because both partners are contributing similar types of resource. The two contributions are therefore likely to be equally difficult to value and to suffer equally from problems relating to property rights. In addition, where both firms are contributing the same type of resource, investors are likely to regard the equity stake as a signal of the relative quality of the resources contributed by the firms, and so both firms will defend their reputations by refusing to accept a minority stake. In the example above, therefore, a horizontal alliance such as R&D collaboration is more likely to lead to a 50:50 joint venture than a vertical alliance such as the distribution arrangement.

Combining these two results suggests that a horizontal alliance involving new investment is far more likely to generate a 50:50 equity joint venture than is a vertical alliance involving the use of existing capacity. A systematic analysis of the interaction between these two project characteristics is presented in Table 2.9. The table examines the motives underlying four combinations of project characteristics and suggests the most likely outcome for equity stakes.

The principles set out above are presented as general principles that apply to all locations, all industries, and all functional areas. This does not mean, of course, that only firm characteristics and project characteristics determine relative equity stakes—quite the contrary. Industries characterized by economies of scale, for example, tend to be dominated by a small number of large firms, all of which have reputations to defend, whereas industries with only limited economies of scale have a larger number of firms with smaller reputations; industries without economies of scale are therefore more likely to develop alliances with unequal equity stakes. Growing industries encourage investments in new capacity, whereas declining industries encourage better use of existing capacity instead; hence growing industries are more likely to require collaboration in the management of new plants and thereby make use of equity joint ventures, whereas declining industries are more likely to have nonequity alliances instead. Because firm characteristics and project characteristics vary systematically across industries, there will be systematic differences between industries in the forms that alliances take. Firm and industry characteristics are therefore "intermediating variables" or "transmission mechanisms" through which industry effects impact upon alliance arrangements.

Other Issues

We have focused our discussion of theory on those topics where the entrepreneurial perspective has most to add. The perspective is useful in other areas too, however.

From a functional perspective, for example, R&D and marketing are both crucial issues for the entrepreneur. As Schumpeter (1934) emphasized, it is vital that R&D is guided by a realistic assessment of the commercial prospects for new products and processes; successful innovation is not a question of technological ingenuity or mere invention. Marketing is crucial because new products have to be designed in a user-friendly way. Entrepreneurs will therefore be particularly keen to hold equity stakes in R&D and marketing. Production, on the other hand, is more a question of routine management, particularly when the basic technology and the market are mature. This suggests that entrepreneurs will be more ready to subcontract production without an equity stake than they will be to outsource R&D or franchise marketing without an equity stake.

Entrepreneurship also affects partner selection. In a horizontal alliance, an entrepreneur will be seeking a partner of similar ability to his or her own but with a different range of personal contacts and a distinctive technological knowledge base. The entrepreneur requires complementary assets of high quality and therefore needs to form a "partnership of equals" with another entrepreneur. Because entrepreneurs are often competitive and aggressive, the relationship may not be an easy one. But a relationship imbued with conflict may be better than one without it, provided that the conflict can be managed, because lack of conflict may signal that one of the entrepreneurs does not have the personal drive that is required. In predicting the emergence of 50:50 equity joint ventures, therefore, the theory does not imply that the venture will necessarily go smoothly; it may thrive on conflict instead.

In a vertical alliance, on the other hand, the entrepreneur is not normally seeking resources similar to his or her own. A more docile and compliant personality may therefore be appropriate. In this case the entrepreneur may set up a nonequity alliance with a passive firm that takes no ownership in the project.

Conclusion

The analysis of alliances presented in top management journals was reviewed in the first part of this chapter. The literature contains a number of generalizations about factors that influence alliance behavior and performance. Because there are many different types of alliance, generalizing across such a heterogeneous set of arrangements is potentially dangerous. The empirical literature does not support the view that all alliances are fundamentally the same. Empirical research often involves studies of specific countries and industries, and when their results are compared, contextual variations appear significant. Alliances vary according to the characteristics of industries, partner firms, type of project, locations, and political regimes; furthermore, they focus on different functional areas and may have either a horizontal or vertical configuration.

Building upon this review, the second half of this chapter attempts to identify the particular forms of alliance that have significant implications for theory, on the grounds that alliance theory should address distinctive issues that are not already fully considered elsewhere. We have argued that cooperative alliances for the coordination of projects should be the primary focus of future theoretical work on alliances. This does not mean that contractual arrangements such as licensing should not be studied from a theoretical point of view, but only that such arrangements are best interpreted as contracts rather than as alliances. In our view, a distinguishing feature of an alliance is that it is not a purely contractual form but must include some cooperative aspects as well.

Provided the concept of alliance is appropriately defined, generalization is possible. Rigorous generalization must be based on explicit assumptions. The key is to draw these assumptions from an appropriate theoretical tradition that addresses key issues head-on instead of (as so often happens) simply assuming them away. We have argued that the modern theory of entrepreneurship provides an appropriate framework with which to generalize about alliances. To support our case, we have shown how the theory of entrepreneurship can be used to develop hypotheses about equity shares in alliances. This analysis treats nonequity alliances as a special case of equity alliances in which one of the partners holds all the equity. A significant advantage of this particular approach is that theory not only predicts the equity shares but also predicts, according to both project and partner characteristics, which partner will hold what share.

The same theoretical tradition can be applied to other issues in the analysis of alliances, such as partner selection, but there is insufficient space to do full justice to these issues here. We hope, however, that our chapter will stimulate other researchers to develop this approach further and test its validity.

References

Barkema, H. G., Shenkar, O., Vermeulen, F., & Bell, J. H. J. (1997). Working abroad, working with others: How firms learn to operate international joint ventures. *Academy of Management Journal, 40,* 426–442.

Barney, J. B. (1999). How a firm's capabilities affect boundary decisions. *Sloan Management Review, 40,* 137–145.

Barringer, B. R., & Harrison, J. S. (2000). Walking a tightrope: Creating value through interorganizational relationships. *Journal of Management, 26,* 367–394.

Beckman, C. M., Haunschild, P. R., & Phillips, D. J. (2004). Friends or strangers? Firm-specific uncertainty, market uncertainty, and network partner selection. *Organization Science, 15,* 259–275.

Brandenburger, A. M., & Nalebuff, B. J. (1996). *Co-opetition.* New York: Doubleday.

Buckley, P. J. (1985). New forms of international industrial cooperation. In P. J. Buckley & M. C. Casson (Eds.), *Economic theory of the multinational enterprise* (chap. 3). London: Macmillan.

Buckley, P. J., & Casson, M. C. (1976). *The future of the multinational enterprise.* London: Macmillan.

Casson, M. (1979). *Alternatives to the multinational enterprise.* London: Macmillan.

Casson, M. (1982). *The entrepreneur: An economic theory.* Oxford: Martin Robertson.

Casson, M. (1985). Multinational monopolies and international cartels. In P. J. Buckley & M. C. Casson (Eds.), *Economic theory of the multinational enterprise* (chap. 4). London: Macmillan.

Contractor, F. J., & Lorange, P. (1988). *Cooperative strategies in international business.* Lexington, MA: Lexington Books.

Doz, Y., & Hamel, G. (1998). *Alliance advantage: The art of creating value through partnering.* Boston: Harvard Business School Press.

Dyer, J. H., & Singh, H. (1998). The relational view: Cooperative strategy and sources of interorganizational competitive advantage. *Academy of Management Review, 23,* 660–679.

Gulati, R. (1995). Does familiarity breed trust? The implications of repeated ties for contractual choice in alliances. *Academy of Management Journal, 38,* 85–112.

Gulati, R., & Westphal, J. D. (1999). Cooperative or controlling? The effects of CEO-board relations and the content of interlocks on the formation of joint ventures. *Administrative Science Quarterly, 44,* 473–506.

Hagedoorn, J., & Schakenraad, J. (1994). The effect of strategic technology alliances on company performance. *Strategic Management Journal, 15,* 291–309.

Hennart, J. F. (1993). Explaining the "swollen middle": Why most transactions are a mix of market and hierarchy. *Organization Science 4*(4), 529–547.

Hickson, D. J., & Pugh, D. S. (1995). *Management worldwide: The impact of societal culture on organizations around the globe.* London: Penguin.

Kale, P., Dyer, J. H., & Singh, H. (2002). Alliance capability, stock market response, and long-term alliance success: The role of the alliance function. *Strategic Management Journal, 23,* 747–767.

Kirzner, I. (1973). *Competition and entrepreneurship.* Chicago: University of Chicago Press.

March, J. G. (1991). Exploration and exploitation in organizational learning. *Organization Science, 2,* 71–87.

Nooteboom, B. (1999). *Inter-firm alliances: Analysis and design.* London: Routledge.

Oman, C. (1980). *Research project on changing international investment strategies: The new forms of investment in developing countries.* Working Document No. 7. Paris: OECD Development Centre.

Osborn, R. N., & Hagedoorn, J. (1997). The institutionalization and evolutionary dynamics of interorganizational alliances and networks. *Academy of Management Journal, 40,* 261–278.

Porter, M. E. (1980). *Competitive advantage.* New York: Free Press.

Quinn, J. B. (1999). Strategic outsourcing: Leveraging knowledge capabilities. *Sloan Management Review, 40*(3), 9–21.

Reuer, J. J. (2000). Parent firms across international joint venture life cycle stages. *Journal of International Business Studies, 31,* 1–20.

Reuer, J. J., & Ariño, A. (2002). Contractual renegotiations in strategic alliances. *Journal of Management, 28,* 47–68.

Ring, P. S., & Van de Ven, A. H. (1994). Developmental processes of cooperative interorganizational relationships. *Academy of Management Review, 19,* 90–118.

Rosenkopf, L., Metiu, A., & George, V. P. (2001). From the bottom up? Technical committee activity and alliance formation. *Administrative Science Quarterly, 46,* 748–772.

Saxton, T. (1997). The effects of partner and relationship characteristics on alliance outcomes. *Academy of Management Journal, 40,* 443–461.

Schumpeter, J. A. (1934). *The theory of economic development* (R. Opie, trans.). Cambridge, MA: Harvard University Press.

Shenkar, O., & Jiatao, L. (1999). Knowledge search in international cooperative ventures. *Organization Science, 10,* 134–143.

Steensma, H. K., Marino, L., Weaver, K. M., & Dickson, P. H. (2000). The influence of national culture on the formation of technology alliances by entrepreneurial firms. *Academy of Management Journal, 43,* 951–973.

Tokuda, A. (2004). *Amending the resource-based view of strategic management from an entrepreneurial perspective.* Discussion Paper 04–018. Reading, UK: University of Reading, Centre for Institutional Performance.

Uzzi, B. (1997). Social structure and competition in interfirm networks: The paradox of embeddedness. *Administrative Science Quarterly, 42,* 35–67.

Young-Ybarra, C., & Wiersema, M. (1999). Strategic flexibility in information technology alliances: The influence of transaction cost economics and social exchange theory. *Organization Science, 10,* 439–459.

Zollo, M., Reuer, J. J., & Singh, H. (2002). Interorganizational routines and performance in strategic alliances. *Organization Science, 13,* 701–713.

3

How Alliances Reshape Competition

Benjamin Gomes-Casseres

Alliances are intended to help firms *cooperate* better and also to help them *compete* better. Are these two objectives always compatible? How are they balanced in alliance strategy? And, more broadly, how does the spread of alliances affect the dynamics of competition? These questions go to the heart of the role of alliances in the organization of industry—a subject that attracted some early research but that has been ignored of late in favor of studies on the internal workings of alliances. These studies have paid off handsomely, but precisely because of this, it is now time to redirect our attention back to the broader questions of how alliances reshape competition.

This chapter proposes a way to think about the interaction between alliances and competition. It begins by reviewing what the literature in industrial organization has had to say about this question. The short answer is "not much"; alliances were a late addition to the research agenda in industrial organization. More recently, alliances have been dealt with routinely in analyses of firm boundaries; this is forcing a new way of thinking about competition. I will argue that competition increasingly takes the form of groups of allied firms against other groups instead of the traditional battle of firm versus firm. This kind of competition is different from that assumed in standard models of industrial organization and of strategy. Understanding this new kind of competition requires us to broaden our unit of analysis and to consider explicitly the various ways in which competition and cooperation interact. (For related work and precursors to this paper, see Gomes-Casseres, 1996 and 2003.)

Comments on a Fragmented Literature

The study of alliances is rooted in the field of industrial organization (IO), much as is the case with the study of strategy and of the multinational enterprise. Our modern understanding of alliances draws on the theory of the firm, a late-developing branch in IO; empirical work on alliance formation and performance often echoes IO studies of firm behavior.

Black Boxes and Contrarians. The IO field was not always fertile ground for students of interfirm alliances. Traditionally, the field of industrial organization studied markets and firms, and nothing in between. In fact, even when it studied firms, it usually treated them as "black box" decision makers that maximize profit subject to external constraints.

One of the most widely used textbooks in the field explains that this is done to simplify the analysis and focus attention on market behavior (Tirole, 1988). The 1989 *Handbook of Industrial Organization* attempts to begin redressing this gap with four opening chapters on the theory of the firm, but even so, most of the rest of this two-volume work reflects the dominant approach in the field at the time (Schmalensee & Willig, 1989). Though I cannot claim to have read this handbook cover to cover, it appears that the only treatment of any form of alliance in this work is a four-page discussion of joint ventures as mechanisms for collusion (pp. 437–441).

Leading IO models of the firm typically assumed away the alliance phenomenon. The classic work by Williamson (1975) and the fundamental paper by Grossman and Hart (1986) explicitly model the choice facing the firm as integration and nonintegration, with no gray zone in between. This, again, is perhaps useful for the analysis at hand and certainly makes the math more tractable. But it did not help those scholars who were puzzled by the empirical evidence that alliances were widespread in business.

As a result, the first IO-oriented papers on alliances have a distinct "contrarian" feel to them. Here is Richardson's plea in 1972:

> I hope to show that the excluded phenomena [various forms of interfirm cooperation and affiliation] are of importance and that by looking at industrial reality in terms of a sharp dichotomy between the firm and market we obtain a distorted view of how the system works.

His paper then makes the argument, still very much alive in the literature today, that alliances are ways for firms with dissimilar capabilities to coordinate production of complementary goods. Richardson's logic and observations notwithstanding, Mariti and Smiley (1983) ten years later still complained that "cooperative agreements have received almost no attention in the academic literature."

This last statement was not altogether true; or rather, it applied only to the academic literature in mainstream IO and microeconomics. Scholars in the field of international business had long since discovered alliances and joint ventures, though their approach was more empirical and eclectic. Stopford and Wells (1972) had the advantage of massive data on the foreign subsidiaries of multinational enterprises, where it could be readily seen that roughly one third of the ventures were jointly owned. They had no data on contractual alliances, but it was clear from the start that most of these joint ventures were not fully controlled by either partner. Their explanation was that the firms sought a delicate balance between a "need for resources" and a "need for control." In a way, this fundamental argument foretold today's seemingly unending debate about what best explains alliances: transaction cost theory (control) or the resource-based view (resources); the answer, clearly, is "both." Scholars in this international business tradition later developed comprehensive approaches to alliances, such as Hennart (1989), Kogut (1988), and others.

Catching up With Reality. By the 1990s, mainstream IO and microeconomics had also begun to "discover" alliances. The theory of the firm branched out to become a field by itself—that of organizational economics. Modern scholars in this field are concerned with transaction costs, contracts, principal-agent relationships, incentives, information, and many other aspects of firm organization. These concepts are equally relevant to the study of alliances, as the work in this volume shows. In their 1998 "revisit" of the boundaries of the firm, Holmstrom and

Roberts proclaim that "investment incentives are not provided by ownership alone" and discuss evidence from Japanese subcontracting, exclusive sourcing, airline alliances, and contractual networks. Shortly thereafter, Baker, Gibbons, and Murphy (2002) provided new impetus for an ongoing stream of theoretical work on alliances as relational contracts. In addition, a stream of new econometric work is testing how alliances act as "intermediate" forms of governance between arm's-length contracts and full integration (e.g., Gomes-Casseres, Jaffe, & Hagedoorn, forthcoming).

This has brought us to a curious juncture. Industrial organization first assumed that firms were black boxes and developed an elaborate set of models around how these boxes behaved in the market. The black boxes are now being opened. Does this new knowledge of the internal workings of firms change our understanding of how firms behave in the market? It should. The histories of large firms and the study of the multinational enterprise have shown that structure can shape strategy, let alone performance. The research agenda here is clear: We must find ways to marry the internal and external workings of firms.

In this marriage of internal and external, alliances play an interesting role. Traditionally, the firm has been one of the standard units of analysis in IO.[1] As we use organizational economics to open this unit, we are also finding that the unit itself may be misleading—instead of firms operating in a market, we now see pairs or groups of allied firms operating in the market. And if the internal workings of a firm can be expected to influence the firm's behavior in the market, would this not be true also of the internal workings of the firm's alliances?

The problem is that while theory is catching up with the reality of how firms and alliances are organized, it is still way behind in explaining how alliances affect market dynamics. And reality is not standing still. In an increasing number of businesses, alliances between firms are transforming the nature of competition and of strategy. Take the case of airlines: Star, Oneworld, and Sky Team are "constellations" of allied firms that compete against each other. Each of these constellations is composed of individual firms, but the firms coordinate their actions when they compete together as a group. There are other contemporary examples in automobiles, telecoms, multimedia entertainment, and elsewhere.

To understand this new kind of industry structure—one where cooperation and competition are combined in complex ways—we need to step back to question our very framework of analysis. Is the firm, even though now an "open box," the right unit of analysis? And is firm-to-firm, oligopolistic competition the right context for this analysis? I will make the case below that the spread of alliances calls for changing both of these elements of the traditional approach to industrial organization.

From Firms to Constellations

The idea that the firm may not be an appropriate unit of analysis is not wholly new. Ronald Coase himself presaged it when he wrote in a footnote in his 1937 article that "it is impossible to draw a hard and fast line which determines whether there is a firm or not. There may be more or less direction" (Coase, 1937, fn. 1, p. 392). Edith Penrose (1995), writing in 1959, clearly recognized the problem of relying on the traditional definition of the firm, but she seemed at a loss as to how to deal with administrative influences that extended beyond firms:

> For an analysis of economic power there is no doubt that the industrial firm is not the most relevant unit; indeed individual men as well as corporations may extend their economic power by extending their ownership interests, [but] an attempt to define the firm according to power groupings would produce too amorphous a concept to handle. (p. 22)

As suggested by Penrose, we may expect that an allied pair or group of firms might behave differently in the market from how a single firm does. To be sure, organizational economists have already shown that there is no such thing as "a single firm"; in their approach, firms are collections of interests and actors held together through authority, ownership, norms, and contracts. In this sense, the difference between a firm and a collection of allied firms may be a matter of degree, not of kind. For example, a firm consisting of loosely controlled units may behave much like a collection of firms in an alliance group. But we do not know this if we do not study such questions; so far, too few researchers have done so.

To avoid confusion, two definitions are in order. An "alliance" is any governance structure to manage an incomplete contract between separate firms and in which each partner has limited control (Gomes-Casseres, 1996). These structures may be more or less formal—it is the degree of incompleteness that determines whether we are dealing with an alliance, not whether or not there is a stand-alone structure to govern the relationship. In fact, alliances may be structured as complex equity joint ventures or they may be looser arrangements for cooperating in research and development (R&D) or marketing or for managing supply and sales relationships. This definition of alliance is akin to that in a line of work by Baker et al. (2002), which stresses the relational nature of the contracts between the firms.

A "constellation" is a set of firms linked together through such alliances and that competes in a particular competitive domain, that is, in a particular business, market, or technology.[2] In this domain, the constellation may compete against other constellations or against single firms (Gomes-Casseres, 1996). It may be a formal structure (as in airlines) or a loose arrangement of companies accustomed to working together (e.g., Starkey, Barnatt, & Tempest, 2000). My definition of constellation, sometimes also referred to as an "alliance group" (Gomes-Casseres, 1994), is akin to that in Jones, Hesterly, Fladmoe-Lindquist, & Borgatti (1998) and is related to what others have called strategic blocks (Nohria & Garcia-Pont, 1992), strategic networks (Jarillo, 1988), webs (Hagel, 1996), and business groups (e.g., Khanna & Rivkin, 2001); for a review, see Gulati (1998). My definition of constellation is more restrictive than these related concepts and closer to the constellations of Lorenzoni and Ornati (1988), who appear to have been the first to use that term, and to those of Normann and Ramírez (1993).[3] Note that a constellation is not the whole network of relationships in an industry. Often, network analysis in alliance research has involved placing firms and alliances in an overall industry network and drawing inferences about a firm's position within that network. There are many studies of this type; an early and good one is by Walker, Kogut, and Shan (1997). This is a perfectly fine approach for what it seeks to answer. But it is not the same as studying the competing networks (plural!) within an industry, which is what I claim is needed. In the language of social network analysis, I am interested here in the identities and workings of the cliques within the network rather than the network as a whole.

Conceptually, a constellation is an alternative to the single firm as a way to govern a bundle of capabilities. Ever since Penrose (1995), the firm has been defined as an administrative mechanism to govern a bundle of capabilities. I agree with this view but turn the question around: Must every bundle of capabilities be governed by a firm? The answer clearly is no—firms, constellations of firms, and no doubt other mechanisms may also be used. This argument is consistent with the view of alliances as an intermediate form of organization between market and hierarchy (Powell, 1990). It also echoes the argument by Lorenzoni and Ornati (1988) that a constellation can be a phase in the growth of small firms or in the dissolution of large firms. Normann and Ramírez (1993) argue that a constellation is an alternative way to organize a value chain, in which links between firms need not follow linearly from up- to downstream firms. The difference, then, between a single firm and a constellation lies in the location of the key capabilities used in competition: in the single firm they are all controlled by one firm; in the constellation they are controlled by several firms that are legally independent from each other but allied with each other.[4] Does recognizing this new unit affect our analysis of industry structures and dynamics? If so, how does the internal design of a constellation affect how it competes? And how does the role of a firm *among* and *within* constellations influence the performance of this firm?

These have not been standard questions in any field of business or economics and indeed lie on the interfaces between several fields. We are only now learning about the market behavior of allied firms, about how value is created and appropriated in constellations, and about how constellations should be managed. But we still lack a framework to analyze this kind of competition; I present one here in the hope of encouraging further research.

From Traditional to Collective Competition

The critical issues in this research agenda revolve around the interplay between alliances and rivalry. Modern analysis suggests that the relationship between competition and cooperation is complex. The rules in the *Antitrust Guidelines for Collaborations Among Competitors* of the Federal Trade Commission and U.S. Department of Justice (2000) reflect this complexity. The document contains two types of rules applying to two separate classes of concerns. One set of concerns revolves around the type of agreement between erstwhile rivals; for example, some types of agreements are seen as more conducive to collusion than others. A second set of concerns focuses on the potential effect of an alliance on market concentration; in other words, even if the partners colluded within their alliance, they may not present a threat to competition if their combined market share is relatively small. In fact, in some situations, suppressing interpartner rivalry in this way may even enhance the competitiveness of an industry, as we shall see below. (See also Bresnahan & Salop, 1986, who attempt to construct a measure that combines these two sets of concerns.)[5]

Another way to say this is that an alliance will affect competition at two levels: *within* the alliance itself (i.e., between the partners) and *outside* the alliance (i.e., between the alliance pair and third parties). To clarify this distinction, consider the PowerPC alliance between Apple, IBM, and Motorola in the early 1990s. This alliance was intended to reduce operating-system rivalry between Apple and IBM as well as microprocessor rivalry between IBM and Motorola. But the U.S. Justice Department did not challenge this alliance, because in effect it aimed to create a stronger rival to the market leaders, Intel and Microsoft. At the level of the Apple-IBM-Motorola alliance, competition was suppressed; but at the level of the battle between PowerPC and Wintel, competition was enhanced.

These multiple levels of analysis have in fact given rise to two approaches in the literature regarding how cooperation and competition interact; here I will call them the "mixing" and "nesting" approaches.

"Mixing" Cooperation and Competition. The first approach describes what happens when competition and cooperation face each other head on. Traditionally, economics viewed the two forces as opposites—one reduces the other. As Adam Smith observed in 1776, "People of the same trade seldom meet together, even for merriment and diversion, but the conversation ends in a conspiracy against the public, or in some contrivance to raise prices." This view has been expanded and deepened over time; until recently, the dominant approach in economics still equated interfirm collaboration with collusion to increase market power (e.g., Baumol, 1992). A more balanced treatment, but still in this general tradition, is Stuckey's (1983) study of the world aluminum industry—a little-known but impressive study of how industry structure generated joint ventures, and how these joint ventures in turn affected firm behavior. In this study, vertical joint ventures are

generated by transaction costs in the supply chain but also generate collusive behavior.

A more recent strand in the "mixing" literature examines competitive tensions that may persist *within* an alliance. Rather than seeing alliances as suppressing competition, as in the collusion tradition, this approach sees the two forces as intertwined inside each alliance. An example of this approach is Hamel's (1991) "race to learn" hypothesis. This approach emphasizes that partners may continue to compete with each other in the market even while allied; even more strikingly, they may use their alliance as a way to acquire competitive capabilities from each other (Hamel, Doz, & Prahalad, 1989). Although the empirical evidence of such behavior in alliances is still thin, some good analytical models have been developed (e.g., Khanna, 1998).

A variant of this approach, formulated as a general model of strategy, is the "co-opetition" model of Brandenburger and Nalebuff (1996). The term *co-opetition* was invented by Silicon Valley entrepreneurs to describe a situation in which firms would cooperate on early R&D or on technology standards while still competing in end-product markets. In the Brandenburger-Nalebuff approach, co-opetition occurs at any interface between suppliers and buyers, or among what they call "complementors." As such, it is used to describe various types of cooperation and competition—from battles over shares in jointly created value to battles around mutual dependence between firms. They do not apply the concept directly to alliances and indeed spend little time on concrete governance of interfirm cooperation; but the potential for extending this approach to alliances is clear.

In all these approaches, the forces of competition and cooperation are not truly "mixed." They meet head-to-head, so to speak, and one outweighs the other or they remain in constant tension, like oil and water. Because of this tension, rivals seeking to cooperate are often advised to *separate* the two forces in their alliance structure (Bamford, Gomes-Casseres, & Robinson, 2003, chap. 6). The well-known history of Xerox and Fuji Xerox is a case in point. These two firms shared technology freely and coöperated on many fronts, but only because the competition between them was tightly circumscribed by territorial licensing contracts. "Good fences make good neighbors," was their motto. Another U.S.-Japanese joint venture failed to separate areas of cooperation and competition; in the Honeywell-Yamatake alliance, interpartner rivalry eventually eroded cooperation between the partners. (Gomes-Casseres, 1996, chaps. 1 and 2.)

The second approach to competition and cooperation does not rely on trying to merge the two forces. Instead, the forces coexist in undiminished form because they meet side by side at different levels in the structure of industry.

"Nesting" Cooperation in Competition. One of the puzzles of modern collaboration is that it generates new forms of rivalry. Often, alliances seem to intensify rather than reduce competition. Adam Smith himself provided a key insight that explains this puzzle: the idea of the division of labor. He argued that factories in which workers specialized in one or a few tasks could be more productive than those in which each worker performed every task. This idea is also at the core of many alliances; frequently, each partner in an alliance specializes in what it does best, thus making the pair more competitive than the members would be each by itself.

In this view, overall competition may be enhanced even when the cooperation within the alliance suppresses rivalry. The suppression of competition is nested inside an organizational unit (the constellation) that in turn competes with other units, perhaps more fiercely than if it did not suppress internal frictions. Separating cooperation and competition in this way can thus lead to the paradox observed in modern high-technology industries: rampant use of alliances combined with cutthroat competition.

I call this kind of rivalry "collective competition" because it refers to the economic behavior of competitors that consist of more than one firm. One way to think about this new type of

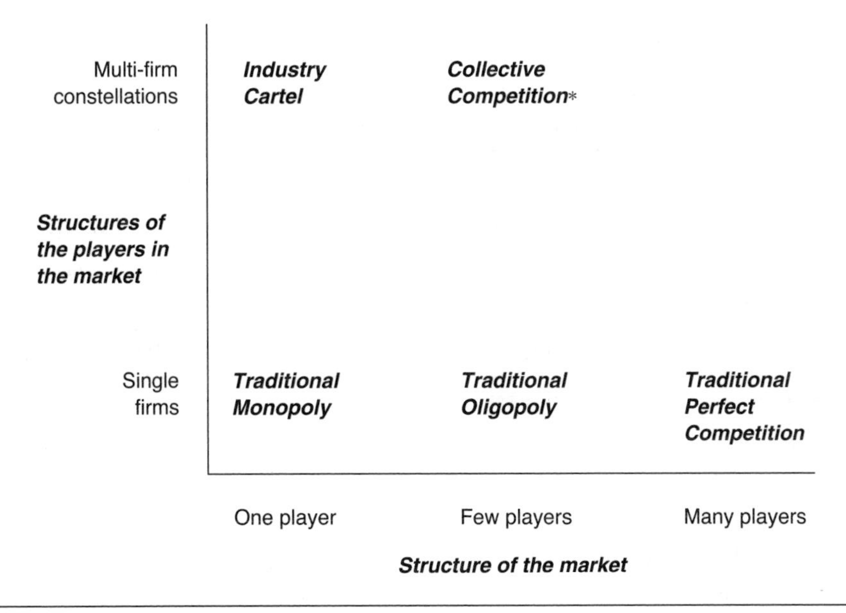

Figure 3.1 Types of Competition

(*) Note: Collective competition may also include single firms in the mix of players, as long as there are one or more constellations.

competition is by considering where it fits on the traditional market-structure continuum in classic IO models. Figure 3.1 is an admittedly oversimplified attempt to map this territory.

The horizontal axis in this figure indicates the *structure of the market;* the distinction between one, a few, or many competitors is a simplified scale reflecting traditional IO market structures. The vertical axis measures the *structures of the players* in the market, specifically, the number of firms in each economic unit. In the traditional approach, this number is always one, that is, each competitor is composed of one firm—in effect, this axis does not exist. I have argued, however, that competitive units come in varying shapes and sizes; firms are not black boxes, and competitors are not always single firms. Our mapping must take account of this fact.

Consider an obvious case of how the vertical dimension in Figure 3.1 matters. At the leftmost end of the horizontal spectrum, a multifirm group will attempt to operate as a single player—a cartel. But there is ample evidence that a cartel usually does not act like a true, single-firm monopolist, because of conflicts of interest among its members. A multifirm cartel is typically more fragile and can be torn apart by internal conflict. Even for the monopolist, therefore, internal structure is critical to its behavior in the market. This is all the more so for groups of firms that compete in oligopolistic markets.

In this two-dimensional figure, collective competition is a variant of oligopoly—it represents competition among "a few" constellations, perhaps also with single firms in the mix.[6] Just as in standard oligopoly, we can expect that the behavior and performance of one constellation is interdependent with those of its rivals. We can expect that constellations display oligopolistic rivalry. Similarly, we can think about strategy in analogous terms, with constellations developing competitive advantages and implementing strategic moves. What we need, then, is a way to think about competition in this context (Silverman & Baum, 2002).

Table 3.1 Differences between Traditional and Collective Competition

	Traditional Competition	*Collective Competition*
Competitive units	Firms	Constellations
Industry structure	Oligopoly of firms	Oligopoly of constellations
Source of competitive differentiation	Firm-based advantage	Group-based advantage
Valuable resources	Controlled by the firm	Assembled by constellation
Governance of resources	Corporate structure	Constellation structure
Source of profit	Rent in the value chain	Rent in the constellation

Even though this figure is useful for indicating the domain of collective competition, it is obviously an oversimplification of the world. In particular, each axis measures only one dimension of, respectively, market and competitor structure. Markets are more complex than that, and so are constellations. Still, it should be clear that collective competition is *akin* to oligopolistic competition but that it differs from it by the nature of the competitive units. As a result, the dynamics of this kind of competition will likely also differ from those of traditional competition, as we shall see next.

Dissecting Collective Competition. Traditional IO and strategy concepts are good starting points for analyzing collective competition, but they need to be amended and expanded. Table 3.1 shows how to translate the concepts of the traditional model to collective competition.

Some concepts from traditional competition have clear analogs in collective competition. In the traditional model, firms are competitive units in an oligopolistic industry. In collective competition, the competitive units are constellations, and industry structure can be conceived of as an oligopoly of constellations. Several studies have used this approach explicitly. Nohria and Garcia-Pont (1992) argued that automobile firms created strategic blocks that mimicked each other's capabilities, much as oligopolistic rivals do; I have described the strategic interaction among RISC microprocessor groups and PDA groups (Gomes-Casseres, 1996); and Suen (forthcoming) explored intergroup rivalry among airline constellations.

In a traditional oligopoly, firms rely on firm-based advantages for differentiation. In collective competition, constellations rely on group-based advantages to differentiate themselves from rivals. The resource-based view helps us think about both firm- and group-based advantages. In fact, there seems to be little in this view that requires capabilities to be controlled by firms—the chief unit of analysis is the bundle of capabilities; I have already noted that this bundle can also be controlled by a constellation. But structure does matter. In the traditional model, firms control resources through ownership and govern them through their corporate structures. A constellation assembles the resources of its members and governs these resources by the way the group is structured and managed.

This approach to defining the relevant units of competition is more relevant to some industries than to others. In some industries, such as in global airlines, major alliances are common, and it is clear that more or less formal constellations compete against others. In other industries, such as in computers, alliances may be looser, but competition is often between different standards or platforms (e.g., Katz & Shapiro, 1994).

The last element of this comparison of traditional and collective competition is the origin of a firm's profit. Simplifying again, the traditional model reasons that firms appropriate a share from the pool of rent in their value chain (Gadiesh & Gilbert, 1998; Saloner, Shepard, & Podolny, 2001). That pool of rent is influenced by industrywide pressures such as those in Porter's five-forces model. The firm earns a piece of this pool by exploiting its valuable resources or, in game-theory language, by bargaining for a share of the value-added that it brings to the pool (Brandenburger & Nalebuff, 1996).

In collective competition, the constellation becomes both a player and a mediator in the bargaining process. Given a pool of rent available in an industry segment, rivalry *among constellations* determines the rent that each group appropriates from the pool, and then bargaining *among the firms in each constellation* determines the share of the constellation's rent that each firm can appropriate for itself. This argument is analogous to the analysis of standards battles in Shapiro and Varian (1999). In sum, the model of collective competition proposed here is one of resources, control mechanisms, and bargaining power operating on at least two levels.[7]

Creation of Group Advantages. The group-based advantage of a constellation differentiates it from rival constellations and determines the share of the industry profits that it can earn. Analogous to the traditional model based on firms, group-based advantage stems from the relative value of the resources controlled by the constellation. Because constellations are groups of allied firms, the resources in the constellation are the sum of the resources contributed to the group by member firms. But these resources are not controlled as tightly as they would be inside a firm, because of the incomplete contracts (and possibly partial ownership) in the alliances that tie the member firms together. Just as in a single alliance, therefore, the potential of a constellation to create joint value is realized only by how well the constellation is structured and managed.

This idea can be illustrated with two cases already cited. The PowerPC alliance of Apple, IBM, and Motorola in fact ended in failure, in large measure because Apple and IBM could not suppress their deep-seated rivalry. In addition, the tripartite nature of the alliance did not make it easy to manage. In other words, on the face of it this group amassed a powerful set of resources that had the potential to threaten the Wintel dominance, but the alliance structure did not allow the partners to marshal these resources properly.

In the case of Xerox and Fuji Xerox, interpartner rivalry also cost the alliance in its battle against Canon in low-end laser printers, a field in which Canon could more efficiently execute a global strategy. This case shows that the advantages of constellations as compared to firms depend critically on the competitive domain. Whereas in laser printers the single firm won out over the alliance, in the traditional copier markets, where global economies of scale were less important, the geographic and technological flexibility enjoyed by the Xerox constellation was a benefit (Gomes-Casseres, 1996, chap. 1). The flexibility of alliances is also a benefit in domains with uncertainty and rapidly changing technologies.

The potential for group advantages hence depends on the industry context and on the nature of the task facing the partners. In their study of business groups ("confederations of legally independent firms") in developing countries, Khanna and Rivkin (2001) find that firms that are members of groups are more profitable than stand-alone firms. They attribute this to the underdeveloped institutional context of these markets, which tends to make market transactions less efficient than "hybrid" transactions inside groups. Chesbrough and Teece (1996) argue that the nature of innovation (systemic vs. autonomous) helps determine whether a "virtual" organization might be an effective competitive unit.

A few papers have measured the effect of group formation on firm performance. Chen and Chen (2003) find that load factors improve in alliances because partners with parallel (overlapping) routes are able to consolidate flights. In our language: Suppression of competition among allies allows the group to function more efficiently as a unit. Brueckner and Whalen (2000) also find that alliances in the airline industry tend to lower prices by about 25%, even if there is some evidence of collusion in markets where the allies formerly competed head-to-head. Again, collusion in overlapping markets within the alliance allows the airline constellations to offer more efficient service overall and hence lower prices in the rest of their networks.[8]

Because group design can affect market behavior of constellations, we can expect that some constellations may decide to modify their design in order to compete better in the market. Depending on the competitive pressures on a constellation, it may be forced to organize either more loosely or more tightly, for example. Airbus is a prime example—to compete better against Boeing, it reorganized itself into a tighter constellation. One obvious and important way for constellations to modify their design and their group advantage is by adding or dropping members. This kind of strategy is analogous to the "patching and restitching" of business portfolios analyzed by Eisenhardt and Brown (1999).

More generally, the competitive rivalry between partners in the market, or between partners and third parties, can either strengthen or weaken the bonds inside a constellation, as suggested by Kogut's (1989) early work on alliances and rivalry. Gimeno (forthcoming) examined the interaction between intragroup and intergroup competition in airline alliances. In his model, the degree of cospecialization among partners inside a constellation drives the extent of rivalry and exclusivity among constellations. In related work, Rowley, Greve, Rao, Baum, and Shipilov (2004) find that complementarity among partners inside a constellation tends to diminish exit. Suen (forthcoming) points out that this kind of interdependence among partners is sometimes inherent in the nature of the industry and technology but can also be created by the mutual commitments in alliance contracts. All in all, these studies show that there is an intimate link between the balance of cooperation and competition *within* constellations and *between* constellations.

Appropriation of Value by Members. Although constellations are created to generate group-based advantages, they must yield value to individual firms in order to attract and retain members. The game of competition may have changed, but we still keep score the old way. What determines the value that a firm can actually appropriate from participation in a constellation? Two strands of work on alliances and networks are relevant to this question. These different approaches are related to the debate in social network analysis between the roles of structural position and of identity (Nohria & Eccles, 1992).

Authors taking a structural approach have argued that the *position of the firm in a network* shapes its power over partners (e.g., Nohria & Garcia-Pont, 1991; Burt, 1992; Lorenzoni & Baden-Fuller, 1995). Rowley, Baum, Shipilov, Greve, and Rao (forthcoming) have conducted a comprehensive test of the relative effects on firm performance of (1) the group's structural position within the industry network; and (2) the firm's structural position inside the group. In their sample of Canadian investment banking firms, the latter matters more than the former. This suggests that the firms may have "matched" each other's alliances and so neutralized any advantage that one group might gain over the other. Comparable patterns have been observed in automobiles (Nohria & Garcia-Pont, 1991) and in semiconductors and personal digital assistants (Gomes-Casseres, 2005).

Others have emphasized that the *scarce resources added by each firm* shape its ability to extract profit from partners (cf. Pfeffer & Salancik, 1978; Brandenburger & Nalebuff, 1996; Ghemawat, 1999). A variant of this approach is that the scarce "resource" in question can be a structural one, such as the role of a firm in setting rules of the game (Baldwin & Clark, 1997) or in fulfilling a unique role in the workings of a constellation (Iansiti & Levien, 2004). Brandenburger and Nalebuff use game theory to make the valuable point that a firm can claim only as much value as it adds to a game. In other words, value creation and appropriation are intimately linked—firms that add great value to a constellation can also claim more value; firms that are marginally important in a constellation can claim little.

A few studies have explored the joint effect of group advantage and firm bargaining. Lazzarini (2003), for example, tried to untangle the effects of group advantages and member power in airline constellations. He finds that group organization seems to affect both sides of the coin but in different sets of circumstances. In formal, explicit constellations, the characteristics of the group seem to matter most to member firm performance; in informal, implicit constellations, firm characteristics seem to have a comparatively greater effect. Further evidence of how value creation and appropriation are intertwined comes from Gulati and Wang (2001), who find that the degree of social embeddedness of a firm affects both the amount of value it can create in alliances (a U-shaped effect), and the amount it claims (a positive effect).

To clarify some of these ideas, consider another Apple-IBM battle, this time in the early 1980s. The IBM PC was launched in 1981 by what we would today call a constellation—led by IBM, it had Intel supplying the microprocessor and Microsoft supplying the operating system. The constellation was held together by technical commitments, equity (IBM owned 20% of Intel), and contracts. As a group, this triad created the microcomputer format that within a few years drove both the Apple II and the previously dominant CPM operating system to the periphery of the market. Later, this IBM PC constellation slowly fell apart, but Microsoft and Intel went on to develop the powerful Wintel alliance. (This story is told well in many places, including in Yoffie, Casadesus-Masanell, & Mattu, 2003.)

The main lesson for us is that although this constellation created tremendous group-based advantages (it established the dominant industry standard), the firms within the constellation benefited to different degrees. IBM, it turned out, ended up with the least claim on the joint value, even though it initiated the constellation, held a central position, and was much larger than its partners.

The key reason for this outcome lies in the nature of the resources each party contributed to the joint enterprise. In IBM's case, its resources were marketing, manufacturing, and the architecture of the product. To IBM's surprise, Compaq and a slew of IBM-clone makers were able to imitate the architecture and then outmanufacture and outmarket IBM. Intel's and Microsoft's resources, however, were protected by copyright and by the firms' efforts to block imitation and stay ahead of clones. Intel and Microsoft also benefited from competition among systems vendors; IBM had no such luck.

Managing Constellation Strategy

How can firms today avoid ending up like IBM (or worse, Apple) and have a better chance at being the Intel or Microsoft of their industry? The approach and research agenda in this chapter may help guide them. Among salient normative questions that need to be addressed in this field are the following (see also Bamford et al., 2003):

- Where in the business value chain and in the market space of the company should the alliances be formed, how many alliances should there be, and of what type?
- What should be the relationship among the various alliances and partners in the constellation?
- How will interactions among alliances of different divisions be identified and managed?
- How should the company's multiple linkages be structured; for example, should there be a loose network, a stand-alone consortium, or an equity joint venture?
- How will the company's constellation compete with rival constellations and to whom will added value ultimately flow?

Although pioneering firms have experimented with alliance constellations in many industries, we do not yet have solid conclusions about what works and what does not. Most of the managerial literature assumes implicitly that the firm is the primary unit of competition; we have seen that this view can be misleading. In businesses where collective competition is important, managers need to govern not only the activities within the strict boundaries of their firm but also their alliances and constellations outside these boundaries. Though the research on constellation strategy is still new, we can already discern a few guidelines.

First, managers need to pay attention to two sets of actions: (1) The initial design of their constellations (i.e., setting goals, choosing partners, and crafting the structure), and (2) the management of the constellation after its start-up (i.e., building relationships, adjusting plans, and making joint decisions). These broad priorities are not different from those present in an individual alliance but they are made more complex by the multiplicity of partners that may exist in a constellation.

Second, constellation designers will face a trade-off between (1) expanding the group in an effort to increase aggregate capabilities, and (2) keeping the group simple to ensure effective governance. The appropriate balance between expansion and governance will likely depend on the competitive context and on the dynamics of the emerging group.

Third, successful management of constellations also requires careful mapping of the competitive landscape and consideration of various options for membership and structure. This is not an activity that currently is regularly done by strategists in many firm. It also requires monitoring and analysis of alliances of the firm's rivals.

Fourth, for a firm to gain from participation in a constellation, it must be able to claim some of the value created by the collective. This means that it needs to control key, scarce resources or otherwise increase its bargaining power vis-à-vis other members in the group. This often raises a catch-22 dilemma. By sharing its capabilities generously, a lead firm in a constellation can attract strong partners and perhaps erode the power of rival constellations. But this growth may well come at the cost of the firm's ability to appropriate value from its constellation.

The right time to address these issues is *before* alliances have spread too far in an industry. Alliances often spread in waves as one firm reacts to its rivals, and before long the whole industry is populated by constellations. When this happens, "strategic gridlock" can preclude new alliances and severely restrict the scope of constellation design (Gomes-Casseres, 2005). So managers need to look ahead. Although it has taken some time for research to catch up with reality in this field, it looks as if managerial practice had best heed the findings of the frontier research in this volume.

At the same time, alliance scholars need to push their research beyond traditional models and approaches. This chapter has tried to map a broad territory that to a large extent remains poorly explored. In short, we now know a lot about what alliances are and how they work as organizational mechanisms, but we still have much to learn about why and how they matter to competition in an industry.

Notes

1. In some analysis, the market as a whole is the unit of analysis, e.g., when investigating the attractiveness of an industry or the degree of competition in a market.

2. The term *competitive domain* is admittedly broad, but it serves to limit the extent of the constellation to the set of alliances that together creates a bundle of assets used in a specific competitive space. I explicitly do not want to include in the constellation *all* alliances of a firm, as alliances in different lines of businesses and different countries are often unrelated to each other competitively. (See also note 3.) Having said this, it is common for there to be overlaps among the competitive domains in which a firm operates, and so among its constellations. This simply means that

management and analysis of these constellations is more complex than otherwise; it does not change the definition itself.

3. In an excellent review, Jones, Hesterly & Borgatti (1997) offer a definition similar to mine, though perhaps a bit more restrictive in that they rule out explicit, legally binding contracts: "Network governance involves a select, persistent, and structured set of autonomous firms . . . engaged in creating products or services based on implicit and open-ended contracts." They then discuss the various forms of social control that are used in network governance.

4. The emphasis on the constellation as simply *an alternative* to the firm is intentional; I do not believe it is the "wave of the future" or that there is some inevitable progression of organizational firms, as Miles, Snow, Mathews, Miles, & Coleman (1997) appear to do.

5. The recognition that alliances, or mergers for that matter, do not necessarily reduce competition even if the number of outright competitors in a market may have diminished, has deep roots in the evolution of antitrust analysis. In the late 1970s and early 1980s traditional structure-conduct-performance models in IO began to give way to a recognition that combinations of companies might enhance efficiency by reducing transactions costs (e.g., Williamson, 1975). The position of the structuralist school was further weakened in the policy arena during the Reagan years, as antitrust authorities began to consider the pro- and anticompetitive effects of mergers and joint ventures in a more balanced way. Joint ventures in R&D, in particular, were seen as procompetitive under many conditions (see Ordover & Willig, 1985; Katz & Ordover, 1990; Jorde & Teece, 1990). Thanks to an anonymous reviewer for this point.

6. In practice, highly competitive markets seldom give rise to alliances, so the top right cell of Figure 3.1 is empty. One reason for this is that in purely competitive markets a firm need not tie up with another to gain access to its capabilities—it can usually acquire the inputs it needs from one of the multiple suppliers in the market. Put another way, the special conditions that give rise to alliances also create barriers to entry that limit the number of competitors.

7. One could generalize this model by adding levels. On one end, one can include units and individuals inside the firm, thus adding layers of resource control and bargaining within the firm; see Rajan & Zingales (2001) and Coff (1999). At the other end, layers can be added by considering the wider game (or industry) in which the game among the rival constellations is nested (i.e., the industry segment); see Slywotzky (1996).

8. Interestingly, they also suggest that their results might change if measured in a world where *all* airlines are allied, compared with the context they observed, in which some airlines were allied and others were not. In other words, the matchup of group vs. firm may well lead to different competitive dynamics from one of group vs. group.

References

Baker, G., Gibbons, R., & Murphy, K. J. (2002). Relational contracts and the theory of the firm. *Quarterly Journal of Economics 117*, 39–83.

Baldwin, C. Y., & Clark, K. B. (1997, September/October). Managing in an age of modularity. *Harvard Business Review*, 84–93.

Bamford, J., Gomes-Casseres, B., & Robinson, M. (2003). *Mastering alliance strategy: A comprehensive guide to design, management, and organization.* San Francisco: Jossey-Bass/Wiley.

Baumol, W. J. (1992). Horizontal collusion and information. *Economic Journal, 102*(410), 129–137.

Brandenburger, A. M., & Nalebuff, B. J. (1996). *Co-opetition.* New York: Currency/Doubleday.

Bresnahan, T. F., & Salop, S. C. (1986). Quantifying the competitive effects of production joint ventures. *International Journal of Industrial Organization, 4*, 155–175.

Brueckner, J. K., & Whalen, W. T. (2000). The price effects of international airline alliances. *Journal of Law and Economics, 43*(2), 503–545.

Burt, R. S. (1992). *Structural holes: The social structure of competition.* Cambridge, MA: Harvard University Press.

Chen, F. C. Y., & Chen, C. (2003). The effects of strategic alliances and risk pooling on the load factors of international airline operations. *Transportation Research, 39*(Pt. E), 19–34.

Chesbrough, H. W., & David J. Teece, D. J. (1996, January/February). When is virtual virtuous: Organizing for innovation. *Harvard Business Review*, 66–73.

Coase, R. (1937). The nature of the firm. *Economica, 4*(16), 386–405.

Coff, R. W. (1999). When competitive advantage doesn't lead to performance: The resource-based view and stakeholder bargaining power. *Organization Science, 10*(2), 119–133.

Eisenhardt, K., & Brown, S. H. (1999, May/June). Patching: Restitching business portfolios in dynamic markets. *Harvard Business Review*, 72–82.

Federal Trade Commission & the U.S. Department of Justice. (2000, April). *Antitrust guidelines for collaborators*. Washington, DC: U.S. Department of Justice.

Gadiesh, O., & Gilbert, G. L. (1998, May/June). How to map your industry's profit pool. *Harvard Business Review*, 139–147.

Ghemawat, P., with Collis, D. J., Pisano, G. P., & Rivkin, J. W. (1999). *Strategy and the business landscape: Text and cases*. Reading, MA: Addison-Wesley.

Gimeno, J. (forthcoming). Competition within and between networks: The contingent effect of competitive embeddedness on alliance formation. *Academy of Management Journal*.

Gomes-Casseres, B. (1994, July/August). Group versus group: How alliance networks compete. *Harvard Business Review*, 62–74.

Gomes-Casseres, B. (1996). *The alliance revolution: The new shape of business rivalry*. Cambridge, MA: Harvard University Press.

Gomes-Casseres, B. (2003). Competitive advantage in alliance constellations. *Strategic Organization, 1*(3), 327–335.

Gomes-Casseres, B. (2005). *The logic of alliance fads: Why collective competition spreads*. Working Paper, Brandeis University.

Gomes-Casseres, B., Jaffe, A., & Hagedoorn, J. (forthcoming). Do alliances promote knowledge flows? *Journal of Financial Economics*.

Grossman, S. J., & Hart, D. O. (1986). The costs and benefits of ownership: A theory of vertical and lateral integration. *Journal of Political Economy, 94*(4), 691–719.

Gulati, R. (1998). Alliances and networks. *Strategic Management Journal, 19*, 293–317.

Gulati, R., & Wang, L. O. (2001). *Size of the pie and share of the pie: Implications of structural embeddedness for value creation and value appropriation in joint ventures*. Working Paper, Northwestern University.

Hagel, J., III (1996). Spider versus spider. *McKinsey Quarterly, 1*, 5–18.

Hamel, G. (1991). Competition for competence and inter-partner learning within international strategic alliances. *Strategic Management Review, 12*, 83–104.

Hamel, G., Doz, Y., & Prahalad, C. K. (1989, January/February). Collaborate with your competitors—And win. *Harvard Business Review*, 133–139.

Hennart, J. F. (1989, July/August). A transaction cost theory of equity joint ventures. *Strategic Management Journal*, 36–47.

Holmstrom, B., & Roberts, J. (1998). The boundaries of the firm revisited. *Journal of Economic Perspectives, 12*(4), 73–94.

Hwang, P., & Burgers, W. P. (1997, Spring). The many faces of multi-firm alliances: Lessons for managers. *California Management Review, 39*, 101–117.

Iansiti, M., & Levien, R. (2004). *The keystone advantage*. Boston: Harvard Business School Press.

Jarillo, J. C. (1988, January/February). On strategic networks. *Strategic Management Journal*, 31–41.

Jones, C., Hesterly, W. S., & Borgatti, S. P. (1997). A general theory of network governance: Exchange conditions and social mechanisms. *Academy of Management Review, 22*(4), 911–945.

Jones, C., Hesterly, W. S., Fladmoe-Lindquist, K., & Borgatti, S. P. (1998). Constellations in professional services: How firm capabilities influence collaborative stability and change. *Organization Science, 9*, 396–410.

Jorde, T., & Teece, D. (1990). Innovation and cooperation: Implications for competition and antitrust. *Journal of Economic Perspectives, 4*(3), 75–96.

Katz, M. L., & Ordover, J. (1990). R&D cooperation and competition. *Brookings Papers on Economic Activity: Microeconomics, 1990*, 137–203.

Katz, M. L., & Shapiro, C. (1994). Systems competition and network effects. *Journal of Economic Perspectives, 8*(2), 93–115.

Khanna, T. (1998). The scope of alliances. *Organization Science, 9*(3), 340–355.

Khanna, T., & Rivkin, J. W. (2001). Estimating the performance effects of business groups in emerging markets. *Strategic Management Journal, 22*, 45–74.

Kogut, B. (1988). Joint ventures: Theoretical and empirical perspectives. *Strategic Management Journal, 9*, 319–332.

Kogut, B. (1989). The stability of joint ventures: Reciprocity and competitive rivalry. *Journal of Industrial Economics, 38*(2), 183–198.

Lazzarini, S. G. (2003). *The performance implications of membership in competing firm constellations: Evidence from the global airline industry*. Unpublished manuscript, Ibmec Business School, São Paolo, Brazil.

Lorenzoni, G., & Baden-Fuller, C. (1995). Creating a strategic center to manage a web of alliances. *California Management Review, 37,* 146–163.

Lorenzoni, G., & Ornati, O. A. (1988). Constellations of firms and new ventures. *Journal of Business Venturing, 3,* 41–57.

Mariti, P., & Smiley, R. H. (1983, June). Co-operative agreement and the organization of industry. *Journal of Industrial Economics, 31*(4), 437–451.

Miles, R. E., Snow, C. C., Mathews, J. A., Miles, G., & Coleman, H. J., Jr. (1997). Organizing in the knowledge age: Anticipating the cellular form. *Academy of Management Executive, 11*(4), 7–24.

Nohria, N., & Eccles, R. G. (1992). *Networks and organizations: Structure, form, and action.* Boston: Harvard Business School Press.

Nohria, N., & Garcia-Pont, C. (1991, Summer). Global strategic linkages and industry structure. *Strategic Management Journal,* 105–124.

Normann, R., & Ramírez, R. (1993, July/August). From value chain to value constellation: Designing interactive strategy. *Harvard Business Review,* 65–77.

Ordover, J., & Willig, R. (1985). Antitrust for high-technology industries: Assessing research joint ventures and mergers. *Journal of Law and Economics, 28*(2), 311–333.

Penrose, E. T. (1995). *Theory of the growth of the firm* (3rd ed.). New York: Oxford University Press.

Pfeffer, J., & Salancik, J. R. (1978). *The external control of organizations: A resource dependence perspective.* New York: Harper and Row.

Powell, W. (1990). Neither market nor hierarchy: Network forms of organization. *Annual Review of Sociology, 24,* 57–76.

Rajan, R. G., & Zingales, L. (2001, August). The firm as a dedicated hierarchy: A theory of the origins and growth of firms. *Quarterly Journal of Economics,* 805–851.

Richardson, G. B. (1972). The organization of industry. *Economic Journal, 82*(327), 883–896.

Rowley, T. J., Baum, J. A. C., Shipilov, A. V., Greve, H. R., & Rao, H. (forthcoming). Competing in groups. *Managerial and Decision Economics.*

Rowley, T. J., Greve, H. R., Rao, H., Baum, J. A. C., & Shipilov, A. V. (2004). *Time to break up: Social and instrumental antecedents of firm exits from exchange cliques.* Unpublished manuscript.

Saloner, G., Shepard, A., & Podolny, J. (2001). *Strategic management.* New York: Wiley.

Schmalensee, R., & Willig, R. (Eds.). (1989). *Handbook of industrial organization* (Vols. 1 and 2). Amsterdam: North Holland.

Shapiro, C., & Varian, H. R. (1999). *Information rules: A strategic guide to the network economy.* Boston: Harvard Business School Press.

Silverman, B. S., & Baum, J. A. C. (2002). Alliance-based competitive dynamics. *Academy of Management Journal, 45*(4), 791–806.

Slywotzky, A. J. (1996). *Value migration: How to think several moves ahead of the competition.* Boston: Harvard Business School Press.

Smith, A. (1776). *The wealth of nations.*

Starkey, K., Barnatt, C., & Tempest, S. (2000). Beyond networks and hierarchies: Latent organizations in the U.K. television industry. *Organization Science, 11*(3), 299–305.

Stopford, J. M., & Wells, L. T. (1972). *Managing the multinational enterprise* (pt. II). New York: Basic Books.

Stuckey, J. A. (1983). *Vertical integration and joint ventures in the aluminum industry.* Cambridge, MA: Harvard University Press, 1983.

Suen, W. (forthcoming). *Non-cooperation: The dark side of strategic alliances.* Houndmills, UK: Palgrave Macmillan.

Tirole, J. (1988). *The theory of industrial organization.* Cambridge: MIT Press.

Walker, G., Kogut, B., & Shan, W. (1997). Social capital, structural holes and the formation of an industry network. *Organization Science, 8*(2), 109–125.

Williamson, O. E. (1975). *Markets and hierarchies: Analysis and antitrust implications.* New York: Free Press.

Yoffie, D. B., Casadesus-Masanell, R., & Mattu, S. (2003). Wintel (A): Cooperation of conflict. Harvard Business School case no. 704419.

4

Opportunism in Cooperative Alliances

Conditions and Solutions

Yadong Luo

Cooperative alliances, broadly defined in this study as equity joint ventures and cooperative arrangements, continue to be a popular vehicle for firms to expand domestically and globally and improve their competitive advantages, but meanwhile, they raise complicated issues of governance as they are "hybrid" organizations that combine elements of both market and hierarchy, and each party has a *de facto* right to manipulate its own contribution and commitment. All alliances, especially equity-based joint ventures, inevitably involve some degree of opportunistic behavior by individual parties or fiduciary risks of interdependence between parties (Das & Teng, 1998; Parkhe, 1993). Any alliance is a loosely coupled system in which investing parties interdependently share existing resources or jointly develop new resources while maintaining their respective parental identities and resource control. This looseness, together with inherent interparty differences in strategic objective, corporate culture, and managerial style plus interparty asymmetry in bargaining power, alliance importance, and parent control, explains why opportunism, or "self-interest seeking with guile" (Williamson, 1979), occurs. Cross-cultural conflicts and environmental uncertainty in a drastically changing environment further increase the likelihood of opportunism (Lyles, Saxton, & Watson, 2004). As a significant obstacle to fostering cooperation, opportunism impairs collaborative effects and synergy creation, hampers interparty confidence, commitment, and reciprocity, impedes alliance evolution and growth by increasing uncertainty, and eventually increases the probability of alliance failure, dissolution, or termination (Deeds & Hill, 1998; Nooteboom, Berger, & Noorderhaven, 1997).

Opportunism is not prefixed but an ex post variable determined by external and internal environments. Extant research, however, has not yet adequately addressed how the external environment influences opportunism in cooperative alliances. Addressing environmental influences is important, because opportunism is a function of uncertainty (Williamson, 1985), and uncertainty is at least partly a function of environmental volatility (Hill, 1990). Opportunism is endogenous, and its strength is largely determined by an investing party's anticipation of its risk-adjusted net returns, which is often discounted by market uncertainty. Thus, to complement existing research on this subject, I seek to elucidate how environmental volatility systematically affects the level of opportunism exhibited by alliance partners.

In this study I explain four interrelated yet distinct constructs that jointly profile volatility in a drastically changing environment: industry structure uncertainty, information unverifiability, environmental changeability, and legal unprotectability. Based on transaction cost and information processing theories, I develop the logic that both transaction cost and information processing complexity increase with industry structural uncertainty, information unverifiability, environmental changeability, and legal unprotectability. Because such volatility hazards are generally beyond organizational control, neither party expects to be able to obviate them by itself or even together, but both do expect that these hazards will deter an alliance's goal achievement and future prospects. Hence, alliance parties may increase opportunistic behavior in joint operations in order to decrease their economic exposure to volatility.

Such opportunism may be even stronger when an alliance participates in a less promising industry or when it has to rely more heavily on the external environment. From the internal lens, I suggest that opportunism exhibited by alliance parties is not isolated from binary relational variables that describe interparty relationships. Relational links, that is, dyadic relations such as resource complementarity, goal congruence, and bargaining asymmetry, are used in this study to address this issue. I view opportunism as a relational variable that changes in a dyadic context, influenced by how exchange partners are interrelated in resources, goals, and bargaining.

More important, deterring opportunism necessitates governance. Although governance has been extensively studied in alliance research, most prior research emphasized governance forms across different alliance types or settings. For instance, Osborn and Baughn (1990) contrasted equity alliances and contractual modes; Walker and Poppo (1991) illustrated coordination mechanisms between and within organizations; Ring and Van de Ven (1992) elucidated the criteria that influence type of governance chosen and nodal forms of broad governance, from discrete contracting and recurrent contracting to relational contracting and hierarchical managerial transactions; Madhok (1995) and Conner and Prahalad (1996) explained the nature of governance and opportunism for firms with different organizational capabilities in organizing economic activity; Nooteboom et al. (1997) documented the effects of governance and trust on relational risk; and finally, Folta (1998) presented the trade-off between administrative control and commitment cost when uncertainty is a factor when choosing governance form.

Thus, although governance has been researched in depth, inquiry into how opportunism in alliances should be deterred remains inadequately studied. This void is largely attributable to the nature of opportunism: it is intricate (multifaceted), intrinsic (difficult to observe), unstable (constantly changing tactics and behavior), and irritable (easily influenced by changes of internal and external environments). Despite these difficulties, understanding how to curb opportunism has theoretical and managerial implications. Theoretically, a counteropportunism framework presents an overarching view that incorporates both economic and social exchange theories in explicating opportunistic incentives, behaviors, and suppressing mechanisms. For managerial implication, understanding counteropportunism tools helps executives to manage alliances effectively, deal with cross-cultural partners, balance cooperation and control, and govern interpartner exchanges.

Theoretical Overview

Williamson defines opportunism as "self-interest seeking with guile. . . . More generally, opportunism refers to the incomplete or distorted disclosure of information, especially to calculated efforts to mislead, distort, disguise, obfuscate, or otherwise confuse" (Williamson, 1985, p. 47). When joined with bounded rationality and asset specificity, the risk of opportunism implies that participants in an exchange may intend to expropriate the *composite quasi-rent* that persuaded others to enter the exchange in the first place (Anderson, 1988; Hill, 1990). A composite quasi-rent is that proportion of the quasi-rent generated by a resource that depends on continued association with the resources of others. Transaction cost theory, which is perhaps the most influential paradigm in articulating the economic rationale underlying opportunism, assumes that the risk of opportunism is inherent in many types of transactions. If asset specificity in one transaction is high, the risk of opportunism is often great enough to warrant replacing the market with a hierarchy. Because Williamson's discussion on opportunism emphasizes how the risk of opportunism can be alleviated by the selection of different governance forms (i.e., market, network, or hierarchy), his definition of opportunism is rather general.

I define opportunism in a cooperative-alliance setting as the act or behavior performed by one party from one country to seek its unilateral gains at the substantial expense of other parties from other countries by breaching contract or agreement, exercising private control, withholding or distorting information, withdrawing commitments or promises, shirking obligations, or grafting joint earnings. Here private control is the process through which one party unilaterally controls certain alliance areas or functions that are critical to the party's private gains. Private control differs from collective control in that the latter is executed jointly by all parties to guide, monitor, and oversee alliance activities and pursue a maximum joint payoff. Unlike collective control, which is always overt, private control is characterized by covert measures and hidden tactics, such as manipulating board decisions, dominating critical value-chain activities, blocking technology transfer, and controlling cash flows. Grafting joint earnings is akin to embezzlement in that it conceals real profit, income, cost, or the price of transactions controlled by the party. For instance, an opportunistic party may overprice an alliance's purchasing costs for buying materials from this party's parent or underprice an alliance's sales to its parent.

Opportunism, irrespective of its forms, exists to varying degrees in almost every alliance because of partners' competitive aims. Joining an alliance is often a means by which a firm pursues strategic goals and competitive advantages; thus, in the course of cooperation, each party still emphasizes its own gains from specific projects in which the parties' needs are frequently not compatible (Jap & Anderson, 2003; Jones, Hesterly, & Borgatti, 1997). Because each party retains its organizational separateness and identity, competitive aims are often fulfilled by opportunistic actions.

Entering an alliance relationship means that the partners will share a future of ongoing mutual dependence, a condition in which one party is vulnerable to another whose behavior is not under the control of the first (Parkhe, 1993; Reuer & Koza, 2000). Thus, no matter what form it takes, opportunism has serious consequences for interparty collaborations. First, opportunism increases transaction costs in repeated exchanges because covert behaviors seeking unilateral gains are difficult to observe and verify. Firms that perceive this threat are faced with a greater need for screening, negotiating, and monitoring the partner firm's behavior, resulting in increased information cost (Hennart, 1988; Nooteboom et al., 1997). Fears of such behaviors are also detrimental to trust-building and forbearance establishment, two important forces driving joint payoff (Buckley & Casson, 1988; Currall & Inkpen, 2002).

Second, opportunism represents a significant obstacle to fostering confidence in partner cooperation, and the risk of opportunism escalates interparty conflicts (Beamish & Banks, 1987; Jehn & Weldon, 1997; Killing, 1983). Opportunistic parties do their own thing and emphasize their own interests, hence weakening the foundation for collaboration. This failure to see beyond the short-term optimization of self-interest inhibits the cooperative effort that is essential to alliance success and is often instrumental in causing alliance dissolution.

Third, opportunism increases coordination difficulty and coupling uncertainty between exchange parties, because joint payoff depends on the extent to which parties can create synergies (Contractor & Lorange, 1988). These synergies are in turn affected by the degree of interpartner coordination and the efficiency of coupling the resources contributed by each party (Dyer, 1997; Khanna, Gulati, & Nohria, 1998; Parkhe, 1991). With high private control by one or two parties, coordination in resource sharing and activity integration becomes more difficult and unstable, thus hindering alliance performance.

Finally, opportunism discourages the development of two critical determinants of superior alliance performance: reciprocity and repeated commitment. In the presence of opportunism, it is difficult to sustain repeated economic exchanges for long because of moral hazards (opportunistic behavior by one party after the other party has already committed to the exchange) or uncertainty about individual and joint payoffs when two parties act simultaneously (Hennart, 1988; Parkhe, 1993). Reciprocity is essential to generating joint payoffs for socially embedded, long-term economic exchanges.

Opportunism, however, is an endogenous variable whose behavior is determined by other variables that crystallize external and internal dynamics (Hill, 1990; Williamson, 1985). According to Williamson (1985), opportunism is a function of a transaction's uncertainty, which is then determined in part by environmental volatility. Environmental volatility curtails a party's expected risk-adjusted net return from the transaction and reduces its anticipated income-stream stability (Dixit & Pindyck, 1994). Logically, when a party anticipates sustained or prolonged uncertainty of gains or income, it tends to behave more opportunistically (Brown, Dev, & Zhou, 2003). Because each party thinks this way, it may anticipate the other party's similarly opportunistic musings; in the face of income uncertainty, both parties become reluctant to be the first to contribute the resources needed to reduce a joint venture's dependence on external uncertainty or to strengthen its operations.

The uncertainty caused by environmental volatility leads to increased information processing and transaction costs, both internally and externally. Internally, uncertainty requires increased monitoring and enforcement costs. Each party must spend more time and resources to monitor the other party and determine if it is abiding by the contract or shirking its obligations. Moreover, each party must spend time and resources on ex post bargaining and haggling over problems that arise over the course of repeated exchange, thus making transaction costs even higher (Dyer & Chu, 2003).

From an information processing perspective, a party that perceives the threat of opportunism must develop information processing mechanisms capable of dealing with the complexity required for such monitoring and enforcement (e.g., efficiently collecting, gathering, and processing relevant information). These information processing requirements increase as internal interdependencies become more uncertain (Tushman & Nadler, 1978, p. 616). Furthermore, uncertainty makes interpartner coordination in resource-sharing and activity integration more difficult and unstable; this also leads to increased information processing requirements and costs (Galbraith, 1977).

Externally, transaction and information processing costs increase when an alliance operates in an uncertain environment; when such costs increase beyond a party's tolerance, opportunism will also increase (Hill, 1990). Environmental volatility increases costs of inbound and outbound value-chain activities (e.g., marketing, promotion, delivery, inventory control) that are susceptible to market conditions and increases the difficulty of anticipating and adjusting to changing circumstances. Environmental volatility also increases the cost of strategic planning, monitoring, and execution, as well as the complexity and uncertainty of task and institutional environments; this all adds to information processing costs. Meanwhile, market volatility influences organizational activities, and executives need more, not less, external information to respond to unexpected situations (Daft, Sormunem, & Parks, 1988). When information processing and transaction costs become unaffordable, opportunism escalates (Anderson, 1988; Johns, 1984).

Each party's opportunism is partially conditional upon relational links that characterize interparty dyadic relationships. Control is the process by which one party influences the behavior and output of another party (the partner firm or alliance) via the use of power or resources. Motive, process, and behavior of control are largely determined by the various bilateral relationships that characterize the firms' integration in resources, value-chain activities, objectives, and even social links. These relational features thus influence opportunism through manipulating, adjusting, and exercising private control. These relational links also determine in part the stability of the interparty relationship, and such stability has strong implications for each party's expected opportunism. For instance, strong binary links between alliance parties increase stake or equity hostage (Williamson, 1985), and this hostage can curtail in part an individual party's opportunistic act (Hill, 1990).

With respect to counteropportunism forces or mechanisms, Williamson (1979, 1985) addresses the importance of "legal ordering" (i.e., contractual monitoring), "equity hostage" (i.e., shared ownership), and "private ordering" (i.e., reputation protection) as primary means of constraining opportunism. His view, and transaction cost theory in general, assumes that interparty exchange is an egotistic process, with each party emphasizing its calculative self-interest. Because this view maintains the centrality of calculativeness, counteropportunism efforts are portrayed mainly as economic ordering, requiring formal governance mechanisms (such as contracts) that explicitly specify each party's liability, responsibility, and rights. This logic is increasingly viewed as incomplete in explaining long-term interparty collaborations whereby firm behavior is also constrained in part by social norms and economic actions are incrementally embedded in the structure of social relations (Granovetter, 1985). According to social exchange theory (Blau, 1964), exchange and cooperation often have a social dimension (intrinsic utility) as well as an economic dimension (extrinsic utility). Specialized investments lose their value when applied to other relationships. Thus, alliance parties become gradually locked into the existing relationship, which furthers continuity (Gulati, 1995; Steensma & Lyles, 2002).

Building on the above logic, this article presents an overarching yet unified framework that articulates both economic exchange– and social exchange–based counteropportunism forces, which together constitute an integrated antiopportunism system. Consistent with several other studies that also portray long-term interpartner exchange as underpinned by both economic and social exchange logics (Biggart & Delbridge, 2004; Das & Teng, 2002; Dyer & Singh, 1998; Gulati & Singh, 1998; Jones et al., 1997; Nooteboom et al., 1997; Poppo & Zenger, 2002; Steensma & Lyles, 2002; Uzzi, 1997), I view counteropportunism forces as being embedded in both economic and social structures. Opportunism is an egotistic as well as nonegotistic act subject to the constraints from both formal structures and social reality (Williams, 1988). Williams argues that neither economic nor social forces by themselves suffice in suppressing opportunism; a mix of both will always be more operative and effective. Material self-interest (e.g., equity participation) and coercion (e.g., contract) are seldom sufficient in inhibiting opportunism or encouraging long-term cooperation due to the fact that one party cannot fully control the other's conduct by threat or reward alone (Axelrod, 1984; Gulati, 1995; Granovetter, 1985). Likewise, intrinsic utility (e.g., social norms and personal bonds) is insufficient in reducing the fiduciary risk of dependence, because alliance formation is economically motivated in the first place, and social constraints make sense only if they go beyond calculative self-interest (Folta, 1998; Nooteboom, 1996; Poppo & Zenger, 2002).

External Determinants of Opportunism

Environmental volatility is a multidimensional concept, and its effects on organizations are context-specific (Bourgeois, 1980; Dess & Beard, 1984; Milliken, 1987). In a general setting, environmental volatility, often synonymous with uncertainty or dynamism, is the rate of change or the degree of instability of factors within an environment (Boyd, Dess, & Rasheed, 1993; Sawyerr, 1993). Its dimensions include changeability, unpredictability, unverifiability, and variability of a group of segments that comprise both micro- (industrial) and macro- (national) business environments (Dess & Beard, 1984; Miller, 1987).

This article emphasizes four interrelated yet distinct dimensions that constitute environmental volatility in a drastically changing environment (such as a typical emerging market): (1) industry structural uncertainty, (2) information unverifiability, (3) environmental changeability, and (4) legal unprotectability. An emerging market is particularly interesting to illustrate this type of environment for three main reasons. First, emerging markets have become a leading host of global cooperative alliances. Second, emerging markets are a rich setting to crystallize environmental volatility. Third, local partners in emerging markets tend to be more opportunistic than foreign counterparts, especially when facing uncertainty (Hoskisson, Eden, Lau, & Wright, 2000).

An emerging market is defined as a country in which the national economy grows rapidly, industries are structurally changing, markets are promising but volatile, the legal protection system is weak, and the regulatory framework undergoes drastic transformations. It is commonly held that industry structural uncertainty and national environmental changeability are major forces that exacerbate environmental volatility in emerging economies (May, Stewart, & Sweo, 2000). Several studies further document that institutional change, especially regulatory transformation at industrial as well as national levels, leads to difficulties in obtaining, interpreting, analyzing, and verifying information pertaining to both task and institutional environments (Hare & Davis, 1997). In particular, government policies shift from overt to covert, thus becoming more opaque, and from simple to complex, thus becoming more heterogeneous (Luo, 2002, pp. 50–60). Finally, legal infrastructure, including legal system development and enforcement, is generally weak in emerging economies (Brown, 1997). Political, social, historical, and cultural factors often impede the implementation and enforcement of commercial laws. Lack of adequate legal protection increases uncertainty with respect to property rights and legitimate returns, disturbs fair competition, and permits unaccountability of regulatory agents' behavior (Hoskisson et al., 2000).

Because industry structural uncertainty characterizes microlevel external constraints immediately imposed on a firm (Boyd & Fulk, 1996), I define it as an objective construct measured by archival information. In contrast, the other three dimensions of environmental volatility are subjective in nature. Perceived levels of general or national environment uncertainty are more appropriate for studying organizational behavior, because decision makers often make decisions based on how they perceive such macrolevel environment (Miller, 1987). Because these perceptions are subjective, they ensure enough observation variance to study macrolevel variables within a country (May et al., 2000; Milliken, 1987). I hence define information unverifiability, environmental changeability, and legal unprotectability as subjective constructs perceived by alliance executives.

Empirical studies validate that objective measures of microbusiness environment and subjective measures of macrobusiness environment are distinct and mutually complementary (Boyd et al., 1993; Buchko, 1994). Whereas industry structural uncertainty mainly captures volatility of market supply and demand, and information unverifiability reflects uncertainty of external information needed for business activities, environmental changeability marks the fluctuation of all environmental segments, and legal unprotectability relates to appropriability hazards and market function completeness. Collectively, these dimensions comprise environmental volatility and individually they affect transaction costs and information processing costs.

Structural Uncertainty and Opportunism

Industrial environment influences the competitive situation that individual organizations face (Scherer & Ross, 1990), and an industry's *structural uncertainty* influences an executive's prospects and decisions (Porter, 1985). Such uncertainty implies an absence of sufficient information about industry structure and executives' inability to predict this structural change and its impact on organizational decision alternatives (Dess & Beard, 1984). In emerging economies in which industries are often undergoing structural transformation and are subject to strong government intervention (Hare & Davis, 1997), structural uncertainty is strikingly high and extremely difficult to manage (Nee, 1992). In such an uncertain context, executives may passively reduce exposure to risk by decreasing resource commitment. This happens because firms have little control over results in the face of industry structural uncertainty caused by government interference during economic transition (Peng, 2000).

Thus, uncertainty translates into immense economic exposure that firms cannot hedge. Joint venture members are unlikely to be able to mitigate the hazards arising from such uncertainty. In fact, foreign joint ventures in most emerging markets face even greater structural uncertainty than do indigenous firms because of the underdevelopment of joint venture law, the immaturity of government policies, and government bodies' lack of experience in dealing with foreign firms (Luo, 2002; May et al., 2000). In response to such uncontrollable factors, joint venture parties are likely to attempt to minimize their respective exposure to external turbulence by behaving more opportunistically. They may reduce their commitment to the joint venture, shirk obligations, or take a "wait and see" attitude toward what the other party or the market does.

I thus anticipate that in a foreign emerging market, alliance parties will behave more opportunistically in response to increased structural uncertainty of the industry in which the joint venture participates, ceteris paribus.

Information Unverifiability and Opportunism

Emerging markets are characterized by a lack of market-economy institutions, regulatory opacity, differing institutional treatment of firms based on location, ownership, or type of business activity, and the nontransparency of government decision-making processes that affect the public (Hoskisson et al., 2000). This makes information about the environment difficult to obtain, analyze, and verify. Opportunism may increase in this situation. First, investing parties may face unclear situations with few well-developed alternatives or clear evaluating criteria on which to base decisions. These factors may force firms to perform limited environmental assessments, take defensive actions to safeguard their existing stakes, and/or hold or reduce their originally planned resource investment (Daft et al., 1988; Miller, 1987; Sawyerr, 1993).

Second, information unverifiability deters environmental munificence, which in turn darkens the outlook for future cooperation and joint gains. A munificent environment is important in fostering continued investment and increased commitment (Dess & Beard, 1984). If a party loses confidence in a joint venture's prospects, it will act more opportunistically and make the other party bear more relational risk (Das & Teng, 1998).

Third, information unverifiability discourages the development of trust, forbearance, and reciprocity; together with goal incongruence (Beamish & Banks, 1987), the discouraging of these behaviors creates more conflict and leads to lower contributions from each party. Similarly, Williamson (1985) holds that when market information is unverifiable, the relational element of the exchange is weakened and the calculative element is magnified.

I thus posit that in a foreign emerging market, alliance parties will behave more opportunistically in response to increased information unverifiability, ceteris paribus.

Environmental Changeability and Opportunism

Emerging markets tend to experience faster economic growth than other types of economies, but this growth is often accompanied by greater environmental changeability. Changeability involves the extent to which the environment's various segments (economic, regulatory, sociocultural, technological, consumer demand, competition, and supply) are variable and unpredictable (Boyd et al., 1993; Dess & Beard, 1984). Changeability captures the instability that makes it difficult to formulate and implement strategic plans (Bourgeois, 1980), deploy and exploit distinctive resources (Keats & Hitt, 1988), and build and upgrade new capabilities (Oliver, 1997). Environmental changeability affects an investing party's perception of host country opportunity and uncertainty, which in turn influences its propensity for risk-taking and futurity (Milliken, 1987).

International joint ventures are often formed in order to share risk (political and operational) and costs (transactional and financial) in a local economy (Contractor & Lorange, 1988). But if environmental changeability prevents investing parties from seeing the prospect of reducing such risks and costs, the parties are more likely to behave opportunistically. In an emerging economy, this changeability is measured largely by how much and how quickly the formal institutional framework changes (Hare & Davis, 1997; Nee, 1992). It is difficult for firms to control or manage such changeability offensively; more often, they react defensively by reducing resource commitment.

I thus envisage that in a foreign emerging market, alliance parties will behave more opportunistically in response to increased environmental changeability, ceteris paribus.

Legal Unprotectability and Opportunism

Legal protection of legitimate business activities and intellectual or industrial property rights is most often weak in emerging economies (Hoskisson et al., 2000; Nee, 1992). "People," rather than the law itself, play a significant role in shaping commercial activities. Although legislative and governmental bodies have began to enact more commercial laws, such as company law, contract law, property right law, and joint venture law, they are not generally strictly enforced for a variety of political, sociocultural, institutional, and historical reasons. This enforcement uncertainty can be partly ascribed to long traditions of untrustworthy legal and governmental systems, lack of independent law enforcement, the deficiency of supervision mechanisms, and frequent unjustified law changes. Institutional doctrine ambiguity, legislative organ behavioral uncertainty, and law inconsistency further aggravate legal unprotectability.

Transaction cost theory posits that opportunism increases when such legal ordering is absent (Williamson, 1979). In Williamson's recent writing, legal unprotectability is part of a locus of shifting parameters that affect legal ordering effectiveness and the comparative costs of governance (Williamson, 1985). Because the shifting of parameters naturally puts at risk a party's legal rights and interests, confidence and commitment decline and the fear of appropriability hazards increases in such an environment. With weak legal protection, a victim of opportunistic conduct has very little legal recourse; this also leads to higher risks and costs, because using an "internal" legal remedy can often cause unanticipated and unwanted consequences. For instance, it may create incentives for an unscrupulous plaintiff party to bring groundless claims; fear of such behavior may cause a victim party to forgo bargaining and a lawsuit. Moreover, this remedy takes some of the risk out of making high-risk moves through transaction-specific investments, thereby dampening their effectiveness as trust-related signals.

I accordingly postulate that, in a foreign emerging market, alliance parties will behave more opportunistically in response to increased legal unprotectability, ceteris paribus.

Internal Determinants of Opportunism

Opportunism is not affected merely by environmental uncertainty external to the firm but also by factors inside the alliance, that is, relational links between exchange parties. External uncertainty increases opportunism because it reduces each party's confidence in ongoing cooperation and darkens alliance outlook. Internal uncertainty arising from dyadic relationships between parties increases opportunism because it reduces each party's commitment to collective activities and weakens joint governance against opportunistic acts. In my view, opportunism in a cooperative alliance is also a relational variable that changes or functions in a dyadic context, influenced by how exchange partners are interrelated in resources, goals, and bargaining.

Resource Complementarity and Opportunism

The complementarity of resources pooled by alliance partners glues them in long-term cooperation, conflict resolution, and forbearance maintenance (Buckley & Casson, 1988; Doz, 1996; Parkhe, 1993). Along with the increase in resource complementarity, more opportunities and benefits will be generated from cooperation. Doz (1996) states that joint payoffs from an alliance are an increasing function of this complementarity. Yan and Gray (1994) suggest that self-interest bargaining may decline if this complementarity is high. In this situation, partners will likely commit more to cooperation and focus less on private control or opportunism. Khanna, Gulati, and Nohria (1998) observe that the scope of competition decreases while the scope of cooperation increases when resource interdependence ascends. Contrarily, more collective control becomes necessary to cope with the growing complementarity and interdependence. More coordination is needed to integrate new resources contributed from different parties and to ensure that all new value-chain functions are efficiently integrated. Resource complementarity cannot create collective values in a vacuum; instead, these values are materialized only if respective resources from different parties are mixed up through collective control such that new operational synergies emerge (Dyer & Singh, 1998). This discussion suggests that as resource complementarity increases, opportunism may decrease.

The link between opportunism and resource complementarity may be further moderated by the economic integration between partners. Economic integration concerns the extent to which resources and functions from different parties are integrated and strategies from these parties harmonized to fulfill a joint target. Economic integration and resource complementarity are two related yet distinct constructs. Contributed resources may be complementary but actual integration may be very low. As a strategic decision, integration mirrors an alliance's status about the depth and extensiveness of interparty fusion in resources, knowledge, inputs, value chains, and business policies. The higher the economic integration, the stronger demand for collectively governing and exploiting complementary resources and capabilities. The heightened integration also ties partner interests more strongly, reducing the private desire for private control and thus propelling a stronger inverse link between private control and complementarity.

Conflicts are more likely to occur if resource complementarity is low (Saxton, 1997). When respective resources are not complementary, both parties tend to anticipate lower synergetic gains from cooperation, thereby plaguing reciprocal commitment or promoting antagonistic behavior (Killing, 1983; Parkhe, 1991). Such self-interest pursuits and related conflicts will in turn increase the probability of response discordance and the level of opportunism. Contrarily, when this complementarity is higher, the alliance may produce stronger competitive advantages than those achievable by the firms operating individually (Dyer & Singh, 1998; Shan, Walker, & Kogut, 1994), and mutual interests will become more inseparable when operational synergies are gradually precipitated in this unique yet ongoing relationship (Hamel, 1991; Harrigan, 1986). Under these circumstances, levels of commitment, tolerance, and forbearance from each party will be higher, intensifying the response conformity between two parties under a given identifier status. This conformity may be even stronger if interparty integration is higher. Integration shortens the deviation between potential value and actual value of resource complementarity and harmonizes individual interests with joint interests, thereby bolstering the accord of strategic response from each party. In sum, the above discussions suggest that opportunism may decrease when resource complementarity increases, and the strength of this link may be stronger when economic integration is higher.

Goal Congruence and Opportunism

Goal congruence in this article is defined as the degree to which each parent's respective goals underlying the establishment of an alliance are compatible or convergent. Research on alliances agrees that the congruity of parental goals affects the extent to which parent firms will behave cooperatively or opportunistically during alliance operations (Beamish & Banks, 1987; Hill, 1990; Inkpen & Beamish, 1997; Lorange & Roos, 1992; Parkhe, 1993; Zaheer, McEvily, & Perrone, 1998). Goal congruity harmonizes the interests of parents that would otherwise give way to the adversary pursuit of divergent goals (Deeds & Hill, 1998; Hennart, 1988; Oxley, 1997; Williamson, 1985). Studies on control concur that goal congruity significantly reduces costs incurred in information exchange between parties, because this congruity reduces each party's perceived uncertainty about what other players will do, which in turn facilitates choosing the best responses that lead to high payoffs at both the joint and individual levels (Eisenhardt, 1985; Flamholtz, Das, & Tsui, 1985; Park, 1996). Thus, opportunism may reduce as congruity increases.

Generally, an individual party's response or behavior is driven by its underlying goals or objectives (Eisenhardt, 1985). For instance, each party in a tightly integrated alliance can consider transmission, cooptation, or assimilation as its strategic response. Goal congruence nurtures response harmony in this situation in which both parties expect compatible aims—which in turn suppresses opportunism. In the absence of goal congruence, cooperation becomes difficult (Geringer & Hebert, 1989) and alliance partners are more likely to engage in dysfunctional activities seeking private interests (Das & Teng, 1998). Research on opportunism holds that goal incongruence is the fertile breeding ground for the pursuit of self-interest with guile (Williamson, 1979). Because none of the collective control mechanisms promises to curb consistently and forcefully all opportunistic behaviors (Birnberg, 1998), goal congruence functions as a deterrent against the incidence of opportunism and as a catalyst for cooperation through harmonizing interests, actions, and responses between parties (Hill, 1990; Nooteboom, 1996; Parkhe, 1993). In sum, as goal congruity increases, opportunism may decrease.

Bargaining Asymmetry and Opportunism

Bargaining power asymmetry between alliance partners can influence the degrees of private control and collective control, because this asymmetry infers an imbalance of interparty dependence in resources and power (Harrigan & Newman, 1990; Inkpen & Beamish, 1997) and an inequality of perceived importance attached to the alliance by different parties (Tallman & Shenkar, 1994; Yan & Gray, 1994). One party's bargaining power is its ability to change the bargaining relationship favorably, to win accommodations from the other party, and to influence the outcomes of bargaining. Bargaining power in alliances arises either from resource-based sources such as possession or control of critical resources (financial, technological, organizational) that are attractive to the partner or indispensable to alliance operations or from context-based sources such as relative urgency of cooperation, alternatives availability, and alliance importance in overall strategic portfolio (Child & Faulkner, 1998; Harrigan, 1986; Yan & Luo, 2001).

Because the level of opportunism is determined by the party's bargaining power such that the dominant bargaining power leads to the dominant private control (Beamish & Banks, 1987; Geringer & Hebert, 1989), bargaining power asymmetry may skew alliance interests and decisions toward the dominant party, thus propelling interest divergence and increasing opportunism. Greater opportunism in corresponding higher asymmetry complies with the logic of mutual hostages: that unless parties share similar power, there will be a strong incentive for parties making less transaction-specific investments to behave opportunistically (Hill, 1990; Williamson, 1979). Asymmetry may also be at odds with cooperation, because this asymmetry may damage commensurate risk structure and reciprocal commitment (Axelrod, 1984). In particular, this asymmetry hampers, at least partly, a weak party's willingness to be vulnerable to relational risks. This, along with reduced confident expectations, may further hinder trust-building between partners and thus reinforce opportunism.

Although it is very possible that two parties may share convergent interests in the founding stage, bargaining power asymmetry causes their interests to diverge over time. This often occurs when one partner acquires sufficient knowledge and skills to eliminate a partner dependency and make the alliance bargain abated or obsolete (Inkpen & Beamish, 1997). In a global setting, for instance, as the foreign partner's local knowledge increases, its dependence on the local partner decreases, leading to a shift in bargaining power and greater divergence of private interests. As this occurs, the alliance will become more unstable, and individual interests will deviate more from joint interests (Ring & Van de Ven, 1994; Yan & Gray, 1994). As different parties are differently susceptible to environmental changes such as drastic decrease in market price due to varying strategic intents and orientations (e.g., the foreign partner may put more emphasis on local sales than the local partner), bargaining power asymmetry may further destabilize the alliance unity and undermine a joint response to environmental hazards. This can enlarge interest gaps and heighten opportunism. In the language of gaming, one player will produce an adverse selection or different response if the other player dominates in the sequential bargaining under asymmetric power—the situation known as the breakdown of a Bayesian equilibrium (Gibbons, 1992, pp. 218–224). Asymmetric information in this sequential bargaining also leads to idiosyncratic responses from different parties to critical decisions (Axelrod, 1984).

Bargaining-power asymmetry also shakes the institutional and cooperative foundations, thus furthering opportunistic effects. Yan and Gray (1994) report that strategic alliances with bargaining power equally matched between partners are equipped with a shared managerial control structure. However, the alliance in which bargaining power is unequally divided adopts an

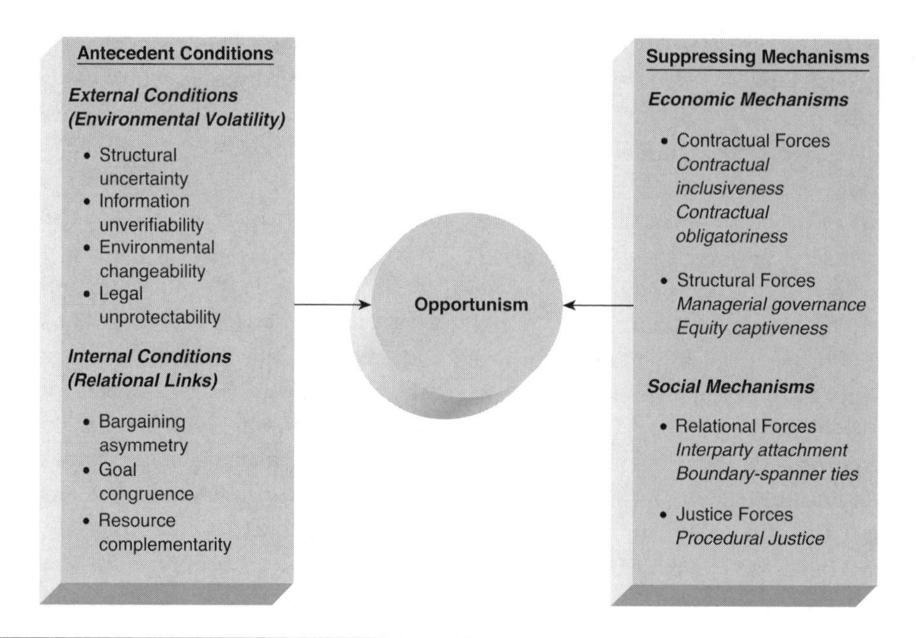

Figure 4.1. Opportunism in Cooperative Alliances: Antecedent Conditions and Suppressing Mechanisms

unbalanced control structure in which the more powerful partner dominates. The power dependence view clearly suggests that a party's ability to control and direct organizational action originates from its bargaining power and that bargaining-power asymmetry will lead to control-ability asymmetry and interdependence asymmetry (Bacharach & Lawler, 1984; Pfeffer & Salancik, 1978). These results can weaken the joint governance structure that couches cooperation and evolution in such a way that a dominant party may threaten to discontinue supplying critical resources to the alliance if the institutional framework is not favorable to it (Schaan, 1988; Saxton, 1997).

Asymmetric power may also escalate the propensity of opportunism because the weak party is likely to attach descended value to the joint payoff (Harrigan & Newman, 1990), and governance safeguards may be unable to detect or correct this behavior (Deeds & Hill, 1998). To conclude, as bargaining-power asymmetry increases, opportunism is expected to increase, ceteris paribus.

Counteropportunism Solutions

Figure 4.1 summarizes an overarching theoretical framework that integrates external and internal conditions that determine opportunism as well as counteropportunism solutions that require both economic and social forces. I suggest that there are four "ordering" systems that restrain opportunism: (1) contractual ordering, (2) structural ordering, (3) relational ordering, and (4) justice ordering. Contractual and structural orderings are derived from economic exchange logic requiring formally stipulated obligation and incentive systems to govern exchange. They share the egotistic assumption that each transacting party aims to maximize its self-interest gains (Williams, 1988). In contrast, relational and justice orderings are affiliated with social exchange logic involving an ongoing reciprocal process in which socially embedded voluntary actions are contingent upon rewarding reactions from others. They share the nonegotistic assumption that each player in a socially embedded exchange needs to follow fundamental principles of social exchange, such as equity (Adams, 1965) and reciprocity (Blau, 1964). "Ordering" is a mandate with which all related actors need to comply, whether compulsorily or voluntarily, in order to create a situation in which exchange between the actors is properly organized, directed, and rewarded.

Economic-based ordering and social-based ordering coexist in relational contracting transactions such as alliances. Economic-based ordering provides a legal and institutional framework within which social-based ordering proceeds, whereas social-based ordering redresses the deficiency of economic-based ordering in a socially confined economic structure. Cooperation between alliance partners is a Pareto-improvement process such that both parties are made better off (Buckley & Casson, 1988, p. 32). Without complementary contributions from justice (equity) and relations (reciprocity), economic-based ordering, no matter how specific or regulative, cannot effectively suppress opportunism (Granovetter, 1985; Poppo & Zenger, 2002). When external disturbances arise, economic-based ordering alone cannot maintain the continuity of the relationship (Folta, 1998). It cannot guarantee mutually acceptable resolutions to cure internal problems such as interparty conflicts, information shirking, and cheating (Lin & Germain, 1998).

Social-based ordering is necessary to overcome economic-based ordering's limitation in the adaptation and execution of long-term relational exchanges and is critical in fostering continuity and reciprocity when disturbances arise. Sociologically, it is ideal for such relational exchanges to be executed within a cooperative culture because "there exist mechanisms within an alliance that favor the creation of an 'internal' social norm of reciprocity" (Granovetter, 1985, p. 501). Cooperation is established by the expectation that beneficial behavior will be reciprocated because of desire to maintain future social exchanges; cooperation will not occur if a party is known as someone who does not reciprocate (Rubin & Brown, 1975). Thus, unless a party seeks only short-term gain, opportunism will not last long due to social exchange constraints that have an enduring "economic" effect on the party's creditability, image, and reputation (Hill, 1990).

Economic Ordering System and Opportunism

In my scheme, economic-based ordering comprises contractual ordering and structural ordering. Contractual ordering is an antiopportunism framework that legally stipulates or codifies each partner's rights, duties, and responsibilities as well as the alliance's major goals, strategies, and policies. It provides a legally bound governance system that contractually monitors interpartner exchanges and dissipates opportunism. Structural ordering, which is akin to Williamson's private ordering (1985), suppresses opportunism by creating an institutional structure that oversees and monitors each party's behavior, commitment, and participation. Such structure can be either interest-based (equity captiveness) or management-based (managerial governance). Equity captiveness captures each partner's motives of self-interested suppression of opportunism in anticipation of future rewards from cooperation. Transaction cost logic assumes that one party is unlikely or unmotivated to cooperate if it has no direct material interest in doing so (Williamson, 1985). Equity captiveness creates a "hostage" situation in which each party's stake and reward are directly tied to alliance development and collective acts. Contractual ordering and structural ordering are supplementary: Contracts specify some important conditions and measures of governance that are not covered in structural ordering; meanwhile, structural ordering describes detailed measures of control and governance for ongoing operations, especially formalized and routinized policies.

Contractual Ordering

Contractual ordering determines and influences the policies and procedures that are to be followed in alliances. It may detail roles, obligations, and processes to be performed, specify procedures for monitoring and penalties for noncompliance, and determine outcomes to be delivered. Williamson (1999, p. 1090) suggests that "credible contracting is very much an exercise in farsighted contracting, whereby the parties look ahead, recognize hazards, and devise hazard mitigating responses—thereby to realize mutual gain." Precodified rigorous contracts are important because they reduce the risk of defection and facilitate legal enforcement. The parties to an alliance contract may mitigate ex post opportunism and investment distortions by using more complete agreements (Williamson, 1979). An incomplete contract creates leeway for opportunism and generates moral hazards for a cooperative relationship (Goldberg, 1976).

Two dimensions of an alliance contract affect opportunism: contractual inclusiveness and contractual obligatoriness. Contractual inclusiveness is the degree to which relevant issues are included and specified in an alliance contract. According to transaction cost economics, incentives for opportunism arise after the investments are sunk (Williamson, 1985). If a mechanism cannot be devised to mitigate each party's ability to act on these incentives, a promising transaction may become unattractive during contract execution (Goldberg, 1976). High contractual inclusiveness reduces the likelihood that the project will deviate from its desired course. Greater coverage of contractual terms guides alliance formation and avoids the creation of loopholes that could hamper alliance performance. It may also alleviate interpartner conflicts that would otherwise jeopardize cooperation. Explicit coverage provides a clear framework that defines each party's rights as well as the principles and procedures of cooperation and conflict resolution. Contractual inclusiveness and specification can also help reduce managerial complexity by coordinating activities for collective goals. It clarifies the rules and responsibilities involved in such issues as project construction, location and size, equity sharing, resource contributions, board composition, nomination of top management, and so on. High inclusiveness further helps each party obtain more accurate information regarding duties, needs, and benefits, which then allows each party to make decisions that benefit both individual payoff and joint reward.

Contractual obligatoriness is the extent to which each party involved in an alliance contract is restrained by the binding force of the contract. An alliance contract cannot be viewed as complete unless it codifies each party's legal obligatoriness (Macneil, 1978). According to a typical contract law, obligatoriness varies according to the contract, because parties have the right to mandate both overall and specific terms that describe a contract's legal effect (Goldberg, 1976). Contractual obligatoriness includes such terms as legal binding force of the overall contract (and applicable laws), penalization against the breaching party, and compensation for the aggrieved party. Without such obligatoriness, the contract is incomplete no matter how inclusive or specific the terms are. Contractual obligatoriness helps mitigate future opportunism because it increases the level of legal obligation that constrains each party during subsequent stages of alliance formation and operations. It also fosters enforcement of the agreement. Having more obligations increases each party's sensitivity to its duties and responsibilities, which in turn improves forbearance. Without obligatoriness, one party may take an opportunistic "wait and see" attitude, avoiding its own responsibilities until the partner firm has fulfilled certain duties. Finally, contractual obligatoriness legally binds each party's behavior and commitment, leading to expected benefits arising from joint operations; this in turn encourages resource contribution and sustained commitment to alliance development.

Structural Ordering

Structural ordering curtails opportunism in two ways: through managerial governance and through equity captiveness. Managerial governance is an antiopportunism subsystem purposely and jointly designed by the parties that establishes formalized and routinized procedures, rules, practices, norms, and policies. Examples of managerial governance include (1) formulating an alliance's various policies and practices (e.g., job descriptions for senior alliance managers, division of labor across functions and hierarchies, joint decision-making processes, procedures for conflict resolution, management of key resources, routinized practices for employee learning, and performance monitoring), (2) developing strategic plans, annual targets, and new projects and jointly monitoring the execution of these plans, targets, and projects, (3) establishing and exercising various information control systems (e.g., marketing, accounting, and inventory information systems), (4) establishing and executing various finance, accounting, budgeting, and auditing control systems (e.g., cash flow management, expenditure approval, dividend policy, budget control, and internal fund control), and (5) instituting a corporate culture that nourishes alliance growth and evolution. Because "all parties in an alliance have an inalienable *de facto* right to pursue their own interests at the expense of others" (Buckley & Casson, 1988, p. 34), managerial governance guides cooperation and reduces opportunism by providing an institutionally bound framework. Managerial governance also narrows the domain and severity of risk to which an exchange is exposed, thereby discouraging opportunistic behavior and private incentive-seeking (Poppo & Zenger, 2002). Moreover, it makes one party's behavior more observable to the other, hence promoting transparency and forbearance, both of which obviate opportunism (Hill, 1990).

A second dimension of structural ordering is equity captiveness: the extent to which the parties' equity ownership is commensurate such that a mutual hostage situation is created. In equity-based alliances, mutual hostage is mainly established through ownership participation. Transaction cost economics advocates the exchange of critical resources between partners in such a way that each partner becomes vulnerable to potential losses, thereby materially demonstrating credible commitment to the other partner and the alliance (Anderson, 1988; Martin, Swaminathan, & Mitchell, 1998). When parties make substantially dissimilar transaction-specific investments, there is a strong incentive for the party making a lower investment to behave opportunistically (Williamson, 1985). If one party's stake is very low, its switching costs will also be very low, hence leading to less captiveness and a smaller potential loss (in case the relationship breaks or the partner takes opportunistic action). Therefore, the possibility of opportunistic behavior is proportional to the difference in transaction-specific investments by alliance members. Mutual assurance through equity captiveness offers a way of diminishing the attractiveness of defection (Deeds & Hill, 1998). Vulnerability on both sides will lessen the incentive to engage in opportunistic behavior for fear of losing critical resources held hostage by the "victim" firm. Unless the perceived gain from opportunism is greater than the loss of the hostage resources, a partner will refrain from opportunistic behavior even if there is scope for it.

Social Ordering System and Opportunism

I have explained that interpartner exchange is largely utilitarian, requiring economic exchange logic to explain individual and joint behaviors and requiring contractual and structural ordering to curb opportunism. However, classical and neoclassical economics assumes that rational, self-interested behavior is only minimally affected by social structure, social norms, and social relations. This is a major limitation, because economic actions, especially long-term, transaction-specific investments, are gradually embedded in social relations, and relationship-specific assets such as trust may be generated (Granovetter, 1985). Interorganizational and interpersonal relationships discourage opportunism and malfeasance. Blau defines social exchange as the "voluntary actions of individuals that are motivated by the returns they are expected to bring and typically in fact bring from others" (1964, p. 91).

Social exchange theorists view social exchange as an ongoing reciprocal process in which actions are contingent on rewarding reactions from others. Reciprocity is hence the fundamental principle of social exchange and the backbone of interpersonal and interorganizational relationships (Das & Teng, 2002). Such relationships, as argued below, improve mutual understanding, trust development, and knowledge sharing, all of which possibly counter opportunism. Social exchange theories address not only how people form reciprocal relationships but also how power is distributed in those relationships. They view fairness and justice as fundamental principles underpinning a repeated exchange. The equity notion (Adams, 1965) in social exchange theory addresses the importance of fair distribution of resources and outcomes in exchange relationships and underscores the link between sharing returns and each party's actual contribution. According to this notion, equity is the basic foundation of social exchange, and inequity leads not only to the dissatisfaction of a suffering party but also to other harmful consequences, such as discontinuity of an ongoing exchange, jeopardy in adaptation, and reduction of commitment, all of which eventually injure the relationship. In light of the above social exchange logic, I propose two social-exchange-based orderings: relational ordering and justice ordering.

Relational Ordering

Relational ordering is a socially based binding force that counteracts the desire for opportunism. It comprises interparty attachment (ties between alliance partners) and boundary-spanner connections (ties between senior alliance executives representing different parties) (Jap & Anderson, 2003; Seabright, Levinthal, & Fichman, 1992). Interparty attachment reflects the history of dyadic organizational investments made since the alliance was formed and it increases with the duration and reciprocity of the relationship. This attachment encourages the exploitation of relationship-specific opportunities and accumulates as the parties invest in developing specialized expertise peculiar to the alliance's needs (Levinthal & Fichman, 1988). These specialized investments lose value when applied to other relationships. Consequently, the parties become locked into the existing relationship, both benefiting from the relationship through joint efforts and coincided responses.

This attachment, rather than institutional arrangement or legal contract, is mainly responsible for the establishing of trust and trustworthy behavior in economic life (Granovetter, 1985). According to economic sociology, individual aggressiveness or opportunistic desire is curbed by the prospect of ostracism by the partner when interfirm attachment supports courtesy between them. Social trust between firms can institutionally undergird market activities and reduce vulnerability to external threats (Emerson, 1976; Powell, 1990). Heightened attachment provides ample opportunity for overt collaboration and restrains covert self-interested behavior (Das & Teng, 1998; Lyles & Salk, 1996), thereby neutralizing the tendency toward opportunism. Furthermore, the interpartner resource-sharing spurred by attachment decreases an alliance's dependence on external resources and reduces its economic exposure to environmental disturbances (Fichman & Levinthal, 1991; Lane, Salk, & Lyles, 2001). Blau (1964) and Cook and Emerson (1978) argue that interorganizational attachment can lead to maintaining a relationship even if the partnership provides fewer necessary resources than it originally did. Seabright et al. (1992) also suggest that attachment counters external hazards that may affect resource fit. Finally, high attachment often means that the parties have passed through a critical "shakeout" period of conflict (Parkhe, 1993). Structural attachments also attenuate interparty incongruities in corporate culture, strategic orientation, and managerial infrastructure (Seabright et al., 1992; Steensma & Lyles, 2002).

Relational ordering at the individual level—interpersonal relationships between boundary-spanners (i.e., senior alliance executives nominated by and representing different parents)—also influences opportunism because the embeddedness of interpersonal connections generates standards of expected behavior that obviate the need for and are superior to purely authoritative relations in discouraging opportunism and malfeasance (Granovetter, 1985). Personal connections reflect socialization by boundary-spanners from each party during their involvement in exchange activities between the partner organizations. Sociologically, these personal bonds can lead to group norms that increase the commitment of the parties to a cooperative relationship (Cook & Emerson, 1978). An alliance's individual boundary-spanning members are a repository of assets created from relationship-specific capital, which may be in the form of personal skills or organizational routines, assets, and technologies (Emerson, 1976). Prisoner's Dilemmas and moral hazards are diminished by the strength of these relations; in other words, the positive result arises not from the transactors themselves but from the strength of their relationships (Granovetter, 1985).

In a collectivism-oriented culture, personal connections have a particularly strong influence on antiopportunism. This is because opportunism, if it occurs, can lead to loss of an individual's social "face," which may lead to the loss of exchange opportunities with all members of that individual's network or even with society overall (Peng & Luo, 2000). Because knowledge concerning the status of each individual's "face" travels quickly through an interpersonal network, an individual's loss of face can result in systemwide negative effects (Luo, 2001). Moreover, personal ties facilitate the convergence of those managerial styles and philosophies that were originally peculiar to the culture of each party. Culture is not a one-time-only experience but a process that is continually reconstructed and refueled through ongoing interaction. It not only shapes network members but is also shaped by them, partly for strategic reasons (Hofstede, 2001). As personal bonds accumulate, the parties develop a common culture that nourishes mutual learning and knowledge exchange; this interpersonal sharing further restrains opportunism.

Justice Ordering

Justice is a foundation for all types of economic transactions. Alliance members are more willing to cooperate and less likely to behave opportunistically if procedural and distributive justice are in play (Johnson, 1997). The equity perspective in social exchange theory suggests that individuals or parties are more likely to commit to the existing relationship, even under uncertainty, if they believe that the decision-making process is fair (procedural justice) and that rewards are commensurate with their efforts (distributive justice) (Lind & Tyler, 1988; Walker & Pettigrew, 1984). In the alliance context, procedural justice involves the extent to which the strategic decision-making processes and procedures that impact each party's gains and interests are perceived by the alliance's boundary-spanners as impartial and fair. "Fair" means that related procedures and criteria are unbiased, representative, transparent, correctable, and ethical (Greenberg, 1987). Each party cares about procedural fairness because of its implications for the tangible outcomes the party will receive, in both the short and the long run.

On the other hand, distributive justice is the extent to which interparty sharing of the rewards from cooperation is fair in light of each party's contribution, commitment, and assumption of responsibility. Rewards include monetary forms such as profit, dividend, and market expansion as well as nonmonetary forms such as knowledge acquisition and reputation improvement. Each party cares about distributive fairness, because inequity in gain-sharing disproportional to a party's contribution will create a significant obstacle to fostering confidence in cooperation. Procedural and distributive justice reinforce each other in fostering overall justice in both the means and ends of fairness in an exchange; they are distinct in that distributive justice is more concerned with reactions to specific outcomes targeted by each party, whereas procedural justice is more strongly related to reactions to the alliance as a whole.

I expect that in an alliance, increased fairness of procedural justice will deter opportunism. A positive perception of procedural justice can improve not only calculative commitment through more active participation in joint decision making and better compliance with alliance rules but also affective commitment through more frequent socialization and heightened membership unity. As a result, incentives for opportunism will decrease. When one party's private interest is better aligned with joint gains from the alliance via heightened procedural justice, that party will attribute greater importance to participatory decision making, resulting in valuable safeguards against opportunism and dysfunction. Participatory decision making underpinned by procedural justice leads to two things: (1) a commitment to and an interest in outcomes, which decrease the perceived likelihood of opportunistic behavior, and (2) the increased likelihood that a partner's opportunistic behavior will be recognized (Saxton, 1997).

Improved procedural justice restrains opportunism through identification and internalization as well. Identification involves group efforts that enhance affiliation, whereas internalization involves group efforts aimed at achieving congruence in the goals and values of each party and the alliance. Both identification and internalization are bases for psychological attachment to organizations (Katz & Kahn, 1978). Increased procedural justice stimulates commitment and loyalty to the joint organization and counteracts the "frustration effect" arising from differences in group norms, values, and cultures (Lind & Tyler, 1988). Stronger group identification helps coordinate responses from different partners via enhanced integrity of alliance identity and improved harmony of individual interests. Procedural justice in the strategic decision-making process also amplifies the acceptance of new internalized norms and alleviates interparty differences in managerial philosophy and style. Through this internalization, both parties may become less opportunistic. Finally, procedural justice reduces the need for interfirm rivalry (Khanna et al. 1998). Once rivalry is reduced, the likelihood of opportunism is reduced accordingly (Deeds & Hill, 1998).

Distributive justice is also important in curbing opportunism. With higher distributive justice, each party's incentive for interpartner exchange becomes stronger because of increased confidence regarding impartial gain-sharing. Due to equity hostage or resource mixture in alliances and the high failure rate of alliances, executives from each party anticipate that nothing is guaranteed with respect to the ultimate outcome of cooperation. As such, when these executives strategically plan their party's commitment to the alliance, they will likely attach greater importance to the fairness of outcome distribution than to the outcome itself. Improved distributive justice can also reduce the hazards of withholding information and shirking obligations, which are common examples of opportunistic behavior. As Barney stated (1999, p. 143), opportunism is part of the cost of gaining access to the special capabilities controlled by another firm that cannot be developed internally or secured through acquisition in a cost-effective way. Enhanced distributive justice can reduce this opportunism, which then facilitates mutual access to and the sharing of the resources pooled for the alliance. Finally, increased distributive justice can foster trust and consequently curtail opportunism. Fair treatment in outcome distribution removes fears of exploitation and stimulates transparency of communication between boundary-spanners (Johnson, 1997; Welbourne, Balkin, & Gomez-Mejia, 1995).

Conclusion

This article seeks to build an overarching and integrated framework for understanding conditions that affect opportunism and mechanisms that restrain opportunism in cooperative alliances. Given the complex, opaque, and covert nature of opportunism, it is difficult for one article to capture every antecedent condition and every counteropportunism force. Nevertheless, this article attempts to address those antecedents, both external and internal, that are particularly influential in affecting the level of opportunism in an uncertain environment and those mechanisms, both economic and social-based, that are particularly essential to preventing, resisting, or reducing opportunism.

To address external antecedents that affect opportunism, this article focuses on how the level of opportunism exhibited by alliance parties copes with environmental volatility, defined as a multivariable concept comprising industry structural uncertainty, information unverifiability, environmental changeability, and legal unprotectability. I conceive of these four variables as individually distinct, each capturing different aspects of volatility, yet jointly picture an overall profile of environmental volatility in an emerging economy. It is widely held that a joint venture party's degree of opportunism is not prefixed but endogenous, contingent on both external and internal factors. I propose that the degree of opportunism is particularly prone to environmental volatility because of the enormous transaction costs and information processing costs that are incurred in dealing with such volatility. Environmental volatility increases transaction uncertainty and information processing difficulty and complexity.

Because environmental volatility in an emerging economy is primarily caused by structural transformation, institutional reforms, and regulatory changes, business executives, with their limited rationality, are generally unable effectively to avoid or control volatility-induced transaction uncertainty and information processing difficulty. Consequently, economic exposure of alliance activities is extremely high. In the absence of well-functioning market institutions, including risk-management agencies and information intermediaries for the public, such economic exposure is almost impossible to hedge via external instruments (contractual and financial instruments such as forwards, futures, options and swaps) or internal instruments (operational and financial initiatives such as leads and lags, netting and matching, and intracorporate arrangements). Compounded by huge sunk and exit costs of alliance investments in which asset specificity is often very high, along with fears of appropriability hazards due to legal unprotectability, investing parties, both foreign and local, are likely to demonstrate more opportunism in reaction to unhedgeable economic exposure arising from environmental volatility.

I elaborate on how dyadic relations between alliance members may also influence opportunism. Dyadic relationships have received increasing attention in alliance literature and are recognized as important predictors of alliance performance (Dyer & Singh, 1998; Khanna et al. 1998; Lado, Boyd, & Hanlon, 1997; Park & Ungson, 1997; Saxton, 1997). Departing from preceding studies, I theorize how such dyadic relationships influence opportunism. I propose that the following influences exist: (1) opportunism is inversely associated with resource complementarity, and such association is further moderated by operational integration, (2) opportunism is increasingly associated with bargaining power asymmetry, and (3) opportunism is also increasingly associated with objective conformity. Although the relational features I cover here are not meant to be exclusive or exhaustive in describing interparty links, they are deemed to be particularly influential in affecting the interparty agreement of strategic intent and strategic behavior. The absence of such agreement propels opportunism.

Although I may not be able to articulate all of the mechanisms that suppress opportunism, I believe that the four ordering systems I propose, including contractual ordering, structural ordering, relational ordering, and justice ordering, are extensive. I explain that each of these ordering systems exists not in isolation but jointly to curtail opportunistic acts. A system comprising more antiopportunism forces will work better than any single force in dispelling opportunism, because each option can discourage only part or some aspect of opportunism. I also suggest that each ordering system is multidimensional, consisting of several specific forces that suppress opportunism.

Although prior studies in the alliance literature have already identified several counteropportunism forces (such as managerial governance, contract inclusiveness, and interparty attachment), other forces, such as organizational justice, contractual obligatoriness, and boundary-spanner ties, are understudied. These underaddressed forces, in conjunction with known antiopportunism levers, are also critical in dissipating opportunism. Justice ordering (both procedural and distributive) is found to have a significant main effect on reducing opportunism for both foreign and local parties. Research on justice has often emphasized the individual level (e.g., employees); I demonstrate that justice is also crucial at the interorganizational level such that improved fairness in the decision process and on outcome distribution alleviates opportunism by both parties. Similarly, alliance research has often emphasized contract specificity or inclusiveness; I document that antiopportunism necessitates high obligatoriness as well. To some extent, obligatoriness is a "coefficient" of contractual function in deterring opportunism because high obligatoriness heightens contractual binding.

Finally, research on cooperation often focuses on interorganizational ties; I show that interpersonal ties between boundary-spanners are also instrumental in attenuating firm-level opportunism. I argue that boundary-spanners are judges who transform perceptual and distributive justice into parent actions; they are representatives of their parent constituents whose decisions are shaped by self-interest of these constituents. Hence, superior personal ties can partly reduce boundary-spanners' role conflicts and increase their commitment to alliance performance.

A growing number of studies share the view that the economic structure of alliance exchange is socially embedded. Central to counteropportunism in alliances is the simultaneous use of both economic mechanisms (contractual ordering and structural ordering) and social mechanisms (relational ordering and justice ordering). Economic and social mechanisms work jointly such that economic-based ordering provides a legal or institutional template within which social-based ordering functions, whereas social-based ordering redresses deficiencies of economic- based ordering in socially confined environments. Opportunism is subject to constraints from both formal structures and social reality. Hence, an integrated antiopportunism system consisting of both economic and social binding forces is more productive in inhibiting opportunism than either mechanism in isolation.

My model also integrates ex ante forces and ex post forces and unites individual-level forces and organizational-level forces. Ex ante forces consist of contractual inclusiveness, contractual obligatoriness, and equity captiveness; ex post forces include managerial governance, relational ordering, and justice ordering. Ex ante forces establish a structural exchange foundation, whereas ex post forces satisfy the need for ongoing reciprocal processes of exchange and evolutionary alliance development. Because much of alliance opportunism is perpetrated by boundary-spanners who represent the parties, an individual-level force such as boundary-spanner ties supplements organizational-level forces in buffering conflict-related opportunism.

References

Adams, J. S. (1965). Inequity in social exchange. In L. Berkowitz (Ed.), *Advances in experimental social psychology* (Vol. 2, pp. 267–299). New York: Academic Press.

Anderson, E. (1988). Transaction costs as determinants of opportunism in integrated and independent sales forces. *Journal of Economic Behavior & Organization, 9*, 247–264.

Ariño, A., & de la Torre, J. (1998). Learning from failure: Towards an evolutionary model of collaborative ventures. *Organization Science, 9*, 306–325.

Axelrod, R. (1984). *The evolution of cooperation.* New York: Basic Books.

Bacharach, S. B., & Lawler, E. J. (1984). *Bargaining: Power, tactics, and outcomes.* San Francisco: Jossey-Bass.

Barkema, H. G., Shenkar, O., Vermeulen, F., & Bell, J. H. J. (1996). Foreign entry, cultural barriers, and learning. *Academy of Management Journal, 40*, 426–442.

Barney, J. B. (1999). How a firm's capabilities affect boundary decisions. *Sloan Management Studies, 40*(3), 137–145.

Beamish, P. W., & Banks, J. C. (1987). Equity joint ventures and the theory of the multinational enterprises. *Journal of International Business Studies, 18*(2), 1–16.

Bies, R. J. (2001). Interactional (in)justice: The sacred and the profane. In J. Greenberg & R. Cropanzano (Eds.), *Advances in organizational justice* (pp. 89–118). Stanford, CA: Stanford University Press.

Biggart, N. W., & Delbridge, R. (2004). Systems of exchange. *Academy of Management Review, 29,* 28–47.

Birnberg, J. G. (1998). Control in interfirm cooperative relationships. *Journal of Management Studies, 35,* 421–428.

Blau, P. M. (1964). *Exchange and power in social life.* New York: Wiley.

Blodgett, L. L. (1992). Factors in the instability of international JVs: An event history analysis. *Strategic Management Journal, 13,* 475–491.

Bourgeois, L. (1980). Strategy and environment: A conceptual integration. *Academy of Management Review, 5,* 25–39.

Boyd, B., & Fulk, J. (1996). Executive practices and perceived uncertainty: A multidimensional model. *Journal of Management, 22*(1), 1–21.

Boyd, B., Dess, G., & Rasheed, M. (1993). Divergence between archival and perceptual measures of the environment: Causes and consequences. *Academy of Management Review, 18,* 204–226.

Brown, C. R. (1997). *Understanding Chinese courts and legal process: Law with Chinese characteristics.* New York: Kluwer Law International.

Brown, J. R., Dev, C. S., & Zhou, Z. (2003). Broadening the foreign market entry mode decision: Separating ownership and control. *Journal of International Business Studies, 34,* 473–488.

Browning, L. D., Beyer, J. M., & Shetler, J. C. (1995). Building cooperation in a competitive industry: SEMATECH and the semiconductor industry. *Academy of Management Journal, 38,* 113–151.

Buchko, A. A. (1994). Conceptualization and measurement of environmental uncertainty: An assessment of the Miles and Snow perceived environmental uncertainty scale. *Academy of Management Journal, 37,* 410–425.

Buckley, P., & Casson, M. (1988). The theory of cooperation in international business. In F. J. Contractor & P. Lorange (Eds.), *Cooperative strategies in international business* (pp. 31–34). Lexington, MA: Lexington Books.

Chi, T., & McGuire, D. (1996). Collaborative ventures and value of learning. Integrating the transaction cost and strategic option perspectives on the choice of market entry modes. *Journal of International Business Studies, 27,* 285–307.

Child, J., & Faulkner, D. (1998). *Strategies of cooperation.* Oxford: Oxford University Press.

Chung, S., Singh, H., & Lee, K. (2000). Complementarity, status similarity and social capital as drivers of strategic JV formation. *Strategic Management Journal, 21,* 1–19.

Conner, K. R., & Prahalad, C. K. (1996). A resource-based theory of the firm: Knowledge versus opportunism. *Organization Science, 7,* 477–502.

Contractor, F. J., & Lorange, P. (1988). The strategy and economic basis for cooperative ventures. In F. J. Contractor & P. Lorange (Eds.), *Cooperative strategies in international business* (pp. 3–28). Lexington, MA: Lexington Books.

Cook, K. S., & Emerson, R. M. (1978). Power, equity and commitment in exchange networks. *American Sociological Review, 43,* 721–739.

Currall, S. C., & Inkpen, A. C. (2002). A multilevel approach to trust in joint ventures. *Journal of International Business Studies, 33,* 479–495.

Daft, R., Sormunem, J., & Parks, D. (1988). Chief executive scanning, environmental characteristics, and company performance: An empirical study. *Strategic Management Journal, 9,* 123–139.

Das, T. K., & Teng, B. (1996). Risk types and inter-firm alliance structures. *Journal of Management Studies, 33,* 827–843.

Das, T. K., & Teng, B. (1998). Between trust and control: Developing confidence in partner cooperation in alliances. *Academy of Management Review, 23,* 491–512.

Das, T. K., & Teng, B. (2002). Strategic alliance constellations: A social exchange perspective. *Academy of Management Review, 27,* 445–456.

Deeds, D. L., & Hill, C. W. L. (1998). An examination of opportunistic action within research JVs: Evidence from the biotechnology industry. *Journal of Business Venturing, 14*(2), 141–163.

Dess, G., & Beard, D. (1984). Dimensions of organizational task environments. *Administrative Science Quarterly, 29,* 52–73.

Dixit, A. K., & Pindyck, R. S. (1994). *Investment under uncertainty.* Princeton, NJ: Princeton University Press.

Doz, Y. L. (1996, Summer). The evolution of cooperation in strategic alliances: Initial conditions or learning processes? [special issue]. *Strategic Management Journal, 17,* 55–83.

Dyer, J. H. (1997). Effective interfirm collaboration: How firms minimize transaction costs and maximize transaction value. *Strategic Management Journal, 18*(7), 535–556.

Dyer, J. H., & Chu, W. (2003). The role of trustworthiness in reducing transaction costs and improving performance: Empirical evidence from the United States, Japan and Korea. *Organization Science, 14,* 57–68.

Dyer, J. H., & Singh, H. (1998). The relational view: Cooperative strategy and sources of interorganizational competitive advantage. *Academy of Management Review, 23*(4), 660–679.

Eisenhardt, K. M. (1985). Control: Organizational and economic approaches. *Management Science, 31,* 134–49.

Emerson, R. M. (1976). Social exchange theory. *Annual Review of Sociology, 2,* 335–362.

Fichman, M., & Levinthal, D. A. (1991). Honeymoons and the liability of adolescence: A new perspective on duration dependence in social and organizational relations. *Academy of Management Review, 16,* 442–468.

Flamholtz, E. G., Das, T. K., & Tsui, A. (1985). Toward an integrative framework of organizational control. *Accounting, Organizations and Society, 10*(1), 35–50.

Folta, T. B. (1998). Governance and uncertainty: The tradeoff between administrative control and commitment. *Strategic Management Journal, 19,* 1007–1028.

Galbraith, J. (1977). *Organizational design.* Reading, MA: Addison-Wesley.

Geringer, J. M., & Hebert, L. (1989). Control and performance of international joint ventures. *Journal of International Business Studies, 20*(2), 235–54.

Gibbons, R. (1992). *Game theory for applied economists.* Princeton, NJ: Princeton University Press.

Goldberg, V. P. (1976). Toward an expanded economic theory of contract. *Journal of Economic Issues, 10*(1), 45–61.

Granovetter, M. (1985). Economic action and social structure: A theory of embeddedness. *American Journal of Sociology, 91,* 481–510.

Greenberg, J. (1987). A taxonomy of organizational justice theories. *Academy of Management Review, 12,* 9–22.

Gulati, R. (1995). Social structure and strategic alliance formation: A longitudinal analysis. *Administrative Science Quarterly, 40,* 619–652.

Gulati, R., & Singh, H. (1998). The architecture of cooperation: Managing coordination costs and appropriation concerns in JVs. *Administrative Science Quarterly, 43,* 781–814.

Gulati, R., Khanna T., & Nohria, N. (1994). Unilateral commitments and the importance of process in alliances. *Sloan Management Review, 35*(3), 61–69.

Hamel, G. (1991). Competition for competence and inter-partner learning within international strategic alliances. *Strategic Management Journal, 12*(1), 83–103.

Hare, P. G., & Davis, J. R. (1997). *Transition to the market economy: Critical perspectives on the world economy.* London: Routledge.

Harrigan, K. R. (1986). *Managing for joint venture success.* Lexington, MA: Lexington Books.

Harrigan, K. R., & Newman, W. H. (1990). Bases of interorganizational cooperation: Propensity, power, persistence. *Journal of Management Studies, 27*(4), 417–434.

Hennart, J. (1988). A transaction cost theory of equity joint ventures. *Strategic Management Journal, 9,* 361–374.

Hill, C. W. L. (1990). Cooperation, opportunism, and the invisible hand: Implications for transaction cost theory. *Academy of Management Review, 15,* 32–44.

Hill, R. C., & Hellriegel, D. (1994). Critical contingencies in strategic alliance management: Some lessons from managers. *Organization Science, 5*(4), 594–608.

Hoskisson, R. E., Eden, L., Lau, C. M., & Wright, M. (2000). Strategy in emerging economies. *Academy of Management Journal, 43,* 249–267.

Inkpen, A. C., & Beamish, P. W. (1997). Knowledge, bargaining power, and the instability of international joint ventures. *Academy of Management Review, 22*(1), 177–202.

Jap, S. D., & Anderson, E. (2003). Safeguarding interorganizational performance and continuity under ex post opportunism. *Management Science, 49,* 1684–1706.

Jehn, K., & Weldon, E. (1997). Managerial attitudes toward conflict: Cross-cultural differences in resolution styles. *Journal of International Management, 34,* 102–124.

Johns, G. R. (1984). Task visibility, free riding, and shirking: Explaining the effect of structure and technology on employee behavior. *Academy of Management Review, 9,* 684–695.

Johnson, J. P. (1997). Procedural justice perceptions among international alliance managers. In P. W. Beamish & J. P. Killing (Eds.), *Cooperative strategies: North American perspectives.* San Francisco: New Lexington Press.

Johnson, J. L., Cullen, J. B., Sakano, T., & Takenouchi, H. (1996). Setting the stage for trust and strategic integration in Japanese-U.S. cooperative joint ventures. *Journal of International Business Studies, 27,* 981–1004.

Jones, C., Hesterly, W. S., & Borgatti, S. P. (1997). A general theory of network governance: Exchange conditions and social mechanisms. *Academy of Management Review, 22*(4), 911–945.

Kale, P., Dyer, J. H., & Singh, H. (2002). Strategic alliance capability, stock market response, and long-term strategic alliance success: The role of the strategic alliance function. *Strategic Management Journal, 23,* 747–767.

Katz, D., & Kahn, R. L. (1978). *The social psychology of organization.* New York: Wiley.

Keats, B. W., & Hitt, M. A. (1988). A causal model of linkage among environmental dimensions, macro organizational characteristics and performance. *Academy of Management Journal, 31,* 570–598.

Khanna, T., Gulati, R., & Nohria, N. (1998). The dynamics of learning joint ventures: Competition, cooperation, and relative scope. *Strategic Management Journal, 19,* 193–210.

Killing, J. P. (1983). *Strategies for strategic alliance success.* New York: Praeger.

Kumar, S., & Seth, A. (1998). The design of coordination and control mechanisms for managing strategic alliance–parent relationships. *Strategic Management Journal, 19,* 579–599.

Lado, A. A., Boyd, N. G., & Hanlon, S. C. (1997). Competition, cooperation, and the search for economic rents: A syncretic model. *Academy of Management Review, 22*(1), 110–141.

Lane, P., Salk, J. E., & Lyles, M. A. (2001). Absorptive capacity, learning, and performance in international alliances. *Strategic Management Journal, 22,* 1139–1159.

Levinthal, D. A., & Fichman, M. (1988). Dynamics of interorganizational attachment: Auditor-client relationships. *Administrative Science Quarterly, 33,* 345–369.

Lin, X., & Germain, R. (1998). Sustaining satisfactory strategic alliance relationships: The role of conflict resolution strategy. *Journal of International Business Studies, 33,* 345–369.

Lind, E. A., & Tyler, T. R. (1988). *The social psychology of procedural justice.* New York: Plenum.

Lorange, P., & Roos, J. (1992). *Strategic alliances: Formation, implementation and evolution.* Cambridge, MA: Blackwell.

Luo, Y. (2001). Antecedents and consequences of personal attachment in cross-cultural cooperative ventures. *Administrative Science Quarterly, 46,* 177–201.

Luo, Y. (2002). *Multinational enterprises in emerging markets.* Copenhagen, Denmark: Copenhagen Business School Press.

Lyles, M. A., & Salk, J. E. (1996). Knowledge acquisition from foreign parents in international alliances: An empirical examination in the Hungarian context. *Journal of International Business Studies, 27,* 877–903.

Lyles, M. A., Saxton, T., & Watson, K. (2004). Venture survival in a transitional economy. *Journal of Management, 30,* 351–370.

Macneil, I. R. (1978). Contracts: Adjustment of long-term economic relations under classical, neoclassical, and relational contract law. *Northwestern University Law Review, 72,* 854–905.

Madhok, A. (1995). Revisiting multinational firms' tolerance for joint ventures. *Journal of International Business Studies, 26,* 117–138.

Majoen, H., & Tallman, S. (1997). Control and performance in international joint ventures. *Organization Science, 8*(3), 257–274.

Martin, X., Swaminathan, A., & Mitchell, W. (1998). Organizational evolution in the interorganizational environment: Incentives and constraints on international expansion strategy. *Administrative Science Quarterly, 43,* 566–601.

May, R. C., Stewart, W. H., & Sweo, R. (2000). Environmental scanning behavior in a transition economy: Evidence from Russia. *Academy of Management Journal, 43,* 403–427.

McFarlin, D. B., & Sweeney, P. D. (1992). Distributive and procedural justice as predictors of satisfaction with personal and organizational outcomes. *Academy of Management Journal, 35,* 626–637.

Miller, D. (1987). The structural and environmental correlates of business strategy. *Strategic Management Journal, 31,* 280–309.

Milliken, F. J. (1987). Three types of perceived uncertainty about the environment: State, effect, and response uncertainty. *Academy of Management Review, 12,* 133–143.

Nee, V. (1992). Organizational dynamics of market transition. *Administrative Science Quarterly, 37,* 1–27.

Nooteboom, B. (1996). Trust, opportunism and governance: A process and control model. *Organization Studies, 17,* 985–1010.

Nooteboom, B., Berger, H., & Noorderhaven, N. G. (1997). Effects of trust and governance on relational risk. *Academy of Management Journal, 40,* 308–338.

Oliver, C. (1997). The influence of institutional and task environment relationships on organizational performance: The Canadian construction industry. *Journal of Management Studies, 34,* 99–124.

Osborn, R. N., & Baughn, C. C. (1990). Forms of interorganizational governance for multinational alliances. *Academy of Management Journal, 33,* 503–519.

Oxley, J. E. (1997). Appropriability hazards and governance in strategic alliances: A transaction cost approach. *Journal of Law, Economics & Organization, 13*(2), 387–409.

Park, S. H. (1996). Managing an inter-organizational network: A framework of the institutional mechanism for network control. *Organization Studies, 17,* 795–824.

Park, S. H., & Russo, M. V. (1996). When competition eclipses cooperation: An event history analysis of strategic JV failure. *Management Science, 42,* 875–890.

Park, S. H., & Ungson, G. R. (1997). The effect of national culture, organizational complementarity and economic motivation on strategic alliance dissolution. *Academy of Management Journal, 40,* 279–308.

Parkhe, A. (1991). Interfirm diversity, organizational learning and longevity in global strategic alliances. *Journal of International Business Studies, 22*(4), 579–601.

Parkhe, A. (1993). Strategic alliance structuring: A game theoretic and transaction cost examination of interfirm cooperation. *Academy of Management Journal, 36,* 794–829.

Peng, M. (2000). *Business strategies in transition economies.* Thousand Oaks, CA: Sage.

Peng, M. W., & Luo, Y. (2000). Managerial ties and firm performance in an emerging economy: The nature of a micro-macro link. *Academy of Management Journal, 43,* 486–501.

Pfeffer, J., & Salancik, G. (1978). *The external control of organizations: A resource dependence perspective.* New York: Harper and Row.

Pisano, G. P. (1989). Using equity participation to support exchange: Evidence from the biotechnology industry. *Journal of Law, Economics, and Organization, 5,* 109–126.

Poppo, L., & Zenger, T. (2002). Do formal contracts and relational governance function as substitutes or complements? *Strategic Management Journal, 23,* 707–725.

Porter, M. E. (1985). *Competitive advantage: Creating and sustaining superior performance.* New York: Free Press.

Powell, W. W. (1990). Neither market nor hierarchy: Network forms of organization. *Research in Organizational Behavior, 12,* 295–336.

Provan, K. G. (1983). The federation as an interorganizational linkage network. *Academy of Management Review, 8,* 79–89.

Provan, K. G., & Skinner, S. J. (1989). Interorganizational dependence and control as predictors of opportunism in dealer-supplier relations. *Academy of Management Journal, 32*(1), 202–212.

Reuer, J. J., & Koza, M. P. (2000). Asymmetric information and alliance performance: Theory and evidence for domestic and international alliances. *Strategic Management Journal, 21,* 81–103.

Reuer, J., Zollo, M., & Singh, H. (2002). Post-formation dynamics in joint ventures. *Strategic Management Journal, 23,* 135–151.

Ring, P. S., & Van de Ven, A. H. (1992). Structuring cooperative relationships between organizations. *Strategic Management Journal, 13,* 483–499.

Ring, P. S., & Van de Ven, A. H. (1994). Developmental processes of cooperative interorganizational relationships. *Academy of Management Review, 19,* 90–118.

Rubin, J. Z., & Brown, B. R. (1975). *The social psychology of bargaining and negotiation.* New York: Academic Press.

Sawyerr, O. O. (1993). Environmental uncertainty and environmental scanning activities of Nigerian manufacturing executives: A comparative analysis. *Strategic Management Journal, 14,* 287–299.

Saxton, T. (1997). The effects of partner and relationship characteristics on joint venture outcomes. *Academy of Management Journal, 40,* 443–461.

Schaan, J. (1988). How to control a joint venture even as a minority partner. *Journal of General Management, 14*(1), 4–16.

Scherer, F. M., & Ross, D. (1990). *Industrial market structure and economic performance.* Boston: Houghton Mifflin.

Schwartz, S. H. (1994). Beyond individualism/collectivism: New cultural dimensions of values. In U. Kim, H. C. Triandis, C. Kagitcibasi, S. C. Choi, & G. Yoon (Eds.), *Individualism and collectivism: Theory, method and applications* (pp. 85–119). Thousand Oaks, CA: Sage.

Seabright, M. A., Levinthal, D. A., & Fichman, M. (1992). Role of individual attachments in the dissolution of interorganizational relationships. *Academy of Management Journal, 35,* 122–160.

Shan, W., Walker, G., & Kogut, B. (1994). Interfirm cooperation and startup innovation in the biotechnology industry. *Strategic Management Journal, 15,* 387–394.

Shenkar, O., & Zeira, Y. (1992). Role conflict and role ambiguity of chief executive officers in international alliances. *Journal of International Business Studies, 23,* 55–75.

Steensma, H. K., & Lyles, M. A. (2002). Explaining joint venture survival in a transitional economy through social exchange and knowledge-based perspectives. *Strategic Management Journal, 21,* 831–851.

Tallman, S., & Shenkar, O. (1994). A managerial decision model of international cooperative venture formation. *Journal of International Business Studies, 25,* 91–114.

Tripsas, M., Schrader, S., & Sobrrero, M. (1995). Discouraging opportunistic behavior in collaborative R&D: A new role for government. *Research Policy, 24,* 367–389.

Tushman, M. L., & Nadler, D. A. (1978). Information processing as an integrating concept in organizational design. *Academy of Management Review, 3,* 613–624.

Tyler, T. R. (1994). Psychological models of the justice motive: Antecedents of distributive and procedural justice. *Journal of Personality and Social Psychology, 67,* 850–863.

Tyler, T. R., & Bies, R. J. (1990). Beyond formal procedures: The interpersonal context of procedural justice. In J. S. Carroll (Ed.), *Applied social psychology and organizational setting* (pp. 77–98). Hillsdale, NJ: Lawrence Erlbaum.

Uzzi, B. (1997). Social structure and competition in interfirm networks: The paradox of embeddedness. *Administrative Science Quarterly, 42,* 35–310.

Walker, G., & Poppo, L. (1991). Profit centers, single-source suppliers and transaction costs. *Administrative Science Quarterly, 36*(1), 66–87.

Walker, I., & Pettigrew, T. F. (1984). Relative deprivation theory: An overview and conceptual critique. *British Journal of Social Psychology, 23,* 301–310.

Welbourne, T. M., Balkin, D. B., & Gomez-Mejia, L. R. (1995). Gainsharing and mutual monitoring: A combined agency-organizational justice interpretation. *Academy of Management Journal, 38,* 881–899.

Williams. B. (1988). Formal structures and social reality. In D. Gambetta (Ed.), *Trust: Making and breaking of cooperative relations* (pp. 3–13). Oxford: Blackwell.

Williamson, O. E. (1979). Transaction-cost economics: The governance of contractual relations. *Journal of Law and Economics, 22,* 233–261.

Williamson, O. E. (1985). *The economic institutions of capitalism.* New York: Free Press.

Williamson, O. E. (1999). Strategy research: Governance and competence perspectives. *Strategic Management Journal, 20,* 1087–1108.

Yan, A., & Gray, B. (1994). Bargaining power, management control, and performance in United States–China JVs: A comparative case study. *Academy of Management Journal, 37,* 1478–1517.

Yan, A., & Gray, B. (2001). Antecedents and effects of parent control in international joint ventures. *Journal of Management Studies, 38*(3), 393–416.

Yan, A., & Luo, Y. (2001). *International joint ventures: Theory and practice.* Armonk, NY: M. E. Sharpe.

Zaheer, A. B., McEvily, B., & Perrone, V. (1998). Does trust matter? Exploring the effects of interorganizational and interpersonal trust on performance. *Organization Science, 9*(2), 141–159.

Zajac, E. J., & Olsen, C. (1993). From transaction cost to transaction value analysis: Implications for the study of interorganizational strategies. *Journal of Management Studies, 30,* 131–145.

Zhang, Y., & Rajagopalan, N. (2002). Inter-partner credible threat in international joint ventures: An infinitely repeated Prisoner's Dilemma model. *Journal of International Business Studies, 33,* 457–479.

5

Understanding Partnering Processes and Outcomes

The Contribution of Evolutionary Theory

Prashant Kale

Maurizio Zollo

Strategic alliances have been the subject of scholarly work for two decades now (Contractor & Lorange, 1988, 2002; Osborn & Hagedoorn, 1997). The phenomenon has been observed in its rapid growth both over time and across geographic and industrial domains using many theoretical lenses. A cursory list would include work in transaction cost economics applied to the choice of the partnering option and the structuring of the partnership (Hennart 1988, 1991; Anderson, 1985), economic sociology leveraged to study issues of power distribution in dyads and networks (Kogut, Shan, & Walker, 1992; Kogut & Walker, 2001; Powell, Koput & Smith-Doerr, 1996), work in strategic management on the analysis of partnering decisions and outcomes from resource- and knowledge-based perspectives (Kogut & Zander, 1993; Inkpen & Beamish, 1997; Inkpen & Dinur, 1988), a whole stream of work on interorganizational trust and postformation interaction leveraging notions borrowed from social psychology (Zaheer, McEvily, & Perrone, 1998; Parkhe, 1993; Gulati, 1995), This chapter takes the specific theoretical perspective of evolutionary theory to summarize the little (and recent) body of work that has explicitly aimed at its application in the context of strategic alliances. More important, though, it also tries to identify areas where its potential application could significantly improve our current understanding of the process as well as the outcomes of strategic alliances.

AUTHOR'S NOTE: We would like to acknowledge and express our gratitude for the research support received from Costas Lioukas as well as for the insightful comments and suggestions by an anonymous reviewer on a previous draft of this paper.

To do so, we first offer a brief recapitulation of the main tenets of the evolutionary approach to the study of managerial phenomena. This emphasizes the work done within the evolutionary economics school (Nelson & Winter, 1982, and subsequent work), because it bridges economic and sociological analysis of organizational change in a theoretical perspective that has gained center stage in the strategic management literature. We then proceed with the analysis of what this approach has produced or could potentially produce in the study of four specific questions that have engaged a large number of alliance scholars over the years. First, when are alliances selected as the appropriate tool to pursue a given strategic objective, and, having decided to form an alliance, how do firms select their alliance partners? Second, once the firm has decided to form an alliance, what determines the structure given to the partnering agreement? Third, beyond the completion of the agreement to cooperate, what factors explain the complex processes through which the two organizations interact and generate the outcomes of their collaboration? Fourth, and last, how do firms develop competencies specific to the management of these complex organizational challenges?

To be clear, an evolutionary perspective can be applied to several constructs relevant at different levels of analysis: at the dyadic partnership itself and its associated partnering process, at the level of the organization(s) involved in the partnership agreement, or at the level of the network of organizations that interact on sometimes a large number of simultaneous partnership agreements. This chapter could therefore be organized either through a taxonomy of managerial questions or according to the different levels of analysis relevant to the phenomenon under study. Because both approaches have their merit, we try to structure the analysis following both criteria, therefore grouping the managerial questions according to the level of analysis that they pertain to most explicitly.

A Primer on Evolutionary Theory Applied to Management Studies

The application of evolutionary theory to the study of economic phenomena dates back a long time. Marshall himself, one of the founding fathers of modern economics, seriously considered adopting Darwinian thinking after the evolutionary revolution it caused in biology, as opposed to the Newtonian model reigning over physics (Nelson, 1995). Despite the fact that he, and the economic science with him, decided to go the Newtonian route, the appeal of evolutionary biology never quite disappeared in the academic discourse and retained both supporters (notably, Veblen and Schumpeter) and detractors (Penrose, 1959). Although most of the concepts that we today consider part of the evolutionary approach were developed by the Carnegie school with its work on the behavioral theory of the firm (Simon, 1945; March & Simon, 1958; Cyert & March, 1963), Campbell (1969) and Aldrich (1979) were the ones who pioneered the explicit application of evolutionary thought in sociology, and of course Nelson and Winter, in their fifteen-year work, culminating in their 1982 book, to undertake a similar venture in the domain of economics.

Of course, the evolutionary perspective to the study of socioeconomic phenomena has itself evolved quite a bit over the last few decades. The key tenets, though, have been relatively stable over the years despite increasing refinement and expansion of work.

Routines. First of all, the theory views an organization as a set of interdependent patterns of repetitive activities (routines), which constitute the "bricks" of the entire construction or, keeping the biological metaphor, the "genes" responsible for the evolution of the organization "being." The evolution of an organization happens through the marginal, continuous adjustment of routines based on performance feedback and following a satisficing principle (Winter, 2003). The constant adjustment of routines occurs through a variation-selection-retention process of novel ideas on how to perform existing tasks better or on the introduction of new tasks (see below, "The Evolutionary Process [V-S-R-R]").

Hierarchies of Routines. An important refinement of the theory, currently well embedded in the knowledge-based view of the firm (Kogut & Zander, 1992) has to do with the distinctive role that different types of routines have in the explanation of how firms evolve. In addition to operating routines, responsible for the stable set of repetitive activities that contribute to the production of services or of products, other routines exist that have the role of adapting operating routines to novel requirements or introducing entirely new ones. This category of routines, which can be labeled "change routines," is the ontological equivalent of dynamic capabilities in strategic management language (Grant, 1996; Teece, Pisano, & Shuen, 1997; Zollo & Winter, 2002) and plays a structural role in explaining organizational evolution (Winter, 2003). A third, and final, element of the hierarchy consists of so-called "learning" routines (Zollo & Winter, 2002; Winter, 2003), that is, stable patterns of repetitive activity that aims at gaining a superior understanding of procedural or causal elements in action-performance linkages.

The Evolutionary Process (V-S-R-R). The way in which the stable elements of an organization change over time is described as a continuous process of generation of ideas for improvement of the status quo (Variation), of evaluation and screening of the change proposals to identify those worthy of implementation (internal Selection), and finally, of translating the selected ideas into either novel or adapted routines (Retention). Some scholars have actually identified a fourth element of the evolutionary process, positioned between selection and retention, related to the diffusion of the selected ideas to all the organizational contexts where the adapted/new routine(s) is of relevance (Szulanski & Winter, 2002; Zollo & Winter, 2002). That process, usually referred to as Replication, goes beyond the standard notions of transfer of best practices; it involves the adaptation of the change proposal to the local context and the progressive discovery of the power and the boundaries of the novel insight (the "Arrow" core).

The Role of Experience. The engine underlying the working of the evolutionary process described above can be identified in the accumulation of experience and the influence it has on the construction and change of routines. In their role as repositories of organizational knowledge (Cohen & Bacdayan, 1994), routines are in fact potentially but marginally reshaped each time they are triggered and enacted. Doing any activity in a stable and predictable pattern is, therefore, conceived as the antecedent rather than the consequence of knowing (Grandori & Kogut, 2002).

Intentionality. Connected with the key role of experience accumulation is the important assumption on the relatively low level of intentionality characterizing the process through which routines and therefore the organization evolve. The marginal adjustments made as a consequence of the observed outcomes of enacted routines are typically performed without a formalized, eventful process.[1] To an extreme, one can even think of "blind" variation processes occurring. Members of the organization involved in a given routine simply change the way they perform it in an effort to improve outcomes. The formal process of change proposals made to higher levels of the hierarchy, followed by analysis, evaluation, and eventual approval of the proposed change, is therefore considered to be an accurate description of only a small fraction of evolutionary processes. Although space for more deliberate mechanisms underlying evolutionary processes is being claimed (Zollo, 1998; Zollo & Winter, 2002) and observed in different empirically contexts (Kale & Singh, 1999; Zollo & Singh, 2004), the current picture of organizational evolution is still one where most of the adaptation happens in an emergent, nondirected process and below the consciousness level of most organizational members and, notably, of the senior management.

Path Dependence. Another important element in this theoretical construction is related to the assumption of the "weight of the past." Given the emphasis on routinized behavior in the description of how organizations evolve, one has to expect that past decisions and actions have a significant explanatory power in any evolutionary model of current decisions and actions. Particularly important is that variation processes generating change in the "genetic" structure of an organization are assumed to be strongly influenced by the existing patterns of behavior. Search for novel solutions tends to be localized close to the existing knowledge domains, because such search will normally build on them and at the same time will be bound by them through the common underlying assumptions and taken-for-granted considerations they normally share. As we shall see, this path-dependence assumption will play an important role in the contribution of evolutionary thinking to the theory of strategic alliances.

To exemplify and apply to the context of interest, two firms engaged in a partnership agreement employ a given set of operating routines to execute the tasks necessary to achieve the strategic objectives of the partnership (develop a new product, manufacture it and distribute it in a new market or to a new typology of clients, etc.). To the extent that the two partners have accumulated experience in working together in prior contexts, they might develop stable patterns of interaction that characterize the way the dyad operates, patterns that have been referred to as interorganizational routines (Zollo, Reuer, & Singh, 2002). Additionally, if they have routines specific to the management of these types of interorganizational interactions, that is, aimed at changing the way they each operate to accommodate the partnering agreement, then these stable patterns of activity can be construed as change routines, or dynamic capabilities (Teece et al., 1997), specialized in the adaptation of interorganizational routines. Finally, assume that the two partners (or any one of them) also have established procedures systematically to extract valuable lessons to learn from their alliance experiences, or so-called deliberate learning processes (Zollo & Winter, 2002). This type of learning behavior would be considered an example of learning routines.

An evolutionary perspective applied to the phenomenon of strategic alliances would then focus on the development of these patterns of routinized behavior both within single firms as well as among them, in dyads and in networks of firms. We are now sufficiently equipped to proceed with the analysis of the application of this particular theoretical approach, beginning with the dyad level of analysis and then proceeding with the firm and the network levels.

The Dyadic Partnership Level

When Do Firms Partner?

This question has been addressed in a large number of prior studies. From a theoretical standpoint, several explanations have been offered based on resource-based theory (Harrigan, 1988), agency theory (Balakrishnan & Koza, 1993), transaction cost economics (Hennart & Reddy, 1997), real options theory (Kogut, 1991), and internationalization theory (Buckley & Casson, 1976). All these perspectives primarily emphasize resource or competitive strategy aspects relevant in a given context to explain when a firm might choose to form an alliance or partnership to achieve its business objectives in that context. In most cases, the empirical test takes the form of a choice model between a partnership and an alternative corporate development mode such as organic internal development or acquisitions (Kogut & Singh, 1988; Balakrishnan & Koza, 1993; Hennart & Reddy, 1997, 2000; Reuer & Koza, 2000).What can evolutionary theory offer to improve our current understanding of this foundational question in strategic alliance research? Based on the path-dependence assumption discussed above, one can argue that the decision to partner and the more general choice of what corporate development mode to use are a function of similar choices a firm has made in other such situations in times prior to the focal one. Essentially, in order to understand fully the choice of partnership as a preferred mode over either internal organic investment or an acquisition to, say, enter a specific market or to achieve any other relevant objective, one needs explicitly to consider the choices made by the same firm in prior instances and, at the very least, control for those decisions in constructing an explanation that is consistent with evolutionary theory.

The rationale is relatively straightforward. Decisions regarding the choice of the corporate development mode, such as alliances, are subject to the same path dependence and routinization processes described above. The weight of the past would play a role in the decision of the present. Whether managers are conscious of it or not, a good part of the explanation of the decision to partner can reside in a firm's natural tendency to replicate past decisions, over and above the analysis of the contextual rationale to choose among the various alternatives that it might have. For example, Corning is a company that traditionally relied on alliances and joint venture to expand into new product or geographic markets and consequently has also developed strong alliance routines over the decades. Thus, according to evolutionary theory, an entry choice by Corning in a new geographic market needs to test forcefully (or at least control) for the simple explanation of a routine response to a well-recognized stimulus before any other resource-based arguments or competitive strategy explanations can be considered. Unfortunately, empirical tests of such a simple explanation are very rare. Some studies that include such explanations focus primarily on testing the path-dependence assumption for the contexts chosen for a given expansion strategy rather than for the corporate development mode that a firm uses. Chang (1996), for example, shows that there is path dependence in the choice of the product domain for entry and exits by firms. Kim and Kogut (1996) uncover similarly strong path dependencies in the choice of technological domains and in the location choice of foreign direct investments. But here we suggest that path-dependence effects in the choice of corporate development modes such as alliances are an important area for further exploration. Specifically, there is need for research that identifies the impact of prior choices on the probability of selecting alliances as the preferred corporate development mode in a given strategic initiative.

An extended application of evolutionary theory to the choice of corporate development mode can move, however, beyond simple path dependence and routinization arguments to provide an explicit consideration of the learning benefits of routinization processes in the context of alliances. If evolutionary theory is right in assuming that the refinement of routines is a key source of adaptation for a firm, then learning should be an outcome of the experience accumulation process. Such learning should lead a firm to improve its performance by choosing the same corporate development mode (e.g., alliance) in future that it has traditionally chosen in the past.

Clearly, there are important counterarguments pointing to the inertial consequences of routinization processes (Leonard-Barton, 1992). Thus, it is inherently interesting to test the validity of the learning assumption on empirical grounds. One simple way of doing it is to set up a test tying the accumulation of experience in alliances to the choice of governance mode and then examine whether this correlates positively with the performance of the alliance agreement. This, we believe, is fertile ground for future empirical work.

With Whom Do Firms Partner?

The second question that is of relevance to firms at the dyadic level is the following: Having chosen the partnering mode, who should the firm partner with? Traditional alliance research has emphasized that firms will choose partners based on a rational and systematic assessment of "fit" between potential partners, given the objectives of a specific strategic opportunity (Doz & Hamel, 1998). Assessment of fit usually emphasizes resource and knowledge complementarity between potential partners (Harrigan, 1988) as well as organizational fit based on the compatibility of their culture and operating styles (Lorange & Roos, 1992). The implicit assumption in most received literature is that a firm treats partner selection in an atomistic or ahistoric manner, that is, a firm chooses its alliance partner based on the merits of that particular partnering situation with limited or no consideration of its own prior partnering history.

However, an evolutionary perspective can call that assumption into question. The tenet of path dependence would suggest that choice of a partner in a particular alliance situation would also be driven partly by a firm's prior partnering experience and partner choices. For instance, a positive partnering experience with another organization would often influence a firm to choose that same partner in future alliance relationships—the opposite would be true for prior partnerships/partners that led to a negative experience. There is already some research that suggests that firms are more likely to partner in the future with those firms they have shared (successful) partnerships with in the past or present (Gulati, 1998).

History can influence future partner choices in another way. In some situations, it is very likely that even though the assessment of resource/capability complementarity and of organizational fit points the firm towards one optimal partner, that particular firm may be a direct "rival" or "threat" to the focal firm's existing alliance partners. In that case, it is possible that the firm may settle for another potential partner, complementarity and fit notwithstanding. Thus, according to evolutionary logic, the history of prior partnerships and the identities of its existing partners will have a profound impact on a firm's choice regarding its partner in a new cooperative venture above and beyond situation-specific considerations of complementarity and fit with that partner. In fact, Li and Rowley (2002) have found that inertia (which could be the result of routines) is an alternative explanation to information asymmetry for the fact that firms tend to choose past partners when forming new alliances.

The implications of considering the role of history and path dependence on research on partner selection are relatively simple. Work that focuses on the nature of complementarity and fit between firms to explain partner choices will also have to account or at least control for the impact of these historical antecedents on partner choice. A count of prior experiences with potential partners, for example, might offer an initial (rough) proxy for this type of evolutionary explanation. Assessments on the (perceived) performance of prior alliances with potential partners would refine this measure considerably, because the degree of success (real or perceived) in prior experiences will significantly influence the sign and the magnitude of the path-dependent effect. Again, we are aware of no work explicitly designed to address these questions empirically.

How Do Firms Structure Their Partnering Agreements?

The third area of inquiry of alliance research focuses on how firms structure their interfirm relationships after they have decided to form an alliance with a particular partner. This topic has received the largest amount of theoretical and empirical attention in the alliance literature. Although surveying this large body of literature is outside the scope of this paper, we briefly review some of the main theoretical arguments that have been made so far to explain an important aspect of alliance structure—namely, the presence or absence of "equity" in such relationships and the level of equity a firm might choose, having made the decision to have an "equity alliance." Following this review we consider the potential contribution of evolutionary theory to explain equity ownership decisions in the context of alliance structure.

Resource-based theory (Barney, 1991) suggests that a firm would like to have an equity ownership with/in its alliance partner if the resources that it seeks from its partner are either significant to the focal firm's own business or significant to its rivals (Dyer, Kale, & Singh, 2004). Ownership under the former condition is useful because it gives the focal firm administrative authority to make decisions regarding the future development of the resource in question in a manner that is critical to its competitive position. Ownership in the latter case would enable the focal firm to exclude or deter rivals from getting easy access to the partner's resources. Real options theory (Kogut, 1991; McGrath, 1997; Folta & Miller, 2002) also examines the impact of the resources in question on equity ownership choices; however, it does not focus on the significance of the resources in place but rather on the uncertainty about the value of those resources. Thus, according to the real options logic, a majority equity ownership in the alliance partner might prematurely increase the commitment costs of the focal firm if there is high uncertainty about the resources being accessed from the partner. A minority ownership in the partner, on the other hand, minimizes commitment costs but also provides the focal firm the "option" and flexibility to increase ownership in the future if necessary.

Transaction cost economics also informs the question of equity ownership in alliance relationships (Williamson, 1991). According to this theory, when firms anticipate high levels of investments in relationship-specific assets and/or high levels of uncertainty regarding future market conditions, they prefer to structure the alliance as an equity alliance. This is because both of the above conditions create the potential for transactional hazards due to likely opportunistic behavior by the alliance partner. Equity ownership and structures mitigate these concerns because they provide the necessary hierarchical means to monitor partner behavior and align incentive by creating mutual hostage situations (Pisano, 1990; Kogut, 1988; Hennart, 1988). The knowledge-based perspective provides an alternative explanation for equity ownership choices in alliance relationships. According to this view, equity ownership decisions are driven by considerations about the level and the nature of coordination that may be called for between alliance partners (Gulati & Singh, 1998). If the expected task interdependence between partners requires a high degree of coordination (of people, information, know-how, etc.) between partners, then equity ownership is preferable because it enables a firm to have the necessary administrative authority to implement the necessary coordination mechanisms and control coordination costs more easily than in the absence of equity ownership.

Although each of the above theoretical perspectives offers valuable insights to understand the choice of equity structures and decisions in alliances, an evolutionary perspective can provide an explanation that is not featured in any of them. From an evolutionary standpoint, the decision to structure a partnership agreement, say, as an equity-based alliance can be explained by path-dependence and routinization processes. If the tenet of path dependence holds true, then according to evolutionary theory the choice of equity ownership and structure in any focal alliance would be strongly influenced by a firm's prior history of making these decisions/choices. Therefore, a firm is more likely to choose an equity-based structure in its focal/present alliances if a greater proportion of its current stock of alliances is accounted for by equity-based alliances. This might be true for two reasons: first, a simple argument that exemplifies the notion of routinized behavior ("This is what we have mostly done in the past"); second, an argument that underscores the fact that by virtue of doing more equity-based alliances in the past, a firm has presumably cultivated a set of routines to form or manage equity alliances (better than nonequity alliances) and/or has at least developed a set of implicit mental heuristics to select only those alliance opportunities where the conditions are suitable for equity structures, given its tacit or explicit skills in forming and managing such structural forms.

Whereas prior history of the "type of alliances" will have an impact on a firm's decision regarding the structure of its present or future alliance relationships, the "history of its alliances with a *particular partner*" would also have an impact on this decision. And, somewhat surprisingly, this latter impact might actually be in a direction opposite to that predicted earlier. Research shows that the presence of prior alliance ties between firms may influence the way they structure their future alliance (Gulati, 1995). However, it has been argued and shown that if a prior alliance between two firms is structured as an equity alliance, it is less likely that a future alliance between those same partners will be structured as an equity alliance. This is because the existence of prior ties provides a basis for the development of mutual trust and relational capital between the two concerned. If such trust exists due to a prior alliance between partners, it reduces the likelihood of firms choosing an equity-based structure for their present/future alliance. Trust-based, relational governance based on prior ties is hence expected to provide an effective substitute for equity-based governance in proposed future ties between the same partners.

Whereas the "familiarity breeds trust" argument is broadly consistent with an evolutionary account because it builds on path-dependency and experience-accumulation processes, another explanation of the substitution effect between partner-specific experience and equity structure is offered by an account linked even more closely to the explanatory power of evolutionary processes: the formation of interorganizational routines. Zollo, Reuer, and Singh (2002) argue that the development of trust might be a sufficient but not a necessary condition for the lowering of the probability of an equity alliance as the stock of partner-specific experience grows. Two firms working together on multiple sequential partnerships are highly likely to develop stable and predictable patterns of interaction to coordinate their activities, prevent or handle conflict situations, assess outcomes, and adapt the cooperative agreement to the ensuing postformation conditions. The presence and constant tacit development of interorganizational routines can therefore act as a buffer against opportunistic behaviors among partners and therefore explain the declining probability of equity-based structures without the assumptions of increasing levels of interpersonal or interorganizational trust among them.

In making this argument, Zollo Reuer, and Singh (2002) exhibit large-scale evidence of the performance impact of the interaction between partner-specific experience and the equity choice of the sign and magnitude predicted by these evolutionary accounts. In addition, they describe qualitative evidence of the higher relevance of routine-based over trust-based explanations of this effect. In a series of interviews with Hewlett-Packard managers responsible for alliance projects, they collected consistent observations of increasing performance outcomes attached to the accumulation of cooperative projects with the same partners (e.g., the company had more than thirty alliances with Microsoft and eighteen with Cisco Systems). When probed as to the likely increase of trust vis-à-vis the familiar partners, though, the response was negative. Performance was rising, according to company managers, because they were learning how to anticipate idiosyncratic issues related to their interactions with a particular partner and how to handle standoffs when they occurred, again given the partner-specific traits that they slowly discovered. The partners in the dyad were developing an implicit understanding of how to work with each other, which was making equity structures redundant to the correct functioning of the partnership agreement.

Although the theoretical argument of experience-based effects on structural decisions is compelling, it rests on limited empirical work. In fact, even the positive impact of partner-specific experience is being challenged by recent work that finds a negative (although marginally significant) effect (Hoang & Rothaermel, in press). Even more important, this line of inquiry needs empirical work to clarify the relative explanatory power of trust-based versus routine-based arguments in explaining alliance structural choices.

How Do Firms Interact During the Alliance Process?

Together with the explanation of important alliance design decisions such as equity arrangements, researchers have been equally interested in understanding the performance drivers of cooperative agreements. To do so, they have focused their attention primarily on specific attributes and their initial conditions to explain differential performance. For instance, extant work shows that alliance performance was strongly influenced by factors such as mutual expectations of the alliance partners (Lorange & Roos, 1992), strategic and organizational fit between partners (Harrigan, 1988), and the governance structure of the alliance (Oxley, 1997). Some recent work has also shown that alliance performance may depend on the presence of trust between alliance partners (Gulati, 1995; Kale, Singh, & Perlmutter, 2000). But this research on alliance performance fails to account for the potential impact on performance of the interaction dynamics between partners following the consummation of the alliance (Doz, 1996). Evolutionary thinking can provide valuable insights in addressing this gap in the literature. Work by Doz (1996) is a good example of such thinking, and we briefly review it here—we also suggest ways to tie it to and extend it with some of the evolutionary theory tenets described above.

Doz (1996) emphasizes the importance of "adaptation," a key element of evolutionary thinking, to explain how cooperation evolves (or fails to evolve) between partners and its impact on eventual outcome of an alliance. He convincingly argues that cooperation evolves between partners based on their learning and adjustment of the cooperation process over time and that this mediates the simplistic relationship, hitherto observed in the extant literature, between the alliance's initial conditions and its performance. The framework he proposes presents a recursive cycle of four main phases: (1) the "initial phase," comprising a set of initial conditions related to the nature of the task to be undertaken, the existing organizational routines of the two partners, the structure of their alliance interface and their mutual expectations (these initial conditions have a profound impact on whether the partners learn about each other and about how to cooperate with each other), (2) the "learning" phase, when partners jointly learn more about the nature of their joint task, the nature of their competitive environment, their respective competencies, and their goals regarding the alliance, (c) the "reevaluation stage," when partners, based on their learning, assess the fit and effectiveness of the alliance, and (4) the "adaptation phase," when partners readjust their initial conditions and operating practices, if necessary, to make the alliance more efficient and effective. In summary, the self-reinforcing evolutionary dynamics based on the adaptation of the alliance to emerging understandings and contextual conditions result in a deeper, wider, and more successful alliance over time.

This framework is consistent with many elements of the evolutionary logic we present above. First, it underscores the incremental nature of the cooperation between alliance partners over time. Second, it stresses the role of "small events" in the early history of the postformation interaction as having an important bearing on its subsequent outcome. Third, the framework reflects the "variation-selection-retention" aspects of the evolutionary perspective. Essentially, when the two partners first begin cooperation, they have fairly different ways (routines) of undertaking their respective activities and consequently different approaches even to interacting with each other. Hence, one normally expects a wide range of diverse possibilities for partners to interact with each other to carry out their joint tasks.

The elaboration of these possibilities constitutes the phase of generative variation in the evolutionary model (V-S-R-R; Zollo & Winter, 2002). To the extent that they invest time and effort to learn and adapt, though, partners are able over time to "select" the optimal and efficient ways of undertaking collaboration. Selected alternatives to current modus operandi that connect with improvements in the outcomes of the cooperation are then retained, whereas outcomes below expectations trigger further search and a new round of generative variation.

Ariño and de la Torre (1998) built on this early evolutionary work by Doz (1996) to enrich our understanding of the development and role of relational capital and trust between partners. They suggest that alliance partners constantly evaluate the efficiency and equity of their relationship, and whenever they perceive a change in these aspects, they either engage in renegotiation of their original partnership terms or modify their behavior unilaterally to restore the balance to the relationship. In this context, prior relational capital between partners determines their willingness to renegotiate and adapt their collaboration—at the same time, successful adaptation and renegotiation strengthen their mutual relationship and trust.

This work highlights the role that the V-S-R-R model plays in the alliance process but also involves other constructs that are part of the theoretical construction developed by scholars of organizational evolution. Path dependence, learning, and adaptation in fact contribute an important piece to the construction of the puzzle explaining alliance performance. But this work also presents some limitations that create opportunities and challenges for future alliance research. For instance, extant evolutionary perspectives examine only the postformation alliance phase. One can argue, however, that evolutionary thinking can also be usefully applied to gain insights about the alliance-formation phase. Second, although frameworks about the evolution of cooperation between partners are intuitively appealing and insightful, it seems challenging to test these frameworks using large-sample empirical data—which is perhaps why we have seen very little work that validates these frameworks and establishes their generalizability. The measurement of relational quality at different stages of the postformation cooperation process, for example, might be particularly challenging across a sufficiently large sample of alliances. In addition, one needs to assess the evolution of the antecedents and consequences of relational quality, with particular regard to the knowledge developed on the nature of the tasks at hand and of the partner with which the focal firm is attempting to execute them.

Alliance Termination

One final line of inquiry in alliance research has to do with the explanation of the termination outcomes of the alliance. This work dates back to the inception of the field, when alliance longevity was viewed as a good proxy for performance (Franko, 1971; see also Pennings, Barkema, & Douma (1994); Barkema, Shenkar, Vermeulen, & Bell, 1997, for some recent examples of empirical work using this assumption). More recently, this assumption has been increasingly challenged on both theoretical and empirical grounds, and evolutionary perspectives have played an important role in those challenges.

In an effort to combine evolutionary explanations with others derived from transaction cost economics, Reuer and Zollo (forthcoming) show that partner-specific experience does influence the likelihood of termination due to success. Not only, therefore, can longevity of alliances hardly be equated with performance, but the development of interorganizational routines can serve to discriminate among the various possible reasons for why alliances terminate, whether these reasons are performance-related or not.

Another result reported by Reuer and Zollo (2005) refers to the fact that the most frequent reason for termination (51% of observations) is related to unilateral withdrawal of one party.[2] In evolutionary terms, this can be interpreted by noting that an inherently dynamic interorganizational process like a strategic alliance is subject to two evolutionary processes that interact with each other. One is the project-level evolution of cooperation, as described above. The other is the evolution of the two organizations that are undertaking the cooperative venture. The drift in one partnering firm's strategic priorities is sufficient to abort even relatively successful alliances. Vice versa, though, the evolution of the alliance program, if of sufficient strategic relevance, can have significant impact on the evolutionary path of either or both partnering organizations.

Studying alliance processes and outcomes in isolation from processes and outcomes in the two organizations, therefore, is a conceptual simplification that we have all been aware of (at least to some extent) and lived with. A coevolutionary perspective serves, in our view, as a powerful signal that the hidden assumption of separating process from organizational evolution is not tenable from both a theoretical and a managerial point of view (Lewin & Koza, 2001). Of course, going from the realization of this important limitation in the strategic alliances literature to the development of work capable of addressing this gap is no small feat. We are aware of no large-scale empirical work dedicated to this problem and would like to propose it as an important avenue for future inquiry stemming from the adoption of an evolutionary perspective. This brings us naturally to the next level of analysis, the evolution of the organization and its implications for the partnership process.

The Organization Level

Recent alliance research has also tried to examine why we observe differential alliance performance across firms. Although alliance success rates are quite low on average (in general, 50% of alliances formed are deemed failures), studies also report a wide variance in firm-level alliance success. Some firms, such as Hewlett-Packard, Pfizer, Corning, and others, seem to consistently enjoy much greater overall alliance success than their peers. Some scholars have suggested that these firms achieve greater alliance success because they possess an "alliance capability" (Kale & Singh, 1999; Anand & Khanna, 2000). But some critical questions remain unanswered in this context, such as what exactly constitutes an alliance capability and what factors explain its development. The evolutionary perspective provides a good theoretical foundation for examining them.

Traditional learning theory has a simple but important explanation. Organizations become better at managing any given task or activity simply by engaging in repetitive experience of that task over time, that is, they "learn by doing" (Huber, 1991). Implicit feedback from the perceived outcomes of accumulated experience helps a firm make incremental improvements in its existing practices or discover new practices through "trial-and-error" search. Traditional experience-curve literature (Ghemawat & Spence, 1985; Argote, 1999) provides strong evidence of such tacit experiential learning in several different contexts. From an evolutionary theory standpoint, too, the role of cumulative experience is central to firms' establishing well-developed routines to manage the task at hand competently. However, the learning-by-doing notion suggests that such routines may often develop in a nondeliberate manner, partly explaining why firms become good at undertaking the task at hand.

Alliance researchers have built on this work to highlight the role of the cumulative alliance experience in explaining a firm's alliance capability and its overall alliance success, and some have also found empirical support for it (Simonin, 1997; Inkpen, 1995; Kale, Dyer, & Singh, 2002). Others have accumulated evidence that is not easily interpretable as a simple learning-by-doing effect; Barkema et al. (1997), for example, observe that parents with greater *domestic* alliance experience produce better results in their international partnerships (IJV) but fail to find a similar effect for the stock of IJV experiences. Similarly,

Anand and Khanna (2000) find that firms with increasing stocks of prior licensing agreements receive a positive response from investors/markets when they announce a new agreement but fail to find the same for joint ventures. Finally, Zollo et al. (2002) fail to detect learning effects for both general alliance experience levels and technology-specific alliance experience but do find positive impacts of partner-specific experience. Even the most recent study to date (Hoang & Rothaermel, in press) on the effect of experience trajectories in alliances finds mixed results. Previous alliance experience accumulated by the biotechnology firm in a pharma-biotech dyad has a significant impact on performance, but the experience accumulated by the pharmaceutical giant does not.

Whereas the importance of tacit experiential learning as a mechanism to explain the development of organizational capabilities in the realm of operating routines is unquestionable, its role in the development of alliance capabilities cannot therefore be taken for granted. Instead, a theory explaining organizational learning in the context of alliances and other comparable corporate development activities needs to invoke mechanisms that go beyond semiautomatic tacit accumulation of experience (Zollo, 1998; Kale, 1999); recent advances in evolutionary theory try to do that. As Zollo and Winter (2002) explain, deliberate learning processes that facilitate articulation and codification of individual and collective knowledge need to be explicitly considered to explain learning in the context of infrequent, heterogeneous, and causally ambiguous tasks such as alliances and acquisitions (Zollo & Winter, 2002). In fact, one of the limitations of the organizational learning literature is the lack of appreciation for the deliberate processes through which individuals and groups figure out what works and what does not in the execution of the task at hand and modify their future behavior accordingly (Narduzzo, Rocco, & Warglien, 2000).

The tenets of organizational evolutionary theory related to change and learning routines are of direct relevance here. In fact, firms use alliances as a vehicle to change and strengthen their competitive position either by accessing new resources/practices or by modifying and improving the use of existing ones. Hence, the routines connected to the management of partnerships can be viewed as an example of a firm's change routines. But how do firms develop the set of alliance practices, skills, and routines? They do that with the help of higher-order routines developed specifically to extract lessons and best practices from their own (or others') prior experience in managing alliances. That is to say, firms can accumulate and leverage alliance management know-how derived from their own prior or ongoing alliance experience or that of others, through a set of established and routinized practices. A brief account of the way these deliberate learning mechanisms work follows.

Articulation. Individuals involved in managing their firm's alliances possess know-how and skills specific to the management of these complex processes and, more important, they have knowledge of the kinds of decisions, actions, and practices that have been deployed in prior instances. In order for this knowledge to have practical utility and for it to develop in magnitude and quality (i.e., in being probed and tested), it needs to go through a process of verbalization and explanation to a plurality of individuals with partly overlapping prior knowledge domains (Nooteboom, 1999). Individuals supposedly learn *as they articulate* their previously tacit and implicit understanding of what to do when, how, and why. In the alliance context, by articulating what decisions they made and what outcomes ensued, alliance managers facilitate their own and others' sense-making of the reasons for the success and failure of the hundreds of events that occur in the course of a strategic partnership.

In addition to this collective sense-making, knowledge articulation produces a refined understanding of patterns of collective activity, thereby enhancing the establishment and adaptation of organizational routines. The combination of this sense-making with a "highly powered" routinization process helps a firm (and its managers) achieve an improved understanding of some of the causal linkages that might exist between actions taken in the alliance context and their associated outcome (Kale & Singh, 1999). The higher-level cognitive effort addresses some of the ambiguity that typically exists between organizational actions and their performance implications in these types of highly complex collective endeavors (Zollo & Winter, 2002).

Codification. Firms can undertake an even higher level of cognitive effort that goes beyond articulation to improve their understanding (and eventual execution) of operating and change routines related to a certain task at hand, together with their performance outcomes. Knowledge codification involves a deliberate effort to create (and use) written artifacts and tools related to the managerial process at hand. The artifacts can potentially inform future decisions or actions based on the reflection, the critical analyses, and the abstraction towards generalizable insights made in the process of developing and using them (Zollo & Winter, 2002). In the alliance management context, codification can involve firms undertaking explicit, organizationwide efforts to develop guidelines, checklists, and manuals to manage different alliance-related tasks better (Kale et al., 2000).

Codification offers several benefits. The obvious one (and the intended objective) is to provide guidelines and directions for the execution of different tasks and decisions in the alliance context. A second has to do with the enhanced diffusion of existing knowledge through these codified resources (Nonaka, 1994; Nonaka & Takeuchi, 1995). We believe, however, that a more durable and often unnoticed (even by the individuals involved) benefit is linked to the actual process of creating codified resources and tools. By involving themselves in writing alliance management guidelines or developing postmortem analyses of partnering processes, managers will emerge with a crisper understanding of the causal linkages between decisions/actions and performance outcomes in the specific context of alliances undertaken by their firm. The process itself of developing these artifacts can uncover hidden assumptions and implicitly challenge imprecise causal linkages. Consequently, the managers involved with these types of routinized learning activities develop an increasingly sophisticated understanding of the causalities, which can translate into the rapid establishment and adaptation of interorganizational (or even general-purpose) partnering routines.

Sharing. Kale and Singh (1999) have suggested that a third learning routine, apart from articulation and codification of knowledge, may be a relevant part of firms' higher-order learning capabilities. This is the process of knowledge-sharing that involves explicit efforts to exchange and disseminate individually and organizationally held knowledge through organizationwide, interpersonal interaction within firms. Patterns of personal interaction, such as formal or informal teams, committees, mentor-mentee relationships, and so on, are a central element of the knowledge-sharing processes within firms. They facilitate the sharing and exchange of not only knowledge that is nontacit but, more important, also knowledge that is still tacit and individually held. In the alliance context, one can find several examples of such knowledge-sharing routines—they range from alliance committees and task forces that meet formally and regularly to exchange alliance management know-how to informal, casual conversations and discussions that take place among the organization's alliance managers. Overall, these learning routines/processes can play a critical role in sharing valuable alliance management knowledge across the firm so as to help build the firm's partnering skills (i.e., the firm's change routines).

Alliance researchers have recently begun undertaking empirical studies to validate the existence and role of the deliberate learning processes described above. Kale (1999) and Kale and Singh (1999) find strong support for the existence of these mechanisms in firms and for their positive impact on firms' eventual alliance performance. In fact, they observe that all the learning processes described above are explained by a common construct that they term a firm's *dynamic learning capability*. This is not surprising, given that all these processes are directed towards explicit efforts to develop, accumulate, and leverage organizational knowledge related to the task at hand. The fact that empirical studies have also found significance for these learning mechanisms in other related corporate development activities, such as acquisitions (Zollo, 1998; Zollo & Singh, 2004), offers some comfort in the generalizability of these findings.

Despite these encouraging beginnings, the road toward a thorough understanding of the learning mechanisms underlying the development of partnering capabilities is still long and poorly lit. For example, we need research on the boundary effects of these mechanisms. When is articulation a more effective learning tool than codification, for example? And when is a simple experience-accumulation process sufficient to develop alliance capabilities, rather than investing in expensive articulation and codification processes? And again, what is the nature of the interdependence among the various learning processes? Are they substitutive or complementary to each other? In a pioneering effort to address some of these questions, Leshchinskii and Zollo (2004) find a significant *and negative* interaction effect between experience-articulation and knowledge-codification processes in the context of acquisitions. Codification is apparently most effective at lower levels of experience, but its impact weakens considerably as experience accumulates. Kale and Singh (1999), on the other hand, find a mediating effect of deliberate learning processes between the experience accumulation and performance in their study of alliances. Clearly, these results are but a mere start. Significant work is necessary before we can feel comfortable in the answers we give to the question of the determinants of alliance capabilities.

The Alliance Network Level

One of the most important implications stemming from a more focused attention dedicated to the interdependence between the process and the firm level of analysis relates to the study of networks of alliances. By elevating the unit of analysis to the network level, one realizes that the study of what happens in the single dyadic relationship cannot be disjointed from the changes occurring within the firm itself in relation to all the other partnerships that the firm is simultaneously entertaining with potentially large numbers of counterparts. For instance, the success or failure of other alliances entertained by the firm for similar strategic purposes will influence the fate of the focal alliance independently from what the partners do or do not do to ensure its success.

Even more broadly, the evolution of the dyadic tie is intuitively and fundamentally linked to the evolution of the entire web of relationships entertained by all the other organizations in the same competitive field. Think about the competitive interactions among the alliances in the airline services industry and what impact actions and outcomes in one consortium can have on the actions and outcomes of the others. A new link between members of different consortia, perhaps related to completely different domains of activity, for example, can put both alliances in disarray, creating trust and procedural issues that might spiral into significant performance decay.

A network essentially refers to the entire set of either direct or indirect relationships that each firm active in a specific market, product, or technological domain entertains with all the other participants in the same domain. In recent years, scholars have called for the study of alliances and partnerships at the level of a broader network of interorganizational relationships (Gulati, 1998; Gulati, Nohria, & Zaheer, 2000) as a priority to add to the collective agenda on the study of cooperative strategies and behavior.

Although the study of the dyad-network interdependencies as well as of the characteristics of network structures is inherently useful to further our understanding of partnering processes and outcomes, we are aware of no work in this area that explicitly undertakes the challenge of understanding the evolutionary processes underlying change in the structure of the entire network of relationships. In fact, we found only two very recent papers (Powell, Koput, & Smith-Doerr, forthcoming; Corrado & Zollo, 2004) that deal with changes over time of large networks of firms. And of the two, only the former focuses on ties related to interorganizational cooperation, whereas the other observes changes in the equity ownership across firms. There have actually been recent calls for work on network dynamics (Gulati, 1998; Gulati et al. 2000).

An evolutionary perspective can in principle add to the richness of insights gained by studying partnering issues at the network level through shifting the emphasis to the dynamics of change in the web of relationship. Just as an individual partnering relationship evolves over time through the constant action of variation, selection, and retention processes on the routinized patterns of activity among the two firms, so does a firm's portfolio of interorganizational relationships and the entire network of relationships within an industry or technological domain. Evolutionary thinking can help the examination of network dynamics through the different theoretical tenets described above applied to the entire dyadic relationship, rather than the interorganizational routine, as the unit of analysis. For example, new ties and partnerships would be influenced by the position of the focal firm within the network, thereby creating a path dependence between past and future positions of firms within the network. By that same logic, however, variation processes in the generation of new ties will alter the structure of the network itself, collaborating to the evolution of its structural properties, such as its density, its degree of clustering, or its average path length, as well as its "strategic" features, such as the form and degree of competition and the patterns of interaction among members of the network. Industry "recipes" (Spender, 1989) on how to behave in a given competitive and cooperative context are thus created and adapted over time.

An evolutionary logic might also apply at the level of the portfolio of partnerships entertained simultaneously by the same firm. This can happen in several ways. First, if a particular new tie or partnership helps a firm achieve certain desired business objectives more effectively or efficiently than some of its prior ties (especially those ties that might have been formed for similar goals), then a firm is likely to shed or at least reconfigure some of those prior partnerships. Second, every time a firm adds a new partner through a new tie/relationship, that partner comes on board with its own network of direct and indirect ties. Consequently, the addition of this new partner and its accompanying network may call for the reconfiguration of a firm's own prior network.

The key, though, is in the ability to say something not so much about the way a portfolio of relationships held by one of the firms evolves but about the development and diffusion of patterns of behavior across relationships with different firms. Experiences accumulated with partners in one context, for example, can be applied (more or less appropriately) to novel ties. Or, more directly, new partners come with their baggage of experiences, heuristics, and established routinized patterns of actions developed in prior alliances, which they might (more or less deliberately) attempt to apply to the focal new tie. Of course, investments in deliberate learning processes might accelerate these evolutionary patterns in the way the focal firm handles its portfolio of alliances.

Despite the intuitive appeal of an evolutionary logic to study the dynamics of change in alliance portfolios as well as overall firm networks, we have no record of studies (or even theoretical treatments) that undertake these quests with an explicit attention to evolutionary mechanisms. We encourage, therefore, future scholars to leverage the available body of knowledge in evolutionary economics and economic sociology to tackle these important questions for the development of the field of study on strategic alliances.

Conclusions

In this chapter we offer a survey of the ways in which evolutionary theory has been applied to the study of interorganizational cooperation and identify several areas where future work can leverage these sets of ideas in order to further the multilevel, multidisciplinary research agenda that distinguishes this field of study. The overarching impression is that an evolutionary perspective can add significant explanatory power to the existing models of partnership selection, alliance governance structure, postformation dynamics, and termination at the dyadic level and firm-level learning and performance, as well as to our current understanding of how networks of interfirm partnerships change over time.

A legitimate question, therefore, is why, if its application offers so much potential, an evolutionary logic has not really taken root (yet) in the study of strategic alliances. One partial answer might be that the theory itself is somewhat new to the field of management, having been utilized so far especially to explain change in the technological innovation trajectories at the firm and industry levels of analysis. Given the role that this perspective has assumed in the strategic management debate (Grant & Spender, 1996; Helfat, 2000), it seems hard to justify further delays in leveraging its potential for the benefit of our common knowledge development in the field.

Another important reason, though, is the heavy requirements that an evolutionary perspective imposes on the nature of the data for empirical analysis. In order to study the evolutionary patterns in the change of interorganizational routines among two partnering firms or industry "recipes" on interfirm cooperation within a network of relationships, one is forced to collect data on the entire history of cooperative agreements within a given pair of firms—or within the portfolio of relationships entertained by the focal firm, or (even more difficult) within the entire network of firms—competing and cooperating within the same domain.

Further, the identification of the history of ties is hardly sufficient to make meaningful observations on the evolutionary processes underlying change at different levels of analysis. One might need additional data for each historical data point, such as the strategic intent of the venture, the structural characteristic of the agreement, its postformation dynamics, and, of course, its performance outcomes. Given the absence of data sets with information on all these aspects of the partnering process, the only solution seems to be the adoption of survey methodologies to collect the required data in sufficient magnitude for generalizable inference. Needless to say, surveys are hardly straightforward processes in this field and are bound to become increasingly difficult as the population of alliance managers is studied with increasing intensity by the growing population of scholars in the field.

These are valid reasons why we are witnessing only a partial application of evolutionary thinking to the study of interorganizational cooperation and why the existing work is focused on only specific questions pertaining primarily to the understanding of postformation dynamics and learning processes. It is also true, though, that we are taking a seemingly unnecessary risk of overstudying well-known questions through well-established theoretical lenses. The keys to many yet unexplored questions, as well as to some of the known ones that have proven particularly hard to crack, might very well be far from the light under the lamppost. We hope we have been able to provide a sufficiently strong and convincing stimulus to scholars in the field to adopt at least some of the theoretical tenets that distinguish evolutionary modeling to exploring the less well-lit knowledge territory. It is easy to predict, at this point, attractive returns to these investments for both the daring explorers and the field of exploration as a whole.

Notes

1. To an extreme, Aldrich (1999) considers the possibility of "blind" variation occurring within organizations.

2. In a nontrivial number of alliances (16%), termination was actually due to the successful completion of the planned task—another reason to suspect the equation of life span with alliance performance.

References

Aldrich, H. (1979). *Organizations and environments.* Englewood Cliffs, NJ: Prentice Hall.

Aldrich, H. (1999). *Organizations evolving.* Thousand Oaks, CA: Sage.

Anand, B., & Khanna, T. (2000). Do firms learn to create value? The case of alliances. *Strategic Management Journal, 21*(3), 295–316.

Anderson, E. (1985). The salesperson as outside agent or employee: A transaction cost analysis. *Marketing Science, 4*(3), 234–246.

Argote, L. (1999). *Organizational learning: Creating, retaining and transferring knowledge.* Boston: Kluwer.

Ariño, A., & de la Torre, J. (1998). Learning from failure: Towards an evolutionary model of collaborative venture. *Organization Science, 9*(3), 306–325.

Balakrishnan, S., & Koza, M. (1993). Information asymmetry, adverse selection, and joint ventures. *Journal of Economic Behavior and Organization, 20,* 99–117.

Barkema, H. G., Shenkar, O., Vermeulen, F., & Bell, J. H. (1997). Working abroad, working with others: How firms learn to operate international joint ventures. *Academy of Management Journal, 40*(2), 426–442.

Barney, J. (1991). Firm resources and sustained competitive advantage. *Journal of Management, 17*(1), 99–120.

Buckley, P. J., & Casson, M. C. (1976). *The future of the multinational enterprise.* London: Homes & Meier.

Campbell, D. (1969). Variation and selective retention in socio-cultural evolution. *General Systems, 16,* 69–85.

Chang, S. J. (1996). An evolutionary perspective on diversification and corporate restructuring: Entry, exit, and economic performance during 1981–89. *Strategic Management Journal, 17,* 587–611.

Cohen, M., & Bacdayan, P. (1994). Organizational routines are stored as procedural memory: Evidence from a laboratory study. *Organization Science, 5,* 554–568.

Contractor, F., & Lorange, J. (1988). *Cooperative strategies in international business.* Lexington, MA: Lexington Books.

Contractor, F., & Lorange, J. (2002). *Cooperative strategies and alliances.* Boston: Elsevier.

Corrado, R., & Zollo, M. (2004). Small worlds evolving: Governance reforms, privatizations and ownership networks in Italy. Working Paper, INSEAD.

Cyert, R., & March, J. (1963). *A behavioral theory of the firm.* Englewood Cliffs, NJ: Blackwell.

Doz, Y. (1996). The evolution of cooperation in strategic alliances: Initial conditions or learning process [special issue]. *Strategic Management Journal, 17,* 55–84.

Doz, Y., & Hamel, G. (1998). *Alliance advantage.* Boston: Harvard Business School Press.

Dyer, J., Kale, P., & Singh, H. (2004). When to ally and when to acquire. *Harvard Business Review, 23*(8), 747–767.

Folta, T. B., & Miller, K. D. (2002). Real options in equity partnerships. *Strategic Management Journal, 23*(1), 77.

Franko, L. G. (1971). *Joint venture survival in multinational corporations.* New York: Praeger.

Ghemawat, P., & Spence, A. M. (1985). Learning curve spillovers and market performance. *Quarterly Journal of Economics, 100*(Suppl.), 839–852.

Grandori, A., & Kogut, B. (2002). Dialogue on organization and knowledge. *Organization Science, 13*(3), 224–231.

Grant, R. (1996). Toward a knowledge-based theory of the firm. *Strategic Management Journal, 17,* 109–122.

Grant, R., & Spender, J. C. (Eds.). (1996). Knowledge and the firm [special issue]. *Strategic Management Journal, 17,* 5–9.

Gulati, R. (1995). Does familiarity breed trust? The implications of repeated ties for contractual choice in alliances. *Academy of Management Journal, 38,* 85–112.

Gulati, R. (1998). Alliances and networks. *Strategic Management Journal, 19,* 293–318.

Gulati, R., & Singh, H. (1998). The architecture of cooperation: Managing coordination costs and appropriation concerns in strategic alliances. *Administrative Science Quarterly, 43,* 781–794.

Gulati, R., Nohria, N., & Zaheer, A. (2000). Strategic networks. *Strategic Management Journal, 21,* 201–215.

Harrigan, K. R. (1988). Joint ventures and competitive strategy. *Strategic Management Journal, 9,* 141–158.

Helfat, C. E. (2000). The evolution of firm capabilities [guest editor's introduction to special issue]. *Strategic Management Journal, 21,* 955–959.

Hennart, J. (1988). A transaction costs theory of equity joint ventures. *Strategic Management Journal, 9*(4), 361–374.

Hennart, J. (1991). The transaction costs theory of joint ventures: An empirical study of Japanese subsidiaries in the United States. *Management Science,* 37(4), 483–497.

Hennart, J., & Reddy, S. (1997). The choice between mergers/acquisitions and joint ventures: The case of Japanese investors in the United States. *Strategic Management Journal, 18,* 1–12.

Hennart, J., & Reddy, S. (2000). Digestibility and asymmetric information in the choice between acquisitions and joint ventures: Where's the beef? *Strategic Management Journal, 21,* 191–193.

Hoang, H., & Rothaermel, F. T. (2005). The effect of general and partner-specific alliance experience on joint R&D project performance. *Academy of Management Journal, 48*(2), 332–345.

Huber, G. P. (1991). Organizational learning: The contributing processes and the literatures. *Organization Science, 2,* 88–115.

Inkpen, A. C. (1995). Organizational learning and international joint ventures. *Journal of International Management, 1,* 165–198.

Inkpen, A., & Beamish, P. (1997). Knowledge, bargaining power, and the instability of international joint ventures. *Academy of Management Review, 22*(1), 177–202.

Inkpen, A., & Dinur, P. (1988). Knowledge management processes and international joint ventures. *Organization Science, 9*(4), 454–468.

Kale, P. (1999). *Building an alliance capability: A knowledge-based approach.* Unpublished dissertation, University of Pennsylvania, Philadelphia.

Kale, P., Dyer, J., & Singh, H. (2002). Alliance capability, stock market response, and long term alliance success: The role of the alliance function. *Strategic Management Journal, 23,* 747–768.

Kale, P., & Singh, H. (1999). Alliance capability and success. *Best Paper Proceedings,* Academy of Management Meetings, Chicago.

Kale, P., Singh, H., & Perlmutter, H. (2000). Learning and protection of proprietary assets in strategic alliances: Building relational capital [special issue]. *Strategic Management Journal, 21*(3) 217–237.

Kim, D. J., & Kogut, B. (1996). Technological platforms and diversification. *Organization Science, 7,* 283–301.

Kogut, B. (1988). A study of the life cycle of joint ventures. In F. K. Contractor & P. Lorange (Eds.), *Cooperative strategies in international business,* 169–186. Lexington, MA: Lexington Books.

Kogut, B. (1991). Joint ventures and the option to acquire and expand. *Management Science, 37,* 19–33.

Kogut, B., Shan, W., & Walker, G. (1992). The make-or-cooperate decision in the context of an industry network. In N. Nohria & R. G. Eccles (Eds.), *Networks and organizations: Structure, form and action,* 348–365. Boston: Harvard Business School Press.

Kogut, B., & Singh, H. (1988). The effect of national culture on the choice of entry mode. *Journal of International Business Studies, 19*(3), 411–432.

Kogut, B., & Walker, G. (2001). The small world of Germany and the durability of national networks. *American Sociological Review, 66,* 317–335.

Kogut, B., & Zander, U. (1992). Knowledge of the firm, combinative capabilities, and the replication of technology. *Organization Science, 3,* 383–397.

Kogut, B., & Zander, U. (1993). Knowledge of the firm and the evolutionary theory of the multinational corporation. *Journal of International Business Studies, 24,* 625–645.

Kogut, B., & Zander, U. (1996). What firms do? Coordination, identity, and learning. *Organization Science, 7*(5), 502–518.

Leonard-Barton, D. (1992). Core capabilities and core rigidities: A paradox in managing new product development. *Strategic Management Journal, 13,* 111–125.

Leonard-Barton, D. (1995). *Wellsprings of knowledge.* Boston: Harvard Business School Press.

Leshchinskii, D., & Zollo, M. (2004). Can firms learn to acquire? The impact of post-acquisition decisions and learning on long-term abnormal returns. Working Paper, INSEAD.

Lewin, A. Y., & Koza, M. P. (Eds.). (2001). Multi-level analysis and co-evolution [editorial in special issue]. *Organization Studies, 22*(6), v–xi.

Li, S., & Rowley, T. (2002). Inertia and evaluation mechanisms in interorganizational partner selection: Syndicate formation among U.S. investment banks. *Academy of Management Journal, 45*(6), 1104–1119.

Lorange, P., & Roos, J. (1992). *Strategic alliances: Formation, implementation, and evolution.* Oxford: Blackwell.

March, J. G., & Simon, H. A. (1958). *Organizations.* New York: John Wiley.

McGrath, R. G. (1997). A real options logic for initiating technology positioning investments. *Academy of Management Review, 22*(4), 974–996.

Narduzzo, A., Rocco, E., & Warglien, M. (2000). Talking about routines in the field. In G. Dosi, R. R. Nelson, & S. G. Winter (Eds.), *The nature and dynamics of organizational capabilities,* 27–50. Oxford, UK: Oxford University Press.

Nelson, R. R. (1995). Recent evolutionary theorizing about economic change. *Journal of Economic Literature, 33*(1), 48.

Nelson, R., & Winter, S. (1982). *An evolutionary theory of economic change.* Cambridge, MA: Harvard University Press.

Nonaka, I. (1994). A dynamic theory of knowledge creation. *Organization Science, 5,* 14–37.

Nonaka, I., & Takeuchi, H. (1995). *The knowledge-creating company.* New York: Oxford University Press.

Nooteboom, B. (1999). *Learning and innovation in organizations and economies.* New York: Oxford University Press.

Osborn, R., & Hagedoorn, J. (1997). The institutionalization and evolutionary dynamics of interorganizational alliances and networks. *Academy of Management Journal, 40,* 261–278.

Oxley, J. (1997). Appropriability hazards and governance in strategic alliances: A transaction cost approach. *Journal of Law, Economics, and Organization, 13,* 387–409.

Parkhe, A. (1993). Partner nationality and structure-performance relationship in strategic alliances. *Organization Science, 4*(2), 301–324.

Pennings, J. M., Barkema, H. G., & Douma, S. W. (1994). Organizational learning and diversification. *Academy of Management Journal, 37*(3), 608–640.

Penrose, E. (1959). *The theory of the growth of the firm.* New York: Wiley.

Pisano, G. (1990). The R&D boundaries of the firm: An empirical analysis. *Administrative Science Quarterly, 35*(1), 124–148.

Powell, W. W., Koput, K. W., & Smith-Doerr, L. (forthcoming). Interorganizational collaboration and the locus of innovation: Networks of learning in biotechnology. *Administrative Science Quarterly, 41,* 116–145.

Powell, W. W., White, D. R., Koput, K. W., & Owen-Smith, J. (forthcoming). Network dynamics and field evolution: The growth of inter-organizational collaboration in the life sciences. *American Journal of Sociology.*

Reuer, J., & Koza, M. (2000). Asymmetric information and joint venture performance: Theory and evidence for domestic and international joint ventures. *Strategic Management Journal, 21,* 81–88.

Reuer, J., & Zollo, M. (2005). Termination outcomes of research alliances. *Research Policy, 34,* 101–115.

Reuer, J., Zollo, M., & Singh, H. (2002). Post-formation dynamics in strategic alliances. *Strategic Management Journal, 23,* 135–151.

Simon, H. (1945). *Administrative behavior.* New York: Free Press.

Simonin, B. L. (1997). The importance of collaborative know-how: An empirical test of the learning organization. *Academy of Management Journal, 40*(5), 1150–1174.

Spender, J. C. (1989). *Industry recipes: An enquiry into the nature and sources of managerial judgement.* Oxford: Basil Blackwell.

Szulanski, G., & Winter, S. (2002). Getting it right the second time. *Harvard Business Review, 80,* 62–69.

Teece, D., Pisano, G., & Shuen, A. (1997). Dynamic capabilities and strategic management. *Strategic Management Journal, 18*(7), 509–533.

Williamson, O. E. (1991). Comparative economic organization: The analysis of discrete structural alternatives. *Administrative Science Quarterly, 36,* 269–296.

Winter, S. G. (2003). Understanding dynamic capabilities. *Strategic Management Journal, 24*(10), 991.

Zaheer, A., McEvily, B., & Perrone, V. (1998). Does trust matter? Exploring the effects of interorganizational and interpersonal trust on performance. *Organization Science, 9*(2), 141–159.

Zollo, M. (1998). *Knowledge codification, process routinization and the creation of organizational capabilities.* Unpublished doctoral dissertation, University of Pennsylvania, Philadelphia.

Zollo, M., Reuer, J., & Singh, H. (2002). Interorganizational routines and performance in strategic alliances. *Organization Science, 13*(6), 701–713.

Zollo, M., & Singh, H. (2004). Deliberate learning in corporate acquisitions: Post-acquisition strategies and integration capability in U.S. bank mergers. *Strategic Management Journal, 25*(12), 1233–1256.

Zollo, M., & Winter, S. (2002). Deliberate learning and the evolution of dynamic capabilities. *Organization Science, 13,* 339–351.

6

What Does a Real Options Perspective Add to the Understanding of Strategic Alliances?

Anju Seth

Tailan Chi

Strategic alliances as a subject of study in international business and strategic management have been examined through a variety of theoretical lenses. In this chapter, we discuss how real options theory contributes to the understanding of the phenomenon. As real options theory has only relatively recently been recognized as a useful tool for analyzing strategic alliances, with considerable prior theoretical work on the phenomenon, our discussion in this chapter will focus on the additional contributions of this perspective.

Real options theory is a very general approach to evaluating decisions under uncertainty and is particularly useful in analyzing decisions involving variables that evolve stochastically over time. As such, it can complement and enrich other theories that were initially developed in a deterministic setting but have the potential of being made dynamic and stochastic. However, not all theories can be fruitfully extended in this manner. We emphasize here that the application of the real options approach requires a careful examination of its commensurability with the assumptions and analytical logic of the theory with which it is being integrated and incorporation of at least some of the theory's key assumptions into the analysis.

AUTHOR'S NOTE: Both authors contributed equally to this chapter. We would like to thank the editors and an anonymous reviewer for valuable comments.

Theories that have been used extensively to examine strategic alliances include the resource- or capability-based view, transaction cost economics, and internationalization theory. All these theories posit uncertainty and potential for learning influence their decision variables (e.g., the choice of mode for exploiting complementary capabilities), even though they vary in the sources of uncertainty being scrutinized. To illustrate the value of the real options approach, we consider a number of controversies that have emerged in the study of strategic alliances and discuss how real options analysis can shed light on these controversies. The real options approach also highlights various critical issues regarding the design of alliance contracts toward aligning the interests of partners and creating appropriate incentives for them to contribute effort to the venture. We describe how different contractual specifications have different incentive effects and outline some key contingencies underlying their use.

The chapter is organized as follows. After a discussion of methods for applying real options analysis to the study of strategic alliances, we highlight its contributions by examining three controversies about strategic alliances and the new insights that can be obtained from a real options analysis. These controversies include (1) the consequences of asymmetric learning by alliance partners, (2) alliance as a transitional mode of operation, and (3) rigidity in the choice of international expansion mode. We then examine the implications of various contractual specifications regarding options in a strategic alliance. The last section summarizes and concludes the paper.

Real Options Analysis

The basic idea of real options analysis is quite straightforward. In the face of uncertainty, the decision maker may acquire new information as time goes by, and the new information may alter his or her assessments of the various alternatives (e.g., different modes of operation). Under such conditions, the option to switch from one alternative to another (i.e., the ability to do so without incurring a significant cost) has value. The application of this approach to the study of strategic alliances basically entails the valuation of the various options embedded in a strategic alliance and its alternatives, together with the expected cash-flow values associated with each of them. Although it is not always the case, one often needs to construct a mathematical model in order to attain a reasonable degree of accuracy in the assessment. In this section, we first provide an overview of how options may add value to alliances in the presence of uncertainty. Next, we consider what sources of uncertainty the partners to a strategic alliance are likely to encounter and how one might model the impact of the uncertainty in a real options model.

Option Value, Uncertainty, and Timing of Exercise

As the most widely understood options are financial options with an explicit exercise price and a definite expiration date that are contractually specified, one might expect that options in strategic alliances also require such contractual stipulations. This turns out not to be the case. Although some alliances may contractually grant an explicit option to restructure the arrangement (e.g., a joint venture [JV] contract may include a clause granting one partner the option to acquire the other partner's stake or the option to sell one's stake to the other partner at an ex ante specified price), this is the exception rather than the rule. The main option that a strategic alliance offers is for the partners to do something different from what is stipulated in the initial contract. So, even in the absence of a contractual specification, the alliance confers the *implicit* option to change the structure of the alliance, with the terms of the restructuring to be negotiated ex post. The exercise of the option typically entails switching to a different mode of operation or at least some restructuring of the alliance (Chi & Seth, 2002). Mode switching or alliance restructuring necessarily involves some exchange of assets (tangible or intangible) between the two parties. The key question then arises: Under what conditions does the option to restructure the alliance create value for the alliance partners?

Before proceeding to a discussion of these conditions, it is important to clarify what we mean by the term "value of the option to the alliance partners." In the general case, when the alliance contains the implicit option to restructure, the partners do not even know whether the option is in the money unless and until they reach agreement on the terms of the restructuring. In the case of a JV that contains the implicit option to acquire or divest at an ex post negotiated price, whether the option to acquire (or divest) is in the money is unknown until the partners reach an agreement on the acquisition price. Only if both parties are better off with one acquiring the other (relative to continuing as partners in the JV) will they be able to reach an agreement on the acquisition price. There is a higher probability that the two parties will reach this agreement (i.e., implying that the call/put option is in the money) when the restructuring maximizes the joint value of the option to restructure. So, at the first level of analysis, the value of the option to both parties considered together is critical to consider. At the next level of analysis, it is also useful to consider the value to each party because they are likely to bargain over how the total gains from exercising the option will be shared between them.

For the value of various options embedded in an alliance to be realized, there must also be some resolution of uncertainty over time. Technically, this resolution of uncertainty can be considered as a shift in the expected value of an uncertain outcome (e.g., the amount of profit a party is likely to earn from the investment project without its partner) or a reduction in its variance. The timing of exercise of the option is associated with the timing of uncertainty resolution (or conversely, if all the uncertain variables remain constant, the option will not be exercised). Because of its influence on the timing of option exercise, it is useful to consider *how* uncertainty is resolved, that is, whether uncertainty is exogenous or endogenous.

Exogenous uncertainty resolves by itself and does not depend on the actions of the focal firm (Dixit & Pindyck, 1994). An example is the future policy of a government that is currently forcing foreign investors to form JVs with indigenous firms. The government may tighten or loosen this policy over the time, but a potential foreign investor can observe the future evolution of the policy without taking any specific actions and is unlikely to find out more by taking any actions. In contrast, endogenous uncertainty is resolved by actions taken by the firm and specifically depends upon "paying running costs to obtain more information about potential benefits" (Roberts & Weitzman, 1981, p. 1262). For example, uncertainty about a potential acquisition target or potential partner's capabilities can be reduced only if action that results in close interactions with the party is taken, such as collaborating with the party in an alliance. This type of uncertainty is hence endogenous to the choice of market entry mode.

In addition to its implications for timing of option exercise, the foregoing discussion has another important implication: When uncertainty is endogenous to the decision to form an alliance, it is an important driver of the value of the option to restructure the alliance. In the absence of this type of uncertainty, but given the presence of exogenous uncertainty, the option to restructure the alliance may still be valuable if partnership in the alliance confers an advantage (relative to other potential parties) in the outcome of the restructuring (e.g., one partner's acquisition of the other's stake in a JV).

Sources of Uncertainty and Options Embedded in Strategic Alliances

Although the real options approach provides a methodology for assessing decisions under uncertainty, it does not, in and of itself, identify the sources of uncertainty that underlie the value of options embedded in a strategic alliance. So it is critical to integrate real options analysis with other theories that specifically identify important sources of uncertainty. Below we present a typology of uncertainty that prior research has used to characterize the conditions under which strategic alliances are formed and review the theoretical lens that helps to identify each source of uncertainty.

Market Uncertainty

As suggested by real options theory, uncertainty about either output or input market can underlie option value (Dixit & Pindyck, 1994). In his pathbreaking paper, Kogut (1991) argued that JVs represent options to expand into new product or geographical markets characterized by uncertain demand. Kogut found evidence that this option is likely to be exercised via acquisition by one JV partner of the other's stake when market demand exceeds a base rate forecast. Market uncertainty can also be associated with uncertainty about the viability of different technologies or the costs of bringing new products to market. Folta's (1998) investigation suggests that technological uncertainty increases the likelihood for a firm to undertake a JV or partial equity investment in another firm as opposed to outright acquisition in the biotechnology industry.

In the context of strategic alliances, one may assume that both partners experience the same level of uncertainty about output and input markets. Under this assumption, it is straightforward to model the uncertainty as a single stochastic variable representing market demand or input cost. If we denote the variable as X_t, we may express the evolution of the variable over time as

$$(X_{t+\Delta t} - X_t)/X_t = \mu(\Delta t) + \sigma(\Delta W_t), \qquad (1)$$

where μ is the expected rate of change in X_t, Δt denotes the length of the time increment, σ measures the size of unpredicted change in X_t, and ΔW_t is a random variable that follows some probability distribution (e.g., binary or normal, with an expectation of zero and a variance dependent on the length of the time increment). Once the stochastic variable is defined, one can use a variety of methods to calculate the value of the option that the variable underlies. We briefly discuss some of the modeling methods toward the end of this section.

Even though a firm's entry into a new market assists the resolution of the uncertainty about the market, the firm can acquire new information by using any mode for its entry. So market uncertainty is exogenous to the choice of mode and will not by itself confer any valuable options on the partners of an alliance if they experience the same level of uncertainty. As shown by Chi and McGuire (1996), any gain a partner may obtain from altering the alliance's structure (e.g., acquiring the other's stake in the alliance) will be entirely at the expense of the other if they experience the same level of market uncertainty, unless there also exists another type of uncertainty (e.g., uncertainty about their respective capabilities).

Uncertainty About Capabilities

Two alliance partners facing the same output and input markets may still differ in their abilities to profit from whatever assets the alliance may eventually accumulate if they acquire the other's control rights to the assets. This differential can result from one partner possessing assets with greater complementarity to those of the alliance or simply being better able to learn the other's capabilities. Given that the evolution of the partners' capabilities is inevitably subject to uncertainty, it is fitting to examine the value of options that their evolving capabilities may underlie—primarily the option to acquire the other partner's control rights.

If we assume that the capabilities of the two parties evolve along separate paths, we need to have two different stochastic variables to model any options embedded in an alliance: one for Party i and the other for Party j. With two

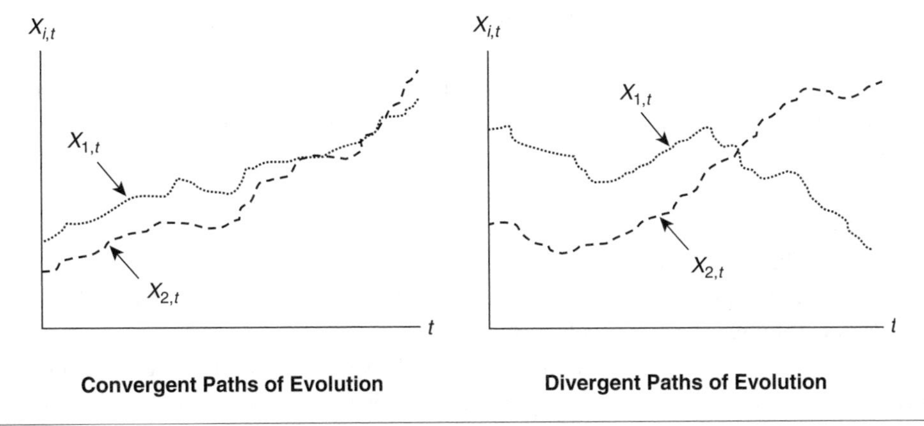

Figure 6.1 Convergent Versus Divergent Evolution of Partner Capabilities

stochastic variables, the evolutionary process can be modeled as

$$\Delta X_{i,t}/X_{i,t} = \mu_i(\Delta t) + \sigma_i(\Delta W_{i,t}) + \rho_i(\Delta W_{j,t}), \quad (2)$$

where $\Delta X_{i,t} = X_{i,t+\Delta t} - X_{i,t}$ and ρ captures the extent of correlation between $\Delta W_{i,t}$ and $\Delta W_{j,t}$. Figure 6.1 illustrates two different patterns of evolution for the capabilities of the partners: one convergent (more likely when ρ is higher) and one divergent (more likely when ρ is lower). When there is more than one stochastic factor, the model becomes complex and difficult to solve. However, because a single-factor model is incapable of analyzing the situation where the capabilities of the partners can diverge, it is our opinion that one needs at least a two-factor model to evaluate properly the options embedded in a strategic alliance. The models developed by Chi and McGuire (1996) and Chi (2000) show that the option to acquire the other partner's stake (or more generally, the option to restructure an alliance so that one party has sole control over its assets) rises as there is a greater likelihood for the partners' capabilities to diverge (i.e., lower ρ). The intuition behind this result can be explained as follows. By definition, the more capable party is better able to earn rent from the alliance's assets and is hence willing to pay a higher price for the assets than the other is [willing].[1] So a greater likelihood of capability divergence means a higher probability for the partners to gain from a mutually beneficial trade in their stakes whereby the more (less) capable party buys the other's stake (sells its own stake to the other) at a favorable price. This is an important result when we consider some of the controversies about strategic alliances in the next section.

Of concern to alliance partners are not only the evolution of their individual capabilities but also those capabilities relative to their joint capabilities that are combined in the alliance. Seth and Kim (2001) show that uncertainty about the synergistic value that can potentially be created via a combination of their capabilities also makes the option to explore the potential synergy in a strategic alliance valuable. If the evolution of their joint capabilities follows a path separate from the evolution of each party's own capabilities, the appropriate model for evaluating the embedded options will require three possibly correlated stochastic variables. One interesting question that can be addressed by such a model is how the correlation of each party's individual capabilities with their joint capabilities affects the probability of alliance dissolution.

Uncertainty and Opportunism

The arguably most influential theoretical perspective on the motivation for strategic alliances (particularly JVs) considers this form of interfirm organization as a way to mitigate various transaction cost problems that plague its alternatives, such as licensing and acquisition (e.g., Hennart, 1988).

As is widely recognized in the literature on the choice of market entry mode, two firms that perceive their assets to be complementary may each know more about the quality of their own assets than those of the other's (Balakrishnan & Koza, 1993; Chi, 1994). This type of information asymmetry can make it difficult for them to evaluate each other's assets and reach a potentially mutually beneficial agreement on the exploitation of the potential synergy due to the adverse selection problem (Akerlof, 1970). Balakrishnan and Koza (1993) suggest that the two firms may be able to mitigate the problem by forming a JV, because a JV involves a contingent claim contract that provides less incentive for them to misrepresent the value of their assets than under acquisition. Nanda and Williamson (1995) further suggest that a potential acquirer can even use a JV with its acquisition target as a vehicle for gaining a more accurate assessment of the target's assets before undertaking a full-scale acquisition. A firm's lack of information about the quality of a potential acquisition target can be represented in a two-factor model with one party's capabilities subject to greater volatility (e.g., σ_i is significantly larger than σ_j). In such a model, as shown by Chi (2000), one can examine how the extent of information asymmetry affects the value of the option embedded in the JV.

The formation and operation of a strategic alliance is also subject to its own set of transaction costs, as clearly recognized in the literature. Particularly important is the potential for one partner to cheat the other or hold up the alliance process (e.g., Chi, 1994). One frequently cited manifestation of such opportunistic behavior is one party's misappropriation of the other's assets by setting up a competing business (or threatening to do so) after acquiring the knowledge that underlies the assets. One can also use a two-factor model to examine what factors affect the likelihood for such opportunistic behavior to occur and the associated cost of forming an alliance. In such a model, $X_{i,t}$ and $X_{j,t}$ can be redefined as each party's ability to gain from setting up a competing business. We expect that both the volatility in and the correlation between the two stochastic variables (i.e., σ_i and ρ) will affect the likelihood of opportunism and the incentive to form strategic alliances.

Model Setup and Solution Methods

The specification of a stochastic process such as the one in equation (1) or (2) above represents only the first step toward examining the options embedded in a strategic alliance and its alternatives. One needs to build a mathematical model that incorporates the specified process in order to assess the options' values and analyze their characteristics. A two-factor process defined in (2) is much more difficult to model than a single-factor process defined in (1), but a single-factor process has serious limitations for modeling options embedded in strategic alliances. As noted earlier, because the assessments of the two alliance partners concerning the value of the alliance's assets can easily differ and most likely evolve separately, a proper evaluation of the options is likely to require the use of a more complex model with two or more factors.

Another challenge in modeling alliance options is to specify whether and how each party will react to the actions of the other. In a straight option model, each party reacts only to the state of nature that is exogenous and purely random. Although useful insights can be derived from such models, clearly the assumption that neither party reacts to the actions of the other represents an oversimplification. A more realistic model requires an integration of the real options approach with the game-theoretic approach, whereby each party plays not only a game with nature but also a game with a thinking opponent that is purposeful and possesses certain foresight. Integration of these modeling approaches can easily make the model intractable, so the challenge is to specify a model that embodies a level of realism that is still tractable. Early models of alliance options that try to incorporate some elements of game theory assume that the partners play a cooperative game under complete information in negotiating the structure of the alliance (e.g., Chi, 2000). This assumption allows the models to examine precisely the characteristics of the options under the restricted conditions, although it limits the models' ability to analyze situations where the partners are more competitive than cooperative. Some researchers have developed models of investment decision making that endogenize responses from competitors on the market (e.g., Joaquin & Butler, 1999). Their work shows that it is possible to model alliance options under a noncooperative framework and raises the prospect for greater insights to be derived from option-based research on strategic alliances.

The dynamic relationships defined in equations (1) and (2) are expressed in discrete time, and models based on such stochastic processes can be solved using decision-tree analysis or Monte Carlo simulation. But one can easily express these relationships in continuous time and solve the resultant models using dynamic programming or contingency analysis. A comparison of these two methods for solving continuous-time models can be found in Dixit and Pindyck (1994). In comparison with discrete-time modeling, the main advantage of continuous-time modeling is the possibility of obtaining closed-form solutions that are more general and less complex in computation, although it requires the use of advanced mathematics that requires specialized training.

An extensive literature on the methods for solving stochastic models has been developed. A commonly used textbook on stochastic modeling in continuous time is by Karatzas and Shreve (1997). Trigeorgis (1991) provides a good explanation of the theoretical linkage between continuous-time and discrete-time models. A recent text on the Monte Carlo simulation method is by Jaeckel (2002). Kamrad and Ritchken (1991) developed a two-factor model in discrete time that is particularly conducive to modeling options in strategic alliances.

Three Controversies and Insights From Real Options Analysis

In this section, we show how the real options approach may shed light on three questions that have been under debate in the study of strategic alliances. These questions are concerned with the consequences of asymmetric learning by alliance partners, alliance as a transitional mode of operation, and rigidity in the choice of international expansion mode.

Consequences of Asymmetric Learning

As discussed in the preceding section, the partners to a strategic alliance may differ in their capacity to absorb the capabilities of the other, resulting in one-sided or asymmetric transfer of knowledge between them. Internalization theory has long recognized the risk in transferring proprietary knowledge to a potential competitor under imperfect intellectual property rights regimes (Buckley & Casson, 1976; Rugman, 1981; Teece, 1986). The intellectual roots of internalization theory include both the theory of firm growth (Penrose, 1959) and transaction cost economics (Coase, 1937, 1960). As a theory that explains the existence of multinational enterprises (MNEs), it posits that an MNE's ability to expand across national boundaries profitably must stem from its possession of some proprietary production knowledge such as technology and marketing know-how. At the same time, it also points out that the possession of such knowledge is not sufficient to explain a firm's preference for owning its production operations overseas, because it can always license the knowledge to a local firm. What motivates the firm to retain ownership must be the existence of difficulties in licensing its knowledge. One of the difficulties highlighted in internalization theory is the imperfection of the intellectual property rights regime that makes enforcement of a licensing contract hazardous. An often-cited hazard is that the licensee, upon acquisition of the licensor's knowledge, may decide to violate the restrictions of the initial licensing contract and compete with the licensor in the face of serious difficulties in enforcing the contractual restrictions.

Using concepts developed under the rubric of the resource- or capability-based view, such as core competencies and inimitability, Hamel, Doz, and Prahalad (1989) urged firms to engage in a learning race with their alliance partners lest they lose their competitive advantage. The rationale behind their prescription is not very different from the misappropriation risk identified in internalization theory, although they do not take intellectual property rights regime as a key variable in their theoretical formulation. The transaction cost analysis that underlies internalization theory, however, only identifies the risk of creating a potential competitor as a possible reason for firms to go it alone and is not concerned about asymmetric knowledge transfer under a strong property rights regime.

More recent extensions of internalization theory's analytical apparatus to the study of strategic alliances question the wisdom of engaging in a learning race in strategic alliances. Zeng and Hennart (2002) argue that it defeats the purpose of undertaking a strategic alliance if both partners concentrate their efforts on acquiring the other's knowledge while trying to withhold knowledge from the other. They suggest that each alliance partner's specializing in its own sphere of expertise is more compatible with the intent of most alliances and that the anticipated joint gains from continued specialization and knowledge-sharing may be sufficient to motivate the partners to do so. In other words, from a game-theoretic perspective, specialization can be a self-enforcing contract for alliance partners to avoid engaging in a value-destroying learning race; as such, the learning-race prescription may be based on an overstated risk of asymmetric learning.

Whereas the debate over the learning race in strategic alliances focuses on how much risk asymmetric learning engenders and what may be the best mechanism for mitigating the risk, analyses using the real options approach discovered a result that may seem surprising to both sides of the debate. As we alluded to in the previous section, the joint gains from the option to acquire the partner's stake in a JV are greater as the changes in their evolving capabilities are less correlated (Chi, 2000). In the specification of equation (2), a lower correlation is represented by a smaller ρ, signifying a higher likelihood that the abilities of the two parties to profit from the venture's assets will diverge—a manifestation of asymmetric learning. This result suggests that asymmetric learning can actually be a source of value creation because the two parties can both benefit from a profitable trade in their respective stakes in the venture when their valuations diverge due to differing abilities to profit from the venture's assets. However, this result does not take into account the risk of misappropriation after the occurrence of asymmetric learning.

Recent work by Chi and Seth (2004) extends this insight by integrating this transaction cost problem into a real options model. They show that asymmetric learning can be value-destroying if the partners are motivated to invest more resources in power-jockeying when they anticipate a significant wealth transfer after the occurrence of asymmetric learning. In other words, whether asymmetric learning is value-enhancing or value-destroying depends on whether the alliance partners can set up mechanisms that prevent asymmetric learning from giving rise to significant wealth transfers between them.

In summary, the application of real options theory to the controversy about the consequences of asymmetric learning in strategic alliances enriches our understanding of the phenomenon. Internalization theory views asymmetric learning as a source of hazard. The learning-race perspective points out that a party may be able to turn the hazard into an opportunity by beating its partner in a learning race but downplays the likelihood that the purpose of the alliance will be defeated if both partners follow this prescription by engaging in such a race. The real options approach views asymmetric learning in a more positive light and considers it a necessary condition for value creation in trading assets between the partners. More important, an integration of real options theory with existing theories not only shows asymmetric learning to be both a potential source of value creation and a potential source of value destruction but also identifies the condition for each of the opposite effects to dominate.

Alliance as a Transitional Mode of Operation

Based on their study of Swedish multinationals, Johanson and Vahlne (1977) suggested that firms tend to follow a staged path of international expansion, starting with simple export, moving onto such intermediate stages as strategic alliances, and reaching the highest stage of solely owned operations. This proposition rests on the assumption that international operation requires certain location-specific knowledge that is tacit in nature and hence has to be acquired gradually over time. For this reason, a firm needs to utilize such intermediate modes as licensing and joint venturing to gain international experience before going it alone. The proposition became known as internationalization theory in the field of international business. It is worth noting that this perspective draws on the work of Penrose (1959), to which the resource- or capability-based view developed later in the field of strategic management also traces its roots (Kor & Mahoney, 2000).

The main proposition of internationalization theory was quickly criticized by the proponents of internalization theory (Rugman, 1980). According to internalization theory, a firm that is able to expand overseas profitability must possess some proprietary assets that are difficult to price or protect due to imperfections under the existing property rights regime. These transactional difficulties would, therefore, motivate the firm to avoid the transfer of its proprietary assets via licensing or joint venturing. Furthermore, one can easily find exceptions to the staged path of expansion posited by internationalization theory, undermining its empirical validity or generality (Benito & Gripsrud, 1992; Fina & Rugman, 1996).

Later extensions of both internationalization theory and internalization theory have, in a way, moved them closer to each other. More recent studies on the influence of a firm's international experience on its choice of expansion mode no longer posit the existence of a rigid expansion path (Johanson & Mattson, 1988). Studies that apply transaction cost analysis to the study of strategic alliances also suggest that the lack of tacit location-specific knowledge can motivate a firm to form alliances in its international expansion (Hennart, 1988). This apparent "reconciliation" is far from complete, however. First, internationalization theory considers the lack of *tacit location-specific knowledge* on the part of the expanding firm to be a sufficient reason for the use of strategic alliances. To those who subscribe to internalization theory, the *transaction costs* of sharing tacit knowledge from two otherwise separate firms are what make strategic alliances a superior modal choice. Second, the lack of tacit location-specific knowledge provides a motivation for only some strategic alliances but would lose its explanatory power if there exists an efficient managerial labor market in which the expanding firm can acquire such knowledge by hiring the appropriate personnel. Third, internationalization theory has a time dimension and considers strategic alliances as a transitional mode, while theories based on transaction cost analysis focus on equilibrium choice and do not leave much room for analyzing transitional modes in a dynamic setting. Even though internationalization theory has a time dimension, the deterministic framework of its original formulation makes it vulnerable to criticism.

Some original proponents of internalization theory have suggested a way to unify the core ideas from both internalization theory and internationalization theory under a real options framework. Buckley, Casson, and Gulamhussen (2002) argue that uncertainty about the foreign market and about the efficacy of the focal firm's own knowledge can make a staged path of foreign expansion economically superior. By initially taking an entry mode that involves low sunk cost such as direct export, licensing, or joint venturing, the firm can gather more information about the market and the efficacy of its own knowledge in serving the market without risking the loss of a large investment. In other words, the low-commitment modes allow the firm to explore the options afforded by its own proprietary knowledge and resolve the initial uncertainty in stages.

The staged path that emerges from the application of real options analysis to existing theories is not rigid and takes into account both the characteristics of the market and the characteristics of the focal firm's resources. The modes that are utilized by a firm in its path of expansion do not have to include strategic alliances. A small-scale wholly owned subsidiary can often serve as a vehicle for gathering information about the new market and the efficacy of the focal firm's own capabilities. Alternatively, as suggested by Nanda and Williamson (1995), a strategic alliance such as a JV can serve as an effective vehicle for the expanding firm to gather more accurate information on the quality of a potential acquisition target's assets. The reason is that a JV with an option to acquire helps reduce the uncertainty that the potential acquirer experiences with regard to the assets in question.

In short, by focusing on the tradeoff between flexibility and commitment, the real options approach helps to integrate the ideas from internalization theory and internationalization theory under a dynamic framework and provides a more precise explanation for the use of strategic alliances as a transitional mode in international expansion. Although both internationalization theory and real options theory take uncertainty as a key determinant, there is an important distinction between them. Internationalization theory views uncertainty as a negative influence in the foreign market entry decision. Under the real options approach, however, greater uncertainty may actually give the firm a stronger reason to enter a foreign country under a low commitment mode (e.g., a strategic alliance), even though a simple discounted cash flow valuation suggests that it is a negative net present value (NPV) project The reason is that the value of the options embedded in a project in general rises with the extent of uncertainty and may outweigh the negative present value of the expected cash flows from the project. The options that may be embedded in foreign market entry include the acquisition of the alliance partner's assets at a favorable price and further expansion of the project in case of positive feedback from the market (Kogut, 1991).

Rigidity in the Choice of International Expansion Mode

The received theory on the choice of foreign market entry mode suggests that the optimal modal choice depends on both the attributes of the expanding firm's own resources and the attributes of any important complementary resources that may be in the possession of other firms (Hennart, 1988; Teece, 1986). Important attributes include the measurability of the resources' quality and of each resource contributor's effort and their vulnerability to opportunistic appropriation (Chi, 1994). As the resources that may be complementary to a firm's own resources can vary from one market to another, one might expect that a firm would use different modes for different markets and that similar firms would choose similar modes for the same market. Recent research by Singh and Zollo (2004) indicates, however, that firms tend to use the same mode regardless of the market being entered and that firms that have similar characteristics often adopt different entry modes in the same market. In other words, many firms apparently exhibit a degree of rigidity in their use of entry modes. Although one cannot rule out the possibility that the perceived rigidity actually reflects a consistency in the characteristics of the requisite resources for profitable operation in different markets, the observed rigidity does raise a puzzle that relates to a broader controversy on the adoption of new institutional forms.

Economic models of organizational choice typically assume that firms are rational in the sense that they make their choices based on an analysis of the marginal benefit from moving to an alternative form of organization against the marginal cost of doing so. The assumption of rational choice is sometimes interpreted imprecisely in the literature as equivalent to the assumption of superrationality, under which the decision maker has complete and perfect information. Sociological studies of organizations uncovered evidence that new organizational forms tend to spread gradually (Scott, 1995). This finding is apparently inconsistent with the assumption of superrationality because under perfect information a firm should know its best form of organization at any given point in time. Granovetter (1985) considers such observed rigidity to refute the assumption of rational choice that most economic models of organizations make. As an alternative to the economic theory of institutional choice, institutional theory in sociology attributes the rigidity that institutions seem to exhibit to their need for legitimacy (Powell & DiMaggio, 1991). According to an often-used definition in institutional theory, legitimacy is "a generalized perception or assumption that the action of an entity is desirable, proper, and appropriate within some socially constructed system of norms, values, beliefs, and definitions" (Suchman, 1995, p. 574). This definition clearly allows factors that are opposed to economic rationality to be dominant forces in organizational choice even though it does not entirely rule out the influence of economic rationality.

An alternative explanation for the reluctance of some firms to adopt new interfirm or intrafirm organizational forms can be derived from option theory under the assumption of economic rationality. The explanation assumes that managers do indeed make rational choices but the efficacy of new organizational form is uncertain to the firm. This uncertainty tends to reduce over time as the performance of other firms that have adopted it becomes known. If the adoption of the new organizational form requires an initial investment that cannot be fully recovered in case it is later found to be inferior and abandoned, then the adoption decision is at least partially irreversible. Under this condition, the option to keep the current organizational form has value, and the option value makes it economically rational to wait until the expected payoff from adopting the new form exceeds, by at least the value of the option, the expected payoff from keeping the current form. In other words, the existence of this option gives rise to a type of rigidity or hysteresis that is economically rational (Dixit & Pindyck, 1994). It should be pointed out that the option-based explanation would suggest a greater retardation in the adoption of new organizational forms in the face of uncertainty and irreversibility than warranted under an institutional economics explanation.

To test whether the apparent rigidity that Singh and Zollo (2004) observed is due to option value or some sociological or psychological condition (e.g., need for legitimacy or cognitive bias), one can investigate whether the extent of rigidity depends on factors that real options theory identifies as important. Specifically, real options theory predicts that the extent of rigidity rises with both the cost of switching organizational form and the level of uncertainty about the new organizational form's economic merit. These factors are not specifically incorporated in sociological or psychological theories that also try to explain the observed rigidity.

Option Clauses in Alliance Contracts

In the preceding sections of the paper, we examined how one may apply the real options approach to the study of strategic alliances and what theoretical insights have been derived from research using this approach. In this section, we discuss how alliance partners can best exploit the value of such embedded options through initial structuring of the alliance. We have shown that the parties can gain from the options embedded in the alliance whether they stipulate any explicit option clauses in their alliance contract. The questions we now turn to are whether it is better for them to specify an explicit option clause in the initial contract and the best way for them to specify such clauses. Because different types of alliances may be structurally designed in myriad ways, our discussion in this section focuses on contractual specifications of options in JVs specifically rather than those contained in alliances more generally.

In order to address these questions, we need to examine the rights and obligations that different kinds of explicit option clauses establish for the JV partners. In general, an explicit option clause represents a contractual stipulation that gives one partner the right to acquire the other's stake or sell its own stake to the other, typically at a value that may be based upon a previously agreed valuation formula or ex post determined by a third-party expert (Chemla, Habib, & Ljungqvist, 2003). This right automatically imposes an obligation on the other party. Although it does not preclude the possibility of the party holding the call (put) option to sell its own stake to the other party (buy the other's stake) at an ex post negotiated price, the explicit option clause creates a measure of asymmetry between the two parties. Specifically, the clause makes it much less costly for the option holder to exercise its option according to the contract than for the option issuer to exercise an unspecified option through negotiation. The explicit option clause protects the value of the specified option from being dissipated by the cost of ex post bargaining.

As we have discussed above, any gain from exercising a put or call option must arise from a differential between the parties' respective valuations of the assets of the alliance. An immediate implication is that the parties can realize more of the value embodied in all the options available from the alliance by giving the call (put) option to the party that is more likely than the other to have a higher (lower) valuation of the alliance's assets (all other things held equal). The reason is that the value of a call (put) option is much more valuable to the party that is more likely to attach a high (lower) value to those assets, presumably due to an expectedly stronger ability to profit from the assets. The question that arises is: Should the parties give the likely "high bidder" a call option or the likely "low bidder" a put option if one is considered more likely to place a higher value on the alliance assets than the other? This depends on which party experiences greater uncertainty about the value of the assets. They can realize more of the value embodied in the options by giving a call or put option to the party that experiences greater uncertainty about the value of the assets than the other, whether the party is likely to be the high or low evaluator. The reason is that the party that has less information on and hence experiences greater uncertainty about the value of the assets can benefit more from holding the right to acquire/divest the assets than the other does (Chi, 2000).

Given that an option clause in the alliance contract can protect the value of the options embedded in an alliance from being dissipated by ex post bargaining, does it mean that the partners should always include such a clause in their contract? A number of authors have found that the percentage of alliance contracts that contain an explicit option clause seems to be below 5% (Reuer & Tong, forthcoming; Richards & Indro, 2002). Why do most alliances seem to omit such a potentially beneficial contractual clause?

To address this question, one needs to examine the costs of including such a clause in the alliance contract. First, note that the option will be exercised when the value created by sole ownership by one party exceeds the value owned by continuing the JV with the original joint ownership. If the value of the assets under Party A' s ownership are expected to be higher than the value of the assets under Party B's ownership, then Party A should have the option to buy Party B's stake (and vice versa). But if, at the time of JV formation, it is unclear which party will have the higher valuation of the JV's assets (as may happen if the two parties bring different but ex ante equally valuable capabilities to the JV), explicit specification of call or put options in the hands of one or the other party may be value-destroying. The implication is that the more similar the value of capabilities that the parties contribute to the JV, the less likely is an explicit option to be included in the JV contract.

Second, note that the parties can negotiate the strike price ex ante (by specifying a valuation formula or agreeing that the "fair price" will be determined by a third-party expert). Imposing these constraints ex ante could reduce the cost of ex post bargaining over the terms of transfer, relative to an implicit option with no previous specifications vis-à-vis the exercise price. However, the cost of negotiating the exercise price depends on the amount of information they have at each point in time. In general, the cost of bargaining is higher when the available information is more imperfect or more asymmetrically distributed (Fudenberg & Tirole, 1991). If the parties expect to have significantly more information about the appropriate price ex post, then the relative cost of negotiating the price ex ante is likely to be higher.

Furthermore, the cost of instituting an explicit option clause includes more than the cost of negotiation, because a price negotiated under more imperfect information is more likely to be inappropriate. The cost of a wrong exercise price will not be too serious if the consequence is simply the price not being used or having to be renegotiated later. The more serious cost may be manifested in the form of perverse incentives for the partners in the operation of the alliance (Chi, 2000). Specifically, if the exercise price of a call option is set too low, then the option issuer is likely to lose incentive to contribute too early, because the assets' value to the call-option holder is likely to exceed the exercise price well before the benefit from the option issuer's effort is fully realized. Similarly, if the exercise price of a put option is set too high, then the option holder is likely to have little incentive to maintain the value of the assets, because the high exercise price already guarantees the party a high return. Given these potential incentive problems stemming from an option clause, it is perhaps reasonable for alliance partners to be reluctant to include such a clause in their initial contract.

Finally, we note that the partners may actually place restrictions on one or both of them with regard to their exercise of the option to acquire the other's stake via ex post negotiation, because the anticipation of such negotiations can motivate them to waste resources in jockeying for power during the alliance process (Klein, 1992; Masten, 1988). Perhaps based on this idea, some alliance contracts hold the parties to certain onerous obligations, such as continued payment of royalty fees to the partner or continued use of the partner's distribution channel, even after the alliance is dissolved (Chi, 2000).

Conclusion

Numerous theoretical perspectives with their roots in economics and sociology have provided valuable insights into our understanding of why strategic alliances are formed and the economic benefits that they provide to the partners in the alliance. These theories, however, are typically cast in a static setting. Although the theories identify different types of uncertainty that confront the alliance partners, their predictions and explanations of alliance behavior do not account for the dynamic evolution of uncertainty and the flexibility of the collaborating parties to modify their decisions as uncertainty is resolved over time. The theories derived from an application of the real options approach to the study of strategic alliances have provided and continue to provide empirical researchers with exciting new challenges.

Note that the assumptions and explanatory logic of real options theory can lead to alternative or complementary explanations of various aspects of the alliance phenomenon. For example, as we have shown above, real options theory exhibits some incommensurability with "behavioral" theories that do not assume economic rationality. Given the incommensurable assumption regarding rationality, we would characterize real options theory as offering an alternative explanation for aspects of the alliance phenomenon that such theories also try to explain. The situation is more complex with regard to economic theories such as property rights and transaction cost economics that also invoke economic rationality. In comparison with such theories, real options theory explicitly assumes uncertainty that is resolvable over time and introduces a unique explanatory factor: the value of options embedded in a course of action. The inclusion of this factor in the explanatory logic may yield very different predictions from those of the "static" economic theories. From the point of view of commensurability of the economic rationality assumption, the real options view could be considered as complementing other economic theories, but from the point of view of the differences in predictions that it potentially yields, it could be considered as an alternative explanation.

We believe that a pluralistic theoretical approach that combines real options modeling with extant theories (with particular attention given to the commensurability of assumptions) has considerable merit for the study of strategic alliances. Such an approach highlights that alliances confer flexibilities for their partners while identifying potential costs and benefits of these flexibilities. So such a pluralistic theoretical approach has the potential to provide a more complete explanation of the total payoffs to the partners in an alliance. When game-theoretic considerations are also incorporated into the analysis, implications for how these payoffs are divided between alliance partners may be derived. As we have shown, the real options approach can represent a way to reexamine the predictions of extant theories in a dynamic framework and to provide a new perspective on existing debates. We also show how such a pluralistic theoretical approach has important implications for the structure of alliance contracts.

Note

1. This assumes that there is no outside party that places an even higher value on the assets.

References

Akerlof, G. A. (1970). The market for "lemons": Quality, uncertainty, and the market mechanism. *Quarterly Journal of Economics, 84,* 488–500.

Balakrishnan, S., & Koza, M. P. (1993). Information asymmetry, adverse selection and joint ventures: Theory and evidence. *Journal of Economic Behavior and Organization, 20*(1), 99–117.

Benito, G. R. G., & Gripsrud, G. (1992). The expansion of foreign direct investment: Discrete rational location choices or a cultural learning process. *Journal of International Business Studies, 23*(2), 461–476.

Buckley, P., & Casson, M. (1976). *The future of multinational enterprise.* London: Macmillan.

Buckley, P., Casson, M., & Gulamhussen, M. (2002). Internationalization—real options, knowledge management, and the Uppsala approach. In V. Havila, M. Forsgren, & H. Håkansson, (Eds.), *Critical perspectives on internationalization.* Amsterdam, Netherlands: Pergamon.

Chemla, G., Habib, M. A., & Ljungqvist, A. P. (2003). *An analysis of shareholder agreements.* Working Paper.

Chi, T. (1994). Trading in strategic resources: Necessary conditions, transaction cost problems, and choice of exchange structure. *Strategic Management Journal, 15,* 271–290.

Chi, T. (2000). Option to acquire and divest a joint venture. *Strategic Management Journal, 21,* 665–687.

Chi, T., & McGuire, D. J. (1996). Collaborative ventures and value of learning: Integrating the transaction cost and strategic option perspectives on the choice of market entry modes. *Journal of International Business Studies, 27*(2), 285–307.

Chi, T., & Seth, A. (2002). Joint ventures through a real options lens. In F. J. Contractor & P. Lorange (Eds.), *Cooperative strategies and alliances.* Amsterdam, Netherlands: Pergamon.

Chi, T., & Seth, A. (2004). *Exploiting complementary capabilities: A dynamic model of the choice of investment mode.* Working paper.

Coase, R. (1937). The nature of the firm. *Economica, 4*(16), 386–405.

Coase, R. (1960). The problem of social cost. *Journal of Law and Economics, 3,* 1–44.

Dixit, A. K., & Pindyck, R. S. (1994). *Investment under uncertainty.* Princeton, NJ: Princeton University Press.

Fina, E., & Rugman, A. M. (1996). A test of internalization theory and internationalization theory: The Upjohn Company. *Management International Review, 36*(3), 199–213.

Folta, T. B. (1998). Governance and uncertainty: The trade-off between administrative control and commitment. *Strategic Management Journal, 19,* 1007–1028.

Fudenberg, D., & Tirole, J. (1991). *Game theory.* Cambridge: MIT Press.

Granovetter, M. (1985). Economic action and social structure: The problem of embeddedness. *American Journal of Sociology, 91*(3), 481–510.

Hamel, G. Y., Doz, Y., & Prahalad, C. K. (1989, January/February). Collaborate with your competitors—and win. *Harvard Business Review, 67,* 133–139.

Hennart, J. F. (1988). A transaction cost theory of equity joint ventures. *Strategic Management Journal, 9,* 361–374.

Jaeckel, P. (2002). *Monte Carlo methods in finance.* London: John Wiley.

Joaquin, D. C., & Butler, K. C. (1999). Competitive investment decisions. In M. Brennan and L. Trigeorgis (Eds.), *Project flexibility, agency, and competition: New developments in the theory and application of real options.* New York: Oxford University Press.

Johanson, J., & Mattson, L. G. (1988). Internationalization in industrial systems—A network approach. In N. Hood & J.-E. Vahlne (Eds.), *Strategies in global competition: Selected papers from the Prince Bertil Symposium at the Institute of International Business, Stockholm School of Economics.* New York: Croom Helm.

Johanson, J., & Vahlne, J. E. (1977, Spring/Summer). The internationalization process of the firm—A model of knowledge development and increasing foreign market commitments. *Journal of International Business Studies, 8,* 23–32.

Kamrad, B., & Ritchken, P. (1991). A lattice claims model for capital budgeting. *Management Science, 37*(12), 140–149.

Karatzas, I., & Shreve, S. E. (1997). *Brownian motion and stochastic calculus.* New York: Springer-Verlag.

Klein, B. (1992). Contracts and incentives: The role of contract terms in assuring performance. In L. Werin & H. Wijkander (Eds.), *Contract economics.* Oxford: Blackwell.

Kogut, B. (1991). Joint ventures and the option to expand and acquire. *Management Science, 37*(1), 19–33.

Kor, Y. Y., & Mahoney, J. T. (2000). Penrose's resource-based approach: The process and product of research creativity. *Journal of Management Studies, 37*(1), 109–139.

Masten, S. E. (1988). Equity, opportunism, and the design of contractual relations. *Journal of Institutional and Theoretical Economics, 144,* 180–195.

Nanda, A., & Williamson, P. J. (1995). Use joint ventures to ease the pain of restructuring. *Harvard Business Review, 73*(6), 119–128.

Penrose, E. T. (1959). *The theory of the growth of the firm.* Oxford: Blackwell.

Powell, W., & DiMaggio, P. (Eds.). (1991). *The new institutionalism in organizational analysis.* Chicago: University of Chicago Press.

Reuer, J. J., & Tong, T. (forthcoming). Real options in international joint ventures. *Journal of Management.*

Richards, M., & Indro, D. (2002). *Why does an option clause exist in a joint venture contract?* Paper presented at the Academy of Management Annual Meetings, Denver, Colorado.

Roberts, K., & Weitzman, M. L. (1981). Funding criteria for research, development, and exploration projects. *Econometrica, 49,* 1261–1287.

Rugman, A. M. (1980). A new theory of the multinational enterprise: Internationalization versus internalization. *Columbia Journal of World Business, 15*(1), 23–29.

Rugman, A. M. (1981). *Inside the multinationals: The economics of internal markets.* London: Croom Helm.

Scott, W. R. (1995). *Institutions and organizations.* Thousand Oaks, CA: Sage.

Seth, A., & Kim, S. M. (2001). Valuation of international joint ventures: A real options approach. In F. J. Contractor (Ed.), *Valuation of intangible assets in global operations.* Westport, CT: Greenwood.

Singh, H., & Zollo, M. (2004). Globalization through acquisitions and alliances: An evolutionary perspective. In H. Gatignon & J. Kimberly (Eds.), *The INSEAD-Wharton alliance on globalizing strategies for building successful global businesses.* Cambridge, UK: Cambridge University Press.

Suchman, M. C. (1995). Managing legitimacy: Strategic and institutional approaches. *Academy of Management Review, 20*(3), 571–610.

Teece, D. J. (1986). Profiting from technological innovation: Implications for integration, collaboration, licensing and public policy. *Research Policy, 15*, 285–305.

Trigeorgis, L. (1991). A log-transformed binomial numerical analysis method for valuing complex multi-option investment. *Journal of Financial and Quantitative Analysis, 26*, 309–326.

Williamson, O. E. (1975). *Markets and hierarchies: Analysis and antitrust implications.* New York: Free Press.

Zeng, M., & Hennart, J.-F. (2002). From learning races to cooperative specialization: Towards a new framework for alliance management. In F. J. Contractor & P. Lorange (Eds.), *Cooperative Strategies and Alliances.* Amsterdam, Netherlands: Pergamon.

7

Networks of Strategic Alliances

Gordon Walker

The intent of this chapter is to lay out in a general way the current state and trends of research on alliance networks as well as the promising paths for future work. The emphasis is primarily on the match between theory, method, and data both for local networks—composed of firms and their partners—and for the network overall. The discussion moves from research on local relational neighborhoods to studies of larger networks defined by industry or geographical boundaries. The chapter ends with current innovations in network analysis, which are numerous and in many ways pathbreaking.

Researchers on strategic alliances frequently include the term *network* to describe the interfirm relationships they analyze. What do they mean by this term? Generally, a network means that the firms are tied to each other just as cities are linked through road systems or people communicate through phone lines. Firms are nodes, as in a lattice, and the alliances connect them. Although many interesting and useful studies on alliances have used the network metaphor, most of this research does not really analyze the network at all. The reason is that the properties of the network—for example, its structure or its density—are not investigated; rather, the alliances are examined not as part of a larger relational system but as if they were independent. The alliances might as well have been formed on different planets. In such studies, referencing a "network" is misleading because it creates the expectation that a network will be analyzed in the research, when in fact this is not the case. More important, if there is in fact a network of alliances among the firms and it is excluded from the analysis, the study's results may be biased. This is so because a large body of research has shown that the properties of a network have a significant influence on the behavior of the firms that compose it, as discussed below.

What, then, does taking a network perspective in alliance research actually mean? At a minimum, it involves analyzing alliances that are at least two steps away from a firm, because networks are systems of serial connections. The closest of these "indirect" ties (see Ahuja, 2000; Uzzi, 1996) connect a firm's immediate partners to each other and to other organizations. The links between the firm and its partners together with the links between the partners themselves constitute the firm's local relational neighborhood. The structure of this neighborhood may be relatively closed when many partners ally with each other or open when they do not. The local neighborhood's degree of closure has been the topic of a great deal of research with broad implications for innovation, performance, and the development of the network itself.

Firms are also connected indirectly across neighborhoods through multiple chains of alliances that together form the network as a whole and whose analysis is more complex than that of local partnerships. Approaches to analyzing the network in full have been based on a variety of concepts, such as centrality and structural equivalence (see Burt, 1980a, for an early review); and studies based on these approaches have generally attempted to show how network structure and firm behavior influence each other. This line of research is rich and growing.

Studies of alliance networks have also taken either a static or dynamic approach. Research on the firm's local neighborhood has primarily examined the network as a static system. Although some studies have looked at changes in the local networks of people (see Burt, 2002), there has been only limited research on the dynamics of local neighborhoods composed of firms. An exception to this trend is the growing research on small worlds that, in a kind of hybrid approach, takes a dynamic perspective on how local structure develops or endures in the larger network context. In contrast, research on the network macrostructure has included both static and dynamic models, and many interesting and potentially fruitful paths of inquiry are currently being followed.

Alliance network studies more generally are a small part of the currently burgeoning research on networks of all kinds. The network literature overall has grown rapidly over the past five years with the availability of new data sources and the development of new network theory and analytical methods. A sample of the new types of network studied includes the Internet (Siganos, Faloutsos, Faloutsos, & Faloutsos, 2003), electricity grids (Watts, 1999a, chap. 5), and neuron linkages in worm brains (Watts, 1999a, chap. 5). Network theory and analysis have likewise expanded, especially with research on small worlds (Watts, 1999a), building in part on earlier work (Milgram, 1967; White, 1970), and scale-free networks (Barabasi & Albert, 1999). How these broad and numerous developments influence research on alliance networks will be discussed at the end of this chapter.

The Network as Local Neighborhood

The vast majority of research on the structure of a firm's local neighborhood has focused on its relative closure. A completely closed structure means that a firm's alliance partners are also partners of each other. A completely open network is one where the partners have no alliances among themselves. The local neighborhood structures of most firms are somewhere in between these two extremes.

Local Closure and Structural Holes. Two competing theories motivate research on the structure of a firm's local neighborhood. The first is Burt's (1992) theory of structural holes. A structural hole exists when a direct relationship is missing between two firms that are not indirectly tied by other firms in the network. When a third firm allies with both firms, the hole is filled, and network connectivity is increased. Burt's argument is that a firm filling a structural hole benefits from acting as a broker that ties together other organizations. Based on its access to diverse resources and sources of information, a broker is able to exploit opportunities for arbitrage and to set terms of trade that favor it over its partners. In Burt's theory, therefore, a firm gains from having an open local neighborhood with disconnected partners.

The second theory is based on the concept of social capital (Bourdieu, 1980; Coleman, 1988). Generally, *social capital* designates the benefits an individual receives from his position in the surrounding social structure, a definition that Coleman (1988) narrows by focusing on the local neighborhood. He argues, in contrast to Burt, that the more closed the network, the stronger the benefits, because in closed networks information about behavior flows faster, norms develop more quickly, and sanctions are imposed more rapidly on firms that violate their partner's expectations. Hence, for Burt, an open local network is good for the central firm because it inspires entrepreneurship and arbitrage; for Coleman, an open local network is bad for the firms that compose it because it creates the opportunity for and sustains exploitative behavior. Whether a closed or open network benefits the central firm therefore depends on whether communication and coordination within the neighborhood help or hinder the firm in achieving its goals.

Extant research generally supports Coleman's view. In a study of Sydney hotels, Ingram and Roberts (2000) show that the more cohesive the managerial friendship network around a hotel, the higher its economic performance, presumably because of reciprocity in sharing customer overflows and norms against price competition. Similarly, Ahuja (2000) finds that closure in the technical collaboration networks of U.S. chemical companies increases the number of patents granted to them; he attributes this result to superior cooperation among partners induced by their ability to monitor each other. Rowley, Behrens, and Krackhardt (2000) test the effect of network closure on firm performance in two industries that differ in their levels of uncertainty; the industries are steel (low uncertainty) and semiconductors (high uncertainty). The authors find that local closure enhances firm performance (return on assets) under low uncertainty when the benefit of interfirm cooperation should exceed the cost of greater redundancy of information but has no effect on performance under high uncertainty. Finally, in a study of alliance formation in the biotechnology industry, Walker, Kogut, and Shan (1997) find that alliances are more likely to be formed by firms located in denser regions of the overall network; they interpret this result as being consistent with Coleman's argument (see also Gulati, 1995). All four of these studies imply that normative pressure within the firm's closed local neighborhood benefits the firm.

In a study that partially supports Burt's structural hole theory, McEvily and Zaheer (1999) find that small, regional job shops whose advisors did not interact with each other were more likely to develop competitive capabilities. The argument here is that a disconnected advice network provides a broader array of information that allows the firm to produce a more robust set of practices. However, McEvily and Zaheer (1999) also find that firms with open networks of advisors are less likely to participate in acquiring knowledge from regional institutions, which in turn reduces the firms' development of capabilities. Presumably, a group of advisors that is less cohesive provides weaker access to public sources of information. In an approach similar to McEvily and Zaheer (1999), Burt (2001a) expands his theory to include both network closure and openness. He extends the frame of the analysis from alliances among the firm's immediate partners to their alliances with organizations outside the local neighborhood. These "indirect" relationships may be with a diverse or narrow set of firms that themselves may be more or less connected. The more diverse and disconnected these firms, the more likely it is that they will have different kinds of information, which leads to higher variance in the information received by the firm's local partners and therefore ultimately by the firm itself. Burt calls the degree of closure of the local neighborhood "internal constraint" and the degree of closure of the broader neighborhood "external constraint." He then argues that the firm achieves its highest performance when internal constraint is high, promoting cooperation within the local neighborhood, and external constraint is low, indicating diverse information sources. This theory is similar to Burt's earlier work on structural autonomy (Burt, 1980b) and is also analogous to Granovetter's (1973) well-known study of weak and strong ties, where high closure is analogous (but not identical) to high tie strength. As yet, Burt's theory of internal and external constraints has not been tested using alliance data.

So far the research discussed has been on static networks and does not address how the microstructure changes over time. Unfortunately, there have been very few studies of how local networks develop. Walker et al. (1997) show that new alliances tend to increase the density of a firm's region in the network, suggesting that firms choose partners within the local neighborhood as opposed to outside it. Burt (2000) points out that this result indicates only that closure persists but shows nothing about the benefit closure might provide.

The persistence of closure as a network develops over time has also been shown by small-worlds research. Small worlds, as discussed in greater detail below, are networks that have dense local neighborhoods and at the same time are tightly connected globally, in the sense that getting from one side of the network to the other takes only a few links. Kogut and Walker (2001), in their small-worlds study of the ownership network among German firms in 1993, demonstrate that the network had high local clustering and that a significant level of clustering remained even after extensive simulated alterations in the relationships among firms. Dense local neighborhoods therefore seem quite impervious to change.

Similarly, in a study of structural holes using data on relationships among managers, Burt (2001b) shows that relationships that span structural holes tend to disappear faster than nonbridging relationships, suggesting that clusters of relationships are more durable. However, the rate at which bridging relationships terminate tends to be lower when the broker is a high-performing manager. Although no research has generalized Burt's result to alliance networks, it is not inconsistent with the logic of the studies discussed above. As a whole, then, it appears that local neighborhoods that are highly clustered are likely to remain so, and brokering positions are rather fragile.

Future Research. Even though it seems that local closure has definitively trumped structural holes as the preferred and more stable microstructure for firms, a host of questions and important projects remain. First, Burt's logic regarding the advantages of brokerage seems unassailable. A firm that acts as a hub connecting disconnected partners simply has more information and therefore more options. Therefore, the key questions are: How do brokers emerge to span structural holes? What forces allow unique brokerage positions to endure? And what types of decision or performance do brokerage positions contribute to most? For example, an open neighborhood may reduce effective price coordination among hotels or further alliance-building in biotechnology but may also lead to more radical innovation by the central firm (see Burt, forthcoming; contrast Ahuja, 2000).

Second, alliance research on the network microstructure has typically obscured asymmetries of power and dependence in the partnerships. Differences between partners in their control over resources and information in the alliance can be salient, because power in a relationship may overwhelm any benefits provided by the firm's position in the network structure (see Cook, Emerson, & Gillmore, 1983). Detailing how asymmetries in interfirm relationships interact with local network structure is an important task.

Third, Burt's (2001) hybrid model, which embeds the local neighborhood in the larger network, may be generalized to alliance networks by identifying both the degree of local closure and the structure of the relationships among all firms in the network. This has not yet been done (Burt, Guilarte, Raider, & Yasuda, 2002).

Fourth, the dynamics of network closure are not well understood. Industry factors—for example, the degree of market uncertainty and shifts in the level of demand—may affect how much value normative constraint contributes to the firms in the network. One possibility is that as uncertainty increases and demand decreases, firms may become more conservative in their partners, increasing the degree of local closure. But when the industry enters a period of expansion, neighborhoods may open up. Exploring this potential dynamic could be useful in future research.

Finally, there has been little study of differences between the neighborhoods of entrants and incumbents over the history of the industry (see Walker et al., 1997). Compared to entrants, incumbents obviously have greater experience of the partnering capabilities of other firms, and this experience may substitute for or complement the structural benefit of a closed neighborhood. Likewise, older firms may have a more stable set of partners. Much new research remains to be accomplished in this area as well.

The Network as Macrostructure

Studies of the total network, comprising all local neighborhoods and the cross-neighborhood connections of firms, are best discussed in terms of how they conceptualize the network macrostructure. Here we identify five current approaches: (1) indirect ties, (2) the centrality of both firms and the overall network, (3) structural and stochastic equivalence, (4) network density and components, and (5) small worlds. These widely differing concepts of the network macrostructure cover almost all of the existing empirical research on this topic. With relatively few exceptions, each provides a unique window onto how characteristics of the network outside the local neighborhood affect firm alliance behavior and outcomes.

Indirect Ties. The most obvious and succinct way to assess the importance of alliances outside the local neighborhood is to measure a firm's number of indirect ties—the firm's relationships with partners two or more steps away in the network. Uzzi (1996), in his seminal study of embeddedness, concludes that the structure of indirect ties has a significant, albeit nonlinear (U-shaped), influence on a firm's chances of failing. He argues that organizations whose suppliers are neither strongly nor weakly connected to their own suppliers will have lower rates of failure, where strong connections are highly concentrated in one or a few partners. A broader concept of indirect ties is developed by Ahuja (2000). His construct includes all the organizations a firm is connected to outside its local neighborhood, not just two steps out as in Uzzi's (1996) study. Ahuja's research shows that the scope of a firm's indirect ties increases its rate of innovation, but this effect is dampened when the local neighborhood is large. His conclusion is that local ties and indirect ties are therefore partly substitutable. It is noteworthy that the way Ahuja measures indirect ties conforms to studies of network components, which are discrete groups of firms that are connected to each other. This topic is discussed later in this chapter.

Firm Centrality. The centrality of network members or of the network overall has long been a focus of network research (see Freeman, 1979, for a classic review). Because this chapter discusses network studies that include indirect relationships only, it will focus only on research that conceptualizes centrality as networkwide and not on those studies that examine "degree centrality," which is the firm's number of alliances. (For research on the determinants and effects of degree centrality, see Gulati & Gargiulo, 1999; Gulati, 1999; Powell, Koput, & Smith-Doerr, 1996; Powell, White, Koput, & Owen-Smith, forthcoming; Walker et al., 1997).

An important measure of firm centrality discussed by Freeman (1979) is "betweenness," which is roughly based on how many geodesics the firm lies on (a geodesic is the shortest path between a pair of firms in the network). Another measure of centrality has been developed by Bonacich (1987). His measure, called "eigenvector centrality" or the eponymous "Bonacich centrality," identifies central firms as those that have relationships with other firms that are themselves central. Finally, Freeman (1979) describes a measure, called "closeness," that can be thought of as the inverse of centrality in general; closeness is defined by the sum of the shortest paths between a firm and other firms in the network. Clearly, the larger this sum, the further the firm is from other firms, and so the lower its centrality.

The meanings of these three centrality measures are based on the common themes of brokerage and information availability. Betweenness characterizes the kind of brokering role Burt ascribes to firms that fill structural holes. Closeness has a slightly different meaning; a higher degree of closeness in the network implies that a firm can reach or be reached by other firms more quickly or more efficiently, in terms of the number of links taken. Finally, the Bonacich measure has elements of both brokering and reachability.

Studies of network centrality have used all three measures. In a study of corporate restructuring in 1990s Germany, Kogut and Walker (2003) construct a network of firm owners based on their overlapping holdings and find that the firms whose owners were more central in the network, in the sense of betweenness, engaged in more merger and acquisition events. Firms with central owners apparently had better access to information and opportunities related to restructuring. Research on centrality as closeness follows the same general logic as betweenness. Powell et al. (1996) predict and show that firms that have higher centrality in terms of shorter path-length connections with other members of the network tend to form more alliances. Gulati's (1999) analysis produced the same result. Gulati (1995) also finds that the shorter the path length between two firms in the network, the more likely they were to form an alliance.

Finally, Bonacich's (1987) measure of centrality has been used primarily to measure what Podolny (1993, 2001) has called "status": the primacy or hegemony of some firms over others. Differences among firms in status, using Bonacich's measure, have been used to predict firm growth (Podolny, Stuart, & Hannan, 1996) and the successful diversification of firms into related markets (Jensen, 2003). Sorenson and Stuart (2001) use Bonacich's measure to indicate superior information-gathering by venture-capital firms. Finally, in their research on alliance formation, Gulati and Gargiulo (1999) argue and find that firms with high Bonacich centrality tend to form alliances with each other, a kind of assortativity that is often found in social networks (Newman, 2002).

A last study that examines the effect of centrality on firm behavior is research by Kogut, Walker, and Kim (1995) on technology-based alliances in the semiconductor industry. Their theory relies on an interpretation of betweenness as brokerage, but with a twist. They studied how the centrality of the network as a whole (see Freeman, 1979) affected entry into the industry.

The empirical results for firm and network centrality are hence rather robust and encourage future research. The assumption of superior information brokerage or access that underlies the theories in these studies seems reasonable. Yet work remains to be done on how relevant information is distributed throughout the network and how this distribution maps onto the firm-level incentives to share or expose the data the firms need to make decisions. We address this issue in greater depth below in our discussion of small worlds.

Network Stratification: Structural Equivalence. A second approach to the network macrostructure is based on the principle of structural equivalence. Structurally equivalent firms have the same (or about the same) set of partners (Lorrain & White, 1971; see also Batagelj, 1997; Nowicki & Snijders, 2001). Firms in a network are typically grouped according to the equivalence of their partner sets, and the groups of structurally equivalent firms are the basis of what

White, Boorman, and Breiger (1976) call a *blockmodel,* a homomorphic reduction of the network in which relationships among the groups (sometimes called positions) indicate the relationships among their member firms.

Blockmodel studies of alliance networks have been motivated by a range of research questions. Several early studies (Knoke & Rogers, 1979; Van de Ven, Walker, & Liston, 1979) found that a blockmodel analysis showed how different types of partnership were distributed across the network and how they affected firm performance. Using a blockmodel analysis of joint ventures among firms in the global aluminum industry, Walker (1988) demonstrates that a search for economies of scale is likely to be the most important factor driving the formation of alliances. Nohria and Garcia-Pont (1991), in an analysis of alliances in the global automobile industry, argue that the structure of partnerships should reflect the structure of competition. In support of their argument, Nohria and Garcia-Pont find that the groups in the blockmodel are centered either on powerful global firms or on collections of regional competitors and are generally highly inbred, meaning that they form alliances more within the group than outside it.

In two papers on the network of alliances in the early years of the biotechnology industry, Walker et al. construct a blockmodel to test two distinct theories. In their first paper (Shan, Walker, & Kogut, 1994), they propose, and the results show, that because firms in different blockmodel groups are likely to give and receive different resources and capabilities, they should have different propensities to form new alliances. The second paper (Walker et al., 1997) shows that firms with alliances in denser regions of the blockmodel tend to have more partnerships.

In addition, Walker et al. (1997) analyze how the network structure in the biotechnology industry develops over time. The blockmodel includes biotechnology start-ups as one dimension and their established firm partners as the second dimension, so that there are both start-up groups and established firm groups. Moreover, as the network evolves, new firms of both types enter the network. Walker et al. (1997) find that membership in start-up groups over time is much more stable than in groups of established firms, primarily because of the latter's higher rate of entry. Furthermore, the trend towards stability in network position becomes more pronounced as the network develops.

Studies of network structure using blockmodels have demonstrated a potential that has yet to be explored fully. Although technical challenges remain in identifying structurally equivalent firms (see Nowicki & Snijders, 2001), these are minor compared to the important questions blockmodeling can address, especially regarding industry evolution. For example, the notion of structural equivalence underlies a major rationale for research on alliances: Firms that share a common set of partners have similar capabilities. How alliances and capabilities in an industry develop over time is therefore a rich area of research that is particularly suited for blockmodel analysis. Further, the structure of intergroup relationships measures differences in organizational status, and the evolution of this structure, as represented by blockmodels of alliances over time, may be a key indicator of status change, an important dimension of firm performance.

Network Components and Density. A fourth perspective on the macrostructure of the alliance network has been the analysis of network density. Denser networks are, almost by definition, more cohesive, which means that in theory, information and resources can move from one side of the network to the other faster and with fewer intermediaries. In an interesting study of cohesiveness in networks over time, Marquis (2003) argues that cohesiveness could be imprinted. He shows that a dense network of firms that are geographically proximate before the advent of extensive air travel to the region tends to remain tightly connected after air travel arrived, suggesting that cohesiveness endures in the face of pressures to break it down. Whether this trend is due to the lasting benefits of cohesiveness, a kind of network externality, or unproductive inertia remains an open question.

A concept related to network density is the partition of the network into discrete, cohesive components. A component is a set of firms that have partnerships only with each other; there are no cross-component alliances. Many networks have a "main" component composed of most of the firms in the network and a number of satellite components containing a few firms each. In their ongoing research on biotechnology alliances, Powell et al. (forthcoming) argue and show that pairs of firms that are in the same component and whose component is highly cohesive are more likely to form an alliance. The two plausible premises behind this finding are, first, that two firms in a cohesive component have lower search costs and so can find each other faster, and second, that cohesiveness induces normative pressure to cooperate, which facilitates alliance-building. This logic is virtually identical to the arguments motivating research on closed and open local neighborhoods discussed above.

Small Worlds. Research on small worlds is a rapidly emerging area of research on alliance networks—in fact, on networks of all kinds. The small-world metaphor was first made popular by Milgram's (1967) search experiments and formalized by White (1970) (see also Kochen, 1989, for a review). Recent research by Watts and his colleagues (Watts, 1999a, 1999b; Newman, Strogatz, & Watts, 2001) has formally refined the small-world concept and led to a rapid increase in empirical studies using interfirm relationships (Baum, Shipilov, & Rowley, 2002; Corrado & Zollo, 2004; Davis, Yoo, & Baker, 2003; Kogut & Walker, 2001). The quickened pace of research over the past four years has introduced such a wealth of approaches to network structure and dynamics that small-world models that were recently seen as standard are now being seriously questioned (Watts, 2004).

In Watt's (1999a, 1999b) model, a small-world network has both dense local neighborhoods and a low average number of paths between any two firms. Watts tests for the existence of a small world through two simple ratios: the first for clustering, and the second for the path length. The clustering ratio has in the numerator the empirical network's average clustering coefficient. In the denominator is the clustering coefficient for a hypothetical network, constructed by randomly assigning ties between firms. The random network has the same number of firms, n, and the same average number of alliances per firm, k, as the empirical network. The clustering coefficient for the random network is k/n. For the network to be a small world, the clustering coefficient of the empirical network should be substantially greater than that of the random network. The ratio for the average path length is constructed similarly. The numerator is the empirical network's value for the average path length, and the denominator is the value for a hypothetical, randomly constructed network of the same size and average outdegree. Watts calculates the denominator as $\log(k)/\log(n)$. Since the average path length in a small world is short, the path-length ratio of empirical to random network values should be around one.

The small world has many similarities with the types of micro- and macrostructure discussed above. There is an obvious correspondence with Burt's (2001) extension of his structural hole theory to include both local clustering and relationships with firms outside the neighborhood. In a small world, firms may experience normative pressure imposed by a closed neighborhood and at the same time benefit from efficient search throughout the network due to its high level of connectivity. Also, the small-world model includes a parameter that is analogous to centrality. To become a small world, a network must contain alliances called shortcuts that tie together otherwise disconnected firms and thus shorten the average distance from one firm to another (Watts, 1999a, p. 71). Shortcuts are therefore likely to lie on geodesics, and firms that are on many shortcuts are likely to be highly central in the network. In addition, the small-world model as a whole resembles Granovetter's (1973) well-known theory of weak ties, in which "strong" ties (within a firm's local neighborhood) enforce norms and "weak" ties (with nonlocal firms) are important for information acquisition.

The small-world model applies primarily to networks that are low-density or sparse, as is typical for alliances. This is important because sparse networks have often been viewed as lacking a meaningful structure. Small-world studies of alliance networks show that they do indeed have structure in spite of their low densities (Baum et al., 2002; Corrado & Zollo, 2004; Davis et al., 2003; Kogut & Walker, 2001). One may say, then, that although an alliance network need not be a small world, recent evidence suggests that it probably is.

The small-world model opens up three clear avenues of research on alliances. First, it raises important questions about network evolution: How does a network become a small world? What factors determine the emergence of firms that are more central, in the sense of lying on numerous shortcuts? How do the local neighborhoods of these firms evolve over time? Second, the small-world model provides a window onto the evolution of empirical networks in specific institutional environments. For example, Corrado and Zollo (2004) examine the network of interfirm ownership in Italy in the 1990s and show that in spite of major national reforms during this period, the small-world structure of the network remained remarkably stable (see also Davis et al., 2003, for similar findings regarding the stability of the U.S. corporate network of board interlocks). Third, the small-world model indicates how one might compare two or more alliance networks, either at one point in time or over multiple time periods. Regional or national networks of partnerships, either within or across industry, are ripe for this kind of analysis.

Problems With the Small-World Model. Although the small-world model shows promise for examining alliance networks, it has several problems (see Watts, 2004). These are created primarily by questions about the behavioral origins of the small-world structure and questions about the identification of the small world in the special case of bipartite networks. The first of these concerns is important not only for clarifying how small worlds evolve but for understanding what the structure implies for the behavior of firms in the network. The second raises the significant issue of how the scope and content of alliances affects network development.

One of the common assumptions about small worlds is that they are created as firms search for and find partners outside the local neighborhood. These cross-neighborhood ties decrease the average path length in the network without reducing the degree of local clustering, thus creating the small world. This assumption need not be true, however. Walker and Kogut (2004) show that the syndication network of venture-capital firms in the United States develops in the opposite way: it is highly integrated with a low average path length first and develops distinct clusters second.

A second important assumption in research on small worlds is that partners are chosen with equal probability (Watts, 1999a). Kleinberg (2000) shows, however, that if the mechanism underlying the creation of a small world is a search process, this assumption is very rarely true. He demonstrates that for a network to be searchable, the likelihood of forming a link with a nonlocal partner must decline exponentially with its distance from the firm, and the exponent must be equal to the number of dimensions used in the search process. This means that the probability distribution of potential partners cannot be uniform.

Therefore, a fundamental tenet of the creation of small worlds—that they emerge through a process of finding partners—is highly dependent on how potential partners are arrayed around each firm. Building on Kleinberg's result, Watts, Dodds, and Newman (2002) show how searchability is affected by the number of dimensions firms use to find partners and how close the firm is to these partners. Like Kleinberg (2000), Watts et al. (2002) find that not all networks can be searched efficiently and so cannot evolve into small worlds, at least through a search mechanism.

A second problem with the small-world model involves how relationships are defined. Many networks, especially those composed of alliances, are bipartite (Borgatti & Everett, 1997; Wasserman & Faust, 1994, chap. 8), which means they are constructed from the joint participation of firms in associations, consortiums, syndicates, or some other form of common affiliation. Firms become allied through shared membership, as, for example, venture-capital firms are tied through their participation in syndications of start-ups. The problem with the bipartite structure as a means of forming small worlds is that the network's local clustering and global connectivity parameters are influenced by the number of members in the partnership.

For example, Newman et al. (2001) show that the clustering coefficient of the small world of interfirm board interlocks in the United States (Davis et al., 2003) is completely due to the sizes of the boards. Hence, to manipulate the degree of local clustering in the network one need only change the distribution of board sizes. Other sources of interlocks, such as reciprocity, social class, or the hegemony of financial firms, can be ignored completely. Small-world research on alliances using bipartite data should therefore be sensitive to characteristics of the affiliations (associations, syndicates) used to build the network. Studies of local neighborhoods should obviously be sensitive to this problem as well.

Some Final Issues

Over the past five years, alliance network research has become a kind of hotbed of new questions and problems:

1. Network evolution: Kogut (2000) has argued that networks develop as firms follow generative rules, such as reciprocity and transitivity, that spring from economic, cultural, and institutional constraints. This line of research has substantial promise for developing testable hypotheses regarding network dynamics. For example, one rule, preferential attachment, has been proposed as the central determinant of network structures that follow a power law distribution (Barabasi & Albert, 1999; Newman, 2001). Another important topic is how adherence to rules changes over time; for example, transitivity may rise and fall with shifts in market uncertainty. Finally, networks evolve as incumbent firms endure and new firms enter. How network structure persists with entry and how entrants gain access to that structure, if at all, are important questions, especially because the rules governing exchange must be learned (Kogut, Urso, & Walker, 2005; Walker et al., 1997; Walker & Madsen, 2004).

2. Bipartite networks: The recent rise in research on bipartite networks suggests a range of questions regarding alliance formation. For example, the investment project that motivates a partnership is almost always ignored as a factor in alliance studies. Yet in any industry the opportunities stimulating joint investment—for example, emerging technology platforms or growing geographical regions—commonly follow a life cycle that is separate from the partnerships formed to exploit them. How these life cycles intersect with the evolution of the alliance network remains an open question.

3. Models of diffusion and catalysis: A traditional and continuously interesting problem in network analysis is diffusion (for a recent study on diffusion through alliances, see Westphal, Gulati, & Shortell, 1997). As Watts (2004) points out, there has been insufficient study of the structure of the network through which diffusion occurs (see Burt, 1987, for a classic study). In this regard, the parameters of network structure in a small world, particularly the number of shortcuts, can clearly affect the rate at which an innovation is adopted (Moore & Newman,

2000). Moreover, in addition to facilitating the diffusion of organizational practices (e.g., Davis, 1991), the network may serve as a conduit for new types of investment projects, which themselves involve further partnering. For example, as a system for funding start-up firms, the existing network structure of syndications may determine the diffusion rate of investment in a new industry; and as investments in the new industry grow, the venture-capital syndication network is rejuvenated. In this way, the speedy rise of e-commerce firms in the 1990s may have been enabled by the existing syndication networks for investment in related industries, such as software.

Conclusion

Research on alliance networks has achieved some robust results, especially regarding the effects of local closure and global centrality. But recent approaches to network structure and analysis present challenges to these conclusions and have opened many avenues of inquiry that are promising. How alliance networks are formed and how they are refreshed with new investment opportunities are key questions that motivate a broad range of study. As new data become available and older data sets yield new insights, alliance network research has an interesting and productive future.

References

Ahuja, G. (2000). Collaboration networks, structural holes and innovation: A longitudinal study. *Administrative Science Quarterly, 45,* 425–455.

Barabasi, A. L., & Albert, R. (1999). The emergence of scaling in random networks. *Science, 286,* 509–512.

Batagelj, V. (1997). Notes on blockmodeling. *Social Networks, 19,* 143–155.

Baum, J., Shipilov, A., & Rowley, T. (2002). Where do small worlds come from? *Industrial and Corporate Change, 12,* 597–725.

Bonacich, P. (1987). Power and centrality: A family of measures. *American Journal of Sociology, 92,* 1170–1182.

Borgatti, S. P., & Everett, M. G. (1997). Network analysis of 2-mode data. *Social Networks, 19*(3), 243–269.

Bourdieu, P. (1980). Le capital social. *Actes Recherches Sciences Sociales, 31,* 2–3.

Burt, R. (1980a). Models of network structure. *Annual Review of Sociology,* Neil Smelser (Ed.), *6,* 79–141.

Burt, R. (1980b). Autonomy in a social topology. *American Journal of Sociology, 85,* 892–925.

Burt, R. (1987). Social contagion and innovation: Cohesion versus structural equivalence. *American Journal of Sociology, 92,* 1287–1335.

Burt, R. (1992). *Structural holes: The social structure of competition.* Cambridge, MA: Harvard University Press.

Burt, R. (2000). The network structure of social capital. In R. I. Sutton & B. M. Staw (Eds.), *Research in organizational behavior* (Vol. 22). New York: Elsevier Science.

Burt, R. (2001a). Structural holes versus network closure as social capital. In N. Lin, K. S. Cook, & R. S. Burt (Eds.), *Social capital: Theory and research.* New York: Aldine de Gruyter.

Burt, R. (2001b). Bridge decay. *Social Networks, 24,* 333–363.

Burt, R. (forthcoming). Structural holes and good ideas. *American Journal of Sociology.*

Burt, R., Guilarte, M., Raider, H. J., & Yasuda, Y. (2002). Competition, contingency, and the external structure of markets. In P. Ingram & B. Silverman (Eds.), *Advances in strategic management.* New York: Elsevier.

Coleman, J. (1988). Social capital in the creation of human capital. *American Journal of Sociology, 94,* S105–S120.

Cook, K. S., Emerson, R. M., & Gillmore, M. R. (1983). The distribution of power in exchange networks: Theory and experimental results. *American Journal of Sociology, 89,* 275–305.

Corrado, R., & Zollo, M. (2004). *Small worlds evolving: Governance reforms, privatizations and ownership networks in Italy.* Working Paper, INSEAD, Fontainebleau, France.

Davis, G. (1991). Agents without principles? The spread of the poison pill through the intercorporate network. *Administrative Science Quarterly, 36,* 583–613.

Davis, G., Yoo, M., & Baker, W. (2003). The small world of the American corporate elite, 1982–2001. *Strategic Organization, 1,* 301–326.

Freeman, L. (1979). Centrality in social networks: Conceptual clarification. *Social Networks, 1,* 215–239.

Granovetter, M. (1973). The strength of weak ties. *American Journal of Sociology, 78,* 1360–1380.

Gulati, R. (1995). Social structure and alliance formation: A longitudinal analysis. *Administrative Science Quarterly, 40,* 619–652.

Gulati, R. (1999). Network location and learning: The influence of network resources and firm capabilities on alliance formation. *Strategic Management Journal, 20,* 397–420.

Gulati, R., & Gargiulo, M. (1999). Where do interorganizational networks come from? *American Journal of Sociology, 4,* 1439–1493.

Ingram, P., & Roberts, P. (2000). Friendships among competitors in the Sydney hotel industry. *American Journal of Sociology, 106,* 387–423.

Jensen, M. (2003). The role of network resources in market entry: Commercial banks' entry into investment banking, 1991–1997. *Administrative Science Quarterly, 48,* 466–498.

Kleinberg, J. (2000). Navigation in a small world. *Nature, 406,* 845.

Knoke, D., & Rogers, D. (1979). A blockmodel analysis of interorganizational networks. *Sociology and Social Research, 64,* 28–52.

Kochen, M. (Ed.). (1989). *The small world.* Norwood, MA: Ablex.

Kogut, B. (2000). The network as knowledge: Generative rules and the emergence of structure. *Strategic Management Journal, 21,* 405–425.

Kogut, B., Urso, P., & Walker, G. (2005). *Generating rules and the emergence of network structure.* Working Paper.

Kogut, B., & Walker, G. (2001). The small world of Germany and the durability of national networks. *American Sociological Review, 66,* 317–335.

Kogut, B., & Walker, G. (2003). *Restructuring or disintegration of the German corporate network: Globalization as a fifth column.* William Davidson Institute Working Papers Series, 2003-591.

Kogut, B., Walker, G., & Kim, D. J. (1995). Cooperation and entry induction as an extension of technological rivalry. *Research Policy, 24,* 77–95.

Lorrain, F., & White, H. (1971). The structural equivalence of individuals in social networks. *Journal of Mathematical Sociology, 1,* 49–80.

Marquis, C. (2003). The pressure of the past: Network imprinting in intercorporate communities. *Administrative Science Quarterly, 48,* 655–690.

McEvily, B., & Zaheer, A. (1999). Bridging ties: A source of firm heterogeneity in competitive capabilities. *Strategic Management Journal, 20,* 1133–1156.

Milgram, S. (1967). The small world problem. *Psychology Today, 2,* 60–67.

Moore, C., & Newman, M. E. J. (2000). Epidemics and percolation in small-world networks. *Physical Review E, 61,* 5678–5682.

Newman, M. (2001). Clustering and preferential attachment in growing networks. *Physical Review E, 64,* 025102.

Newman, M. (2002). Assortative mixing in networks. *Physics Review Letters, 89,* 208701.

Newman, M., Strogatz, S., & Watts, D. (2001). Random graphs with arbitrary degree distributions and their applications. *Physical Review E, 64,* 026118.

Nohria, N., & Garcia-Pont, C. (1991). Global strategic linkages and industry structure. *Strategic Management Journal, 12,* 105–124.

Nowicki, K., & Snijders, T. A. B. (2001). Estimation and prediction for stochastic blockstructures. *Journal of the American Statistical Association, 96,* 1077–1087.

Podolny, J. (1993). A status-based model of market competition. *American Journal of Sociology, 98,* 829–872.

Podolny, J. (2001). Networks as the pipes and prisms of the market. *American Journal of Sociology, 107,* 33–60.

Podolny, J., Stuart, T., & Hannan, M. (1996). Networks, knowledge and niches: Competition in the worldwide semiconductor industry, 1984–1991. *American Journal of Sociology, 102,* 659–689.

Powell, W., Koput, K., & Smith-Doerr, L. (1996). Interorganizational collaboration and the locus of innovation: Networks of learning in biotechnology. *Administrative Science Quarterly, 41,* 116–145.

Powell, W., White, D., Koput, K., & Owen-Smith, J. (forthcoming). Network dynamics and field evolution: The growth of interorganizational collaboration in the life sciences. *American Journal of Sociology.*

Rowley, T., Behrens, D., & Krackhardt, D. (2000). Redundant governance structures: An analysis of structural and relational embeddedness in the steel and semiconductor industries. *Strategic Management Journal, 21,* 369–386.

Shan, W. J., Walker, G., & Kogut, B. (1994). Interfirm cooperation and startup innovation in the biotechnology industry. *Strategic Management Journal, 15*(5), 387–394.

Siganos, G., Faloutsos, M., Faloutsos, P., & Faloutsos, C. (2003). Power laws and the AS-level Internet topology. *IEEE/ACM Transactions on Networking, 11*(4), 514–524.

Sorenson, O., & Stuart, T. (2001). Syndication networks and the spatial distribution of venture capital investments. *American Journal of Sociology, 106,* 1546–1588.

Uzzi, B. (1996). The sources and consequences of embeddedness for the economic performance of organizations: The network effect. *American Sociological Review, 61,* 674–698.

Van de Ven, A., Walker, G., & Liston, J. (1979). Coordination patterns within an interorganizational network. *Human Relations, 32,* 19–36.

Walker, G. (1988). Network analysis for cooperative interfirm relationships. In F. Contractor & P. Lorange (Eds.), *Cooperative strategies in international business.* Lexington, MA: Lexington Books.

Walker, G., & Kogut, B. (2004). The early small world of venture capital in the United States. Working Paper presented at the Utah Strategy Conference, Park City, Utah.

Walker, G., Kogut, B., & Shan, W. (1997). Social capital, structural holes and the formation of an industry network. *Organization Science, 8,* 109–125.

Walker, G., & Madsen, T. (2004). *Incumbent stratification, interfirm mobility and organizational growth in the foreign exchange market, 1973–1993.* Paper presented at the Annual Meeting of the Academy of Management, New Orleans.

Wasserman, S., & Faust, K. (1994). *Social network analysis.* New York: Cambridge University Press.

Watts, D. (1999a). *Small worlds.* Princeton, NJ: Princeton University Press.

Watts, D., (1999b). Networks, dynamics, and the small-world phenomenon. *American Journal of Sociology, 105,* 493–527.

Watts, D. (2004). The "new" science of networks. *Annual Review of Sociology, 30,* 243–270.

Watts, D., Dodds, P. S., & Newman, M. (2002). Identity and search in social networks. *Science, 296,* 1302–1305.

Westphal, J., Gulati, R., & Shortell, S. (1997). Customization or conformity? An institutional and network perspective on the content and consequences of TQM adoption. *Administrative Science Quarterly, 42,* 366–394.

White, H. C. (1970). Search parameters for the small world problem. *Social Forces, 49,* 259–264.

White, H., Boorman, S., & Breiger, R. (1976) Social structure from multiple networks. I. Blockmodels of roles and positions. *American Journal of Sociology, 81,* 730–780.

PART III

Alliance Management

Opening the "Black Boxes"

8

Structuring and Restructuring Alliances

A Theory-Based Process Model

Stephen Tallman

Anupama Phene

Most discussions of alliances and alliance structure address in largest part the organizational, contractual, and relational structures of an alliance or alliance type as though these structures were determined by a set of transactional conditions. Rather, alliances, whether we are considering actual, real-world deals or conceptual, "ideal types" of alliances, are more usefully and realistically seen as the outcomes of lengthy processes involving both economic and social considerations and subject to many external pressures. This chapter describes the process of alliance structuration in hopes of tying together the various topics in this section of the book, showing how the various theories described above (and others that have been left to their own devices) work together to predict what alliances might issue from such a process, and demonstrating how the alliance processes discussed in subsequent chapters constantly support and threaten the existence and effectiveness of the alliances in which they take place.

The process of forming an alliance is messy and complex, involving as it does at least two and perhaps many more already messy and complex organizations as partners and (perhaps) owners. Depending on previous and existing transactions, relationships, skills, strategies, and various other contextual conditions, any description of such a process must be seen as stylized and frequently violated. In reality, the process of cooperation is likely to be compressed in some stages, extended in others, simultaneous when predicted to be sequential, and otherwise unwilling to be placed on a neat timeline. We believe that understanding such a complex process requires the abstraction of a stylized model if we hope to understand the strategic considerations behind alliances and the pressures that twist these considerations into unexpected forms. This chapter is organized around a step-by-step process model, although we also try to point out opportunities to violate the specifics of our model even as we propose it. We also believe that considerations from organizational theories—both sociological and economic—are both useful approaches for understanding alliance structures, as is done throughout this volume, and for understanding the process of alliance structuring. Therefore, the steps in the alliance-formation process that is proposed here will be delineated by theoretical considerations as well as practical concerns.

The Process of Structuring Alliances

The process of structuring alliances involves initiation, operation, and restructuring or termination. The initiation of alliances falls into three stages, based on Williamson's (1985) idea of the fundamental transformation from large- to small-numbers bargaining in transactional analysis. The first stage involves a choice regarding the organizational form, at which point cooperation through an alliance (and perhaps even the type of alliance) is selected. From a resource-based (or knowledge-based) perspective, alliances are ideally structured to maximize the synergy effects of combining complementary operating capabilities and other resources. The second stage represents the partner search and selection process. Although alliances may be theoretically structured to gain synergistic advantages, the outcome of the effort to create an alliance is subject to the careful screening and subsequent choice of a valuable and complementary alliance partner. The third stage comprises negotiations with the selected partner to create a framework that establishes complementarities and fosters the development of synergies. The alliance management capabilities of the potential partners (familiarity and competencies in setting up alliances as opposed to acquisitions and in setting up equity-based ventures as opposed to contractual deals) play an important role at this stage. Reduced uncertainty about success and lower transaction costs are the results of capabilities for creating and managing alliances as opposed to operational skills for conducting the business of the alliance.

Once an alliance is organized, new structural issues arise that are not tied closely to transaction cost economic models but, rather, relate more to agency issues and to the social processes of organizations. A fourth stage is defined as the operating stage, where firms are involved in the day-to-day management of the alliance. The internal processes of organizations are never fully aligned and efficient but are subject to political pressures, individual shirking, power and influence of units, communication design, and a host of other issues. Alliances, with their dual (or multiple) allegiances and competing concepts of ends, means, and relationships, are even more vulnerable to such organizational inefficiencies.

These operational stresses often lead to a fifth stage in which the alliance is either restructured or terminated. Following Zajac and Olsen's (1993) model of transactional value, this stage reflects the assessment that the costs of the alliance are or have become higher than its benefits. This stage is the result both of unanticipated outcomes from the alliance and of the evolution of resources and capabilities on the parts of the partners, and possibly on the part of the alliance itself, that make the original bargain unsatisfactory to one or both partners. As a natural consequence of firms operating a venture and learning from these operations, the fifth stage may arise regularly, resulting in reconsideration of the negotiated arrangement for the alliance and a newly structured approach to operations. This cycling through stages three, four, and five seems to be an expected outcome of bargaining power models in dynamic environments (Gray & Yan, 1992).

The Stages of Structuring Alliances

The Alliance Choice

The key decision in the process of structuring an alliance is the decision to use an alliance. In most cases of organizational or market expansion, the firm has opportunities to expand organically through internal growth; to expand by purchasing necessary assets and capabilities in the marketplace; to expand via merger with or acquisition of another firm; or finally, to undertake an alliance (whether contractual or equity based) with another firm or firms. A variety of considerations can move the firm to choose an alliance over other structural forms (Tallman & Shenkar, 1994). A first key concern is the lack of critical resources. Madhok and Tallman (1998) proposed a four-part analytic path to make this decision:

1. The firm does not have the necessary capabilities and assets available internally so that some internal reorganization will not permit it to pursue the new strategic direction without adding resources, and
2. The firm cannot purchase the needed resources in the open marketplace, generally because critical skills and capabilities are often not available for sale but are tied to organizations, but
3. The firm cannot access these critical skills by purchasing another firm. Often, another firm does have the capabilities that are lacking, but the actual competency of a firm may be obscured by its many other activities, the cost may be excessive, and there is often concern that an outright acquisition will drive off the very human and group assets that are critical to the expansion, so that
4. The firm may seek an alliance or joint venture with a firm that has the assets that are lacking. Not upsetting the target organization means critical assets are less likely to be lost, the need for extensive integration is avoided, and flexibility is retained for future moves.

In essence, we are describing a make, buy, or lease decision targeted at organizational capabilities rather than pieces of equipment. The firm either creates new competences itself, buys them (usually through acquiring another firm or a unit of another firm), or leases them through some extended contractual arrangement—an alliance.

The decision regarding the choice of an alliance strategy generally focuses on tacit organizational knowledge and capabilities rather than simple commodities or hard assets that can be found in the marketplace but typically do not offer significant advantage—everyone else can buy them too. Technological dynamism, reflected in an environment punctuated by competence-destroying technologies, forces firms to maintain a wide range of technological knowledge and skills (Tushman & Anderson, 1986). However, very few firms can develop this wide range of knowledge internally (Lane, Lyles, & Salk, 1998). Alliances are an alternative mode through which firms can gain access to external knowledge resources (Almeida & Phene, 2004). Further, sharing knowledge with alliance partners can result in the creation of new capabilities that cannot be developed in isolation (Colombo, 2003).

Strategic alliances are even more important as sources of external knowledge in the international context. The global environment contains a diversity of knowledge embedded in national systems of innovation. Firms face disadvantages from lack of local knowledge relating to social, political, and economic conditions in foreign markets (Beamish, 1994). One option of dealing with the lack of knowledge about the local environment is the incremental approach to internationalization (Johanson & Vahlne, 1977); another is a strategic alliance. Chang (1995) suggests that firms can learn from experience or from other firms. Whereas the incremental approach focuses on learning from experience, the strategic alliance concentrates on learning new skills from other firms—but on a temporary basis, as opposed to an acquisition (Hamel, Doz, & Prahhalad, 1989). International alliances offer firms an opportunity to transfer technology and know-how (Mjoen & Tallman, 1997) across firm and country boundaries while providing access to location tied knowledge, such as governmental access, labor relations, or market characteristics (Makino & Delios, 1996).

Resource scarcity must generally be tied to additional considerations if the alliance decision is to be the choice. One key issue is the need for speed, combined with capital constraints. Forming an alliance is likely to be faster than establishing a wholly owned start-up organization and less expensive and less risky than an acquisition. Schilling (1998) suggests that a technology producer having alliances with distributors or users of its technology may have the edge in quickly establishing an installed base for the technology. Alliances, like acquisitions, bring access to complete organizational architectures and complex capabilities in one transaction. Alliances, however, are typically much less expensive up front. The firm will typically arrange payments from ongoing revenues that would not otherwise be available to either partner, with perhaps a small initial payment, rather than making a large capital investment in acquiring the other firm. Alliances, too, usually avoid bidding processes, are less subject to oversight and regulation, and require less internal adjustment—all factors in speeding up the transaction.

Another concern that can encourage alliance rather than more expensive and permanent arrangements is a sense of potential risk in the transaction. Alliances leave assets available for other purposes in addition to the alliance and also keep capital free to respond to other opportunities, so presenting lower opportunity costs. They also reduce exposure of capital and other valuable assets to risk of loss, for instance in the case of an investment in a volatile foreign market or in the case where the sought-after assets and capabilities are not fully understood, exposing the firm to performance risk. Yet another issue arises when the firm is trying to learn new skills. Alliances can open up opportunities to learn from partners in a cooperative environment rather than through subterfuge or enforced seizure of assets. If these skills are truly new, the firm may wish to retain flexibility in case its first learning effort does not work out and an alternative source of knowledge (a new partner) is needed quickly. In all these cases, we see the firm, under conditions of time and capital constraints and when risk control is an important consideration, looking for resources that it is lacking.

The issues addressed above suggest that certain theoretical perspectives would be most relevant to the initial choice of organizational structure. Resource-based theory and related knowledge- or capability-based approaches suggest, as discussed above, that under conditions of resource scarcity, alliances may be more effective than internalization in providing access to critical resources. Use of alliances in risky or uncertain situations has been tied to real options theory (Kogut & Kulatilaka, 1994), as alliances can provide multiple approaches to a new market or technology at a relatively low cost. Transaction cost models suggest also that alliances may be more appropriate than market transactions in situations where a firm is investing in a transaction with potential opportunism risks. Organizational learning theory suggests that close organizational ties (as opposed to markets) are needed to transmit tacit, organizationally embedded knowledge (which may be hard to develop internally). Transaction value analysis favors alliances when a cooperative form provides joint value maximization (Zajac & Olsen, 1993)—when the net present value of the payoff (revenues less production and transaction costs) that partners expect from collaboration exceeds that of proceeding alone (Colombo, 2003). Other theoretical perspectives provide further reasoning to justify alliances, but one clear message is that alliances can often be the preferred alternative in an investment, not a second-best fit.

Partner Search and Selection

Once the decision for alliance is made (or at least given serious consideration), the firm must begin to consider partners—with whom we ally is of vital concern and perhaps even more important than the general decision to pursue an alliance. Geringer (1991) suggests that this stage of the alliance process is critical because partner choice influences resource availability and the viability of the collaboration. This is also the stage at which real costs begin to be incurred, as the focal firm approaches potential targets to evaluate their true value as partners. Search costs can vary widely, depending on the experience of the firm, the complexity of the assets that it is trying to access, the number of possible partners, and related concerns. These costs are a key part of the transaction costs of forming an alliance. This stage still represents a large-numbers situation in which the focal firm has not yet committed to a particular partner and so has some advantage in any bargaining—prospective partners will presumably be generous while competing for an opportunity.

The screening process is critical, as the focal firm must evaluate its prospective partners regarding their actual asset and capability bases and their prospects for transactional integrity—strategic rather than financial due diligence. Das and Teng (1999) define the operational skills and capabilities that manifest from the asset base as the resource fit between partners. They suggest that resource fit can take two forms—complementary fit, which implies sharing of different resources, represented in alliances between large pharmaceutical firms with financial and marketing resources and small biotechnology firms with innovation resources; and supplementary fit, which implies pooling of similar resources to reduce costs and improve efficiencies. Evaluation of resource fit may be relatively easy if the emphasis is on basic competency in a relevant core technology. Further, fit or overlap between knowledge bases of partners can facilitate shared learning (Dyer & Singh, 1998). In effect, partners' absorptive capacities are able to substitute for physical and personnel resources that may otherwise need to be dedicated to facilitating shared learning (Cantwell & Colombo, 2000).

At times asset and capability evaluation may be difficult, particularly when unique or complex capabilities are needed with which the firm has had little or no experience. Hitt, Dacin, Levitas, Arregle, and Borzac (2000), in their study of international partner selection of firms from emerging and developed countries, indicate that developed market firms' criteria for partner choice often emphasized unique competencies and local market knowledge. The selection of an unskilled partner, or a partner with incompatible systems, or a partner that is unwilling to expose its critical assets will not add value to the alliance but will still be costly. Bleeke and Ernst (1991) suggest that alliances between strong firms are likely to be successful and alliances between strong and weak firms or between weak firms tend to fail. Thus, identification of strong and capable partners is critical.

The other aspect of the screening process involves transactional integrity, or the ability of the prospect to be a reliable partner. These are transactional or process complementarities between the firm and the prospective partner. The firm must evaluate prospective partners for transactional integrity—are they likely to become opportunistic, what reputations can they present, are they likely to be misrepresenting their skills (leading to adverse selection problems) or be unreliable as partners (leading to shirking or other moral hazard concerns), and how much monitoring might be needed? It is often the case that prospects with necessary technical skills fail as partners because of conflicting objectives, policies, cultures, or other "peripheral" skills (Tallman & Shenkar, 1994).

Balakrishnan and Koza (1993) emphasize the need for information about reliability of potential partners, due to moral-hazard concerns that arise from the unpredictability of the behavior of partners and the likely costs to a firm from opportunistic behavior by a partner, if such behavior occurs. Another part of the transactional or process complementarities is reflected in strategic fit or the extent of compatible goals. Partners often overlook the strategic-fit issue and assume that partners share similar objectives (Das & Teng, 1999). Difficulties in identifying true strategic objectives increase due to their changing nature over time. Thus, a partner may often be preferred due to prior relationships or ties that have demonstrated strategic fit, in contrast to other potential partners that may demonstrate better resource fit. The network of prior alliances often serves as an information guide in the choice of potential partners (Gulati, 1995).

Careful search processes are needed to evaluate both strategic and resource fit. Kale, Dyer, and Singh (2002) highlight the need for identification of potential partners to assess whether they can effectively work together. They offer the example of Eli Lilly's process of sending a due diligence team to a potential alliance partner to assess the partner's resources, capabilities, and culture. The team's mandate includes scrutiny of the potential partner's financial condition, information technology, research capabilities, and health and safety record. The team also places special emphasis on cultural assessment of the partner, examining corporate values and expectations, organizational structure, reward systems and incentives, leadership styles, decision-making processes, patterns of human interaction, work practices, history of partnerships, and human resources practices, because Lilly's experience suggests that culture clash is a key contributor to alliance failure. Adverse selection can be technical or organizational in nature. The latter is more difficult to identify and is also likely to be more costly over time.

The successful final outcome of this stage is the choice of an appropriate partner. Partner choice effectively locks the firm into a particular path and reduces the situation to one-on-one bargaining leading to the negotiation stage. Failure requires the firm to return to the field but is not typically very costly at this stage—few transaction-specific investments have been made.

Negotiation

The negotiation stage involves the process of establishing actual complementarities in the collaboration and careful definition of those resources that will be available to the partnership, as well as agreement on the ownership (or lack thereof), organization, and structure of the alliance. This stage is fraught with difficulty due to potential partner opportunism in designing the alliance. The bargaining process should identify a poorly selected partner (preferably early in the process) and should also build safeguards against opportunistic behavior or moral hazard, but must do so in a reasonably efficient manner and without destroying a sense of cooperation and mutual goals.

From a transaction cost economics perspective, a "fundamental transformation" has taken place in the transaction once a specific partner is selected and the transaction becomes a one-on-one negotiation. Prior to this transformation, the focal firm has a relatively small and quite general investment in the process and is in the position to investigate various potential partnerships at relatively low cost until the best apparent partner is identified. As soon as the partner is selected and negotiations begin, though, all investment becomes highly transaction-specific, and failure results in near-total loss of this investment. This condition results in a basic paradox—as the negotiation proceeds, the putative partners learn more about each other but they also become more committed to proceeding in order to protect sunk costs—pressures for a successful outcome to the negotiation grow with time, no matter the emerging face of the partner.

What issues should be of concern to firms bargaining over an alliance? First are the actual operating capabilities of the partner. If, per the resource-based view of alliances, both sides are looking for resource complementarities, this is the opportunity to discover whether the apparent assets and skills identified in the search phase are real and whether an agreement can be reached by which the combinatory effort can proceed. As the two sides consider relative input values, relative importance of resources, relative financial investments, roles and responsibilities, and so on, they must also determine a fair ownership arrangement in equity alliances or a fair allocation of proceeds in a contractual alliance. Bargaining-power models, in particular, propose that greater resource commitments bring greater control and, when appropriate, a larger ownership share (Gray & Yan, 1992). A second set of complementarities that must be considered at this time are those related to organizational systems, expectations, cultures, goals, and so forth in determining management control systems. Clarifying *how* the alliance relationship will work is as important as determining what its inputs and outputs should be. Indeed, most alliance failures relate more to incompatibilities in organization and lack of agreement on management responsibilities than to technical resources (Tallman & Shenkar, 1994).

These complementarities are also likely to have a heavy influence on the eventual terms of the agreement. A lack of agreement may ruin the negotiation and terminate the transaction or may result in more intense bargaining over protective terms, punitive terms, control of the alliance or specific resources, and so on. High compatibility or an existing (positive) relationship between the firms will tend to lead to less-specified contracts, fewer punitive clauses, and a general substitution of "trust," or confidence in a lack of opportunistic goals on the part of the partner, for specific contractual safeguards. Likewise, firms with experience in setting up alliances, and especially those with a formal alliance management structure (Kale et al., 2002), are more likely to conclude a successful negotiation and produce an agreement that will benefit the firm.

A particular aspect of negotiations in technology-focused industries is the competition for ideas. Alliances have been termed "learning races" (Khanna, Gulati, & Nohria, 1998; Hamel, 1991), in which partners vie in attempts to outlearn each other, creating significant tension. A learning race can result in the firm either absorbing and learning critical capabilities from its partner or losing its own capability to its partner. The negotiation task is therefore charged with creating a balance between learning and protection. Simonin (1999) indicates that effective negotiation is underlaid by the larger ability to understand the partner's stance and by the more narrowly defined ability to evaluate legal, tax, and financial implications of the collaboration. The ability to understand a partner's stance derives from the concept of relational capital, which reflects the level of mutual trust, respect, and friendship that arise out of close interaction at the individual level between alliance partners, whether from previous interaction or from well-developed skills at organizing alliances.

Kale, Singh, and Perlmutter (2000) suggest that relational capital can help companies successfully balance the acquisition of new capabilities and the protection of existing proprietary assets in alliance situations by facilitating better learning through interaction and minimizing the likelihood that an alliance partner will engage in opportunistic behavior to absorb unilaterally or steal information or know-how that is core or proprietary to its partner. If the partners are both aware of the risks of exposing knowledge to a potentially opportunistic partner, negotiations over sharing knowledge will be closely tied to governance mechanisms to protect knowledge. This situation generates a second paradox, in that some knowledge must be exposed to allow a fair agreement to be reached—presenting a risk of exposure of valuable resources in itself. Potential alliances can flounder at this stage if one or both partners refuse to reveal enough information about their inputs to permit a proper valuation and an equitable arrangement for management control and financial allocations. Das and Teng (1999) suggest that firms can employ scenario analyses to help assess how the alliance and the partner firms may evolve over time and how the evolution may change the relative positions of each partner and adjust operational strategies.

In addition to the use of relational capital to deal with difficulties of opportunism, adequate control mechanisms, which can ensure coordination of tasks, must be organized. These may include the use of formal mechanisms such as definition of authority, allocation of responsibility, standardization, and informal modes such as transfer of personnel (Inkpen & Dinur, 1998; Gulati & Singh, 1998). The governance structure of the alliance is a significant determinant of the learning process. Alliances that are closer to hierarchies, such as equity joint ventures, perform better at interorganizational learning (Oxley, 1997), especially in the transfer of complex capabilities (Kogut, 1988), than do less formal alliances. These alliances reflect greater commitment of the partners and larger resources vested in the venture. As a result, the incentives to learn and to earn within the alliance, rather than race to absorb know-how and exit, may be stronger for both partners. Recent research (Poppo & Zenger, 2002) shows that more complete contracts strengthen relational governance, and both improve performance in operating alliances, suggesting that relationships complement rather than substitute for well-designed, complete contracts during the negotiation stage.

The negotiation task must balance the benefits of unitary control with the advantages of flexibility to maximize the value from collaboration and to capture the benefits of using the alliance as an alternative to hierarchy. The final paradox of the negotiation phase is that the more organizationally embedded and tacit are the knowledge resources that the partners hope to share, the greater the potential value of the alliance, but the more difficult is a complete contract to negotiate. Prior relationships that provide a degree of "trust" between the partners may smooth over the difficulties and risks of such an agreement, but the degree of uncertainty that seems to be an inherent aspect of sharing complex knowledge resources also makes a successful conclusion to the bargaining session more difficult and the coordinating mechanisms that result more complex. Failure at the negotiation forces the firms to reconsider their cooperative strategies and renew the search for partners. A successful negotiation will at last deliver an alliance to the partners. Unfortunately, this only sets the stage for the real work of the transaction—managing the alliance operation—and if the bargaining session is forced to yield an alliance even in the face of problems, it may only set up more costly failure later in the life cycle.

Operations

The next stage of the alliance process involves monitoring and managing the ongoing collaboration. The alliance process has moved beyond the quasimarket condition of seeking partners and agreeing on the exchange of value to a quasi-hierarchical condition of managing a (more or less formal) organization. The operational stage ultimately determines the success or failure of the collaboration—even a good negotiation has no value if the resulting alliance fails to function (Van de Ven & Polley, 1992). Bamford, Ernst, and Fubini (2004) assert that the high risk of failure for alliances and joint ventures can be attributed to the stage following the signing of the memorandum of understanding and that lack of attention during this stage can result in strategic conflicts between the allied companies, governance gridlock, and missed operational synergies. Desai, Foley, and Hines (2004), in their analysis of American transnational corporations, find an increased utilization of wholly owned subsidiaries, in contrast to alliances. They suggest that this may be due to conflicts that occur in the operational stage of an alliance in the context of structuring production, finances, and risk of intellectual property theft.

Managing alliances is a difficult process and often leads to poor results and failure. Success is possible, though, and the evidence suggests that experience and dedicated alliance management functions in the parent firms (Kale et al., 2002), complete contracts and solid relation governance (Poppo & Zenger, 2002), appropriate resource contributions (Robins, Tallman, & Fladmoe-Lindquist, 2002), the right balance of control and ownership, compatible cultures, and joint learning all encourage success and longevity.

Conflict is inherent in alliances because of partner opportunism, goal divergence (Doz, 1996), and cross-cultural differences (Kale et al., 2000). Das and Teng (1999) argue that relational risk, reflected in partner opportunism and goal divergence, is an unavoidable and problematic element of strategic alliances. Alliance partners are typically focused on their self-interest at the cost of the partner firms and even the alliance. Partners may engage in shirking, appropriating the partner's resources, distorting information, harboring hidden agendas, delivering unsatisfactory products and services, and other types of moral hazard, thereby jeopardizing the success of the alliance. On the other hand, partners may be well chosen, honest, and cooperative, but the difference is not necessarily easy to determine, and either under- or overcontrolling an alliance can lead to unacceptable costs.

It is also the case that the more complex the relationship and the more embedded the assets and capabilities that are shared, the more potential value can be derived, but the more difficult and costly the management effort. Simple contractual alliances with narrow objectives and short expected life spans may require only that the contractual agreement be followed in order to be successful. Long-term and complex agreements and joint ventures may need to be managed essentially as independent firms, requiring dedicated management teams over long periods of time. The more open-ended the potential benefits an alliance or joint venture provides to the partners, the higher the likely cost of management, so that the actual return on investment may be no higher than for smaller, simpler arrangements.

Cultural distance in international alliances exacerbates these difficulties. The problem of cultural distance between allying firms is supported in research determining that U.S. firms learned less in alliances with non-U.S. firms (Mowery, Oxley, & Silverman, 1996). National culture creates various obstacles to collaboration and simultaneously increases the opportunity for learning from collaboration, because alliance partners have to contend with new and different institutional contexts. Firms use low-cost governance structures to overcome the costly information disadvantage as cultural distance increases (Fladmoe-Lindquist & Jacque, 1995). Empirical studies bear out the idea that cultural distance between the firm's home country and the foreign location in which it is operating leads to a greater incidence of cooperative modes as opposed to equity ownership (Kogut & Singh, 1988). Thus, greater cultural distance increases the propensity for alliance formation even as it makes alliances more difficult to operate (Almeida, Grant, & Phene, 2002). A partial explanation is that knowledge is inextricably bound in the local context and can be accessed only through a partner that is also embedded in the context.

Alliances that are intended to share complex knowledge suffer from technical difficulties, in that the absorptive capacity of partners for such know-how may be limited (Simonin, 1999). Not only do partners have different organization concerns, as above, but even if intentions are positive and aligned, some uncertainty typically exists about the actual ability of the two sides to create synergies on a technical operating level—even the most careful selection and negotiation have inherent risks of poor selection of partner. At this level, too, cultural distance (both organizational and national) limits the ability of the partners to learn from each other (Fiol & Lyles, 1985).

Madhok (1997) theorizes that in situations of high sociocultural distance, partner routines might be substantially different, resulting in an inability to absorb and exploit know-how efficiently. These differences in routines are demonstrated in Appleyard's (1996) survey of employees of semiconductor companies, indicating differences in patterns of learning across nationalities—Japanese employees relied on public channels of learning, whereas U.S. employees depended on private channels. Certain countries have specific institutional environments that foster goodwill, trust, and cooperation (Hill, 1995); for instance, such an environment enables Japanese firms to generate relational rents through cooperative alliances (Dyer, 1996). Firms from countries that do not possess these supportive, socially complex institutions will have distinctly different routines for accessing knowledge, and a mix of the two is likely to create operating difficulties.

Besides relying on the social context, firms can develop the wide variety of skills, including staffing, trust-building, resolving conflicts, transferring resources, training, and renegotiating agreements, that are required at this stage (Simonin, 1999). The creation of dedicated teams (Bamford et al., 2004) to manage this phase, with responsibilities in creating strategic alignment, a shared governance system, and managing interdependencies between the firms, can build cohesive and high performing alliances. Similarly, Dyer, Kale, and Singh (2001) argue that a dedicated strategic-alliance function that coordinates all alliance-related activity within the organization and is charged with institutionalizing processes and systems to teach, share, and leverage prior alliance-management experience and know-how throughout the company will improve performance. Indeed, Kale et al. (2000) argue that firms need to employ a variety of contractual and organizational mechanisms (formal and informal) to manage conflict. Further, experience with alliances can translate into specific skills for the formation and management of alliances (Lyles, 1988). Thus, experienced firms can internalize and refine specific routines associated with forming collaborations.

Further, proper structuring of organizational responsibilities in the economic value-adding activities of the alliance seems to enhance performance and longevity. Robins et al. (2002) find that international alliances perform better when the international partner provides strategic resources and the local partner provides access to local institutions, but also when the alliance itself is responsible for providing operating resources. Mjoen and Tallman (1997) show that when partners feel that they control the application of those strategic resources that they have provided to the alliance, they develop a sense of overall control of and satisfaction with the alliance. Madhok and Tallman (1998) propose that as alliances persist, the partners commit to alliance-specific investments in both relationships and operations that will generate rents that are highly specific to the particular alliance and will disappear if that partnership fails, thus providing a strong economic incentive to maintain the relationship.

These studies, and those cited above that focus more on relational success, presume that the objective of the alliance is to gain increased rents from the unique combination of resources that is the alliance. If Hamel (1991) and others interested in learning aspects of alliances are correct, though, many firms see success as internalizing the know-how of their alliance partners for independent use. In such cases, even strong economic gains may seem inadequate to maintain the alliance, and relationships are created only for exploitation. Given the importance of reputation and future prospects (Parkhe, 1993) to the possibility of future collaborations, opportunistic learning strategies seem to be self-limiting, even if some degree of learning from the partner (as opposed to learning about the partner) is probable in any alliance. Only careful controls, established in the negotiation phase and pursued during the operation phase of the alliance process, can keep learning from being destructive.

And why are all these complex mechanisms needed to control what was supposed to be a faster, cheaper means of accessing resources and capabilities? Simple economic analysis of alliances seems to expect that up-front costs may be significant but that once the deal is signed, the venture will require only normal operating costs and will begin to yield benefits. This is unlikely. Developing actual complementarities between disparate resource stocks is an involved process, and the more complex and embedded the involved capabilities, the more difficult, costly, and uncertain the process (Madhok & Tallman, 1998). Thus, we see that the setup costs of alliances do not end with the final agreement; they just transform and become ever more specific to the transaction and partner. All the experience and mechanisms described above can help to create real complementarity and synergy, and experience may also keep capital patient. At the same time, actual synergies and associated rents begin to appear only when real integration of complementary assets develops, and this *must* take time—and the more the alliance is dependent on the close cooperation of individuals, the longer that time (Tallman, 2000). The most likely outcome is always that costs are greater and benefits further in the future than expected. Under such circumstances, the potential for a partner to act opportunistically in order to gain earlier or greater benefits must increase, further stressing the alliance and possibly entailing the need for sanctions, arbitration, or legal action.

Because managers involved with alliances typically also retain their identity with and allegiance to their original parent firm, social controls that suppress such behavior may be weaker than in other organization forms, and international alliances are likely to face both increased communication problems and even lower loyalty to the alliance venture. Given the opportunities for opportunism and the incentives to extract returns by some means, we should perhaps be more surprised that so many alliances do function successfully than that so many fail or must be renegotiated. Failure after operations begin is an expensive outcome, particularly if investment has been made in developing the systems and relationships to operate the venture, because these have little salvage value (Madhok & Tallman, 1998). A good contract and skills at building alliances can prevent considerable losses. Success at this stage is generally seen as longevity, stability, and the ability to fulfill the objectives of the original alliance strategy. However, even successful alliances may need to undergo changes as the relationship evolves, and we see the need to describe a fifth phase of the alliance process.

Termination/Renegotiation

Alliances continue to evolve throughout the operational stage in response to the pressures outlined above. Zajac and Olsen (1993) emphasize the renegotiation stage of alliance transactions. As the partners and the alliance itself evolve over time, their relative contributions also change, and the original deal, even if successful, becomes no longer acceptable. Indeed, bargaining-power models suggest that a successful cooperative venture is really just a succession of renegotiations of a dynamic economic and social relationship (Gray & Yan, 1992). Research suggests the existence of three evolutionary paths for alliance systems. The first is the termination of the collaboration, often due to achievement of partner objectives but also often reflecting a failure to manage complementarity and develop synergies, an inability to adjust to evolving roles, or an inability to manage the interfirm relationship. Serapio and Cascio (1996) suggest that knowing when and how to exit can be critical to a firm's achieving its original objectives without compromising other competitive aspects of its operations. Simonin (1999) asserts that organizations that do not prepare for this eventuality and do not learn how or when to exit may either fall into competency traps (Levitt & March, 1988) or find that their collaborators are ready to exit when they are not (Reich & Mankin, 1986).

The second path is the acquisition of the alliance partner. Vanhaverbeke, Duysters, and Nooderhaven (2002) suggest that firms use incremental strategies in exploring and gaining control over external resources and capabilities. Research draws an analogy between an investment in a strategic alliance and an option on technological know-how of uncertain value with the shift from a strategic alliance to an acquisition similar to the striking of that option (Bowman & Hurry, 1993, Haspeslagh & Jemison, 1991). Thus, firms move from a strategic alliance to an acquisition as soon as the interaction within the alliance has sufficiently dissolved the information asymmetry and mitigated the managerial indigestibility problem (Hagedoorn & Sadowski, 1999). The real options model of alliances (Kogut, 1991) ties strategic success to alliance failure—real call options are either discarded by terminating alliances or exercised by acquisition. This model takes a rather one-sided approach to the concept of alliance strategies (what does the partner think about being a quasifinancial option, after all?), and tends to ignore the potential for greater rents through maintaining the alliance (Madhok & Tallman,

1998), although newer models suggest that options can be held rather than exercised in the absence of an expiration date.

The third path reflects a reevaluation of the alliance and adjustments in its structure and objectives. Gray and Yan (1992) suggest that at least for equity joint ventures, evolving capabilities in the parents and a changing balance of resource dependencies lead to restructuring of the venture as relative bargaining power changes over time. Ring and Van de Ven describe "a repetitive sequence of negotiation, commitment, and execution stages, each of which is assessed in terms of efficiency and equity" (1994, p. 97). Doz (1996) posits a model in which the initial conditions for alliance formation influence learning, which then leads to an evaluation of the alliance and subsequent adjustments. A recent study by Reuer, Zollo, and Singh (2002) identifies determinants of postformation governance changes in the alterations in alliances' contracts, boards of oversight committees, and monitoring mechanisms. However, because governance by managerial fiat may be impossible, coordination in strategic alliances must be sustained by discrete renegotiation over specific contractual conditions or by mutual expectations of reciprocity (Osborn, Denekamp, Duysters, & Baughn, 1998). Thus, Vanhaverbeke et al. (2002) argue that managing strategic alliances calls for management skills that differ from those in traditional hierarchical firms, such as lateral communication, openness, and conflict resolution (Larsson, Bengtsson, Henriksson, & Sparks, 1998).

The incompatibility of corporate cultures is one of the most important reasons why alliances fail (Segil, 1988). Whereas Meschi's (1997) findings indicate that all cultural differences between partners recede over time, Simonin (1999) finds organizational culture a bigger and more enduring obstacle than national culture. One device for overcoming incompatibility of corporate culture is to build on alliances with existing partners. Gulati (1995) demonstrates that the social context resulting from prior alliances between two partners leads to increased alliance formation in the future. As alliance partners work together, they develop joint or interorganizational routines and greater cultural alignment, resulting in a greater ability to learn from each other. The greater the experience of a firm in collaborating with partners with varied and diverse organizational cultures, the greater its ability to learn and adapt to new situations. With experience should come recognition that if the transactional value of the alliance is still positive, renegotiation in the face of an obsolete initial agreement is a positive outcome, even if a firm's decreased resource input value must result in its accepting a reduced level of control and benefit. So long as the rate of return is superior, economic rationality should drive the firm to accept this outcome, when refusal to renegotiate will lead to termination of the alliance and acceptance of a second-best alternative strategy.

This is not to say that termination is always a failed outcome—if the objectives of the alliance are accomplished or a changing market or evolving capabilities have made the venture no longer rational, then termination is the preferred outcome. Likewise, if the venture has greater value for one partner than the other, whether due to differential learning, changing strategies, new opportunities, or simply different assessments of value, then an acquisition is the proper outcome. It is the breakdown of an economically viable, even preferred, alliance due to distrust, control disputes, impatience, or other relational problems that is real alliance failure. Experience, contractual mechanisms for renegotiation, mediation, or arbitration, organizational units with specific responsibilities for maintaining alliances, and the like all contribute to greater understanding of the problems and more effective solutions to alliance agreements that are no longer comfortable fits. The end of a particular agreement may not mean the end of the alliance but in any case must be recognized as a logical phase of the process of structuring—and restructuring—an alliance.

Conclusion

This chapter views structuring alliances as a multistage process in which each stage has its own set of pressures and demands. Different theoretical approaches to alliances offer different degrees of insight at each stage, but none explains the entire process fully. Our intent has been to provide theoretical and empirical evidence about the process of structuring alliances as an effort to integrate some the various theories and also to show how their application can lead to practical insights and recommendations about designing and managing alliances both for managers and for researchers.

References

Almeida, P., & Phene, A. (2004). Subsidiaries and knowledge creation: The influence of the MNC and host country on innovation. *Strategic Management Journal, 25,* 847–864.

Almeida, P., Grant, R., & Phene, A. (2002). Knowledge transfer through alliances: The role of culture. In M. Gannon & K. Newman (Eds.), *Handbook of cross-cultural management.* Oxford: Blackwell.

Appleyard, M. (1996). How does knowledge flow? Interfirm patterns in the semiconductor industry [special issue]. *Strategic Management Journal, 17,* 7–154.

Balakrishnan, S., & Koza, M. (1993). Information asymmetry, adverse selection and joint ventures. *Journal of Economic Behavior and Organization, 20*(1), 99–118.

Bamford, J., Ernst, D., & Fubini, D. (2004). Launching a world-class joint venture. *Harvard Business Review, 82*(2), 90–101.

Beamish, P. (1994). Joint ventures in LDCs: Partner selection and performance. *Management International Review, 34,* 60–75.

Bleeke, J., & Ernst, D. (1991). The way to win in cross-border alliances. *Harvard Business Review, 69*(6), 127–135.

Bowman, E., & Hurry, D. (1993). Strategy through the options lens: An integrated view of resource investments and the incremental choice process. *Academy of Management Review, 18*(4), 760–783.

Cantwell, J., & Colombo, M. (2000). Technological and output complementarities and inter-firm cooperation in information technology ventures. *Journal of Management and Governance, 4*(1/2), 117–147.

Chang, S. (1995). International expansion strategy of Japanese firms. *Academy of Management Journal, 38*(2), 385–410.

Colombo, M. (2003). Alliance form: A test of contractual and competence perspectives. *Strategic Management Journal, 24*(12), 1209–1229.

Das, T., & Teng, B. (1999). Managing risks in strategic alliances. *Academy of Management Executive, 13*(4), 50–63.

Desai, M., Foley, C., & Hines, J. (2004). Venture out alone. *Harvard Business Review, 82*(3), 22–23.

Doz, Y. (1996). The evolution of cooperation in strategic alliance: Initial conditions or learning processes? *Strategic Management Journal, 17,* 55–79.

Dyer, J. (1996). Does governance matter? Keiretsu alliances and asset specificity as sources of Japanese competitive advantage. *Organization Science, 7*(6), 649–666.

Dyer J., & Singh, H. (1998). Relational advantage: Relational rents and sources of interorganizational competitive advantage. *Academy of Management Review, 23,* 660–679.

Dyer, J., Kale, P., & Singh, H. (2001). How to make strategic alliances work. *MIT Sloan Management Review, 42*(4), 37–44.

Fiol, M., & Lyles, M. (1985). Organizational learning. *Academy of Management Review, 10*(4), 803–814.

Fladmoe-Lindquist, K., & Jacque, L. (1995). Control modes in international service operations: The propensity to franchise. *Management Science, 41*(7), 1238–1249.

Geringer, M. (1991). Strategic determinants of partner selection criteria in international joint venture. *Journal of International Business Studies, 22*(1), 41–63.

Gray, B., & Yan, A. (1992). A negotiations model of joint venture formation, structure and performance. *Advances in Comparative Management, 7,* 41–75.

Gulati, R. (1995). Social structure and alliance formation patterns: A longitudinal analysis. *Administrative Science Quarterly, 40*(4), 619–645.

Gulati, R., & Singh, H. (1998). The architecture of cooperation: Managing coordination costs and appropriation concerns in strategic alliances. *Administrative Science Quarterly, 43*(4), 781–815.

Hagedoorn, J., & Sadowski, B. (1999). The transition from strategic technology alliances to mergers and acquisitions. *Journal of Management Studies, 36*(1), 87–107.

Hamel, G. (1991). Competition for competence and interpartner learning within international strategic alliances [special issue]. *Strategic Management Journal, 12,* 83–103.

Hamel, G., Doz, Y., & Prahalad, C. K. (1989). Collaborate with your competitors—and win. *Harvard Business Review, 67*(1), 33–139.

Haspeslagh, P., & Jemison, D. (1991). *Managing acquisitions: Creating value through corporate renewal.* New York: Free Press.

Hill, C. (1995). National institutional structures, transaction cost economizing and competitive advantage: The case of Japan. *Organization Science, 6*(1), 119–142.

Hitt, M., Dacin, T., Levitas, E., Arregle, J., & Borzac, A. (2000). Partner selection in emerging and developed market contexts: Resource-based and organizational learning perspectives. *Academy of Management Journal, 43*(4), 449–468.

Inkpen, A., & Dinur, A. (1998). Knowledge management processes and international joint ventures. *Organization Science, 9*(4), 454–469.

Johanson, J., & Vahlne, J. E. (1977). The internationalization process of the firm—A model of knowledge development and increasing foreign market commitment. *Journal of International Business Studies, 8*(2), 23–32.

Kale, P., Dyer, J., & Singh, H. (2002). Alliance capability, stock market response and long-term alliance success: The role of the alliance function. *Strategic Management Journal, 23*(8), 747–767.

Kale, P., Singh, H., & Perlmutter, H. (2000). Learning and protection of proprietary assets in strategic alliances: Building relational capital. *Strategic Management Journal, 21*(3), 217–237.

Khanna, T., Gulati, R., & Nohria, N. (1998). The dynamics of learning alliances: Competition, cooperation, and relative scope. *Strategic Management Journal, 19*(3), 193–210.

Kogut, B. (1988). Joint ventures: Theoretical and empirical perspectives. *Strategic Management Journal, 9*(4), 319–332.

Kogut, B. (1991). Joint ventures and the option to expand and acquire. *Management Science, 37,* 19–33.

Kogut, B., & Kulatilaka, N. (1994). Options thinking and platform investments: Investing in opportunity. *California Management Review, 36*(2), 52–72.

Kogut, B., & Singh, H. (1988). The effect of national culture on the choice of entry mode. *Journal of International Business Studies, 19,* 411–432.

Lane, P., Lyles, M., & Salk, J. (1998). Relative absorptive capacity, trust and interorganizational learning in international joint ventures. In M. Hitt, J. E. Costa, & R. Nixon (Eds.), *Managing strategically in an interconnected world.* London: Wiley.

Larsson, R., Bengtsson, L., Henriksson, K., & Sparks, J. (1998). The interorganizational learning dilemma: Collective knowledge development in strategic alliances. *Organization Science, 9,* 285–305.

Levitt, B., & March, J. G. (1988). Organizational learning. *Annual Review of Sociology 14,* 319–340.

Lyles, M. (1988). Learning among joint venture sophisticated firms. *Management International Review, 28,* 85–98.

Madhok, A. (1997). Cost, value and foreign market entry mode: The transaction and the firm. *Strategic Management Journal, 18*(1), 39–61.

Madhok, A., & Tallman, S. (1998). Resources, transactions and rents: Managing value through interfirm collaborative relationships. *Organization Science, 9,* 326–339.

Makino, S., & Delios, A. (1996). Local knowledge transfer and performance: Implications for alliance formation in Asia. *Journal of International Business Studies, 27*(5), 5–27.

Meschi, P. (1997). Longevity and cultural differences of international joint ventures: Toward time-based cultural management. *Human Relations, 50*(2), 211–229.

Mjoen, H., & Tallman, S. (1997). Control and performance in international joint ventures. *Organization Science, 8,* 257–274.

Mowery, D., Oxley, J., & Silverman, B. (1996). Strategic alliances and interfirm knowledge transfer [special issue]. *Strategic Management Journal, 17,* 77–91.

Osborn, R. N., Denekamp, J. G., Duysters, G., & Baughn, C. (1998). Embedded patterns of international alliance formation. *Organization Studies, 19,* 617–638.

Oxley, J. E. (1997). Appropriability hazards and governance in strategic alliances: A transaction cost approach. *Journal of Law, Economics, and Organization, 13,* 387–409.

Parkhe, A. (1993). Strategic alliance structuring: A game theoretic and transaction cost examination of interfirm cooperation. *Academy of Management Journal, 36,* 794–829.

Poppo, L., & Zenger, T. (2002). Do formal contracts and relational governance function as substitutes or complements? *Strategic Management Journal, 23,* 707–726.

Reich, R., & Mankin, E. (1986). Joint ventures with Japan give away our future. *Harvard Business Review, 64*(2), 78–87.

Reuer, J., Zollo, M., & Singh, H. (2002). Post-formation dynamics in strategic alliances. *Strategic Management Journal, 23*(2), 135–151.

Ring, P. S., & Van de Ven, A. H. (1994). Developmental processes of cooperative interorganizational relationships. *Academy of Management Review, 19,* 90–118.

Robins, J. A., Tallman, S., & Fladmoe-Lindquist, K. (2002). Autonomy and dependence of international cooperative ventures. *Strategic Management Journal, 23,* 881–902.

Schilling, M. (1998). Technological lockout: An integrative model of the economic and strategic factors driving technology success and failure. *Academy of Management Review, 23*(2), 267–285.

Segil, L. (1988). Strategic alliances for the 21st century. *Strategy and Leadership, 26*(4), 12–17.

Serapio, M., & Cascio, W. (1996). End games in international alliances. *Academy of Management Executive, 10*(1), 62–74.

Simonin, B. L. (1999). Ambiguity and the process of knowledge transfer in strategic alliances. *Strategic Management Journal, 20,* 595–623.

Tallman, S. (2000). Forming and managing shared organization ventures: Resources and transaction costs. In D. Faulkner & M. de Rond (Eds.), *Cooperative strategy: Economic, business, and organizational issues* (pp. 96–118). Oxford: Oxford University Press.

Tallman, S., & Shenkar, O. (1994). A managerial decision model of international joint venture formation. *Journal of International Business Studies, 25*(1), 91–114.

Tushman, M., & Anderson, P. (1986). Technological discontinuities and organizational environments. *Administrative Science Quarterly, 31,* 439–465.

Van de Ven, A., & Polley, D. (1992). Learning while innovating. *Organization Science. 3*(2), 92–116.

Vanhaverbeke, W., Duysters, G., & Noorderhaven, N. (2002). External technology sourcing through alliances or acquisitions: An analysis of the application-specific integrated circuits industry. *Organization Science, 13*(6), 714–734.

Williamson, O. E. (1985). *The economic institutions of capitalism.* New York: Free Press.

Zajac, E. J., & Olsen, C. P. (1993). From transaction cost to transactional value analysis: Implications for the study of interorganizational strategies. *Journal of Management Studies, 30*(1), 131–145.

9

Alliance Contractual Design

Africa Ariño

Jeffrey J. Reuer

Alliance partners are exposed to uncertainties about future states of nature (i.e., environmental uncertainty) and about the future behavior of the counterpart once in the alliance (i.e., behavioral uncertainty). Contracts that govern alliances are therefore useful in providing "guidance to the courts on partner intentions should the alliance break down" (Ryall & Sampson, 2003, p. 3). However, contracts do something more than safeguard partners against unforeseen events or partner opportunism. There is empirical evidence that alliance contracts include terms that are legally unenforceable, such as business plans (Ryall & Sampson, 2003). Thus, it seems that alliance contracts provide an opportunity to define partner expectations and to help them plan activities.

Our purpose in this chapter is to provide an overview of what we know about alliance contracts from the alliance management literature. Despite their importance, formal contracts have received scarce attention from alliance researchers. Those concerned with alliance design have focused mainly on the broader choice of governance form. For example, the conditions under which an alliance is the most efficient governance form have been studied extensively (e.g., Hennart, 1988; Balakrishnan & Koza, 1993; Chi, 1994; Hennart & Reddy, 1997; Reuer & Koza, 2000). This work has compared alliances with acquisitions as well as with the decision to develop new markets or technologies in-house.

Along similar lines, the choice of alliance form has received attention as well, with some studies addressing the question of when an equity alliance is preferable to a nonequity structure (e.g., Pisano, 1989, 1990; Osborn & Baughn, 1990; Gulati, 1995; Oxley, 1997; Kale & Puranam, 2004). Of the few empirical studies that consider alliance contracts, the earlier ones do so using contract-related variables as explanatory variables of other alliance attributes or outcomes (Parkhe,

AUTHOR'S NOTE: We gratefully acknowledge the financial support of the Anselmo Rubiralta Center for Research on Globalization and Strategy at IESE and of the Spanish Ministerio de Ciencia y Tecnología (grant SEC2003–09533).

1993; Deeds & Hill, 1998; Reuer & Ariño, 2002). The study of contract characteristics as dependent variables to be explained is very recent (Luo, 2002; Poppo & Zenger, 2002; Mayer, 2004; Reuer & Ariño, 2003; Reuer, Ariño, & Mellewigt, forthcoming; Ryall & Sampson, 2003).

This chapter is organized as follows. After a short introduction to the contents of alliance contracts, we start by contrasting alliance contractual form and governance form. Next, we focus on two related concepts: contractual complexity and contractual completeness. We suggest that contractual complexity is a theoretically more appropriate construct to investigate in the absence of detailed information about the transaction contemplated in the contract. After that, we present the measures of contractual complexity used in past studies. We then go over the determinants of contractual complexity by considering their influence on contracting costs and benefits in light of the environmental and behavioral uncertainties that collaborators face. Conclusions and suggestions for future research are offered at the end. Although we focus here on the management literature, we also draw some ideas from the literature on the economics of contracting.

Research on Alliance Contracts

Until recently, little was known about the contents of alliance contracts, primarily due to the difficulties entailed in accessing this kind of data (Ring, 2002; Ryall & Sampson, 2003). There is scant secondary data on such detailed information on alliances and limited data available from the government, and confidentiality considerations can preclude access to contractual information for a sufficiently large number of agreements to study.

Typically, a contract outlines the roles and responsibilities of each party, the allocation of decision and control rights, the planning for various contingencies, how the parties will communicate, and how to resolve disputes (Argyres & Mayer, 2004). In an article aimed at practitioners, Campbell and Reuer (2001) offer a comprehensive overview of the basic legal issues an alliance contract should contemplate (see Box 9.1 for an outline). Although they focus on bilateral equity joint ventures (JVs), they make clear that many of the same considerations apply to nonequity alliances—except for issues associated to share-related provisions and so on—and to multilateral alliances—except that negotiating these contracts is probably more complex than negotiating bilateral agreements. Many law firms now provide detailed checklists for clients and cover similar items for contracting parties. For instance, Freshfields Bruckhaus Deringer highlights eighteen broad legal issues that parties must consider, and within each of these broad categories there are a dozen or more legal considerations to which alliance partners must attend.

Contractual Form and Governance Form: Disentangling the Two

An important distinction that must be made at the outset concerns the contractual forms of alliances and the governance forms that firms also employ in shaping their economic exchanges. Based on Williamson (1979, 1985) and other authors, James (2000, p. 48) states that "the specific exchanges negotiated by trading partners and the allocation of risks and trading gains resulting from them . . . constitute a *contract*" [emphasis in original], whereas *governance* refers to "alternative institutional modes for organizing transactions" (Williamson, 1979, p. 234). Hence, we use the broader term *governance form* to refer to the chosen institutional context in which transactions take place—be this the market, the hierarchy, or any hybrid form. Governance form is to be distinguished from governance mechanisms within a particular governance mode, such as the presence of a board of directors, which in fact could be the object of contractual specification. In this sense, governance form solves the boundary problem,

Box 9.1 Basic Legal Issues Included in Typical Alliance Contracts

- *Establishment issues:*
  - *Preliminary issues:*
    - confidentiality or nondisclosure agreement,
    - "lockout" provision preventing the parties from conducting parallel negotiations with a competitor.
  - *Setting up the alliance:*
    - shareholdings (applicable to equity alliances only):
      - partners' contributions deemed as equal (50:50 ownership and control structure): provisions to break potential deadlocks,
      - partner's contributions not deemed as equal: provisions establishing the need to have the minority partner's approval on crucial decisions.
    - board of directors and staffing (applicable to equity alliances only):
      - proportion of managers that should come from each company,
      - what their minimum qualifications should be,
      - whether the other party may object to any individual,
      - what the level and source of remuneration should be,
    - articles of association (applicable to equity alliances only): shareholders' agreement on issues such as:
      - passing resolutions,
      - share issuance, transfer, and disposal,
      - appointment of directors, and so on.
    - place of incorporation (applicable to equity alliances only) and advisors such as lawyers or accountants.
  - *Parties and framework of contract:*
    - identification of the parties,
    - purpose of the agreement,
    - main body of the agreement specifying the obligations and restrictions on the parent companies,
    - "boilerplate" clauses or standard provisions around a variety of issues,
    - signature and data clauses,
    - schedules that detail elements of the agreement,
    - "all agreement" clause indicating that no other documents or oral agreements are part of the enforceable contract. If there is a document intended to be part of the contract, it should be clearly incorporated within it.
  - *Performance clauses:*
    - duties and obligations of the partners,
    - timing of any performance.
  - *Restrictions on the partners:*
    - noncompetition or nonsolicitation clauses,
    - confidentiality agreements, possibly including that any public statements about the alliance must be approved by both parties,
    - ownership and licensing of intellectual property rights.

- *Liability:*
    - agreement on the extent to which they will be liable, possibly settling a certain amount of money,
    - in case of force majeure, agreement on how long the situation may last before a new partner is sought or the alliance dissolved.

➢ *Postestablishment issues:*

- *Changes to the contract:*
    - a clause establishing that changes to the contract will be written and signed by both parties is common,
    - change control procedure: schedule, level of management that can agree to a contractual change,
    - minimum number of formal meetings to review issues concerning the alliance,
    - consideration of the transfer of the agreement and the obligations within it to another party.
- *Dispute resolution:*
    - escalation procedure: usually a dispute is first referred to the partners' operational managers, then to senior management, then to an outsider for assistance, then to a mediation or arbitration procedure.
    - recourse to the courts:
        - which courts would have jurisdiction,
        - whose laws will govern the agreement.
- *Share disposal* (applicable to equity alliances only):
    - circumstances in which new shares will be issued and to whom,
    - transfer of shares between the partners or to an outside party; advice notice; preemption rights,
    - what happens with JV's subsidiaries,
    - all shares of one partner to be dealt with in a block,
    - restrictions on transfer of shares to outsiders,
    - how the shares are to be valued,
    - circumstances that trigger the transfer of shares.
- *Termination:*
    - share disposal issues (applicable to equity alliances only),
    - circumstances under which the agreement will be terminated, including what constitutes a serious breach leading to alliance terminations,
    - consequences of termination: what will happen to personnel, intellectual property rights, assets, and contracts and obligations.

whereas contractual form specifies terms of trade including allocation of decision rights.

Although governance form and contractual form are related, there is not necessarily a one-to-one relationship between the two. Empirical evidence suggests that significant contractual heterogeneity within types of governance form exists. In their study of 200 contracts of biotechnology nonequity alliances, Lerner and Merges (1998) report 25 types of control rights. They analyze the incidence of these control rights, excluding from their sample terms that appear in less than 5% or more than 95% of the contracts. Their findings show that some of the controls appear in as few as 6% of the contracts, and some in as many as 93%, with a mean number of 9.3 control rights per contract.

Reuer and Ariño (2003) collected data on eight types of contractual terms in 91 alliances across a variety of industries. In the case of equity alliances, the incidence of each type of terms ranges between 39% and 82% of the contracts. The range varies from 26% to 58% in the case of nonequity alliances. In a related study of alliances in the German telecommunications industry (Reuer et al., forthcoming), the same eight types of terms were analyzed. In this case, the incidence varies between 33% and 100% of the equity alliance contracts and between 11% and 93% of the nonequity alliance contracts.

There is also emerging evidence that the incidence of contractual terms does not vary significantly between equity and nonequity alliances as might be expected. For example, Ariño and Reuer (2004) report no significant differences in the mean incidence of particular contractual provisions between equity and nonequity alliances, with the exception of auditing-rights provisions, which appear in 82% of the equity-alliance contracts and in only 26% of the nonequity ones. The same result (44% vs. 11%) holds in their study with Mellewigt (Reuer et al., forthcoming).

Furthermore, contractual and governance forms have some common and some different determinants, as Table 9.1 shows. Asset specificity and prior ties appear as the only common determinants of governance form (Reuer & Ariño, 2002; Reuer et al., forthcoming) and of contractual complexity (Poppo & Zenger, 2002; Reuer & Ariño, 2003; Reuer et al., forthcoming). Other determinants of governance form include transaction activities (Oxley, 1997; Pisano, 1989), technology scope (Oxley, 1997), the existence of potential alternative partners (Reuer & Ariño, 2002), and partner search costs (Reuer et al., forthcoming). On the other hand, contractual complexity seems associated with technological change (Poppo & Zenger, 2002), performance measurement difficulty (Poppo & Zenger, 2002), the alliance being time-bound (Reuer & Ariño, 2003), the strategic importance assigned to the alliance (Reuer & Ariño, 2003; Reuer et al., forthcoming), and the firm's age (Reuer et al., forthcoming).

Confusion between contractual and governance forms results in a simplified depiction of managerial control increasing as one moves from market-based to fully internalized exchanges. In the context of alliance research, it is often assumed that equity alliances confer greater control than nonequity alliances because shared ownership and the presence of a joint board serve as incentive alignment mechanisms in the former arrangement (e.g., Hennart, 1993; Chi, 1994). However, contracts of nonequity alliances can also incorporate numerous controls as specified in contracts. For instance, the 25 different types of control rights reported by Lerner and Merges (1998) provide evidence for this. Practitioners considered that the key control rights are those terms that relate to the management of the alliance: management of clinical trials, control of the initial manufacturing process, control of manufacturing after product approval, creation of exclusive territory for research and development (R&D) firms, and the creation of comarketing rights for R&D firms.

In sum, contractual form and governance forms serve different purposes. There is substantial contractual heterogeneity within particular governance forms, whereas some clauses are as likely to appear in equity as in nonequity alliance contracts. Furthermore, based on some recent research, it appears that contractual and governance forms share few determinants. The two are distinct features of alliance design, and subsuming contractual features within discrete governance structures may be misleading. Thus, alliance research delving into contractual characteristics is worth the effort in better understanding alliance design and the negotiation of collaborative relationships.

Table 9.1 Illustrative determinants of alliance contractual complexity and governance form

Determinants of contractual complexity and/or governance form:	*Contractual complexity*	*Governance form*	*Studies*
Asset specificity	X	X	Reuer and Ariño, 2002; Reuer, Ariño and Mellewigt, 2005
Prior ties	X	X	Poppo and Zenger, 2002; Reuer and Ariño, 2003; Reuer, Ariño and Mellewigt, 2005
Transaction activities		X	Oxley, 1997; Pisano, 1989
Technology scope		X	Oxley, 1997
Alternative partners		X	Reuer and Ariño, 2002
Partner search costs		X	Reuer, Ariño and Mellewigt, 2005
Technological change	X		Poppo and Zenger, 2002
Performance measurement difficulty	X		Poppo and Zenger, 2002
Alliance time-boundedness	X		Reuer and Ariño, 2003
Alliance strategic importance	X		Reuer and Ariño, 2003; Reuer, Ariño and Mellewigt, 2005
Firm age	X		Reuer, Ariño and Mellewigt, 2005

Contractual Complexity and Contractual Completeness: The Constructs

Contractual complexity and contractual completeness are two related concepts that are often used interchangeably in the literature or are confused. We start by putting forward our definitions of both terms and then we review the use of the terms in the literature.

We define *contractual complexity* as a design feature of firms' contractual agreements that reflects the number and stringency of the provisions employed (Reuer & Ariño, 2003). A contract with many, highly stringent provisions is more *complex* than one with few, less stringent provisions. Based on Luo (2002, pp. 904–905), we define *contractual completeness* as a design feature of firms' contractual agreements that reflects the extent to which all relevant terms and clauses are specified and the extent to which the contract accounts for unanticipated contingencies and delineates relevant guidelines for handling these contingencies.

Williamson (1985, p. 20) states that drafting, negotiating, and safeguarding an agreement,

> can be done with a great deal of care, in which case a complex document is drafted in which numerous contingencies are recognized, and appropriate adaptations by the parties are stipulated and agreed to in advance. Or the document can be very incomplete, the gaps to be filled in by the parties as the contingencies arise.

Implicitly, he is contrasting *complexity* and *incompleteness.* Later on in his book, Williamson (1985, p. 178) suggests that *complexity* and *completeness* do not necessarily go hand in hand:

"Complex contracts are invariably incomplete, and many are maladaptive."

In the context of air force engine procurement agreements, Crocker and Reynolds (1993, p. 126) describe *incomplete* exchange agreements as those in which "contracting parties intentionally leave unspecified their duties in certain contingencies." A totally *complete* contract is one in which all potential contingencies are covered; a totally *incomplete* contract places no strictures at all on the terms under which subsequent trade may be effected. Intermediate degrees of contractual completeness specify duties for some contingencies, leaving the other possibilities to future resolution as events unfold. Clearly, term specificity is contemplated here explicitly, whereas contingency adaptability is contemplated only implicitly.

Along these lines, Luo (2002, pp. 903–904) describes a *complete* contract as one that "simultaneously obviates opportunism through term specificity and bolsters adaptation through contingency adaptability." Term specificity and contingency adaptability are two dimensions of contract completeness. This characterization of contract *completeness* is consistent with Williamson's description of contractual *complexity*.

Poppo and Zenger (2002) consider more *complex* contracts to be ones that have a more elaborate specification of promises, obligations, and processes for dispute resolution. *Complex* contracts offer details on roles and responsibilities to be performed, specify procedures for monitoring and penalties for noncompliance, and determine outcomes or outputs to be delivered. Their treatment of the concept captures the term-specificity dimension appearing in Williamson's description of *complexity* and in Luo's (2002) characterization of *completeness*.

Ryall and Sampson (2003, p. 12) refer to contract *completeness* as "the degree to which required inputs, expected outputs and division of intellectual property rights are fully specified." This depiction focuses on the term-specificity dimension, but it does not consider the contingency-adaptability component of contractual completeness (Luo, 2002). In fact, they consider contract *completeness* as a single dimension reflecting contract "tightness," which they characterize as being correlated with the number of terms in the contract.

From this brief review we may infer that contract *complexity* and contract *completeness* are used in very different ways in the literature. We submit that whereas contract *complexity* is a feature of a contract per se, contract *completeness* is relative to the particular attributes of a transaction. For instance, a contract put in place for a simple transaction may not be *complex* but may be *complete,* just as a contract for a more elaborate exchange relationship may be *complex* but not *complete.* For a given transaction, we safely may say that a contract with more specific and detailed terms is more *complete* than one with less specific and detailed terms. However, when comparing contracts across different transactions, such a statement could not be affirmed: A contract with few terms might be more *complete* than one with more detailed terms if the former specifies all terms and clauses that are relevant to the transaction while the latter does not. Although *completeness* is a relevant feature of contracts, researchers may have to yield to studying contractual *complexity,* as assessing the former requires very detailed information about the transaction in question—information that researchers often lack.

Contractual Complexity and Contractual Completeness: The Measures

In this section, we review measures of contractual complexity and contractual completeness used in alliance studies (see Table 9.2). Although we believe they are all measures of contractual complexity, we respect the authors' labels, be they complexity, completeness, or something else.

In his study of a cross-section sample of alliances, Parkhe (1993) developed a measure of contractual safeguards. Specifically, he developed a checklist of contractual safeguards obtained from a computer-assisted search of the legal literature (cf. Macneil, 1978, 1981; Narasimhan, 1989;

Table 9.2 Measures of alliance contractual complexity used in the literature

Study	*Measure*
Parkhe (1993)	Contractual safeguards $= \frac{1}{36}\sum_{i=1}^{8} D_i$, D_i = i if provision i exists; $D_i = 0$ otherwise. Provisions: (1) periodic written reports of all relevant transactions; (2) prompt written notice of any departures from the agreement; (3) the right to examine and audit all relevant records through a firm of CPAs; (4) designation of certain information as proprietary and subject to confidentiality provisions of the contract; (5) non-use of proprietary information even after termination of agreement; (6) termination of agreement; (7) arbitration clauses; and (8) lawsuit provisions.
Deeds & Hill (1998)	Contractual safeguards $= \frac{1}{8}\sum_{i=1}^{8} D_i$, $D_i = 1$ if provision i exists; $D_i = 0$ otherwise Provisions: same as Parkhe (1993)
Poppo & Zenger (2002)	Contractual complexity: 1-item (7-point scale): "the formal contract is highly customized and required considerable work"
Reuer & Ariño (2002)	Contractual complexity: same measure as Parkhe (1993)
Luo (2202)	Two dimensions of contract completeness confirmed through factor analysis: • Term specificity: mean of responses assessing the degree to which a JV contract specifies relevant terms and clauses concerning the following (5-point scale) (detailed terms and clauses were listed under each of these categories, but are not reported): (1) how to set up the JV; (2) how to operate and manage the JV; and (3) how to cooperate and resolve conflict between partners; (4) how to terminate the JV. • Contingency adaptability: mean of responses to the extent to which (5-point scale): (1) term specification is adaptive for issues that are particularly vulnerable to an uncertain environment or resource availability; (2) the contract has specified major principles or guidelines for handling unanticipated contingencies as they arise; and (3) the contract has provided alternative solutions for responding to various contingencies that are likely to arise.
Reuer & Ariño (2003)	Contractual complexity: • same measure as Parkhe (1993) • modified measure: $\sum_{i=1}^{8} X_i$, $X_i = 1$ if provision i exists; $X_i = 0$ otherwise Two dimensions of contractual complexity identified through factor analysis of tetrachoric correlations among provisions (same mathematical formulas as before): • Partner control: provisions (4) to (8) (see Parkhe, 1993) • Operations control: provisions (1) to (3) (see Parkhe, 1993)

Study	*Measure*
Ryall & Sampson (2003)	Contract completeness: • $\sum_{i=1}^{6} X_i$, X_i = 1 if completeness clause i exists; X_i = 0 otherwise • dummy variable = 1 if the contract contains three or more completeness clauses; 0 otherwise Completeness clauses: (1) development specifications (such as tolerances) included; (2) time frame for completion of each stage specified; (3) number of employees to be contributed specified; (4) specific persons stipulated for management or other development work; (5) specific technologies to be contributed described; and (6) intellectual property rights defined over specific technologies.
Reuer, Ariño & Mellewigt (2005)	Contractual complexity: same measures as Parkhe (1993) and Reuer & Ariño (2002)

Practicing Law Institute, 1986) and documented eight provisions (see Table 9.2). These different types of alliance safeguards are arrayed in increasing order of strength or severity, so a weighting scheme for the stringency of contractual provisions can be adopted to arrive at the global measure of contractual complexity that appears in Table 9.2. This measure works as follows. D_i equals 1 if the first provision was employed, 0 otherwise; 2 if the second provision was employed, 0 otherwise; and so on (i = 1–8). All of the D_i's are summed up, so the summation term ranges from 0 to 36, and division by 36 yields a measure ranging from 0 to 1. When the variable takes on a value of 0, none of the eight provisions listed above are in place. When the variable assumes its maximum value of 1, all of the eight provisions appear in the alliance agreement.

Deeds and Hill (1998) modify Parkhe's measure in the following way: They asked respondents representing research alliances in the biotechnology industry to report on the inclusion in the contract of the same provisions as used by Parkhe (1993). However, they use as a measure of contractual safeguards the proportion of the total items included in the alliance (see Table 9.2), so they do not weight individual provisions by their stringency.

Reuer and Ariño (2002) use Parkhe's measure of contractual safeguards. In later articles (Reuer & Ariño, 2003; Reuer et al., forthcoming) they refer to this measure as contractual complexity. The first two articles by Reuer and Ariño (2002, 2003) are based on a sample of both equity and nonequity alliances across a number of industries, whereas their joint work with Mellewigt (Reuer et al., forthcoming) uses a sample of alliances in the telecommunications industry. For comparative purposes, Reuer and Ariño (2003) also assigned each provision the same weight (see this modified measure in Table 9.2). The authors obtain the same results with this unweighted measure—similar to the one used by Deeds and Hill (1998)—as with Parkhe's original weighted measure, which provided evidence that the stringency weights did not influence interpretations of the antecedents of more or less complex alliance agreements.

More important, however, is that Reuer and Ariño (2003) explore whether contractual complexity is in fact a unidimensional or multidimensional construct. They use exploratory factor analysis of tetrachoric correlations among the provisions used in Parkhe's measure. They find that the provisions load on the two factors in accordance with their order of stringency, and none of the provisions load in a manner inconsistent with their ranked stringency. They label the first factor *partner control,* as provisions loading highly on it deal with concerns about the partner's behavior outside the alliance itself, such as the use of information outside of the scope of the alliance, the ending of the collaborative agreement, and the use of outside parties to resolve disputes. The authors label the second factor *operations control,* as it relates more directly to the monitoring of the collaborative agreement during its life span (i.e., including contractual provisions such as rights to reports of relevant transaction, notification rights for departures to the agreement, and auditing rights).

In their study of information service exchanges, Poppo and Zenger (2002) measure contractual complexity by asking respondents to indicate their level of agreement with the following statement: The formal contract is highly customized and required considerable work (1 = strongly disagree, 7 = strongly agree).

As noted earlier, Luo (2002) identifies two dimensions of contract completeness: term specificity and contingency adaptability. These dimensions are measured as specified in Table 9.2. Factor analysis of data from a sample of manufacturing JVs confirmed the existence of term specificity and contingency adaptability as two factors. Luo explains that informants were asked to assess contract completeness, benchmarking with the industry's standard regarding the desired level of this completeness. However, it looks as though this instruction referred only to term specificity but not to contingency adaptability. If this is so, Luo's measures are measures of contractual completeness; otherwise, they measure contractual complexity.

Ryall and Sampson (2003) examine technology alliance contracts in the telecommunications equipment and microelectronics industries. They examine contract terms using a coding scheme that considers contract completeness as a characteristic not of the entire contract but just of some of the terms considered in it. More specifically, their coding scheme considers three dimensions that are mutually exclusive: contract completeness, monitoring, and penalties. For instance, the existence of a term related to *content of reviews specified* contributes to the monitoring dimension but does not add to contract completeness. The terms considered to affect contract completeness and the measures for this construct appear on Table 9.2. Terms excluded from the measure of contract completeness comprise monitoring terms (reviews of development work required, timing of reviews specified, content of reviews specified, physical audits of development work permitted, and reviews required of both firms), and penalty terms (financial penalties for underperformance and right to terminate for underperformance—as distinct from "material breach"). In this way, although they acknowledge that contracts are multidimensional, contract completeness is considered as unidimensional.

Despite the variety of labels used, all these measures capture the domain of the contractual complexity concept; although to different extents, they capture the number and stringency of the provisions used. However—with the possible exception of Luo's (2002) measure, as discussed above—they do not capture the contractual completeness concept as they do not depict whether all relevant terms and clauses are specified. The identification of distinct dimensions in some of the analyses (Luo, 2002; Reuer & Ariño, 2003) allows more fine-grained analyses than can be performed with more global or unidimensional measures. Most measures may be applied across a broad spectrum of alliance contracts as they are not specific to the alliance purpose, an exception being the measure used by Ryall and Sampson (2003), which is quite particular to technology alliances.

So far, we have discussed in this chapter that selecting contractual forms and governance forms are two distinct issues in alliance management. We have dug into the contents of alliance contracts and have argued that contractual complexity and contractual completeness are two separate constructs. We suggest that researchers may have to submit to studying contractual complexity instead of focusing on contractual completeness, as detailed knowledge of firms' exchange relationships is often lacking. Our review of contract-related measures shows that in fact they are generally measures of contractual complexity, not of contractual completeness. We turn now to the conditions identified in the literature that drive contractual complexity. We introduce them with a brief consideration of the nature of contracting costs and benefits.

Determinants of Contractual Complexity

Contractual provisions may be costly to negotiate, monitor, and enforce. If they were not, firms would strive to negotiate extremely detailed contracts for all of their alliances. At the same time, however, these costs can be efficient for firms to bear when the safeguards reduce the costs and performance losses from exchange hazards that stem from both environmental and behavioral uncertainties (Ring & Van de Ven, 1992).

Contracting involves both ex ante and ex post costs (Williamson, 1985). Ex ante costs include those of formalizing the agreement—determining a partner's legal competence to contract, reaching agreement on corresponding rights and responsibilities, conducting a legal search, and finding a means of legally employing the resources (Ring, 2002). They also include costs associated with gathering information about and crafting optimal responses to a potentially large set of feasible contingencies (Crocker & Reynolds, 1993). Ex post costs are often associated with contract renegotiation (Ring, 2002): legal fees, reorganization expenses, and opportunity costs due to management time (Reuer & Ariño, 2002).

Ex ante and ex post contracting costs are interdependent (Williamson, 1985), and the two are to be considered interactively (Ring, 2002). Conditions "that generate increased contracting costs should result in efficient contracts being less complete, whereas conditions that exacerbate the potential for ex post inefficiencies should lead to more exhaustive agreements" (Crocker & Reynolds, 1993, p. 127). On the one hand, as suggested by Crocker and Reynolds (1993), conditions increasing the likelihood of opportunistic behavior augment the potential losses from misbehavior and would result in more complex contracts. On the other hand, conditions leading to higher environmental uncertainty augment ex ante contracting costs, as foreseeing future contingencies is more difficult than if environmental uncertainty is low. The parties may prefer to design less complex agreements—thus reducing actual ex ante costs—and to renegotiate the contract if needed in the future—possibly incurring in ex post costs.

In this section, we review a number of conditions that may affect ex ante and ex post contracting costs, as well as contracting benefits. The illustrative conditions are the level of transaction-specific investments, the existence of prior ties between the parties, whether the alliance is time-bound or open-ended, the strategic importance partners assign to the alliance, and the level of the costs associated to searching for alternative partners (see Table 9.1 above). For each condition, we elaborate briefly on how it influences contractual complexity, and we present germane research results.

Transaction-Specific Investments

When asset specificity is low, resources can be deployed to other relationships or businesses without difficulty and partner identity is not important (Klein, Crawford, & Alchian, 1978; Williamson, 1991). As the partner cannot threaten to hold up the firm under this condition, the firm has little incentive to bear the costs associated with designing a more complex contract in an attempt to stabilize the relationship. However, when a firm makes transaction-specific investments in an alliance, the partner can jeopardize the alliance by threatening dissolution, which would mean the firm would lose the value of specialized assets. Faced with such threats, managers must evaluate the value losses and ex post renegotiation costs they would experience from holdup behavior against the additional costs of negotiating safeguards into their alliance contracts ex ante. As the potential value loss increases with investments in specific assets, managers will find it advantageous to negotiate more complex contracts to cover the consequences of breach and termination as well as designing the processes by which such threats will be handled (Dyer, 1997; Poppo & Zenger, 2002; Reuer & Ariño, 2003).

Poppo and Zenger (2002) find support for this proposition, as their results indicate an increased usage of more customized, complex contracts as asset specificity increases. Reuer and Ariño (2003) present similar findings: The greater the transaction-specific investment in an alliance, the greater the number and stringency of contractual provisions built into the alliance contract. This result holds using unidimensional, both weighted and nonweighted, measures of contract complexity. Their disaggregate analysis contemplating two dimensions of contract complexity—partner-control provisions and operations-control provisions—suggests that firms use the more stringent provisions oriented to control the partner as asset specificity increases, but the presence or absence of transaction-specific investments has no apparent influence on the usage of weaker contractual provisions designed for monitoring an alliance's operations.

In contrast, Reuer, Ariño, and Mellewigt (forthcoming) find no significant influence of asset specificity on contractual complexity, whereas asset specificity relates instead to the decision to adopt an equity alliance over a nonequity alliance. In order to examine whether asset specificity leads to greater contractual complexity in alliances without additional governance mechanisms in place, they performed their analyses in a subsample of nonequity alliances, obtaining similar insignificant results. The authors attribute their findings to the empirical setting—German telecommunications companies. Given the high technological uncertainty present in this environment, the likelihood of contractual renegotiation is very high, so complex contracts are also likely to require costly renegotiations. Faced with the risk of holdup under these circumstances, managers may prefer to protect themselves by turning to a governance solution instead of a contractual solution (e.g., Poppo & Zenger, 2002).

Previous Ties

Although the threat of opportunism will be a function of the particular attributes of the alliance in question, it can also be shaped by firms' prior collaborative histories with one another. Relational contracts are possible because repeated exchanges between firms induce cooperation, as the possibility of putting an end to relations acts as a self-enforcing sanction (e.g., Telser, 1980). By contrast, firms entering into relationships with new partners support these relationships with formal contractual provisions and rely upon the court system for enforcement (Johnson, McMillan, & Woodruff, 2002). Thus, on the one hand, the existence of prior relationships among the partners reduces behavioral uncertainty and may allow for a lower level of contractual complexity. On the other hand, those prior relationships may result in lower contracting costs, hence allowing the partners to put in place more complex contracts without incurring higher contract negotiation costs. Which of these effects dominates will dictate the use of complex contracts as substitutes or complements to trust.

There are two mechanisms by which successive collaborative relationships between firms can reduce behavioral uncertainty and hence make possible that firms avoid the costs of designing more complex alliances. The first mechanism is the trust that emerges from successive collaborative relationships between firms, which may substitute for more elaborate governance because the firms have already invested in relationship building and have borne setup costs, which would need to be incurred for alternative safeguards (e.g., Klein, 1980). Dyer (1997) suggests that Japanese automakers' networks have lower transaction costs than their U.S. counterparts because they engage in repeated exchanges. Related evidence from buyer-supplier relations confirms that interorganizational trust allows firms to economize on negotiation costs (Zaheer, McEvily, & Perrone, 1998). In sum, repeat alliances pose less moral-hazard concerns (Gulati, 1998) than first-time alliances because a partner's behavior is more predictable, as is its competence for delivering the expected contributions (Ring, 2002).

A second mechanism by which successive collaborative relationships between firms reduce behavioral uncertainty is the development of interorganizational routines. Such routines allow firms to avoid the costs of detailing mechanisms for monitoring and coordination (Gulati, 1998; Zollo, Reuer, & Singh, 2002). Parkhe (1993) shows that partners' cooperative history reduces coordination efforts and compliance costs; in turn, these diminish the need for contractual safeguards. Similarly, Dyer and Singh (1998) suggest that the relationship-specific knowledge that emerges from frequent and intense partner interactions builds a firm's relational capabilities, which can improve the efficiency of alliances.

However, as already anticipated, when the parties share a history of frequent exchange in which promises have been fulfilled, contract negotiation costs are lower (Ring, 2002). Thus, prior ties may allow for the design of complex contracts without incurring costs that partners transacting for the first time need to bear for a similar level of contractual complexity. Ring (2002) suggests that when partners have worked together in other alliances, they have discussed certain conditions and agreed on them already; to the extent that some of these conditions are "boilerplate" or common terms, including them in a new alliance contract entails no additional cost. Furthermore, partners with prior relationships have developed a mutual knowledge that allows them to discuss behavioral uncertainty issues that would be extremely costly for newly transacting partners to identify or address:

> Previous cooperation fosters a climate of openness that is essential to discussing behavioral problems. . . . By the same token, two parties that have cooperated earlier tend to be more collaborative in adapting to unanticipated environmental hazards. In order to jointly gain greater rents from cooperation and adaptation, they are likely to keep a contract's contingency adaptability at a high level. (Luo, 2002, p. 907)

Previous relationships allow partners to learn what they need to specify and what contingencies to consider (Mayer, 2004).

Reuer and Ariño (2003) find that in the presence of prior alliances, firms specify fewer provisions relating to alliance operation control. However, the existence of prior ties does not influence the use of provisions concerning partner control. These results support the argument that the routines built through past relationships preclude the need to use contracts in order to set up coordination mechanisms, hence resulting in less-complex contracts. Conversely, these findings undermine the argument that contracts are used as substitutes for trust. Along the same lines, Luo (2002) finds no significant association between prior cooperation and the use of specific terms to obviate opportunism in the contract.

Ryall and Sampson (2003) show that when firms are engaged in multiple alliances with the same partner, some boilerplate provisions, such as arbitration clauses, are identical between alliance contracts. This provides evidence that partners economize contracting costs by incorporating into their new contracts clauses already negotiated and agreed-upon for past contracts. Reuer, Zollo, and Singh (2002) also find that firms tend to be more apt to alter alliance contracts when they have collaborated with each other in the past.

Poppo and Zenger (2002) find that prior relationships between firms lead to more detailed contracts. Ryall and Sampson (2003) interpret this result to provide evidence that prior relationships allow partners to learn more about each other and draft better and, perhaps, tighter contracts. Consistent with this, Luo (2002) shows that prior cooperation is significantly and positively associated with contingency adaptability. Ryall and Sampson (2003) find that contracts are more detailed when firms have allied with each other previously; however, contracts are less complex in the case of concurrent alliances with the same partner, even when alliance duration and technology breadth are controlled for. Their interpretation of these findings is that:

> firms gain experience in drafting effective collaborative agreements with prior alliances, which allows these firms to specify rights, obligations and development costs at lower cost. In contrast, concurrent alliance relationships with the same partner may operate as an informal means to deter noncooperative behavior, because such behavior can affect the future prospects not only of the current alliance, but also of the concurrent alliance. (Ryall & Sampson, 2003, p. 4)

This interpretation is consistent with the fact that learning about what to specify and what contingencies to consider may be derived from prior ties, whereas concurrent ties may provide this learning opportunity only at a later time. Luo's (2002) argument that prior cooperation allows the companies to discuss—and agree upon—issues that newly transacting partners would not be able even to identify is in consonance with this set of research findings. Case study research by Mayer and Argyres (2004) also supports this reasoning.

Time-Boundedness

Strategic alliances designed to operate for a prespecified length of time experience lower environmental uncertainty than alliances with open-ended durations. In the former case, partners are in better position to anticipate different future states and efficiently specify their duties and rights under these different states (e.g., Noldeke & Schmidt, 1995). As partners have negotiated explicit time bounds on their alliances, they are also more likely to be aware of related issues covered in alliance contracts, such as ownership of proprietary technology, disclosures of confidential information, and the alliance's termination. On the contrary, when firms place no bounds on the duration of the alliance, it can be costly to anticipate future economic conditions and craft contractual provisions that provide adequate responses. So as to avoid these transaction costs, firms tend to rely on incomplete contracts under these conditions (Crocker & Reynolds, 1993).

The presence or absence of time bounds on alliances can affect not only the level of environmental uncertainty faced by the partners but also the level of behavioral uncertainty. Open-ended alliances are self-enforcing agreements in that the potential gains from future collaboration provide a safeguard against opportunistic behavior meant to appropriate more immediate payoffs (Telser, 1980). As suggested by Hill (1990), opportunism is viable if the future is *not* important to the provoker. By contrast, the shadow of the future is shorter in time-bound alliances, and these do not support a tit-for-tat equilibrium of cooperation that can protect against opportunism (Axelrod, 1984). Given these characteristics, time-bound alliances do not lend themselves to acting as self-enforcing agreements, and formal contractual provisions may be required to safeguard them.

In sum, alliances with a prespecified duration entail lower environmental but higher behavioral uncertainty than open-ended alliances. Lower environmental uncertainty entails lower contracting costs, which would result in more complex contracts, and higher behavioral uncertainty provides incentives to design more complex contracts as well. Thus, it is to be expected that alliances with a prespecified duration have more complex contracts than open-ended alliances.

Turning to the empirical evidence, Crocker and Reynolds (1993) find—although in a nonalliance context—that more distant dates of contract performance lead to more incomplete exchange agreements because of the higher environmental uncertainty and the consequently increased costs of implementing more complete contracts. Luo (2002) shows that the longer a JV is expected to last, the higher it ranks in terms of contingency adaptability, resulting in more complex contracts along this dimension of contract that deals with environmental uncertainty.

Focusing on the impact of behavioral uncertainty, Parkhe (1993) shows that longtime horizons decrease uncertainty regarding potential opportunism, which in turn diminishes the need for complex contracts. Luo (2002) finds a negative impact of expected duration on term specificity, and Reuer and Ariño (2003) provide evidence that alliance agreements with specified durations tend to rely more heavily on the partner-control provisions but less on operation-control provisions.

Strategic Importance of the Alliance

Increasingly, alliances are between actual or potential competitors, involve two-way knowledge transfers, and have global market aspirations (e.g., Hagedoorn, 1993; Gomes-Casseres, 1996). As a reflection of these changes, firms are applying more disciplined processes for selecting partners and negotiating collaborative agreements (e.g., Harbison & Pekar, 1998) and are implementing positions or functions dedicated to managing their strategic alliances (e.g., Kale, Dyer, & Singh, 2002). As a result, partners are more exposed to the hazards such alliances involve (Koza & Lewin, 1998; Singh & Mitchell, 1996), which include the risk of having a competitor appropriate key strategic resources (Khanna, Gulati, & Nohria, 1998; Branstetter & Sakakibara, 2002). Firms are therefore justified in bearing additional costs to clarify rights and obligations concerning the scope of the alliance (Borys & Jemison, 1989), ownership claims on proprietary technology provided to or created during the alliance, and the management of the alliance's termination.

In light of these risks, managers will also have an incentive to detail the ways in which strategically important alliances will be monitored and any disputes that arise will be resolved as the alliance evolves (Ring & Van de Ven, 1994; Doz, 1996). Additionally, strategically important alliances tend to involve more complexity (Hagedoorn, 1993), making it more costly to reach agreement for establishing mutual consent (Ring, 2002). The strategic importance a firm assigns to an alliance reflects the firm's attitude and commitment to it (Deeds & Hill, 1998). The more valuable the contributed resources, the more extended contract negotiations will be (Ring, 2002). Thus, managers will be more willing to dedicate the additional resources that negotiating a complex contract entails when it refers to a strategically important alliance.

Reuer and Ariño (2003) and Reuer et al. (forthcoming) demonstrate that the greater the strategic importance of an alliance, the more complex the alliance contract is. These results hold when using a unidimensional measure of contractual complexity, both weighted and nonweighted. However, when using disaggregate measures, Reuer and Ariño (2003) find that the strategic importance of alliances shapes the usage of partner-control provisions in alliance contracts but has no impact on firms' adoption of the provisions for alliance operation control. These results speak of the importance that behavioral uncertainty takes on for agreements that firms view as strategically important.

Search Costs

Searching for potential exchange partners can be costly, given the various expenses incurred when scrutinizing potential partners and the need to involve agents in the process (e.g., Arrow, 1974). Screening potential exchange partners takes time and negotiation entails delays, and these costs are nontrivial (Wernerfelt, 2004).

These inefficiencies in the market for alliance partners suggest that alliance termination may affect firms unfavorably, even if their commitments to a collaborative arrangement are not entirely partner-specific. Because search costs for an alliance partner would need to be incurred in locating a new partner, the firm has an incentive to design a more complex contract to allocate duties, design processes for unforeseeable outcomes, and specify exchanges and remedies in more precise terms.

The greater the search costs involved in locating a partner for a particular transaction, the greater the firm's incentive to bear the costs in designing more complex contractual arrangements. By contrast, if the firm can find an alternative partner with relative ease, the contract can be comparatively simple because the costs of switching to another exchange partner are lower, and it is therefore more likely that the relationship will be self-enforcing. Empirical evidence on the incidence of search costs on alliance contractual complexity is scarce, with Reuer et al. (forthcoming) finding that the greater the search costs for an alliance partner, the greater the complexity of the alliance contract.

Conclusion

Our purpose in this chapter is to offer an overview of management research on strategic alliance contracts, which is still relatively scarce given the difficulties in accessing this kind of data. We distinguish alliance contractual form and governance form, as these are often confused in the literature even if they serve different purposes. We also trace the distinction between two related constructs frequently mixed in the literature: contractual complexity and contractual completeness. It seems to us that in the absence of detailed knowledge about transaction attributes, it is more appropriate to consider and refer to contractual complexity than to contractual completeness. In fact, most of the measures used in the literature—even if labeled in different ways—assess contractual complexity and not completeness. Finally, we examine the conditions that may warrant the design of more or less complex alliance contracts depending on the effects of those conditions on environmental and behavioral uncertainties and hence on the costs of and benefits from contracting.

More work remains to be done. We need to understand better how ex ante and ex post contracting costs interact in the presence of various levels of behavioral and environmental uncertainties, and what the implications are for decisions concerning contractual complexity. In a related vein, we need to understand whether decisions regarding contractual complexity and governance form are made simultaneously or sequentially, and the extent to which one and another type of uncertainty influences those decisions may offer interesting suggestions for management practice.

One area that has received virtually no empirical attention is that of contracting as a process, the outcome of which goes beyond a legal document. This is an important area of research, as the contracting process may have an influence on the behavioral uncertainty the partners will face once in the alliance. "In contracting, the legal requirement of mutual consent and commitment—a meeting of the minds—is achieved by [a] process of sense making" (Ring & Van de Ven, 1994, p. 100). And sense-making may result in a psychological contract that may complement or substitute the formal document.

In Ring and Van de Ven's (1994) framework, contracting is a part of the commitments stage of alliances, a stage in which "the 'wills of the parties meet' (Commons, 1950) when they reach an agreement on the obligations and rules for future action in the relationship" (p. 98). Sense-making will occur only if the parties interact intensively. Through these interactions, the parties assess their possible compatibility and they start forming perceptions about one another. The parties may develop a psychological contract about the terms of the relationship (Ring & Van de Ven, 1994), a benefit of the contracting process that is not considered in current discussions of contracting costs and benefits.

Arguably, both a sound legal contract and a psychological contract are necessary for an alliance to develop favorably. On the one hand, an excessive focus on legal issues may lead to distrust among parties. On the other hand, the absence of formal legal structures paves the way to an abuse of trust. Thus, a balance between formal and informal aspects on contracting may be desirable. A well-managed contracting process centered in sense-making and mutual understanding can produce both a tight legal contract that sets specific terms and plans ways to adapt to a number of contingencies, as well as a psychological contract that allows the parties to reach mutually satisfactory agreements when facing unforeseen circumstances. We believe that research into alliance contracts along these lines will be important for moving beyond the literature's emphasis on discrete governance structures and for providing more detailed guidance to managers designing and negotiating collaborative agreements.

References

Argyres, N., & Mayer, K. J. (2004). *Contract design capability and contract performance by high technology firms: Implications for the roles of managers, engineers, and lawyers.* Working Paper, Boston University School of Management.

Ariño, A., & Reuer, J. J. (2004). Designing and renegotiating strategic alliance contracts. *Academy of Management Executive, 18,* 37–48.

Arrow, K. J. (1974). *The limits of organization.* New York: W. W. Norton.

Axelrod, R. (1984). *The evolution of cooperation.* New York: Basic Books.

Balakrishnan, S., & Koza, M. P. (1993). Information asymmetry, adverse selection and joint ventures. *Journal of Economic Behavior and Organization, 20,* 99–117.

Borys, B., & Jemison, D. B. (1989). Hybrid arrangements as strategic alliances: Theoretical issues in organizational combinations. *Academy of Management Review, 14,* 234–249.

Branstetter, L. G., & Sakakibara, M. (2002). When do research consortia work well and why? Evidence from Japanese panel data. *American Economic Review, 92,* 143–159.

Campbell, E., & Reuer, J. J. (2001). International alliance negotiations: Legal issues for general managers. *Business Horizons, 44,* 19–26.

Chi, T. (1994). Trading in strategic resources: Necessary conditions, transaction cost problems, and choice of exchange structure. *Strategic Management Journal, 15,* 271–290.

Commons, J. R. (1950). *The economics of collective action.* Madison: University of Wisconsin Press.

Crocker, K. J., & Reynolds, K. (1993). The efficiency of incomplete contracts: An empirical analysis of air force engine procurement. *RAND Journal of Economics, 24*(1), 126–146.

Deeds, D. L., & Hill, C. W. L. (1998). An examination of opportunistic action within research alliances: Evidence from the biotechnology industry. *Journal of Business Venturing, 14,* 141–163.

Doz, Y. L. (1996). The evolution of cooperation in strategic alliances: Initial conditions or learning processes? [special issue] *Strategic Management Journal, 17,* 55–84.

Dyer, J. H. (1997). Effective interfirm collaboration: How firms minimize transaction costs and maximize transaction value. *Strategic Management Journal, 18,* 535–556.

Dyer, J. H., & Singh, H. (1998). The relational view: Cooperative strategy and sources of interorganizational competitive advantage. *Academy of Management Review, 23,* 660–679.

Gomes-Casseres, B. (1996). *The alliance revolution: The new shape of business rivalry.* Cambridge, MA: Harvard University Press.

Gulati, R. (1995). Does familiarity breed trust? The implications of repeated ties for contractual choice in alliances. *Academy of Management Journal, 38,* 85–112.

Gulati R. (1998). Alliances and networks. *Strategic Management Journal, 19,* 293–317.

Hagedoorn, J. (1993). Understanding the rationale of strategic technology partnering: Interorganizational modes of cooperation and sectoral differences. *Strategic Management Journal, 14,* 371–385.

Harbison, J. R., & Pekar, P., Jr. (1998). *Smart alliances: A practical guide to repeatable success.* San Francisco, CA: Jossey-Bass.

Hennart, J. F. (1988). A transaction cost theory of equity joint ventures. *Strategic Management Journal, 9,* 361–374.

Hennart, J. F. (1993). Explaining the swollen middle: Why most transactions are a mix of "market" and "hierarchy." *Organization Science, 4,* 529–547.

Hennart, J. F., & Reddy, S. (1997). The choice between mergers/acquisitions and joint ventures: The case of Japanese investors in the U.S. *Strategic Management Journal, 18,* 1–12.

Hill, C. W. L. (1990). Cooperation, opportunism, and the invisible hand: Implications for transaction cost theory. *Academy of Management Review, 15*(3), 500–513.

James, H. S., Jr. (2000). Separating contract from governance. *Managerial and Decision Economics, 21,* 47–61.

Johnson, S., McMillan, J., & Woodruff, C. (2002). Courts and relational contracts. *Journal of Law, Economics, and Organization, 18,* 221–277.

Kale, P., Dyer, J. H., & Singh, H. (2002). Alliance capability, stock market response, and long-term alliance success: The role of the alliance function. *Strategic Management Journal, 23,* 747–767.

Kale, P. & P. Puranam. 2004. Choosing equity stakes in technology-sourcing relationships: An integrative framework. *California Management Review, 46*(3): 77–99.

Khanna, T., Gulati, R., & Nohria, N. (1998). The dynamics of learning alliances: Competition, cooperation, and relative scope. *Strategic Management Journal, 19,* 193–210.

Klein, B. (1980). Transaction cost determinants of "unfair" contractual arrangements. *American Economic Review, 70,* 356–362.

Klein, B., Crawford, R. A., & Alchian, A. (1978). Vertical integration, appropriable rents, and the competitive contracting process. *Journal of Law and Economics, 21*(2), 297–326.

Koza, M. P., & Lewin, A. Y. (1998). The co-evolution of strategic alliances. *Organization Science, 9*(3), 255–264.

Lerner, J., & Merges, R. P. (1998). The control of technology alliances: An empirical analysis of the biotechnology industry. *Journal of Industrial Economics, 46,* 125–156.

Luo, Y. (2002). Contract, cooperation and performance in international joint ventures. *Strategic Management Journal, 23,* 903–920.

Macneil, I. R. (1978). Contracts: Adjustments of long-term economic relations under classical, neoclassical, and relational contract law. *Northwestern University Law Review, 72,* 854–902.

Macneil, I. R. (1981). Economic analysis of contractual relations: Its shortfalls and the need for a "rich classificatory apparatus." *Northwestern University Law Review, 75,* 1018–1063.

Mayer, K. J. (2004). *The role of prior relationships on contract design: An analysis of early termination provisions.* Working Paper, Marshall School of Business.

Mayer, K. J., & Argyres, N. S. (2004). Learning to contract: Evidence from the personal computer industry. *Organization Science, 15*(4), 394–410.

Narasimhan, S. (1989). Relationship or boundary? Handling successive contracts. *California Management Review, 77,* 1077–1122.

Noldeke, G., & Schmidt, K. (1995). Option contracts and renegotiation: A solution to the hold-up problem. *Rand Journal of Economics, 26,* 163–179.

Osborn, R. N., & Baughn, C. C. (1990). Forms of interorganizational governance for multinational alliances. *Academy of Management Journal, 33,* 503–519.

Oxley, J. E., (1997). Appropriability hazards and governance in strategic alliances: A transaction cost approach. *Journal of Law, Economics, and Organization, 13,* 387–409.

Parkhe, A. (1993). Strategic alliance structuring: A game theoretic and transaction costs examination of interfirm cooperation. *Academy of Management Journal, 36,* 794–829.

Pisano, G. P. (1989). Using equity participation to support exchange: Evidence from the biotechnology industry. *Journal of Law, Economics, and Organization, 5,* 109–126.

Pisano, G. P. (1990). The R&D boundaries of the firm: An empirical analysis. *Administrative Science Quarterly, 35,* 153–176.

Poppo, L., & Zenger, T. (2002). Do formal contracts and relational governance function as substitutes or complements? *Strategic Management Journal, 23*(8), 707–725.

Practicing Law Institute. (1986). *Corporate partnering: Advantages for emerging and established companies.* New York: Practicing Law Institute.

Reuer, J. J., & Ariño, A. (2002). Contractual renegotiations in strategic alliances. *Journal of Management, 28*(1), 47–68.

Reuer, J. J., & Ariño, A. (2003). Strategic alliances as contractual forms. *Academy of Management Best Paper Proceedings.*

Reuer, J. J., A. Ariño, & T. Mellewigt. (forthcoming). Entrepreneurial alliances as contractual forms. *Journal of Business Venturing.*

Reuer, J. J., & Koza, M. P. (2000). Asymmetric information and joint venture performance: Theory and evidence for domestic and international joint ventures. *Strategic Management Journal, 21,* 81–88.

Reuer, J. J., Zollo, M., & Singh, H. (2002). Post-formation dynamics in strategic alliances. *Strategic Management Journal, 23,* 135–151.

Ring, P. S. (2002). The role of contracts in strategic alliances. In F. Contractor and P. Lorange (Eds.), *Cooperative strategies and strategic alliances* (pp. 145–162). London: Elsevier Science.

Ring, P. S., & Van de Ven, A. H. (1992). Structuring cooperative relationships between organizations. *Strategic Management Journal, 13,* 483–498.

Ring, P. S., & Van de Ven, A. H. (1994). Developmental processes of cooperative interorganizational relationships. *Academy of Management Review, 19,* 90–118.

Ryall, M. D., & Sampson, R. C. (2003). *Do prior alliances influence contract structure? Evidence from technology alliance contracts* (Simon School of Business Working Paper No. FR 03-11). Abstract retrieved March 7, 2005, from http://ssrn.com/abstract=396601.

Singh, K., & Mitchell, W. (1996). Precarious collaboration: Business survival after partners shut down or form new partnerships [special issue]. *Strategic Management Journal, 17,* 99–116.

Telser, L. G. (1980). A theory of self-enforcing agreements. *Journal of Business, 53,* 27–44.

Wernerfelt, B. (2004). Governance of adjustments. *Journal of Business, 77*(2), 3–24.

Williamson, O. E. (1979). Transaction-cost economics: The governance of contractual relations. *Journal of Law and Economics, 22,* 233–261.

Williamson, O. E. (1985). *The economic institutions of capitalism.* New York: Free Press.

Williamson, O. E. (1991). Comparative economic organization: The analysis of discrete structural alternatives. *Administrative Science Quarterly, 36,* 269–296.

Zaheer, A., McEvily, B., & Perrone, V. (1998). Does trust matter? Exploring the effects of interorganizational and interpersonal trust on performance. *Organization Science, 9,* 123–141, 141–159.

Zollo, M., Reuer, J. J., & Singh, H. (2002). Interorganizational routines and performance in strategic alliances. *Organization Science, 13,* 701–713.

10

Interorganizational Trust

Akbar Zaheer

Jared Harris

It has become increasingly clear that interorganizational trust is an important factor affecting the actions and performance of organizations engaged in dyadic and network relationships such as strategic alliances. Scholars from a number of disciplines—from strategic management and organization theory to economics and marketing—have conceptually and empirically addressed the role that interorganizational trust, as well as trust in general, plays in firm behavior and performance. In this chapter, we look broadly at the scholarship in the area of interorganizational trust, with special attention to the extant empirical work. We take a broad-brush approach to the literature, aiming to be inclusive but focusing primarily on the burgeoning literature on the topic within the strategy and organizational literature.

The goal of the chapter is to provide a comprehensive, high-level, definitive statement on interorganizational trust, an area of particular interest to both scholars and practitioners of strategic alliances. Specifically, in the following sections of the chapter, we survey the literature on interorganizational trust, identify and integrate the key themes that emerge from the empirical contributions on the subject, and explore theoretical issues around conducting research in this domain, concluding with directions for future research in both theoretical and methodological areas.

Interorganizational Trust: The State of the Art

Issues associated with organizational trust have generated a great deal of broad scholarly interest in the field, as evidenced by the dozens of articles and special issues of the leading journals that have been devoted to the theme of trust. Yet, although there exists a significant amount of literature on trust in an organizational context—as well as research in related areas such as alliances, social networks, and interpersonal trust—scholarly work specifically dealing with interorganizational trust is a more limited area of research. Empirical

AUTHORS' NOTE: We are grateful for review comments from Andy Van de Ven, Bill McEvily, David Souder, Andy Wicks, and an anonymous reviewer. Although their input has greatly improved the paper, all errors remain our own.

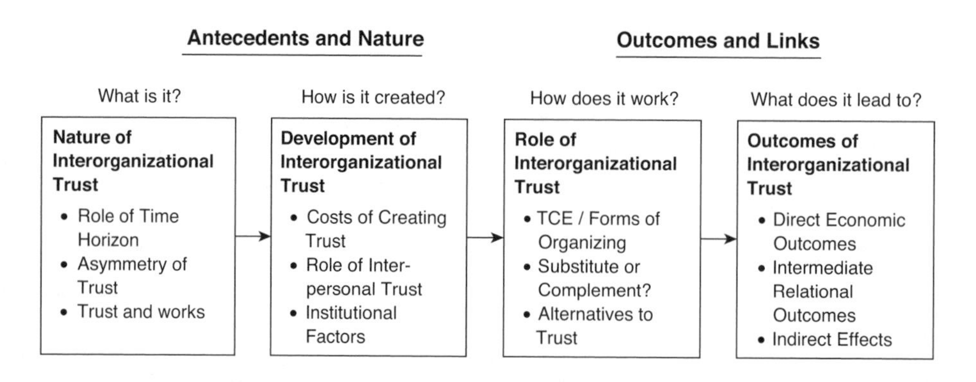

Figure 10.1 A Staged Model of Interorganizational Trust: Four Empirical Themes

work on the topic is an even smaller—yet growing—subset of this literature; a grasp of the existing empirical findings is crucial to understanding and taking stock of the current state of the field. In this section, we focus on synthesizing the empirical research on the subject in an effort to establish both what we know and what we do not about interorganizational trust, thereby identifying areas for future research.

In surveying the empirical work on interorganizational trust, individual findings tend to fall into one of four primary areas of inquiry. We use these areas in turn to formulate a staged model of interorganizational trust. These areas are the nature of interorganizational trust, the development of interorganizational trust, the role of interorganizational trust, and the outcomes of interorganizational trust. These four areas can be seen as exploring the following four questions, with respect to interorganizational trust: What is it? How is it created? How does it work? What does it lead to?

We further divide each of these topic areas into several subcategories that have occupied the primary interest of empirical research in each area (see Figure 10.1). We discuss the empirical findings and implications from the organizational literature according to these four themes in the conceptual order of the staged model, addressing the nature of trust and its development, role, and outcomes. In addition to the synopsis of empirical work and theoretical discussion of the themes, also see Table 10.1 for an article-by-article summary of empirical work on interorganizational trust in the organizational literature.

Nature of Interorganizational Trust

What is the nature of trust between organizations? The pursuit of an answer to this question remains the focal subject of much interorganizational trust research. We begin our discussion by defining interorganizational trust. A commonly used definition of interorganizational trust is the extent to which members of one organization hold a collective trust orientation toward another organization (Zaheer, McEvily, & Perrone, 1998). Relatedly, Currall and Inkpen (2002) draw attention to the socially constructed shared history within an organization toward another organization that constitutes a collective orientation. In this vein, it is important to avoid anthropomorphizing the organization by treating interorganizational trust as equivalent to an individual trusting another individual.

The fact that trust is such a broad concept, complicated by its various connotations in common usage, results in researchers parsing trust into a variety of finer-grained dimensions, teasing out various aspects of trust. These dimensions

(Text continues on page 181)

Table 10.1 Empirical Research on Interorganizational Trust

Study	*How Interorg. Trust is Defined/ Measured*	*Findings: Antecedents*	*Findings: Consequences*	*Non Findings or Mixed Results*	*Relation Between Interorg. and Interpers. Trust*	*Theoretical Framework*
1. Van de Ven and Walker (1984)	'Norms of equity': satisfaction with the other party's commitment fulfillment, fairness, and distributive justice.Measured via survey.	N/A	N/A	No support for claim that monitoring and formalization destroy trust; no support for claim that trust leads to increased resource dependence.	N/A	Exchange theory and distributive justice.
2. Anderson & Narus (1990)	Trust: a firm's belief that another organization will act to create positive outcomes for the firm. Cooperation: coordinated interdependent action with expected reciprocity. Measured via survey.	Cooperation builds trust.	Trust leads to satisfaction with the relationship. (Which presumably would increase propensity to cooperate, making the causal chain circular.)	N/A	N/A	Various management theories.
3. Heide & John (1990)	Joint action: the degree of interpenetration of organizational boundaries. Measured via survey.	Continuity expectations, verification efforts, and specific investments positively influence joint action (cooperation).	N/A	None with respect to joint action.	Implied close link; concept of joint action strongly parallels the idea of 'closeness' in interpersonal relationships.	TCE and various other management theories.

(Continued)

Table 10.1 (Continued)

Study	*How Interorg. Trust is Defined/ Measured*	*Findings: Antecedents*	*Findings: Consequences*	*Non Findings or Mixed Results*	*Relation Between Interorg. and Interpers. Trust*	*Theoretical Framework*
4. Heide & John (1992)	Supportive relational exchange norms: expectations of mutuality of interest that prescribe stewardship behavior designed to enhance the wellbeing of the relationship as a whole. Measured via survey.	N/A	Relational norms (flexibility, information exchange, solidarity) mediate the positive relationship between investment in specific assets and vertical control.	N/A	N/A	TCE and social norms.
5. Heide and Miner (1992)	Four dimensions of 'interorganizational cooperation': flexibility, information exchange, shared problem solving, restraint in use of power.	Relationship extendedness linked to all dimensions of cooperation. Frequency of interaction linked to some dimensions.	N/A	No support for the claim that performance ambiguity reduces interorganizational cooperation.	N/A	Game theory
6. Larson (1992)	Trust: expectations of high reliability and low opportunism.	History of interaction builds trust between organizations. Building trust also requires significant resource allocation.	Trust appears to be related to the successful governance of entrepreneurial firm networks.	N/A	Implied close relationship, given the context of small, entrepreneurial firms.	Exploratory inductive study. Uses network perspective and new institutional theory.
7. Moorman, Zaltman, & Deshpande (1992)	Trust: willingness to rely on an exchange partner in whom one has confidence. Measured via survey.	N/A	Trust increases the quality of interactions, cooperative involvement, and commitment to the relationship.	Trust is not shown to increase utilization of information.	Distinguishes between the two; trust examined in intra- and interorg. relationships, with slightly different results.	Various management theories.

Study	*How Interorg. Trust is Defined/ Measured*	*Findings: Antecedents*	*Findings: Consequences*	*Non Findings or Mixed Results*	*Relation Between Interorg. and Interpers. Trust*	*Theoretical Framework*
8. Seabright et al. (1992)	Not directly addressed; main focus on the dissolution of dyadic relationships. Attachment in the dyad affects continuity of the relationship.	Diminishing 'resource fit' in the dyad leads to dissolution; attachment between boundary spanners lessens the likelihood of dissolution.	Decreased interpersonal commitment between boundary spanners can lead to the demise of the relationship.	None	Suggests that boundary spanner attachments may be "critical," and that such attachments "may rely on personal knowledge and trust."	Resource dependence perspective and org. theory related to commitment.
9. Moorman, Deshpande, & Zaltman (1993)	Trust: willingness to rely on an exchange partner in whom one has confidence. Measured via survey.	Perceptions of the other party's expertise, sincerity, integrity, tact, timeliness, and confidentiality increase trust. Perceived congeniality and org. formalization decrease trust.	N/A	Factors such as perceived dependability, collective orientation, culture, location, and various moderating variables are not found to boost trust. Mixed results for organizational power.	Implied close link; surveys sent to key boundary spanners.	Various management theories.
10. Ganesan (1994)	Trust: willingness to rely on an exchange partner in whom one has confidence; includes expectations of credibility and benevolence. Measured via survey.	Perceptions of specific investments increase trust. Also, positive reputation fosters credibility-based trust in that partner.	Credibility-based trust is positively related to a long-term relationship orientation.	Amount of– and satisfaction with– past interactions not shown to build trust.	N/A	TCE and various other management theories.

(Continued)

Table 10.1 (Continued)

Study	*How Interorg. Trust is Defined/ Measured*	*Findings: Antecedents*	*Findings: Consequences*	*Non Findings or Mixed Results*	*Relation Between Interorg. and Interpers. Trust*	*Theoretical Framework*
11. Mohr and Spekman (1994)	Trust: belief that a party's word is reliable, and that a party will fulfill its obligations in an exchange.Measured via survey.	N/A	Trust (along with communication quality, info sharing, commitment) predicts partnership success (measured as sales and satisfaction).	None related to trust.	N/A	Various management theories.
12. Morgan & Hunt (1994)	Trust: confidence in an exchange partner's reliability and integrity. Measured via survey.	Shared values and communication lead to trust; opportunism decreases trust.	Trust leads to relation-ship commitment, cooperation, and functional conflict. Trust decreases uncertainty.	None related to trust.	N/A	Commitment-trust theory of relationship marketing.
13. Gulati (1995)	Trust: expectation of low opportunism. Assumed to exist in repeated alliances; represented by absence of equity arrangement.	History of interaction and familiarity lead to trust. Repeat partners and those from the same country are less likely to safeguard.	N/A	Number of partners does not affect governance form. Prior nonequity alliances don't impact equity use in new ventures.	N/A	TCE and sociological theory
14. Zaheer and Venkatraman (1995)	Trust: predictable, fair, and reciprocal action with respect to commitments. Measured via survey.	N/A	Trust is significantly associated with hierarchical forms of organizing. Trust increases the explanatory power of TCE factors.	None	Identified as an area or future research.	TCE and sociological exchange theory

Study	*How Interorg. Trust is Defined/ Measured*	*Findings: Antecedents*	*Findings: Consequences*	*Non Findings or Mixed Results*	*Relation Between Interorg. and Interpers. Trust*	*Theoretical Framework*
15. Aulakh et al. (1996)	Trust: "the degree of confidence the individual partners have on the reliability and integrity of each other." Measured via survey.	Flexibility, expectation of continuity, and open information exchange lead to greater trust in cross-border dyads.	None found.	No support for link between trust and performance (measured by increased sales and market share of the partnership).	Close relationship is implied	Relational norms, social control, and TCE
16. Sapienza and Korsgaard (1996)	Undefined but implied; specific focus is on whether relationship partners act 'justly.' Trust measured via survey and initial lab experiment.	Timely feedback (i.e. communication from entrepreneur to investor) leads to greater trust in the entrepreneur.	N/A	Mixed results for the claim that investor influence also leads to greater trust in the entrepreneur.	Tightly linked–interorg. trust is essentially equated with trust between entrepreneurial CEO and lead investor.	Procedural justice theory
17. Nooteboom, Berger, & Noorderhaven (1997)	Trust: confidence in another's reliability in fulfilling expectations (competence-based trust) as well as in the another's benevolence (intentional trust). Measured via survey.	N/A	Trust reduces risk, envisioned as the perceived probability of loss rather than the perceived size of the loss.	Indications that only intentional trust (habitualization) reduces perceived risk, and not competence trust, although the concepts are difficult to disentangle.	Implied close relationship.	TCE, other management theories.
18. Gulati & Singh (1998)	Trust: confidence in the predictability of each other's actions. Three proxies used to 'measure' trust: repeated ties, regional commonality, bilateral relationship.	Repeated interactions, commonality of national location, and bilateral relationship are all assumed to be measures of trust, but not directly tested.	Trust (repeated ties) leads to hierarchical alliances.	Mixed support (among regions) for regional commonality leading to hierarchy. No support for claim of multi-partner alliances reducing trust.	N/A	Coordination costs (TCE) and interdependence perspective.

(Continued)

Table 10.1 (Continued)

Study	*How Interorg. Trust is Defined/ Measured*	*Findings: Antecedents*	*Findings: Consequences*	*Non Findings or Mixed Results*	*Relation Between Interorg. and Interpers. Trust*	*Theoretical Framework*
19. Sako (1998)	Trust: expectation that a party will behave in a mutually acceptable manner; distinguishes between competence and goodwill trust. Measured via survey.	Customer service, informal commitment and info exchange lead to trust.	Trust is positively related to performance (continuous improvement and just-in-time delivery).	Mixed support for formal contracts leading to increased trust. (Results varied by international region.)	N/A	Various management theories.
20. Zaheer, McEvily, and Perrone (1998)	Trust: relational concept that incorporates reliability, predictability, and fairness. Measured via survey.	N/A	Interorg. trust associated with higher performance (four-item measure of goal fulfillment in the dyadic relationship).	No support for the claim that interpersonal trust leads to less conflict in the interorganizational relationship.	Highly correlated but distinct.	Psychological and sociological theories of trust and conflict; organization economics.
21. Young-Ybarra and Wiersema (1999)	Trust: dependability, predictability, good faith. Measured via survey.	Shared values and communication increase trust. Economic hostages increase trust. Relationship asymmetry discourages trust.	Trust leads to two kinds of strategic flexibility (measured in terms of exit opportunity and modification).	No support for the claims that previous relations or length of time in the relationship would both be positively correlated with trust.	N/A	TCE, social exchange theory.
22. Dyer and Chu (2000)	Trust: one party's confidence that the other party in the exchange relationship will not exploit its vulnerabilities. Measured via survey.	Consistency and routines highly correlated with trust. Institutional factors affect trust; results mixed across three cultural settings. Quantified costs of creating trust.	N/A	No support for the claim that trust can be produced through economic ties or hostages.	They suggest that high stability of personnel at both organizations may be "necessary to produce relationship-based trust," suggesting a close tie to interpersonal trust.	Relationship-based view, process-based view, and economic (hostage-based) view.

Study	*How Interorg. Trust is Defined/ Measured*	*Findings: Antecedents*	*Findings: Consequences*	*Non Findings or Mixed Results*	*Relation Between Interorg. and Interpers. Trust*	*Theoretical Framework*
23. Fryxell, Dooley, & Vryza (2002)	Trust: willingness to be vulnerable, based on perception of the qualities of the other party. Measured via survey.	N/A	Social controls positively influence performance if affect-based trust is present; without such trust, social controls have the opposite effect.	None related to trust.	N/A	Various management theories.
24. Luo (2002)	Cooperation: exchange process that acts as a safeguard mechanism—essentially, calculative trust. Measured via survey.	Contingency adaptability in contracting increases cooperation. Trust and contracting are complements.	Cooperation leads to contract adaptability. Cooperation improves performance (sales, ROI); this relationship improves if the contract is more complete.	No support for the claim that term of contract influences, or is influenced by, cooperation.	N/A	Relational governance, TCE.
25. Poppo and Zenger (2002)	Trust: norms of flexibility, solidarity, and information exchange. Measured via survey.	Increase in level of contract complexity is associated with increased relational governance (trust).	Increase in level of trust associated with increased contract complexity. Both are associated with higher performance.	No support for the claim that contractual complexity and trust are substitutes. (Whereas complementarity view supported.)	N/A	TCE and sociological embeddedness.
26. Zaheer, Lofstrom, and George (2002)	Trust: expectation that other party will fulfill obligations, behave predictably, and negotiate fairly. Examined in inductive multiple case studies.	Interpersonal trust among CEOs a key factor in alliance formation and issue resolution. Trust among mid-level managers impacts day-to-day efficiency.	Loss of trust results in alliance dissolution.	N/A	Interorganizational trust not mere aggregation of interpersonal trust. Decline in interorg. trust also related to decline in interpersonal trust.	Grounded theory building.

(Continued)

Table 10.1 (Continued)

Study	*How Interorg. Trust is Defined/ Measured*	*Findings: Antecedents*	*Findings: Consequences*	*Non Findings or Mixed Results*	*Relation Between Interorg. and Interpers. Trust*	*Theoretical Framework*
27. Dyer & Chu (2003)	Trust: one party's confidence that the other party in the exchange relationship will not exploit its vulnerabilities. Measured via survey.	N/A (although they acknowledge that causality could be reversed or reciprocal).	Trust significantly lowers transaction costs. Trust tied to information sharing. Trustworthiness brings higher performance.	Mixed results for findings grouped by individual country supporting the idea of national variation in trust norms.	N/A	TCE
28. Carson et. al. (2003)	Trust: confidence in expected behavior and goodwill of other party regarding business actions. Measured via survey.	Client skill level, teachability of the task, co-location, and task overlap (parallel execution) all increase trust-based governance.	Trust-based governance positively relates to task performance. This relationship is also magnified by client's skill level, task teachability, and task overlap.	No support for claim that co-location of client and supplier increases positive effect of trust on task performance.	N/A	Information processing, relational governance.
29. Hagen and Simons (2003)	Trust: willingness to accept vulnerability. Measured via survey–distinguishing between interpersonal trust vs. trust in the organization.	Interpersonal justice leads to interpersonal trust. Procedural justice leads to interorganizational trust.	Interorganizational trust associated with higher performance (four dimensions measured by survey).	Mixed results for interpersonal trust leading to better performance.	Reinforces idea of separate constructs; relationship not directly explored.	Procedural justice theory; interpersonal justice theory.
30. Jap & Anderson (2003)	Trust: interpersonal willingness to be vulnerable to the actions of another party, with the expectation of reliability. Measured via survey.	N/A	Trust improves partner performance, competitive advantage, joint profits, and relationship extendedness. These positive effects decrease as ex post opportunism rises.	N/A	Interpersonal trust has less of a positive effect on performance as organization-level opportunism rises.	Relational governance.

Study	*How Interorg. Trust is Defined/ Measured*	*Findings: Antecedents*	*Findings: Consequences*	*Non Findings or Mixed Results*	*Relation Between Interorg. and Interpers. Trust*	*Theoretical Framework*
31. McEvily, Zaheer, & Perrone (2003)	Trust: expectation that other party will fulfill obligations, behave predictably, and negotiate fairly. Measured via survey.	Vulnerability generally reduces trust in the partner. Buyer vulnerability increases supplier trust in buyer.	N/A	No support for claims that vulnerability increases trust in the partner, or that supplier vulnerability increases buyer trust.	Distinct but positively correlated.	TCE and exchange theory.
32. Perrone, Zaheer, & McEvily (2003)	Trust: expectation that other party will fulfill obligations, behave predictably, and negotiate fairly. Measured via survey.	N/A	Interorg. trust mediates the relationship between an individual's firm's clan culture and the trust placed in that individual by other boundary spanners.	None related to interorganizational trust.	Interorg. Trust mediates the relationship between an organizational trait and the interpersonal trust between boundary spanners.	Various management theories.
33. Poppo, Zhou, and Zenger (2003)	Relational governance: composite concept that includes promise-keeping, information sharing, and open communication. Measured via survey.	History of social contact and longer contract duration are associated with increased relational governance (an indicator of trust).	Relational governance mitigates the detrimental effect of historical social contact on performance.	No support for the claim that higher exchange hazard levels are associated with greater relational governance (an indicator of trust).	N/A	Game theory, TCE, and social relations perspectives.
34. Howorth, Westhead, & Wright (2004)	Trust: perception of fairness and justice.	N/A	Trust reduces info asymmetry and competitive negotiation between entrepreneurial firm owners and MBO successors.	N/A	Implied close relationship, given the context of small, entrepreneurial firms.	Agency theory, negotiation theory. Qualitative, multiple case studies.

(Continued)

Table 10.1 (Continued)

Study	*How Interorg. Trust is Defined/ Measured*	*Findings: Antecedents*	*Findings: Consequences*	*Non Findings or Mixed Results*	*Relation Between Interorg. and Interpers. Trust*	*Theoretical Framework*
35. Lui & Ngo (2004)	Trust: expectation that other party intends to fulfill their role in the relationship. Composed of goodwill trust and competence trust. Measured via survey.	N/A	Trust moderates the relationship between contractual safeguards and performance. Goodwill trust is a safeguard substitute; competence trust a complement.	Although prior relations are sometimes used as a proxy for trust, they find only mild correlation between prior relations and trust.	Goodwill trust arises from interpersonal trust. Competence trust may derive from things such as reputation effects.	TCE, social relations perspectives.
36. Mayer & Argyres (2004)	Trust: not explicitly defined, but encompasses vulnerability and expectation of reliability.	Appears that contract completeness increases trust.	Completeness may contribute to the positive effects of contracts on trust.	N/A	N/A	TCE.
37. Mellewigt, Madhok, & Weibel (2004)	Trust: willingness to be vulnerable, based on a positive expectation of partner's intentions. Measured via survey.	N/A	The effect of transaction hazard on contract complexity is weakened by trust, whereas trust boosts the effect of strategic importance on contract complexity.	None related to trust.	N/A	TCE, RBV, and inter-organizational relations perspectives.
38. Saparito, Chen, & Sapienza (2004)	Relational trust: confidence that other party will act beneficially out of consideration for the trustor's welfare. Distinct from calculative trust. Measured via survey.	N/A	Trust mediates the relationship between bank customer service efforts and customer loyalty, even after self-interest assumptions are accounted for.	N/A	N/A	Relational and self interest perspectives.

often frame very different descriptive views of trust; for example, interorganizational trust can be seen as goodwill-based (Saparito, Chen, & Sapienza, 2004) or competence-based (Lui & Ngo, 2004). Because trust has developed into a multidimensional construct, researchers both conceive of and measure trust in various ways (Table 10.1). A major, economics-derived stream on trust views it as a quasirational calculation of the probability of another's future benevolent actions (Gambetta, 1988) or as a dispositional characteristic of the trustor (Dasgupta, 1988).

A more organizationally oriented view is that trust is reciprocal or relational in nature (Hardin, 1991; Zaheer & Venkatraman, 1995). The term *relational* as it applies to trust has at least two implications: relational as social, and relational as dyadic. First, relational-as-social trust, in contrast to "calculative" trust or trust as quasirational choice, implies the inclusion of relational elements, or possessing a social orientation. Macneil (1980) draws attention to relational contracting as a contrast to more explicit classical and neoclassical contracting. Relational contracting includes social elements such as norms and expectations as well as encompassing long-time horizons. Relational-as-dyadic trust suggests trust relative to an identified other and favors a dynamic and reciprocal—rather than dispositional—view of trust. In this way, a relational view of interorganizational trust implies that a specific organization is the object of trust (Zaheer et al., 1998). Yet this does not preclude organizations from possessing or acquiring reputations for being trustworthy; to that extent, interorganizational trust is not *exclusively* dyadic or relational but can be network-based as well. Reputations may be more easily spread when the firm is embedded in a dense network of ties.

The relational issue in trust naturally raises the question of time horizons, as it implies that one is prepared to defer reciprocation in some way. The reciprocal relationship between trust and trustworthiness also brings up the issue of possible asymmetries in trust between parties. Finally, as mentioned above, network membership may influence the nature of interorganizational trust. In the rest of this section, we consider the empirical research and raise theoretical issues around the role of time horizons in relational trust, as well as the notion of asymmetries in dyadic interorganizational trust and the nature of trust within networks.

Role of Time Horizon. It has often been noted, perhaps apocryphally, that for sociologists trust is only about the past, whereas for economists it is only about the future. In other words, the history of past relations is what a sociologist might use to explain trust. An economist, on the other hand, is concerned only with the prospects for future gain or loss—the past is merely sunk cost.

One of the original, forward-looking frameworks commonly employed in thinking about trust was the game-theoretic view on the evolution of cooperation proposed by Axelrod (1984), who showed that expectations of continued interaction change the behavior of relationship partners. Organizational scholars have built upon this game-theoretic framework (Doz, 1996; Parkhe, 1993), finding that organizational perceptions of the interfirm relationship continuing into the future encourage cooperation between the organizations involved (Heide & Miner, 1992). The valuation of the future is where the issue of the organization's time horizon, or rate of time discount, becomes salient. If the organization's rate of time discount is low, it will value the future more than will one with a higher rate of time discount. In the former case, the potential benefits of future trust and cooperation will be valued higher than will the immediate benefits of opportunism (Axelrod, 1984, 1997), because from this perspective an organization will cooperate with another only if the prospective gains from cooperation exceed those from opportunism. Accordingly, one would expect organizations that have a lower rate of time discount to be more trusting and trustworthy than organizations with a higher rate of time discount. However, the implicit rate of organizational time discount is clearly a deep-seated cultural assumption (Schein, 1992) that would be difficult to surface empirically.

On the other hand, studies emphasizing the role of the past in the creation of trust show that the history of previous interaction between the organizations—including familiarity as well as relationship history—leads to increased trust (Gulati, 1995), and some research goes so far as to use repeated ties as a proxy for interorganizational trust (Gulati & Singh, 1998). However, other research (Lui & Ngo, 2004; Young-Ybarra & Wiersema, 1999) has found that the length of time the partner organizations have been together or even the mere presence of prior relations between two organizations is unrelated to trust. Although previous history clearly does not equate exactly to prospects for extended future collaboration, the question of how past ties and history serve as a signal of the "shadow of the future," and the associated trust or cooperation emanating from it, appears to be an unresolved issue. A way to reconcile the divergent sociological and economic perspectives is to look to the past history of the relationship as well as casting an eye toward prospects for future cooperation.

Asymmetry of Trust. Trust research usually assumes that trust between two alliance or exchange partners is symmetrical. If "trust begets trust" in a virtuous cycle, this implies a close relationship between trust and trustworthiness, potentially creating a self-reinforcing cycle of trusting and being trusted. The extent of trust on either side of the dyad is often assumed to be approximately the same. Yet it is by no means self-evident that trust should in fact be symmetric across the dyad; if anything, a symmetric alignment in trust may be the exception rather than the rule, because the bases of trust across the dyad may differ (McEvily, Zaheer, & Perrone, 2003).

Although the effects of interorganizational trust are generally assumed to arise from bilateral, essentially equivalent norms of cooperation (e.g., Aulakh, Kotabe, & Sahay, 1996), some research has started to examine the potentially asymmetric nature of interfirm trust. Although overall relationship asymmetry appears to discourage the formation of interorganizational trust (Young-Ybarra & Wiersema, 1999), other research indicates that vulnerability is an important aspect of trust creation (McEvily et al., 2003). If vulnerability leads to trustworthiness, this may have indirect implications for organizational performance, because trustworthiness and performance have been shown to be linked (Dyer & Chu, 2003).

The exploration of dyadic trust asymmetry evokes notions of power and resource dependence (Pfeffer & Salancik, 1978), because asymmetric trust is likely to arise from the presence of greater vulnerability on the part of one of the alliance partners. Wicks, Berman, and Jones (1999) suggest that such an imbalance of power and trust may result in negative performance outcomes for the alliance, but there remains great potential for this issue to be explored empirically. Trust asymmetry is also likely to be part of a dynamic cycle of trust creation and development and may shift as the interorganizational relationship matures (Narayandas & Rangan, 2004).

Interorganizational Trust and Networks. Numerous points of convergence exist between research on interorganizational trust and research on interorganizational networks. However, little cross-fertilization has occurred between the two fields. This is surprising, because trust is recognized as a major element of social capital and is often invoked as the logic for the benefits of cohesive networks. Research, for example, shows that relational flexibility in a dyad—a norm strongly associated with interfirm trust—can affect the norms of firms throughout the dyad's larger supply-chain network (Wathne & Heide, 2004). Husted's (1994) inductive research suggests that the density of individual social network ties is positively related to interfirm trust. A number of network effects rely fundamentally on the mechanism of trust. For instance, the notion of closure is fundamentally based on the idea that tightly knit cliques are strongly undergirded by trust. Similarly, "structural embeddedness" (Gulati &

Gargiulo, 1999) refers to third-party reputation effects that are again mainly trust-based—that is, reputations for trustworthy behavior. High trust is thought to be associated with strong ties (Wicks et al., 1999).

Yet this research leaves specific questions about interfirm trust and networks unanswered; for example, would a network rich in structural holes discourage trust more than a network that is more dense? This seems plausible, because the theorized value of structural holes arises from, among other things, the ability of an organization to play one network relationship against another, a strategy that is inherently Machiavellian. In situations where trust matters, such as with the exchange of tacit knowledge, one would expect to find, as Ahuja (2000) does, that closure counts for more than holes. Thus, interorganizational trust becomes an important contingency mechanism that influences the relative benefits or detriments of different forms of network structure.

Although Larson's (1992) inductive study indicates that interorganizational trust generally has positive effects on the successful governance of firm networks, this relationship has been little researched. As mentioned above, Gulati (1995) suggests that repeat alliance partners are more likely to trust; and Lui and Ngo (2004) suggest that competence-based trust can arise from reputation effects—results with important ramifications for network governance. McEvily and Zaheer (2004) explore the central role an institutional "network facilitator" plays in creating trust in geographical industrial networks. Overall, the nature of interorganizational trust presents a number of open questions for future research.

Development of Interorganizational Trust

A fundamental question that researchers have attempted to answer is how interorganizational trust is created and developed (e.g., Ring & Van de Ven, 1994). There are several lines of inquiry into this question that occur throughout the literature, including the costs of creating trust, the role of interpersonal trust in the development of interorganizational trust, particularly questions about the unit and level of analysis, and the influence of institutional factors such as geographic region or culture in promoting or hindering trust creation.

Costs of Creating Trust. An examination of the costs of trust creation is an obvious counterpoint and complement to an analysis of the *benefits* arising from trust. (Our attention to the benefits arising from interorganizational trust comes later in our staged model, when we consider the outcomes of trust.) It is worth noting that a focus on the beneficial effects of trust underlies the majority of scholarly research on the topic, and this is precisely what makes an inquiry into the costs associated with trust's development so interesting.

Research largely treats trust creation costs as implicit rather than as quantifiable expenditures, difficult trade-offs, or opportunity costs. For example, in the exploratory inductive study cited above involving network dyads of entrepreneurial firms, Larson (1992) shows that the development of trust between organizations requires significant time and resources—in other words, costs. Other research identifies specific organizational actions and behavior leading to trust creation, such as flexibility and information exchange in the case of cross-border partnerships (Aulakh et al., 1996), the provision of timely feedback in entrepreneur-funder relations (Sapienza & Korsgaard, 1996), and co-location in the case of interfirm research and development (R&D) collaboration (Carson, Madhok, Varman, & John, 2003). For example, Sako (1998) finds that customer-service efforts lead to trust creation between buyer and supplier firms. These organizational actions all have economic costs associated with them but are not explicitly treated as such.

An important consideration in analyzing the costs of trust creation is the notion that the process of interorganizational trust creation and commitment is likely to be a sequential and gradual one, with each following the other to higher and higher levels, rather like the creation of interpersonal trust itself (Blau, 1964). As Ring and Van de Ven (1994) argue, the development of trust is a cyclical process of recurrent bargaining, commitment, and execution events among the organizational parties. Das and Teng (1998, p. 499) note that "only if partner firms have a fairly high level of confidence in partner cooperation would they be willing to enter into a JV," which suggests that interorganizational trust may need to be in place before any formal commitments are made—a concept that is well established with respect to interpersonal trust (e.g., Lewicki & Bunker, 1996).

This provides a good starting point for further theorizing about the mechanisms for creating interorganizational trust. Because of the potentially reciprocal nature of trust, there are several paths to trust creation, which may involve differential costs. At least two approaches to trust creation may be identified in the literature. First, to demonstrate that an organization trusts another, it may take a large and clearly costly (if not reciprocated) gamble with a new or potential alliance partner—typically conceived of as a "unilateral commitment" (Gulati, Khanna, & Nohria, 1994). By obviously placing itself in a position of vulnerability (Mayer, Davis, & Schoorman, 1995) the organization invites the alliance partner to reciprocate its trust. In other words, such voluntary vulnerability may be predicated on the hope that "trust begets trust." A second path to establishing interfirm trust is to demonstrate that one is trustworthy (rather than trusting); for example, an organization might focus on scrupulously honoring commitments and making sure to commit to only what is within the firm's power to execute. It would be interesting to work through the contingencies when one or the other path to trust creation is more "optimal," although clearly other routes to trust creation exist.

This consideration of different trust creation mechanisms brings us to another reason why organizations may sometimes behave in more quasirational ways than individuals acting alone when it comes to trusting another organization: The higher level of risk associated with organizational commitment may make the costs of additional information collection both necessary and worthwhile. The costs of conducting background checks, which could be included in the overall cost of trust creation, are more easily amortized over the higher volume and value of transactions between organizations in an alliance than they would be in the simple case of lone individuals trusting each other. Again, such costs lend themselves to quantification, and further research along these lines stands to greatly enhance our understanding of interorganizational trust.

In addition to these indirect examinations of costs, an area that researchers have more directly considered recently is the relationship between contracts and trust, in the transaction cost economics (TCE) tradition. Along these lines, one study (Poppo & Zenger, 2002) links an increase in general contract complexity with increased trust. Other research indicates that specific attributes of formal contracting increase trust, such as contingency adaptability (Luo, 2002) and contract duration (Poppo, Zhou, & Zenger, 2003). If, as seems clear, greater complexity or specificity in a contract represents increased transaction costs, to the extent that these contractual attributes lead to greater trust, they represent the costs of trust creation.

In this vein, Dyer and Chu (2003) find no support for their alternative hypothesis that trust lowers ex ante contracting costs; however, they do find that trustworthiness lowers ex post contracting costs, suggesting that once trust is established, transaction costs may in fact decline (Bromiley & Cummings, 1995). This has implications for the costs of maintaining trust in an ongoing relationship, where initial costs of trust creation may be viewed as an investment the value of which can be realized over time.

These results resonate with others that, although not explicitly addressing trust, show that transaction costs are also lower in the presence of relational norms commonly associated with trust (Artz & Brush, 2000). It also appears that the development of trust might depend upon the creation of trustworthiness or vulnerability (McEvily et al., 2003), which in turn entail their own tangible and intangible costs. In sum, whether achieved through explicit contracting provisions or through organizational attributes, the establishment of interorganizational trust can require time, effort, and resource allocations that represent real and significant economic costs to the organizations involved.

Making judgments about the costs of building trust and assessing the value of trust can also be envisioned as a question of "fit" between trust and other organizational attributes such as the relationship's interdependence (Wicks et al., 1999). The greater the interdependence between two organizations, the greater the need for trust. Other scholars make a "fit" argument between trust and trustworthiness (Perrone, Zaheer, & McEvily, 2003). Essentially, these scholars argue that because the creation of trust is costly, organizations should trust only as much as is necessary. Of course, determining just how much trust is "optimal" and whether creating an advance reservoir of trust is wise, and if so how to do it, are nontrivial issues both substantively and empirically.

In addition, other researchers (Wicks & Berman, 2004) have begun to explore the role that institutional context plays in the ability of firms to create trusting relationships with other organizations; key elements of this context include formal institutions, sociocultural values, and industry norms—which may all have a direct impact on the costs of creating trust within that context. Ring (1996) suggests that the requirements—and therefore costs—of creating interorganizational trust actually depend upon whether the type of trust being created is situation-specific ("fragile") or more resilient—for which greater attention and resources may be required to create a lasting trust relationship. In conclusion, the actions that lead to trust creation have associated costs, and these costs will vary depending on the nature of the trust being created and the institutional context for the interfirm relationship.

Role of Interpersonal Trust. There is a wealth of research in the area of interpersonal trust in organizational contexts (Becerra & Gupta, 2003; Dirks & Ferrin, 2001; Kramer, 1999; Malhotra & Murnighan, 2002). Uncovering the precise relationship between interorganizational and interpersonal trust is an important line of inquiry because, although the two forms of trust are shown to be related phenomena (Zaheer et al., 1998), they are clearly not the same thing. Studies show significant differences between interpersonal trust and interorganizational trust in predicting outcomes (Hagen & Simons, 2003).

Nevertheless, interpersonal trust appears to be important in the development of interorganizational trust (Zaheer et al., 1998). In other empirical studies, the influence of interpersonal trust on interorganizational trust is not directly analyzed but rather has implied significance. In studies of interorganizational trust within the context of small entrepreneurial firms, for example, interfirm trust appears to be tightly linked to trust between individuals in those organizations (Howorth, Westhead, & Wright, 2004; Larson, 1992; Sapienza & Korsgaard, 1996). Even in the context of relations between larger organizations, stability of personnel appears to be an important factor in the development of interorganizational trust (Dyer & Chu, 2000), suggesting the importance of trust between boundary-spanners (Currall & Judge, 1995). This idea is reinforced by research showing that interpersonal trust between boundary-spanners decreases the likelihood of interfirm relationship dissolution (Seabright, Levinthal, & Fichman, 1992). John (1984) finds that boundary-spanner attitudes have a profound effect on norms of interfirm opportunism or cooperation, suggesting the importance of interpersonal trust; indeed, a multiplicity of interpersonal factors have been shown to heighten interorganizational trust (Moorman, Deshpande, & Zaltman, 1993).

In addition, there are performance implications for the relationship between interpersonal and interorganizational trust. For example, Jap and Anderson (2003) find that interpersonal trust between boundary-spanners has a positive effect on organizational performance measures, but this effect diminishes as ex post opportunism rises. Some effects of interpersonal trust are less clear, such as the inconclusive link between interpersonal trust and decreased organizational conflict (Zaheer et al., 1998). It does appear, however, that interpersonal trust at different levels of the organization has different effects; interpersonal trust among executives is a key factor in alliance formation and issue resolution, whereas interpersonal trust among midlevel managers has a greater impact on day-to-day efficiency of alliance operations (Zaheer, Lofstrom, & George, 2002).

Several studies attempt to gain more fine-grained insight into the nature of the tie between interpersonal and interorganizational trust. Lui and Ngo (2004) discover a strong empirical distinction between two different dimensions of trust—goodwill trust and competence-based trust, each with different outcomes—finding that goodwill trust arises from interpersonal trust, whereas competence trust may derive from more general reputation effects. In addition, although most of these studies examine the role of interpersonal trust in creating interorganizational trust, research has also found support for interorganizational trust's mediating influence on the relationship between organizational characteristics and the interpersonal trust between boundary-spanners (Perrone et al., 2003). Overall, the relationship between interpersonal and interorganizational trust has received abundant research attention, but unanswered questions remain about the contingencies under which it influences interorganizational trust and its outcomes.

Institutional Factors. Another area explored by empirical research is the theorized influence of location and national culture (Fukuyama, 1995) on the development of trust and its associated relational norms. Dyer and Chu (2000) study trust in buyer-supplier relationships in the automotive industry, finding that the antecedents of trust differ depending on the national setting. For example, the length of time since the first interaction is found to influence interorganizational trust positively in Japan but not in the United States or Korea. In contrast, repeated exchange is correlated with trust in Korea and the United States but not in Japan. Other researchers have also investigated the variability of interorganizational trust across different national contexts (Husted, 1994; Lane, 1997; Lane & Bachmann, 1996), in particular finding support for the notion that trust-producing mechanisms vary according to the cultural context.

There are also indications that regional and cultural differences impact the effects and consequences of interorganizational trust. Sako (1998) examines the relationship between interorganizational trust and performance outcomes by surveying component suppliers in the automotive industry across different countries. She finds that the cultural context gives rise to differences in the effects of trust, a finding echoed by Dyer and Chu (2003). Using a transaction cost framework, Gulati and Singh (1998) study governance structures of strategic alliances and find that trust behavior and its consequences differ according to national or regional differences in alliance location, consistent with findings in the alliance literature (e.g., Parkhe, 1993). In general, as Kramer (1999) asks, to what extent are such trusting actions also influenced by social, institutional, and psychological norms? This stream of research indicates that cultural, regional, or institutional forces can have a powerful effect on the antecedents, nature, and consequences of interorganizational trust (Wicks & Berman, 2004).

Although the role of industry-level institutions in creating trust has been examined in a case study (McEvily & Zaheer, 2004), the influence of institutional context has been most extensively examined with respect to international settings and cultural influences. If the exchange partners have dissimilar cultural or national origins, the whole process of trust creation, the nature of trust itself, and the costs of trust creation are markedly different (Child & Mollering, 2003; Dyer & Chu, 2003). Nationality impacts how individuals perceive trustworthiness (Caldwell & Clapham, 2003). Gulati (1995) finds that partners from the same country have fewer safeguards because they trust each other more. On the other hand, certain collectivist societies, such as Japan, display a strong in-group orientation (Huff & Kelley, 2003) and relate differently to in-group and out-group members. Lincoln (1990) argues that the important task for researchers is not merely to demonstrate that received theory applies differently in different cultural contexts but also to extend theory by identifying new boundary conditions within such contexts. For example, Lincoln observes that the assumptions of TCE theory may have to be modified in the Japanese context due to institutional pressures for long-term employment and supplier relationships, which suggest that trust might characterize relationships to a greater extent in Japan than elsewhere. More broadly, "cross-cultural differences constitute empirical variance to be explained and thus an opportunity for theory" (1990, p. 256).

In summary, issues around the development of interorganizational trust present numerous opportunities for scholarly inquiry. In particular, although the benefits of trust have been extensively studied, corresponding interest in the costs of trust creation, both transaction costs and actual costs, has been lacking. The prospects for research into the relationship between interorganizational and interpersonal trust are also vast as they span questions of construct validity and levels of analysis, in addition to the influence of the one on the other, as well as the contingent role of interpersonal trust in affecting the outcomes of interorganizational trust. Finally, research is also needed into the role the institutional context plays in the development of interorganizational trust.

Role of Interorganizational Trust

Many empirical studies look at the relationship between trust and organizational governance. This stream typically draws upon the TCE framework to examine the role of interorganizational trust in choosing an organizational form, safeguarding against opportunism, or reducing transaction costs. These ideas have also expanded into a debate as to whether formal governance mechanisms serve as substitutes, complements, or alternatives to interorganizational trust.

TCE and Forms of Organizing. Research suggests that trust plays a constitutive role in the structuring of alliance relationships (Ring & Van de Ven, 1992). It is well founded that interorganizational trust arises from the need to compensate for the inherent incompleteness of contracts (e.g., Lane & Bachmann, 1998; Williamson, 1985) and implies the incorporation of relational elements into contracting (Macneil, 1980). For example, Heide and John (1992) study interfirm relationship governance structures, finding trust-related relational norms to be highly influential on those structures.

In particular the relationship between trust and transaction-specific assets has been the subject of considerable research, although the link is a complex one. Trust can easily be viewed as a safeguard and a substitute for hierarchy—which would imply that trust and asset specificity have a positive relationship because higher asset specificity requires higher safeguarding and trust would complement asset specificity (Zaheer & Venkatraman, 1995). However, trust may also serve other roles. One such role may be that of trust as a hostage, or signal of commitment to the relationship, in which case trust may demonstrate a negative relationship with asset specificity because it would serve as a substitute for it. The exact nature of the relationship between trust and governance is the subject of mixed results; whereas Anderson and Narus (1990) find support for cooperative action leading to interorganizational trust, other research indicates that trust acts as a mediator between concrete financial costs and cooperative outcomes (Morgan & Hunt, 1994).

Several empirical studies examine the role trust plays in the formation of interorganizational structure. For instance, Gulati and Singh (1998) directly address the impact of interorganizational trust on organization structure, finding that trust (measured via repeated ties) is related to hierarchical alliances. Zaheer and Venkatraman (1995) find interfirm trust to be positively correlated to asset specificity, suggesting that such investments are a signal of good faith in the relationship. Some scholars find support for the idea that economic hostages lead to trust (Young-Ybarra & Wiersema, 1999), whereas others find no support for such a connection (Dyer & Chu, 2000). These findings illustrate the possibility that trust may play an important role in how interorganizational relationships are structured, although research in this area has produced conflicting results.

Other research focuses specifically on the impact of interorganizational trust on the nature of the relational contracts themselves, finding a positive link between interorganizational trust and contract complexity (Poppo & Zenger, 2002). Although some scholars have searched fruitlessly for a positive relationship between exchange hazard levels and increased interfirm trust (Poppo et al., 2003), others have found evidence of a more complex relationship. For example, Mellewigt, Madhok, and Weibel (2004) find a moderating role of trust—that the effect of exchange hazard level on contract complexity is weakened by interorganizational trust, whereas trust boosts the effect of strategic importance on contract complexity. On the other hand, because Dyer and Chu (2003) find that interorganizational trust increases dyadic information sharing *in addition* to significantly lowering transaction costs, they argue that trust is a unique governance mechanism in its ability to create value beyond transaction cost minimization. This idea is supported by their finding that trustworthiness correlates with several different performance measures, building upon previous work that initially conceived of trust as a self-reinforcing safeguard (Dyer, 1997). The impact of trust on contracting appears to have effects far beyond simple minimization of contracting costs.

Substitute or Complement? The discussion about trust and contracting leads to generalized questions regarding their relationship in an attempt to determine whether formal relationship governance mechanisms are complements to or substitutes for interfirm trust. Early theorizing envisioned trust as a substitute for control, an argument that has in various settings proven inconclusive (Van de Ven & Walker, 1984), shown mixed results (Sako, 1998), and found strong empirical support (Dyer & Chu, 2003). On the other hand, some initial trust research supporting a complementary view of trust and contracting (Zaheer & Venkatraman, 1995) has been repeatedly reinforced (Fryxell, Dooley, & Vryza, 2002; Luo, 2002; Mayer & Argyres, 2004; Poppo & Zenger, 2002). The question remains: Are interfirm trust and contracting mechanisms substitutes or complements?

One way researchers have begun to reconcile these conflicting views is through the use of a contingency framework, as shown in recent empirical studies. This contingency view indicates a more finely parsed relationship between contract safeguards and interorganizational trust than that of generalized concepts of substitutability or complementarity. One empirical study (Lui & Ngo, 2004) bifurcates interfirm trust into its goodwill- and competence-based aspects, showing that these different types of trust have different effects on the relationship between safeguards and performance, suggesting that trust and contracts can serve as substitutes *or* complements, depending upon other contingent factors.

More specifically, there are at least two contingencies on which the relationship between trust and contracting might depend: the stage of the relationship and the complexity of the contract. In the early stages of the relationship, for example, contracts may substitute for trust and regulate behavior to the extent that such substitution is possible, given the difficulty of writing completely contingent contracts. In later stages of an interorganizational relationship, as trust develops, contracts may merely serve to specify the outer bounds of relational governance, complementing the trust that has since developed. These potential effects of the dynamic nature of relationship formation and development may also be influenced by contract complexity (Sampson, 2000). The greater the contract complexity, and the more the contract represents and reflects actual working conditions, the greater the ability of the contract to substitute for trust. A consideration of these contingencies, illuminating the potential substitutability of other governance mechanisms for trust, leads us to a fuller theoretical discussion of alternatives to interorganizational trust.

Alternatives to Trust. One of the basic theoretical issues about the nature of trust is whether calculativeness in fact plays a role in trust or if it is an alternative, substitute mechanism. As such, a key part of TCE-oriented work in interorganizational trust is the scholarly debate regarding whether or not trust is calculative in nature (Craswell, 1993; Williamson, 1993). Is trust subsumed by calculativeness, or is calculativeness a sometimes closely related but distinct idea? Recent empirical work by Saparito et al. (2004) draws a clear distinction between goodwill-oriented "relational trust" and calculative trust, finding that relational trust mediates the relationship between supplier-firm customer service and customer-firm loyalty, even after calculative assumptions are controlled for. Interorganizational trust, then, appears to be a powerful mechanism in interorganizational relationships even when it does not derive from calculative motivations; such trust can lead to a variety of desirable outcomes and have a significant influence on the very nature and structure of the interorganizational relationship.

This supports the argument that organizational trust is indeed distinct from calculativeness (Bromiley & Harris, 2005). In this sense, teasing out calculativeness from trust involves attending to the concept of opportunism itself; John (1984) explores the antecedents of opportunism, and Wathne and Heide (2000) examine its complexity, resulting in a more fine-grained parsing of the concept of opportunism and its outcomes. Although it may be considered unrealistic to expect organizations or the people in them to act against their own self-interest (Dasgupta, 1988; Hardin, 1991), research has begun to show clearly that trust explains a variety of interorganizational actions much more plausibly than calculative self-interest does. More research is required to better understand the difference between trust and calculativeness as distinct and alternative mechanisms for organizational action.

There is also some discussion in the literature about the role of routines in managing interorganizational relations and the degree to which such routines can serve as alternative mechanisms to trust. The extent to which expectations, behaviors, actions, and outcomes at the interorganizational interface are influenced or determined by trust rather than merely by interorganizational routines is important both theoretically and empirically for understanding the nature and role of interorganizational trust. In essence, the question is whether interorganizational trust exists independent of interorganizational routines, and if not, how the two are related. For example, theorists have raised important theoretical questions about the relationship between trust and organizational routines, envisioning trust *as* routines (Zollo, Reuer, & Singh, 2002).

Clearly, routines significantly influence interorganizational workings, behaviors, relations, and governance—and in fact in many cases are likely to be the very means by which trust and trustworthiness are manifested. However, much like calculativeness, we also view routines as being distinct from trust and believe that drawing out the differences between them and clarifying their relationship is key. To begin with, interorganizational trust is an expectation in a partner organization's reliability, predictability, and fairness. Interorganizational routines, on the other hand, are institutionalized, regularized, formal or informal processes that govern interactions between the two organizations. These routines can arise from trusting expectations, certainly, but may also arise from other behavioral expectations that have very little to do with trust or trustworthiness. The existence of routines does not eliminate the fundamental need to uncover and understand interorganizational trust as a mechanism that potentially influences those routines and vice versa. As such, we see several ways in which trust and routines may be interrelated: routines as an antecedent to trust, routines as a consequence of trust, and routines as a moderator of trust relationships.

Empirical work has only very slightly addressed the tie between trust and routines; Dyer and Chu (2000) find that consistency and routines are highly correlated with interorganizational trust, and other research indicates that trust arises in part from norms of procedural justice—which could be envisioned as routinized processes (Hagen & Simons, 2003; Sapienza & Korsgaard, 1996). Trust and routines have been examined together only in these few studies, leaving many unanswered questions about the relationship between trust and routines.

Overall, the role that trust plays in governance of interfirm relationships is centrally tied to issues about the extent to which it serves as a substitute for or a complement to elements such as asset specificity, contracts, calculativeness, and routines. The many different roles that trust can play and the many conflicting findings in this area create numerous avenues for theoretical and empirical resolution.

Outcomes of Interorganizational Trust

A great deal of research interest exists regarding whether interorganizational trust leads to desirable business outcomes, and if so, what those are. Although in some instances evidence of a relationship between interorganizational trust and performance has proven inconclusive (e.g., Aulakh et al., 1996), a variety of studies focus on this connection with interesting results. Although some research emphasizes direct outcomes, other work examines more complex, indirect effects. Most of the research, however, focuses on only the positive outcomes of interorganizational trust.

Direct Economic Outcomes. Interorganizational trust has been shown to positively influence a number of recognizable economic outcomes, such as lowered transaction costs (Dyer & Chu, 2003), increased sales (Mohr & Spekman, 1994), and increased return on investment (ROI) (Luo, 2002). In addition, interfirm trust has a positive effect on project management measures, such as task performance (Carson et al., 2003), and operational measures, such as continuous improvement and just-in-time delivery (Sako, 1998). In general, this evidence indicates that interorganizational trust can help achieve advantageous economic performance outcomes.

Intermediate Relational Outcomes. Research on interorganizational trust suggests that it also leads to a variety of outcomes that are less directly economic but are nevertheless desirable outcomes for the relationship. At one extreme, a loss of trust can lead to the dissolution of the relationship entirely (Seabright et al., 1992); in fact, it appears that undesirable performance outcomes and loss of trust can escalate into a self-reinforcing downward spiral (Zaheer et al., 2002). On the other hand, increasing interfirm trust can lead to increased strategic flexibility (Young-Ybarra & Wiersema, 1999), greater information-sharing (Dyer & Chu, 2003), lowered perceptions of relational risk (Nooteboom, Berger, & Noorderhaven, 1997), heightened contingency adaptability (Luo, 2002), and improved knowledge transfer (Szulanski, Cappetta, & Jensen, 2004). Several studies also indicate that trust strongly increases satisfaction with various aspects of the interfirm relationship, including joint goal fulfillment (Hagen & Simons, 2003; Zaheer et al., 1998), expectation of relationship continuation (Jap & Anderson, 2003), and positive perceptions of exchange success (Mohr & Spekman, 1994; Poppo & Zenger, 2002).

Several studies focus on the performance outcomes that are of particular importance to buyer-supplier relationships, suggesting both that trust plays a key role in determining the long-term orientation of both organizations (Ganesan, 1994) and also that trust in a supplier greatly impacts the actual product utilization of the buyer

(Moorman, Zaltman, & Deshpande, 1992). In addition, Wathne and Heide (2004) find that interfirm flexibility—a relational norm often associated with trust—has the potential to affect relational norms beyond the dyad in other parts of the supply chain.

Indirect Effects. In addition to these direct effects, scholars are starting to investigate more complex relationships between interorganizational trust and performance, including interaction effects and mediation models. Fryxell et al. (2002) discover that the presence of interfirm trust affects the influence of social-control mechanisms on performance; in the presence of trust, social controls positively influence performance, but without trust, social controls have the opposite effect. High interorganizational trust tends to mitigate the detrimental effect of historical social contact on exchange performance (Poppo et al., 2003), and different types of trust moderate the relationship between contractual safeguards and performance in different ways (Lui & Ngo, 2004). Whereas Jap and Anderson (2003) find that rising ex-post opportunism decreases the positive effects of interorganizational trust on performance, Saparito et al. (2004) discover that interfirm trust can help minimize the negative effects of opportunism.

Overall, research on interorganizational trust has revealed a wide range of positive outcomes for interfirm relationships such as alliances and buyer-supplier relationships. These include a variety of direct effects on performance, such as lowered transaction costs and increased ROI, but also a large set of indirect benefits through the mediating or moderating roles of interorganizational trust.

Directions for Future Research

Building upon the rich foundation of the empirical findings described and the theoretical discussion and extension of the themes we have surfaced—from questions about what trust is, to an examination of what it leads to—we now turn to the issues that merit further discussion and hold the most promise for future research. Some of these areas of potential research arise directly from the research streams we have discussed, although others are notable primarily due to the lack of research attention paid to them, in particular trust repair and the downside of trust. After considering these promising areas arising from theoretical considerations, we consider some methodological issues, because it is difficult to discuss theory development without also considering the corresponding methodological implications and challenges.

Theoretical Directions

Costs of Creating Trust. Extant trust research has tended to adopt an optimistic, even Panglossian perspective on trust, focusing almost exclusively on the benefits trust provides rather than the costs of producing those benefits via the creation of trust. Yet, as we have discussed, further research into the costs of trust creation holds great potential for advancing our knowledge about trust. Costs in this regard extend beyond transaction costs to actual resource and time costs. Even though existing research largely stops short of quantifying trust creation costs, such quantification seems eminently possible and is necessary to advance work in the domain, particularly because the field is otherwise open to the charge of taking a one-sided and incomplete view of the phenomenon.

Trust, Calculativeness, and Opportunism. Another potential opportunity for trust researchers is to explore further the relationship between trust, calculativeness, and opportunism. Although we assert that trust and calculativeness are indeed distinct concepts (Bromiley & Harris, 2005), more research along these lines is necessary to establish the distinction. Further, interesting questions arise, such as: To what extent does calculativeness encourage trustworthy behavior on the part of the exchange partner, ultimately helping to create trust? Moreover, even in situations where opportunistic motives are inconsequential to a particular organization's pursuit of trust and trustworthiness, calculativeness may still have a part to play in deciding what resources to commit to trust creation.

Role of Time Horizon. Research linking time horizons with trust will help answer questions about whether organizations with longer time horizons and a lower rate of time discount tend to be more trusting and trustworthy. What sorts of organizations will have low rates of time discount? Perhaps organizations that have had a long history, are more stable, and have low employee turnover. Although time horizon in an interorganizational relationship appears to have the potential to influence trust in that relationship, does trust have the reciprocal ability to influence the perceptions of the time horizon within the relationship? If time horizon is short, is there a heightened need for reliance on institutional trust rather than relational trust?

Role of Interpersonal Trust. In addressing the question of how interorganizational trust is formed, the importance of interpersonal trust appears to be obvious, but are there situations in which it matters less or more? In other words, can interorganizational trust form in a way that precludes or enhances the need for interpersonal trust between specific boundary-spanning individuals? From a contingency perspective, how might context affect the need for interpersonal trust and its role in interorganizational trust formation?

Institutional Factors. As we noted earlier, empirical work has established that there are differences in norms of interorganizational trust across national and cultural contexts. However, future research not only needs more systematic examination of the differences across such contexts, it needs to explain the theoretical underpinnings of such differences and subsequently to extend our theoretical understanding (Lincoln, 1990). In addition, greater attention could be paid to contextual factors arising not only from national or cultural influences but also from formal institutions (North, 1990) or industry norms (Wicks & Berman, 2004), from regulatory entities and quasigovernmental organizations to industry norms and tacit practices of interfirm interaction that may be idiosyncratic to particular geographies or economic segments. What happens to interorganizational trust when firm alliances cross these boundaries?

Interorganizational Trust and Governance. Aside from the basic question of whether trust serves to substitute or complement the contract, scholars have begun to examine more nuanced relationships between trust and governance. One direction that may be worthwhile in this regard is to continue to split trust into different dimensions or forms, such as goodwill-based and competence-based trust. Each of these forms of trust may play quite different roles in governance and in influencing relationship outcomes. Another potential direction is to expand the inquiry into more complex mediating or moderating relationships between trust and contracting by including factors such as organizational context, structure, transparency, knowledge characteristics of the alliance and the alliance partners, and the past history of the alliance, including its performance. Further, the conflicting findings regarding the relationship between trust and asset specificity represent an avenue ripe for empirical resolution. Finally, because governance can play a role in minimizing corporate misconduct, the role of interfirm trust in facilitating or discouraging such misconduct needs to be examined.

Interorganizational Trust and Networks. Given that the network implications for trust research have been little explored, a basic question that arises is how the antecedents, concomitants, and consequences of trust change when trust is no longer simply dyadic but is network-based. How might network trust affect the dyadic interorganizational relationship? Moreover, other mechanisms besides trust also operate in networks, such as sanctioning and reputation effects, and disaggregating those from trust-based explanations of outcomes would be important.

Asymmetry of Trust. As discussed earlier, an implicit assumption in the literature is that trust between the alliance partners is essentially symmetric. However, research has not examined the empirical validity of this assumption nor the antecedents and the outcomes of asymmetric trust in interorganizational relationships. Moreover, there may be performance implications of trust symmetry and asymmetry, and furthermore, the implications may vary by the directionality of the asymmetry (i.e., *which* partner trusts more).

Rebuilding Interorganizational Trust. The topic of trust repair is notably absent from the empirical research on interorganizational trust. Although trust scholars have declared a theoretical interest in the problem of rebuilding relationships of trust, discussion of trust repair has been isolated mainly to the interpersonal level of analysis; there has been virtually no formalized research investigating the topic of trust repair at the interorganizational level.

Downside of Trust. Another theoretical area that is notably absent in our empirical survey is research on the downside of interorganizational trust, which could include at least two primary areas of inquiry. First, theorists have pointed to the importance of studying the negative consequences of trust, including the lock-in from unproductive high-trust relationships (Gargiulo & Benassi, 2000). Second, scholars have pointed out that situations of high trust inherently contain the conditions for trust's abuse or betrayal (Granovetter, 1985; Shapiro, 1987). Studying the costs of misplaced trust may involve examining whether greater fraud takes place between exchange partners in high-trust alliance relationships. Relatedly, research may investigate whether high interorganizational trust leads to collusion; as Baier (1986, p. 253) points out, a trust-tied community "without justice" may be little more than a "group of mutual blackmailers and exploiters." Interorganizational trust, then, may indeed possess a dark side for the community at large and may need to be pursued with caution (Husted, 1998).

Methodological Research Issues

In addition to theoretical directions for future research, several methodological issues emerge from an examination of the empirical work on interorganizational trust. As such, we identify three key methodological challenges that face trust researchers: decoupling interorganizational trust from interpersonal trust, observing and measuring trust, and accounting for endogenous choice with respect to trust.

Decoupling Interpersonal and Interorganizational Trust. In considering the connection between interorganizational and interpersonal trust, one is led to questions of unit of analysis, which in turn are inextricably tied to the construct definition itself. At what point does interpersonal trust between boundary-spanners become interorganizational trust? Under what circumstances does one moderate the effects of the other? How might this differ when the referent interpersonal trust exists at different organizational levels? Does trust between organizational subunits constitute trust between entire organizations? It is important to consider when it would matter to illuminate such a distinction and how such research might avoid the "cross-level fallacy" identified by Rousseau (1985).

Observing Interorganizational Trust. How is interorganizational trust defined and therefore observed? What are the relative advantages or disadvantages of using secondary data versus primary data? For instance, if secondary data is to be used in operationalizing interorganizational trust, it might be done by envisioning repeated interaction between organizations as some indication of trust—but what are the implications of using proxies such as this? Research, for example, has employed various proxies for trust, but research has also shown that these commonly accepted proxies may not necessarily correlate with trust (Lui & Ngo, 2004). Furthermore, trust is a dynamic and continuous variable, not an either/or phenomenon (Flores & Solomon, 1998), providing an additional challenge to analyses that attempt to place interorganizational trust in a two-by-two framework.

Trust and Endogenous Choice. One of the aspects of interorganizational trust that researchers are keenly interested in is the relationship between trust and organizational (or alliance) performance. One of the challenges of studying such a connection, however, is the possibility of endogeneity—performance may affect trust, too. In such cases models that account for endogeneity, such as Two Stage Least Squares, would be important to consider. As well, unobserved factors might be driving performance measures rather than the interorganizational trust itself. Because organizations are typically large complex entities, making attributions of interorganizational-trust causes and organizational-performance effects is a much more difficult undertaking than drawing inferences between trust and behavior at the individual level. Researchers may also consider using multiple methods to more convincingly establish the causal chains through methodological triangulation.

Conclusion

The objective of this chapter is to consolidate, synthesize, and integrate the wide stream of empirical work on interorganizational trust. Four major themes emerge from our survey: the nature of interorganizational trust, its development, its role, and the outcomes of trust. For each theme we explore the relevant theoretical issues, leading to the identification of a promising research agenda for scholars of interorganizational trust. This agenda includes ten central theoretical avenues—as well as three key methodological challenges—that hold high potential for scholarly inquiry into this important phenomenon.

References

Ahuja, G. (2000). Collaboration networks, structural holes, and innovation: A longitudinal study. *Administrative Science Quarterly, 45*(3), 425–455.

Anderson, J. C., & Narus, J. A. (1990). A model of distributor firm and manufacturer firm working partnerships. *Journal of Marketing, 54,* 42–58.

Artz, K. W., & Brush, T. H. (2000). Asset specificity, uncertainty and relational norms: an examination of coordination costs in collaborative strategic alliances. *Journal of Economic Behavior & Organization, 41,* 337–362.

Aulakh, P. A., Kotabe, M., & Sahay, A. (1996). Trust and performance in cross-border marketing partnerships: A behavioral approach. *Journal of International Business Studies, 27*(5), 1005–1032.

Axelrod, R. (1984). *The evolution of cooperation.* New York: Basic Books.

Axelrod, R. (1997). *The complexity of cooperation.* Princeton, NJ: Princeton University Press.

Baier, A. (1986). Trust and antitrust. *Ethics, 96*(2), 231–260.

Becerra, M., & Gupta, A. K. (2003). Perceived trustworthiness within the organization: The moderating impact of communication frequency on trustor and trustee effects. *Organization Science, 14*(1), 32–44.

Blau, P. M. (1964). *Exchange and power in social life.* New York: Wiley.

Bromiley, P., & Cummings, L. L. (1995). Transactions costs in organizations with trust. In R. Bies, B. Sheppard, & R. Lewicki (Eds.), *Research on negotiation in organizations* (Vol. 5, pp. 219–247). Greenwich, CT: JAI Press.

Bromiley, P., & Harris, J. (2005). Trust, transactions cost economics, and mechanisms. In R. Bachmann & A. Zaheer (Eds.), *Handbook of trust research.* Northampton, MA: Edward Elgar.

Caldwell, C., & Clapham, S. E. (2003). Organizational trustworthiness: An international perspective. *Journal of Business Ethics, 47,* 349–364.

Carson, S. J., Madhok, A., Varman, R., & John, G. (2003). Information processing moderators of the effectiveness of trust-based governance in interfirm R&D collaboration. *Organization Science, 14*(1), 45–56.

Child, J., & Mollering, G. (2003). Contextual confidence and active trust development in the Chinese business environment. *Organization Science, 14*(1), 69–80.

Craswell, R. (1993). On the uses of "trust": Comment on Williamson. *Journal of Law & Economics, 36,* 487–500.

Currall, S. C., & Inkpen, A. C. (2002). A multilevel approach to trust in joint ventures. *Journal of International Business Studies, 33*(3), 479–495.

Currall, S. C., & Judge, T. A. (1995). Measuring trust between organizational boundary role persons. *Organizational Behavior and Human Decision Processes, 64*(2), 151–170.

Das, T. K., & Teng, B. S. (1998). Between trust and control: Developing confidence in partner cooperation in alliances. *Academy of Management Journal, 23*(3), 491–512.

Dasgupta, P. (1988). Trust as a commodity. In D. Gambetta (Ed.), *Trust: Making and breaking cooperative relations.* Cambridge, MA: Basil Blackwell.

Dirks, K. T., & Ferrin, D. L. (2001). The role of trust in organizational settings. *Organization Science, 12*(4), 450–467.

Doz, Y. L. (1996). The evolution of cooperation in strategic alliances: Initial conditions or learning processes? *Strategic Management Journal, 17,* 55–83.

Dyer, J. H. (1997). Effective interfirm collaboration: How firms minimize transaction costs and maximize shareholder value. *Strategic Management Journal, 18*(7), 535–556.

Dyer, J. H., & Chu, W. (2000). The determinants of trust in supplier-automaker relationships in the U.S., Japan, and Korea. *Journal of International Business Studies, 31*(2), 259–285.

Dyer, J. H., & Chu, W. (2003). The role of trustworthiness in reducing transaction costs and improving performance: Empirical evidence from the United States, Japan, and Korea. *Organization Science, 14*(1), 57–68.

Flores, F., & Solomon, R. C. (1998). Creating trust. *Business Ethics Quarterly, 8*(2), 205–232.

Fryxell, G. E., Dooley, R. S., & Vryza, M. (2002). After the ink dries: The interaction of trust and control in U.S.-based international joint ventures. *Journal of Management Studies, 39*(6), 865–886.

Fukuyama, F. (1995). *Trust: The social virtues and the creation of prosperity.* New York: Free Press.

Gambetta, D. (1988). Can we trust trust? In D. Gambetta (Ed.), *Trust: Making and breaking cooperative relations.* Cambridge, MA: Basil Blackwell.

Ganesan, S. (1994). Determinants of long-term orientation in buyer-seller relationships. *Journal of Marketing, 58,* 1–19.

Gargiulo, M., & Benassi, M. (2000). Trapped in your own net: Network cohesion, structural holes, and the adaptation of social capital. *Organization Science, 11*(2), 183–196.

Granovetter, M. (1985). Economic action and social structure: The problem of embeddedness. *American Journal of Sociology, 91*(3), 481–510.

Gulati, R. (1995). Does familiarity breed trust? The implications of repeated ties for contractual choice in alliances. *Academy of Management Journal, 38*(1), 85–112.

Gulati, R., & Gargiulo, M. (1999). Where do interorganizational networks come from? *American Journal of Sociology, 104*(5), 1439–1493.

Gulati, R., Khanna, T., & Nohria, N. (1994). Unilateral commitments and the importance of process in alliances. *Sloan Management Review, 35*(3), 61–69.

Gulati, R., & Singh, H. (1998). The architecture of cooperation: Managing coordination costs and appropriation concerns in strategic alliances. *Administrative Science Quarterly, 43*(4), 781–814.

Hagen, J. M., & Simons, T. (2003). *Differentiating trust-in-the-company from trust-in-the-executive in supply chain relations.* Paper presented at the Academy of Management 2003 Annual Meetings, Seattle, WA.

Hardin, R. (1991). Trusting persons, trusting institutions. In R. J. Zeckhauser (Ed.), *Strategy and choice.* Cambridge: MIT Press.

Heide, J. B., & John, G. (1990). Alliances in industrial purchasing: The determinants of joint action in buyer-supplier relationships. *Journal of Marketing Research, 27,* 24–36.

Heide, J. B., & John, G. (1992). Do norms matter in marketing relationships? *Journal of Marketing, 56,* 32–44.

Heide, J. B., & Miner, A. S. (1992). The shadow of the future: Effects of anticipated interaction and frequency of contact on buyer-seller cooperation. *Academy of Management Journal, 35*(2), 265–291.

Howorth, C., Westhead, P., & Wright, M. (2004). Buyouts, information asymmetry and the family management dyad. *Journal of Business Venturing, 19*(4), 509–534.

Huff, L., & Kelley, L. (2003). Levels of organizational trust in individualist versus collectivist societies: A seven-nation study. *Organization Science, 14*(1), 81–90.

Husted, B. W. (1994). Transaction costs, norms, and social networks: A preliminary study of cooperation in industrial buyer-seller relationships in the United States and Mexico. *Business & Society, 33*(1), 30–57.

Husted, B. W. (1998). The ethical limits of trust in business relations. *Business Ethics Quarterly, 8*(2), 233–248.

Jap, S. D., & Anderson, E. (2003). Safeguarding interorganizational performance and continuity under ex post opportunism. *Management Science, 49*(12), 1684–1701.

John, G. (1984). An empirical investigation of some antecedents of opportunism in a marketing channel. *Journal of Marketing Research, 21,* 278–289.

Kramer, R. M. (1999). Trust and distrust in organizations: Emerging perspectives, enduring questions. *Annual Review of Psychology, 50,* 569–598.

Lane, C. (1997). The social regulation of inter-firm relations in Britain and Germany: market rules, legal norms and technical standards. *Cambridge Journal of Economics, 21,* 197–215.

Lane, C., & Bachmann, R. (1996). The social constitution of trust: Supplier relations in Britain and Germany. *Organization Studies, 17*(3), 365–395.

Lane, C., & Bachmann, R. (1998). *Trust within and between organizations.* New York: Oxford University Press.

Larson, A. (1992). Network dyads in entrepreneurial settings: A study of the governance of exchange relationships. *Administrative Science Quarterly, 37,* 76–104.

Lewicki, R. J., & Bunker, B. B. (1996). Developing and maintaining trust in work relationships. In R. M. Kramer & T. R. Tyler (Eds.), *Trust in organizations: Frontiers of theory and research.* Thousand Oaks, CA: Sage Publications.

Lincoln, J. R. (1990). Japanese organization and organization theory. *Research in Organizational Behavior, 12,* 255–295.

Lui, S. S., & Ngo, H. Y. (2004). The role of trust and contractual safeguards on cooperation in non-equity alliances. *Journal of Management, 30*(4), 471–486.

Luo, Y. (2002). Contract, cooperation, and performance in international joint ventures. *Strategic Management Journal, 23*(10), 903–919.

Macneil, I. R. (1980). *The new social contract.* New Haven, CT: Yale University Press.

Malhotra, D., & Murnighan, J. K. (2002). The effects of contracts on interpersonal trust. *Administrative Science Quarterly, 47,* 534–559.

Mayer, K. J., & Argyres, N. (2004). Learning to contract: Evidence from the personal computer industry. *Organization Science, 15*(4), 394–411.

Mayer, R. C., Davis, J. H., & Schoorman, F. D. (1995). An integrative model of organizational trust. *Academy of Management Review, 20*(3), 709–734.

McEvily, B., & Zaheer, A. (2004). Architects of trust: The role of network facilitators in geographical clusters. In R. M. Kramer & K. S. Cook (Eds.), *Trust and distrust in organizations* (pp. 189–213). New York: Russell Sage Foundation.

McEvily, B., Zaheer, A., & Perrone, V. (2003). *Vulnerability and the asymmetric nature of trust in interorganizational exchange.* Paper presented at the European Academy of Management Annual Meeting, Milan, Italy.

Mellewigt, T., Madhok, A., & Weibel, A. (2004). *Trust and formal contracts in interorganizational relationships—Substitutes and complements!* Paper presented at the Brigham Young University/University of Utah 2004 Winter Strategy Conference, Park City, UT.

Mohr, J., & Spekman, R. (1994). Characteristics of partnership success: Partnership attributes, communication behavior, and conflict resolution techniques. *Strategic Management Journal, 15*(2), 135–152.

Moorman, C., Deshpande, R., & Zaltman, G. (1993). Factors affecting trust in market research relationships. *Journal of Marketing, 57,* 81–101.

Moorman, C., Zaltman, G., & Deshpande, R. (1992). Relationships between providers and users of market research: The dynamics of trust within and between organizations. *Journal of Marketing Research, 29,* 314–328.

Morgan, R. M., & Hunt, S. D. (1994). The commitment-trust theory of relationship marketing. *Journal of Marketing, 58,* 20–38.

Narayandas, D., & Rangan, V. K. (2004). Building and sustaining buyer-seller relationships in mature industrial markets. *Journal of Marketing, 68,* 63–77.

Nooteboom, B., Berger, H., & Noorderhaven, N. G. (1997). Effects of trust and governance on relational risk. *Academy of Management Journal, 40*(2), 308–338.

North, D. (1990). *Institutions, institutional change and economic performance.* New York: Cambridge University Press.

Parkhe, A. (1993). Partner nationality and the structure-performance relationship in strategic alliances. *Organization Science, 4*(2), 301–324.

Perrone, V., Zaheer, A., & McEvily, B. (2003). Free to be trusted? Organizational constraints on trust in boundary spanners. *Organization Science, 14*(4), 422–439.

Pfeffer, J., & Salancik, G. R. (1978). *The external control of organizations.* New York: Harper & Row.

Poppo, L., & Zenger, T. (2002). Do formal contracts and relational governance function as substitutes or complements? *Strategic Management Journal, 23*(8), 707–725.

Poppo, L., Zhou, K. Z., & Zenger, T. (2003). *The economic and social embeddedness of relational governance: An empirical study exploring origins and effectiveness.* Paper presented at the Academy of Management 2003 Annual Meetings, Seattle, WA.

Ring, P. S. (1996). Fragile and resilient trust and their roles in economic exchange. *Business & Society, 35*(2), 148–175.

Ring, P. S., & Van de Ven, A. H. (1992). Structuring cooperative relationships between organizations. *Strategic Management Journal, 13,* 483–498.

Ring, P. S., & Van de Ven, A. H. (1994). Developmental processes of cooperative interorganizational relationships. *Academy of Management Review, 19*(1), 90–118.

Rousseau, D. M. (1985). Issues of level in organizational research. In L. L. Cummings & B. M. Staw (Eds.), *Research in organizational behavior* (Vol. 7, pp. 1–37). Greenwich, CT: JAI Press.

Sako, M. (1998). Does trust improve business performance? In C. Lane & R. Bachmann (Eds.), *Trust within and between organizations.* Oxford: Oxford University Press.

Sampson, R. C. (2000). The role of lawyers in strategic alliances. *Case Western Reserve Law Review, 53,* 909–927.

Saparito, P. A., Chen, C. C., & Sapienza, H. J. (2004). The role of relational trust in bank–small firm relationships. *Academy of Management Journal, 47*(3), 400–411.

Sapienza, H. J., & Korsgaard, A. (1996). Procedural justice in entrepreneur-investor relations. *Academy of Management Journal, 39*(3), 544–574.

Schein, E. (1992). *Organizational culture and leadership* (2nd ed.). San Francisco: Jossey-Bass.

Seabright, M. A., Levinthal, D. A., & Fichman, M. (1992). Role of individual attachments in the dissolution of interorganizational relationships. *Academy of Management Journal, 35*(1), 122–160.

Shapiro, S. P. (1987). The social control of impersonal trust. *American Journal of Sociology, 93*(3), 623–658.

Szulanski, G., Cappetta, R., & Jensen, R. (2004). When and how trustworthiness matters: Knowledge transfer and the moderating effect of causal ambiguity. *Organization Science, 15*(5), 600–613.

Van de Ven, A., & Walker, G. (1984). The dynamics of interorganizational coordination. *Administrative Science Quarterly, 29*(4), 598–621.

Wathne, K. H., & Heide, J. B. (2000). Opportunism in interfirm relationships: Forms, outcomes, and solutions. *Journal of Marketing, 64,* 36–51.

Wathne, K. H., & Heide, J. B. (2004). Relationship governance in a supply chain network. *Journal of Marketing, 68,* 73–89.

Wicks, A. C., & Berman, S. L. (2004). The effects of context on trust in firm-stakeholder relationships: The institutional environment, trust creation, and firm performance. *Business Ethics Quarterly, 14*(1), 141–160.

Wicks, A. C., Berman, S. L., & Jones, T. M. (1999). The structure of optimal trust: Moral and strategic implications. *Academy of Management Review, 24*(1), 99–116.

Williamson, O. E. (1985). *The economic institutions of capitalism.* New York: Free Press.

Williamson, O. E. (1993). Calculativeness, trust, and economic organization. *Journal of Law & Economics, 36,* 453–486.

Young-Ybarra, C., & Wiersema, M. (1999). Strategic flexibility in information technology alliances: The influence of transaction cost economics and social exchange theory. *Organization Science, 10*(4), 439–459.

Zaheer, A., Lofstrom, S., & George, V. P. (2002). Interpersonal and interorganizational trust in alliances. In F. J. Contractor & P. Lorange (Eds.), *Cooperative strategies and alliances.* London: Pergamon.

Zaheer, A., McEvily, B., & Perrone, V. (1998). Does trust matter? Exploring the effects of interorganizational and interpersonal trust on performance. *Organization Science, 9*(2), 141–159.

Zaheer, A., & Venkatraman, N. (1995). Relational governance as an interorganizational strategy: An empirical test of the role of trust in economic exchange. *Strategic Management Journal, 16*(5), 373–392.

Zollo, M., Reuer, J. J., & Singh, H. (2002). Inter-organizational routines and performance in strategic alliances. *Organization Science, 13*(6), 701–713.

11

Exploring Dark Corners

An Agenda for Organizational Behavior Research in Alliance Contexts

Kwok Leung

Steven White

As a context for organizational behavior phenomena, alliances remain largely unexplored territory. To date, alliance research has been dominated by strategy scholars drawing primarily on economics and focusing on structure and control as antecedents and intermediary outcomes, and alliance or partner performance as the dependent variable of interest. Even studies of trust and cooperation are actually extensions of the structure and control focus (i.e., what types of structures create or support interorganizational trust) and are justified by their impact on alliance performance in terms of achieving one or both partners' task objectives for the alliance.

The resulting list of explanatory and outcome variables and the underlying processes is relatively limited. The most typical variables are fundamentally structural (see Table 11.1), such as organization form, ownership (equity and nonequity alliances) and control (e.g., Dyer, 1997; Gulati & Singh, 1998; Reuer, Zollo, & Singh, 2002), task interdependence and division of labor (e.g., Bensaou & Venkatraman, 1995; Garrette & Dussauge, 1995; Gulati & Singh, 1998), prior relationships between the partners (e.g., Gulati, 1995; Gulati & Gargiulo, 1999), and goals of the alliance and/or partners. Outcomes are largely limited to alliance formation, achievement of alliance or partner goals, and alliance termination. Processes are also limited, including exchange, reciprocity, opportunism, trust, and negotiation of contribution and distribution of outcomes. As a result, in spite of decades of research, alliances remain unexplored in terms of the cognitive, social-psychological phenomena falling under the broad category of organizational behavior (OB).

AUTHOR'S NOTE: This chapter is partly supported by a grant from the Research Grants Council of Hong Kong.

Table 11.1 Expanded List of Salient Variables in Alliance Contexts

	Antecedents	*Processes*	*Outcomes*
Structural (strategy)	Resources, power, dependence, (a)symmetries, knowledge, goals.	Exchange, reciprocity, trust (as predictable behavior), opportunism, control, learning, collaboration, (re)negotiation (of structural features).	Task accomplishment, alliance formation, and termination.
Social Cognitive (OB)	Personality traits, cognitive style, frames and schemata, (sub)cultures, individual and group identity, goals, and affectivity.	Interpretation, sense-making, dissonance, attribution, (re)negotiation (of culture, values, and objectives), interpersonal and intergroup dynamics such as trust, communication, and leadership behavior.	Job attitudes and performance, work motivation, commitment, emotional and affective quality of relationships, changes in identities and cultures, group (re)definition.

Research on prealliance negotiation and partner selection has explored a number of social and cognitive variables. As our following literature review shows, however, existing research on post-formation alliances is surprisingly circumspect in its consideration of OB variables and processes as either antecedents or outcomes. Even when they are included, as with, for example, "trust," they are pitched at the group and organization levels of analysis, not at the individual level. Indeed, there seems to be a tacit view among many alliance scholars that analysis at the individual or interpersonal level is not necessary for understanding phenomena and outcomes at the alliance, firm, and interfirm levels. In the rare cases in which OB variables are included in research designs and analyses, such as when culture is used as predictor of outcomes, conceptualization is usually simplistic compared to OB-based research, and measures are only rough proxies (e.g., Anderson & Gatignon, 1986; Barkema, Shenkar, Vermeulen, & Bell, 1997; Li & Guisinger, 1991). Although strategy process researchers often go the furthest in incorporating OB constructs and phenomena into their models of alliance formation and postformation dynamics (e.g., Ariño & de la Torre, 1998; Doz, 1996; Hamel, 1991; Kumar & Nti, 1998), the range of constructs they draw on is still quite limited compared to those available in the OB literature, and outcomes are typically restricted to task performance variables.

The purpose of this paper is to build on de Rond's (2003) broad thesis that alliances are inherently social phenomena and, to understand better their dynamics and performance, to stimulate further research on and in alliances that draws on OB research literature's rich stock of constructs and processes. Strategy-based research on alliances so far has largely ignored the interpersonal dynamics that underlie any alliance or interorganizational relationship, although a number of strategy scholars have ventured further afield into OB phenomena in their analyses of alliances, addressing such issues as the "social fit" and affective elements of relationships (Artz & Brush, 2000; Child & Faulkner, 1998; Mohr & Spekman, 1994; Jemison & Sitkin, 1986; White, forthcoming; Lui & Ngo, forthcoming), as well as dependence, conflict, and perceptions of equity (Ariño & de la Torre, 1998; Das & Teng, 2000; Doz, 1996; Kogut, 1989; Inkpen & Beamish, 1997; Madhock & Tallman, 1998; Ring & Van de Ven, 1994). While such work is moving in the right direction, there are still great conceptual and phenomenological expanses that remain largely unexplored.

At the same time, we also identify features of alliances that constitute particularly rich contexts for studying variables and processes central to OB research. After reviewing the dimensions defining the alliance context, we review literature that has explored OB variables and processes in this context and suggest a research agenda to address the under- or unexplored "dark corners." We bring together constructs and issues suggested by the albeit limited past research and this research agenda in the form of a behavioral model of alliances in which integration vigilance plays a key moderating role between diverse antecedents and outcomes that are salient in an alliance.

Alliances as Contexts: Structural and Social Cognitive Dimensions

Although scholars have proposed various definitions of alliances or cooperative interorganizational relationships (e.g., Parkhe, 1993; Ring & Van de Ven, 1992, 1994), two features are common to them all. First, they involve two or more organizational actors, and separately defined identities, interests, and power are either implied or explicitly stated. In other words, each actor is able to make decisions regarding the formation of and behavior within an alliance. Second, the partners form an alliance in order to achieve specific goals, which may be the same for all partners or different across partners and of varying degrees of compatibility. These two features of alliances—relationships and goals—have been central to management research in alliances, and that research has been the nearly exclusive domain of strategy scholars. As dicussed before, their primary interest in alliances has been the performance implications of alliance structures and subsequently the structuring and management of alliance relationships as antecedents to goal achievement.

Alliances, however, present a much richer area for research than that already charted by strategy and a few OB scholars. The first and most obvious area for expanding our research horizons vis-à-vis alliances emerges once we recognize the range of relationships within an alliance. Strategy researchers typically limit their analyses to two types of relationships: between parent organizations, and between the parent and the alliance (*g* and *h* in Figure 11.1). As Figure 11.1 shows, however, there are nine additional relationships that are relevant for alliances when different levels of analysis (individual, group, organization) and boundaries (organization, various subunits) are considered. At the individual and group levels, they include relationships among individuals from the same parent (*b*), different parents (*a*), outside of either parent organization (*c*), or among all three (from either parent or outsiders, i.e., the alliance, *e*). This may also include interpersonal relationships between the leader of an alliance and a senior executive to whom they report in a parent organization (*k*).

At the intergroup level, there are interactions between groups from the different parents (*d*), and between the alliance (or subgroups within the alliance) and groups within either parent organization (*f*). Finally, an alliance may also affect the relationship between a parent organization and another (nonpartner) organization (*i*), and the alliance itself may have important interactions with nonparent organizations (*j*). The number of relationships is even greater if we include those across levels of analysis, that is, between an individual and a group or organization or between a group and an organization.

The nature, quality, and dynamics of each of these relationships may themselves be important focal issues in addition to their potential impact on a focal alliance's dynamics and outcomes. Accordingly, each of these relationships and levels of analysis represents possible areas of study within a widened definition of "alliance" research. However, such complex intergroup

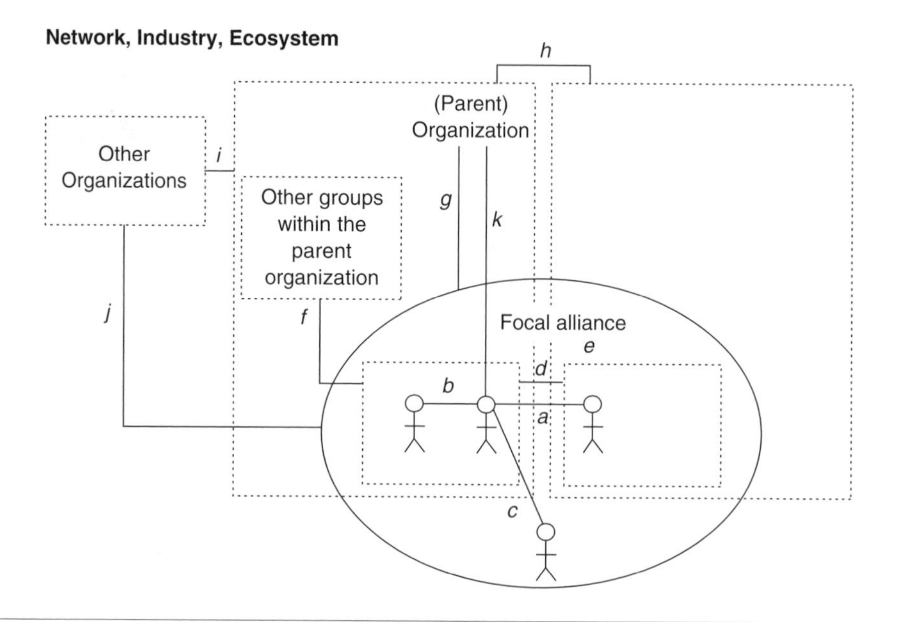

Figure 11.1 Salient Relationships in and Surrounding an Alliance

Relationships and levels of analysis

a: Dyads: individuals from each partner
b: Dyads and groups: individuals from same partner in same alliance
c: Dyads and groups: individual from a partner and from outside
d: Groups: alliance groups from each partner
e: Group: multiparty relationships among members (combination of *a*, *b* and *c*)
f: Groups: alliance group and non-alliance group within same parent organization
g: Groups: alliance (or alliance group) and parent organization
h: Organizations: parent organizations involved in alliance
i: Organizations: alliance partners and nonpartners within a network, industry, or ecosystem
j: Organizations: alliance and nonparent organization in a network, industry, or ecosystem
k: Dyads: leader of alliance and direct superior in parent

dynamics have rarely been addressed in OB research. Alliances therefore provide an excellent context for examining these complex issues that, in the end, could deepen our understanding of the dynamics associated with complex interpersonal and intergroup relationships.

In addition to recognizing a broader range of salient relationships, a second way to expand our alliance research horizons is to recognize a broader range of variables and constructs. As already discussed, alliance research is now largely restricted to what may be categorized as structural variables describing the antecedents, processes, and outcomes of interest (Table 11.1). OB research, however, suggests a much broader range of variables and processes that could help understand alliance outcomes, and most of these are unexplored by existing alliance research (Table 11.1). The impact of multiple role identities among individuals in an alliance, for example, will influence both the interpretation and effort exerted towards achieving diverse goals, in addition to communication among individuals who must collaborate, as well as attributions made of other individuals' actions. A number of OB outcome variables, such as motivation, commitment, and identification, could also be important mediating variables affecting alliance performance or goal achievement of partner organizations. Such social cognitive characteristics of individuals and groups and the processes and outcomes resulting from them are largely unexplored in existing alliance research.

In the following section, we review the albeit limited research that has incorporated OB variables into studies of alliances or investigated OB phenomena in alliance contexts. We find that the key themes and foci of these studies fall into a limited number of categories: identity and intergroup dynamics, culture clash, third culture emergence, and interunit conflict (between partner organizations and between alliance and parent). These categories actually correspond to the categories of specific problem issues that Bailey and Shenkar (1993) identify in their earlier review of research on international joint ventures (IJVs), a formally structured and integrated alliance form. Intergroup issues they identify included staffing friction, blocked promotions, split loyalties, compensation gaps, and blocked or incomplete information. Cultural issues arise from blurred organizational cultures and lack of familiarity with a new culture. Finally, interunit conflict is identified in the form of limited delegation by the parent to the alliance. Our review casts a wider net by reviewing work done in diverse forms of alliances, not just IJVs, in order to identify areas into which a few scholars have tentatively entered, as well as the major gaps in research in and about alliances.

Taking Inventory of OB Research in Alliances

As mentioned above, most research involving alliances is at the alliance, firm, or interfirm level, and we know relatively little about behavioral issues within an alliance, such as decision making, communication, and conflict processing. Werner's (2002) conclusion from his review of international management research trends from 1996 to 2000 in 20 top management journals reflects this lack of attention and understanding. Of the twelve major categories he identifies, only two categories pertain to our review: IJVs and strategic alliances, and networks. The research in these two categories is primarily at the firm level, addressing such issues as partner selection and relations and outcomes of alliances. In two other categories that have some relevance to our review—subsidiary and multinational team management and expatriate management—there is some research on organizational behavior, but many gaps are evident. Werner concludes, "international micro level research seems to be overlooked in the leading management journals" (2002, p. 293). While no one has undertaken a systematic analysis of research on domestic alliances, a casual scan of the literature suggests that Werner's conclusion applies equally well to this area of inquiry. In short, we know surprisingly little about how interpersonal processes play out in an alliance context.

The lack of organizational behavior research in an alliance context is unsettling. So much is at stake in an alliance, as reflected by the voluminous firm-level research on this topic, but we know so little about the relevant people issues that may make or break an alliance. The complexity and difficulty of managing an alliance is widely acknowledged, and there are many books detailing the dos and don'ts in managing people issues in alliances (e.g., Spekman, Isabella, & MacAvoy, 2000; Yoshino & Rangan, 1995), but this advice rests primarily on conjectures rather than on empirical evidence.

The following sections present the results of our inventory of the existing literature on organization behavior in alliance contexts, drawing on firm-level findings as well as theoretical and empirical work in intergroup behavior, social identity, and diversity management. The aim is to provide a coherent account of what we know about the people issues involved in alliances and to develop a framework for guiding future research in this important but underdeveloped area. We focus on the processes and dynamics of ongoing alliances, for the purposes of this analysis excluding behavioral research on preformation processes, such as the negotiation of an alliance contract.

Identity and Intergroup Issues

As introduced above, a major challenge in alliances emerges from the fact that two or more distinct groups of employees from parent firms must work together. Drawing on prior work on intergroup behavior and social identity (Ashforth & Mael, 1989; Sherif & Sherif, 1953; Tajfel, 1978; Turner, 1987), many researchers have studied the sources and impact of mistrust, in-group favoritism, and rigid group boundaries on collaboration. For example, in a survey of a multiethnic company in the United States, Barak, Cherin, and Berkman (1998) identify two diversity dimensions: fairness, which refers to the fairness with which management treats different ethnic groups, and inclusion, which refers to the inclusion of different ethnic groups in management processes. These two dimensions highlight the intergroup tension salient in a multigroup context, in which people worry about injustice and exclusion as a result of negative intergroup dynamics.

Identity Issues. Empirical findings in an alliance context generally corroborate the hurdles suggested by intergroup, social identity, and diversity management theories. Salk and Shenkar (2001), for example, find that identities are fixed relatively early in the life of an alliance and persist as a frame through which individuals interpret others and events in the alliance. In a survey of local and expatriate members of the management teams of IJVs located in Canada and the United States, Johnson (1999) finds that they are more committed to the IJV than to the parent firms. However, about 32% of the respondents reported conflicting loyalties, with 21% showing high commitment to the IJV but low commitment to the parents, and 11% showing high commitment to the parents but low commitment to the IJV. In a multigroup context, split loyalty is always an issue that may stifle commitment and productivity. Based on a case involving the alliance of three American companies for designing advanced robotics devices, Gould, Ebers, and Clinchy (1999) note that the intergroup dynamics inherent in alliances are often characterized by anxiety and defensive reaction to such anxiety, including rigid group boundaries and out-group distrust.

Trust. Madhok (1995) argues that trust is important to the continuation of an alliance and further suggests that there are two components of trust in this context: structural and social. The structural component of trust refers to the complementarity and synergy of the resources contributed by both sides, and the social component refers to the quality of the relationship between employees of the two sides. Rephrased, structural trust relates to the task interdependence between the partners, while social trust is interpersonal and affective. Consistent with the social-trust argument, in a survey of local managers of IJVs in China, Chen and Boggs (1998) find that perceived mutual trust between the partners is related to the possibility of continued cooperation. Similarly, in a survey of managers who worked for alliances in the United States, Kale, Singh, and Perlmutter (2000) find that relational capital, defined in terms of respect, trust, friendship, and reciprocity, is related to learning between the partners. Luo (2001) describes these outcomes as being dependent on the development of "personal attachment" between individuals in an alliance, in turn dependent on factors at the individual, organizational, and environmental levels.

Trust and relational capital do not arise spontaneously (Inkpen & Beamish, 1997). Indeed, it should not be surprising that mistrust is common in alliances, especially when goals and objectives are different or competing (Zeng & Chen, 2003). Research shows that one reason that alliances are shaky is the inherent difficulty in building trust among individuals and groups in an alliance. In a survey of local employees of four JV factories in South China, Wong, Ngo, and Wong (2003) find that job security is related to trust in the organization, whereas supervisor-subordinate *guanxi* is related to trust in supervisors. Their findings suggest that job security and positive superior-subordinate relationships contribute through different processes to building trust among individuals in an alliance.

Currall and Inkpen (2002) propose that trust should be conceptualized as multilevel: personal, group, and firm, resulting in nine types of trust when these three types of trust for the trustors and trustees are crossed. They also propose ways to measure these nine types of trust, providing a useful starting point for future research to decipher the precise nature of trust in an alliance context.

In-Group Favoritism. The tendency to favor employees of one's side, or in-group favoritism, is another common problem in alliances. In a study of managers in a Japanese-German IJV in Germany, Salk and Brannen (2000) identify in-group favoritism as leading to more advice-related and task-related ties with coworkers of the same national background. Furthermore, the Japanese managers had a better-connected network for private communication than the German managers, which seems consistent with the clear distinction between work and private life salient in the German culture. In another alliance, Salk and Shenkar (2001) show the deleterious effects that in-group favoritism and bias can have on collaboration and alliance outcomes when such favoritism and bias challenge notions of fairness in, for example, personnel appointments.

Divergent Perception. Differences may be manifest as divergent perceptions by individuals within an alliance, and these may (but do not necessarily) lead to significant intergroup problems. In a study of American expatriate and local Chinese managers in American multinationals in Taiwan, Chang (1985) found that compared with local employees, American expatriates were more satisfied with job security, prestige inside the company, autonomy in decision making, personal development, and chances for advancement but less satisfied with physical surroundings. In addition, American expatriates reported higher satisfaction with friendliness of colleagues and friendship with people of different nationalities, while Chinese managers reported higher satisfaction with friendship with people of the same nationality.

At-Twaijri (1989) replicated this study with managers from fifty U.S. joint business ventures in Saudi Arabia and found that compared with Saudi managers, American expatriates were more satisfied with pay and benefits, prestige inside the company, autonomy in decision making, personal development, and chances for advancement but less satisfied with physical surroundings. In addition, American expatriates reported higher satisfaction with friendships with people of different nationalities, while Saudi managers reported higher satisfaction with friendliness of colleagues and friendships with people of the same nationality. Expatriates in these two studies were generally more satisfied with their compensation, status, and job content than local employees, and this could further accentuate the boundary between them in an alliance and become an impediment to collaboration.

It should be noted that these problems do not necessarily plague all alliances, even if there are distinctions between groups, such as asymmetries in outcomes. Chiah-Liaw, Petzall, and Selvarajah (2003), for example, studied six Australian-Malaysian joint ventures (JVs) in Malaysia and found that the compensation gap between the two groups of staff was problematic but did not seem to be a major problem in these alliances' performance, and other problems were seen as mild.

Positive Interaction and Alliance Performance

Because identity and intergroup issues may threaten the viability of an alliance, an obvious prediction from this perspective is that alliances that are able to avoid or overcome these divisive forces are more likely to be successful. In line with this reasoning, Aulakh, Kotabe, and Sahay (1996) argue that positive interaction is conducive to the success of IJVs. Li, Xin, Tsui, and Hambrick (1999) analyze the problems in JV leadership teams in China and propose a number of practical guidelines for effective team-building. Many of their suggestions center on the idea of enhancing a strong team identity and improving the group dynamics within the team. In a survey of alliances in the United States, Saxton (1997) finds that prior relationships between the partners are associated with initial satisfaction with an alliance but not with alliance outcomes. While prior relationships likely reduce mistrust and group boundaries separating the partners and contribute to initial satisfaction, alliance outcomes are probably more dependent on subsequent interactions between the partners.

A number of studies suggest that positive interaction and engagement in the form of communication and commitment to the partnership are effective in breaking down intergroup barriers. In a study of chief executive officers (CEOs) in IJVs in China, Gong, Shenkar, Luo, and Nyaw (2001) find that communication within an IJV and between an IJV and its parents are negatively related to role conflict and ambiguity of these CEOs. In a study of a retail network resulting from the merger of two different firms in Norway, Nygaard and Dahlstrom (2002) find that personal communication is associated with low role ambiguity, but no such effect is found for group and impersonal modes of communication. In a survey of computer dealers and suppliers who formed a strategic partnership in the United States, Mohr and Spekman (1994) find that trust, commitment to the partnership, coordination, communication, and participation in planning are associated with partnership success. In a survey of alliances in the United States, Saxton (1997) finds that the degree of shared decision making is associated with successful alliance outcomes. Lin and Germain (1999) surveyed a group of Chinese and American managers from Sino-American JVs in China and found that at the firm level, relationship commitment—the desire to maintain a relationship—was positively related to cross-cultural adaptation and interaction frequency. Luo (2001) finds that personal attachment and positive working relationships develop as individuals work together longer, parental goals are congruous, and cultural gaps are smaller. He also finds that environmental factors that challenged the alliance (market disturbances and regulatory deterrence) also enhance personal attachment. Finally, Brannen and Salk (2000) find that although differences in identity persist across groups, in the German-Japanese JV that they studied the individuals are able to develop shared work norms that facilitate their collaboration.

As in overcoming negative intergroup dynamics, studies have also shown the benefits of commitment, trust, and cooperation for conflict resolution and subsequently for alliance performance. In their study of computer dealers and suppliers, Mohr and Spekman (1994) find that in resolving conflicts, problem solving is related positively and severe resolution (harsh words and domination) and smoothing over problems are related negatively to partnership success. In a survey of managers who worked for alliances in the United States, Kale et al., (2000) find that a communication- and contact-intensive conflict management process is positively related to learning between the partners. In a survey of U.S. and Chinese managers in IJVs in China, Lin and Miller (2003) find that commitment to the partnering relationship is positively related to problem solving and compromising but negatively related to forcing and legalism in resolving conflict between the two partners. Lui and Ngo (forthcoming) similarly find that the degree of trust is an antecedent to conflict response modes and outcomes. Specifically, in relationships characterized by high trust, the cooperation process is characterized by more acquiescence to a partner, a more limited range of actions, and less reciprocal, tit-for-tat behavior.

In contrast, perceived power asymmetries seem to suppress productive conflict-resolution approaches. In their survey of U.S. and Chinese managers in IJVs in China, Lin and Germain (1998) find that a high level of perceived relative power is related to less compromising and more forcing. They also find that perceived power is related to higher satisfaction with the partnership.

Promoting justice is a powerful way to reduce the intergroup schism in an alliance. Perceptions of justice corresponded with positive job attitudes, positive evaluation of expatriate managers, and low intention to quit among local employees working for IJVs in China (Leung, Smith, Wang, & Sun, 1996; Leung, Wang, & Smith, 2001). Wong et al. (2002) find that for local employees in IJVs in China, procedural and distributive justice is associated with more trust in the IJV. Johnson, Korsgaard, and Sapienza (2002) surveyed senior management teams of IJVs located in the United States and Canada and found that perceived procedural justice and the extent of decision control by the IJV were related to organizational commitment to the IJV by the management team. Interestingly, the positive effect of procedural justice on organizational commitment to the IJV was more pronounced when decision control was perceived as low. In other words, if managers in an IJV cannot make decisions on their own, justice becomes even more important in elevating commitment to the IJV.

In a survey of local employees who worked for IJVs in China, Chen, Choi, and Chi (2002) find that they perceive their compensations as unfair when compared with expatriates. However, if they perceive expatriates as beneficial to China as a whole and recognize that they deserve a higher pay because of higher living standards at home, the perceived fairness of the compensation of expatriates is higher. These findings suggest that it is essential to maintain a high level of justice perception in an alliance context to minimize negative reactions to injustice, which can swiftly drag an intergroup relationship down into a negative spiral (Salk & Shenkar, 2001; Leung & Stephan, 1998).

Cultural Clash

It is well known that clashes in organizational, national, or other spheres of culture (e.g., Schneider & Barsoux, 2003) may pose a serious threat to an alliance, and cultural dissimilarity between the partners is usually assumed to be detrimental to an alliance as incompatible values, priorities, and practices clash. For example, Hitt, Dacin, Tyler, and Park (1997) find that Korean and American executives use different criteria in decision making. Koreans emphasize growth and hence emphasize industry attractiveness, sales, and market share, whereas Americans emphasize profitability and hence emphasize projected demand, discounted cash flow, and return on investment (ROI). In a scenario study of U.S.-Japanese JVs, Sullivan, Peterson, Kameda, and Shimada (1981) find that Japanese managers prefer conferment to resolve a conflict, whereas American managers prefer binding arbitration. In a survey of managers working for American multinational corporations (MNCs) in Taiwan, Chinese managers were found to endorse paternalistic values more than American managers, believing that firms should take care of employees both inside and outside the workplace (Chang, 1985). At-Twaijri (1989) conducted a similar survey in U.S. joint business ventures in Saudi Arabia and found that Saudi managers also endorsed paternalistic values more than American managers. Local employees were also likely to expect more care, concern, and help than what their expatriate managers would provide, and disappointment due to higher expectations of this type may lead to dissatisfaction among local staff.

In line with the cultural dissimilarity argument, Hambrick, Li, Xin, and Tsui (2001) advance the notion of a compositional gap—resulting from diversity among managers—to explain the problems confronting management groups in IJVs. A compositional gap emerges from a number of compositional characteristics, such as demographics, values, personality, and cognitive styles. These compositional differences of management groups in IJVs are likely to lead to relationship and substantive conflict. On the positive side, these compositional differences may stimulate cognitive diversity that is beneficial to the effectiveness of IJVs, but the authors suggest that the relationship between compositional differences and cognitive diversity is unstable and may not occur regularly.

The empirical literature provides considerable support for the detrimental effects of cultural dissimilarity. In their study of CEOs in IJVs in China, Gong et al. (2001) find that role conflict is positively related to objective distance between the two partners in terms of goals. Lyles and Salk (1996) find that at the firm level in Hungary, cultural conflict is related to lower knowledge acquisition from foreign parents and hence lower performance of IJVs. In structured interviews with executives in IJVs in India, Pothukuchi,

Damanpour, Choi, Chen, and Park (2002) find that differences in organizational culture between the two partners based on the dimensions of organizational culture identified by Hofstede, Neuijen, Ohayv, and Sanders (1990) are negatively correlated with their satisfaction with the JV. In a survey of alliances in the United States, including some multinational firms, Saxton (1997) finds that similarity in strategic content (e.g., technology and marketing) and organizational processes (e.g., structure and human relations) between the partners is associated with initial satisfaction with the alliances, although no such effect was found for alliance outcomes. Perhaps alliance outcomes are influenced more strongly by variables other than similarity in these two domains.

Empirical results from studies addressing national culture have also found a positive correlation between cultural similarity and collaboration. The value of similarity is demonstrated in a study of managers in a Japanese-German JV in Germany by Salk and Brannen (2000). They find that the factors determining one's influence in this setting are quite similar for both the Japanese and German managers, and this similarity is attributed to the high performance of this IJV team. In a survey of local managers in IJVs in China, Chen and Boggs (1998) find a positive relationship between cultural similarity (defined by the foreign partner being from a Chinese society: Hong Kong, Singapore, and Taiwan) and likelihood of continued cooperation. In a survey of U.S. and Chinese managers in IJVs in China, Lin and Germain (1998) find that in resolving intercultural conflict, perceived cultural similarity between the two conflicting parties is associated with the use of problem solving and satisfaction with the partnership.

Other studies suggest that the relationship between (national) cultural similarity and conflict or other outcomes is not straightforward. For example, Shenkar and Zeira (1992) find that the role conflict and ambiguity of CEOs of IJVs in Israel are not related to characteristics of the parent firms of the IJVs, such as the number of parent firms involved and their size. Rather, differences in power distance and masculinity/femininity of the parent firms are positively related to role ambiguity, but differences in collectivism/individualism and uncertainty avoidance are negatively related to role ambiguity. Such results suggest that cultural differences may not always lead to problems in an alliance. We revisit the cultural-dissimilarity argument with regard to national culture in a later section as we propose a behavioral model of alliances to try to reconcile such complex and sometimes inconsistent empirical results.

Third Culture

Some scholars have argued that one way to minimize cultural clash in an alliance is to form a new culture for the alliance. Brannen and Salk (2000) propose that the organizational culture of an IJV should be conceptualized as a "negotiated culture" that results from the cultures of the two parents, the idiosyncratic elements of the IJV, and negotiations and compromises of senior members of the IJV. Dynamic and emergent in nature, this negotiated culture does not relate to the culture of the parents in a simple, mechanistic way, and is subject to the influence of a whole host of contextual factors. This view of a negotiated culture is supported by results obtained in semistructured interviews of the top management team of a German-Japanese JV located in Germany. The negotiated culture of this IJV was well defined and widely shared by both Germans and Japanese. While this emergent culture shared elements of German and Japanese cultures, it also differed in many features that the authors traced to salient contextual factors impinging on this IJV. A number of strategies were adopted to forge endorsement of this culture, involving compromise by one group (one group adopted the norms of the other group), meeting in the middle (compromises by both sides), innovation (new for both groups), and division of labor (one group was responsible for a particular task).

In analyzing Sino-American JVs in China, the idea of a third culture is also proposed by Hui and Graen (1997). They suggest that the best integrative strategy for these IJVs is to combine elements from both cultures. Specifically, the Chinese concept of *guanxi* (relationships), which is holistic and emphasizes loyalty, should be integrated with the American notion of leader-member exchange (LMX), which is work-oriented and emphasizes performance. For American managers to succeed in these IJVs, emphasizing both a long-term relationship (*guanxi*) and competence (LMX) is important and represents an endorsement of a third culture derived from the two constituent cultures.

Parent Firms, Alliances, and Their Relationships

The complexity of an alliance goes beyond typical intergroup issues because there are two parent firms with impinging influences on the alliance. For example, based on a detailed analysis of four Sino-U.S. JVs in China, Yan and Gray (1994) find that the relative bargaining power of a partner is related to management control of the IJV, such as the nomination of directors to its board of directors and the general manager as well as the adoption of management systems from the parent.

Ring and Van de Ven (1992) propose four types of governance structures for cooperative relationships based on the degree of risk involved and the reliance on trust. When risk is high but trust between the two sides is low, hierarchical governance structures with clear authority lines are likely to be adopted and the autonomy accorded to an alliance is likely to be low. In contrast, if the risk involved is low and the trust is high, a governance model based on recurrent contracting transactions that involve repeated exchanges with moderate degrees of transaction specificity is likely to be adopted. The autonomy accorded to such an alliance is likely to be high.

Several studies have focused on the relationship between risk, especially in the form of asset specificity, and governance structure. In their study of architect and contractor relationships, Lui and Ngo (forthcoming) find that asset specificity and governance mechanism have an effect on relationship quality (e.g., trust) and type of response to conflict. These findings are similar to those of Dyer's (1997) study of supplier relationships among Japanese firms.

Other studies have focused on the nature of the relationship between parent and alliance. In a detailed analysis of a U.S.-European JV by means of interviews and archival data, Lyles and Reger (1993) find that JV managers employ a variety of tactics to obtain autonomy from their parents. The process is complex, dynamic, and nonlinear, and much of it is unplanned and opportunistic. Leadership of the JV also plays a significant role in shaping the degree of autonomy granted by its parents. JV managers are accountable to two parents, and their skill in balancing the demands of the parents and maintaining positive relationships with them helps increase their autonomy.

It would seem that as long as there is agreement regarding the degree of control over the alliance by the parents and in the goals and directions between the parents and alliance, then the rift between the parents and an alliance should be immaterial. However, we know very little about how these agreements come about and the factors that influence these agreements, an area urgently in need of research.

Research Agenda

Our review of the OB literature in alliance contexts suggests clear directions for future research on and in alliances. First, there is a need to expand the range of relationships studied under the rubric of "alliances." Besides the relationships between partners and parent-alliance (*g* and *h* in Figure 11.1), we have identified nine others that represent either potentially important antecedents to alliance performance or performance itself.

Second, there is a need to explore and incorporate more social-cognitive variables and processes in studying alliance phenomena. Those listed in Table 11.1 are only for illustrative purposes, and more constructs will certainly emerge as more OB research is undertaken in alliance contexts. We also argue that a number of these variables are not alliance or partner-firm performance outcomes themselves, but are antecedent and intermediary variables and processes that we should expect to have an impact on performance outcomes. Examples include satisfaction (with relationships, personal goals, etc.), stress, affectivity, work motivation, commitment, attitudes towards the partner organization and its members, salient bases of identity, and interpersonal and intergroup dynamics.

More specifically, the integration of constructs from OB with strategy researchers' concern for task performance holds particular promise. For example, issues of identities and roles are critical for understanding alliance performance because they have a direct impact on cooperation and goal attainment, and the alliance context creates strong forces affecting these issues. Individuals must manage multiple identities and roles, a task that is especially challenging when those are in conflict (dissonance). As two individuals or groups come together, their respective identities may clash or overlap to varying degrees, their identities evolve, and new identities possibly emerge.

Other OB variables that are important in an alliance context include the distribution and bases of power among individuals and groups in an alliance, which have clear implications for cooperation and goal achievement. How these actors perceive, respond, and attempt to gain power interacts with the quality of their interaction and ability to achieve their goals. Similarly, perceptions of equity and fairness regarding processes and outcomes also affect relationship quality and ability to work together. The frames and schemata that participants bring to an alliance and develop during the course of an alliance drive interpretation and sense-making, and the outcomes of these processes have a direct impact on interactions among alliance participants. These issues represent an important set of antecedents for alliances as well as a set of outcomes as they evolve in the process of interaction among participants in an alliance and in response to external changes in the alliance.

Finally, the complexities of alliances make them fertile but virgin territory for leadership research. Leadership in such contexts may be by a representative from one partner, by a top management team representing each parent organization, or by an outsider without prior ties to either partner organization. A leader faces the challenge of managing multiple and sometimes conflicting identities and goals among representatives of each partner as well as relationships between the alliance and the parent organizations. There is a clear need to have a better understanding of the types of leaders who can manage such challenges effectively or what kinds of leadership structures are most effective.

In addition to being a source of new research topics, research from OB traditions could enrich research on and in alliance contexts in more general ways. First, there should be more models that include feedback loops, building on insights from case-study-based process studies and perhaps incorporated into statistical models predicting various outcomes. For example, performance at a previous point in time may be an important predictor of alliance restructuring or interpretation of performance (and thereby motivation or other intermediary outcomes) at a subsequent point in time. This analysis also suggests that multiple time-point sampling of alliances and participants in alliances is preferable to one-time sampling.

Second, political perspectives on organizational dynamics suggest research designs that account for the various stakeholders in an alliance, not just the parent or partner firms. Examples of stakeholders defined by interpersonal, intergroup, and interorganizational relationships are suggested by Figure 11.1, which depicts formally defined stakeholders. Others may be identified by particular interests vis-à-vis an alliance and they may not correspond to any formal groups. These stakeholders use their power to pursue their interests, and this in turn drives alliance evolution and whether (or which) goals of an alliance are achieved. At the same time, these stakeholders may change over time (in terms of their interests, power, coalitions, and new emergence) in response to external events as well as developments within the alliance.

Third, alliances also represent a key context for studying interface processes as two or more individuals, groups, or organizations interact, both as phenomena of interest in themselves as well as drivers of collaboration and performance. For example, as Brannen and Salk (2000) find, cultures change as they interact, either by a merging of the cultures, creation of a "third" culture, or hardening of boundaries between the original cultures. Similarly, identities of individuals and groups may blend and combine or they may harden and form impenetrable intergroup boundaries. Diversity and cohesiveness within a group may also affect the interaction between groups and have important implications for cooperation as well as management across such groups.

Understanding such interface processes, however, requires a deeper understanding of negotiation processes in alliance contexts. While there is some OB research on negotiation between potential partners at the search and formation stages of an alliance, there is little such research on the postformation stage of an alliance. For example, how do partner characteristics (e.g., gaps and overlaps in cognitive and cultural variables, definitions and perceptions of risk, conflict resolution approaches, and others) interact and affect the formal and implicit negotiation processes? We would also expect fundamental differences between negotiating a market transaction and negotiating a relationship, extending the extensive research on the difference in governance structures among different types of relationships.

Integration Vigilance and a Behavioral Model of Alliances

As a first step in exploring the dark corners that we have identified, we introduce and develop the construct *integration vigilance*, placing it within the context of a behavioral model of alliances and making specific recommendations for further research. Integration vigilance is meant to capture the awareness and extra effort that prior literature (e.g., Draulans, deMan, & Volberda, 2003; White, forthcoming) suggests may enable managers to balance the tensions and overcome the challenges inherent in alliances. The model also draws attention to the range of outcomes—affective, relational, and task performance—that are salient in practice and, as our review suggests, understudied.

Researchers have identified elements that contribute to integration vigilance, which may be broadly categorized as cognitive and manifest vigilance. Kale, Dyer, and Singh (2002), for example, find that alliance experience and the existence of a dedicated alliance function (a formal position within a firm to manage issues related to alliances) are positively related to the long-term success of the firm's alliances. Such structures represent not only the cognitive aspect—namely, the recognition that such preparation and processes are necessary—but also the manifest aspect, which refers to conscious effort to facilitate the functioning of an alliance. It is conceivable, however, that some firms are high in cognitive vigilance but lack concrete initiatives for promoting the success of an alliance.

We expect managers and parent organizations with higher integration vigilance to structure a relationship ex ante in a way that would reduce the likelihood of subsequent conflict, whether by reducing competing interests or role ambiguity. This is one way to frame the findings of Gong et al. (2001), in which the completeness of the contract for an IJV was negatively related to role conflict and ambiguity of the CEOs of IJVs in China, and the degree of the parents' formalization of management structure and regulations was also negatively related to their role conflict. We argue that the completeness of an IJV contract and the formalization of management structures and regulations are indicators of a higher level of integration vigilance on the part of the senior management of the parent firms, and that these vigilant executives are in turn more effective in helping the CEOs of their IJVs reduce and cope with role ambiguity and conflict. Integration vigilance is related to competence, as suggested by findings from research on mergers and acquisitions. For instance, Nygaard and Dahlstrom (2002) studied a retail network resulting from the merger of two different firms in Norway, and found that managerial competence was related to lower role ambiguity. Perhaps integration vigilance is able to enhance managerial competence capable of enhancing performance in an alliance context.

A few studies also show that extra effort can reduce the intergroup friction between different groups in an alliance. In a survey of local employees who worked for IJVs in China, Chen et al. (2002) found that they perceived their compensations as unfair when compared with expatriates. However, interpersonal sensitivity shown by expatriates toward locals moderated the negative influence of compensation disadvantages vis-à-vis the expatriates on perceived fairness of their compensation. In other words, when interpersonal sensitivity of expatriates was high, the negative effect of compensation disadvantage vis-à-vis the expatriates was reduced. Doucet and Jehn (1997) found that American expatriates working in IJVs in China reported more hostile conflict with other American expatriates than with Chinese employees. Intercultural accommodation seems to be able to explain why the American expatriates behaved less aggressively toward Chinese, because they seemed to accommodate the Chinese cultural norms of harmony and face-saving in interacting with Chinese.

In contrast, the insensitivity of some expatriate managers to accommodate local norms is demonstrated by a survey of American and Chinese managers working for MNCs in Taiwan by Chang (1985). He found that Chinese managers perceived a higher need to accommodate local needs in management issues than did American expatriates. For example, compared with American expatriate managers, Chinese managers were more likely to agree with the view that expatriates would be more effective if they were familiar with Chinese culture. Such results suggest integration vigilance in terms of the accommodation of local norms and practices is not always easy, even if obvious.

Particular approaches to conflict resolution between partners are another example of the manifestation of integration vigilance that could have a positive impact on alliance outcomes. In their scenario study of U.S.-Japanese JVs, for example, Sullivan et al. (1981) found that Japanese managers perceived more future trust if the American partner requested conferment to resolve a conflict than binding arbitration. However, if an American partner was the president of the IJV, the Japanese managers perceived more future trust if binding arbitration rather than conferral was used in conflict resolution. This latter finding suggests that the Japanese managers were willing to accommodate the preferences of the American president.

Cultural Distance and Integration Vigilance

Integration vigilance may provide an explanation for inconsistent findings regarding the relationship between cultural dissimilarity and alliance effectiveness. Although some have questioned its validity as a construct and its measurement in practice (Shenkar, 2001; Veiga, Lubatkin, Calori, & Very, 2000; Au, 2000), *cultural distance* has been proposed to capture the difference between partners from two countries in terms of national or society-level differences along demographic as well as cultural dimensions, including values and norms. Much of the research we have reviewed earlier did find that cultural dissimilarity had negative consequences for alliances.

Those findings, however, are not always supported. Li, Karakowsky, and Lam (2002), for example, fail to find any greater success among Japanese firms in China when compared with U.K. and U.S. firms, despite the smaller cultural distance between Japan and China. In a survey of U.S.-Japan and U.S.-U.S. JVs, Park and Ungson (1997) even find that U.S.-Japan JVs last longer than U.S.-U.S. JVs. The authors argue that trust, learning, and a long-term perspective may be more prevalent in cross-border alliances, which explains their higher stability.

Gong et al. (2001) are also surprised to find that, contrary to their prediction, cultural distance is negatively related to role conflict and ambiguity. That is, the greater the cultural distance, the lower the role conflict. These authors speculate that cultural distance may lead to complementarity effects between the two partners, which reduces role conflict and ambiguity. Similarly, in structured interviews with executives of IJVs in India, Pothukuchi et al. (2002) find that, contrary to their expectations, differences in the national culture of the two partners based on Hofstede's four dimensions of national culture are positively related to efficiency and competitiveness of the JVs. Finally, Leung and his associates (Leung et al., 1996, 2001) surveyed local employees of IJVs in China who work with different groups of expatriate managers. Locals who work with Chinese expatriates from Hong Kong and Taiwan report less positive job attitudes than locals working for expatriates from the West and from other parts of Asia. Their results also show that the fairness of the expatriate managers, not the cultural distance, was important in influencing the job attitudes of locals.

Pothukuchi et al. (2002) argue that how cultural distance is managed affects the outcome of the performance of an IJV, and a simple relationship between cultural distance and IJV performance is unlikely. Building on this, we propose that integration vigilance may moderate the relationship between cultural distance and alliance outcomes. Leung et al. (2001) argue that when managers need to work with colleagues who are culturally different, the cultural distance perceived may trigger anticipatory adjustment behaviors, which render them more effective in a culturally diverse environment. Cultural distance, coupled with high integration vigilance, can actually lead to better alliance outcomes. Cultural distance takes its toll on an alliance only when integration vigilance is low.

Behavioral Model

We propose a behavioral model of alliances (Figure 11.2) that takes into account the findings as well as the gaps identified in the course of our review and that also incorporates specific propositions about the role of integration vigilance. Central to our model is interpersonal and intergroup collaboration, which we maintain is the cornerstone for alliance success. Positive interpersonal and intergroup collaboration engenders a high level of trust, good communication and flow of information, mutual support and teamwork, and productive conflict resolution. Specifically, collaboration has an impact on three different types of outcomes—affective, relational, performance—that are salient in alliances. *Affective outcomes* refers to job affect variables such as satisfaction, work motivation, and stress. *Interpersonal and intergroup outcomes* refers to quality of interpersonal and intergroup relationships and satisfaction with these relationships. *Performance outcomes* refers to joint or individual task performance and productivity. We expect a positive relationship between interpersonal and intergroup collaboration and these three types of outcomes.

Given the central role of interpersonal and intergroup collaboration on alliance outcomes, the natural question is: What factors are critical antecedents to collaboration? As the studies in our review have shown, collaboration is challenged by the interpersonal and intergroup tensions inherent in an alliance (e.g., Das & Teng, 2000; de Rond & Bouchikhi, 2004; Zeng & Chen, 2003). Prior research, not only from alliance contexts, suggests three major antecedents of interpersonal and intergroup collaboration. First is identity conflict, referring to an individual's split loyalty to a parent firm and to an alliance. Strong identification with the parent firm and weak

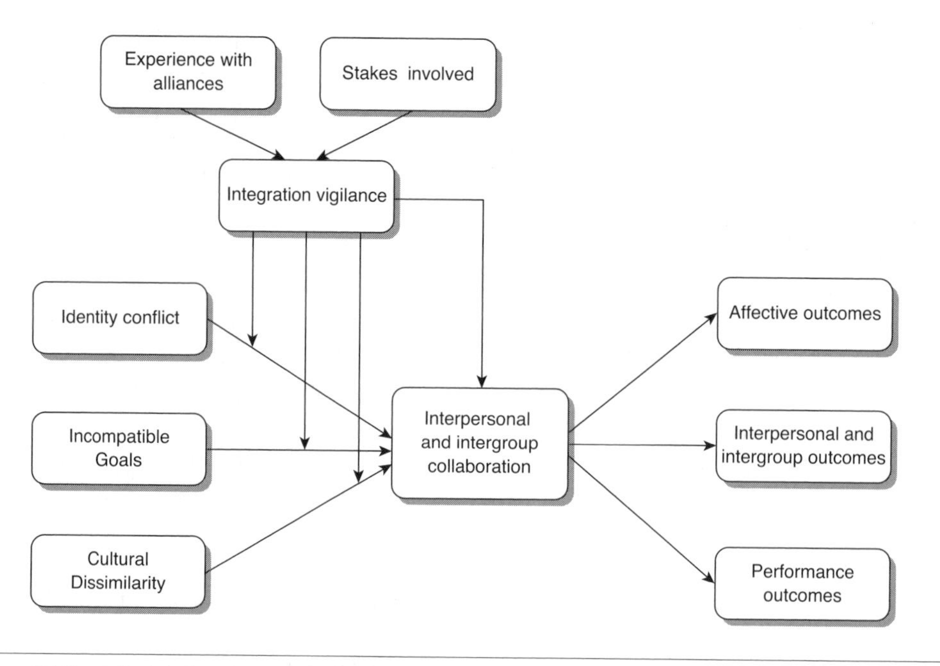

Figure 11.2 A Behavioral Model of Alliances

identification with the alliance will result in unfavorable interpersonal and intergroup collaboration. Second is incompatible goals, referring to unaligned or competing goals for employees from the two sides of an alliance, which inhibits information-sharing and other activities necessary for effective collaboration. Third is cultural dissimilarity, referring to the degree of difference between employees of the two sides of alliance in terms of their values, norms, beliefs, assumptions, and practices (whether representing national, organizational, or other spheres of culture). Greater cultural dissimilarity would likely result in unfavorable interpersonal and intergroup collaboration.

We propose integration vigilance to be a critical moderator, mitigating the negative impact of these three major impediments to interpersonal and intergroup collaboration. Integration vigilance provides the knowledge and motivation to exert the appropriate effort and introduce the appropriate mechanisms to reduce the destructive impact of identity conflict, incompatible or competing goals, and cultural dissimilarity. We also expect a direct, positive effect of integration vigilance on interpersonal and intergroup collaboration. Finally, we argue that integration vigilance is in turn influenced by the stakes involved (e.g., Ring & Van de Ven, 1992) and the amount of experience with alliances (e.g., Kale et al., 2002).

The constructs and relationships included in our model are grounded in the OB and strategy literature related to alliances. To develop and test the construct of integration vigilance further, the next step is to develop an operationalization and method for measuring it. A valid instrument will provide the basis for assessing its impact on processes and outcomes in alliances as well as for identifying its antecedents.

Conclusions

Research on alliances and in alliance contexts has been dominated by strategy researchers with a focus on structural features and task-related performance. This paper argues that research in organizational behavior with a more social-cognitive focus could enrich our understanding of the dynamics and performance of alliances. Furthermore, alliances also represent a rich yet largely ignored context for studying a range of phenomena central to organizational behavior. To further such objectives, and based on a review of the existing research on alliances, we propose a research agenda that incorporates a wider range of OB constructs. We also introduce the construct of integration vigilance within a behavioral model that relates OB variables to collaboration and subsequently an expanded range of outcomes that are salient in alliance contexts.

References

Anderson, E., & Gatignon, H. (1986). Modes of foreign entry: A transaction cost analysis and propositions. *Journal of International Business Studies, 17,* 1–26.

Ariño, A., & de la Torre, J. (1998). Learning from failure: Towards an evolutionary model of collaborative ventures. *Organization Science, 9,* 306–325.

Artz, K., & Brush, T. (2000). A transaction cost examination of performance in collaborative strategic alliances. *Journal of Economic Behavior and Organization, 41,* 337–362.

Ashforth, B., & Mael, F. (1989). Social identity theory and the organization. *Academy of Management Review, 14,* 20–39.

At-Twaijri, M. (1989). A cross-cultural comparison of American-Saudi managerial values in U.S.-related firms in Saudi Arabia: An empirical investigation. *International Studies of Management & Organization, 19,* 58–73.

Au, K. Y. (2000). Inter-cultural variation as another construct of international management: A study based on secondary data of 42 countries. *Journal of International Management, 6,* 217–238.

Aulakh, P. S., Kotabe, M., & Sahay, A. (1996). Trust and performance in cross-border marketing partnerships: A behavioral approach. *Journal of International Business Studies, 27,* 1005–1032.

Bailey, E. K., & Shenkar, O. (1993). Management education for international joint venture managers. *Leadership & Organization Development, 14,* 15–20.

Barak, M. E. M., Cherin, D. A., & Berkman, S. (1998). Organizational and personal dimensions in diversity climate: Ethnic and gender differences in employee perceptions. *Journal of Applied Behavioral Science, 34,* 82–104.

Barkema, H., Shenkar, O., Vermeulen, F., & Bell, J. (1997). Working abroad, working with others: How firms learn to operate international joint ventures. *Academy of Management Journal, 40,* 426–442.

Bensaou, B., & Venkatraman, N. (1995). Configurations of interorganizational relationships: A comparison between U.S. and Japanese automakers. *Management Science, 41,* 1471–1492.

Brannen, M. Y., & Salk, J. E. (2000). Partnering across borders: Negotiating organizational culture in a German-Japanese joint venture. *Human Relations, 53,* 451–487.

Chang, S. K. C. (1985). American and Chinese managers in U.S. companies in Taiwan: A comparison. *California Management Review, 27,* 144–156.

Chiah-Liaw, G., Petzall, S., & Selvarajah, C. (2003). The role of human resource management (HRM) in Australian-Malaysian joint ventures. *Journal of European Industrial Training, 27,* 244–262.

Chen, C. C., Choi, J., & Chi, S. C. (2002). Making justice sense of local-expatriate compensation disparity: Mitigation by local references, ideological explanations, and interpersonal sensitivity in China-foreign joint ventures. *Academy of Management Journal, 45,* 807–817.

Chen, R. R. X., & Boggs, D. J. (1998). Long term cooperation prospects in international joint venture: Perspectives of Chinese firms. *Journal of Applied Management Studies, 7,* 111–126.

Child, J., & Faulkner, D. (1998). *Strategies of co-operation.* Oxford: Oxford University Press.

Currall, S. C., & Inkpen, A. C. (2002). A multilevel approach to trust in joint ventures. *Journal of International Business Studies, 33,* 479–495.

Das, T., & Teng, B. (2000). Instabilities of strategic alliances: An internal tensions perspective. *Organization Science, 11,* 77–101.

de Rond, M. (2003). *Strategic alliances as social facts.* Cambridge, UK: Cambridge University Press.

de Rond, M., & Bouchikhi, H. (2004). On the dialectics of strategic alliances. *Organization Science, 15,* 56–69.

Doucet, L., & Jehn, K. A. (1997). Analyzing harsh words in a sensitive setting: American expatriates in communist China. *Journal of Organizational Behavior, 18,* 559–582.

Doz, Y. (1996). The evolution of cooperation in strategic alliances: Initial conditions or learning processes? [special issue]. *Strategic Management Journal, 17,* 55–83.

Draulans, J., deMan, A., & Volberda, H. (2003). Building alliance capability: Management techniques for superior alliance performance. *Long Range Planning, 36,* 151–166.

Dyer J. (1997). Effective interfirm collaboration: How firms minimize transaction costs and maximize transaction value. *Strategic Management Journal, 18,* 535–556.

Garrette, B., & Dussauge, P. (1995). Patterns of strategic alliances between rival firms. *Group Decision and Negotiation, 4,* 429–452.

Gong, Y., Shenkar, O., Luo, Y., & Nyaw, M. K. (2001). Role conflict and ambiguity of CEOs in international joint ventures: A transaction cost perspective. *Journal of Applied Psychology, 86,* 764–773.

Gould, L. J., Ebers, R., & Clinchy, R. M. (1999). The systems psychodynamics of a joint venture: Anxiety, social defences, and the management of mutual dependence. *Human Relations, 52,* 697–722.

Gulati, R. (1995). Does familiarity breed trust? The implications of repeated ties for contractual choice in alliances. *Academy of Management Journal, 38,* 85–112.

Gulati, R., & Gargiulo, M. (1999). Where do interorganizational networks come from? *American Journal of Sociology, 104,* 1439–1493.

Gulati, R., & Singh, H. (1998). The architecture of cooperation: Managing coordination costs and appropriation concerns in strategic alliances. *Administrative Science Quarterly, 43,* 781–814.

Hambrick, D. C., Li, J., Xin, K., & Tsui, A. S. (2001). Compositional gaps and downward spirals in international joint venture management groups. *Strategic Management Journal, 22,* 1033–1053.

Hamel, G. (1991). Competition for competence and interpartner learning within international strategic alliances. *Strategic Management Journal, 12,* 83–103.

Hitt, M. A., Dacin, M. T., Tyler, B. B., & Park, D. (1997). Understanding the differences in Korean and U.S. executives' strategic orientations. *Strategic Management Journal, 18,* 159–167.

Hofstede, G., Neuijen, B., Ohayv, D. D., & Sanders, G. (1990). Measuring organizational cultures: A qualitative and quantitative study across twenty cases. *Administrative Science Quarterly, 35,* 286–316.

Hui, C., & Graen, G. (1997). Guanxi and professional leadership in contemporary Sino-American joint ventures in mainland China. *Leadership Quarterly, 8,* 451–465.

Inkpen, A., & Beamish, P. (1997). Knowledge, bargaining power, and the instability of international joint ventures. *Academy of Management Review, 22,* 177–202.

Jemison, D. B., & Sitkin, S. B. (1986). Corporate acquisitions: A process perspective. *Academy of Management Review, 11,* 145–163.

Johnson, J. P. (1999). Multiple commitments and conflicting loyalties in international joint venture management teams. *International Journal of Organizational Analysis, 7,* 54–71.

Johnson, J. P., Korsgaard, M. A., & Sapienza, H. J. (2002). Perceived fairness, decision control, and commitment in international joint venture management teams. *Strategic Management Journal, 23,* 1141–1160.

Kale, P., Dyer, J. H., & Singh, H. (2002). Alliance capability, stock market response, and long-term alliance success: The role of the alliance function. *Strategic Management Journal, 23,* 747–767.

Kale, P., Singh, H., & Perlmutter, H. (2000). Learning and protection of proprietary assets in strategic alliances: Building relational capital. *Strategic Management Journal, 21,* 217–237.

Kogut, B. (1989). The stability of joint ventures: Reciprocity and competitive rivalry. *Journal of Industrial Economics, 38,* 183–198.

Kumar, R., & Nti, K. (1998). Differential learning and interaction in alliance dynamics: A process and outcome discrepancy model. *Organization Science, 9,* 356–367.

Leung, K., Smith, P. B., Wang, Z. M., & Sun, H. F. (1996). Job satisfaction in joint venture hotels in China: An organizational justice analysis. *Journal of International Business Studies, 27,* 947–962.

Leung, K., & Stephan, W. G. (1998). Perceptions of injustice in intercultural relations. *Applied and Preventive Psychology, 7,* 195–205.

Leung, K., Wang, Z. M., & Smith, P. B. (2001). Job attitudes and organizational justice in joint venture hotels in China: The role of expatriate managers.

International Journal of Human Resource Management, 12, 926–945.

Li, J., & Guisinger, S. (1991). Comparative business failures of foreign-controlled firms in the United States. *Journal of International Business Studies, 22,* 209–224.

Li, J., Karakowsky, L., & Lam, K. (2002). East meets east and east meets west: The case of Sino-Japanese and Sino-West joint ventures in China. *Journal of Management Studies, 39,* 841–863.

Li, J., Xin, K. R., Tsui, A., & Hambrick, D. C. (1999). Building effective international joint venture leadership teams in China. *Journal of World Business, 34,* 52–68.

Lin, X., & Germain, R. (1998). Sustaining satisfactory joint venture relationships: The role of conflict resolution strategy. *Journal of International Business Studies, 29,* 179–196.

Lin, X., & Germain, R. (1999). Predicting international joint venture interaction frequency in U.S.-Chinese ventures. *Journal of International Marketing, 7,* 5–23.

Lin, X., & Miller, S. J. (2003). Negotiation approaches: Direct and indirect effect of national culture. *International Marketing Review, 20,* 286–303.

Lui, S., & Ngo, H. (forthcoming). An action pattern model of interfirm cooperation. *Journal of Management Studies.*

Luo, Y. (2001). Antecedents and consequences of personal attachment in cross-cultural cooperative ventures. *Administrative Science Quarterly, 46,* 177–201.

Lyles, M. A., & Reger, R. K. (1993). Managing for autonomy in joint ventures: A longitudinal study of upward influence. *Journal of Management Studies, 30,* 383–404.

Lyles, M. A., & Salk, J. E. (1996). Knowledge acquisition from foreign parents in international joint ventures: An empirical examination in the Hungarian context. *Journal of International Business Studies, 27,* 877–903.

Madhok, A. (1995). Revisiting multinational firms' tolerance for joint ventures: A trust-based approach. *Journal of International Business Studies, 26,* 117–137.

Madhock, A., & Tallman, S. (1998). Resources, transactions rents: Managing value through interfirm collaborative relationships. *Organization Science, 9,* 326–339.

Mohr, J., & Spekman, R. (1994). Characteristics of partnership success: Partnership attributes, communication behaviour, and conflict resolution techniques. *Strategic Management Journal, 15,* 135–152.

Nygaard, A., & Dahlstrom, R. (2002). Role stress and effectiveness in horizontal alliances. *Journal of Marketing, 66,* 61–82.

Park, S. H., & Ungson, G. R. (1997). The effect of national culture, organizational complementarity, and economic motivation on joint venture dissolution. *Academy of Management Journal, 40,* 279–307.

Parkhe, A. (1993). Strategic alliance structuring: A game theoretic and transaction cost examination of interfirm cooperation. *Academy of Management Journal, 36,* 794–829.

Pothukuchi, V., Damanpour, F., Choi, J., Chen, C. C., & Park, S. H. (2002). National and organizational culture differences and international joint venture performance. *Journal of International Business Studies, 33,* 243–265.

Reuer, J., Zollo, M., & Singh, H. (2002). Post-formation dynamics in strategic alliances. *Strategic Management Journal, 23,* 135–151.

Ring, P. S., & Van de Ven, A. H. (1992). Structuring cooperative relationships between organizations. *Strategic Management Journal, 13,* 483–498.

Ring, P. S., & Van de Ven, A. H. (1994). Developmental processes of cooperative interorganizational relationships. *Academy of Management Review, 19,* 90–118.

Salk, J., & Brannen, M. Y. (2000). National culture, networks, and individual influence in a multinational management team. *Academy of Management Journal, 43,* 191–202.

Salk, J., & Shenkar, O. (2001). Social identities in an international joint venture: An exploratory case study. *Organization Science, 12,* 161–178.

Saxton, T. (1997). The effects of partner and relationship characteristics on alliance outcomes. *Academy of Management Journal, 40,* 443–461.

Schneider, S. C., & Barsoux, J. L. (2003). *Managing across cultures.* New York: Financial Times/Prentice Hall.

Shenkar, O. (2001). Cultural distance revisited: Towards a more rigorous conceptualization and measurement of cultural differences. *Journal of International Business Studies, 32,* 519–535.

Shenkar, O., & Zeira, Y. (1992). Role conflict and role ambiguity of chief executive officers in international joint ventures. *Journal of International Business Studies, 23,* 55–75.

Sherif, M., & Sherif, C. (1953). *Groups in harmony and tension.* New York: Harper and Row.

Spekman, R., Isabella, L., & MacAvoy, T. (2000). *Alliance competence: Maximizing the value of your partnerships.* New York: John Wiley.

Sullivan, J., Peterson, R. B., Kameda, N., & Shimada, J. (1981). The relationship between conflict resolution approaches and trust—A cross cultural study. *Academy of Management Journal, 24,* 803–815.

Tajfel, H. (1978). *Differentiation between social groups.* London: Academic Press.

Turner, J. (1987). *Rediscovering the social group: A self-categorization theory.* Oxford: Blackwell.

Veiga, J., Lubatkin, M., Calori, R., & Very, P. (2000). Measuring organizational culture clashes: A two-nation post-hoc analysis of a culture compatibility index. *Human Relations, 53,* 539–557.

Werner, S. (2002). Recent developments in international management research: A review of 20 top management journals. *Journal of Management, 28,* 277–305.

White, S. (forthcoming). Cooperation costs, governance choice and alliance evolution. *Journal of Management Studies.*

Wong, Y. T., Ngo, H. Y., & Wong, C. S. (2002). Affective organizational commitment of workers in Chinese joint ventures. *Journal of Managerial Psychology, 17,* 580–598.

Wong, Y. T., Ngo, H. Y., & Wong, C. S. (2003). Antecedents and outcomes of employees' trust in Chinese joint ventures. *Asia Pacific Journal of Management, 20,* 481–499.

Yan, A., & Gray, B. (1994). Bargaining power, management control, and performance in United States–China joint ventures: A comparative case study. *Academy of Management Journal, 37,* 1478–1517.

Yoshino, M. Y., & Rangan, S. U. (1995). *Strategic alliances: An entrepreneurial approach to globalization.* Boston: Harvard Business School Press.

Zeng, M., & Chen, X. (2003). Achieving cooperation in multiparty alliances: A social dilemma approach to partnership management. *Academy of Management Review, 28,* 587–605.

12

Alliance Forms and Human Resource Issues, Implications, and Significance

Randall S. Schuler

Ibraiz Tarique

Alliances are increasingly important forms of organization for many companies (Osborn & Hagedoorn, 1997; Inkpen, 2002; Luo, 2002; Schuler, 2001; Narula & Duysters, 2004; Ernst & Halevy, 2004; Yeheskel, Newburry, & Zeira, 2004; Bouchet, Soellner, & Lim, 2004). There is no apparent reason for this trend not to continue as pressures from global competition, the need to learn quickly, and the need to use valued scarce resources wisely are likely to be with us for some time (Ariño & Reuer, 2004). But, as organizations know, it is one thing to form an alliance and quite another thing to make it succeed (Isabella, 2002), and with so many reasons for forming alliances, organizations want them to be as successful as possible. Examination of many alliance failures in conjunction with the reasons for their establishment indicates that the quality of human resources management (HRM) can be critical (Schuler, Jackson, & Luo, 2004; Briscoe & Schuler, 2004). Much of what we know about alliance success and failure, however, comes from the research on international joint venture (IJV) alliances. And although this form of alliance is used extensively throughout the world and has many implications for HRM, there are many other forms of alliances that are equally prevalent (Narula & Duysters, 2004).

Thus, the purpose of this chapter is to extend our knowledge of HRM in all forms of alliances

AUTHOR'S NOTE: The authors wish to thank S. Jackson, M. Moelleney, B. Kugler, G. Bachtold, W. Harry, J. Ettlie, D. Osborn, and O. Shenkar for their suggestions and commentary in the development of this chapter.

(O. Shenkar, personal communications on the lack of research, theory, and discussion about the role of HRM in alliances other than IJVs, August and September, 2004). We propose to do this by expanding from our understanding of HRM in IJV alliances. But we first describe the several forms of alliances and then describe in more detail a four-stage model of HRM in IJVs. We suggest that these four stages can be adapted to all forms of alliances because all share varying amounts of complexity and complications and the potential for conflict, uncertainty, and instability. These in turn can serve as roadblocks and barriers to three needs common to all forms of alliances: the needs for learning, economies and efficiencies, and control. And because these conditions are amenable to HRM activities, as the form of alliance goes from relatively simple to much more complex, the significance and importance of HRM increases. Using three theoretical perspectives, we offer five testable propositions for further research on HRM in alliances.

Alliances

Alliances in general involve two or more firms agreeing to cooperate as partners in an arrangement that is expected to benefit both firms (Hagedoorn, 1993). Sometimes alliances involve one firm agreeing to cooperate with another firm, and sometimes the result is the creation of a third company, a joint venture (JV) (Gulati, 1998; Koka & Prescott, 2002).

A *nonequity alliance* is an investment vehicle in which profits and other responsibilities are assigned to each party according to a contract. Each party cooperates as a separate legal entity and bears its own liabilities. Nonequity alliances have great freedom to structure their assets, organize their production processes, and manage their operations. This form of alliance can be developed quickly to take advantage of short-term business opportunities and then dissolved when their tasks are completed. Among the many types of nonequity alliances are joint exploration projects, research and development consortia, coproduction agreements, comarketing arrangements, and long-term supply agreements (Osborn & Hagedoorn, 1997; Child & Faulkner, 1998; Luo, 2002; Ariño & Reuer, 2004).

Equity-based alliances can be classified as domestic and international. Such arrangements typically represent a long-term collaborative strategy (Luo, 2002; Ariño & Reuer, 2004). Furthermore, equity-based alliances require active day-to-day management of a wide variety of human resource (HR) issues (Isabella, 2002). Some of the HR issues that are critical to the success of equity-based international or cross-border alliances may also arise in nonequity alliances, but they may be less central to the success of the alliance. In equity-based alliances, however, long-term success is impossible unless HR issues are managed effectively (Child & Faulkner, 1998). There are many lessons, however, that *may* be transferable from our discussion of equity-based alliances to managing HR issues in nonequity alliances.

Because the bulk of the research on alliances vis-à-vis HRM is based on international alliances or IJVs we wish to investigate the extent to which HRM lessons in IJVs are transferable to other forms of alliances. We propose to do this by extending our discussion of HR issues and implications in alliances more broadly by back-filling on domestic equity and nonequity alliances using an existing model of HRM in IJVs and three theoretical perspectives. We first review the existing work on IJVs and the work specifically about HRM in IJVs and then extend this knowledge to HRM in alliances more broadly. Throughout this chapter the term *HRM* refers to the organizational function of managing people assets within organizations, whereas *HR* identifies issues, implications, policies and practices that are relevant to and should be addressed by HRM.

International Joint Ventures

IJVs are legally and economically separate organizational entities created by two or more parent organizations that collectively invest financial as well as other resources to pursue certain objectives (Luo, 2002; Schuler et al., 2004). IJVs are typically used when the required integration between the partners is high and the venture business is characterized by uncertainty and decision-making urgency (Doz & Hamel, 1998; Ariño & Reuer, 2004). Although an overwhelming majority of IJVs involve only two parent firms (one from a foreign country and the other from the local country), some ventures may consist of multiple participants and multiple countries (Schuler & Tarique, 2005). JVs that are launched by home-country-based (foreign) and host-country-based (local) firms appear to be the dominant form of JV partnership (Luo, 2002). Because the creation of an IJV involves establishing an independent organization, the need to establish effective HR practices capable of dealing with two or more organizational cultures and national cultures is particularly evident in this type of alliance (Schuler, 2001; Schuler et al., 2004).

Reasons for International Joint Ventures

IJVs have become a major form of entry into global markets (Evans, Pucik, & Barsoux, 2002; Luo, 2002; Barkema, Shenkar, Vermeulen, & Bell, 1997). Harrigan (1986) and Luo (2002) argue that there also are many other reasons that companies form IJVs. The most common reasons include capturing increased economies of scale (Newburry & Zeira, 1997), being cost-effective and efficient in the height of the globalization of markets (Datta, 1988; Harrigan, 1985, 1986), gaining local knowledge and local market image and channel access (Gomes-Casseres, 1989; Harbison, 1996), learning and transferring that knowledge (Mudambi, 2002; Cyr, 1995; Lei, Slocum, & Pitts, 1997; Inkpen, 2002), and supporting company strategies for internationalization (Evans, et al., 2002) (see Schuler et al., 2004, for a more detailed treatment).

Knowledge and Learning

Of the above, a reason that has gained heightened recognition is learning and knowledge, sharing and transfer (Inkpen & Tsang, forthcoming; Foss & Pedersen, 2002; Inkpen, 2002; Reid, Bussier, & Greenway, 2001; Child & Faulkner, 1998; Shenkar & Li, 1999). In many industries, increasing global competition and unabated technological advancement have resulted in a wide range of international collaborative alliances intended to access knowledge, skills, and resources that cannot be internally produced by organizations in a timely or cost-effective fashion. Companies that are capital/resource-rich but knowledge-poor are particularly attracted to this type of venture.

Organizational learning has long been considered a key building block and major source of competitive advantage (Badaracco, 1991). A global alliance is not only a means by which partners trade access to each other's skills but also a mechanism for actually acquiring a partner's skills. In bringing together firms with different skills, knowledge bases, and organizational cultures, IJVs create unique learning opportunities for the partner firms. By definition, alliances involve a sharing of resources. This access can be a powerful source of new knowledge that in most cases would not have been possible without the formal structure of an IJV. As such, IJVs are no longer a peripheral activity but a mainstay of competitive strategy. IJVs forge new knowledge-transfer pathways across both technologically and traditionally linked positions (Cyr & Schneider, 1996; Luo, 2002).

Using and relying on external learning and knowledge transfer are challenging and complex (Mudambi, 2002; Inkpen, 2002; Barkema et al., 1997). A fundamental impediment to interpartner learning and knowledge transfer originates from the nature of the knowledge involved. Codified explicit knowledge is generally transparent and readily accessible and transferable, but many elements of knowledge transferred between IJV partners are tacit. *Tacit* means that the knowledge is deeply embedded in organizational routines (e.g., structure, rules, and policies) and difficult to codify and teach. In organizations, tacit knowledge involves intangible factors embedded in personal beliefs, experiences, and values. It is also stored organically in team relationships. If two firms seek transfer of the knowledge that is explicitly codifiable (e.g., patents), they normally choose international licensing instead of the IJV. When the knowledge is tacit and thus uncodifiable in the license contract, the IJV becomes a better device for transferring or sharing this type of knowledge (Ariño & Reuer, 2004).

Certainly, behaviors and styles of managers in organizations have a significant impact on the ability and willingness of a firm to learn (Frayne & Geringer, 2000). For example, learning requires managers to be open and willing to suspend their need for control. Although firms and individuals need the ability and willingness to learn as they enter into the IJV formation process, they also need to be transparent so that others may learn as well (Child & Faulkner, 1998; Hamel, 1991). Thus, both partners need to have similar qualities that support learning if the partnership is to have a longer-term success (Doz & Hamel, 1998; Hamel, 1991; Lyles, 1987; Parkhe, 1991; Pucik, 1988). Because learning capability can quickly lead to attaining competitive advantage (Prahalad & Hamel, 1990), asymmetry in learning capability can soon lead to partnership instability and dissolution (Inkpen, 2002).

Efficiencies and Economies

In addition to the growing importance of learning from IJVs and alliances more generally is another significant reason, and that is to gain and retain management and organizational efficiencies and economies. These economies and efficiencies can result from combining operations, building upon the experiences of existing management, and taking advantage of the latest in technologies, e.g., when establishing a new facility (Luo, 2002; Newburry & Zeira, 1997; Datta, 1988).

Although there are several other reasons for establishing and operating IJVs, we propose to use efficiencies and economies as a basis for our initial extension of the relationship between IJVs and HRM to other forms of alliances. But in proposing these two reasons, we are obliged to incorporate another consideration into our extension, and this consideration is the need for the parent(s) to exercise control over the IJV (Luo, 2002; Geringer & Frayne, 1990, Frayne & Geringer, 1990).

Control

Without the ability to exercise control, it can be more difficult for a parent to establish conditions to maximize learning for itself or perhaps even the IJV system, also gain and retain the managerial and organizational economies of scale and efficiencies, and also protect shareholders' assets and "brand image," as in the very unfortunate situation at the Union Carbide Corporation (UCC) operation in Bhopal, India, which was an IJV (50% UCC) in which the parent company's shareholder value and its reputation, as well as thousands of lives, were lost (W. Harry, personal communication, November 9, 2004). As a consequence, parent companies engage in numerous strategies to maintain control (Narula & Duysters, 2004; Luo, 2002).

Thus, our proposed description of the general relationship between HRM and alliances is based on what we refer to as three needs in alliances: (1) learning and knowledge transfer, (2) management and organizational economies of scale and efficiencies, and (3) controlling. The utility of these three will hopefully become more apparent in the discussion below of the four-stage model IJVs and the associated HRM and organizational issues and implications.

Human Resources Management in International Joint Ventures

The organizational and HR issues in IJVs are clearly very extensive (Child & Faulkner,

1998; Schuler, 2001). They can be refined and categorized, however, into several stages, which begin with the development of the IJV itself by the two (or more) parents and go through the advancement of the IJV itself (Evans et al., 2002; Schuler, 2001; Pucik, 1988; Makhija & Ganesh, 1997; Lei et al., 1997; Lorange & Roos, 1992). The four stages of the IJV process are shown in Exhibit 12.1, representing the entire IJV system. Shown in each stage are the organizational and HR issues most applicable to the IJV system. These in turn become the basis for identifying the HR implications for each stage. We propose that aspects of these stages are applicable in varying degrees to other forms of alliances as well (Isabella, 2002). That is a reason we describe them in some detail; even greater detail is provided in Schuler (2001). Another reason is to review the existing literature on HRM in IJVs. Future research can tailor these HR implications to the organizational and HR issues that are uniquely associated with other forms of alliances.

Stage 1–Formation: The Partnership

To manage an IJV for success, it is important to understand JV formation as including the seven aspects shown in the Stage 1 section of Exhibit 12.1. Potential partners in an IJV need to determine separately their reasons for using an IJV as part of their business strategy. Also noted above, these include several reasons within the major categories of: (1) minimizing the sum of production and transactions costs (Hennart, 1991), (2) improving one's competitive position (Gomes-Casseres, 1989), (3) acquiring knowledge (Kogut, 1988), (4) increasing one's acceptance and legitimacy (Pfeffer & Cohen, 1984), and (5) gaining a new source of skills to improve one's human capital (Cascio, 1991).

Early planning in JVs is especially important in order that differences in cultural and management styles between the parents and the venture are considered (Datta & Rasheed, 1993). Without planning, the likelihood of reaping the gains from the IJV is diminished (Cyr, 1995; Pucik, 1988). Differences between partners in such qualities as culture, managerial styles, intentions, absorptive capacity, objectives of the IJV, and even the role of the HR department can be part of an HR plan that includes an audit of these qualities (Pucik, 1988).

Selecting the manager for new business development is important. These managers are the linkages between the two parents and the linkages with the JV itself. Although the chief executive officer (CEO) or chief operating officer (COO) of the parent may spot IJV opportunities, it is the manager for new business development within an organization who is responsible for making the IJV happen (Schuler, Jackson, Dowling, & Welch, 1991). In this capacity, this manager is likely to interact with a counterpart in the other parent. Together, these two may begin the activities remaining in Stage 1. Thus, they set the stage to link with the IJV itself. Consequently, the selection of this person is critical to the entire IJV process, including the contract negotiation process (Ariño & Reuer, 2004). The more knowledge and experience this individual has, particularly in IJVs, the more likely the IJV will be a success.

Potential partners can come from past JVs, suppliers, competitors, and other firms, but potential partners from past alliances or JVs offer more information about themselves (Child & Faulkner, 1998). Past experience enables the organization to learn not only about the IJV process itself but also about the styles, operations, goals, and practices of the other potential partner and build upon previously created trust (Isabella, 2002). Similar patterns of familiarity may exist with suppliers, but in those relationships the amount of control over the supplier has often been substantially greater than over another past partner. Thus, there is likely to be a smaller amount of IJV-relevant knowledge about suppliers. Increasingly, competitors are a major source of potential partners (Pucik, 1988; Cyr, 1995; Lei et al., 1997). These potential partners are likely to offer knowledge complementarily instead of only compatibility; hence the potential for learning may be greater. The relationship, however, may thus be more unstable, particularly if the

Exhibit 12.1 Organizational/HR Issues and HR Implications in the Four Stages of the IJV System

Organizational/HR Issues	*HR Implications*
Stage 1–Formation • Identifying reasons • Planning for utilization • Selecting dedicated manager • Finding potential partners • Selecting likely partners • Handling issues of control, trust and conflict • Negotiating the arrangement	• The more important learning is, the greater the role for HRM • Knowledge needs to be managed • Systematic selection is essential • Cast a wide net in partner search • Be thorough for compatibility • Ensure procedures and communications • More skilled negotiators are more effective
Stage 2–Development • Locating the IJV • Establishing the right structure • Getting the right senior managers	• Concerns of multiple sets of stakeholders need to be considered for long term viability and acceptance • The structure will impact the learning and knowledge management processes. These are impacted by the quality of IJV managers • Recruiting, selecting, and managing senior staff can make or break the IJV
Stage 3–Implementation • Establishing the vision, mission, values, the strategy and structure • Developing HR policies and practices • Dealing with unfolding issues • Staffing and managing the employees	• These will provide meaning and direction to the IJV and employees • These will impact what is learned through trust, control and conflict management • Need to design policies and practices with local–global considerations • The people will make the place
Stage 4–Advancement and Beyond • Learning from the partner • Transferring the new knowledge to the parents • Transferring the new knowledge to other locations	• Partners need to have the capacity to learn from each other • HR systems need to be established to support knowledge flow to the parent and learning by the parent • Sharing through the parent is critical

motivation of the partners is competitive rather than collaborative (Doz & Hamel, 1998).

Partner selection determines an IJV's mix of skills, knowledge, and resources, its operating policies and procedures, and its vulnerability to indigenous conditions, structures, and institutional changes (Luo, 2002; Child & Faulkner, 1998; Geringer & Herbert, 1991). In a dynamic, complex, or hostile environment, the importance of local partner selection to IJV success is magnified, because the right partner can spur the IJV's adaptability, strategy-environment configuration, uncertainty reduction, and contract negotiation process (Luo, 1998; Ariño & Reuer, 2004). Lei et al. (1997) hypothesize that the selection of the partner should include an analysis of the nature or importance of the JV's task to the partner, the type of knowledge involved, and the nature of the partners' reward system. These factors are central to promoting alliance-based learning for one or both partners. Again, the analysis of these factors has different implications depending upon whether the organization is selecting for longer-term cooperative partners or shorter-term competitive partners (Child & Faulkner, 1998; Doz & Hamel, 1998). The implications for HRM are substantially different in these two scenarios (Pucik, 1988).

The perspective on IJVs reflected in the discussion and propositions in this chapter and the current literature is that alliances are intended for the longer term (Doz & Hamel, 1998; Child & Faulkner, 1998). Although alliances may involve cooperative or competitive partners, it appears that cooperative partners may help increase the chances of success and the effectiveness of the learning process itself (Isabella, 2002; Child & Faulkner, 1998; Doz & Hamel, 1998; Pucik, 1988; Cyr, 1995). Consensus has it that the very nature of JVs contributes to their failure: they are a difficult and complex form of enterprise (Shenkar & Zeira, 1987), and many companies initiate IJVs without fully recognizing and addressing the major issues they are likely to confront (Morris & Hergert, 1987; Ariño & Reuer, 2004).

Success requires adept handling of three key issues: control, trust, and conflict. Control, along with trust and learning, is one of the most important and most studied topics in the alliance literature (Luo, 2002; Schuler et al., 2004; Geringer & Hebert, 1989; Yan & Gray, 1994; Inkpen & Currall, 1997). Control is defined as a purposeful and goal-oriented activity that influences the acquisition, interpretation, and dissemination of information within an organizational setting (Simons, 1987). This definition highlights the information/knowledge qualities of IJVs. Thus, not surprisingly, Hamel (1991) and Doz & Hamel (1998) suggest that learning can be the most important lever in IJV control.

Makhija and Ganesh (1997) suggest that learning is a central process in IJVs and that IJV control mechanisms directly impact the learning processes. They suggest that IJV control mechanisms have unique information-processing properties that encourage certain flows of information (Child & Faulkner, 1998; Luo, 2002). Nooteboom, Berger, and Nooderhaven (1997) suggest that trust may become a substitute for control and that as trust increases, the need for formal control mechanisms decreases. Who actually controls the operation can depend on who is responsible for the day-to-day management of the IJV (Baliga & Jaeger, 1984). Ownership distribution may matter less than how operating control and participation in decision making are actually apportioned (Harrigan, 1986). For a parent with minority ownership, for example, the right to appoint key personnel can be used as a control mechanism (Schaan, 1988). Control can be achieved by appointing managers loyal to the parent company and its organizational ethos (Killing, 1983). Of course, loyalty to the parent cannot be guaranteed: "The ability to appoint the joint venture general manager increases the chances that the parent's interests will be observed, but it is no guarantee that the joint venture general manager will always accommodate that parent's preferences" (Schaan, 1988, p. 14).

Top managers, however, will be expected to make decisions that deal with the simultaneous demands of the parents and their employees in the enterprise. At times, such decisions will by necessity meet the demands of some parties better than those of other parties. If the partners do not anticipate such decisions, they may fail to build in control mechanisms, for example in the contract itself, to protect their interests (Isabella, 2002; Luo, 2002; Schuler et al., 2004; Ariño & Reuer, 2004). Weak control can also result if parent-company managers spend too little time on the IJV, responding to problems only on an ad hoc basis. Finally, control-related failures are likely to occur if control practices are not reevaluated and modified in response to changing circumstances (Doz & Hamel, 1998; Inkpen & Currall, 1997; Ariño & Reuer, 2004).

Inkpen and Currall (1997) define trust as a reliance on another partner under a condition of risk. Four dimensions of trust include (1) communication and information exchange, (2) task coordination, (3) informal agreements, and (4) surveillance and monitoring which indicate the absence of trust. Trust is positive because it strengthens interorganizational ties (Fichman & Levinthal, 1991), speeds contract negotiations (Reve, 1990), and reduces transactions costs (Bromiley & Cummings, 1993). Trust is not only a control concept in the alliance relationship, but a dynamic and potentially unstable one as well. Many researchers state that alliances should be established in the spirit of trust and commitment (Yan & Gray, 1994; Parkhe, 1991). Yan and Gray (1994), for example, note that disasters occur when both sides distrust each other's intentions and start doing things that cause distrust.

It appears that learning and trust are positively related, whereas trust and the use of informal and formal controls are negatively related (Sabel, 1993; Yan, 1998; Dyer, 1997; Nooteboom, et al., 1997). Because learning is a critical component of alliance longevity and stability, establishing mechanisms to ensure that trust increases benefits the relationship between alliance partners (Child & Faulkner, 1998; Doz & Hamel, 1998). Thus, a partner needs to reduce the likelihood of engaging in opportunistic behavior when the balance of power shifts in its favor (Inkpen & Currall, 1997). Partners need to resist the "race to learn" at differential rates, because this will shift the balance of power and the focus of dependencies.

Because alliances are inherently unstable relationships, they require a delicate set of organizational and management processes to create trust and the ongoing capacity to collaborate (Isabella, 2002; Johnson, Cullen, Sakano, & Takenouchi, 1996). This means that senior executives must be involved in designing management processes, which might be explicitly outlined in contract negotiations, that (1) provide effective ways to handle joint strategy formulation, (2) create structural linkages, (3) provide adequate day-to-day coordination and communication, and (4) establish a win-win culture (Child & Faulkner, 1998; Ariño & Reuer, 2004). It is also important that senior executives establish mechanisms to manage conflict.

Differences in such parent qualities as relative power, levels of commitment, experience with IJVs, goals, size, location of parents, and cultural similarity can lead to complications, uncertainty, and conflict (Killing, 1983; Anderson & Weitz, 1989; Parke, 1991; Lin & Germain, 1998). Many misunderstandings and problems in alliances are rooted in managerial differences (Datta, 1988). Differing approaches to managerial style are one area that can create problems. For example, one party may favor a participative managerial style, whereas the other may believe in a more autocratic style of management. Another area that can be problematic is acceptance of risk-taking when one parent is prepared to take more risks than the other. Such differences often make the process of decision making slow and frustrating. The resulting conflict can be dysfunctional and can diminish control, learning, and efficiencies.

Differing levels of commitment from the two parents provide yet another source of difficulty (Datta, 1988). The commitment of each partner reflects the project's importance to the partner. When an imbalance exists, the more-committed partner may feel frustrated by the other partner's apparent lack of concern; or the less-committed partner may feel frustrated by demands and time pressures exerted by the other, more-committed partner. The level of commitment by parties to the alliance can contribute to conflict and even to success or failure (Inkpen & Crossan, 1995).

In resolving conflicts, Lin and Germain (1998) found that a problem-solving strategy seems to be more effective than strategies involving compromise, force, or legalisms. They also found that parents with more experience in IJVs with each other tended to codify few understandings and so relied on their knowledge of and trust in each other rather than detailed contracts intended to deal with all eventualities. With experience, the IJV parents get to know each other better and develop ways of resolving differences (Inkpen & Crossan, 1995).

Not surprisingly, the quality of IJV contract negotiations during the IJV formation can have an impact upon three consequences of importance: IJV formation satisfaction, IJV process performance, and IJV overall performance (Luo, 1999; Lei et al., 1997; Ariño & Reuer, 2004). Central to the quality of the contract negotiations are the bargaining processes and strategies used by each of the partners (Aldrich, 1979; Green & Welsh, 1988; Yan & Gray, 1994; Ariño & Reuer, 2004). For partners interested in learning, approaching the negotiations with a problem-solving strategy would appear to be effective. The need for this strategy to be carried out by the negotiators would therefore be important. Establishing trust and mutual understanding, perhaps through previous experience, would aid in establishing the culture for the problem-solving strategy. Here HR activities can play an instrumental role, for example, in the selection of the negotiator (Child & Faulkner, 1998; Ariño & Reuer, 2004). The characteristics of the contract negotiator(s) can also have an impact on the success of the IJV. These characteristics include cultural similarities, personality and skills, and loyalty. Selecting for these characteristics and ensuring they are supported and rewarded are important HRM contributions (Ariño & Reuer, 2004).

Stage 2–Development: The International Joint Venture Itself

Once the IJV process has been formed, there are several important activities that must be addressed in the development of the IJV itself, as shown in Exhibit 12.1 (Isabella, 2002; Child & Faulkner, 1998). Where to locate is an important decision. It can be decided to locate the IJV itself in a third country or in the country of one of the partners. Locating in a third country may diminish the "home-field advantage" for either partner; however, it may increase the complexity and complications and need for more information-gathering and broader expertise, because several of the local stakeholders, for example, trade unions, political officials, members of society, and regulators, may be unknown to foreign partners (Schuler & Tarique, 2005). Locating in the country of one partner, however, may give a "local knowledge" and control advantage. If, however, this knowledge is shared with the other partner, the advantage can move to the partnership and the IJV itself rather than remaining with one partner.

In developing the IJV, a major consideration is providing appropriate structure. Two aspects of structure are particularly important; one is the extent to which the IJV will be able to make its own decisions, adapt to the local environment, and operate on its own, and the second includes the methods or processes by which the IJV will be attached or integrated into the parent(s) in order to provide a transfer of knowledge, learning, and other resources (Hill & Hellriegel, 1994; Doz & Prahalad, 1981; Doz & Hamel, 1998). If the design grants a great deal of autonomy to the IJV, the parents confront the question of how to control the IJV and integrate the IJV with the parents in order to provide the parents with the opportunity to learn and transfer information and knowledge from the IJV and yet enable the IJV to be effective locally. Such control, information, and knowledge flow can be facilitated by formal methods, such as detailed documents of conduct and agreed-upon exchanges of specific information, and/or by informal means, such as the selection processes used by the IJV and/or personnel transfers and assignments between the IJV and the parents (Makhija & Ganesh, 1997). Used in combination, the formal and informal methods may facilitate the transfer of both explicit and tacit knowledge as well as control of the IJV by the parents.

The positions of the IJV top team include the board of directors, the managing director (general manager), and the COO. The selection of the various members of the IJV is an important process in itself, in combination with the design of the appropriate structure (Harvey, Speier, & Novicevic, 1999; Hamel, 1991; Makhija & Ganesh, 1997; Pucik, 1988; Cyr, 1995). Together, these activities highlight the interdependence of individual and organizational capabilities and characteristics for the IJV to be locally effective and for the parents to be globally effective as well as have information and knowledge transfer occurring in order to build absorptive capacity and social capital in the IJV (Inkpen & Tsang, forthcoming). Extending the arguments of Beamish (1985), Hergert and Morris (1988), and Lorange and Roos (1992), without the development of a learning (absorptive) capability in the IJV itself, the IJV process will be come unstable. Just as distrust will develop between partners who are asymmetric in learning, so will it develop between the IJV itself and the parents. The impact will be a greater desire by the IJV for independence from the parents, thereby reducing the parent's control, global effectiveness, and opportunity for learning (Child & Faulkner, 1998).

When both parents are interested in the IJV and want it to succeed, they will probably get involved in all the key decisions made early on, as reflected in the contract negotiation (Ariño & Reuer, 2004). Under these conditions, the board of directors is likely to be composed equally of representatives of the parents and the IJV (internal and external to these entities). The COO, if not the managing director/general manager, may be selected from the source providing the most experience with the operation of the IJV.

Stage 3–Implementation: The International Joint Venture Itself

The implementation stage of the IJV process involves the four sets of activities shown in the Stage 3 section of Exhibit 12.1. The vision, mission, values, strategy, and structure of the IJV need to support, encourage, and reward learning and the sharing of knowledge (Slocum & Lei, 1993). They also need to support the other needs of the business, the needs of the parents, and the needs of the other multiple stakeholders—in other words, the IJV system. With a high-quality top management team in the IJV, the vision, mission, values, strategy, and structure are more likely to be crafted to fit local needs as well as those of the parents. At this point, it is clearly not in the interest of the IJV to ignore the linkages with the parents. For the parents, willingness to trust the IJV top management team to act in their interests, and at the same time, the interests of the IJV are critical (Child & Faulkner, 1998; Schuler, Dowling, & DeCieri, 1992; Schuler & Van Sluijs, 1992; Van Sluijs & Schuler, 1994; Inkpen & Dinur, 1998).

The entire set of HR policies and practices needs to be created for the IJV. The factors that these policies and practices need to reflect include the IJV's (1) vision, mission, values, culture, structure, strategy, (2) labor market, (3) need for global integration with parent(s) such as for knowledge transfer, and (4) differences between the country cultures of the parents and the IJV (Schuler & Tarique, 2005). Who actually develops the HR policies and practices can range from one of the parents to the IJV exclusively. The more the development is left with the IJV, the greater likelihood the practices will be effective for local adaptation but not as effective for the parents, for global integration, and for learning transfer (Child & Faulkner, 1998). High-quality top managers, however, are likely to develop locally responsive HR policies and practices with sensitivity to the parents' considerations. Possibly some policies will be nonnegotiable and have to meet parents' standards (e.g., ethical, safety/ environmental), whereas other policies (e.g., working hours, compensation, and benefits) can be much more locally adaptable.

There are many organization and HR issues that unfold as the IJV gets set up, including the assignment of managers, managers' time-spending patterns, top management evaluation, managing loyalty issues, and career and benefits planning (Briscoe & Schuler, 2004; Shenkar & Zeira, 1990; Dowling, Welch, & Schuler, 1999). The substance of these issues needs to be addressed explicitly by any IJV (Luo, 2002; Lorange, 1986). Each partner may place differing priorities on the JV; therefore, a partner may assign relatively weak management resources to the venture. To be successful, not only should the assigned managerial resources have relevant capabilities and be of adequate quality, but the overall blend of these managerial resources should reflect a balance of the interests of both parents and of the IJV. Because these assignments could be perceived as attempts to control the IJV (Pucik, 1988), it could be argued that the IJV's top management should have the final say in the staffing of any positions within the IJV itself. Where trust needs are high, however, and the parents have the needed competencies, the parents may be able to dictate initial and temporary staffing needs.

The IJV has to carry out a set of operating duties simultaneously with its development of new strategies. This raises the issue of the appropriate emphasis to give to operating tasks and strategic tasks and the need to allocate sufficient human resources to both. The situation is similar to that of an independent business organization: the IJV must be able to draw sufficient human resources from the operating mode to develop its strategy further. If the parent organizations place strong demands for short-term results on the IJV, this may leave them with insufficient resources to staff for strategic self-renewal. This is likely to be intensified if the IJV has to look for a customer base to support its existence. Over time, the balance between focus on operations versus strategic planning may shift as the IJV becomes more independent and the short-term operating tasks become more manageable.

Deciding how to evaluate IJV managers is another major challenge. It has been claimed that several JVs have failed because of inappropriate staffing (Lorange, 1986). Myopic, biased parent organizations may make poor selection decisions or may be tempted to use the IJV to off-load surplus. Performance evaluation of the top IJV management team, therefore, is important (Child & Faulkner, 1998). Parents and the IJV need to be sensitive to the potential need for dual loyalties. For short-term expatriate assignments, the potential may be moot, but for longer-term expatriates, parents may have to expect, even desire, to have their employees develop dual loyalties. Dual loyalties may help facilitate control and the transfer and sharing of knowledge, because the employees can be trusted by the parents and the IJV itself.

It has been reported that more than 50% of expatriates feel their overseas assignments are either immaterial or detrimental to their careers (Briscoe & Schuler, 2004)—a finding that indicates the potential motivational problems any IJV may encounter. The motivation of executives assigned to an IJV can be enhanced by the creation of a clear linkage between the assignment and an assignee's future career. Some assurance of job security may be needed to offset perceived risks. As with any overseas assignment, assignment to a JV may make the manager's future career appear uncertain. If the parent company has not thought this issue through, this uncertainty may be justified. Thus, parent organizations should offer career planning to counter the ambiguity and risks associated with an IJV assignment and to limit the potential for unsatisfying repatriation experiences. (Shenkar, 1995; Brewster & Harris, 1999; Black, Gregersen, Mendenhall, & Stroh, 1999; Caligiuri & Lazarova, 2000). They can also keep regular contact with the IJV, possibly through the use of mentors or even a specific department within the parent organizations.

Finally, the success of the IJV rests upon getting the right people at the right place at the right time. Sources of staffing for the IJV include parents, local-country nationals, third-country nationals, international itinerants (independent expatriates for hire), competitors, suppliers, customers, and universities (Harry & Banai, 2005). The selection criteria should include ability to perform the job, acceptance of the mission, values, strategy, structure, policies, and practices of the IJV, motivation, and ability to learn and share knowledge (Harvey et al., 1999; Child & Faulkner, 1998).

Stage 4—Advancement: The International Joint Venture and Beyond

The advancement stage of the IJV process involves learning from the partner, transferring knowledge and learning to the parents, and transferring knowledge and learning to other locations. As the IJV becomes established, the partners' relationship continues to evolve (Child & Faulkner, 1998). In the views of Luo (2000) and Doz and Hamel (1998), learning and adjustment by the partners are the key to alliance longevity and the avoidance of premature dissolution. If partners learn at unequal rates, the relationship will be inherently and inevitably unstable (Makhija & Ganesh, 1997; Inkpen & Beamish, 1997). As partner A's learning surpasses partner B's, the bargaining power of partner A increases. At this stage, partner A can engage in opportunistic, self-interested behavior or engage in forbearance (Inkpen & Currall, 1997). As partner B sees partner A engaging in forbearance, partner B's need for control decreases and the level of trust between the two partners grows. If partner A engages in opportunistic behavior, partner B attempts to increase control, and thereby the level of trust diminishes (Inkpen & Currall, 1997). Thus, when both partners trust each other, learning and knowledge transfer can continue (Schuler et al., 2004; Inkpen & Tsang, forthcoming).

Parents may still find that building trust with the IJV itself is important. Without trust, the IJV may try to avoid transferring learning and knowledge to the parent. What is transferred instead is merely information. This may be more likely as the IJV grows, establishes its own identity, and seeks independence from the parents. In general, mechanisms for knowledge and information transfer that can be used include top management support, staff rotation, staff training and development, site visits, rewards and recognition, and repatriation management (Lei et al., 1997; Inkpen & Currall, 1997; Inkpen & Crossan, 1995; Cyr, 1995; Collins & Doorley, 1991).

So far, learning and knowledge transfer have occurred from one partner to another and from the IJV itself to the parent. In both cases, the parent organization is gaining new learning and knowledge that can be used for its internal operations or for its next IJV process (Child & Faulkner, 1998; Doz & Hamel, 1998). Although consideration of transferring this learning and knowledge to future IJVs will enter into the complexities of partner selection described in the first stage, transferring learning to and building social capital in other units within the organization is more straightforward and more under the control of the organization (Inkpen & Tsang, forthcoming). Nonetheless, managers are involved and need to be encouraged to behave in ways that facilitate learning and knowledge transfer, for example, cooperative, team-oriented behaviors. To continue to get these needed behaviors, performance management (including selected performance measures) *and* reward systems (including nonfinancial rewards) need to be aligned with those behaviors. Thus, there are both organizational-level and individual/group–level implications in transferring learning and knowledge of other locations.

Proposed Application of the Four-Stage Model to Human Resources Management in Alliances

We suggest that the four-stage model we have used to describe the IJV alliance can be extended to apply to any type of alliance. It may be likely, however, that other forms of alliances, for example, nonequity licensing agreements between two firms or even equity agreement in domestic JVs, may involve fewer organizational and HR issues and perhaps even fewer stages. Nonetheless, we submit that these differences among the alliances are more in degree than in kind, as described more fully below (Das & Teng, 2002). Thus, we propose that models similar to Exhibit 12.1 can be developed for several forms of alliances. Propositions can also be created using common theoretical perspectives.

There may be an inflection point, however, with alliances involving only two separate companies that do not join together to create a separate third entity, a JV. In creating a JV alliance, a JV system is created with two or more parents and the JV itself. Consequently, all issues involved in creating, controlling, and managing at least three organizations come into being. Consequently the levels of complexity and complications increase and so also the potential for conflict, uncertainty, and instability that is likely to be much greater than in alliances in which there are only two organizations. Furthermore, alliances in which there is an international dimension rather than solely a domestic one are also likely to have significantly more complexity and complications and thus potential for conflict, uncertainty, and instability (Luo, 2002; Schuler et al., 2004; Briscoe & Schuler, 2004; Mallik, Zbar, & Zemmel, 2004).

As the above stages suggest, the formation and operation of an IJV raise many HR issues that have implications for how the IJV system (the IJV parents and the IJV itself) manage their human resources. Many of these implications are grounded in the assumption that IJV parents and the IJV itself have needs for learning, maintaining control, and gaining and retaining management efficiencies and economies. Organizations can support learning, knowledge flow, and sharing and transfer with HRM practices (Jackson & Schuler, 2003; McGill, Slocum, & Lei, 1992; Inkpen & Tsang, forthcoming). Organizations can also maintain control via HRM using their own selection, appraisal, and compensation practices in the JV and can gain and retain economies and efficiencies through their compensation and training practices.

These three major needs in and for the IJV system—learning, control, and efficiencies, with their associated HR issues and implications for HRM—appear also to have application for all forms of alliances (Inkpen, 2002; Reid, Bussiere, & Greenway, 2001). Their application to and future research suggestions for all forms of alliances can be based upon three theoretical perspectives, transaction cost theory, agency theory, and learning theory, because they all are closely aligned with the rationale that links and differentiates varying forms and type of alliances, as stated above. Yet other theoretical perspectives, such as resource dependence, institutional strategic human capital, collaboration, negotiation, and social capital, have relevance but are more extensive than we have space for here (Narula & Duysters, 2004). They are, however, worth utilizing in an extension of this chapter (Osborn & Hagedoorn, 1997; Schuler, 2001). These three theoretical perspectives are briefly described here. Then their application to and research suggestions for all forms of alliances are presented.

Theoretical Perspectives for Understanding Human Resources Management in Alliances

Although there are many theoretical perspectives that are used to explain various aspects of alliances, there are three that appear to be particularly applicable when discussing HRM and organizational issues (Inkpen & Tsang, 2005).

Transaction Cost Theory

Transaction cost economics assumes that business enterprises choose governance structures that economize transaction costs associated with establishing, monitoring, evaluating, and enforcing agreed-upon exchanges (Williamson 1979, 1981). Predictions about the nature of the governance structure an alliance will use incorporate two behavioral assumptions: bounded rationality and opportunism (i.e., the avoidance of forbearance). These assumptions mean that the central problem to be solved by alliances is how to design governance structures that take advantage of bounded rationality while safeguarding against opportunism. To solve this problem, implicit and explicit contracts are established, monitored, enforced, and revised. For example, the theory has direct implications for understanding how HR activities are used to achieve a governance structure for managing the myriad implicit and explicit contracts between employers and employees in an IJV system (Schuler & Tarique, 2005; Wright & McMahan, 1992). IJV partners try to establish contractual relationships with each other to reduce their transaction costs. They find this process, however, easier to do vis-à-vis explicit, visible resources than with invisible assets such as competencies and knowledge (Ariño & Reuer, 2004).

Agency Theory

Agency theory focuses attention on the contracts between a party (i.e., the principal) that delegates work to another (i.e., the agent) (Jensen & Mecklin, 1976). Agency relations are problematic to the degree that (1) the principal and agent have conflicting goals, and (2) it is difficult or expensive for the principal to monitor the agent's performance (Eisenhardt, 1989). Contracts are used to govern such relations. Efficient contracts align the goals of principals and agents at the lowest possible cost (Ariño & Reuer, 2004). Costs can arise from providing incentives and obtaining information (e.g., about the agent's behavior and/or the agent's performance outcomes). Agency theory appears to be particularly useful for understanding executive and managerial compensation practices, which are viewed as a means for aligning the interests of the owners of a firm (i.e., principals) with the managers in whom they vest control (Reuer & Miller, 1997). It is also useful in gaining insights into how venture partners can control the behaviors of the general manager of the IJV, or how the acquiring firm can control the behaviors of the managers in the acquired firm and any other form of alliance with JVs as well as of the key individuals in nonequity forms of alliances.

Organizational Learning Theory

According to the organizational learning theory perspective (Kogut, 1988; Teece, 1986), prior learning facilitates the learning and application of new, related knowledge (Cohen & Levinthal, 1990). This idea can be extended to include the case in which the knowledge in question is itself a set of learning skills constituting an alliance's absorptive capacity. This capacity increases as a function of the previous alliance formation's experience, its learning processes, and the need for information the alliance considers lacking in order to attain its strategic objectives (Lane, Salk, & Lyles, 2001; Steensma & Lyles, 2000). In foreign market entry, advocates of the internationalization-process school (Johanson & Vahlne, 1977) have argued that firms expand slowly from their domestic bases into progressively distant areas. Learning from previous expansions is the driving force behind new investments, whether in JVs or other forms of alliances (Barkema et al., 1997). Learning and the transfer of learning can serve to benefit organizations in any form of alliance.

Human Resources Management in Varying Forms of Alliances

As suggested above, the four-stage model of the IJV alliance may have application to many forms of alliances because the differences among them are more of degree rather than of kind—with one exception. Further illustrating this is Figure 12.1, which depicts the relationship between HR policy and practice significance and implications and type of alliance. These relationships are proposed because as the alliance form moves from nonequity to international alliance

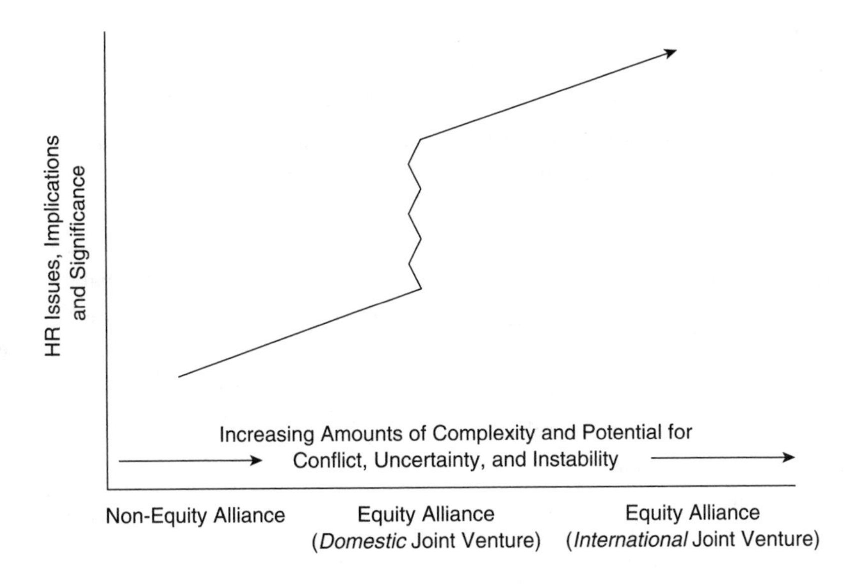

Figure 12.1 Relationships Between Human Resources Issues, Implications, and Significance and Alliance Forms

SOURCE: R. S. Schuler & I. Tarique, 2004

(IJV), complexity and complications increase and the potential for conflict, uncertainty, and instability also increase (Bouchet et al., 2004; Luo 2000; Schuler et al., 2004; Osborn & Hagedoorn, 1997). These result in challenges and roadblocks to learning, control, and management/organizational efficiencies, all needs that can be addressed by HR policies and practices, as discussed above (Schuler, 2001).

These relationships are proposed to have a one-to-one relationship as we move from the simplest alliance to the most complex alliance, an IJV with one major inflection or disruption point (Luo, 2002). Indeed, as shown in Figure 12.1, there is a significant distinction between alliances that create a third organization (equity alliance), a JV, and those that do not create a JV. Alliances without a JV (nonequity alliances) still have many implications for HR policies and practices, but they are proposed to be fewer than those with JVs. Many of the specific steps in the four-stage model for IJVs (Exhibit 12.1) are still likely to exist, but their complexity and complications are expected to be significantly less (Luo, 2002), thus their significance and importance are substantially less.

Propositions and Research Directions

Based upon the description of Figure 12.1, we propose five general propositions based upon the three theoretical perspectives to suggest future research.

> Proposition 1: Complexity, complications, and the potential for conflict, uncertainty, and instability increase as the form of alliance moves from nonequity alliance to an international alliance (an IJV).

As Osborn and Hagedoorn (1997) suggest, varying forms of alliances are linked and differentiated by their amount of uncertainty and complexity and, with these, the amount of control that can be exerted over the alliance system (the companies involved in the alliance itself). As the alliance form moves from a nonequity status to an international alliance status, as depicted in Figure 12.1, we propose that complexity, complications, and the potential for conflict, uncertainty, and instability increase.

> Proposition 2: The challenges to learning, gaining, and retaining efficiencies and exercising control increase as the form of alliance moves from nonequity alliance to an international alliance (an IJV).

As a consequence of the relationships described in Proposition 1, we further propose that increasing amounts of complexity, complications, and potential for conflict, uncertainty, and instability will become challenges and potential roadblocks (1) to managing the learning processes in the alliance system, (2) to gaining and retaining efficiencies and economies of scale, and (3) to exercising control over the alliance system activities.

> Proposition 3a: The implications for and significance of HRM increase as the form of alliance moves from nonequity alliance through the several stages of alliance activity to an international alliance (an IJV).
>
> Proposition 3b: The implications for and significance of HRM are much greater for equity alliances than nonequity alliances.

HR policies and practices have the ability to provide clarity, organizational and management, to organizational and HR phenomena. Done effectively, they are able to contribute to the three needs for managing the learning processes, gaining and retaining efficiencies and economies of scale, and exercising control over the alliance system activities. And as the alliance system moves from nonequity to an international alliance form, these three needs increase, and hence the implications for and significance of HRM will increase. Although the separate HR polices and practices will all be individually and uniquely important, it is proposed that the nature of their significance will increase when done systematically across the forms of alliances. Furthermore, it is proposed that the nature of the contributions of the HR polices and practices will vary by the stage of the alliance. This is particularly likely to be the case in comparing the two major sections shown in Figure 12.1 as created by the inflection point between alliances, with and without an independent third entity, the JV. This is proposed to be due to far fewer complexities and complications and reduced potential for conflict, uncertainty, and instability associated with non-JV situations compared to JV situations that create a third organizational entity.

> Proposition 4: HR issues and implications can be developed into four stages similar for all types of alliances, although the specific content will vary.

Whether an alliance is in nonequity or equity form, alliance activity can be categorized or staged in similar ways, each with issues and implications for HRM. For example, the formation of any alliance should be based on identifiable reasons, most of which will have implications for HRM. Partners will also have to be found and selected for the various forms of alliances; learning and knowledge are important, and selecting partners one can learn from is important. In the development of any alliance, activities around where and how the alliance will be located and staffed will arise. A manager for an alliance or new business for a nonequity licensing arrangement may be necessary to ensure that the alliance activity is managed in order to benefit the relationship. In the implementation phase, additional staff may need to be added, either to staff the JV (domestic or international) or to staff a company's nonequity alliances with growing number of companies throughout the world. Finally, in the advancement stage, all forms of alliances can be seen (should be seen) as providing learning opportunities, and this needs to be done systematically whether it is from a JV and/or other parent, or whether from the units or individuals within a company that are managing the nonequity alliance activities.

Conclusion

Alliances of all forms are growing in their importance for organizations, and concern to understand and manage them as well as possible is increasing. In this chapter we try to highlight the role of HRM in alliances. Because the existing body of work in this area has largely focused on international alliances (IJVs), this chapter seeks to extend this focus by describing the potential relationships between HR policies and practices and several forms of alliances, from the simplest nonequity alliance to the most complex IJV. For this, we utilize the four-stage model to describe the issues and implications for HRM in IJVs.

Along with this model, the key underlying phenomena in alliances are identified, those being complexity and complications, along with the potential for conflict, uncertainty, and instability, all of which are proposed to increase as the form of alliance moves from a nonequity alliance to an international alliance, as illustrated in Figure 12.1. The organizational and HR issues that arise in alliances result because these underlying phenomena become challenges and roadblocks to what are important needs in all forms of alliances, that is, learning, efficiencies, and control. In turn, all of them have implications for HRM that increase in significance from nonequity to equity alliances because more is at stake as the alliances become more complex, particularly when the alliance creates another separate organizational form, the venture itself.

There may, however, be an exception to the relationships proposed in Figure 12.1. It is argued by some that it may be more difficult to manage nonequity arrangements with reciprocal product/knowledge flows than JVs (Osborn & Hagedoorn, 1997). If this is the case, then it might be argued that this special type of nonequity alliance should be placed to the right of the IJV alliance illustrated in Figure 12.1. Alternatively, the horizontal axis might be based upon what is exchanged rather than the form of ownership. This being the case, then, this axis might have "pure supply arrangements" to the left, and to the right might be "reciprocal product/knowledge flow" alliances (R. N. Osborn, personal communication, October 26, 2004). This, however, is for another paper to explore in more depth.

Based upon the relationships shown in Figure 12.1, propositions are offered that could form the basis for further research in the area of HRM in alliances. These propositions reflect the three theoretical perspectives of learning theory, agency theory, and transaction cost theory. Future research might reflect other theoretical perspectives as well as these three. Future research might also be based upon a generic four-stage model of HRM in alliances that is similar yet distinct from that shown in Exhibit 12.1. Of course, it is also plausible to see Exhibit 12.1 tailored to different forms of alliances, particularly distinguishing between nonequity alliances and equity alliances, where the implications and significance to HRM might be expected to be substantially different, at least in degree.

References

Aldrich, H. (1979). *Organizations and environments.* Englewood Cliffs, NJ: Prentice Hall.

Anderson, E., & Weitz, B. (1989). Determinants of continuity in conventional industrial channel dyads. *Marketing Science, 8,* 310–323.

Ariño, A., & Reuer, J. (2004). Designing and renegotiating strategic alliance contracts. *Academy of Management Executive, 3,* 37–48.

Badaracco, J. (1991). *The knowledge link.* Boston: Harvard Business School Press.

Baliga, R., & Jaeger, A. (1984). Multinational corporations: Control systems and delegation issues. *Journal of International Business Studies, 3,* 25–40.

Barkema, H., Shenkar, O., Vermeulen, F., & Bell, J. (1997). Working abroad, working with others: How firms learn to operate international joint ventures. *Academy of Management Journal, 40,* 426–443.

Beamish, P. (1985). The characteristics of joint ventures in developed and developing countries. *Columbia Journal of World Business, 3,* 13–19.

Black, J., Gregersen, H., Mendenhall, M., & Stroh, L. K. (1999). *Globalizing people through international assignments.* Reading, MA: Addison-Wesley.

Brewster, C., & Harris, H. (1999). *International HR.* London and New York: Routledge.

Briscoe, D. R., & Schuler, R. S. (2004). *International human resource management: Policies and practices for the global enterprise* (2nd ed.). New York: Routledge.

Bromiley, P., & Cummings, L. (1993). *Organizations with trust: Theory and measurement.* Paper presented at the meeting of the Academy of Management Meetings, Atlanta, GA.

Bouchet, G., Soellner, F. N., & Lim, L. H. (2004). Check your mindset at the border. *Worldview, 3,* 57–67.

Caligiuri, P. M., & Lazarova, M. (2000). Strategic repatriation policies to enhance global leadership development. In M. Mendenhall, T. Kuehlmann., & G. Stahl (Eds.), *Developing global business leaders: Policies, processes, and innovations.* New York: Quorum Books.

Cascio, W. (1991). *Costing human resources: The financial impact of behavior in organization.* Boston: PWS-Kent.

Chi, T., & McGuire, D. (1996). Collaborative ventures and value of learning: Integrating the transaction cost and strategic option perspectives on the choice of market entry modes. *Journal of International Business Studies, 27,* 285–307.

Child, J., & Faulkner, D. (1998). *Strategies of cooperation.* Oxford and London: Oxford University Press.

Collins, T., & Doorley, T. (1991). *Teaming up for the 90s: A guide to international joint ventures and strategic alliances.* Homewood, IL: Business One Irwin.

Cohen, W. M., & Levinthal, D. A. (1990). Absorptive capacity: A new perspective on learning and innovations. *Administrative Science Quarterly, 35,* 128–152.

Cyr, D. (1995). *The human resource challenge of international joint ventures.* Westport, CT: Quorum Books.

Cyr, D., & Schneider, S. (1996). Implications for learning: Human resource management in east-west joint ventures. *Organization Studies, 17,* 207–226.

Das, T., & Teng, B. (2002). Alliance constellations: A social exchange perspective. *Academy of Management Review, 3,* 445–456.

Datta, D. (1988). International joint ventures: A framework for analysis. *Journal of General Management, 14,* 78–91.

Datta, K., & Rasheed, A. (1993). Planning international joint ventures: The role of human resource management. In R. Culpan (Ed.), *Multinational strategic alliances* (pp. 251–271). New York: International Business Press.

Doz, Y., & Hamel, G. (1998). *Alliance advantage: The art of creating value through partnering.* Boston: Harvard Business School Press.

Doz, Y., & Prahalad, K. (1981). Headquarters influence and strategic control in MNCs. *Sloan Management Review, 23,* 15–29.

Dowling, P., Welch, D., & Schuler, R. (1999). *International human resource management* (3rd ed.). Cincinnati, OH: South-Western Publishing.

Dyer, J. (1997). Effective interfirm collaboration: How firms minimize transaction costs and maximize transaction value. *Strategic Management Journal, 18,* 535–556.

Eisenhardt, K. (1989). Agency theory: An assessment and review. *Academy of Management Review, 14,* 57–74.

Ernst, D., & Halevy, T. (2004). Not by M&A alone. *McKinsey Quarterly, 1,* 6–10.

Evans, P., Pucik, V., & Barsoux, J. (2002). *The global challenge: Frameworks for international human resource management.* Boston: McGraw-Hill.

Fichman, M., & Levinthal, D. (1991). Honeymoons and the liability of adolescence: A new perspective on duration dependence in social and organizational relationships. *Academy of Management Review, 6,* 442–468.

Foss, N., & Pedersen, T. (2002). Transferring knowledge in MNCs: The role of sources of subsidiary knowledge and organizational context. *Journal of International Management, 8,* 49–67.

Frayne, C., & Geringer, J. (1990). The strategic use of human resource management practices as control mechanisms in international joint ventures.

Research in Personnel and Human Resources Management (Suppl. 2), 53–69.

Frayne, C., & Geringer, J. (2000). *Challenges facing general managers of international joint ventures.* Unpublished paper, San Diego State University.

Geringer, J., & Frayne, C. (1990). Human resource management and international joint venture control: A parent company perspective. *Management International Review, 30,* 37–52.

Geringer, J., & Hebert, L. (1989). Control and performance of international joint ventures. *Journal of International Business Studies, 20,* 235–254.

Geringer, J., & Herbert, L. (1991). Measuring performance of international joint ventures. *Journal of International Business Studies, 22,* 253–267.

Green, S., & Welsh, A. (1988). Cybernetics and dependence: Reframing the control concept. *Academy of Management Review, 13,* 287–301.

Gomes-Casseres, B. (1989). Joint ventures in the face of global competition. *Sloan Management Review, 30,* 17–26.

Gulati, R. (1998). Alliances and networks. *Strategic Management Journal, 19,* 293–317.

Hagedoorn, J. (1993). Understanding the rationale of strategic technology partnering: Interorganizational models of co-operation and sectoral differences. *Strategic Management Journal, 14,* 371–386.

Hamel, G. (1991). Competition for competence and inter-partner learning within international strategic alliances. *Strategic Management Journal, 12,* 83–104.

Harbison, J. (1996). *Strategic alliances: Gaining a competitive advantage.* New York: Conference Board.

Harrigan, K. (1985). Managing joint ventures. *Management Review, 76,* 24–42.

Harrigan, K. (1986). *Managing for joint venture success.* Boston: Lexington.

Harry, W., & Banai, M. (2005). International itinerants. In M. Morley (Ed.), *International human resource management and international assignments.* Basingstoke, UK: Palgrave Macmillan.

Harvey, M., Speier C., & Novicevic M. (1999). The impact of emerging markets on staffing the global organization: A knowledge-based view. *Journal of International Management, 5,* 167–186.

Hennart, J. (1991). The transaction costs theory of joint ventures: An empirical study of Japanese subsidiaries in the United States. *Management Science, 37,* 483–497.

Hergert, M., & Morris, D. (1988). Trends in international collaborative agreements. In F. Contractor & P. Lorange (Eds.), *Cooperative strategies in international business* (pp. 1–28). Toronto, Canada: Lexington Books.

Hill, R., & Hellriegel, D. (1994). Critical contingencies in joint venture management: Some lessons from managers. *Organizational Science, 5,* 594–610.

Inkpen, A. (2002). Learning, knowledge management, and strategic alliances: So many studies, so many unanswered questions. In F. Contractor & P. Lorange (Eds.), *Cooperative strategies and alliances* (pp. 267–289). Amsterdam: Pergamon.

Inkpen, A., & Beamish, P. (1997). Knowledge, bargaining power and international joint venture stability. *Academy of Management Review, 22,* 177–202.

Inkpen, A., & Crossan, M. (1995). Believing is seeing: Joint ventures and organizational learning. *Journal of Management Studies, 32,* 595–618.

Inkpen, A., & Currall, S. (1997). International joint venture trust: An empirical examination. In P. W. Beamish & J. P. Killing (Eds.), *Cooperative strategies: North American perspectives* (pp. 308–334). San Francisco: New Lexington Press.

Inkpen, A., & Dinur, A. (1998). Knowledge management processes and international joint ventures. *Organization Science, 9*(4), 454–468.

Inkpen, A., & Tsang, E. (forthcoming). Social capital, networks, and knowledge transfer. *Academy of Management Review.*

Isabella, L. (2002). Managing an alliance is nothing like business as usual. *Organizational Dynamics, 31,* 47–59.

Jackson S., & Schuler, R. (2003). *Managing human resources: A partnership perspective* (8th ed.). Cincinnati, OH: South-Western Publishing.

Jensen, M., & Mecklin, W. (1976). Theory of the firm: Managerial behavior, agency costs and ownership structure. *Journal of Financial Economics, 2,* 305–306.

Johanson, J., & Vahlne, J. E. (1977). The internationalization process of the firm: A model of knowledge development and increasing foreign market commitments. *Journal of International Business Studies, 8,* 23–32.

Johnson, J., Cullen J., Sakano T., & Takenouchi H. (1996). Setting the stage for trust and strategic integration in Japanese-U.S. cooperative alliances. *Journal of International Business Studies, 27,* 981–1004.

Killing, J. (1983). *Strategies for joint venture success.* New York: Praeger.

Kogut, B. (1988). Joint ventures: Theoretical and empirical perspectives. *Strategic Management Journal, 9,* 319–332.

Koka, B., & Prescott, J. (2002). Strategic alliances as social capital: A multidimensional view. *Strategic Management Journal, 23,* 795–816.

Lane, P., Salk, J., & Lyles, M. (2001). Absorptive capacity, learning, and performance in international joint ventures. *Strategic Management Journal, 22,* 1139–1161.

Lei, D., Slocum, J., & Pitts, R. (1997). Building cooperative advantage: Managing strategic alliances to promote organizational learning. *Journal of World Business, 32,* 202–223.

Lin, X. & Germain, R. (1998). Sustaining satisfactory joint venture relationships: The role of conflict resolution strategy. *Journal of International Business Studies, 29*(1), 179–196.

Lorange, P. (1986). Human resource management in multinational cooperative ventures. *Human Resource Management, 25,* 133–148.

Lorange, P., & Roos, J. (1992). *Strategic alliances, formation, evolution, and implementation.* London: Basil Blackwell.

Luo, Y. (1998). Joint venture success in China: How should we select a good partner. *Journal of World Business, 33,* 145–166.

Luo, Y. (1999). Toward a conceptual framework of international joint venture negotiations. *Journal of International Management, 5,* 141–165.

Luo, Y. (2002). Contract, cooperation, and performance in international joint ventures. *Strategic Management Journal, 23,* 903–919.

Lyles, M. (1987). Common mistakes of joint venture experienced firms. *Columbia Journal of World Business, 22,* 79–85.

Makhija, M., & Ganesh, U. (1997). The relationship between control and partner learning in learning related joint ventures. *Organizational Science, 8,* 508–524.

Mallik, A., Zbar, B., & Zemmel, R. W. (2004, November 4). Making pharma alliances work. *McKinsey Quarterly, 1,* 12–18.

McGill, M., Slocum, J., & Lei, D. (1992, Summer). Management practices in learning organizations. *Organizational Dynamics, 21,* 5–17.

Morris, D., & Hergert, M. (1987). Trends in international collaborative agreements. *Columbia Journal of World Business, 22,* 15–21.

Mudambi, R. (2002). Knowledge management in multinational firms. *Journal of International Management, 8,* 1–9.

Narula, R., & Duysters, G. (2004). Globalization and trends in international R&D alliances. *Journal of International Management, 10,* 199–218.

Newburry, W., & Zeira, Y. (1997). Implications for parent companies. *Journal of World Business, 32,* 87–102.

Nooteboom, J., Berger, H., & Noorderhaven, N. (1997). Effects of trust and governance on relational risk. *Academy of Management Journal, 40,* 308–338.

Osborn, R. N., & Hagedoorn, J. (1997). The institutionalization and evolutionary dynamics of interorganizational alliances and networks. *Academy of Management Journal, 40,* 261–278.

Parkhe, A. (1991). Interfirm diversity, organizational learning, and longevity in global strategic alliances. *Journal of International Business Studies, 22,* 579–602.

Pfeffer, J., & Cohen, Y. (1984). Determinants of internal labor markets in organization. *Administrative Science Quarterly, 29,* 550–572.

Prahalad, C., & Hamel, G. (1990). The core competence of the corporation. *Harvard Business Review, 68,* 79–91.

Pucik, V. (1988). Strategic alliances, organizational learning and competitive advantage: The HRM agenda. *Human Resource Management, 27,* 77–93.

Reid, D., Bussiere, D., & Greenway, K. (2001). Alliance formation issues for knowledge-based enterprises. *International Journal of Management Reviews, 3,* 79–100.

Reuer J., & Miller, K. (1997). Agency costs and the performance implications of international joint venture internalization. *Strategic Management Journal, 18,* 425–438.

Reve, T. (1990). The firm as a nexus of internal and external contracts. In M. Aoki, B. Gustafson, & O. Williamson (Eds.), *The firm as a nexus of treaties* (pp. 133–161). Newbury Park, CA: Sage.

Sabel, C. (1993). Studied trust: Building new forms of cooperation in a volatile economy. *Human Relations, 46,* 1133–1170.

Schaan, J. (1988). How to control a joint venture even as a minority partner. *Journal of General Management, 14,* 4–16.

Schuler, R. S. (2001). HR issues in international joint ventures. *International Journal of Human Resource Management, 12,* 1–50.

Schuler, R. S., Dowling, P. J., & DeCieri, H. (1992, September). The formation of an international joint venture: Marley Automotive Components Ltd. *European Management Journal,* 304–309.

Schuler, R., Jackson, S., Dowling, P., & Welch, D. (1991). The formation of an international joint venture: Davidson instrument panel. *Human Resource Planning, 15,* 50–60.

Schuler, R., & Jackson, S., & Luo, Y. (2004). *Managing human resources in cross-border alliances.* New York: Routledge.

Schuler, R. S., & Tarique, I. (2005). HRM and international joint venture variation. In I. Björkman & G. Stahl (Eds.), *Handbook of research in IHRM.* London: Edward Elgar.

Schuler R. S., & Van Sluijs, E. (1992). Davidson-Marley BV: Establishing and operating an international joint venture. *European Management Journal, 10,* 28–37.

Shenkar, O. (1995). *Global perspectives of human resource management.* Englewood Clifts, NJ: Prentice Hall.

Shenkar, O., & Li, J. (1999). Knowledge search in international cooperative ventures. *Organizational Science, 10,* 34–44.

Shenkar, O., & Zeira, Y. (1987). Human resource management in international joint ventures: Direction for research. *Academy of Management Review, 12,* 546–557.

Simons, R. (1987). Accounting control systems and business strategy: An empirical analysis. *Accounting, Organizations and Society, 4,* 357–374.

Slocum J., & Lei, D. (1993). Designing global strategic alliances: Integrating cultural and economic factors. In G. P. Huber & W. H. Glick (Eds.), *Organizational change and redesign: Ideas and insights for improving performance* (pp. 295–322). New York: Oxford University Press.

Steensma, H., & Lyles, M. (2000). Explaining IJV survival in a transitional economy through social exchange and knowledge-bases perspective. *Strategic Management Journal, 21,* 831–851.

Teece, D. (1986). Profiting from technological innovation: Implications for integration, collaboration, licensing and public policy. *Research Policy, 15,* 785–805.

Van Sluijs, E., & Schuler, R. (1994). As the IJV grows: Lessons and progress at Davidson-Marley BV. *European Management Journal, 12,* 315–321.

Williamson, O. (1979). Transaction cost economics: The governance of contractual relations. *Journal of Law and Economics, 22,* 233–262.

Williamson, O. (1981). The economics of organization: The transaction cost approach. *American Journal of Sociology, 87,* 548–577.

Wright, P., & McMahan, G. (1992). Theoretical perspectives for strategic human resource management. *Journal of Management, 18,* 295–320.

Yan, A. (1998). Structural stability and reconfiguration of international joint ventures. *Journal of International Business Studies, 29,* 773–796.

Yan, A., & Gray, B. (1994). Bargaining power, management control and performance in United States–China joint ventures: A comparative case study. *Academy of Management Journal, 37,* 1478–1517.

Yeheskel, O., Newburry, W., & Zeira, Y. (2004). Significant differences in the pre- and post-incorporation stages of equity international joint ventures (IJVs) and international acquisitions (IAs), and their impact on effectiveness. *International Business Review, 13,* 613–636.

13

Learning and Knowledge Development in Alliances

Marjorie A. Lyles

Siegfried P. Gudergan

This chapter addresses the dynamic learning capabilities of firms within the context of alliances and associated alliance management processes. We focus our discussion on routine processes underlying learning in alliances and start exploring routine adjustments, instances of improvisation, new adaptations under conditions of novelty, and the dynamic integration of the new learning to the knowledge base of the firm. Our discussion centers on types of knowledge, specifically alliance management, knowledge characteristics, cognitive and social dimensions of learning processes, and the organizational setting of the alliance. Our goal is to explore the state of the art of research addressing how firms learn while they are in alliances and how they access the knowledge of others. We aim neither to provide an eclectic model of learning in alliances nor to offer a full-blown model containing a comprehensive set of possible relationships, as has been done previously by authors such as Salk and Simonin (2003) and Inkpen (2002). However, we intend to shed some light on how learning processes in alliances might differ under conditions of novelty. The logic of the latter focus is based on Eisenhardt and Martin's (2000) argument that the role of dynamic capabilities such as learning capabilities depends on the degree of volatility in the environment in which a firm operates, in that learning processes in more volatile environments are associated with adjustments and improvisation.

The organizational learning literature, and the literature on learning and knowledge management in alliances in particular, is characterized by a perplexing abundance of definitions and approaches, of which not all are consistent. It is helpful for us to begin this chapter with our definitions. Learning has been defined as "the development of insights, knowledge, and associations between past actions, the effectiveness of those actions, and future actions" (Fiol & Lyles, 1985). Typically knowledge has been classified as *explicit* knowledge, which can be written and easily communicated, or *tacit* knowledge, which is somewhat unconscious and difficult to communicate. Alliances, which are "relatively enduring interfirm cooperative arrangements" (Parkhe, 1991), are frequently formed with an intent of gaining access to new knowledge from the partner firm. This new type of knowledge would be related either to the business or task being conducted or to the alliance management process. Joint ventures, licensing agreements, contractual agreements, and networks are among the most common types of alliances.

For firms relying on knowledge and innovation for their competitive edge, the use of alliances to improve innovation and performance is significant and increasing. Gudergan, Devinney, and Ellis (2003) note that,

> alliances account for more than 15% of turnover generated by the top 1,000 U.S. firms (Harbison & Pekár, 1998) and for an average 26% of *Fortune* 500 companies' revenues, a proportion that has more than doubled over five years (Andersen Consulting, 1999). Moreover, business consultants such as Margulis and Pekár (2001) expect the percentage of revenues generated from alliances to climb to 33% in the United States and to 40% in Europe by 2005.

These statistics support the notion that alliances are of importance to the innovativeness and competitiveness of their parent firms because of the dispersion of capabilities across firms (Powell, Koput, & Smith-Doerr, 1996; McEvily & Chakravarthy, 2002). The consequences are that corporations will engage in alliances more and may also partner with the same firm more than once. In fact, it seems likely that if a corporation has good experiences with another firm as a partner, it will pursue partnering with that firm again (Lyles, 1988). Barkema, Shenkar, Vermeulen, and Bell (1997) explain how firms learn to operate business relationships. The extent to which the partners handle the process of alliance management and learn over time how to be a better partner will create value for the partner firms (Anand & Khanna, 2000). As a result of the alliance, the partners attempt to build organizational processes that enhance their knowledge development and longevity (Szulanski, 1996; Kogut & Zander, 1992; Lyles, Dhanaraj, & Steensma, 2004; Steensma & Lyles, 2000). Building on Simonin (1997), we define the knowledge of alliance management as an organization's abilities to identify and select potential alliance partners, negotiate and structure an effective alliance agreement, monitor and manage ongoing alliances, and know when and how to terminate an alliance.

Even multinational corporations that build upon an extensive alliance experience base are subject to failures and disappointing outcomes. Shenkar and Yan (2002) show that escalation of partner political behavior plays a key role in the failure of collaborative ventures. Each alliance is unique, and much of the knowledge about how to manage alliances is tacit and therefore difficult to transfer (Szulanski, 1996). Reuer, Park, and Zollo (2002) refer to this as "experience heterogeneity and venture novelty." They find that creativity accrues from prior alliance experience and is important to performance. At the same time, because each alliance is unique, knowledge transfer and access to a partner's knowledge base are often difficult to copy and assimilate. Firms build experience-based knowledge when they have entered into several alliances, and they also bring their own intangible and explicit knowledge to the relationship.

Consequently, the routines built to support alliance management and the knowledge acquired from partners are always subject to questions of adaptation, reevaluation, improvisation, and mutation (Lyles, 1988; Miner, Bassoff, & Moorman, 2001). It is the distinctiveness of many alliance management experiences that requires organizations constantly to adapt their alliance management process to new circumstances. The uniqueness of each alliance also requires management to recognize that adaptation of best practices or of the knowledge acquired will often not transfer easily (Szulanski, 1996).

Companies pursue alliances for a range of purposes, such as strengthening their market position, developing new products, increasing access to markets, increasing their technology base, and reducing costs or risk; related circumstances are not only likely to be heterogeneous within a portfolio of alliances an organization is engaged with, but also characterized by constant change. Through alliances, companies intend to learn how to improve management practices, learn new technologies, or learn to partner better so they can enhance the organizations' performance. Developing new knowledge about management or other operational processes is therefore an important rationale for forming alliances (e.g., Kogut, 2000; Lyles & Salk, 1996; Parkhe, 1991) and the associated learning facilitates innovation and competitiveness (Gudergan, Devinney, & Ellis, 2002).

Doz and Hamel (1998) outline five key areas in which learning occurs within alliances: (1) the *environment*—includes both the external environment, such as customers, competition, technology, society, culture, and so on, and internal environment, that is, the strategic circumstances relevant to each partner, (2) the *task*—alliance tasks the partners engage in to accomplish their aims, such as managing the interface in joint activities, (3) the *process*—decisions and operations that are necessary to carry out the alliance tasks successfully, as well as structures and routines that shape the alliancing process, (4) the *skills*—alliance partner skills comprise both easily transferred skills and the more tacit or embedded skills, and (5) the *goals*—individual partner goals that take into account their motives and agendas that they pursue in the alliance. Sharing and developing knowledge in these areas and, more important, implementing it within the context of the alliance and the partners' organizations can lead to better performance of the partners (Grant & Baden-Fuller, 2004).

Learning in alliances embodies different *types of knowledge, knowledge characteristics, knowledge of learning processes, cognitive* and *social dimensions,* and the *organizational setting* of the alliance. These features have been examined in various interorganizational structures where they represent different learning and knowledge management challenges. For example, authors such as Simonin (1999a) examine ambiguity and the process of knowledge transfer in strategic alliances; Zollo, Reuer, and Singh, (2002) examine interorganizational routines, learning, and performance in strategic alliances; Inkpen and Dinur (1998) look at knowledge management processes in international joint ventures; Lyles and Salk (1996) study knowledge acquisition from foreign parents in international joint; Beckman and Haunschild (2002) examine the effects of partner heterogeneity and experience on network learning; and Reagans and McEvily (2003) study network structure and knowledge transfer.

We now aim to explain relevant matters associated with the different features of learning in alliances. Figure 13.1 provides a simple illustration of our conceptualization of the features that affect learning in alliances. The remaining sections of this chapter are organized along the five features of influencing interorganizational learning—*types of knowledge,* specifically *alliance management, knowledge characteristics, cognitive dimensions, social dimensions,* and the *organizational setting*—and summarize key contributions. These categories provide the basis for a structured discussion. We conclude with suggestions about further research opportunities in general, and those that are of interest when alliances operate in volatile environments requiring creativity processes such as improvisation.

Types of Knowledge: Alliance Management

Theorists have identified that firms utilize their experience and vicarious learning from others to build routines, adaptations, and standardizations that can be transferred (Argote, 1999; Baum, Li, & Usher, 2000). Organizations can create new knowledge by combinative capabilities and

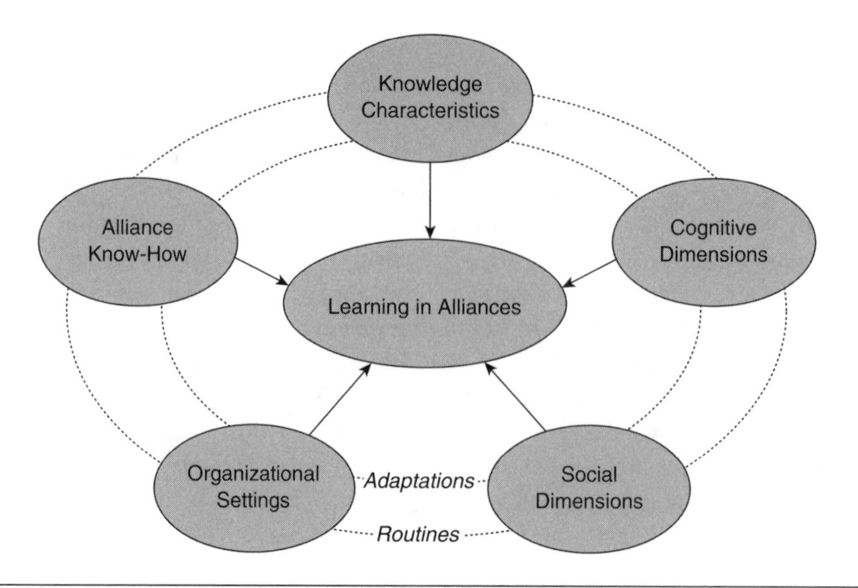

Figure 13.1 Conceptualization of Alliance Learning

different pieces of existing knowledge (Kogut & Zander, 1992; Van den Bosch, Volberda, & de Boer, 1999; Zander & Kogut, 1995), which presents a powerful motive or learning intent for seeking alliances for innovation. An organization might expect that the more experience it has at a particular activity, such as partnering and managing alliances, the more likely it would be that it would be able to repeat the action in a similar fashion and that it would be successful (Winter, 1987). In fact, research suggests firms can learn from their prior alliance experience and that this aids in alliance performance (Anand & Khanna, 2000; Kale, Singh, & Perlmutter , 2000; Lane, Salk, & Lyles , 2001). Simonin (1997, 1999a) argues that collaborative know-how can be considered a unique type of competence, one that may help explain why some alliances succeed brilliantly while others fail spectacularly and why some organizations are able to leverage their network of collaborative arrangements more effectively than others.

Yet, learning from experience is especially difficult and problematic when the repetition of comparable circumstances is rare—as in alliances. Thus, because of the uniqueness of each alliance, learning from experience may be learning under conditions of ambiguity or novelty (Zollo et al., 2002). Consequently, knowledge of alliance management needs to provide a flexible basis and embrace novelty associated with improvisation and other creative aspects in the learning process (Argote, 1999; Gudergan et al., 2002; Herriott, Levinthal, & March, 1985; Levinthal & March, 1981; Miner et al., 2001; Dyer & Singh, 1998; Reuer et al., 2002). Given this, knowledge transfer is often difficult, and it is unlikely that there are standardized routines for managing the specific intricacies of individual alliances that would apply to all alliances of a firm (Doz & Hamel, 1998; Szulanski, 1996). Understanding routines and processes that are transferable across different alliances, representing standardized routines, those that require adaptation, and those that are unique to a particular alliance, can assist in allocating appropriate learning efforts within alliances.

March (1991) suggests two types of learning: *exploitation,* in which the processes and outcomes are more certain and the time horizon is shorter, and *exploration,* in which the outcomes are unpredictable and there are longer time horizons. Explorative learning is highly uncertain and can be enhanced by nonredundant ties such that the partners are exposed to different knowledge domains (Nakamura, Shaver, & Yeung, 1996; Grant & Baden-Fuller, 2004). Exploitive learning is an extension of the current knowledge domains and is strengthened by repeated ties (Mowery, Oxley, & Silverman, 1996).

Knowledge of alliance management seems to be produced most by explorative learning. Because of the novelty of each alliance, the relationship between alliance know-how and performance may vary for different kinds of alliances (Reuer et al., 2002). Anand and Khanna (2000) find that firms create more value from their joint venturing experience than from their licensing experience, and the effects of learning are greater for research and development (R&D) and production joint ventures than for marketing. One avenue for future research may be to analyze for what length of time particular knowledge of alliance management is useful as compared to other know-how that is based on more of an exploitative nature.

Furthermore, the applicability of this alliance knowledge is also affected by the durability and stability of the alliance itself. Therefore, being able to measure the extent to which alliance know-how is transferable and adaptable and explain the effects of alliance know-how transferability and adaptability conditioned on the levels of durability and stability would assist in explaining learning in alliances. Within this context, the dimensions of accidental and intentional learning, as well as the exploitative and explorative nature of the latter, can be explored to examine more comprehensively the role of alliance know-how in interorganizational learning conditioned on the degree of volatility in the environment in which the alliance operates.

Knowledge Characteristics

Knowledge characteristics, most commonly found to be *tacitness, complexity,* and *ambiguity,* influence learning in alliances (Simonin, 1999a, 1999b; Anand & Khanna, 2000). Alliances are often seen as efficient vehicles for knowledge transfer across organizational boundaries, especially for knowledge that is difficult to transfer because of its tacitness (Kogut, 2000). It has been argued that managerial and marketing expertise is more tacit than product development, production, and technology (Shenkar & Li, 1999) because science and technological knowledge may be recorded, diagrammed, or configured. Management and marketing skills are embedded and not easily codified in formulae or manuals. They cannot be reverse engineered easily (Zander & Kogut, 1995). In comparison, quantifiable technologies and processes are more explicit and more easily transferred (Von Glinow & Teagarden, 1988). In addition, transactional concerns are quite intense in alliances (Mowery et al., 1996; Inkpen & Beamish, 1997), and this could potentially make learning in an alliance a competitive process, as partners race to learn each other's domain of knowledge (Hamel, 1991; Khanna, Gulati, & Nohria, 1998; Anand & Khanna, 2000).

Knowledge complexity in alliances can be linked to the level of interdependency of different knowledge components related to areas such as production systems and supply-chain structures or marketing routines and new product development processes of the partners. Although greater complexity of knowledge is assumed to impede transferability, Zander and Kogut (1995) do not identify a significant effect of complexity on the transfer of knowledge of manufacturing processes. Yet, although Simonin (1999a) shows that knowledge complexity plays a role in transferring knowledge related to manufacturing processes in alliances, in another study Simonin (1999b) does not observe a relationship between knowledge complexity and the transfer of marketing knowledge. These inconclusive findings about the effect of knowledge complexity on its transfer in alliances are likely to be related to the tacitness of the knowledge and possible difficulties in imitations that are the result of knowledge ambiguity (Reed & DeFillippi, 1990).

The complexity and ambiguity of knowledge are likely to increase with greater change in the external environment in which the partners operate and with the variations in the alliances that are formed. Yet little is known about the interplay of routine adjustments and improvisations in learning and knowledge ambiguity and complexity in alliances. Given the lack of conclusive and consistent research results regarding the impact of knowledge characteristics on learning in alliances, it seems there are many avenues open for future research. Future studies could also, therefore, examine the interplay of knowledge complexity, tacitness, and ambiguity in explaining knowledge transfer and adaptability in alliances under conditions of novelty.

Cognitive Dimensions

In their seminal papers, Cohen and Levinthal define absorptive capacity as the "ability to identify, assimilate, and exploit knowledge from the environment" (1989, p. 589, also 1990, 1994). They argue that this ability is largely dependent on a firm's prior knowledge endowments. Several empirical studies have been conducted in support of this notion and its significance to strategic alliance capabilities such as learning and innovation (Lane & Lubatkin, 1998; Van den Bosch et al., 1999; Lane, Lyles, & Salk, 1998; Mowery et al., 1996; Pisano, 1990; Powell et al., 1996; Tsai, 2002; Bucic & Gudergan, 2003). Furthermore, absorptive capacity is important for mediating explorative and exploitative adaptations (March, 1991).

Most studies, however, focus on outcomes of absorptive capacity. Thus, absorptive capacity is seen as an explanation for innovation (Cohen & Levinthal, 1990; Bucic & Gudergan, 2003), business performance (Lane et al., 2001; Tsai, 2002), and interorganizational learning (Lane & Lubatkin, 1998). Several studies have applied the concept to alliances and dyads (Lane & Lubatkin, 1998; Lane et al., 2001; Mowery et al., 1996; Bucic & Gudergan, 2003). Conceptually, some light has been shed on the different components, respectively, of recognition, assimilation, and application of new external knowledge. In this vein, Zahra and George (2002) have introduced a "dynamic capabilities" perspective of absorptive capacity and distinguish between potential and realized absorptive capacity.

Grant and Baden-Fuller (2004) suggest that the important capability should be accessing the alliance partner's knowledge bases, not necessarily trying to transfer the knowledge or to replicate it. Building upon March's (1991) distinction between knowledge exploration and knowledge exploitation, they argue that knowledge acquisition (or transfer) and access (or application and leverage) play distinct roles in different contexts. Knowledge transfer in alliances is more relevant when routines and their outcomes are certain, whereas accessing knowledge seems more appropriate when consequences of processes are difficult to predict.

In spite of all these important forward strides, much work of a conceptual, theoretical, and empirical nature remains. For example, an area for future research may be to examine the intricacies of absorptive capacity within the context of knowledge acquisition and access to explain more comprehensively the role of absorptive capacity in facilitating learning in alliances. Within the context of acquiring and accessing knowledge, it is also important to understand how the absorptive capacity of the alliance facilitates adaptations of the learning required for adjusting knowledge in volatile situations. For instance, research could evolve around examining the factors that make up an effective absorptive capacity in multipartner alliances in which peripheral partners of various kinds change constantly so that relevant new knowledge can be accessed successfully. Or in a similar vein, building on the work of Zahra and George (2002), future work could focus on learning processes associated with improvisation and creativity that underlie the "dynamic capabilities" of the alliance, of which its absorptive capacity is a part. An explicit understanding about the nature of an absorptive capacity in alliances that operate in volatile environments and its impact on the development of knowledge under conditions of novelty would both shed light on the concepts of dynamic capabilities and absorptive capacity in alliances and advance our insight about learning and knowledge development in alliances.

Social Dimensions

Research on the role of the social aspects of alliances suggests that relational embeddedness, as evidenced by parent support to the international joint venture (IJV), trust, and socialization between the parent firms and the IJV all enhance interfirm learning (Brown & Duguid, 2001; Dyer & Singh, 1998; Lyles & Salk, 1996; Parkhe, 1991; Uzzi, 1997). In an alliance, whether a nonequity partnership or joint venture in the case of IJV, relational embeddedness between managers of parent firms and that of the IJV creates a common identity that helps to "motivate members to participate and openly share valuable knowledge—while preventing undesirable spillovers to competitors—prevent free riders, and reduce the costs associated with finding and accessing different types of valuable knowledge" (Dyer & Nobeoka, 2000, p. 348; see also Dhanaraj, Lyles, Steensma, & Tihanyi, 2004).

Kogut and Zander (1996) suggest that firm boundaries provide in essence a context for knowledge to be developed and exploited; they emphasize the role of coordination, identity, and learning as key activities of the firm. In a similar vein, Nonaka (1994) emphasizes the role of "socialization" in the diffusion of knowledge within organizations. His perspective suggests that social relations enhance the emergence of new knowledge and facilitate the transformation of tacit to explicit knowledge and vice versa. Kale et al. (2000) suggest that relational capital between partners enhances learning capability, simultaneously mitigating the transactional concerns.

Embeddedness creates the "logic of confidence and good faith" (Meyer & Rowan, 1977) and provides the "cohesive force" (Orton & Weick, 1990) that is imperative for creating an environment in which knowledge can flow. Likewise, Brown and Duguid (2001) find that in communities of practice, identity provides the bond that determines whether knowledge is "sticky," making its flow difficult, or "leaky," allowing generous flow. Recent research supports this argument, showing that social capital, a measure of embeddedness, positively impacts innovation (Shan, Walker, & Kogut, 1994). In alliances, informal communication promotes interorganizational learning (Bucic & Gudergan, 2003; Gudergan et al., 2002) and knowledge acquisition (Lyles & Salk, 1996), and social networking facilitates sharing of tacit knowledge (Makhija & Ganesh, 1997).

All these conceptual ideas refer to the central role of social or community orientation of knowledge, an aspect that Cohen and Levinthal's (1990) conceptualization of absorptive capacity does not explicitly mention. Cohen and Prusak (2001) suggest trust, loyalty, and membership as three dimensions of social capital and provide a conceptual framework:

> Social capital consists of the stock of active connections among people, the trust, mutual understanding, and shared values and behaviors that bind the members of human networks and communities and make cooperative action possible. (2001, p. 4)

However, cognitive aspects such as absorptive capacity and its relationship to social capital and learning processes need to be further explored. More important, social capital and its associated concepts of trust, loyalty, and membership evolve over time. This has notable implications in situations in which an alliance and its partners are confronted with constant change of the external environment in which they operate or varying compositions in complex multipartner alliances. For instance, although we know that trust among partners facilitates learning, trust is likely to be weaker in alliances characterized by greater instability that can originate from an unpredictable external environment or fluctuations in the involvement of partners in the alliance. In a similar vein, loyalty to the alliance and membership in the partnership are less developed in situations that are more volatile. Thus, the social foundations underlying learning in alliances suggest that knowledge access and development would be less effective under conditions of novelty. Yet little is known about how learning can be strengthened in alliances when social capital is low so that learning routines can be adjusted and partners can improvise.

Organizational Setting

A theoretical basis for knowledge development and sharing builds on the notion of internalization of processes and systems, which includes intangible knowledge-based assets (Buckley & Casson, 1988; Martin & Salomon, 2003). Within alliances, the partner firms face a dual dilemma; they aim to learn while in the alliance and they also desire to protect their highly valuable intangible knowledge. Parkhe (1991) suggests that partner diversity will enhance learning. Supporting this, Bucic and Gudergan (2003) show that diversity of the members of an alliance team facilitates learning, and Anand and Khanna (2000) identify firm-specific differences that allow some firms to benefit more from alliances and to capitalize on their experience-based learning and the transfer of know-how between the partners. Dussauge, Garrette, and Mitchell (2000) suggest that learning and skill transfer occur more often in alliances in which most of the contributions of a particular type come from one partner rather than in a "scale" alliance in which the contributions overlap.

Others find that ownership and control structures influence learning. For example, Lyles and Salk (1996) find that 50:50 joint ventures with little conflict can have the greatest knowledge transfer. In general, a balanced approach to decision-making power reduces the level of conflict between the parents and increases the likelihood of IJV learning and IJV survival in transitional economies (Steensma & Lyles, 2000). Some research addresses the importance of coordinating the alliance activities. Kale, Dyer, and Singh (2002) suggest that centralized coordination enhances the firm's ability to utilize its alliance experience to build new capabilities, including learning capabilities. Bucic and Gudergan (2004) also show that formal and centralized alliance structures impede learning in the alliance team. These various research studies suggest that ownership, structure, control, and the organizational systems will influence knowledge development and transfer.

The notion of "centrality" is also important in assessing the central position in a network of partnerships among multiple firms. The central player can serve as a "broker" of knowledge and information and can also be the first to know of new knowledge (Hargadon & Sutton, 1997). Particularly when a firm is attempting explorative learning that results in technological development or innovations, the development of diverse ties in a network avoids the hazard of overembeddedness. Overembeddedness can result in repeated ties that carry few new learning opportunities (Burt, 1992). It permits a firm to combine its partnering capabilities with technological competence and absorptive capacity and thus enhances the firm's attractiveness as a strategic partner (Ahuja, 2000; Roijakkers, Hagedoorn, & Van Kranenburg, 2003).

Yet Das and Teng (2002) warn that a network of multiple-partner firms also requires a greater competence in alliance management if the central firm is to capitalize on its central role as the broker. There can be barriers that occur as a result of the network itself that can minimize knowledge transfer, such as the number of partners in the network, the possibilities of noise in the transfer of knowledge, and maintaining the relationship that encourages tacit knowledge transfer.

Far less is known about the organizational aspects shaping absorptive capacity and how it influences strategy and performance in alliances. Because absorptive capacity results from prior knowledge, Cohen and Levinthal (1990) point out that aspects that are "distinctly organizational" shape a firm's absorptive capacity beyond the sum of employees' individual absorptive capacities. Yet understanding of the organizational determinants of absorptive capacity remains limited. Furthermore, although we know that mechanistic structures in alliances hinder the development of dynamic capabilities evident in weaker learning and creativity processes in the alliance, whereas organic structures are more conducive in alliances (Bucic & Gudergan, 2004), we lack research that explicitly examines the interplay of the alliance's organizational setting and other alliance features such as the partnership's social capital and absorptive capacity under conditions requiring constant improvisation and adjustment of routines.

Conclusions and Key Questions for Future Research in Organizational Learning in Alliances

In the preceding sections we discuss learning processes in alliances in general and reflect on routine adjustments, instances of improvisation, new adaptations under conditions of novelty, and the dynamic integration of new learning to the knowledge base of the firm—processes that ultimately impact on innovation in alliances. Although there are significant contributions that shed light on learning processes in alliances, there are also several avenues for future research that we suggest within the context of our conceptualization, in which we examine the role of knowledge of *alliance management, knowledge characteristics, cognitive dimensions, social dimensions,* and the *organizational setting* of learning in alliances.

Table 13.1 provides some exemplar areas for future research closely tied to the individual features of learning in alliances. For example, it is important to explain how alliance know-how is affected by the durability and stability of the alliance; related to knowledge characteristics, research could focus on the interplay of knowledge complexity, tacitness, and ambiguity in explaining knowledge transfer and adaptability in alliances under conditions of novelty. Within the context of the cognitive dimension, an area for future research may be to study the intricacies of absorptive capacity, such as the ability to exploit knowledge, within the context of knowledge acquisition and access to explain more comprehensively the role of absorptive capacity in facilitating learning in alliances. In addition, it is relevant to examine the interplay of cognitive aspects such as absorptive capacity and its relationship to social capital and learning processes in alliances. Finally, there are opportunities for exploring the effects on absorptive capacity of different organizational structures in alliances.

Although individually these are important areas for future research, understanding how the various aspects related to alliance know-how, knowledge characteristics, cognitive dimensions, social dimensions, and organizational settings interact with each other becomes more perplexing but can explain important processes that affect learning and knowledge development in alliances in general and under conditions of novelty in particular. For instance, how does organizational structure in alliances interact with particular aspects of social embeddedness in strengthening absorptive capacity in alliances? What roles do structural centralization and formality play in developing informal interactions in volatile alliance environments and how does this differ for knowledge acquisition and access in alliances? What particular alliance management processes are required to support these learning processes in alliances? Or, with a different emphasis, are there distinct dimensions embedded in absorptive capacity at the alliance level that have differential effects on the use of knowledge characterized by distinctive levels of complexity, tacitness, and ambiguity for unsteady contexts in which an alliance operates? If so, how does this relate to exploitive and explorative learning in alliances requiring improvisation and routine adjustments? Taking another focus, how

Table 13.1 Exemplar Areas for Future Research

Research Area	*Focus of Research*	*Research Questions*
Knowledge of Alliance Management	• the usefulness of particular alliance know-how for a shorter time period of an explorative nature versus other know-how based on more of an exploitative nature • the effects of durability and stability of the alliance on alliance know-how in context characterized by change • the effects of alliance know-how transferability and adaptability conditioned on the levels of durability and stability • the effect of accidental and intentional learning, as well as the exploitative and explorative nature of the latter, on alliance know-how transferability and adaptability	o How does alliance durability moderate the relationship between alliance know-how transferability and improvised alliance learning? o What are the differential effects of exploitative and explorative learning on alliance know-how in stable versus instable alliances? o How does alliance longevity influence the impact of alliance know-how transferability on non-routine alliance learning? o What particular alliance know-how can be standardized and how does alliance know-how standardization affect alliance learning under conditions of novelty?
Knowledge Characteristics	• the interplay of knowledge complexity, tacitness and ambiguity in explaining knowledge transfer and adaptability under conditions of novelty in alliances	o How does knowledge complexity influence the effect of knowledge ambiguity on knowledge adaptability in alliances operating under condition of flux? o How does knowledge ambiguity affect the relationship between tacitness and knowledge transfer in multi-partner alliances with constantly changing peripheral members?
Cognitive Dimensions	• the intricacies of absorptive capacity within the context of knowledge acquisition and access to explain more comprehensively the role of absorptive capacity in facilitating learning in alliances that requires improvisation and routine adjustments	o What are the differential effects of particular dimensions of absorptive capacity on knowledge acquisition and access in alliances operating highly volatile environments?
Social Dimensions	• the cognitive aspects such as absorptive capacity and its relationship to social capital and the learning in alliances operating in constant flux	o How does absorptive capacity affect the effect of social capital on alliance learning under conditions of novelty? o How does relational embeddedness influence an alliance's absorptive capacity?
Organizational Settings	• the effects of organizational aspects in alliances on absorptive capacity and learning and knowledge development requiring routine adaptations and the dynamic integration of acquired or accessed knowledge • the organizational determinants of absorptive capacity in alliances and their effect non-routine learning	o What are the differential effects of particular organizational structures in alliances on an alliance's social capital and absorptive capacity? o How does absorptive capacity influence non-routine learning and knowledge adaptation in alliances?

do the stability and durability of the alliance affect the development of social capital and absorptive capacity at the alliance level? What are related implications for learning in alliances operating in constantly changing sets of relationships? We could identify a range of additional areas for possible future research. However, such a list would be too long for the purpose of this chapter.

In conclusion, we endeavor to explore the state of the art of research addressing how firms learn while they are in alliances and how they access the knowledge of others. This discussion stresses aspects of several routine learning processes and alludes to some intricacies related routine adjustments, instances of improvisation, new adaptations under conditions of novelty, and the dynamic integration of new learning to the knowledge base of the firm. Our chapter focuses on five features that play a role in learning in alliances: alliance know-how, knowledge characteristics, cognitive dimensions, social dimensions, and organizational settings. Around those features we present key contributions relevant to learning alliances. In spite of all these important advances, much research of a conceptual, theoretical, and empirical nature remains; this is the case in particular for contexts in which learning in alliances occurs under conditions of novelty. In order to provide direction for future research related to learning in alliances, we have discussed and identified some exemplary areas.

References

Ahuja, G. (2000). The duality of collaboration: Inducements and opportunities in the formation of inter-firm linkages. *Strategic Management Journal, 21,* 317–343.

Anand, B. N., & Khanna, T. (2000). Do firms learn to create value? The case of alliances [special issue]. *Strategic Management Journal, 21,* 295–315.

Argote, L. (1999). *Organizational learning: Creating, retaining, and transferring knowledge.* Boston: Kluwer Academic.

Barkema, H., Shenkar, O., Vermeulen, F., & Bell, H. J. (1997). Working abroad, working with others: How firms learn to operate international joint ventures [research forum on alliances and networks]. *Academy of Management Journal, 40*(2), 426–442.

Baum, J. A., Li, S. X., & Usher, J. M. (2000). Making the next move: How experiential and vicarious learning shape the locations of chains' acquisitions. *Administrative Science Quarterly, 45*(4), 766–801.

Beckman, C., & Haunschild, P. (2002). Networks of learning: The effect of partners' heterogeneity of experience on corporate acquisitions. *Administrative Science Quarterly, 47,* 92–124.

Brown, J. S., & Duguid, P. (2001). Knowledge and organization: A social-practice perspective. *Organization Science, 12*(2), 198–213.

Bucic, T., & Gudergan, S. (2003). *A componential model of collaborative innovation in alliances.* Working Paper, University of Technology, Sydney. Presented at the 4th European Conference on Organizational Knowledge, Learning and Capabilities, Barcelona, Spain.

Bucic, T., & Gudergan, S. (2004). The impact of organisational settings on creativity and learning in alliances. *M@n@gement, 7*(3), 257–273.

Buckley, P., & Casson, M. (1988). A theory of cooperation in international business. In F. Contractor & P. Lorange (Eds.), *Cooperative strategies in international business* (pp. 31–53). Lexington, MA: Lexington.

Burt, R. (1992). *Structural holes: The social structure of competition.* Cambridge, MA: Harvard University Press.

Cohen, D., & Prusak, L. (2001). *In good company: How social capital makes organizations work.* Boston: Harvard Business School Press.

Cohen, W. M., & Levinthal, D. A. (1990). Absorptive capacity: A new perspective on learning and innovation. *Administrative Science Quarterly, 35,* 128–152.

Cohen, W., & Levinthal, D. (1994). Fortune favors the prepared firm. *Management Science, 40*(2), 227–251.

Das, T. K., & Teng, B. (2002). Alliance constellations: A social exchange perspective. *Academy of Management Review, 27*(3), 445–456.

Dhanaraj, C., Lyles, M., Steensma, K., & Tihanyi, L. (2004). Managing the dynamics of tacit and explicit learning in IJVs: The role of relational embeddedness and the impact on performance. *Journal of International Business Studies, 35,* 428–442.

Doz, Y., & Hamel, G. (1998). *Alliance advantage: The art of creating value through partnering.* Boston: Harvard Business School Press.

Dussauge, P., Garrette, B., & Mitchell, W. (2000). Learning from competing partners: Outcomes and durations of scale and link alliances in Europe, North America and Asia. *Strategic Management Journal, 21*(2), 99–126.

Dyer, J. H., & Nobeoka, K. (2000). Creating and managing a high-performance knowledge-sharing network: The Toyota case [special issue]. *Strategic Management Journal, 21,* 345–367.

Dyer, J., & Singh, H. (1998). The relational view: Cooperative strategy and sources of interorganizational competitive advantage. *Academy of Management Review, 23*(4), 660–679.

Eisenhardt, K. M., & Martin, J. A. (2000). Dynamic capabilities: What are they? *Strategic Management Journal, 21*(10/11), 1105–1121.

Fiol, C. M., & Lyles, M. A. (1985). Organizational learning. *Academy of Management Review, 10*(4), 803–813.

Grant, R. M., & Baden-Fuller, C. (2004). A knowledge accessing theory of strategic alliances. *Journal of Management Studies, 41,* 61–84.

Gudergan, S. P., Devinney, T., & Ellis, R. S. (2002). An integrated theory of alliance governance and performance. In M. A. Trick (Ed.), *Mergers, acquisitions, alliances and networks.* Pittsburgh, PA: Carnegie Mellon University Press.

Gudergan, S. P., Devinney, T., & Ellis, R. S. (2003). *A competence-innovation framework of non-equity alliance performance.* Institute for the Study of Business Markets Working Paper, Pennsylvania State University.

Hamel, G. (1991). Competition for competence and inter-partner learning within international strategic alliances [special issue]. *Strategic Management Journal, 12,* 83–103.

Hansen, M. T. (1999). The search-transfer problem: The role of weak ties in sharing knowledge across organization subunits. *Administrative Science Quarterly, 44,* 82–111.

Hargadon, A., & Sutton, R. (1997). Technology brokering and innovation in a product development firm. *Administrative Science Quarterly, 42,* 716–749.

Herriott, S. R., Levinthal, D. A., & March, J. (1985). Learning from experience in organizations. *American Economic Review, 75*(2), 298–302.

Inkpen, A. C. (2002). Learning, knowledge management and strategic alliances: So many studies, so many unanswered questions. In F. Contractor & P. Lorange (Eds.), *Cooperative strategies and alliances.* Amsterdam, The Netherlands: Elsevier.

Inkpen, A. C., & Beamish, P. W. (1997). Knowledge, bargaining power, and the instability of international joint ventures. *Academy of Management Review, 22,* 177–202.

Inkpen, A. C., & Dinur, A. (1998). Knowledge management processes and international joint ventures. *Organization Science, 9,* 454–468.

Kale, P., Dyer J. H., & Singh, H. (2002). Alliance capability, stock market response, and long-term alliance success: The role of the alliance function. *Strategic Management Journal, 23,* 747–767.

Kale, P., Singh, H., & Perlmutter, H. (2000). Learning and protection of proprietary assets in strategic alliances: Building relational capital. *Strategic Management Journal, 21*(3), 217–237.

Khanna, T., Gulati, R., & Nohria, N. (1998). The dynamics of learning alliances: Competition, cooperation, and relative scope. *Strategic Management Journal, 19,* 193–210.

Kogut, B. (2000). The network as knowledge: Generative rules and the emergence of structure [special issue]. *Strategic Management Journal, 21,* 405–425.

Kogut, B., & Zander, U. (1992). Knowledge of the firm, integration capabilities, and the replication of technology. *Organization Science, 3,* 383–397.

Kogut, B., & Zander, U. (1996). What firms do? Coordination, identity, and learning. *Organization Science, 7*(5), 502–518.

Lane, P. J., & Lubatkin, M. (1998). Relative absorptive capacity and interorganizational learning. *Strategic Management Journal, 19,* 461–477.

Lane, P. J., Lyles, M. A., & Salk, J. E. (1998). Relative absorptive capacity, trust, and learning in international joint ventures. In M. A. Hitt, J. E. Ricart, & R. D. Nixon (Eds.), *Managing strategically in an interconnected world* (pp. 373–397). New York: Wiley.

Lane, P., Salk, J., & Lyles, M. A. (2001). Knowledge acquisition and performance in transitional economy international joint ventures. *Strategic Management Journal, 22*(12), 1139–1162.

Levinthal, D., & March, J. G. (1981). A model of adaptive organizational search. *Journal of Economic Behavior & Organization, 2*(4), 307–333.

Lyles, M. A. (1988). Learning among joint-ventures sophisticated firms. *Management International Review, 28*(4), 85–98.

Lyles, M., Dhanaraj, C., & Steensma, K. (2004). Critical issues in learning processes. In S. W. Floyd, J. Roos, C. Jacobs, & F. W. Kellermanns (Eds.), *Innovating strategy processes.* Oxford: Blackwell.

Lyles, M. A., & Salk, J. E. (1996). Knowledge acquisition from foreign parents in international joint ventures: An empirical examination in the Hungarian context. *Journal of International Business Studies, 29*(2), 154–174.

Makhija, M. V., & Ganesh, U. (1997). The relationship between control and partner learning in learning-related joint ventures. *Organization Science, 8,* 508–527.

March, J. G. (1991). Exploration and exploitation in organization learning. *Organization Science, 2,* 71–87.

Martin, X., & Salomon, R. (2003). Tacitness, learning, and international expansion: A study of foreign direct investment in a knowledge-intensive industry. *Organization Science, 14*(3), 297–311.

McEvily, S., & Chakravarthy, B. S. (2002). The persistence of knowledge-based advantage: An empirical test for product performance and technological knowledge. *Strategic Management Journal, 23*(4), 285–305.

Meyer, J., & Rowan, B. (1977). Institutionalized organizations: Formal structure as myth and ceremony. *American Journal of Sociology, 83,* 340–363.

Miner, A. S., Bassoff, P., & Moorman, C. (2001). Contours of organizational improvisation and learning. *Administrative Science Quarterly, 46,* 304–337.

Mowery, D. C., Oxley, J. E., & Silverman, B. S. (1996). Strategic alliances and interfirm knowledge transfer [special issue]. *Strategic Management Journal, 17,* 35–39.

Nakamura, M., Shaver, J. M., & Yeung, B. (1996). An empirical investigation of joint venture dynamics: Evidence from U.S.-Japan joint ventures. *International Journal of Industrial Organization, 14,* 521–541.

Nonaka, I. (1994). A dynamic theory of organizational knowledge creation. *Organization Science, 5*(1), 14–37.

Orton, J. D., & Weick, K. E. (1990). Loosely coupled systems: A reconceptualization. *Academy of Management Review,* 15(2), 203–223.

Parkhe, A. (1991). Interfirm diversity, organizational learning, and longevity in global strategic alliances. *Journal of International Business Studies, 22*(4), 579–602.

Pisano, G. P. (1990). The R&D boundaries of the firm: An empirical analysis. *Administrative Science Quarterly, 35*(1), 153–176.

Powell, W., Koput, K. W., & Smith-Doerr, L. S. (1996). Interorganizational collaboration and the locus of innovation: Networks of learning in biotechnology. *Administrative Science Quarterly, 41,* 116–145.

Reagans, R., & McEvily, B. (2003). Network structure and knowledge transfer: The effects of cohesion and range. *Administrative Science Quarterly, 48*(2), 240–267.

Reed, R., & DeFillippi, R. (1990). Causal ambiguity, barriers to imitation, and sustainable competitive advantage. *Academy of Management Review, 15,* 88–102.

Reuer, J., Park, K., & Zollo, M. (2002). Experiential learning in international joint ventures: The roles of experience heterogeneity and venture novelty. In F. Contractor & P. Lorange (Eds.), *Cooperative strategies and alliances.* Amsterdam, The Netherlands: Elsevier.

Roijakkers, N., Hagedoorn, J., & Van Kranenburg, H. (2003). Multiple partnering capabilities, technological competences, and repeated high-tech partnering. Working Paper, Maastricht University. Presented at the Strategic Management Society 23rd Annual Conference, Baltimore, MD.

Salk, J. E., & Simonin, B. L. (2003). Beyond alliances: Towards a meta-theory of collaborative learning. In M. Easterby and M. A. Lyles (Eds.), *The Blackwell handbook of organizational learning and knowledge management.* Oxford: Blackwell.

Shan, W., Walker, G., & Kogut, B. (1994). Inter-firm cooperation and startup innovation in the biotechnology industry. *Strategic Management Journal, 15,* 387–394.

Shenkar, O., & Li, J. (1999). Knowledge search in international cooperative ventures. *Organization Science, 10*(2), 134–143.

Shenkar, O., & Yan, A. (2002). Failure as a consequence of partner politics: Learning from the life and death of an international cooperative venture. *Human Relations, 55*(5), 565–583.

Simonin, B. L. (1997). The importance of developing collaborative know-how: An empirical test of the learning organization. *Academy of Management Journal, 40*(5), 1150–1174.

Simonin, B. L. (1999a). Ambiguity and the process of knowledge transfer in strategic alliances. *Strategic Management Journal, 20*(7), 595–623.

Simonin, B. L. (1999b). Transfer of marketing know-how in international strategic alliances: An empirical investigation of the role and antecedents of knowledge ambiguity. *Journal of International Business Studies, 30*(3), 463–490.

Steensma, K., & Lyles, M. A. (2000). Explaining IJV survival in a transitional economy through social exchange and knowledge-based perspectives. *Strategic Management Journal, 21*(8), 831–852.

Steensma, H. K., Tihanyi, L., Lyles, M. A., & Dhanaraj, C. (forthcoming). The evolving value of foreign partnerships in transitional economies. *Academy of Management Journal.*

Szulanski, G. (1996). Exploring internal stickiness: Impediments to the transfer of best practice within the firm [special issue]. *Strategic Management Journal, 17,* 27–43.

Tsai, W. (2002). Social structure of "coopetition" within a multiunit organization: Coordination, competition, and intraorganizational knowledge sharing. *Organization Science, 13,* 179–190.

Uzzi, B. (1997). Social structure and competition in interfirm networks: The paradox of embeddedness. *Administrative Science Quarterly, 42,* 35–67.

Van den Bosch, F., Volberda, H. W., & de Boer, M. (1999). Coevolution of firm absorptive capacity and knowledge environment: Organizational forms and combinative capabilities. *Organization Science, 10,* 551–568.

Von Glinow, M. A., & Teagarden, M. (1988). The transfer of human resource management technology in Sino-U.S. cooperative ventures: Problems and solutions. *Human Resource Management, 27*(2), 201–229.

Winter, S. G. (1987). Knowledge and competence as strategic assets. In D. J. Teece (Ed.), *The competitive challenge: Strategies for industrial innovation and renewal.* Cambridge, MA: Ballinger.

Zahra, S. A., & George, G. (2002). Absorptive capacity: A review, reconceptualization, and extension. *Academy of Management Review, 27*(2), 185–203.

Zander, U., & Kogut, B. (1995). Knowledge and the speed of the transfer and imitation of organizational capabilities: An empirical test. *Organization Science, 6*(1), 76–92.

Zollo, M., Reuer, J. J., & Singh, H. (2002). Interorganizational routines and performance in strategic alliances. *Organization Science, 13*(3), 339–351.

PART IV

Cross-Border Collaborations

14

Alliances and International Business Theory

Andrew Delios

Strategic alliances and international business theory have been almost inseparable from the early days of the study of each. Early research on international business theory received some of its strongest grounding in internalization theory (Buckley & Casson, 1976; Rugman, 1982) and the eclectic paradigm (Dunning, 1988). These early theories considered the question of why firms would engage in internalized cross-border transactions for intermediate products instead of market-based transactions for these products. These approaches considered that any one of a variety of modes could be used for these transactions, including licensing, franchising, nonequity alliances, equity alliances, and wholly owned subsidiaries. In this sense, the study of strategic alliances was embedded in the foundations of international business theory.

Even noneconomic approaches to international business theory addressed the issue of strategic alliances. Perhaps the best-known early behavioral theory of international expansion has been internationalization theory (Johanson & Vahlne, 1977), which describes the internationalization process as one rooted in uncertainty reduction through the accumulation of relevant types of experience. Organizational decisions about when to enter a particular market and how to enter a market are contingent on a firm's experiential learning and the uncertainty in a market. For the How? question, internationalization theory considers nonequity alliances, joint ventures, and wholly owned subsidiaries among the choices for a firm for its mode of entry to a foreign market. Again, we find that strategic alliances are embedded in a core theory in international business.

The developments in international business theory since the 1970s have included a deepening of our understanding of many of the core issues in internalization, eclectic, and internationalization theories. These developments have also included the introduction of new conceptual and theoretical frameworks for understanding new and emerging phenomena that have become prevalent in international business. Such theories

AUTHOR'S NOTE: This research was supported by an NUS Academic Research Grant (R-313-000-052-112).

include organizational learning, neoinstitutional theory, institutional economics, social network theory, and resource-based theory, to name a few.

At the same time, work on strategic alliances has continued to evolve. Research on strategic alliances has included a similar deepening and broadening of the research scope in terms of the theoretical frameworks employed. Chapters 2 and 3 in this book identify two of the core theories used for examining strategic alliances, namely transaction cost economics and an industrial organization approach. Chapters 3 through 7 bring forward new theoretical perspectives such as real options theory, evolutionary economics, institutions and organization coevolution theory, and a networks approach. In addition to these new theoretical viewpoints, organization learning theory, a bargaining power approach, and neoinstitutional theory have also been applied to improve our understanding of the formation and management of strategic alliances.

As the preceding discussion implies, although research in international business and strategic alliances began as heavily overlapping areas of research, since the onset of the 1990s, these two areas of research have become more and more distinct. Part of this divergence was initiated by volumes of work devoted exclusively to strategic alliances. One such landmark publication was Contractor and Lorange's (1988) edited collection on cooperative strategies. This edited volume had several key pieces, such as Gomes-Casseres (1988), Hergert and Morris (1988), and Kobrin (1988), that collectively set the agenda for international alliance research for the decade of the 1990s.

Aside from this brief mention of divergence, in this chapter I concentrate on identifying areas of past, present, and future convergence in international business theory and strategic alliance research. As necessitated by the scope of a chapter, this identification is necessarily bounded to a few well-defined research streams. The exclusion of other viewpoints on international business theory or international alliances, such as culture and international alliances, the eclectic theory, or the resource-based view, does not signify that I consider these to be outside the realm of the topic of international alliances and international business research. Rather, these areas rest just outside the bounds of the discussion in this chapter.

This chapter has a focus on identifying past, present, and future points of alignment between research on alliances and international business theory. I make this identification by describing how international business theory and research on alliances had common conceptual antecedents (the past), I then look at how these fields are currently intertwined (the present), and how these two areas of research might converge or diverge (the future).

The Past

Alliances and International Business Theory

A variety of theoretical viewpoints have spoken to issues prevalent in international alliances. Several of these viewpoints have been at the core of international business theory. Even with early roots in the core, viewpoints on alliances have transitioned from the core of international business theory, as situated in internalization theory and internationalization theory, to positions that are much more diverse.

International business theory and research on international alliances had their earliest intersection when researchers considered the mode by which firms expanded into international markets. The entry-mode choice has long been considered one of the most critical decisions for a firm making an expansion into international markets (Stopford & Wells, 1972; Wind & Perlmutter, 1977). The critical nature of the entry-mode choice emerges from the idea that the entry-mode choice can have critical implications for the performance of a foreign entry (Root, 1987; Geringer & Hèbert, 1991; Woodcock, Beamish, & Makino, 1994; Delios & Beamish, 2004). A variety of mode choices exists for a firm:

no international involvement, licensing and franchising, exporting, direct investment via a joint venture (minority-owned, co-owned, or majority-owned), or wholly owned subsidiary. One of the principal issues faced by early researchers in international business was understanding why differing degrees of ownership were utilized by multinational enterprises when making a foreign entry (Vernon & Wells, 1976; Gatignon & Anderson, 1988).

Internalization Theory and International Alliances

Internalization theorists concentrated much of their early work on international business activity on understanding the determinants behind the choice between licensing and direct investment (Buckley & Casson, 1976; Rugman, 1982). Subsequent work by international-business scholars soon began to look at the level-of-ownership question, which at that time had at its focus the choice between wholly owned subsidiaries and joint ventures (Hennart, 1982). In studies situated in the internalization stream, scholars principally associated the level of ownership as stemming from the levels of a firm's proprietary, firm-specific knowledge: higher ownership (entry by wholly owned subsidiary) was a response to the need to protect firm-specific knowledge (essentially technological and research-and-development expertise) from unwanted dissemination. Hence, internalization theory stated that full ownership and high control would be observed when a firm transferred unique, firm-specific knowledge to the host country when making its foreign direct investment. The converse of this, of course, is that shared ownership would be more prevalent the lower a firm's possession of unique, firm-specific knowledge.

The ideas of internalization theorists ran parallel to the precepts of transaction cost (TC) theory (Williamson, 1975, 1985). TC theory is concerned with explaining what the most efficient governance structure—markets, hierarchies, or a hybrid—is under which to govern a specific set of transactions. TC theory enriched internalization theory by providing several key concepts by which the entry-mode choice could be more rigorously modeled. Scholars writing on the theory of multinational enterprise (Teece, 1986a), on theories of joint ventures (Beamish & Banks, 1987; Hennart, 1988; Kogut, 1988) and on entry-mode strategies (Anderson & Gatignon, 1986) melded the ideas of TC theory with the previous work of internalization theorists.

In the 1980s, in conceptual and empirical studies situated in the internalization paradigm, TC theory was particularly useful in understanding the determination of ownership levels (Anderson & Gatignon, 1986; Gatignon & Anderson, 1988; Gomes-Casseres, 1989). Anderson and Gatignon (1986) brought the ideas of TC theory to the international business literature in their extensive review of the ownership strategy literature.

In Anderson and Gatignon (1986), the amount of equity ownership was equated with the amount of control that a firm could exert over its subsidiary's operations. Control is important because it provides a foreign parent with the ability to influence the systems, methods, and decisions implemented in its foreign subsidiaries (Anderson & Gatignon, 1986) and with a means to resolve disputes that could arise in a joint venture (Davidson, 1982). The trade-off for a foreign firm when making a decision about ownership levels is that with greater control come an increased resource commitments and increased risk. In this sense, the ownership decision, and the choice of whether to enter by a joint venture or not, involves a trade-off between control and resource commitments made under different levels of risk and uncertainty (Anderson & Gatignon, 1986).

In parallel, although not identical to the work of Anderson and Gatignon (1986) and the idea of the influence of proprietary firm-specific knowledge, was the basic tenet of TC theory that as asset specificity increases, the greater will be the hazards associated with market-based exchange and the greater the incentives to internalize the transaction (Williamson, 1975, 1985). Anderson and Gatignon (1986) considered the optimal degree of control (level of ownership) to be positively related to the degree of possession of proprietary assets (Caves, 1996). Davidson and McFetridge (1985), in comparing the option of licensing versus direct investment, provided some of the earliest evidence that the possession of firm-specific knowledge/assets leads to higher ownership levels. Gatignon and Anderson (1988), in an empirical study of many of the propositions outlined in Anderson and Gatignon (1986), found that in industries characterized by high levels of firm-specific knowledge, a smaller number of entries was by the joint venture mode.

Other studies found similar relationships. For example, Kim and Hwang (1992) and Erramilli and Rao (1993) observed a positive relationship between a firm's possession of proprietary knowledge/assets and its level of ownership in its foreign subsidiaries. Meanwhile, these basic ideas about the choice to enter by wholly owned subsidiary or joint venture were supported by empirical work on the ownership strategies of U.S. firms investing in developed and developing economies (Gatignon & Anderson, 1988; Gomes-Casseres, 1989) and Japanese firms investing in the United States (Hennart, 1991).

Although the need to safeguard a firm's proprietary knowledge and the assets transferred to a foreign subsidiary in its foreign direct investment (FDI) is an important determinant of foreign ownership levels, international business theorists identified a second knowledge/asset–related influence. This second influence does not concern the assets transferred to a foreign subsidiary, instead, it concerns the need to acquire complementary assets on foreign entry.

When a firm expands into international markets, it is often faced with the need to acquire new assets (Stopford & Wells, 1972). Similar to the knowledge/assets a foreign firm transfers to a foreign subsidiary, the knowledge/assets it needs to acquire to mount a successful entry might also be subject to market inefficiencies that make the cost of market-based exchange prohibitive. Hence, a common strategy of a foreign firm on foreign entry is to form a joint venture with a local partner to secure locally based assets.

Hennart (1988) wrote the definitive statement on how the resources and assets provided by foreign and local partners contributed to the prevalence of various types of joint venture entries. Hennart (1988) and Beamish and Banks (1987) argue that joint ventures are organizational modes that combine the complementary assets of two partners when the exchange for these assets in factor markets is subject to high transaction costs. Put another way, joint ventures are an efficient organizational structure for acquiring assets for which there are factor market imperfections. Consequently, multinational firms are motivated to structure foreign entries as joint ventures, and to take lower equity positions, when faced with the need to acquire complementary assets that cannot be obtained efficiently in factor markets.

Hennart (1988) distinguishes between two basic types of joint ventures. One is a link joint venture. A link joint venture is one in which the local and foreign partners contribute different resources. These resources can be capital, technology, country knowledge, market knowledge, distribution, nationality, and raw material or other forms of inputs. The other basic type is a scale joint venture. A scale joint venture is one in which the two partners contribute a similar resource. The purpose of a scale joint venture is to achieve advantages through an increase in size, such as the competitive gains that can come from economies of scale. The motivation to form a scale joint venture to achieve economies of scale is pronounced when small firms must match the scale advantages of large firms.

Hennart's (1988) research marked one of the first points of divergence between research on international alliances and that on international business. It marked this divergence by beginning to explore issues that are directly relevant to the field of international alliances but somewhat tangential to core international business theory, even though the work was still grounded in an internalization paradigm. Other work that extended or was developed at the same time as Hennart's explored the influence of required and contributed assets/knowledge to provide empirical support for the idea that a foreign firm's propensity to enter via a joint venture increases with the need to source complementary host-country assets (Beamish & Banks, 1987; Gomes-Casseres, 1989, 1990; Hennart, 1991; Delios & Beamish, 1999).

Subsequent work enriched our conceptions about what constitutes the types of knowledge/assets sought by a foreign firm on entry. This work merits mention at this point as it relates to research conducted in the late 1990s and early 2000s on international alliances, international business, and national institutional environments. One area of research concerned identification of knowledge of the host-country environment as a critical locally based asset. Early research on multinational firms identified deficiencies in knowledge of the local environment as a significant competitive disadvantage for a foreign firm (Hymer, 1976). Local knowledge of a host-country environment encompasses information about an array of host-country characteristics—political and legal rules and the social norms for business transactions—which define the conditions under which business transactions occur (North, 1990).

Some characteristics of a host-country environment can have a direct effect on a foreign firm's decision about whether to implement a joint venture on entry. For example, legal restrictions on the foreign ownership of domestic enterprises establish definitive limits on foreign equity holdings and induce entry by joint ventures (Contractor, 1990; Gomes-Casseres, 1990).

Other aspects of the host-country environment have an indirect effect on the propensity to enter by joint ventures. These aspects relate to hazards that can accompany transactions because of weaknesses in the transactional environment in the host country (North & Weingast, 1989). These weaknesses can undermine property rights and increase risks in exchange. Where property rights are weaker and environmental risks are greater, firms are less likely to make investments because assets face greater transactional hazards and returns are less predictable and certain (Williamson, 1996). These weaknesses can exacerbate the propensity to avoid joint venture entries when the entering firm is transferring proprietary assets to the host country (Henisz, 2000).

One such weakness is the level of volatility in the political environment. In externally uncertain and volatile environments, firms are better off utilizing joint ventures instead of wholly owned subsidiaries because of the increased flexibility provided to the firm by a low-control mode (Anderson & Gatignon, 1986, p. 15). Hennart (1988) and Hill, Hwang, and Kim (1990) have also argued that firms can reduce their exposure to host-country risk by utilizing joint venture entries in host countries with high political risk and uncertainty. Empirical studies by Vernon (1983), Shan (1991), and Kim and Hwang (1992) identified a positive relationship between political and economic risk and the propensity to enter by a joint venture.

Other host-country characteristics, such as the level of intellectual property rights protection, can be an important concern for foreign entrants (Oxley, 1995). If there is weak property-rights protection, for example, and the value of assets that should be protected by patents and trademarks cannot be fully realized by the owner, then the incentives to make investments involving these technological or marketing-based assets are reduced (Teece, 1986b). In such an institutional setting, the cost of contracting and the cost of using a hybrid such as a joint venture increases because of the increased risk of leakage or unwanted dissemination of proprietary technological and marketing assets to rivals, suppliers, and buyers (Williamson, 1996). Consistent with the need to protect proprietary knowledge and minimize transaction costs when constructing institutional arrangements for foreign entry, a firm's entry propensity to use joint ventures varies with the need to safeguard assets and minimize risks across countries with different institutional environments.

The Internationalization Approach and International Experience

A multinational firm is exposed to potential liabilities and uncertainties different from local firms because it is foreign and because it lacks experience in and knowledge of the host country market. Although being foreign and lacking knowledge of a market might seem like synonymous concepts, in international business theory they are not. Being foreign means a firm might be discriminated against by public policy makers, employees, or buyer and supplier firms because of its nationality. Being foreign can also mean that a firm lacks knowledge of a host-country market, but this aspect of a firm's foreignness can be overcome through the accumulation of experience either internationally or in its host-country markets.

This idea that the accumulation of host-country (international) experience can alleviate a foreign firm's local-knowledge disadvantages is at the heart of the internationalization approach to understanding international business (Johanson & Wiedersheim-Paul, 1975; Johanson & Vahlne, 1977). The internationalization approach argues that a firm's level of commitment to its investments in its foreign markets increases with greater knowledge of a market. In this case, *commitment* refers to the types of entries a firm makes in its foreign markets. Exporting is a low-commitment entry, a joint venture involves a modest commitment, and a wholly owned subsidiary is a high-commitment entry.

International expansion in the stages model is a process rooted in uncertainty reduction through the accumulation of relevant types of experience (Johanson & Vahlne, 1977). Experience in a host country, for example, provides important information about its business environment (Luostarinen, 1980), thereby reducing uncertainty and enabling a firm to make a better evaluation of potential future expansions (Barkema, Shenkar, Vermeulen, & Bell, 1996). Investment experience broadens a firm's perception of its alternatives and increases the extent of its search (Cyert & March, 1963). The accumulation of international investment experience is reflected in two sequences of foreign entry: one from culturally and geographically close countries to more distant ones (Davidson, 1980), and one for a firm's investment path in a country, from exporting to distribution, to joint venture manufacturing, and finally to wholly owned manufacturing (Davidson, 1980).

In this way, the internationalization approach is linked to the choice to utilize a joint venture. The use of a joint venture depends to a large extent on the level of a firm's experience internationally and in its host-country markets. This dependence extends from the view that a firm's internationalization process is one of experience and knowledge accretion. When firms make international investments, specific knowledge of the host country is gained, as is more general knowledge of conducting international operations (Barkema, Bell, & Pennings, 1996). As argued by the internationalization theorists, firms with more experience in a host country have developed organizational capabilities suited to that country and are able to make greater commitments to foreign investments (Johanson & Vahlne, 1977). Firms are able to make greater commitments as experience and knowledge are gained in a host country because managers in a firm can make better strategic decisions as they develop the capability to operate independently in the host country. Even so, given the difficulty of acquiring local knowledge, firms with little host-country experience must often acquire local knowledge by partnering with local firms in a joint venture entry (Barkema et al., 1996).

These arguments are supported by Chang (1995), who suggested that more internationally experienced firms face fewer local knowledge disadvantages. Further, Makino and Delios (1996) found that the gains from making an FDI as a local-partner joint venture, as opposed to a wholly owned subsidiary, decreased with greater levels of international experience because of the foreign firm's development of local knowledge. Finally, other empirical research points to a negative relationship between a firm's propensity to use joint ventures and its level of host-country experience (Davidson, 1980; Li, 1995).

Previous research has also demonstrated that experience gained in specific settings, such as a subsidiary's industry or the nation in which a subsidiary is sited, minimizes the deterring influence of elements of the institutional environment, such as political hazards, on wholly owned entry (Delios & Henisz, 2000). It also reduces a firm's tendency to follow the FDI entry-location and entry-mode decisions of other firms (Henisz & Delios, 2001; Lu, 2002). This issue of imitation of the prior mode choices of other firms and international alliance and international business research forms part of the core of present-day work in these areas.

The Present

The transitions made in the directions of present-day conceptual and empirical work on international alliances and international business have led to a much greater variety in the types of studies and types of phenomena explored and a much more fine-grained analysis of many of the issues involved in international business and international alliances. In the preceding section ("The Past"), our discussion of international alliances was restricted to just the case of joint ventures. Joint ventures were not the only mode of international alliances implemented in the 1970s and 1980s, yet a joint venture was the dominant mode of investment. One of the transitions in present-day research on international alliances has been to consider many more forms of alliances other than joint ventures (Oxley, 1995). Indeed, even a joint venture is no longer considered to be divisible into just one of three types of joint ventures (co-owned, majority-owned, or minority-owned). Finer distinctions exist, based on the number of partners, the nationality of partners, and the organizational affiliation of partners (Makino & Beamish, 1998).

These thrusts into refining the types of organizational forms in international alliance research represent just a small part of the developments in this field. A complete elucidation of all the trends is beyond the scope of this chapter, but such insights are highlighted in other chapters in this book as well as by Beamish and Killing (1997a, 1997b; 1997c).

By a similar token, research in international business has become much more varied and rich. Recent reviews of the international business (management) literature (Werner, 2002; Lu, 2003) identify the important domains in research on international business. These reviews show the topics that have gained prominence but also illustrate how research on international business has undergone a transition from economics and behavioral approaches, as in, respectively, internalization theory and internationalization theory, to core theories emerging from other disciplines, most notably a sociological approach as found in neoinstitutional theory. Finally, research on host-country environments has been reenergized by a stronger grounding in an institutional economics approach. The remainder of this section covers the two institutional perspectives.

Institutional Economics and Institutional Environments

An "institutional" perspective can refer to both institutional theory (Scott, 1995) and institutional economics (North, 1990). The institutional environment characterized in the institutional economics literature is critical in shaping economic activity and firm behavior. North (1990) conceptualizes a nation's institutions as the rules of the game that comprise informal constraints (sanctions, taboos, customs, traditions, and codes of conduct) as well as formal rules (constitutions, laws, property rights).

A "formal rules" perspective of a nation's institutions emphasizes political (Henisz, 2000) and legal (Greif, 1993; La Porta, Lopez-de-Silanes, Shleifer, & Vishny, 1998 Levine & Zervos, 1998) aspects of institutions.

One of the major challenges to a multinational firm when it is operating in its varied host-country markets is how to adapt its systems, structures, and strategies, including its international alliance strategy, to nations that have a different set of institutions from those in the home country. As this institutional distance increases, the challenges similarly increase (Xu & Shenkar, 2002). As a first step in successfully deploying its resources in a new country, managers in a multinational firm must identify and contend with these points of difference in institutional environments between the host country and the other-country markets in which it has previously sited operations (Martin, Swaminathan, & Mitchell, 1998; Zaheer, 1995). Cross-national differences in laws and regulations for purchasing property, licensing new businesses, hiring workers, imports and exports, capital repatriation, contracting with suppliers and buyers, obtaining licenses, and paying taxes can increase the costs and risks of doing business in a country.

Other forms of institutional differences that are manifest as regulatory or political hurdles to doing business can also influence the costs of doing business. Aside from the political and regulatory realm, research on the cultural dimension of national institutional environments points out how cross-national differences in culturally rooted business practices can create difficulties in transferring one model of management from one country to another (Guillén, 2000).

One consequence of institutional distance is that as it increases, a firm becomes less likely to enter a particular country. If an investment occurs, another consequence is that a firm becomes more likely to enter by a joint venture the greater the institutional distance between its existing markets and that which it is entering.

The reasons for using a joint venture, or a non-equity alliance, when entering an institutionally distant nation involve issues of overcoming knowledge disadvantages as well as overcoming the liability of being foreign. A host-country (local) partner can provide a valuable service in exchange for ownership in a multinational firm's subsidiary. Because of its links to local suppliers, it can increase the local content involved in the subsidiary's production. It can increase the levels and efficiency of local labor, via both connections and knowledge of local employment practices. Further, it can provide insight into the local political and regulatory environment. As with early work in internalization theory, work grounded in institutional economics identifies how a joint venture fits into the overall framework of a firm's foreign-market entry strategy.

The advantage of an institutional economics approach as opposed to earlier work is that it provides a multidimensional view of a nation's institutional environment. Further, it helps develop more precise predictions based on the mechanisms that connect a particular dimension of the institutional environment to a particular mode of international alliance. The major difference with an institutional economics approach is that the joint venture and international alliance issue exists as a peripheral question in a broad field instead of existing as a core question in a narrow field, as it was with internalization theory. This trend is similar to what one observes when looking at the intersections between institutional theory, international business, and international alliances.

Institutional Theory

Institutional theory is rooted in a sociological perspective on organizations. Sociological perspectives have been applied to a variety of strategic issues in firms to overcome limitations inherent in rational choice models (Fligstein & Dauber, 1989). Unlike institutional economics, sociology-based institutional theory conceptualizes institutions as rules and norms that define legitimate behavior (DiMaggio & Powell, 1983; Zucker, 1987). In an institutional theory perspective, organizations conform to the prevailing belief systems of the society to obtain legitimacy (Deephouse, 1996; Suchman, 1995)—and hence resources and social-psychological support (D'Aunno, Sutton, & Price, 1991)—from the external environment, even if such behavior may sometimes be at odds with efficiency requirements of the firm (DiMaggio & Powell, 1983; Meyer & Rowan, 1977). Organizational survival and effectiveness, however, cannot last long without attention to technical considerations (Meyer & Scott, 1983). Therefore, institutional theory has often been combined with efficiency-based theories to explain firm behavior and strategy (Eisenhardt, 1988; Oliver, 1997).

Like an institutional economics perspective, when applied to questions relevant to international business an institutional theory perspective is used to emphasize the importance of the "formal rules" of a nation in regulating or influencing organizational behavior. Consistent with institutional economics, institutional theorists embrace coercive isomorphism (DiMaggio & Powell, 1983), or rules supported by the force of law and the government (Scott, 1987; Starbuck, 1976), as an important force defining appropriate and legitimate behavior for a firm. The isomorphic forces are supported by the "three pillars" of institutions—regulatory, normative, and cognitive—found in Scott's (1995) conceptualization. The regulatory pillar corresponds to the "formal rules" definition of institutions in institutional economics. The institutional environment of a multinational firm consists of these multiple but separate and distinctive domains (Kostova & Zaheer, 1999).

External legitimacy can hence be obtained by a foreign subsidiary if it conforms to the regulatory rules of the political-legal institutions in its host country. Across nations, however, institutions differ from each other in the level of support for business organizations. Strong institutions provide legitimacy and social-psychological support, as well as material benefits such as reductions in transaction and production costs, that are conducive to the efficient operations of a firm. Weak institutions can provide legitimacy and social-psychological support for firms that conform to local rules and norms, but with fewer material benefits (King & Levine, 1993; Levine & Zervos, 1998). Furthermore, laws and rules in institutionally weak countries can be incompatible, from an efficiency perspective, with the requirements of a firm, such as protection of property rights (La Porta et al., 1998) and freedom from government corruption (Henisz, 2000).

An important theme in institutional theory is that organizations can be situated in multiple institutional fields (Hoffman, 1999) under multiple institutional pressures (D'Aunno et al., 1991; Singh, Tucker, & House, 1986) but respond to these pressures strategically (Oliver, 1988, 1991). Researchers in international business who have grounded their work in an institutional theory perspective view subsidiaries as subject to two groups of institutional forces: those that emanate from local firms and organizations in the host country and those that come from the parent firm and other units in a multinational firm (Westney, 1993; Rosenzweig & Singh, 1991). Scholars emphasize the importance of conforming to local rules and norms to obtain external legitimacy for a subsidiary (Kostova & Zaheer, 1999; Rosenzweig & Nohria, 1994), while also considering the need for internal coordination and efficiency within a multinational firm's system (Ghoshal & Bartlett, 1990; Westney, 1993).

The isomorphic forces facing a multinational firm and its subsidiaries have been studied primarily in two contexts. One is the choice of which market to enter (Mayer & Mucchielli, 1998; Ford & Strange, 1999; Guillén, 2000; Henisz & Delios, 2001); the other is the choice of entry mode (Davis, Desai, & Francis, 2000; Lu, 2002; Yiu & Makino, 2002). The latter, again, is the point at which research on international business intersects with research on strategic alliances.

Prominent themes in these entry-mode studies are the issues of institutional pressures from one or all of the three pillars, the role of uncertainty, and the prevalence of imitation, even given countervailing economic pressures for a particular entry-mode decision. As mentioned earlier, isomorphic pressures to conform to the expectations of key actors or to the actions of peers in a market can lead to imitation of the actions of other firms and subsequent conformity in organizational structures and strategies. Host-country governments, through laws, regulations, and political sanctions, are an institutional regulatory force that can lead to conformity and similarity in the structure and strategies of multinational firms (Kostova, 1999; Kostova & Zaheer, 1999; Guillén, 2000).

The pressure for conformity in the entry-mode choice can come from the regulatory environment (Yiu & Makino, 2002); it can also extend from the extent of uncertainty in an environment. Prior research on organizations has shown that uncertainty, such as that encountered in an international plant location, can increase the importance of social considerations relative to technical considerations (Festinger, 1954; DiMaggio & Powell, 1983; Haunschild & Miner, 1997). When a decision is marked by uncertainty, a prominent social influence is the set of actors in the immediate interorganizational environment (Hannan & Carroll, 1992). Given uncertainty, an organization looks to the decisions of other organizations to provide a guide (Tolbert & Zucker, 1983), with the result being that as a large number of organizations engage in a decision, it becomes common knowledge or a rule of thumb to implement the same decision (March, 1991).

In terms of international alliances, there has certainly been an increased prevalence of this organizational form from the onset of the 1990s to the mid-2000s. Part of the reason for this could be an imitative effect, particularly if an environment is highly uncertain. Research on the entry-mode choice provides good evidence that a firm's propensity to utilize joint ventures is jointly dependent on the frequency of use of joint ventures by peer firms as well as the level of uncertainty in an environment (Lu, 2002). If either of these decreases, then the prevalence of joint venture entry by new entrants also declines.

The Future

When identifying trends in research streams, it is difficult to separate the past from the present and the present from the future. Perhaps one way to make this separation is to consider the maturity of a stream of research in a particular area in terms of identifying whether it is in the past, present, or future. If we use this criterion, it is clear that internalization theory and internationalization theory rest in the past. The two institutional approaches can be considered to be in the present, as the body of work situated in international business and international alliance questions for these two areas has begun to mature. Where, then, rests the future?

The near future, at least, can come from the continued application of institutional approaches to finer-grained analyses of questions pertinent to the fields of international business and international alliances. It can also come from the application of conceptually well-developed fields to phenomena directly related to international business and international alliances.

Social Networks

One such perspective is a social networks approach. Social networks theory (Granovetter, 1985) has recently become widely used to study issues on organizations, strategy, and international alliances (Nohria, 1992). The latter, international alliances, is a natural phenomenon for the application of social network theory, because alliances are just one form of interfirm relationship that can be part of a firm's social network (Dyer & Singh, 1998). Although social network theory has been successfully applied to international business theory (Bruton, Lohrke, & Lu, 2004), in studies by Andersson and Forsgren (2000) and Salk and Brannen (2000), it has not been applied specifically or extensively to the study of international business and international alliances. This is somewhat surprising, given the rising prevalence of social network theory and its natural application to international alliances. On the other hand, it is not surprising, given the substantial data demands frequently necessitated for a rigorous social network analysis and the compounding of those demands if one conducts such a study in multiple countries.

Resource and Knowledge Acquisition

Another area of rich research in the strategy and organizations field is the resource-based view (Wernerfelt, 1984; Barney, 1991). Resource-based approaches have been advocated strongly in the strategy literature in particular, although less strongly in the international business literature. The distinct lack of application of a resource-based approach to international business could come from the difficulty of operationalizing a firm's resources (Priem & Butler, 2001); it could also come from the seeming conceptual overlaps between a resource-based approach and an internalization approach.

The conceptual overlaps coupled with the difficulty in measurement of resources mean that the predictions and subsequent empirical tests of a study rooted in the resource-based view can yield empirical results that would also support an internalization theory perspective. Both sets of studies, for example, would suggest that wholly owned entries would prevail over joint venture entries where a firm possessed unique resources (assets). Although the causal mechanisms for the resultant entry-mode choice would be different, a typical empirical study would not be able to distinguish between one and the other.

A similar claim could be made for the knowledge-based view of a firm, at least as captured in the writings of Kogut and Zander. According to Kogut and Zander (1993), inefficiencies in the interfirm transfer of firm-specific knowledge, not imperfections in the transactional market for knowledge, lead firms to select wholly owned entries over joint ventures or other forms of international alliances when making a foreign entry. Again, measurement, particularly if done at an archival-data level, does not permit the empirical evidence to provide a clear distinction between the predictions of an internalization theory perspective and those of a knowledge-based perspective.

The phenomenon of international alliances sits at the resolution nexus of this triumvirate of theories. Examining observable organizational-mode choices, including equity and nonequity forms of alliances, can provide the kind of variegated setting that might be necessary to distinguish among the predictions of a knowledge-based approach, a resource-based view, and internalization theory. In particular, doing so in the setting of international business might help with such an examination. The reason for this is the emergence of a new form of FDI, namely asset-seeking FDI (Wesson, 1993). Asset-seeking FDI tends to occur as a firm attempts to build its overall competitiveness by investing in foreign markets with the purpose of sourcing and internalizing new technologies, new management skills, or other sources of competitive advantage (Kuemmerle, 1999; Frost, 2001; Makino & Inkpen, 2003).

The phenomenon and prevalence of asset-seeking FDI present a challenge to internalization theory simply from the perspective that the motivation to make a direct investment does not stem from the need to internalize the cross-border transfer of a firm's proprietary knowledge/asset advantages. Joint ventures and other forms of international alliances are also prevalent as modalities in asset-seeking FDI and asset-seeking international activities. A careful application of internalization theory, the resource-based view, or a knowledge-based approach might lead to conflicting sets of predictions that would help resolve issues of how well one theory or another explains phenomena particular to the intersection of international business and international alliances. At the same time, it might feed back into core developments in these theoretical streams. This last point also relates to issues covered in the concluding comments, namely, that international business and international alliances are no longer joined by a unique, theoretical base.

Concluding Comments

Research on international alliances and on international business was tightly intertwined in the formative years of these two fields. This intertwining came about because the question being asked by international business researchers—Why do firms engage in foreign direct investment as opposed to other modes for entering foreign markets?—forced an explicit consideration of the joint venture mode of entry. These formative studies provided a substantial base for subsequent work in both of these fields.

The work in these two areas in the past two decades has brought these fields to a mature state. International business research has become more varied in the questions it asks and more sophisticated in the methods employed to investigate phenomena. Research on alliances has progressed similarly, obviating the need for more exploratory studies on alliances, single-case studies, or repetitions of the types of messy research described by Parkhe (1993).

As these streams of research have matured, there has been an untwining of these fields from one another. Work on international alliances has become much more multifaceted, whereas research on international business has expanded in terms of the types of questions explored and the conceptual footings for the studies. At times, research on international business and international alliances does intersect, but the trends in present-day research and those I expect to see in future research suggest these fields are becoming increasingly distinct.

This separation of research on international alliances and international business is, as one would expect, occurring as these fields become more isolated in terms of studying phenomena unique to the field. That said, the prevalence of using a unique theory base, as in the past of the research for both of these streams, is becoming less common. What has happened and what will continue to happen is that we will see stronger ties between research on international business and international alliance phenomena, but this intersection will be situated in mainstream theoretical bases and research in other organizational fields, such as strategy and organization theory.

Perhaps the largest question related to these two fields is whether the unique nature of the phenomena in each field will continue to drive research. Certainly, the trends in foreign direct investment activity and foreign trade indicate that international business will become a more prominent aspect of business activities in tomorrow's world than it is in today's. Will the same hold true for alliances, particularly international joint ventures? As more and more firms become widely familiar with countries in different regions of the world, as investment policies and other aspects of national economies are increasingly harmonized, and as regulations regarding local participation in foreign-owned enterprises are loosened in countries such as China and Thailand, the prevalence of international joint ventures is likely to decline. Will such a decline precipitate a similar decline in research, just as the downturn in the Japanese economy and the growth of the mainland Chinese economy sparked respective downturns and surges in research on business in Japan and China (White, 2002)? If it does, then the cores of research on international business and international alliances will become even further distanced from one another in future work.

References

Anderson, E., & Gatignon, H. (1986). Modes of foreign entry: A transaction cost analysis and propositions. *Journal of International Business Studies, 17*(3), 1–26.

Andersson, U., & Forsgren, M. (2000). In search of centres of excellence: Network embeddedness and subsidiary roles in multinational corporations. *Management International Review, 40*(4), 329–350.

Barkema, H. G., Bell, J. H. J., & Pennings, J. M. (1996). Foreign entry, cultural barriers, and learning. *Strategic Management Journal, 17,* 151–166.

Barkema, H. G., Shenkar, O., Vermeulen, F., & Bell, J. H. J. (1996). Working abroad, working with others: How firms learn to operate international joint ventures. *Academy of Management Journal, 40,* 426–442.

Barney, J. (1991). Firm resources and sustained competitive advantage. *Journal of Management, 17,* 99–120.

Beamish, P., & Banks, J. (1987). Equity joint ventures and the theory of the multinational enterprise. *Journal of International Business Studies, 17,* 1–16.

Beamish, P. W., & Killing, J. P. (1997a). *Cooperative strategies: Asian perspectives.* San Francisco: New Lexington Press.

Beamish, P. W., & Killing, J. P. (1997b). *Cooperative strategies: European perspectives.* San Francisco: New Lexington Press.

Beamish, P. W., & Killing, J. P. (1997c). *Cooperative strategies: North American perspectives.* San Francisco: New Lexington Press.

Bruton, G. D., Lohrke, F. T., & Lu, J. W. (2004). The evolving definition of what constitutes international strategic management research. *Journal of International Management, 10,* 413–429.

Buckley, P. J., & Casson, M. (1976). *The future of multinational enterprise.* London: MacMillan.

Caves, R. E. (1996). *Multinational enterprise and economic analysis* (2nd ed.). New York: Cambridge University Press.

Chang, S. (1995). International expansion strategy of Japanese firms: Capability building through sequential entry. *Academy of Management Journal, 38,* 383–407.

Contractor, F. J. (1990). Ownership patterns of U.S. joint ventures abroad and the liberalization of foreign government regulation in the 1980s: Evidence from the benchmark surveys. *Journal of International Business Studies, 21*(1), 55–73.

Contractor, F. J., & Lorange, P. (Eds.). (1988). *Cooperative strategies in international business.* Lexington, MA: Lexington Books.

Cyert, R. M., & March, J. G. (1963). *A behavioral theory of the firm.* Englewood Cliffs, NJ: Prentice Hall.

D'Aunno, T., Sutton, R. I., & Price, R. H. (1991). Isomorphism and external support in conflicting institutional environments: A study of drug abuse treatment units. *Academy of Management Journal, 34*(3), 636–661.

Davidson, W. H. (1980). The location of foreign direct investment activity: Country characteristics and experience effects. *Journal of International Business Studies, 11*(1), 9–22.

Davidson, W. H. (1982). *Global strategic management.* New York: John Wiley.

Davidson, W. H., & McFetridge, D. G. (1985). Key characteristics in the choice of international technology transfer. *Journal of International Business Studies, 16*(2), 5–21.

Davis, P., Desai, A., & Francis, J. (2000). Mode of international entry: An isomorphism perspective. *Journal of International Business Studies, 31*(2), 239–258.

Deephouse, D. L. (1996). Does isomorphism legitimate? *Academy of Management Journal, 39*(4), 1024–1039.

Delios A, & Beamish P. W. (1999). Ownership strategy of Japanese firms: Transactional, institutional and experience influences. *Strategic Management Journal, 20*(10), 915–933.

Delios A, & Beamish P. W. (2004). Joint venture performance revisited: Japanese foreign subsidiaries worldwide. *Management International Review, 44*(1), 69–91.

Delios, A., & Henisz, W. (2000). Japanese firms' investment strategies in emerging economies. *Academy of Management Journal, 43,* 305–323.

DiMaggio, P. J., & Powell, W. W. (1983). The iron cage revisited: Institutional isomorphism and collective rationality in organizational fields. *American Sociological Review, 48,* 147–160.

Dunning, J. (1988). The eclectic paradigm of international production: A restatement and some possible extensions. *Journal of International Business Studies, 19*(1), 1–31.

Dyer, J., & Singh, H. (1998). The relational view: Cooperative strategy and sources of interorganizational competitive advantage. *Academy of Management Review, 23,* 660–679.

Eisenhardt, K. M. (1988). Agency- and institutional-theory explanations: The case of retail sales compensation. *Academy of Management Journal, 31*(3), 488–511.

Erramilli, M. K., & Rao, C. P. (1993). Service firms' international entry-mode choice: A modified transaction-cost analysis approach. *Journal of Marketing, 57*(3), 19–38.

Festinger, L. (1954). A theory of social comparison processes. *Human Relations, 7,* 117–140.

Fligstein, N., & Dauber, K. (1989). Structural change in corporate organization. *Annual Review of Sociology, 15,* 73–96.

Ford, S., & Strange, R. (1999). Where do Japanese manufacturing firms invest within Europe and why? *Transnational Corporations, 8,* 117–142.

Frost, T. (2001). The geographic sources of foreign subsidiaries' innovations. *Strategic Management Journal, 22,* 101–123.

Gatignon, H., & Anderson, E. (1988). The multinational corporation's degree of control over foreign subsidiaries: An empirical test of a transaction cost explanation. *Journal of Law, Economics, and Organization, 4,* 305–336.

Geringer, J. M., & Hèbert, L. (1991). Measuring performance of international joint ventures. *Journal of International Business Studies, 22*(2), 249–263.

Ghoshal, S., & Bartlett, C. A. (1990). The multinational corporations as an interorganizational network. *Academy of Management Review, 15*(4), 603–625.

Gomes-Casseres, B. (1988). Joint venture cycles: The evolution of ownership strategies of U.S. MNEs. In F. J. Contractor & P. Lorange (Eds.), *Cooperative strategies in international business.* Lexington, MA: Lexington Books.

Gomes-Casseres, B. (1989). Ownership structures of foreign subsidiaries: Theory and evidence. *Journal of Economic Behavior and Organization, 11*(1), 1–26.

Gomes-Casseres, B. (1990). Firm ownership preferences and host government restrictions: An integrated approach. *Journal of International Business Studies, 21,* 1–22.

Granovetter, M. (1985). Economic action and social structure: The problem of embeddedness. *American Journal of Sociology, 91*(3), 481–510.

Greif, A. (1993). Contract enforceability and economic institutions in early trade: The Maghribi traders' coalition. *American Economic Review, 83*(3), 525–548.

Guillén, M. F. (2000). Business groups in emerging economies: A resource-based view. *Academy of Management Journal, 43*(3), 362–380.

Hannan, M. T., & Carroll, G. R. (1992). *The dynamics of organizational populations.* New York. Oxford University Press.

Haunschild, P., & Miner, A. (1997). Modes of interorganizational imitation: The effects of outcome salience and uncertainty. *Administrative Science Quarterly, 42*(3), 472–500.

Henisz, W. J. (2000). The institutional environment for economic growth. *Economics and Politics, 12,* 1–31.

Henisz, W., & Delios, A. (2001). Uncertainty, imitation, and plant location: Japanese multinational corporations, 1990–1996. *Administrative Science Quarterly, 46*(3), 443–475.

Hennart, J. F. (1982). *A theory of multinational enterprise.* Ann Arbor: University of Michigan Press.

Hennart, J. F. (1988). A transaction cost theory of equity joint ventures. *Strategic Management Journal, 9,* 483–497.

Hennart, J. F. (1991). The transaction cost theory of joint ventures: An empirical study of Japanese subsidiaries in the United States. *Management Science, 37*(4), 483–497.

Hergert, M., & Morris, D. (1988). Trends in international cooperative agreements. In F. J. Contractor & P. Lorange (Eds.), *Cooperative strategies in international business.* Lexington MA: Lexington Books.

Hill, C. W. L., Hwang, P., & Kim, W. C. (1990). An eclectic theory of the choice of international entry mode. *Strategic Management Journal, 11*(2), 117–128.

Hoffman, A. J. (1999). Institutional evolution and change: Environmentalism and the U.S. chemical industry. *Academy of Management Journal, 42*(4), 351–371.

Hymer, S. H. (1976). *International operations of national firms—A study of direct foreign investment.* Cambridge: MIT Press.

Johanson J., & Vahlne, J. E. (1977). The internationalization process of the firm—A model of knowledge development and increasing foreign market commitments. *Journal of International Business Studies, 8*(1), 23–32.

Johanson, J., & Wiedersheim-Paul, F. (1975). The internationalization of the firm: Four Swedish cases. *Journal of Management Studies, 12*(3), 305–322.

Kim, W. C., & Hwang, P. (1992). Global strategy and multinationals' entry mode choice. *Journal of International Business Studies, 23*(1), 29–53.

King, R. G., & Levine, R. (1993). Finance and growth: Schumpeter might be right. *Quarterly Journal of Economics, 108*(3), 717–737.

Kobrin, S. J. (1988). Trends in ownership of U.S. manufacturing subsidiaries in developing countries: An interindustry analysis. In F. J. Contractor & P. Lorange (Eds.), *Cooperative strategies in international business.* Lexington, MA: Lexington Books.

Kogut, B. (1988). Joint ventures: Theoretical and empirical perspectives. *Strategic Management Journal, 9,* 319–332.

Kogut, B., & Zander, U. (1993). Knowledge of the firm and the evolutionary theory of the multinational corporation. *Journal of International Business Studies, 24*(4), 625–645.

Kostova, T. (1999). Transnational transfer of strategic organizational practices: A contextual perspective. *Academy of Management Review, 24*(2), 308–324.

Kostova, T., & Zaheer, S. (1999). Organizational legitimacy under conditions of complexity: The case of the multinational enterprise. *Academy of Management Review, 24,* 64–81.

Kuemmerle, W. (1999). The drivers of foreign direct investment into research and development: An empirical investigation. *Journal of International Business Studies, 30,* 1–24.

La Porta, R., Lopez-de-Silanes, F., Shleifer, A., & Vishny, R. W. (1998). Law and finance. *Journal of Political Economy, 106*(6), 1113–1155.

Levine, R., & Zervos, S. (1998). Stock markets, banks, and economic growth. *American Economic Review, 88,* 537–558.

Li, J. T. (1995). Foreign entry and survival: Effects of strategic choices on performance in international markets. *Strategic Management Journal, 16,* 333–351.

Lu, J. (2002). Intra- and inter-organizational imitative behavior: Institutional influences on Japanese firms' entry mode choice. *Journal of International Business Studies, 33*(1), 19–39.

Lu, J. (2003). The evolving contributions in international strategic management research. *Journal of International Management, 9*(2), 193–215.

Luostarinen, R. (1980). *Internationalization of the firm.* Helsinki, Finland: Helsinki School of Economics.

Makino, S., & Beamish, P. W. (1998). Performance and survival of joint ventures with non-conventional ownership structures. *Journal of International Business Studies, 29*(4), 797–818.

Makino, S., & Delios, A. (1996). Local knowledge transfer and performance: Implications for alliance formation in Asia. *Journal of International Business Studies, 27*(5), 905–927.

Makino, S., & Inkpen, A. (2003). Knowledge seeking FDI and learning across borders. In M. Easterby-Smith & M. Lyles (Eds.), *Handbook in organizational learning and knowledge management* (pp. 233–252). Oxford: Blackwell.

March, J. G. (1991). Exploration and exploitation in organizational learning. *Organization Science, 2,* 71–87.

Martin, X., Swaminathan, A., & Mitchell, W. (1998). Organizational evolution in the interorganizational environment: Incentives and constraints on international expansion strategy. *Administrative Science Quarterly, 43,* 566–601.

Mayer, T., & Mucchielli, J. L. (1998). Strategic location behavior: The case of Japanese investments in Europe. *Journal of Transnational Management, 3,* 131–167.

Meyer, J., & Rowan, B. (1977). Institutionalized organizations: Formal structure as myth and ceremony. *American Journal of Sociology, 83*(2), 340–363.

Meyer, J. W., & Scott, W. R. (1983). *Organizational environments.* Beverly Hills, CA: Sage.

Nohria, N. (1992). Is a network perspective a useful way of studying organizations? In N. Nohria & R. Eccles (Eds.), *Networks and organization: Structure, form and action* (pp. 1–22). Boston: Harvard Business School Press.

North, D. (1990). *Institutions, institutional change, and economic performance.* Cambridge, UK: Cambridge University Press.

North, D., & Weingast, B. (1989). Constitutions and commitment: The evolution of institutions governing public choice in 17th century England. *Journal of Economic History, 49,* 803–832.

Oliver, C. (1988). The collective strategy framework: An application to competing predictions of isomorphism. *Administrative Science Quarterly, 33,* 543–561.

Oliver, C. (1991). Strategic responses to institutional processes. *Academy of Management Review, 16*(1), 145–179.

Oliver, C. (1997). Sustainable competitive advantage: Combining institutional and resource-based views. *Strategic Management Journal, 18*(9), 697–713.

Oxley, J. E. (1995). *International hybrids: A transaction cost treatment and empirical study.* Unpublished doctoral dissertation, University of California, Berkeley.

Parkhe, A. (1993). "Messy" research, methodological predispositions, and theory development in international joint ventures. *Academy of Management Review, 18*(2), 227–268.

Priem, R., & Butler, J. (2001). Is the resource-based "view" a useful perspective for strategic management research? *Academy of Management Review, 26*(1), 22–40.

Root, F. R. (1987). *Entry strategies for international markets.* Lexington, MA: Lexington Books.

Rosenzweig, P. M., & Nohria, N. (1994). Influences on human resource management practices in multinational corporations. *Journal of International Business Studies, 25*(2), 229–251.

Rosenzweig, P., & Singh, J. (1991). Organizational environments and the multinational enterprise. *Academy of Management Review, 16,* 340–361.

Rugman, A. M. (1982). *New theories of multinational enterprise.* London: Croom Helm.

Salk, J., & Brannen, M. (2000). National culture, networks, and individual influence in a multinational management team. *Academy of Management Journal, 43*(2), 191–202.

Scott, W. R. (1987). The adolescence of institutional theory. *Administrative Science Quarterly, 32,* 493–511.

Scott, W. (1995). *Institutions and organizations.* Thousand Oaks, CA: Sage.

Shan, W. (1991). Environmental risks and joint venture sharing arrangements. *Journal of International Business Studies, 22*(4), 555–578.

Singh, J. V., Tucker, D. J., & House, R. J. (1986). Organizational legitimacy and the liability of newness. *Administrative Science Quarterly, 31,* 171–193.

Starbuck, W. H. (1976). Organizations and their environments. In M. D. Dunnette (Ed.), *Handbook of industrial and organizational psychology* (pp. 1069–1123). New York: Rand McNally.

Stopford, J. M., & Wells, L. T., Jr. (1972). *Managing the multinational enterprise: Organization of the firm and ownership of the subsidiaries.* New York: Basic Books.

Suchman, M. C. (1995). Managing legitimacy: Strategic and institutional approaches. *Academy of Management Review, 20*(3), 571–610.

Teece, D. J. (1986a). Transactions cost economics and the multinational enterprise: An assessment. *Journal of Economic Behavior and Organization, 7*(1), 21–45.

Teece, D. J. (1986b). Profiting from technological innovation. *Research Policy, 15,* 285–305.

Tolbert, P., & Zucker, L. (1983). Institutional sources of change in the formal structure of organisations: The diffusion of civil service reform, 1880–1935. *Administrative Science Quarterly, 28,* 22–39.

Vernon, R. (1983). Organizational and institutional responses to international risk. In R. J. Herring (Ed.), *Managing international risk.* Cambridge, UK: Cambridge University Press.

Vernon, R., & Wells, L. T. (1976). *Manager in the international economy.* Englewood Cliffs, NJ: Prentice Hall.

Werner, S. (2002). Recent developments in international management research: A review of the top 20 management journals. *Journal of Management, 28*(3), 277–306.

Wernerfelt, B. (1984). A resource-based view of the firm. *Strategic Management Journal, 5*(2), 171–180.

Wesson, T. (1993). *An alternative motivation for foreign direct investment.* Unpublished doctoral dissertation, Harvard University, Boston.

Westney, D. E. (1993). Institutionalization theory and the multinational corporation. In S. Ghoshal & D. E. Westney (Eds.), *Organization theory and the multinational corporation* (pp. 53–76). New York: St. Martin's Press.

White, S. (2002). Rigor and relevance in Asian management research: Where are we and where can we go? *Asia Pacific Journal of Management, 19,* 287–352.

Williamson, O. E. (1975). *Markets and hierarchies: Analysis and antitrust implications.* New York: Free Press.

Williamson, O. E. (1985). *The economic institutions of capitalism.* New York: Free Press.

Williamson, O. E. (1996). *The mechanisms of governance.* New York: Oxford University Press.

Wind, Y., & Perlmutter, H. (1977). On the identification of frontier issues in international marketing. *Columbia Journal of World Business, 12*(4), 131–139.

Woodcock, C. P., Beamish, P. W., & Makino, S. (1994). Ownership-based entry mode strategies and international performance. *Journal of International Business Studies, 25*(2), 253–273.

Xu, D., & Shenkar, O. (2002). Institutional distance and the multinational enterprise. *Academy of Management Review, 27,* 608–618.

Yiu, D., & Makino, S. (2002). The choice between joint venture and wholly owned subsidiary: An institutional perspective. *Organization Science, 13*(6), 667–685.

Zaheer, S. (1995). Overcoming the liability of foreignness. *Academy of Management Journal, 38*(2), 341–363.

Zucker, L. G. (1987). Institutional theories of organization. *Annual Review of Sociology, 13,* 443–464.

15

Nurturing Successful Alliances Across Boundaries

Piero Morosini

A Ray of Hope

It was late March 1999. As a seasoned executive of a global corporation, General Motors vice-chairman Bob Lutz knew that well over 50% of alliances were destined for failure. Especially those taking place across such distant—and distinctive—national cultures as the French and the Japanese. These thoughts were undoubtedly in his mind as he learned that the French company Renault had just bought a 36.6% stake in Japanese Nissan for $5.4 billion to form an alliance between the two companies. His remark to a journalist became instant news: "Renault would be better off buying $5 billion of gold bars, putting them on a ship and dumping them in the middle of the Pacific" (Mackintosh, 2004).

Bob Lutz was not alone in his opinion. The international media, company executives, management academics, and consultants all over the world were nearly unanimous in their disapproval of the Renault-Nissan alliance. A sample of their comments gives a sense of their main concerns:

> Much has been made of the culture clash between [the May 1998 merging partners] Daimler and Chrysler but it will be nothing compared to Nissan and Renault. At their core, they are both nationalistic and patriotic, and each believes its way is the right way to do things. We will have quite a teething period for the first year or two as they feel each other out.

> Two mules don't make a race-horse.

> I would have preferred Renault to take 51 percent even if it meant having to assume Nissan's debt on its balance sheet. That way Renault could have become the real boss and set some firm direction, rather than having to negotiate.

> French taxpayers might be left footing the bill for Renault, whose top managers were perhaps blinded by the brilliance of their own vision.

> Even the most optimistic observers reckon that the payoff horizon—assuming that the alliance could overcome its enormous business and cultural hurdles—would be long-term, not short. (Ghosn, 2002a; Hughes, Barsoux, & Manzoni, 2003)

Not only did mainstream managerial theories support these concerns fully; so did Renault and Nissan themselves. On the one hand, Renault had only just been taken off the losers' league of automakers following a remarkable comeback that was turning losses of $680 million in 1996 into combined profits of $1.65 billion in 1998 and 1999. In addition, Renault was still recovering from a highly publicized failure to merge with Volvo in 1995. A distinctively French and European carmaker, Renault had never run a global operation; in 1998 the company sold no cars in the United States and only 2,476 units in Japan, the world's two largest automotive markets.

On the other hand, Nissan was nearly bankrupt in 1999. Since 1991 it had been losing money and market share continuously, and car production had dropped by 600,000 units. The latter meant that Nissan's factories were running at 53% utilization of capacity. The company's product portfolio was aging, and it had ten times the number of suppliers and four times the number of manufacturing platforms as Ford and Volkswagen respectively. Its $20 billion debt mountain was more comparable to that of a medium-sized developing country than that of a large automaker.

The joining companies were quite complementary in geographic scope and skills: Renault had a flair for marketing and design and was strong in Europe and Latin America; Nissan was an engineering powerhouse with a strong market presence in Japan, North America, and Asia. However, these two companies had no history of working together. To complicate matters, in March 1999 the French state had a 44% controlling stake in Renault, and Nissan, as Japan's second-largest automaker, was a highly emblematic symbol of that country's industrial strength. Not surprisingly, after its alliance with Nissan was publicly announced, Renault's share price fell, and three separate rating agencies issued negative reviews of the company's debt.

On a sunny afternoon in mid-March 2004 in Paris, almost five years to the day since the Renault-Nissan alliance had been so universally written off, Renault's president Louis Schweitzer was preparing to retire. Seated comfortably behind his office desk at Renault's headquarters, he told a journalist:

> The future is rosy. Clearly we have the pieces in place that are required for growth. . . . Renault-Nissan has been an incredible, and in many ways unexpected, success. . . . Someday, maybe—I hope so—Nissan may help [Renault's re-entry into] the United States [market]. (Phelan, 2004)

Renault's original $5.4 billion investment in Nissan was worth $18.4 billion in March 2004. This made Renault's 36.6% stake in Nissan (which Renault increased to 44.4% in 2003), worth more than the total market value of the French carmaker itself. Nissan's head of Europe (and former Renault executive), Patrick Pelata, called it: "the biggest return on investment in the history of the automotive industry" (Morosini, 2004b). The Japanese company's profits of $7.6 billion and 11% operating margins were the highest in the automotive industry. As indicated by these results, in March 2004 the Renault-Nissan alliance was universally regarded as a successful model by competitors, practitioners, and business schools around the world.

March 2004 marked the end of an era for the Renault-Nissan alliance. Both companies announced they would share a single chief executive officer (CEO) starting in 2005 in the person of Carlos Ghosn, a former Renault executive who, as Nissan CEO, had presided over the company's remarkable revival since May 1999. Renault and Nissan jointly announced financial results for the first time in 2004. Their combined $109 billion in sales and $9.4 billion in profits catapulted both companies from the bottom of the automakers' leagues to the world's fifth-largest car manufacturer and one of the most profitable.

The immense success of Renault-Nissan against nearly insurmountable odds holds enormous implications for the theory and practice of corporate alliances. In an area where poor performance results have been systematically recorded over the last three decades of the twentieth century, this alliance provides an opportunity to look at the field with new eyes. The way in which the Renault-Nissan alliance was formed and managed has in fact run counter to what most mainstream academic tenets had maintained so far. In this chapter I hence attempt to draw inspiration from Renault-Nissan's success during the 1999-to-2004 period and find new patterns that might contribute to a better understanding and management of all international alliances.

Renault-Nissan: The Paradoxical Alliance

There is a well-known paradox at the heart of our subject matter. On the one hand, strategic alliances and international joint ventures (IJVs) experienced such explosive growth during the last three decades of the twentieth century that they came to be regarded as the dominant organizational form of global business.[1] On the other hand, an abundant empirical literature suggests that well over 50% of all alliances and IJVs fail (Morosini, 1998; Das & Teng, 2000). The specialized academic literature refers to the *instabilities of strategic alliances,* a more technical term for alliance failure, defined as *major changes or dissolutions of alliances that are unplanned from the perspective of one or more partners* (Inkpen & Beamish, 1977). Before looking at alliances with new eyes, let us therefore examine what the mainstream academic theories have maintained regarding the reasons behind the dismal performance record of alliances.

Researchers suggest that the degree of stability of alliances depends upon the balance of power between the joining companies and the type of strategic contributions that the partners seek. Hence, alliances can be classified according to the controlling powers of the partners (i.e., "double-parenting" or "multiple-parenting" management structures) or the nature of the partners' strategic contributions (i.e., technological know-how, skills, market entry).

A number of theories have been advanced to explain the instabilities of all these types of alliances. They can be divided into six major categories. A first group of theories regards alliances as relational contracts, where instability stems from a lack of historical, trusting involvement between the allies (Macneil, 1974, 1980). The second set of theories maintains that alliances allow the joining firms to achieve lower transaction costs vis-à-vis the marketplace, with instability arising as a result of the opportunistic behavior of the allies (Williamson, 1975, 1985). A third category of theories views alliances as bargaining negotiations and business games that the allies play for market advantage, where instability arises whenever cheating an ally or acting based on self-interest provides greater payoffs than cooperative behavior (Axelrod, 1984; Bacharach & Lawler, 1981; Jensen & Meckling, 1976). The strategic management school of thought regards alliances as a company's means to achieve superior strategic positioning vis-à-vis its rivals, with instability stemming from setting unrealistic strategic goals (Porter, 1980, 1985, 1990). The resource-dependence and transitional theories maintain that the instability of alliances is to be expected after the allies achieve the kind of resources they wanted from each other or as a result of alliances naturally evolving into different organizational forms (Pfeffer & Salancik, 1978; Franko, 1971; Kogut, 1989). Lastly, the internal-tensions perspective suggests that the instability of alliances stems from the development of pairs of competing forces, that is, cooperation versus competition, rigidity versus flexibility, and short-term versus long-term orientation (Das & Teng, 2000).

It is striking how little these theories help us understand what really happened in the case of the Renault-Nissan alliance that made it so stable and successful during the 1999-to-2004 period. Relational contract theorists would find the stability of Renault-Nissan difficult to explain in the absence of any historical involvement between the two companies prior to the formation stages of the alliance. Opportunistic behavior according to the transaction-costs theories is hard to imagine within such an efficient and global industry as the automotive sector, where company reputation and brand image play such an important role. A game-theoretical or bargaining approach would be at odds to explain the stability of Renault-Nissan, especially during the 2001-to-2004 time period when Nissan—initially a much weaker partner compared to Renault—became by far the alliance's main driving force for revenue growth and profits. Strategic-management theorists are doubtless puzzled when considering that Renault-Nissan's strategic goals—universally deemed to be "unrealistic"—nonetheless drove the stability of the alliance from the outset, whereas much more "realistic" strategic goals behind alliances such as DaimlerChrysler-Mitsubishi (or the DaimlerChrysler combine itself) led to disastrous results. Resource-dependent and transitional pundits would find it surprising that Renault-Nissan remained stable during the 1999-to-2004 period, even after the allies achieved all of their initial objectives in 2001 and in spite of massive transfer of key resources—managerial, technological, functional, financial—between the allies. Finally, the internal-tensions theorists might find it challenging to corroborate that it was the development of tremendous internal tensions and pairs of competing forces that from the outset provided stability to the Renault-Nissan alliance, not the other way around. Table 15.1 summarizes the disturbing paradoxes posed by the Renault-Nissan alliance when confronted with the relevant theories.

The inadequacy of the mainstream theories to explain alliance instability has been highlighted before (Das & Teng, 2000), leading some researchers to propose generic and *prescriptive* responses to this issue based on empirical studies. Some of these authors maintain that alliance stability stems from the managerial ability to judge when to use acquisitions and when to enter alliances (Dyer, Kale, & Singh, 2004). Thus, equity alliances are to be favored when modular synergies are expected, when there is a relatively high value of soft to hard resources, where the extent of redundant resources is medium, the degree of market uncertainty is high, and the level of competition is low. However, the success of the Renault-Nissan alliance does not easily fit these prescriptions. From the outset, it promised (and achieved) modular, sequential, as well as reciprocal synergies between the allies. It can certainly be argued that the automotive industry has a particularly high level of market uncertainty or that it faces an especially high level of relative value of soft to hard resources. But Renault's and Nissan's resources prior to their alliance surely were complementary rather than redundant within an industry regarded at that time as "hypercompetitive."

Other prescriptive authors have looked at the financial and strategic performance of cross-border alliances (Ernst & Bleeke, 1994). They have found that cross-border alliances performed better when one partner is a strong performer in its industry and the other is at least average. Moreover, the better-performing cross-border alliances were those taking place in the joining companies' core businesses and between geographically complementary allies. The latter was certainly the case of the Renault-Nissan alliance. However, in March 1999 both Renault and especially Nissan were very far from winners in any respect. "Two mules don't make a race-horse" was, as we have seen, the memorable way in which one critic echoed most people's expectations of the future of this alliance.

Why Are Conventional Theories Inadequate?

In my view, three main drawbacks have prevented previous theories from providing deeper insights into what drives the stability of alliances

Table 15.1 The Theoretical Paradoxes Posed by the Renault-Nissan Alliance

Theory and Authoritative Reference	*Central Tenet of the Theory*	*Main Source of Alliance Stability According to Theory*	*The Renault-Nissan Paradox*
Relational contract (Macneil 1974, 1980)	Alliances are relational (as opposed to discrete) exchanges, based on a history of trusting interactions between the allies.	Instability occurs when there is no history of trusting relationships prior to the alliance deal or whenever a lack of trust arises between the allies.	Renault and Nissan had *no history* of working together nor any significant interaction whatsoever prior to negotiating their March 1999 alliance deal.
Transaction costs (Williamson, 1975, 1985)	Alliances allow firms to minimize transaction costs stemming from the assumption that economic actors are boundedly rational and often exhibit opportunistic behavior in the marketplace.	Opportunistic behavior on the part of the allies is costly and difficult to control, undermining the stability of strategic alliances.	Opportunistic behavior highly discouraged within relatively efficient and global industries such as the automotive sector, where *company reputation* and *brand image* play such a crucial role.
Games and negotiations • Game theory (Axelrod, 1984) • Bargaining power (Bacharach and Lawler, 1981)	Alliances are a series of choice outcomes that partners make over time, each partner fearing that the other will get the larger payoff by acting opportunistically while it cooperates in good faith. Alliances are a series of bargaining negotiations over time, where each party's bargaining power is wielded and manipulated constantly.	Alliance instability arises when payoffs from cheating a partner are greater than those of cooperating with it. Alliance instability arises when the partners' relative bargaining power shifts significantly in the life of the partnership.	Opportunistic behavior highly discouraged within relatively efficient and global industries such as the automotive sector, where *company reputation* and *brand image* play such a crucial role. Renault-Nissan alliance highly stable over the 1999–2004 period in spite of the initial (and very large) assiymetry of bargaining power between the allies shifting *both* dramatically and diametrically during 2001–2004.
Strategic management (Porter, 1980, 1985, 1990)	Alliances are one of a company's means to achieve superior strategic positioning *vis-à-vis* its rivals.	Instability stems from setting unrealistic strategic goals within the alliance.	Renault's and Nissan's strategic goals *universally* heralded as unrealistic in March 1999.
Time and resource dependence • Resource dependence (Pfeffer and Salancik, 1978) • Transitional (Franko, 1971. Kogut, 1989)	Alliances result from firms' willingness to control other firms' resources that are highly critical to their survival and performance. Alliances essentially are transitional forms because - due to internal managerial difficulties - they are unable to carry out long- term projects.	Alliances are terminated after the partners acquire the kind of resources they need from each other. Alliance instability is to be expected as they are intrinsically transitional organizational forms.	The Renault-Nissan alliance has remained stable during 1999–2004 in spite of a massive transfer of key resources between the allies by 2002, and even though *all* of the alliance's initial strategic objectives were attained by the same year. Renault-Nissan alliance highly stable organizationally even though *all* of the alliance's initial strategic objectives were attained by 2002. It paradoxically moved to broader, longer-term goals after March 2004.
Internal Tensions (Das and Bing-Sheng Teng, 2000)	Alliances are sites in which conflicting forces develop and which can be viewed as being constituted by a specific number of pairs of competing forces.	Instability of alliances stems from the development of three pairs of competing forces: cooperation versus competition, rigidity versus flexibility and short-term versus long-term orientation.	It was the development of tremendous internal tensions along these three pairs of competing forces that provided stability to the Renault-Nissan alliance during the 1999–2004 period.

(or rather the lack thereof). First, these theories often look at alliances as discrete, one-shot events largely motivated by synergistic payoffs. Second, they usually take an analytical perspective that overlooks the challenges of *socially* amalgamating people from diverse backgrounds to collaborate throughout the life span of the alliance. And third, these theories tend to take a prescriptive approach to addressing alliance stability that might appear simplistic in the "real world."

A closer look at the successful Renault-Nissan alliance allows us to address these issues with new eyes. It suggests that forming and managing stable alliances is not to be conceived as a discrete, one-shot analytical undertaking. Rather, it is a continuous and holistic challenge to creating a living *social* entity. Moreover the success of Renault-Nissan highlights that the payoffs of alliances stem from the allies' ability jointly to imagine, share, and build a common future rather than from their capacity to leverage upon past strengths. The Renault-Nissan experience also underlies the importance of the allies being able to amalgamate people socially from the outset in order to collaborate, learn, and share knowledge and resources across each other's cultural and organizational boundaries. Finally, Renault-Nissan's success suggests that company executives ought to emphasize organic rather than prescriptive approaches in order to drive alliance stability over time.

In the past, the lifetime of alliances has often been segmented in sequential stages underlying the formation, contractual, and implementation steps (Korine, Asakawa, & Gomez, 2002). By contrast, in the next sections we will follow a *social-capabilities* framework (Morosini, 2004b), grounded in the Renault-Nissan data during the 1999-to-2004 period, that apprehends international alliances as the organic, holistic, and continuous experiences they actually are. We therefore refer to a period of social initiation between top representatives of the prospective allies, followed by a process of social commitment that immediately precedes a process of intense social amalgamation within Nissan—and more restrictively between specific areas of Renault's and Nissan's operations. The organic, social process of nurturing an international alliance is represented in Figure 15.1.[2]

Servinacuy, or the Art of Social Initiation

Servinacuy is a Kichua word denoting an ancient conjugal practice of social initiation in Peru's Andean civilizations of millennia in age. Within certain Andean communities, whenever a young couple contemplates future marriage, they move in together for a number of months. If the experience of living together is satisfactory, they go on to marry. In any other case, the couple gives up their marriage hopes to become single individuals once more, ready for *servinacuy* with another partner in the community.[3]

There is more than what meets the eye in *servinacuy.* The partners expect—and are expected by the community—to marry, and so they prepare mentally and emotionally as individuals beforehand. Then both partners give the best to each other openly, truthfully, and respectfully to experience life together and share their dreams as a married couple. *Servinacuy* thus resolves, for the Andean people, the timeless paradox of building solid conjugal relationships. On the one hand, the two do get the chance of building their shared dreams together. On the other, they get to know, take risks, and experience firsthand the practicalities and uncertainties of cooperating with each other as a couple before entering a life-long commitment.

The Renault-Nissan alliance was called a "marriage of desperation for both parties" when it was announced in March 1999 (Edmondson, 1999). A more precise description, however, should have heralded a successful corporate *servinacuy* period turning into a long-term marriage. During the period from July to December 1998, Renault's and Nissan's top executives (joined by a number of selected managers from both companies) went through a six-month living experiment of working together with the aim of forging a formal alliance between the two

Nurturing alliances across boundaries

 Servinacuy: Social Initiation	Social Committment	Common Glue
Enacting a living experiment to test the prospective allies' ability to work together to create a shared future:	*Negotiating further and codifying contractually the pledges initiated during servinacuy:*	*Developing five social capabilities that foster a flow of knowledge, learning and resources across cultural and organizational boundaries:*
• *Developing trusting and truthful social relationship at the top* • *Establishing joint study teams to discover opportunities for future collaboration* • *Carrying out an actual experience of cooperative work* • *Creating social networks amongst key managers from both sides*	• *Maintaining continuity of purpose* • *Establishing multiple connections with the social initiation stage* • *Leveraging upon the trust built during the social initiation stage* • *Closing a deal that fosters reciprocity between the allies*	• *Boundary-spanning leadership* • *Company-wide building blocks* • *Knowledge interactions* • *Communication rituals* • *Cross-boundary rotations*

Figure 15.1 Nurturing Alliances Across Boundaries

companies. What these companies did during this period of social initiation explains much of the subsequent success of their alliance. It is revealing to compare this to what other (more unstable) alliances have—and have not—done during their initial stages of building a partnership.

In June 1998, Renault's Schweitzer disregarded advice from investment bankers against a direct approach and wrote to Nissan's President Yoshikazu Hanawa proposing broad strategic cooperation. He sent a similar letter to the president of Mitshubishi Motor Cars (MMC). Unlike MMC, Hanawa's answer was quick and enthusiastic. A framework for cooperation was sketched by an internal support team in July 1998. Schweitzer and Hanawa met a dozen times over the ensuing months to learn to trust each other and imagine a future alliance between their companies. Hanawa gives an insight into the atmosphere the two leaders created during these initial stages:

> With many people around, it is difficult to tell each other the truth, that is why I decided to negotiate alone. . . . I believe the process leading up to an alliance is all about telling the truth; dishonesty only makes the process longer. . . . I was impressed with Mr. Schweitzer's courageous decision to embrace a new business opportunity. (Korine et al., 2002)

As a next step Schweitzer and Hanawa picked 100 engineers and managers from both companies to work together in joint study teams without any formal objective. Instead, these people were encouraged to drop their mental stereotypes about France and Japan and concentrate on hard business fact-finding. Freed from cultural stereotypes and from following preconceived goals, the teams set a discovery trip of sorts in motion. Some of the executives involved in the teamwork recall the prevailing feelings:

> The kind of information that we were sharing with each other prior to the alliance agreement was a very rare case . . . since both sides had strong individual needs to make themselves stronger, the joint study took place sincerely.

> It was extraordinary in terms of synergies. We really believed in it. . . . Quite frankly, we were so complementary in terms of geography, products, personality . . . so we had great confidence. (Korine et al., 2002)

By working together with neither prejudices nor preestablished goals, the teams found a common ground as well as concrete opportunities for collaboration between the two companies. Armed with this hard business data, in October 1998 Schweitzer prepared a two-page mock press release entitled "Nissan and Renault join forces." Schweitzer explained:

> We had to move closer strategically, but it could not be a simple acquisition or a merger, because a Franco-Japanese merger is no easy matter. . . . I suggested to him [Hanawa] that three people from Renault should become members of the Nissan board of directors: the COO [chief operating officer], the vice-president product planning and the deputy chief financial officer. I only asked for those three. (Korine et al., 2002)

Hanawa observed, "I did not agree with it [the mock press release] from the start, of course. But I was not surprised. Through our discussions, I felt that Mr. Schweitzer always had a more comprehensive view of the partnership than I did" (Edmondson, 1999).

On November 10, Renault's Schweitzer, Ghosn (who would become COO, and later on, in 2000, CEO of Nissan), and Douin made a presentation to the Nissan board of directors describing the benefits of a large-scale collaboration between the two companies. The presentation drew heavily on the findings of the joint study teams. No formal commitment was yet in sight, but it was decided that the work of the joint study teams would continue until December 1998.

Both Renault's Schweitzer and Nissan's Hanawa had clear ideas of what they wanted out of a strategic alliance. But they were unfamiliar to each other and had no history of working together. As in *servinacuy,* they set a living process of social initiation in motion to test their companies' ability to work cooperatively and deliver on the promise of a shared future. The process itself had useful outcomes, for example, allowing for joint discoveries, developing the ability to share knowledge trustingly and openly, and developing social capital in the form of valuable social networks between the two companies. The six-month social-initiation process gave Renault an advantage over competitive suitors such as Ford or DaimlerChrysler. The latter companies resorted to a more conventional "due-diligence" process. In other words, they carried out static analytical evaluations rather than an actual experiment of social collaboration and focused on finding synergies based on past and current strengths, rather than on jointly imagining a shared future.

Social Commitment Is Not About the Contract

March 1999 saw two archetypal approaches to alliance negotiation and closure at play in the automotive industry. On the one hand, DaimlerChrysler CEO Juergen Schrempp had a two-month due diligence carried out to assess the prospect of an alliance with Nissan. Then, on March 9, he met at length with his management board in a hotel on the shores of Lake Geneva.

A "green team" of company managers focused on the likely benefits of an alliance with Nissan. A "red team" focused on the drawbacks. After listening to both sides, Schrempp and his management team made a decision. The next day, Schrempp flew to Tokyo and met for three hours with Nissan's Hanawa. DaimlerChrysler broke off alliance talks with Nissan after that meeting. Soon after, following a similar process, DaimlerChrysler entered into an equity alliance with Mitsubishi Motor Corporation (MMC). When signing that deal, Schrempp remarked: "They [MMC] are the ideal partner for us" (Morosini, 2004a).

Renault's approach to negotiating an alliance with Nissan was different. In their case, both the substance and the style of their alliance negotiations were an organic result of what the two companies achieved during their social-initiation stages. The level of confidence in their ability to work cooperatively, the mutual trust that had been created, and the informal pledges that had been jointly formulated played a critical role in the final outcome of the negotiations. In other words, these negotiations were not just about signing an alliance deal following a sound due-diligence assessment. Rather, the prospective allies enacted a process of *social commitment* that codified the mutual pledges stemming from their earlier experiment of working together. This is made evident from an examination of the negotiations of the Renault-Nissan alliance in greater detail.

Already in August 1998 Schweitzer had proposed to Hanawa: "We have a firm and trusting relationship. To make our relationship stronger, why not think about holding each other's shares?" To this Hanawa replied, "Nissan, frankly, has no money to spend on buying Renault stock." "We can talk about this again in the future," replied the Frenchman. "From Renault's point of view, there is no future for us if we cannot work together with Nissan" (Edmondson, 1999).

The proposal soon became that Renault would buy a stake in Nissan. Hanawa outlined four conditions any foreign buyer had to meet: to keep the Nissan name, protect jobs, promote restructuring under the lead of Nissan, and pick a CEO from inside Nissan. Schweitzer did not object. At the same time, Hanawa told Schweitzer that Nissan would need to raise $6 billion in cash. This was well above Schweitzer's $3 billion limit. In November 1998, Hanawa visited DaimlerChrysler's headquarters and was greeted with a proposal to invest in Nissan itself. He flew to Paris the next day to inform Schweitzer that he planned to continue negotiations with the German-American automaker. A disappointed Schweitzer remarked, "We cannot provide the amount of cash Nissan needs. If Renault cannot tie up with Nissan we will eventually be driven out of the market" (Edmondson, 1999).

However, on March 10, 1999, DaimlerChrysler's Schrempp abruptly called off alliance talks with Nissan. Hanawa considered his options. He decided to approach Ford's CEO, Jacques Nasser, with whom he had had earlier contacts. However, Schweitzer sent Hanawa a confidential note saying that there was hope that Renault could make a much larger investment in Nissan than he had proposed earlier. But Schweitzer requested that no later than March 13, Hanawa sign a "freeze" agreement preventing Nissan from approaching other carmakers until talks with Renault were completed or called off. Hanawa flew to Paris. After inspecting the "freeze" agreement, he still could not pin down the exact amount of Renault's investment in Nissan. "Please trust me," said Schweitzer (Edmondson, 1999).

Hanawa signed the "freeze" agreement. On March 16, 1999, Renault's board approved a $5.4 billion investment in Nissan. The following day, Renault and Nissan announced a signed alliance agreement that closely resembled the two-page mock press release that had been written back in October 1998 during the social initiation process of the alliance. Schweitzer said,

> The decision we made during the final negotiations was not to change our position. It was an important choice on our part to say: "It's not because DaimlerChrysler is not around that we are changing our proposal." I decided not to [change the

> proposal] because I felt it would destroy the relationship of trust which was indispensable for us to work together. (Korine et al., 2002)

Hanawa added, "The fact that we agreed on the terms of equal position was important for me, as dominance destroys motivation" (Korine et al., 2002).

The Glue That Keeps Alliances Together

An abundant literature has documented the detrimental effects of cultural, professional, and organizational boundaries on the performance of alliances, especially as their scale and scope increase in size, complexity, and international coverage (Beamish & Killing, 1997). Here, the capacity to amalgamate the allies' resources across boundaries is crucial to turn cultural and organizational differences into performance advantages during alliance implementation. At the leadership level, I call this amalgamation capacity the "common glue" of organizations (Morosini, 2004b).

The common glue represents the social capabilities that build cohesiveness among a company's pivotal executive cadres and the unique way in which cooperative relationships between key members are created, nurtured, and transformed into valuable products and services in the marketplace.

I have found that a company's common glue is made up of five distinct social capabilities, which together have a strong, positive impact on the competitive performance of organizations (refer to Figure 15.2). These five social capabilities can be defined as:

1. *Boundary-spanning leadership*—the extent to which an organization's key leadership cadre—typically numbering a few hundred executives from many nationalities—possesses boundary-spanning character traits such as tolerance, patience, the ability to "walk the talk," a giver's mentality, and wholeness. It also includes the extent to which this key leadership cadre is managed as a truly global, cohesive, and trusting group.

2. *Companywide building blocks*—an organization's capability to develop a set of shared commonalities among its members. These commonalities include a common language, a set of shared business values, global career development paths for the boundary-spanning leadership group, and a common companywide approach to internal reporting and performance measurement.

3. *Knowledge interactions*—an organization's capability to put in place cross-boundary teams, dialogues, processes, projects, and communities of practice—to exchange know-how—in support of compelling, companywide business cases.

4. *Communication rituals*—an organization's capability to carry out a set of frank, compelling, regular, and companywide communication interactions that instill common leadership behavior in its boundary-spanning leadership group.

5. *Cross-boundary rotations*—an organization's capability to develop and implement global personnel policies—for example, expatriate and repatriate programs, executive performance evaluations, and incentives—that foster the smooth and continual rotation of its key executives across boundaries.

Building Renault-Nissan's "Common Glue"

The Renault-Nissan alliance provides a prime example of how—even across extreme cultural and organizational boundaries—a determined group of leaders can build a strong common glue that drives superior organizational stability and competitive performance. At Renault-Nissan, the building of this corporate common glue was

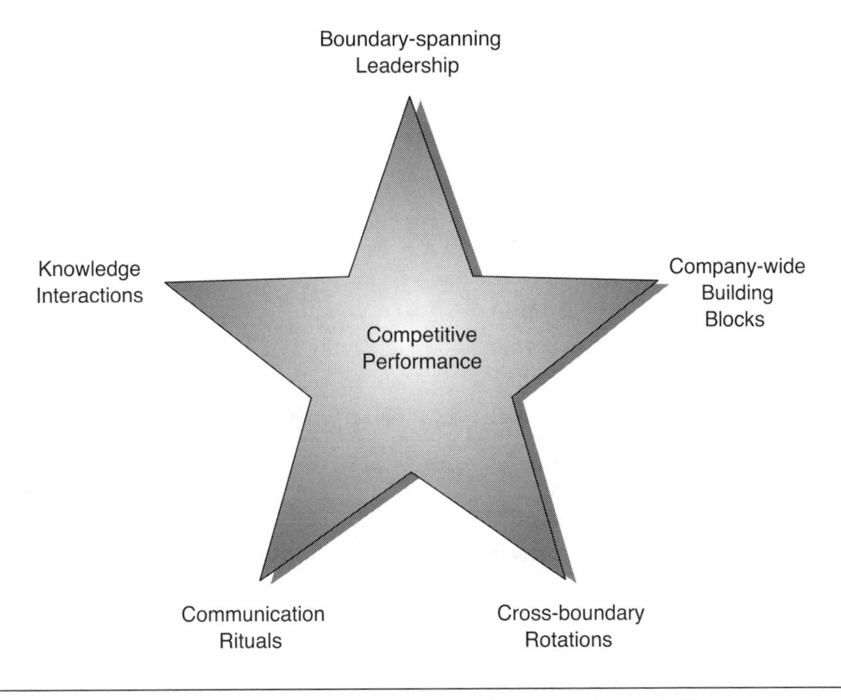

Figure 15.2 What Is the "Common Glue"? A Set of Five Social Capabilities

carried out simultaneously at two levels. First, eighteen Renault expatriates took key leadership positions in Nissan on July 1 and helped build a strong common glue within the Japanese company. As a result, Nissan was able to implement a revival plan successfully and went on to become the world's most profitable automaker in the 2002-to-2004 period. The common glue that Nissan's leaders built within the company from July 1999 reflected not only many of the carmaker's historical roots but also the new realities of Nissan's alliance with Renault.

Second, a common glue of sorts was also built between Renault and Nissan from July 1999. Initially it involved a reduced number of key executives from both companies and was centered on very specific knowledge exchanges and functional collaboration projects. However, it is very noticeable that over the 1999-to-2004 period, collaboration between Renault and Nissan grew in scale and importance, gradually but relentlessly, to the extent that in March 2004 the companies reported key financial results jointly and announced that they would share a single CEO in 2005. This had never been contemplated in the original 1999 alliance agreement. Hence, the common glue that was built between Renault and Nissan does not appear to have followed the milestones of any preconceived strategic plan. Rather, it seems to have been a case of previous successes feeding ever greater dreams of a shared future.

By contrast, similar combines, such as the DaimlerChrysler-Mitsubishi alliance (or the Daimler and Chrysler combine itself), decided not to build a strong common glue between the joining companies during the implementation stages. In fact, when the DaimlerChrysler-Mitsubishi alliance was dissolved in 2004, most observers duly pointed out the profound differences in implementation approach vis-à-vis the Renault-Nissan. Regarding the DaimlerChrysler combine, in a previous work I highlighted that,

> After achieving their early [postmerger integration synergies in 1999] it was

> decided that the former Daimler Benz and Chrysler were to be managed as separate entities in order to maintain the integrity of their brands and their distinct pre-merger corporate cultures. Therefore, the new company was *not* to implement a common global management overlay across the former Daimler Benz and Chrysler, no common organizational blueprint, no major know-how exchanges, no single set of global personnel policies and no unified building blocks. In the absence of a strong "common glue," DaimlerChrysler's attempts [over the 1999-to-2002 period] to gain competitive advantages by combining both merging companies' strengths, were lost along the cultural, functional and organizational divides in place. (Morosini, 2004a)

In the following subsections I illustrate the way in which Renault and Nissan went about building a strong common glue after their March 1999 alliance deal.

Boundary-Spanning Leadership

Carlos Ghosn became COO of Nissan on July 1, 1999. From the outset, this South American of Lebanese descent and French education provided an example of boundary-spanning leadership traits at work in Nissan. At the time of his COO appointment, Carlos Ghosn did not speak Japanese, but he addressed the people in Japan directly, without preexisting mental models, cultural prejudices, or preconceptions. Said Ghosn, "I am not going [to Japan] with any preconceived ideas" (Woodruff, 1999).

Ghosn encouraged the expatriates he brought with him to Japan to do the same thing:

> [In July 1999] I handpicked 17 [French executives] from Renault and brought them to Nissan. I chose people who were around 40 years old, experts in their field, very open minded and coaches, not people who wanted to play it solo. . . . [Before coming to Japan I told them:] we are not missionaries. We are not going there to teach the Japanese [about] the role of women in Japanese business. We are there to help fix Nissan, that's all. Any issue that does not contribute to that is of no concern to us. (Ghosn, 2002a; Hughes et al., 2003)

Amongst the 17 Renault expatriates whom Ghosn brought to Japan were Patrick Pelata and Thierry Moulonguet, who, as heads of Nissan product development and finance, respectively, would play a critical role in the company's revival. Once in Japan, Ghosn oversaw the reduction of Nissan's board of directors from 37 members to 10. When Nissan's Hanawa asked him whom he wanted as Japanese members on the executive committee board, Ghosn replied, "I don't know. You choose. You know me so please, you pick them—knowing what you know of me" (Ghosn, 2002a; Hughes et al., 2003).

Immediately after this, Ghosn formed the company's boundary-spanning leadership team:

> I requested that 1,500 profiles of Nissan employees be posted in headquarters to select about 200 people for nine cross-functional teams. I was looking for young mavericks who would be the backbone of the next Nissan leadership generation. Multicultural experience was not considered an absolute requirement for success, but it was a value-added. I think that the basic personal qualities of an individual can always overcome any lack of experience. It is important how you handle small frustrations. And when you have taken time to understand and accept that people don't think or act the same way in France or in Japan, then the cultural differences can become seeds for innovation as opposed to seeds for dissention. (Thornton, 1999; Miller & Zaun, 2002)

By early 2000, Nissan's new leadership cadre was in place. It was a reduced group of 200 executives not permanently housed at the company's Tokyo headquarters, as had been the case until then, but spending time there on a project-by-project basis. Together with this newly formed boundary-spanning leadership team, Carlos Ghosn began patiently crafting building blocks inside Nissan and made "walk the talk" and transparent communication his leadership trademark. As a result, the company's executive team presided over one of the fastest, most successful turnarounds ever.

Companywide Building Blocks

Building blocks are the "Forrest Gump of management"; they denote managerial aspects that are obvious to the intellect but very hard to find in a functioning state in most companies. For example, although most multinational companies I studied had an official internal company language, such as English, the same companies demonstrated extremely weak levels of mutual understanding across organizational and cultural boundaries.

One of the first things that Nissan's boundary-leadership team did was to set companywide building blocks such as a common language in place. Says Ghosn,

> I told the old guard [of Nissan managers from the outset]: You speak English. Learn it immediately if you must or you're out. But some key words were not understood in the same way by different Japanese people or even different French people. So I asked a mixed Renault-Nissan team to establish a dictionary of essential terms. The 100 or so entries included clear definitions for terms like "commitment," "authority," "objectives," "transparency" and "targets." (Emerson, 2001)

A common language helped Nissan work effectively in cross-functional and cross-company teams, with Renault and Nissan executives from different functions and nationalities working together to achieve challenging business objectives. Examples of the latter include: "launch 22 new car models in the next three years"; "improve manufacturing capacity utilization in Japan from 53% in 1999 to 82% in 2002"; and "cut automotive debt in half, to $5.8 billion net in the next three years" (Morosini, 2004b).

Another building block that Ghosn instilled in Nissan early on was to look for and encourage certain common character traits in the company's employees, especially among those who played—or were expected to assume—leadership roles. One such character trait was "walk the talk" behavior. Explains Ghosn, "What we think, what we say, and what we do must be the same. We have to be impeccable in ensuring that our words correspond to our actions. If there are discrepancies between what we profess and how we behave, that will spell disaster" (Emerson, 2001).

Companywide Business Cases

In a previous work, I described a "companywide business case" as a central element of one of the common glue's constituent social capabilities that I have defined above as *knowledge interactions:*

> A companywide business case is a business initiative with clear quantitative and qualitative targets, which requires the involvement of—and has a strong impact on—most of a company's component areas, and which the company executives feel passionate about. A [company] executive . . . summarized it as: *An exciting business initiative that connects everybody and brings forward the performance of the entire organization.* (Morosini, 2004b)

Nissan's Revival Plan (NRP) was the companywide business case that Ghosn introduced in July 1999 as the company's COO. With Nissan on the brink of complete financial and market collapse, the plan aimed to strengthen radically the company's common glue around the mission of revival. Some of the main strategic goals in the plan read:

- Return to profitability during the year March 2000 to March 2001. The [annual] net income after tax of the Nissan Group will be positive.
- An [annual] operating margin superior to 4.5% of sales during the year March 2002 to March 2003.
- A 50% decrease in net debt, from $12.6 billion today to $6.3 billion by March 2003.
- Reduce purchasing costs by 20% by March 2003.
- Reduce 21,000 jobs (from 148,000 to 127,000) by March 2003. (Ghosn, 1999)

When Ghosn unveiled the plan at the Tokyo Motor Show on October 18, 1999, few people believed Nissan would achieve its ambitious goals. A Japanese analyst captured the prevailing mood: "It is impossible for Japanese managers to carry out such a drastic restructuring program" (Hirano, 1999).

Nissan's stock, already at record lows at the time of the October 1999 Tokyo Motor Show, fell a further 5% less than two weeks following the NRP announcement. However, Nissan achieved—and in many cases exceeded—all of the NRP's stated goals, contrary to every expectation. When asked how Nissan managed to do this, Ghosn often responded that knowledge interactions such as cross-functional teams were a key ingredient for success. Many of these teams had already been in place during the social initiation stages of the alliance and were utilized to design the NRP without resorting to outsiders such as consultants or industry experts. At the October 18 Tokyo Motor Show Ghosn explained:

> How did we elaborate the Nissan Revival Plan? On July 5 we established nine cross-functional teams. Each one was led by two Executive Committee members and headed by a pilot. Team members were selected by the leaders and the pilot from the company's managerial ranks. The composition had to be cross-functional and international. It is not top-down. It is not bottom-up. It is both. Each team had one topic. One goal: Make proposals to develop the business and reduce costs. One deadline: This morning's Board meeting for final decisions. One rule: No sacred cows, no taboos, no constraints. One belief: The solutions to Nissan's problems are inside the company. Only one issue is non-negotiable: The return to profit. (Ghosn, 1999)

Not all of the NRPs involved painful restructuring goals; there was also room for dreams. When announcing the NRP in October 18, 1999, Ghosn had concluded by saying:

> I know and I measure how much effort, how much sacrifice and how much pain we will have to endure for the success of the NRP. But believe me, we don't have a choice and it will be worth it. We all shared a dream; a dream of a reconstructed and revived company, a dream of a thoughtful and bold Nissan on track to perform profitable growth in a balanced alliance with Renault to create a major global player in the world car industry. This dream today becomes a vision with the NRP. This vision will become a reality as long as every single Nissan employee will share it with us. (Ghosn, 1999)

Rather than one-sided restructuring, the key to the success of the NRP was product development. At the very heart of the plan was in fact the company's commitment to launch 22 entirely new car models over the ensuing three years, something that very few automotive companies had attempted to do before. This was the task of a dedicated cross-functional team and the reason behind many of the company's new hires and investments from 1999 on. Isuzu Motors star designer Shiro Nakamura was recruited in September 1999 to restore allure to Nissan's tarnished brand image vis-à-vis the customers. This meant heavy discounts on Nissan's car models compared to competitors with better brand reputations. In 2000, all of Nissan's design teams scattered worldwide under Nissan's regional engineering functions were already unified under Nakamura's leadership. R&D investments rose from 3.7% of net sales in 1998 to 5%. A significant amount of the increased budget went to support the recruitment of 1,000 new engineers for leading-edge projects such as fuel-cell-powered cars.

Moreover, in 1999 Ghosn approved a $930 million new assembly plant in central Mississippi to supply the key U.S. market—representing one third of Nissan's sales—with new pickup trucks, minivans, and sport-utility models starting in mid-2003. In May 2000, Nissan also announced a $300 million investment to produce new Nissan car models in Brazil, an effort headed by a former Renault executive. Explained Ghosn,

> People need to know what the prize is, what are they aiming for, what are the benefits or the advantage to them of changing some established tradition. When this is clearly spelled out, people will be motivated to follow. . . . [We are like] a Formula One pilot, [who is] constantly using the accelerator and the brakes. He uses them at the same time to go to the max. We are at the same time accelerating and braking. (Emerson, 2001; Shirouzu, White, & Zaun, 2000)

Braking and accelerating at the same time also proved useful in dealing with Nissan's army of 5,000 auto-parts suppliers and 600 dealers, all of which had long-standing cross-shareholding ties with Nissan. This system, called *keiretsu,* had a long tradition in Japanese capitalism. It had provided an environment of mutual loyalty, stability, and low risk that had nurtured the growth of most of Japan's large corporations since the mid-nineteenth century. However, *keiretsu*'s intrinsic lack of flexibility was proving to be one of its most serious shortcomings within the rapidly changing global business milieu of the twenty-first century. In the case of Nissan, *keiretsu* meant that even though many of the company's networks of suppliers and dealers had overgrown costs and low productivity compared to their competitors, they were kept in place because of long-dated shareholding ties. When unveiling the NRP, Ghosn made it clear to journalists, dealers, and suppliers that maintaining *keiretsu* was not among the company's objectives:

> With the exception of four companies, none is considered to be indispensable for the future. This means we will be unwinding most of our shareholdings strictly on the basis of a cost/benefit analysis. . . . Our objective is to free all capital resources from non-strategic, non-core assets and to invest more in our core business while at the same time significantly reducing our debt. (Ghosn, 1999)

The day after the unveiling of the NRP, Nissan's suppliers and dealers were given a deadline of January 2000 to submit bids for new contracts that would be in line with the restructuring targets that had been announced. It was made clear that not all of the bids would be accepted—but it was equally transparent that the selected companies would gain a much greater access to Nissan's business.

Companywide business cases are continuous features within most high-performing organizations. They become central elements of those organizations' common glue driving their leadership cohesiveness and competitive performance across functional and cultural boundaries. Thus, in 2001, after the NRP's goals had been achieved and the company had revived, Nissan launched "180," another companywide business case where "1" stands for one million additional car units sold, "8" denotes 8% margin, and "0" stands for zero debt, all to be achieved by 2005. As the goals of "180" were met before schedule, in June 2004 Ghosn started to publicize "Value Up," yet another companywide business case that was going to turn Nissan's and Renault's brands and product portfolio into higher-value-added items in the consumer's minds. The cross-functional teams became a permanent supporting feature in all of Nissan's companywide business cases. Said Ghosn, "In my experience, executives in a company rarely reach across boundaries. Working together in cross-functional teams helps managers to think in new ways, challenge existing practices, explaining the necessity for change and projecting difficult messages across the entire company (Ghosn, 2002a; Hughes et al., 2003).

Building Glue Between Renault and Nissan

The implementation stages of the Renault-Nissan alliance did not only contemplate French executives helping Nissan strengthen its common glue. Parallel to this process, the social amalgamation process between Renault and Nissan themselves continued gradually and inexorably. An example of this was given by the knowledge interactions between the two companies that took place over the 1999-to-2004 period via the so-called "cross-company teams." Explains Ghosn,

> The experience of the Mexico regional "cross-company team" is a good example [of cooperation between Renault and Nissan. In early 1999] Nissan was suffering from overcapacity in the Mexican market. Renault had abandoned this market since 1986. Putting managers from both companies together meant that they immediately recognized the synergy opportunity. In just five months they put together a plan for producing Renault cars in Nissan plants. A year later, in December 2000, the first Renault models rolled off the production lines. The improvement in Nissan's manufacturing position has been dramatic. At the Cuernavaca plant, capacity utilization went from 56% to nearly 100% by January 2002. And this greatly accelerated Renault's re-entry into Mexico. What's more, Renault could use Nissan's local dealers as distributors. (Ghosn, 2002b)

Cross-company teams provided an approach that allowed Renault and Nissan to go through a social initiation experience first and then move into more formal frameworks of collaboration and knowledge exchanges on a case-by-case basis. This social approach was found to be so effective in nurturing collaboration between Renault and Nissan, that all other formal aspects—that is, legal, structural, organizational—were made secondary to it. Observed Ghosn,

> At a certain point in negotiations between the two companies [in July 1998], there was a discussion about how they would work together. Renault's negotiators assumed that the best way forward would be to set up a series of joint ventures, and they wanted to discuss all legal issues surrounding a joint venture: who contributes what and how much, how the output is shared and so forth. The Nissan team pushed back; they wanted to explore management and business issues, not legal technicalities. As a result, negotiations were stalled. . . . I recommended abandoning the joint venture approach. If you want people to work together, the last thing you need is a legal structure that gets in the way. My solution was to introduce informal cross-company teams (CCTs). Some teams focused on specific aspects of automobile manufacturing and delivery. . . . Others focused on a [geographic] region. . . . All told, we created 11 such cross-company teams. . . . Through these teams, Renault and Nissan managers have found many ways to leverage the strengths of both companies. (Ghosn, 2002b)

Communication Rituals

From the outset Ghosn instilled a culture of extremely transparent, open, precise, and factual communications, both inside Nissan and with outside parties such as the media. In 2002, Ghosn reflected back upon what Nissan's leadership set out to do in this area: "If you want to mobilize 130,000 people in different cultures and different countries you have to be precise, you have to be factual, and you have to base everything you say on hard evidence that people can measure" (Ghosn, 2002a; Hughes et al., 2003).

In 2001, Thierry Moulonguet—a former Renault executive who became Nissan's vice-president of Finance in June 1999—characterized this new approach to communications further: "With Carlos Ghosn the rules of the game are simple and clear. That was perfectly understood by the young generation of Japanese managers. He is very approachable. Anyone can send him an e-mail, he looks at all of them. He reacts in an open and straightforward way" (Hauter, 2001).

A year later, addressing an audience of business school students, Ghosn provided additional arguments supporting the need for total clarity in communications:

> If people don't know the priority, don't understand the strategy, don't know where they're going, don't know what is the critical objective, you're heading for trouble. Confusion is the first sign of trouble. It's [the leader's] duty to clarify the environment, to make sure there is the maximum light in the company. (Ghosn, 2002a; Hughes et al., 2003)

Nissan's new culture of transparent and factual communications was instilled by its top leaders' habit of "walking the talk." In other words, it was made alive within the company through the top leaders' daily behavior, interactions, and practices. In 2001, Ghosn's response to a journalist summarized this approach. Asked how much time he spent in communications, he replied, "Even in brainstorming sessions, even when we elaborate strategy, you communicate all the time" (Nuss, 2001).

Some of these daily events and practices became powerful and visible rituals that made the new walk-the-talk approach to communications come alive within the company. For example, in order to communicate his conviction that the solutions to Nissan's problems were inside the company, Ghosn would make surprise visits to Nissan's research facilities and production plants, gathering input from senior managers and line workers alike. The decision to make English Nissan's common official language was backed up with intensive language courses for all the company's employees, regardless of level. In spite of the company's critical state in 1999, Ghosn also started the practice of inviting the media to Nissan's annual shareholder meetings and gave them complete freedom to report what they saw. He explained the rationale behind this new transparency: "[People say] you cannot criticize your own company, but if you don't look at reality as it is, even being harsh at yourself, you'll never fix it" (Ghosn, 2002a; Hughes et al., 2003).

Ghosn's reactions to critical observations by journalists and other similar outsiders often puzzled them. Far from being defensive, Ghosn would talk candidly about the company's shortcomings while pointing the way out of them. For instance, a journalist who in 1999 expressed disbelief that Nissan lacked even the most basic competitive marketing data, received the following reply from Ghosn: "You laugh, [but] it's real. We had no substantial analysis, segment by segment [of] what was going on" (Shirouzu et al., 2000).

His choice to communicate the NRP to the outside world at the same time as Nissan employees were learning about it—at the Tokyo Motor Show on October 18, 1999—was a powerful sign of the company's determination to establish transparent, reliable goals and achieve them in a no-nonsense fashion. Ghosn explained, "Credibility has two legs . . . the first is performance, but [we have nothing to show at the start]; the second leg of credibility is transparency—what I think, what I say, what I do is the same thing. So we have to be extremely transparent" (Ghosn, 2002a; Hughes et al., 2003).

Supporting this, following the public announcement of Nissan's NRP in October 1999,

Ghosn stuck to the revival plan's ambitious goals even though these were regarded as unrealistic by an overwhelming majority of competitors, industry experts, the international media, and most qualified observers. Said Ghosn, "The big risk is that if you announce ambitious [goals], people will not believe you. They'll say, 'He said 100 percent, but if he gets 50 percent he'll be happy.' . . . Well, we want 100, and we're going to get 100. If we don't get it next year [2000], that's it. We will resign" (Peterson, 2000).

Instilling this new culture of transparent communications was not easy. In 1999, Ghosn had found a rather compartmentalized culture within Nissan that prevented the flow of communications across the company's various functions, borders and hierarchical lines. He observed, "Country organizations were not talking to each other, people were not talking to each other. I want to destroy this spirit" (Burt & Harney, 1999). The "cross-functional teams" were crucial to turning the prevailing culture into a more open spirit that fostered cross-boundary communications. But there were other organizational changes that provided further support to the new culture. In late March 2000, Ghosn—in one of the few unilateral decisions he had made since his arrival in Japan—replaced the company's divisional presidencies in North America and Europe with four cross-functional management teams that met monthly. He remarked, "Each time you have a regional president, you start to have problems of communication and retention of information, either from headquarters to the region or from the region to the headquarters. We don't want that. This is a killer for the global performance of the company" (Ghosn, 2002b).

Cross-Boundary Rotations

Nissan used personnel and career-growth policies effectively in order to break boundaries, rotate key executives around, and create a truly global leadership cadre inside the company. For example, a new stock-option plan for all of Nissan's managers worldwide was set in place in July 1999. It helped in moving key development, design, and purchasing executives to centralized, global locations that facilitated cross-functional knowledge interactions. To support this further, in 2000 a new global promotion and compensation system was rolled out. Based on the employees' profit contribution, it broke an old tradition of incentives based on seniority at Nissan and throughout corporate Japan. Nissan also established and led a Nomination Advisory Committee to review promotion recommendations. Since 2000, no leadership promotions have been made at Nissan without a performance review by this committee, which uses a performance rather than seniority criterion to endorse its recommendations.

However, preparing the mind-sets and attitudes of its employees was a key step that preceded the rollout of Nissan's sweeping changes in personnel, career-growth, and incentives policies. Ghosn had made this clear when unveiling the NRP in October 1999:

> Performance-based career advancement will be established at the latest by the end of 2000 to make sure we act in a coherent manner across the company. Concretely, some of the changes will not be implemented before ensuring that the people in charge have changed their attitude, and that the clear performance indicators for which they are accountable exist. (Ghosn, 1999)

Preparing mind-sets and molding attitudes were made challenging due to the magnitude of the changes involved. One Nissan manager commented, "There is a schism [inside Nissan]. We've told those who are resisting the changes that they have one year to change their attitude" (Larimer, 2001). At first Nissan employees were disoriented by the changes and complained, "We attend meetings late into the night, and the next morning we are requested to come in at 6 A.M. If this goes on for days and days, it just won't work, unless we get paid more" (Kawato & Ikematsu,

2000). However, Carlos Ghosn was unwavering and demanded total commitment to the implementation of these changes by Nissan's boundary-spanning leadership cadre. In December 1999, he had already told the press, "There is a group in the company who still think this will blow over, though their number grows smaller by the day" (Taylor, 1999).

Nissan's new global promotion criterion put into place in 2000—based on performance—was ruthlessly showcased in March 2001. On that date, Nissan announced a series of high-profile casualties affecting executives who had repeatedly failed to meet their targets, including one company vice-president and twenty subsidiary presidents. Said Ghosn, "Accountability has to start at the top [otherwise] it is very difficult to push a company at all levels [and] make sure everybody is committed to the subject" (Nuss, 2001).

However, the benefits of the new personnel and career-growth policies were showcased in other ways as well. Challenging long-dated boundaries of gender, in 2001 a high-profile female Japanese executive was hired from JP Morgan Securities to head Nissan's communications department, becoming the first woman ever to lead a function within the company. The move grabbed widespread attention from the Japanese media, which commented that up until then ambitious Japanese female executives had had to switch from domestic to foreign-owned companies in order to make progress in their careers. Boundaries of age and seniority were also challenged by Nissan's new policies. In 2000, Nissan executives in their early forties were for the first time promoted to very senior positions based on their profit-contribution performance rather than their seniority. Likewise, many of the best-performing heads of Nissan's cross-functional teams were promoted rapidly. Said one of them,

> In the old system everyone could be promoted, so there was no pressure. . . . For many employees it was a good system but for those with good skills, it was no good. If I [had] been replaced by a younger man in the past I would have been shocked. But now I don't think I would care, because clearly the person has better skills than mine. (Ibison, 2001)

Conclusion

As he contemplated retirement in his Paris office in March 2004, Renault's president made statements that mystified most outsiders who came to visit him. This did not seem to trouble Schweitzer. Looking back at the Renault-Nissan alliance, he simply said, "We did not try to forge a common culture. . . . We never talked about an alliance of equals" (de Saint-Seine, 2004). Anyone hearing his declarations without knowing much about the alliance would probably predict a corporate disaster story. But Renault-Nissan was exactly the opposite. Not only had this alliance been the largest corporate marriage between a Western and an Eastern partner to that date, but it was also one of the very few examples of successful international alliances in any major global industry. Nevertheless, to most people this marriage had looked as odd as could possibly be imagined and its chances of success hopelessly slim from the outset.

This feeling of oddity would intensify after learning *how* the Renault-Nissan alliance attained success. This in itself countered much of the prevailing theories—but then, the perplexing facts of this alliance were far too compelling to be ignored. Not forging a common culture did not prevent Renault and Nissan from nurturing a strong common glue between themselves. Even if these companies did not talk about an alliance of equals, they nevertheless created an environment of genuine trust, loyalty, and reciprocity. Although neither of them were particularly strong industry players—Nissan actually being nearly bankrupt at the time of the alliance—these two companies managed to forge a top-performing global partnership in less than five years. Most surprisingly, French and Japanese managers cooperated effectively across national and corporate cultural divides that most pundits could only characterize as gaping. The list of oddities could continue; it is in fact described in more detail in the preceding sections.

The odd facts of the Renault-Nissan alliance nevertheless provide valuable lessons and data to all executives and academics intent on looking at the field with new eyes. Let us start with the latter.

The Renault-Nissan combine opens new research vistas across the entire range of theories that in the past have emphasized rather mechanistically the strategic, tactical, transactional, optimizing, or relational aspects of alliances (refer to Figure 15.1). I elicit some of the most obvious ones. Relational-contract theories have emphasized a history of trusting interactions between the prospective allies as a key determinant of alliance stability. However, the Renault-Nissan alliance suggests that the quality of relationships developed between the partners might be the key predictor of stability during the alliance formation stages.

Moreover, when assessing the quality of relationships between the prospective allies, time may not be the key dimension. Rather, we might need to look at the intrinsic truthfulness that the potential allies exhibit in disclosing each other's real motives from the outset. As Renault-Nissan demonstrates, truthful interactions between the partners can build trust and motivation in a relatively short time and across formidable cultural and organizational divides. In turn, a strong relational trust and motivation developed during the alliance formation stages may be a critical predictor of alliance stability.

The Renault-Nissan alliance also highlights that transactional, game-theoretical, and bargaining approaches may have overemphasized certain assumptions that look at alliances as a series of competitive choice outcomes played mechanistically between utilitarian and opportunistic agents. Instead, these theorists might find greater predictive insights by looking at alliances as intrinsically cooperative forms developed between organizations that operate as social actors within well-established, diverse, and complex communities. Researching the conditions of collaborative behavior and cooperative choice outcomes between the allies may serve to unveil crucial predictors of alliance stability from transactional and tactical viewpoints.

Similarly, when it comes to predicting alliance stability, strategic management pundits might find it fruitful to include the social-capabilities perspective as the necessary complement of strategic goal-setting. Whereas the latter provides analytical and linear strategic positioning with clues for predicting alliance stability, the former gives an insight into how likely the allies are to work together and actually achieve the desired strategic positioning. Hence, both strategic goals and social capabilities ought to be regarded jointly as strategic predictors of alliance stability. Explicitly including the variables that determine the social context and social capabilities of the allies could also inform the predictive power of the time-dependence, internal-tension, and resource-dependence perspectives. In particular, including the degree to which the partners create a strong common glue for cohesive, cooperative leadership might help to predict alliance stability even in cases when massive transfers of resources take place effectively between the allies and in spite of conflictive tensions between the partners arising from time to time.

Overall, the Renault-Nissan alliance underlies the value of working toward an epistemology of socially constructed knowledge within and across organizations. Such an endeavor would provide the necessary complement to the prevailing more mechanistic theoretical perspectives on alliances. On the one hand, certain academics suggest that such mechanistic approaches have so far proved insufficient to explain the instability of alliances (Dyer et al., 2004). On the other, certain executives might regard the same mechanistic perspectives as useful in addressing only about "5%" of the challenges involved in conceiving, negotiating and managing alliances (Ghosn, 1999), the remaining 95% being—as the Renault-Nissan alliance demonstrates—the social challenge of creating and nurturing an atmosphere of collaboration, where ideas, knowledge, and resources flow across boundaries and get transformed into products and services that customers find economically useful (Morosini, 2004b).

As shown in this chapter, such a social perspective might inform the phenomenon of alliances in its entirety, from the formation to the negotiation and implementation stages. No less important, the "make-or-break" of an alliance might be better explained and predicted from the perspective of its social fabric rather than by looking exclusively at its more mechanistic aspects, as has been the case so far. As it intrinsically looks at organizations as holistic and organic phenomena, a social research perspective of alliances might benefit from interdisciplinary collaboration as well as from adopting methods of inquiry that are directly grounded on empirical data and observations (Glaser, 1978, 1992; Glaser & Strauss, 1967).

Executives and practitioners may find it valuable to move slightly away from a process mind-set and to think of international alliances more in terms of organic endeavors to nurture both the conditions and the social capabilities for cooperative work across cultural and organizational boundaries. Evidence that such a mind-set (outlined in more detail in the Appendix) is behind the superior stability and performance of certain alliances stems not only from the Renault-Nissan combine but also from Fuji-Xerox, its Japanese-American forerunner in the office equipment industry—as well as from a number of other similar international alliances taking place over the last three decades of the twentieth century (Morosini, 1998). By contrast, executives who overemphasize the mechanistic aspects of an alliance to the detriment of its social facets, might end up with brilliantly conceived alliances that are nevertheless poorly executed. Or perhaps, even worse, they might end up leveraging mechanistically upon the current strengths of the allies while missing out on the enormous benefits of imagining a shared future and delivering on that promise together through truthful and trustful cooperation.

In short, we have drawn inspiration from the Renault-Nissan alliance to propose new insights that might explain and predict better the stability and performance of all international alliances. Against the background of a dismal performance track record, we have found that nurturing an alliance organically and holistically to develop the social capabilities for trustful and truthful cooperation between the allies can lead to superior performance even across the most challenging cultural and organizational divides.

Appendix

Corporate alliances have had a dismal performance record over the last three decades of the twentieth century. Conventional mainstream theories are at odds to explain the reasons behind such poor performance results, especially in the case of alliances occurring across cultural and organizational divides. However, the success of the alliance between French Renault and Japanese Nissan provides a fresh view of these issues that might help other similar international partnerships achieve success across cultural and organizational boundaries. Renault-Nissan's experiences suggest three critical stages to build successful alliances across boundaries: *Servinacuy,* or social initiation; social commitment; and the building of a "common glue." (See Figure 15.1). In essence, this is a more holistic, organic, and continuous approach to alliance formation, negotiation, and implementation that pays special attention to the issues of social amalgamation between the joining companies.

1. *Servinacuy,* or social initiation, is about enacting a living experiment to test the allies' ability to collaborate and build a shared future

A number of companies carry out a "due diligence" evaluation of the potential synergy payoffs before signing an international alliance deal. However, these companies often find it difficult to achieve the expected synergies due to difficulties managing the cultural and organizational barriers in place during implementation. Instead, the Renault-Nissan approach was to carry out a rigorous, living experiment of collaboration and mutual discovery *before* starting negotiations. This provided a test of the allies' abilities to develop mutual trust, work cooperatively, imagine a future together, and deliver on the shared promises. This is a social initiation approach akin to *servinacuy,* the practice of cohabitation before marriage in ancient Peru.

2. Social commitment is *not* about signing a contract but rather about negotiating and formalizing the pledges made during *servinacuy*

Prospective allies from different cultural and organizational backgrounds that have not gone through *servinacuy* and have no history of working together would do well to incorporate the perceived implementation risks of their partnership into the negotiation phase. However, this often leads to a competitive negotiation spirit, with each partner seeking dominance over the other while at the same time avoiding domination by the other. By contrast, Renault's and Nissan's social initiation meant that they went to the negotiation table having already developed valuable assets in the form of mutual trust, social networks, the ability to work collaboratively, and the belief in a shared future that had been jointly imagined.

3. Building a "common glue" is about the allies developing the social capabilities to collaborate across boundaries

An abundant literature has documented the detrimental effects of cultural, professional, and organizational boundaries on the performance of alliances, especially as their scale and scope increase in size, complexity, and international coverage. Against this background, the common glue represents the social capabilities that build cohesiveness among an organization's pivotal executive cadres. An organization's common glue is made up of five distinct social capabilities, which together have a strong, positive impact on the competitive performance of organizations. The Renault-Nissan alliance provides a prime example of how a determined group of leaders can build a strong common glue that drives superior competitive performance across cultural and organizational boundaries. By contrast, similar combines, such as the DaimlerChrysler-Mitsubishi alliance (or the Daimler and Chrysler combine itself), decided not to build a strong common glue between the joining companies during the implementation stages, leading to disastrous performance results.

Notes

1. The term *alliances* is often given diverse meanings by different individuals, groups, and organizations. The uninhibited use of qualifying adjectives, e.g., "strategic alliances," "global alliances," or "cross-cultural alliances," only adds to the prevailing confusion. Therefore, from the outset an important consideration is terminology. No precise definition for the term "alliance" exists in international-management, business-law, or accounting literature. The best approximation to a definition is by contrasting and comparing alliances with international joint ventures (IJVs). On the one hand, IJVs are usually characterized as separate organizational and legal entities made up of parts of the parent companies' assets and headquartered in countries that are foreign from the perspective of at least one of the parents. The distribution of equity among the parent companies ranges from 50:50 IJVs to reduced-minority or dominant-majority stakes. On the other hand, alliances encompass a broader range of *collaborative* agreements from the point of view of both the assets that are committed to the partnership as well as the legal and organizational forms that can be found (e.g., with or without equity participation, and not necessarily involving separate legal entities). Thus, multiple networks of "strategic alliances," and "cross-cultural alliances" (that is, alliances taking place across culturally distant countries) are seen as comprising the global constellation of resources available to the multinational firm. The *collaborative* purpose of

alliances usually involves transaction-specific investments that are nonredeployable and nonsalvageable. The strategic aims of alliances have been categorized within the superordinate levels of management of the multinational firm. The taxonomies that are more often used range from "heterarchical" forms to "transnational corporations" and "multifocal" or "horizontal" multinationals.

2. In developing the approach suggested in Figure 15.1, I have followed methodological tenets that are akin to those of grounded theory. As the name itself suggests, this approach, introduced by the sociologists Barney Glaser and Anselm Strauss in 1967, is a qualitative methodology that generates theory from research that is "grounded" in data. Within the social sciences, grounded theory emerged as an alternative strategy to more conventional research approaches that relied heavily on hypothesis testing, verification techniques, and quantitative analysis. Grounded theory proposes a flexible, direct approach to research where both the subject under inquiry and the hypotheses emerge naturally and without much interference from a preestablished investigative framework on the part of the researcher. Hence, grounded theory tenets are particularly well suited to the task of looking at the phenomenon of international alliances–or any such subject, as a matter of fact—with new and fresh eyes. See Glaser, 1978, 1992; Glaser, & Strauss, 1967.

3. *Servinacuy* is still practiced in a number of Andean communities within Peru. Since antiquity, *servinacuy* has been assisted by phytotherapeutical contraceptive practices, and it was the man who had the formal prerogative of renouncing the subsequent step of marriage. However, in such cases he had to provide adequate compensation to his *servinacuy* partner. See Soriano, 1997. A modern, perhaps more liberal and egalitarian version of *servinacuy*-like practices was pioneered in Scandinavia during the late 1950s. It has become widespread in most Western societies ever since, not only as a social practice but also enshrined in many of these countries' codes of civil law.

References

Axelrod, R. (1984). *The evolution of cooperation.* New York: Basic Books.

Bacharach, S. B., & Lawler, E. J. (1981). *Bargaining power, tactics and outcomes.* San Francisco, CA: Jossey-Bass.

Beamish, P. W., & Killing, J. P. (Eds.). (1997). *Cooperative strategies,* vol. 3, *Asian Pacific Perspectives.* San Francisco: New Lexington Press.

Burt, T., & Harney, A. (1999, November 9). Le cost-killer makes his move. *Financial Times,* 19.

Das, T. K., & Teng, B. S. (2000). Instabilities of strategic alliances: An internal tensions perspective. *Organization Science, 11,*(1), 77–101.

de Saint-Seine, S. (2004). Interview with Renault's CEO Schweitzer. *Automotive News Europe, 9*(7), 10.

Dyer, J. H., Kale, P., & Singh, H. (2004, July/August). When to ally and when to acquire. *Top-Line Growth,* 109–115.

Edmondson, G. (1999, March 29). Dangerous liaison: Renault and Nissan. *Business Week.*

Emerson, V. (2001, Spring). An interview with Carlos Ghosn. *Journal of World Business,* 3–11.

Ernst, D., & Bleeke, J. (1994). *Collaborating to compete.* New York: John Wiley.

Franko, L. G. (1971). *Joint venture survival in multinational corporations.* New York: Praeger.

Ghosn, C. (1999, November 8). We don't have a choice [speech transcript]. *Automotive News,* 36–44.

Ghosn, C. (2002a, September 24). Global Leader Series, Speech at the European Institute of Business Administration, Fontainebleau, France.

Ghosn, C. (2002b). Saving the business without losing the company. *Harvard Business Review, 80*(1), 3–11.

Glaser, B. G. (1978). *Theoretical sensitivity.* Mill Valley, CA: Sociology Press.

Glaser, B. G. (1992). *Basics of grounded theory analysis.* Mill Valley, CA: Sociology Press.

Glaser, B. G., & Strauss, A. L. (1967). *The discovery of grounded theory: Strategies for qualitative research.* Chicago: Aldine.

Hauter, F., & Ghosn, C. (2001, July 2). En situation de crise, la transparence s'impose. *Figaro Enterprises,* 28–29.

Hirano, K. (1999, October 19). Tokyo stocks close mixed in thin trading. *Japanese Economic Newswire,* 1.

Hughes, K., Barsoux, J., & Manzoni, J. (2003). Redesigning Nissan (A): Carlos Ghosn takes charge. European Institute of Business Administration 303-044-1; (B): Leading change. European Institute of Business Administration 303-045-12003.

Ibison, D. (2001, July 27). Nissan puts merit before service. *Irish Times,* 63.

Inkpen, A. C., & Beamish, P. W. (1977). Knowledge, bargaining power, and the instability of international joint ventures. *Academy of Management Review, 22,* 177–202.

Jensen, M. C., & Meckling, W. H. (1976). Theory of the firm: Managerial behavior, agency costs and ownership structure. *Journal of Financial Economy, 3,* 305–360.

Kawato, N., & Ikematsu, H. (2000, January 27). Feelings mixed on "Ghosn reform." *Daily Yomiuri,* 18.

Kogut, B. (1989). The stability of joint ventures: Reciprocity and competitive rivalry. *Journal of Industrial Economics, 38,* 183–198.

Korine, H., Asakawa, K., & Gomez, P. Y. (2002). Partnering with the unfamiliar: Lessons from the case of Renault and Nissan. *Business Strategy Review, 13*(2), 41–50.

Larimer, T. (2001, January 15). Rebirth of the Z. *Time,* 18–20.

Mackintosh, J. (2004, March 29). Renault's long shot romps home. *Motor Industry,* 13–15.

Macneil, I. R. (1974). The many futures of contracts. *Southern California Law Review, 47,* 691–816.

Macneil, I. R. (1980). *The new social contract.* New Haven, CT: Yale University Press.

Miller, Z., & Zaun, T. (2002, April 5). Nissan intends to return favor to a French ally. *Asian Wall Street Journal,* A1.

Morosini, P. (1998). *Managing cultural differences.* Oxford: Pergamon Press.

Morosini, P. (2004a). Are mergers and acquisitions about creating value? In P. Morosini & U. Steger (Eds.), *Managing complex mergers.* Oxford: Financial Times/Prentice Hall.

Morosini, P. (2004b). Competing on social capabilities. In S. Chowdhury (Ed.), *Next generation business handbook,* (pp. 248–271). New York: Wiley.

Nuss, E. (2001). Why should we change? The Nissan revival plan. European Institute of Business Administration, *Business Link, 3,* 18–22.

Peterson, T. (2000, January 18). Nissan's Carlos Ghosn: "No ifs, no ands, no buts." *Business Week.*

Pfeffer, J., & Salancik, G. R. (1978). *The external control of organizations: A resource dependence perspective.* New York: Harper and Row.

Phelan, M. (2004, March 17). Retiring CEO says Renault-Nissan are poised for growth. *Tribune Business News.*

Porter, M. E. (1980). *Competitive strategy: Techniques for analyzing industries and competitors.* New York: Free Press.

Porter, M. E. (1985). *Competitive advantage: Creating and sustaining superior performance.* New York: Free Press.

Porter, M. E. (1990). *The competitive advantage of nations.* New York: Free Press.

Shirouzu, N., White, J. B., & Zaun, T. (2000, November 17). A revival at Nissan shows there's hope for Japan Inc. *Asian Wall Street Journal,* 1.

Soriano, W. E. (1997). *Los Incas, economia, sociedad y estado en la era del tahuantinsuyo.* Lima, Peru: Amaru Editores.

Taylor, A. (1999, December 20). The man who vows to change Japan Inc. *Fortune,* 73–77.

Thornton, E. (1999, November 15). Remaking Nissan. *Business Week,* 70–74.

Wickens, M. (2002, March 16). Nissan saviour a comic-book hero. *Toronto Star,* 25.

Williamson, O. E. (1975). *Markets and hierarchies: Analysis and anti-trust implications.* New York: Free Press.

Williamson, O. E. (1985). *The economic institutions of capitalism.* New York: Free Press.

Woodruff, D. (1999, March 31). Cultural chasm: Renault faces hurdles in bid to turn Nissan around. *Asian Wall Street Journal,* 1.

16

International Joint Ventures in Emerging Economies

Past Drivers and Emerging Trends

Jaideep Anand

Prashant Kale

International joint ventures (IJVs) are an important class of strategic alliances. In the past, IJV research has often led to important and general insights into issues of formation, dynamics, and success factors of strategic alliances. IJVs have also formed an important area of inquiry in the field of international business, particularly the study of emerging economies. Since the late 1980s and early 1990s, such joint ventures have been a particularly important element in the international strategies of many firms seeking entry into emerging economies (Beamish, Delios, & Lecraw, 1997). As a matter of fact, until recently, IJVs were the most common form of foreign direct investment (FDI) in emerging economies, accounting for over 50% of the total FDI in these regions (Contractor & Lorange, 1988; Beamish et al., 1997). International business and strategy literatures generally view interfirm joint ventures as a means to access and combine resources from different firms so as to achieve a set of individual and joint objectives for the partners (Beamish, 1985; Hennart, 1988).

In this chapter, in order to synthesize previous research and to understand current trends with respect to IJVs in emerging economies, we address the main motivations for the formation of these IJVs and examine the trends of driving forces. Research suggests that IJVs in emerging economies potentially depend on the need to meet government regulations or the need to access and combine resources that individual firms lack internally (Beamish, 1985; Contractor & Lorange, 1988). For instance, multinational partners seeking to enter emerging economies potentially depend on the local partner for local downstream resources, such as knowledge of the

AUTHOR'S NOTE: We are very grateful to Oded Shenkar for comments on an earlier draft.

local market, local distribution channels, and so on, and/or a means to meet local regulatory norms. On the other hand, local partners rely on their foreign counterparts for upstream resources, such as product technology and know-how. Because resource access and dependence lie at the heart of these ventures, the fate of future IJVs of this type and the survival of existing IJVs rest upon the salience and value of the resources of the respective partners in the IJV.

Recently, academic research (Desai, Foley, & Hines, 2002) as well as the popular press (*Economic Times,* 2003) has observed an increase in the termination of existing IJVs and a decrease in the formation of new IJVs as a mode of FDI. Extant research (Adarkar, Adil, Ernst, & Vaish, 1998) as well as our fieldwork indicates that IJV survival has become a particularly thorny issue following the liberalization of foreign entry and investment norms in emerging economies. India is a good example of such occurrence; increased termination of existing IJVs and a reduction in the formation of new IJVs have been observed in India, which began its liberalization in 1991 (*Business Today,* 1996; *Economic Times,* 2003; Ghoshal, 1998; Mukund, 2002; Vachani, 1995).

Building on this basic observation, we propose, first, that the forces of government regulation and resource complementarity have been weakening in the last few years. Economic liberalization of the business environment in emerging economies reduces the salience of the resources contributed by the local partner. Second, asymmetry in interpartner learning enables one of the partners, usually the multinational company (MNC) partner, to learn and acquire the resources provided by the other and thus reduce its dependence on the partner. As a result, both of these factors will adversely impact survival of existing IJVs and reduce the formation of new IJVs.

In the last few years, emerging economies such as China, India, and others have become an increasingly important part of the global business landscape. These economies have not only become important providers of low-cost goods and services, they have also provided large and rapidly growing markets. Because IJVs have been the most dominant form through which MNCs have joined hands with local players to exploit these opportunities, they have garnered a lot of attention from both practitioners and academics alike.

Our chapter helps understand the growth and decline of IJVs in emerging economies and, more broadly, sheds light on multinational business activity in these economies. We also draw out the implications of this trend for the study of international business and strategic alliances in general. For example, the arguments of our chapter also help to illustrate how the liability of foreignness, typically associated with MNCs or foreign companies entering emerging economies, has become less of an issue in the context of the ongoing liberalization of the business environment in most emerging economies.

International Joint Ventures in Emerging Economies

Often, organizations are not internally self-sufficient in terms of the resources that are necessary for successfully undertaking their businesses. In such cases, they access these resources through other organizations in their external environment. They often formalize these relationships by creating interfirm joint ventures when the resources in question are important or difficult to access or when there is some uncertainty regarding their access (Pfeffer & Nowak, 1976). Joint ventures are useful devices for mobilizing resources from other organizations in the environment and managing the subsequent resource interdependence with the environment.

Emerging-market IJVs are essentially the result of such resource interdependence between the foreign and local partners engaged in them. IJVs are formed between MNCs and their local counterparts. These ventures are formed when each partner firm possesses some but not all of the requisite resources and capabilities to compete in a market. The two IJV partners may contribute distinct and complementary resources to the IJV (Beamish, 1985). A large proportion of these IJVs, however, are not formed solely to access complementary resources of the partner firm. Many emerging markets have traditionally had severe government restrictions on foreign entry, ownership, and control; therefore, joint ventures have often been the only viable mechanism for MNCs wishing to do business in such markets (Beamish, 1985; Blodgett, 1991; Contractor & Lorange, 1988; Gomes-Casseres, 1990). Prior research has not examined these issues in detail, despite some comparison of "restrictive" and "nonrestrictive regimes" in the literature (Gomes-Casseres, 1987).

Firms form IJVs in emerging markets for a variety of reasons. For example, IJVs may be formed to facilitate entry into these markets, to access local capabilities to compete in these markets, to reduce potential competition, to access low-cost factor inputs from these economies, and so on (Contractor & Lorange, 1988). Although strategic alliances and joint ventures can facilitate entry into all kinds of markets, the inefficiency of markets and the salience of local connections in IJVs play an even more important role in emerging economies. Based on these objectives, two broad classes of IJVs are observed in these economies: (1) market-entry IJVs that are formed between foreign firms and local players to facilitate entry of foreign players into these markets, and (2) export-oriented IJVs that are formed by foreign companies with local partners to access low-cost factor inputs from these markets (Anand & Delios, 1996). Other kinds of IJVs with more than two partners or formed between two foreign partners also exist, but rarely.

Local Regulations and Liberalization

International Joint Venture Formation as a Response to Regulation

Governments of most emerging economies have traditionally placed many restrictions on foreign firms' entry and ownership in their economies. Generally, these restrictions first existed at the economywide level, whereby foreign ownership and investment were discouraged across most industries or sectors (Ahluwalia & Little, 1998). In cases where entry was permitted, foreign firms were not able to have 100% or majority control of the business; instead, regulations required them to enter only through joint ventures with local companies as partners (Blodgett, 1991). Other restrictions included limitations on repatriation of profits, employment of expatriates, majority control or positions on IJV boards, and so on. The period when such regulations existed in emerging markets is generally referred to as the preliberalization period (Ghemawat & Khanna, 1998). Although these restrictions were generally present at the economywide level, there were some differences across industry sectors. But although such intersector variations did exist, the general trend across sectors exhibited severe regulatory constraints on foreign entry and ownership.

Given these restrictions in most emerging economies, MNCs keen to enter these economies during their preliberalization period formed IJVs with local partners to meet the regulatory norms guiding foreign entry and participation in local business (Blodgett, 1991; Kobrin, 1982). Foreign partners were able to operate in such an environment only through the local partner's statutory participation and presence in their business. The ability to help the foreign partner meet entry norms was, in fact, one of the most critical resources provided by local partners to the IJV. Local partners also provided the local regulatory know-how necessary to run a business. Consequently, these IJVs also provided legitimacy to the foreign partner in local markets (Baum & Oliver, 1991), especially with respect to the regulatory and bureaucratic apparatus in these economies. In summary, before liberalization, the emphasis was on meeting the requirements imposed by local regulations and obtaining local access.

Recent Liberalization and Its Effects

Recent liberalization in many of these economies has generally entailed the lessening of restrictions on trade and business investment. In this chapter, we refer to liberalization as the opening of foreign direct investment and the removal or dilution of restrictions on foreign entry and ownership in the economy (Ahluwalia, 1994; Ahluwalia & Little, 1998; Ghemawat & Khanna, 1998). In many cases, such as India in 1991, the liberalization was economywide; it seems that most industries experienced this liberalization, although its extent and rate may have varied somewhat across different sectors (Ahluwalia & Little, 1998). In some cases, such liberalization was also accompanied by a reduction in barriers allowing local firms to expand further within their existing businesses or enter into new businesses. Many economies in Asia, Latin America, and Eastern and Central Europe have recently experienced such liberalization, and some are undergoing this process presently. Liberalization, in effect, increases the salience of economic considerations over political ones, and the implications of these reforms for firms (and their IJVs) cannot be underestimated or trivialized (Carman & Dominguez, 2001).

The implications for MNCs' entry-mode choices are that IJVs are no longer mandated in many of these economies and are therefore likely to become less popular, even though local governments may continue to encourage local participation by providing other incentives. MNCs may prefer to make acquisitions of local firms or set up de novo investments. But the implications of this fundamental regulatory change are not limited to new IJVs; it may also adversely impact the survival of existing IJVs. For example, recent experiences in China reveal that many state-owned enterprises (SOEs) can now sell out their stakes in IJVs to the foreign partners in response to financial constraints. The liberalized environment permits the foreign partner to take over the IJV.

North (1990) points out that there has to be a correspondence between the external environmental conditions and firms' internal organizational attributes. This interaction between the external environment and organizations plays an important role in shaping the governance and growth of organizations (North, 1990). The ability of firms, including IJVs, to "achieve congruence with the changing business environment" (Teece, Pisano, & Shuen, 1997, p. 515) is key to the transformation in emerging economies. Organization theorists (e.g., Stinchcombe, 1965; Mitchell, 1994) have argued that changes in the external environment may adversely impact organizational survival by creating a mismatch between firms' resources and the external environment.

We believe this is likely to be the case for some IJVs in emerging economies. Following liberalization it became easier for MNCs, from a regulatory standpoint, to enter and do business in emerging economies on their own. In many cases, they were not required to have local ownership and participation in their business. In a few cases, if local participation was still required, foreign partners were permitted to hold majority (greater than 50%) ownership in these ventures or at least a much greater stake than previously permitted. Liberalization, therefore, suddenly reduced the salience of an important resource traditionally contributed by local partners, namely, the ability to meet regulatory norms on foreign entry/investment. This has undermined the value added by many local partners and reduced the dependence of the foreign partner on them. Effectively, there is a mismatch between the needs of the new, external environment and one of the main resources provided by local IJV partners. This was particularly true of preliberalization IJVs. Consequently, if local partners have little to offer besides the ability to meet regulatory norms, the survival of many IJVs, especially those formed in the preliberalization period, is threatened.

Liberalization of the economy is generally also accompanied by an increase in competition in that economy (Mukherjee & Sengupta, 2001; Carman & Dominguez, 2001). This happens for two reasons. First, liberalization makes it easier for new entrants to enter any industry or business because of the removal or easing of regulatory restrictions on entry. Second, liberalization permits existing players to expand further into their existing industries or businesses. In emerging-economy contexts, these two factors give rise to an increase in competition of two kinds: increase in foreign competition, and increase in competition from local players. Lifting the barriers to foreign entry, investment, and ownership makes it easier for MNCs and foreign firms to participate in the economy. Therefore, we may observe a marked increase not only in the absolute number of foreign competitors in various industries but also in the proportion of foreign competition in the industry.

Following liberalization more foreign players are likely to enter the market, not only as an immediate response to the regulatory relaxation that permits such entry, but also because liberalization sends a positive signal about the future. Foreign entrants may perceive the decision to liberalize as a precursor to a more open and fair business environment that fosters higher-growth opportunities in the local market. It may also create confidence that if liberalization creates higher economic growth, as is expected (Mukherjee & Sengupta, 2001), local government is less likely to roll back many of the relaxations put in place. In the longer term, liberalization may lead to the evolution of more competitive local firms.

Resource Complementarity and Learning Races

In the section above, we highlight the role of the local firms' presence and participation in order to meet regulatory norms as a resource that creates interfirm dependence between local and foreign firms. Other resources, however, may also create interdependence between IJV partners, and it may be useful to examine their role in IJV survival. For instance, prior research has indicated that resource complementarity between partners positively influences alliance formation and success (Harrigan, 1988; Contractor & Lorange, 1988; Parkhe, 1991).

Resource Complementarity as a Driver of International Joint Venture Formation

One firm may lack all the necessary resources or capabilities across the business value chain and therefore may form a partnership with another firm to access the necessary resources that it lacks. When joint venture partners contribute distinct resources or capabilities relevant to managing adjoining aspects of the value chain, they are said to exhibit resource complementarity (Contractor & Lorange, 1988; Parkhe, 1991). An example of this would be when one partner provides the product or product technology and the other partner provides resources to market that product.

FDI theory reveals that MNCs typically have advantages in globally fungible resources, such as technology, product know-how, and other intangibles such as brand equity (Hymer, 1976; Caves, 1996), which they exploit to enter or expand into overseas markets. But if they lack a local presence in these markets, they cannot fully exploit these advantages (Hymer, 1976; Zaheer, 1995; Kostova & Zaheer, 1999). By partnering with local firms through IJVs, however, they can access downstream resources they lack, such as local channels of distribution (Killing, 1983; Anand & Delios, 2002) and local market know-how (Blodgett, 1991; Inkpen & Beamish, 1997). Such partnerships also help foreign firms overcome their liability of newness or foreignness in these markets (Zaheer, 1995) and reduce the risk of failure associated with the entry.

Conversely, IJV researchers have also argued that local firms in emerging economies often lack key resources, such as capital, technology, and managerial expertise (Peng, 1999), and often partner with foreign MNCs to access these resources (Pan, 1996; Lyles & Steensma, 1997; Lyles, Sulaiman, Barden, & Kechik, 1999). Collectively, the foreign and local partners potentially contribute distinct resources required to successfully manage the upstream and downstream parts of the value chain respectively. These resource contributions complement each other so as to create mutual benefits for the partners and cement a mutual interdependence between them that leads to a continued relationship.

Firms need adequate amounts of both upstream and downstream resources to compete successfully and survive in their markets (Teece, 1986). Therefore, MNCs will continue with IJVs only if their local partner provides valuable complementary resources and/or skills, and vice versa. However, if the partners feel that the resource complementarity is not sufficiently high, they will be inclined to terminate their partnership. This will be particularly true when IJVs operate in a postliberalization business environment in emerging economies (Shenkar & Luo, 2004). This is because in such contexts, resource complementarity is a more important and salient aspect driving interfirm IJVs as compared to the salience of regulatory restrictions that mandate IJVs between foreign partners and their local counterparts. In the absence of regulatory constraints, firms are more likely to form and remain in IJVs only if there is high resource complementarity between them. On the other hand, if resource complementarity is low, they have less incentive to continue with the IJV. For example, we observed that out of 17 prominent IJVs terminated in India after liberalization began in 1991, all but one were from the preliberalization period.

Interpartner Learning

Although IJV partners may contribute distinct but complementary resources to the IJV, their respective resources can evolve over time. One partner may potentially acquire the resources provided by the other through other means, such as internal development or purchase of discrete resources (Capron, Dussauge, & Mitchell, 1998), or, more important, by learning and internalizing them from its counterpart in the joint venture. In fact, many scholars view joint ventures and alliances as de facto learning opportunities to acquire and internalize valuable capabilities and skills possessed by the partner (Hamel, 1991; Lane & Lubatkin, 1998; Inkpen & Beamish, 1997). If such learning takes place across IJV partners, it can reduce the resource dependence between them and subsequently lead to termination of the relationship.

Organizational learning theory suggests that learning (in alliances) depends on several factors. It is linked not only to partners' learning intent (Hamel, 1991) but also to their respective learning capacity (Khanna, Gulati, & Nohria, 1998). Thus, asymmetrical outcomes are not uncommon in the case of IJVs (Luo, Shenkar, & Nyaw, 2001). Learning capacity comprises several factors. It includes processes that firms use to facilitate learning, such as assigning individuals clear roles and responsibilities to learn specific things (Ghoshal, 1987; Gupta & Govindarajan, 1991; Inkpen, 1998), rotating managers between the IJV and parent (Gupta & Govindarajan, 2000), and implementing systems to share internally and disseminate the information and know-how learned from the IJV or partner (Hamel, 1991; Inkpen, 1998). It also includes the firm's managerial and technical competencies necessary to learn from the partner, as well as investments by the firm to build the skills that enable learning from the partner.

Because learning may be an important objective for partners in emerging-economy IJVs that bring together complementary resources of partners (Dussauge, Garrette, & Mitchell, 2000), these IJVs may often degenerate into a "learning race" between them. Scholars argue that partners often exhibit significant asymmetry or difference in their respective learning rates based on their respective intents and capacities (Khanna et al., 1998). Generally, one partner may have greater ability to learn from the alliance and its counterpart than the other does. *Learning differential* refers to the difference in partners' respective learning intent and capacity. The greater the learning differential between partners, the greater the asymmetry in their learning and subsequently the more likely that one partner will soon outlearn the other. Subsequently, when one partner learns the resources and capabilities of the other, it alters the state of interdependence between partners. The partner that eventually wins this learning race will have little incentive to continue the alliance.

A liberalized business environment, with its lack of regulatory requirements for foreign and local partners to remain in the IJV, will witness such learning races. This environment provides an incentive for a learning race to unfold in both pre- and postliberalization IJVs because a partner with greater learning intent/capacity can abandon the IJV relationship and proceed alone once it learns key resources from its counterpart. Of course, this learning may not be useful if the economy continues to experience arbitrary changes in regulation. In that case, the foreign firm's local connections and social capital may be more relevant sources of advantage.

In our field studies we find that the foreign partner wins such learning races in emerging-market IJVs. This is because, as we observed in our fieldwork, the MNC partner generally scores much higher on learning capacity and intent as compared to the local partner. Also, because the IJV resides in the local market, it may be easier for the foreign partner to learn context-specific capabilities of its counterpart. In contrast, the local player may often not be in a similar position to learn and internalize technological know-how, which resides primarily with the foreign parent outside the IJV (Gupta & Govindarajan, 2000). Also, as some researchers have suggested, local players simply lack the absorptive capacity (Cohen & Levinthal, 1990) to internalize such knowledge (Lane & Lubatkin, 1998). Consequently, in most emerging market IJVs, the foreign partner outlearns its local partner and, having done so, has little incentive to remain in the IJV.

Control and Survival of Existing International Joint Ventures

In the section above we discuss how resource contributions by IJV partners and resource dependence, or lack thereof, between them influence the survival of these ventures. According to IJV literature, resource contributions and resource dependence also influence the amount of relative control partners can or would like to exercise in a particular IJV (Killing, 1983). We believe that this relationship between contributions and control in turn has the potential to influence the survival propensity of these ventures.

Researchers have generally shown great interest in studying the distribution of IJV control between partners.[1] Attention has been placed on studying both factors that influence the distribution of IJV control and the subsequent impact of that control. Two sets of factors seem to influence IJV control. First, the nature of the regulatory regime that might lay down specific guidelines regarding control and may be subject to unanticipated changes (Blodgett, 1991), which is a particularly salient aspect of emerging economies; and second, the nature or magnitude of resources contributed by IJV partners (Harrigan, 1988; Yan & Gray, 1994). We argue that in the absence or weakening of the first factor, that is, when there are no or less regulatory restrictions on how much control any one partner could have, the second factor, namely the resources contributed by respective partners, will become a more salient factor in the consideration of IJV control.

The resource-dependence perspective (Pfeffer & Salancik, 1978) and its extension, the bargaining power perspective (Yan & Gray, 1994), have been very relevant in explaining IJV control. These theories have argued that power in interorganizational relationships such as IJVs stems from resources possessed and contributed by respective partners. The relative bargaining power of IJV partners presumably rests upon two aspects of their resource contributions: the nature of the resources contributed by the respective partners, and/or the relative magnitude of their resources contributions (Blodgett, 1991). A partner that contributes resources that are more critical or salient in the context of the relationship and/or that contributes greater resources to it will perceive itself as having greater bargaining power. Consequently, it will seek greater control over the IJV. Greater control can provide several benefits. First, if a firm has greater control over the IJV, it can better ensure that the resources it contributes are being appropriately used in the IJV and/or are not being misappropriated by the partner. Second, by virtue of gaining greater control over the IJV, the firm can earn proportional returns for the resources that it contributes.

In the case of IJVs in emerging economies, this has two implications. First, some prior researchers have suggested that foreign partners that generally contributed upstream resources such as technology, product, or product know-how provided more critical resources to the IJV than the local partner that provided mainly the downstream resources (e.g., Lecraw, 1984; Blodgett, 1991; Gomes-Casseres, 1990). Therefore, the foreign partners would have greater bargaining power and subsequently greater control over the IJV. Many emerging economies, by virtue of their severe restrictions on the extent of foreign ownership and control before liberalization, limited the amount of decision-making control that foreign partners could exercise. In such environments, higher bargaining power based on more critical resource contributions did not necessarily translate into greater IJV control. Consequently, if a particular foreign partner was keen to enter this market, it might still form an IJV and continue with it in spite of lesser control because it had limited alternatives for entering that market. If the business environment is liberalized, however, foreign partners would wish to increase their control over IJVs, given the nature of their resource contributions; and if unable to get commensurate control, they might even be willing to discontinue the IJV because they may now have alternatives to doing business in that market.

The above argument, based on the differences in the "nature" of resource contributions, can also be extended to difference in the "magnitude" of resource contributions made by partners. If for instance, one partner makes greater contribution of resources into the IJV than its counterpart, it would expect commensurate, that is, greater control, over the IJV. If a foreign partner, however, were to make greater resource contributions while regulatory restrictions on foreign ownership and control were present, its control would be limited irrespective of its actual contributions. But once the market is liberalized, foreign partners in both types of IJVs—those that were formed before liberalization and those that were formed later—would seek greater control if they made greater resource contributions; and if such commensurate control were not possible, they might terminate their IJVs.

Implications

Implications for New and Existing International Joint Ventures

We discuss above two broad drivers of IJV formation in emerging economies—government regulation and complementary resources. Both these aspects have significant implications for both existing IJVs and new IJVs.

From a regulatory standpoint, as government regulations become less stringent with liberalization in many of the emerging economies, the survival of many existing IJVs will be threatened. This is because liberalization has clearly obviated the role of the local partner in helping MNC entrants meet traditional entry and ownership restrictions in many emerging economies—hence foreign partners may not wish to continue partnering with local players for this reason and thereby adversely affect the survival of their IJVs with such partners. In addition, in many such situations, foreign partners may not continue to invest new resources in their extant IJVs, thus hurting the competitiveness of these ventures and threatening their survival. Relaxation of regulatory norms also has implications for future IJVs in that, absent the pressure of regulatory restrictions on forming JVs for entry into emerging economies, MNCs will simply be reluctant to form new IJVs for this purpose in the future—thus formation of new IJVs is likely to decrease in the future. Further, the formation of IJVs may also diminish from a real options point of view if the market evolution of an economy presents less uncertainty than that inherent in changes in regulation or politics.

From the point of view of complementary resources, if local partners' resources, apart from their ability to help the foreign partner meet local regulatory norms, are complementary and important to the foreign partner in any particular venture, the foreign partner will help such an IJV survive. Such resources would generally include local market know-how, access to local distribution channels, and so on that complement the foreign partners' resource contributions in terms of its product know-how, technology, and so on. Contribution of these complementary resources relevant to adjoining aspects of the value chain increases resource dependence between partners and consequently will increase the likelihood of existing IJV survival. But, as we also discuss above, for existing IJVs to survive, it is important for IJV partners to distribute control commensurate with their contributions. With liberalization, and possibly due to local learning by the foreign partner, the relative contribution of the local partner is likely to diminish. Flexibility in negotiating or renegotiating control of the IJV may enhance the chances of survival for the IJV. As far as new IJVs are concerned, they will be formed only based on genuine complementarity of resources between the proposed partners.

Implications for Multinational Companies

The factors of regulatory liberalization, resource complementarity, and learning in IJVs also have several implications for both MNCs and local emerging-economy firms. For MNCs, liberalization has not only opened up more choices for investments in emerging economies but also has reduced their reliance on local firms. First, due to ongoing liberalization, many MNCs can now enter most emerging markets without having to form JVs with local players. However, MNCs may still want to form JVs, lack of regulatory restrictions notwithstanding, because such ventures do offer MNCs a temporary opportunity to learn and acquire the resources/skills of their partner so as to alter the resource dependence between them over time; and once they have completed such learning, they can terminate their IJVs.

But MNCs also need to recognize that there are subsequent implications of this approach. Many local firms have been aware of the "learning race dynamics" in emerging-economy IJVs and thus have become more hostile and wary of forming new IJVs with MNCs. Hence, even if MNCs are keen to form IJVs with local players going forward, they will have to be ready for a hostile/cold response to such actions on the local players' part.

Due to the continuing changes in emerging economies, MNCs are better able to integrate their country operations with their global network (Anand & Delios, 1996). Greater ownership stakes, liberalization of trade, and superior communication infrastructure in recent years has meant that MNCs do not need self-contained local operations that were once the norm in restrictive economies. Instead, these firms can now optimize across their global supplier and customer chains more easily. Smaller international firms without the resources to manage local regulations and IJVs may also now participate in emerging-economy opportunities.

Implications for Local Firms

There are several implications for local firms are several. First, they need to recognize that one of their primary contributions, that is, ability to help the MNC partner meet local regulatory norms, has clearly become less salient following liberalization. Hence, MNCs will form IJVs with them only if they offer meaningful, complementary assets to their foreign partner. Second, in such cases, however, local players clearly need to recognize the dangers of an asymmetric learning race between the MNC and local partner in such IJVs—and many local players increasingly recognize this; in response, they have two options; either they can avoid forming such IJVs in the future or they can take proactive steps to *win the learning race that they have traditionally lost* or at least try to keep it more symmetrical. Here, local players in emerging markets can benefit by learning from the IJVs between U.S./Western MNCs and their Japanese or Korean partners during the late 1980s (Hamel, 1991).

In contrast to what has happened in emerging-market IJVs, in those 1980s IJVs the local Japanese/Korean companies seemed to learn more and faster than their MNC counterparts. One can speculate that this difference among countries is linked to the operating environments and management philosophies of these companies respectively. Prior research has documented that Japanese/Korean companies were very keen to establish international presence and leadership in their business. Therefore, they often formed IJVs with MNCs explicitly to learn from them and invested effort in developing their learning capacities for this purpose and adopting an export-oriented strategy (Hamel, 1991). In contrast, at least until recently, local companies in many current emerging economies seemed content with doing business within their long-protected local markets without a sufficiently strong desire to build superior capabilities or operating efficiencies to compete extensively in international markets (Ghoshal, 1998; Adarkar et al. 1998). This in turn influenced the development of their competencies and their focus on building a strong capacity to learn from their foreign counterpart. Thus, local players not only need to realize their learning disadvantage but, more important, they need to address this shortcoming either by increasing their own learning capacity so as to win the learning race or at least by devising means to control their partners' learning opportunities through governance, contracts, or regulatory arrangements and preserve their mutual resource dependence.

Of course, there is another way to view this whole "learning race" situation in IJVs. In the discussion so far, we suggest that when one partner has a much higher learning-intent capacity than its counterpart (i.e., there is a high learning differential between them), it can use that to reduce its resource dependence on the partner and thereby threaten IJV survival. But what happens if both partners have high learning intent and capacity, and the learning differential between them, as a result, is relatively low? It is possible that in such situations, too, IJV survival might be threatened; in fact, if both partners learn to perform the best capabilities of their counterpart, the IJV might end even faster than otherwise. However, in such situations, other interpartner dynamics might also hurt IJV survival. If both partners fiercely engage in the learning race, it might create more tensions/conflicts between them, accelerate the growth of mistrust, and so on.

Implications for International Business and Strategic Alliances

In a more general sense, this study also sheds some light on theory and practice in international business and strategic alliances. The study of IJVs in emerging economies has been an important area of study in international business and strategic alliances. This research has led to important developments in theories of multinational management and strategy. It is interesting to note the response of IJVs to reduced regulation in emerging economies—it provides a natural experiment to weigh the relative effects of regulation and complementarity in capabilities and reveals the large impact that government regulations have had on the formation and continued use of IJVs. This natural experiment also reveals that although previous political and government policy uncertainties in these economies had a large effect on the nature and magnitude of FDI, present economic uncertainties due to the rapid pace of changes in many of these emerging economies is less of a deterrent to investment.

At the same time, this natural experiment fosters understanding of the contributions provided by local partners other than helping to meet regulatory demands. We continue to witness the formation and survival of IJVs in the liberal environment of Hong Kong—not in response to government regulation but due to a true complementarity in capabilities. It is possible that some MNCs may not want to play the learning race and may prefer instead to use the division of labor between the two partners to specialize. The changes in many emerging economies also provide a fertile setting to test many aspects of changes in contributions and control by local and international partners. For example, are IJVs with more asymmetrical control more likely to survive than those with symmetrical control by partners?

Scholars have often observed that foreign entrants are handicapped by a *liability of foreignness* in international domains (Zaheer, 1995). We observe that in emerging economies, MNCs have been able to reduce their liability of foreignness in two different ways. First, the ongoing relaxation of regulatory restrictions on foreign entry and ownership implies that as far as local regulatory/political authorities are concerned, they increasingly view MNCs more positively, thereby reducing the likelihood of any adverse impact that MNCs' "foreign origin" might have on MNCs' business prospects in the country. Second, the learning-race dynamics shows us that from a resource and capability standpoint, too, if MNCs use these IJVs as a means to quickly learn and acquire locally relevant knowledge and skills from their local joint venture partner, they can operate in the local market on their own at a later stage. Both these factors show that even in emerging-economy contexts, the liability of foreignness typically perceived for MNC entrants has become a less relevant and/or more temporary phenomenon.

The reduced salience of the liability of foreignness also implies that firms are less devoted to local issues and proportionately are more involved with global optimization of their business operations. Because less attention is needed for country-specific barriers and regulations, firms are better able to function as a seamless unit, being able to exploit arbitrage opportunities arising due to differences in country endowments and markets (Anand & Delios, 1996).

Further, the nature of this liability of foreignness is also likely to change: emphasis on meeting regulatory norms and procedures to seek legitimacy is diminishing, while emphasis on good management of the subsidiaries and integration with the global network is enhanced. As the emerging economies become more familiar to MNCs and the observed cultural, socioeconomic, and institutional barriers recede, one would expect the liability of foreignness to continue to decrease as well. But this does not imply that we shall necessarily see the complete disappearance of IJVs in these contexts. IJVs could remain quite popular even in some economies that otherwise provide unrestricted access and do not require local ownership. These contexts would include those, for example, where the cultural, institutional, or socioeconomic conditions continue to require unique resources. These may also include specific societies characterized by thicker interpersonal or interfirm networks and where access to these networks plays an important role in doing business.

Fewer IJVs in emerging economies does not necessarily imply fewer strategic alliances between MNCs and local firms. In fact, the number of strategic alliances might increase. In other words, although equity-oriented arrangements such as IJVs may be diminishing, partnerships with local firms for procuring local supplies and inputs, technology (both for global exploitation and local customization), and horizontal partnerships may increase substantially. Such changes imply that governance mechanisms are shifting toward nonequity contractual arrangements. This trend is also consistent with the perception of greater transparency and fewer appropriation hazards in emerging economies, because equity arrangements have been one way to mitigate such hazards (Gulati & Singh, 1998).

A critically important feature of emerging economies is greater uncertainty. This includes greater behavioral, legal, and political uncertainty, among others, and is at least one dimension that separates emerging-economy contexts from others. In the past, this emphasis on uncertainty has led to adoption of opportunism and transaction-cost-based frameworks, not only in emerging economies but in international business in general. For example, theories of FDI and international strategic alliances generally emphasize the potential hazards of opportunism and safeguards against appropriation (Caves, 1996; Gulati & Singh, 1998). With regulatory reform and reduced information asymmetry, it seems that the emphasis on these elements may also diminish. Instead, researchers are beginning to emphasize the role of capabilities and coordination (Kogut & Zander, 1996). In this sense, theories of international business and FDI are now beginning to converge with other theories of the growth of firms.

Conclusions

IJVs have traditionally been an important organizational form of doing business in most emerging economies. This has been true for both regulatory reasons and resource-based reasons, and MNCs that wish to enter these markets and local players that are from these markets have relied on this organizational form. But recent trends show that most extant IJVs between MNCs and local players are increasingly becoming unstable and often end up in termination, and that new IJVs are being formed at a lower rate than before. This paper explores how relaxation of the regulatory environment in these markets and the asymmetrical learning-race dynamics between MNCs and local partners in these IJVs both explain these trends and show how both these factors, at least until now, have stacked up mostly in favor of MNCs.

In exploring these aspects, this paper also sheds light on two other important topics traditionally discussed in the international business and alliance literature in general. From an international business perspective, it shows how the liability of foreignness typically associated with foreign firms' entry in new markets is increasingly becoming a less relevant phenomenon in emerging economies.

As far as the general alliance research is concerned, although this article discusses emerging-market IJVs, it contributes to understanding some important alliance dynamics in general. It shows that to understand the evolution of alliances in general, it is very important to examine how both external market factors (the regulatory liberalization of emerging markets in this case) and internal firm factors (the asymmetrical learning capabilities in this case) have a joint impact on how an alliance evolves over time and how and why it might lead to termination eventually.

Note

1. IJV control has been studied in terms of partners' relative control over IJV equity and, more important, control over important or strategic decisions in the IJV. Some researchers also view equity control as a proxy for decision-making control.

References

Adarkar, A., Adil, A., Ernst, D., & P. Vaish. (1998). Emerging market alliances: Must they be win-lose? *McKinsey Quarterly, 4,* 121–137.

Ahluwalia, M. S. (1994). India's quiet economic revolution. *Columbia Journal of World Business, 29*(1), 6–12.

Ahluwalia, I. J., & Little, I. M. D. (1998). *India's economic reforms and development: Essays for Manmohan Singh.* Delhi: Oxford University Press.

Anand, J., & Delios, A. (1995). India: A dream deferred or a dream shattered. *Business Quarterly, 60*(2), 22–27.

Anand, J., & Delios, A. (1996). Competing globally: How Japanese MNCs have matched goals and strategies in India and China. *Columbia Journal of World Business, 31*(3), 50–62.

Anand, J., & Delios, A. (2002). Absolute and relative resources as determinants of international acquisitions. *Strategic Management Journal, 23*(2), 119–134.

Baum, J. A., & Oliver, C. (1991). Institutional linkages and organizational mortality. *Administrative Science Quarterly, 36,* 187–219.

Beamish, P. (1985). The characteristics of joint venture in developed and developing countries. *Columbia Journal of World Business, 20*(3), 13–19.

Beamish, P., & Banks, J. C. (1987). Equity joint ventures and the theory of the multinational enterprise. *Journal of International Business Studies, 18,* 1–17.

Beamish, P., Delios, A., & Lecraw, D. J. (1997). *Japanese multinationals in the global economy.* Basingstoke, UK: Edward Elgar.

Bleeke, J., & Ernst, D. (1993). *Collaborating to compete.* New York: Wiley.

Blodgett, L. (1991). Partner contributions as predictions of equity share in international joint ventures. *Journal of International Business Studies, 22,* 63–78.

Bradach, J. L., & Eccles, R. G. (1989). Markets versus hierarchies: From ideal types to plural forms. *Annual Review of Sociology, 15,* 97–118.

Business Today. (1996). Why the P&G and Godrej alliance broke up.

Capron, L., Dussauge, P., & Mitchell, W. (1998). Resource redeployment following horizontal acquisitions in Europe and North America, 1988–1992. *Strategic Management Journal, 19*(7), 631–661.

Carman, J., & Dominguez, L. (2001). Organizational transformations in transition economics: Hypotheses. *Journal of Macromarketing, 21*(2), 164–180.

Caves, R. (1996). *Multinational enterprise and economic analysis* (2nd ed.) Cambridge, UK: Cambridge University Press.

Cohen, W. M., & Levinthal, D. A. (1990). Absorptive capacity: A new perspective on learning and innovation. *Administrative Science Quarterly, 35*(1), 128–153.

Contractor, F. J. (1990). Ownership patterns of U.S. joint ventures abroad and the liberalization of foreign government regulations in the 1980s: Evidence from the benchmark surveys. *Journal of International Business Studies, 21*(1), 55–73.

Contractor, F., & Lorange, P. (1988). Why should firms cooperate? The strategy and economics basis for cooperative ventures. In F. Contractor & P. Lorange (Eds.), *Cooperative strategies in international business.* Lexington, MA: Lexington Books.

Desai, M., Foley, F., & Hines, J. (2002). *International joint ventures and the boundaries of the firm.* Working Paper, Harvard Business School.

Dhanaraj, C., & Beamish, P. W. (2001). *Legitimacy and mortality in overseas subsidiaries.* Working Paper, Indiana University.

Doz, Y. (1996). The evolution of cooperation in strategic alliances: Initial conditions or learning processes? [special issue]. *Strategic Management Journal, 17,* 55–83.

Dussauge, P., Garrette, B., & Mitchell, W. (2000). Learning from competing partners: Outcomes and durations of scale and link alliances in Europe, North America and Asia. *Strategic Management Journal, 21*(2), 99–126.

Economic Times. (2003, April 16). Finmin to make it tougher for foreign companies to exit local JVs.

Geringer, J., & Hebert, L. (1989). Control and performance of international joint ventures. *Journal of International Business Studies, 20*(2), 235–254.

Ghemawat, P., & Khanna, T. (1998). The nature of diversified business groups: A research design and two case studies. *Journal of Industrial Economics, 44*(1), 35–61.

Ghoshal, S. (1987). Global strategy: An organizing framework. *Strategic Management Journal, 8,* 425–440.

Ghoshal, S. (1998). Don't get taken for a ride. Corporate dossier. *Economic Times.*

Gomes-Casseres, B. (1987). Joint venture instability: Is it a problem? *Columbia Journal of World Business, 2,* 97–102.

Gomes-Casseres, B. (1990). Firm ownership preferences and host government restrictions. *Journal of International Business Studies, 21*(1), 1–23.

Gulati, R. (1995). Does familiarity breed trust? The implications of repeated ties for contractual choice in alliances. *Academy of Management Journal, 38,* 85–112.

Gulati, R. & Singh, H. (1998). The architecture of cooperation: Managing coordination costs and appropriation concerns in strategic alliances. *Administrative Science Quarterly, 43*(4), 781–814.

Gupta, A. K., & Govindarajan, V. (1991). Knowledge flows and the structure of control within multinationals. *Academy of Management Review, 16*(4), 768–792.

Gupta, A. K., & Govindarajan, V. (2000). Knowledge flows within multinational corporations. *Strategic Management Journal, 21,* 473–496.

Hamel, G. (1991). Competition for competence and interpartner learning within international strategic alliances. *Strategic Management Journal, 12*(1), 83–103.

Harrigan, K. R. (1988). Joint ventures and competitive strategies. *Strategic Management Journal, 9,* 141–159.

Hebert, L., & Beamish, P. (1997). Characteristics of Canada-based IJVs. In P. Beamish & P. Killing (Eds.), *Cooperative strategies.* San Francisco: New Lexington Press.

Hennart, J. (1988). A transaction cost theory of equity joint ventures. *Strategic Management Journal, 9,* 361–374.

Hitt, M., Dacin, M. T., Levitas, E., Arregle, J. L., & Borza, A. (2000). Partner selection in emerging and developed market contexts: Resource-based and organizational learning perspectives. *Academy of Management Journal, 43,* 449–467.

Hymer, S. (1976). *The international operations of national firms: A study of direct foreign investment.* Cambridge: MIT Press.

Kale P., Dyer, J. H., & Singh, H. (2002). Alliance capability, stock market response, and long-term alliance success: The role of the alliance function. *Strategic Management Journal, 23*(8), 747–767.

Inkpen, A. (1998). Knowledge management processes and international joint ventures. *Organization Science, 9*(4), 454–468.

Inkpen, A., & Beamish, P. (1997). Knowledge, bargaining power, and the instability of international joint ventures. *Academy of Management Review, 22*(1), 177–203.

Kale, P., & Singh, H. (1999). Building alliance capability: A knowledge-based approach. *Academy of Management Best Paper Proceedings.* Chicago: Academy of Management.

Kale, P., Singh, H., & Perlmutter, H. (2000). Building relational capital: Learning and the protection of proprietary assets. *Strategic Management Journal, 21*(3), 217–238.

Khanna, T., Gulati, R., & Nohria, N. (1998). The dynamics of learning alliances: Competition, cooperation and relative scope. *Strategic Management Journal, 19*(3), 193–210.

Khanna, T., & Palepu, K. (1999, July). The right way to restructure conglomerates in emerging markets. *Harvard Business Review,* 125–134.

Killing, P. (1983). *Strategies for joint venture success.* London: Croom Helm.

Kobrin, S. (1982). *Managing political risk assessment: Strategic response to environmental change.* Berkeley and Los Angeles: University of California Press.

Kogut, B., & Zander, U. (1996). What firms do? Coordination, identity, and learning. *Organization Science, 7*(5), 502–518.

Kostova, T., & Zaheer, S. (1999). Organizational legitimacy under conditions of complexity: The case of the multinational enterprise. *Academy of Management Review, 24*(1), 64–81.

Lane, P. J., & Lubatkin, M. (1998). Relative absorptive capacity and interorganizational learning. *Strategic Management Journal, 19,* 461–477.

Lecraw, D. J. (1984). Bargaining power, ownership, and profitability of transnational corporations in developing countries. *Journal of International Business Studies, 1,* 27–43.

Lin, J., Yu, C. M., & Seetoo, D. (1997). Motivations, partner contributions and control of international joint ventures. In P. Beamish & P. Killing (Eds.), *Cooperative strategies.* San Francisco: New Lexington Press.

Luo, Y., Shenkar, O., & Nyaw, M. K. (2001). A dual parent perspective on control and performance in international joint ventures: Lessons from a developing economy. *Journal of International Studies, 32*(1), 41–58.

Lyles, M. A. (1988). Learning among joint venture sophisticated firms. *Management International Review, 28,* 85–99.

Lyles, M. A., & Steensma, H. (1997). *An examination of social exchange and knowledge based theories in explaining IJV performance and survival in a transitional economy.* Research Papers in Management Studies. Working Paper 38/97, Cambridge University.

Lyles, M. A., Sulaiman, M., Barden, J., & Kechik, A. (1999). Factors affecting international joint venture performance: A study of Malaysian joint ventures. *Journal of Asian Business, 15,* 1–20.

Macaulay, S. (1963). Non-contractual relations in business. *American Sociological Review, 28,* 55–70.

Manral, L. (2001). Technology transfer and the spillover effect to local firms: Evidence for India. *Academy of Management Executive, 15*(2), 129–130.

Mitchell, W. (1989). Whether or when? Probability and timing of incumbents' entry into emerging industrial subfields. *Administrative Science Quarterly, 34,* 208–230.

Mitchell, W. (1994). The dynamics of evolving markets: The effects of business sales and age on dissolution and divestiture of start up firms and diversifying entrants. *Administrative Science Quarterly, 39,* 575–602.

Mjoen, H., & Tallman, S. (1997). Control and performance in international joint ventures. *Organization Science, 8*(3), 257–273.

Mowery, D. C., Oxley, J. E., & Silverman, B. S. (1996). Strategic alliances and interfirm knowledge transfer [special issue]. *Strategic Management Journal, 17,* 77–92.

Mukherjee, A., & Sengupta, A. (2001). Joint ventures versus fully owned subsidiaries: Multinational strategies in liberalizing economies. *Review of International Economics, 9*(1), 163.

Mukund, A. (2002). *Kinetic Honda–the break-up.* European Case Clearing House Case Collection.

North, D. (1990). *Institutions, institutional change, and economic performance.* Cambridge, UK, and New York: Cambridge University Press.

Pan, Y. (1996). Influences of foreign equity ownership level in joint ventures in China. *Journal of International Business Studies, 27,* 1–26.

Park, S., & Russo, M. (1996). When competition eclipses cooperation: An event history analysis of joint venture failure. *Management Science, 42*(6), 875–891.

Parkhe, A. (1991). Interfirm diversity, organizational learning, and longevity. *Journal of International Business Studies, 22,* 579–602.

Peng, M. (1999). *Business strategies in transition economies.* Thousand Oaks, CA: Sage.

Pfeffer, J., & Nowak, P. (1976). Joint-ventures and interorganizational interdependence. *Administrative Science Quarterly, 21*(3), 398–413.

Pfeffer, J., & Salancik, G. (1978). *The external control of organizations.* New York: HarperCollins.

Reich, R. B., & Mankin, E. (1986, January/February). Joint ventures with Japan give our future away. *Harvard Business Review,* 45–53.

Reuer, J., & Koza, M. (2000). Asymmetric information and joint venture performance: Theory and evidence for domestic and international joint ventures. *Strategic Management Journal, 21*(2), 195–197.

Ring, P. S., & Van de Ven, A. H. (1992). Structuring cooperative relationships between organizations. *Strategic Management Journal, 13,* 483–499.

Schendel, D. E., & Hofer, C. W. (1979). *Strategic management: A new view of business policy and planning.* Boston: Little, Brown.

Shenkar, O., & Luo, Y. (2004). *International business.* Hoboken, NJ: Wiley.

Shenkar, O., & Zeira, Y. (1992). Role conflict and role ambiguity of chief executive officers in international joint ventures. *Journal of International Business Studies, 23*(1), 55–87.

Stinchcombe, A. L. (1965). Social structure and organizations. In J. G. March (Ed.), *Handbook of organizations.* Skokie, IL: Rand McNally.

Teece, D. J. (1986). Profiting from technological innovation. In D. J. Teece (Ed.), *The competitive challenge: Strategies for industrial innovation and renewal.* New York: Harper & Row.

Teece, D. J., Pisano, G., & Shuen, A. (1997). Dynamic capabilities and strategic management. *Strategic Management Journal, 18*(7), 509–533.

Thomas, A. S., & Annamma, P. (1994). India: Management in an ancient and modern civilization. *International Studies of Management & Organization, 24*(1,2), 91–115.

Tushman, M. L., & Anderson, P. (1986). Technological discontinuities and organizational environments. *Administrative Science Quarterly, 31,* 439–466.

Vachani, S. (1995). Enhancing the obsolescing bargain theory: A longitudinal study of foreign ownership of U.S. and European multinationals. *Journal of International Business Studies, 26*(1), 159–180.

Wernerfelt, B. (1984). A resource-based view of the firm. *Strategic Management Journal, 5,* 171–180.

Yan, A. (1998). Structural stability and reconfiguration of international joint ventures. *Journal of International Business Studies, 29*(4), 773–796.

Yan, A., & Gray, B. (1994). Bargaining power, management control and performance in United States-China joint ventures: A comparative case study. *Academy of Management Journal, 37*(6), 1478–1517.

Zaheer, S. (1995). Overcoming the liability of foreignness. *Academy of Management Journal, 38,* 341–363.

Zaheer, A., McEvily, B., & Perrone, V. (1998). Does trust matter? Exploring the effects of interorganizational and interpersonal trust on performance. *Organization Science, 9,* 1–10.

PART V

Nontraditional Strategic Alliances

17

Alliances in the New Economy

Lalit Manral

Kathryn Rudie Harrigan

Does the rationale and role of alliances in the "new economy" differ from those in the "old economy"? The answer to this question assumes fundamental importance in light of the lack of clear understanding among academic researchers and practitioners alike regarding the optimal strategies and structures underlying competitive advantage in the "new economy." The genesis of this lack of consensus is traceable to two unrelated and unresolved issues. First, the conceptualization of "new economy" vis-à-vis the "old economy" is quite vague.[1] Although the distinction has been a major issue in the practitioner literature since the early 1990s, the academic literature has not accorded it a formal acceptance. The attribute of "new economy" industries of greatest interest herein is the nonphysical nature of assets. Second, the narrow range of theoretical/analytical tools not only restricts the classification of only certain types of hybrid organizational structures as alliances but also constrains the detailed exposition of the underlying rationale for their existence.

The extant literature on alliances—which straddles disciplinary and functional boundaries that separate sociology of organizations, transaction cost economics, strategy, and organizational theory—provides the objectives and consequences of alliances. The "strategic behavior" perspective addresses the strategic concern of a firm, wherein the decision to form an interfirm alliance is often the outcome of the make-or-buy decision arising due to various reasons, such as the need to access complementary assets, reduce risk due to environmental uncertainty, and so on (e.g., Williamson, 1975, 1991; Teece, 1986; Harrigan, 1986). On the other hand, the "social structural" perspective addresses the choice of partners by focusing on the firm's social context, which internalizes the information on the availability, competencies, and reliability of prospective partners (Granovetter, 1985, 1992; Useem, 1984; Palmer, Friedland, & Singh, 1986; Mizruchi & Stearns, 1988; Gulati, 1995b; Walker, Kogut, & Shan, 1997). In this perspective, alliances are influenced by interdependence and network embeddedness, contingent on the level of structural differentiation of the social system in which the firms are embedded (Gulati & Gargiulo, 1999).

However, the literature fails to provide a logical explanation for the paradoxical behavior of many de novo Internet-based firms. While suggestive of the "new economy" imperatives for firm strategy and structure, this paradoxical behavior is aided by a particular mode of organizing, which corresponds to the level of opportunism that a focal firm is willing to embrace. During the initial (formative) stage of their life cycles, a large number of Internet-based firms are embedded in a network of opportunistic alliances, which is paradoxical. It is so because by indulging in opportunistic alliances—to harness the power of market forces to develop, manufacture, market, distribute, and support their products—they erode their value as collaborators. But in contrast to conventional theories of strategy and organization, by resorting to multiple opportunistic partnerships these de novo Internet-based firms develop collaborative capabilities. These collaborative capabilities enable the de novo Internet-based firms not only to establish themselves at the center of a network of opportunistic alliances but also possibly to convert it into a network of long-term strategic alliances.

In light of the emergent phenomena, we seek to provide, in addition to the above-mentioned supply-side arguments, an additional "demand-side" explanation to account for the myriad ephemeral alliances formed by such Internet-based firms. To do so, we borrow extensively from network economics, which explains how demand-side industry conditions—of increasing returns to adoption—tend to make some products more attractive the more they are adopted. The increased demand at individual product level due to increased consumption of the same product is referred to as direct network effect, whereas it is referred to as indirect network effect when it is due to increased consumption of the whole cluster with which the product is associated. Hence, we argue that Internet-based firms act to exploit the inherent indirect network externalities at the product-cluster level by forming as many opportunistic alliances with as many firms as possible. By doing so, they seek to achieve costless coordination and influence consumer expectations about the potential size of the network of consumers to influence market outcome in their favor. There are also issues of "virtuality"—easy entry via outsourcing of tasks to form a spider's web with a conceptual firm at the hub.

First, we briefly explain how digitization of firm processes, a salient feature of Internet-based firms, has transformed the way firms do business. This new way of doing business has been referred to as the "new economy" in the popular press. Second, we review the literature that explains how firms use alliances to cope with complexity and/or uncertainty in their technological environment. The literature explains how and why alliances are critical for the coevolution of organizational form with the environmental context. Third, we analyze why the relevance of this predominantly supply-side literature seems to blur when applied to the context of a large number of Internet-based firms. We conclude that explaining the paradoxical structure and conduct of these Internet-based firms requires some modification of the assumptions underlying the broad perspectives in this literature. Fourth, we explain the opportunistic strategy underlying the structure and conduct of Internet-based firms. Fifth, we provide a unique alternate explanation for the opportunistic alliances formed by Internet-based firms. According to this perspective, Internet-based firms form short-term opportunistic alliances to exploit the demand-side externalities. Finally, we discuss the implications of this study and future of research on alliances within the broader context of strategy research.

Digitization of Firm Processes

The incorporation of Internet technologies into organizational routines has indubitably transformed and significantly broadened the strategic options of Internet-based firms. The competitiveness of Internet-based firms stems from reduced transaction costs, increased global market reach, and new ways to create mass customization and personalization of products and services (Choi, Stahl, & Whinston, 1997). For instance, electronic commerce (e-commerce), which represents just one aspect of how the Internet has transformed the way Internet-based firms do business, has extended the reach (local to global), increased response speed (customer and partner interaction), and reduced transaction costs (search, coordination, and contracting) of firms, as information flows through the Internet are richer and faster.

The most important technological feature that characterizes the Internet-based firms and underlies their competitiveness in e-commerce is the digitization of firm processes. Digitization of firm processes is an evolutionary transformation of the processes both inside and outside the firm through the incorporation of Internet technologies into organizational routines. It means transformation from "managing atoms to managing bits, where managing atoms involves manipulation of physical assets: stockpiling inventory, shipping products, buying equipment, installing machinery, building factories, etc., and managing bits involves manipulation of information: gathering, analyzing, modeling, sorting, sharing & replicating data" (Slywotzky & Morrison, 2000). Firms differ in terms of the extent of digitization of their business processes. For instance, one firm may concentrate on just online interaction with customers through digital order processing, another may use the Internet to streamline its production system, yet another may do so for inventory management, and some may do so for a combination of these activities.

The benefits of digitization of firm processes also depend upon whether a firm transacts fully on the Internet; that is, whether the focal firm is an Internet pure play. For instance, the Internet-based firms that transact fully on the Internet reap the benefits of not only capturing demand in real time but also transmitting the same digitally to other participants in the value net (Slywotzky & Morrison, 2000; Barua, Pennell, Shutter, & Whinston, 2000).[2] Doing so enables them to exploit economies of both scale and scope. On the other hand, Internet-based firms that use the Internet as a complementary/supplementary medium in addition to (or in place of) existing channels and offline processes do so to develop and maintain a learning (or experience) curve by establishing strong linkages with other firms in their value network (Bovet & Martha, 2000).

Effective digitization of business processes requires that firms develop or adopt applications that facilitate electronic linkages for coordination and collaboration with partners (Slywotzky & Morrison, 2000).[3] This is because digitizing isolated firm processes that do not have any interface with other firm processes or activities defeats the very spirit underlying digitization—real-time information management across intra- and inter-firm boundaries. It therefore corresponds to an increased ability of a firm to form multiple opportunistic alliances. This is because once the processes themselves are modular, a firm's choice concerning make-or-buy decisions is dictated by the efficiency and value generated by the combination of such processes within a value network of opportunistic partners.

It then becomes imperative to understand how Internet-based firms cope with the paradoxical requirement imposed by their desire to digitize their processes. It would be interesting to know not only how digitization has contributed to this unexplored transformation of firm structure and conduct but also the strategy that underlies the choice of digitization. In this chapter, we propose that the choice of extent (or level) of digitization is indeed endogenous and depends on the propensity of firms to embrace opportunism in the e-space.

Strategy in the New Economy

The structure and conduct of Internet-based firms pose a challenge to researchers in strategic management for more reasons than one. First, both the success and the failure of Internet-based firms in terms of their ability to generate wealth have been attributed to technology more than any other factor, as compared to firms in any other industrial sector. This implies that much is not known about the structural and behavioral factors that underlie the success of some Internet-based firms and not others. Further, researchers have also not adequately explored the specificity of mechanisms that underlie the success of Internet-based firms in generating wealth. That is, why have some firms succeeded in generating wealth under conditions of inescapable and rapid technological change, while others perished?

The contribution of technology to creation of wealth has been acknowledged ever since Adam Smith theorized the generation of wealth as that occurring through economic growth; the technical basis of growth was the existence of a mechanism whereby output progressively increased (e.g., Caton, 1985). Recognizing a fundamental feature of the industrial era—that of falling price per unit output based on exponential growth obtained by technological applications—Schumpeter (1934) postulated that wealth is generated through the accumulation of entrepreneurial profit, which occurs due to a recombination of the means of production. The ability of firms to survive, grow, and create wealth in a complex technological environment—characterized by continuously evolving consumer preferences and technological capabilities—depends on its capability to develop new products and new methods of organizing (Schumpeter, 1942).

The efficacy of a particular mode (or method) of organizing is jointly determined by "local efforts," that is, self-help, craft mechanisms, and as a function of the "institutional environment," that is, polity, judiciary, property rights laws, and contract (Williamson, 1999). The governance perspective (Coase, 1937; Williamson, 1975, 1985, 1991, 1999) describes strategy as choosing between three distinct modes of economic organization of firm activities: market, hybrid, and hierarchy. The three generic forms are distinguished by different (1) coordination and control mechanisms, (2) abilities to adapt to environmental disturbances, and (3) underlying contract law. A firm chooses a particular form of governance depending upon the characteristics of the particular transaction(s). The basic idea behind choosing a particular governance mode is to minimize transaction costs.

However, what is important and remains largely unexplained is how firms cope with the complexity of their technological and demand environment in the short run. That is, how do de novo entrants in nascent industries choose the appropriate mode of organizing under conditions of high technological and demand uncertainty? The total effect of the complexity of the technological and demand environment on firms at any instant can be attributed to two sets of contrasting forces. The factors that contribute to the complexity—which are discussed in the next section—constantly and continuously undermine and erode the distinct processes underlying the success of competing Internet-based firms. On the other hand, the complexity is attenuated by the cumulative and specific nature of the processes of learning and development of organizational competencies on both the supply and demand side. In the long term, firms manage the complexity of their technological and demand environment—the contextual condition of firms—by rapidly coevolving their organizational form with technological change and demand shift.

Complexity of the Technological Environment

The environmental context of a firm changes continuously (Emery & Trist, 1965) due to the impact of such forces: technological change, global competition, policy, and shifting consumer preferences (e.g., Levinthal, 1997; Singh, 1997). The literature in organization theory uses the term *complex environment* loosely to refer to the combined system of internal and external environment of a firm, characterized by rapid technological change and, consequently, adoption of complex structural features resulting in heterogeneous organization types (Dill, 1958; Thompson, 1967; Terreberry, 1968; Dess & Beard, 1984; Meyer & Scott, 1983).

The complexity of a firm's technological environment is attributable to the occurrence and possibility (existing and future states) of many factors that constantly and continuously undermine and erode the distinct processes underlying its success. First, rapid technological change in the form of technological discontinuity, which could be "competence enhancing" or "competence destroying," affect incumbent firms' long-term performance by enhancing environmental uncertainty (e.g., Tushman & Anderson, 1986). Second, even continuous innovation in product and process technologies by competitors could slowly erode a firm's existing market position (e.g., Balkin, Markman, & Gomez-Mejia, 2000). Third, emergence of disruptive technologies that originate outside the existing technological paradigm could in the long run challenge incumbent firms' market position by triggering new markets altogether (e.g., Bower & Christensen, 1995; Christensen, 1997). Fourth, a difficult learning environment—due to the complexity of the knowledge requirement—may obfuscate the critical issues required for success (e.g., Cohen & Levinthal, 1990). Finally, the context specificity of firm competencies not only undermines their ability to adapt to radical or disruptive technological changes (Nelson, 1991), but also prevents the latter from being easily transferred and used in other problems and applications (Winter, 1987).

The failure of firms to manage the increased complexity of the technological environment is attributable to such factors as organizational inertia, marketing myopia, or insufficient resources (Christensen & Bower, 1996). A major reason is that incumbent firms hesitate to invest in development of new routines—to negotiate the complexity of their technological environment—because of a fundamental disconnect with the existing market-based resource-allocation process (Christensen, 1997). Further, even if successful firms may have financial resources to invest in development or even outright adoption of new routines, they may find themselves at a disadvantage—vis-à-vis new entrants—to the extent that the new routines are not based on existing competence (Tushman & Anderson, 1986; Winter, 1987; Nelson, 1991).

Managing the complex technological environment involves developing efficient and highly effective monitoring, screening, and information-processing systems (Ashby, 1956). This not only enables firms to manage the environmental uncertainty, but also enhances their ability to scan a greater environment. This ability helps firms to anticipate, react, and respond to environmental change by reassessing their organizational goals (Thompson & McEwen, 1958) and aligning their structures with the changed environment (Katz & Kahn, 1966). In simple words, in the long term, firms come to terms with the complexity of their technological environment due to the coevolution of their organizational forms with the technological environment (Tushman & Anderson, 1986).

Coevolution of Technology and Organizational Form

Technology is a fundamental force that contributes not only to environmental variation but also in shaping organizational forms (Tushman & Anderson, 1986). Extraordinary challenges posed by the environment in the form of rapidly changing technology force firms to respond in terms of reevaluating and repackaging their set of capabilities (Levinthal, 1997). Firms reconfigure their organizational forms to increase their ability to respond to changes in the external environment brought about by technological developments both within and outside. One should not confuse this reconfiguration—of, say, the asset structure, or even internal and external transformation by successful firms in dynamic environments—as a series of temporally independent short-term strategic maneuvers. In doing so, the organizational life cycle of such firms can be thus mistakenly viewed as a sum of various short-run survivals with different alliance partners, products, technologies, markets, and organizational forms.

The dynamic capabilities approach (Teece, Pisano, & Shuen, 1997)[4] hits the nail on the head precisely by highlighting the competitive advantages of successful firms stemming from their capacity to renew competences in response to the rapidly changing contextual condition. It attributes the difference in the abilities of firms to create and capture wealth to the "distinctive processes" shaped by the firms, "asset positions," and the "evolution paths adopted." The strategic management of successful firms in a complex technological environment therefore involves adapting, integrating, and reconfiguring internal and external organizational skills, resources, and functional competences to match the requirements of a changing environment (Teece et al., 1997). Similarly, the strategic flexibility approach is characterized by the ability of firms to shape and reshape clusters of assets in distinct and unique combinations needed to serve ever-changing customer needs (Harrigan, 1985, 1988). However, according to both the above-mentioned perspectives, a critical condition that underlies the ability of firms to manage the complexity of their technological environment is guaranteed access to valued resources.

Collaborative Capabilities

A firm's access to valued resources is determined by the structural context of its network relationships (e.g., Kogut, Shan, & Walker, 1992; Podolny, 1993; Han, 1994; Gulati, 1995b; Gulati & Gargiulo, 1999). Embeddedness not only enhances a firm's probability of survival but also enables it to shape economic action by creating unique opportunities and obligations and access to those opportunities (Uzzi, 1996). Firms that are centrally located within the web of interaction have greater control over relevant resources and enjoy a broad array of benefits and opportunities unavailable to those on the periphery of the network (Ahuja, 2000).

Businesses developing products based on complex technologies face a higher risk of failure in the short-term—ceasing operations and exiting their industry—than businesses developing less technologically complex products (Singh, 1997). This is due to the systemic nature of complex technologies, wherein the entire system may become obsolete due to obsolescence of a few components. However, organizational form can influence business survival by assigning or outsourcing some activities to other organizations. This approach to complex technologies simplifies intraorganizational processes, replacing them with interorganizational ones. The internal simplification for the focal organization comes at the expense of introducing external and more complex interorganizational relationships (Singh, 1997).

A large number of firms in the high-technology sector outsource most of their manufacturing to ensure strategic flexibility so that they can quickly ramp up production without having to worry about building factories or hiring people. They can also ramp down more easily if demand slackens, reducing the need for layoffs during hard times. Companies are increasingly outsourcing even such activities as customer-management functions, including billing and customer help-desk operations, in order to focus on their core competencies and reduce investment in rapidly changing technologies. This serves the purpose of both the suppliers and buyers quite well.

In other words, a critical capability required of a firm for managing the complexity of its technological environment in the short-term is collaborative capability. Collaborative capabilities define a firm's value and ability as a collaborator by instantiating and refining routines for synergistic partnering (Powell, Koput, & Smith-Doerr, 1996). In simple words, a firm's competence in forging alliances with all and sundry leads to what can be defined as its collaborative capability. The ability of firms to build alliances at a rapid pace depends on the extent to which they have routinized the process of forming interfirm linkages and the ease with which these routines can be replicated and transferred to new contexts. What are the capabilities, if any, required of a firm to be able to routinize the replication of the routines that underlie its portfolio of successful interfirm alliances?

The Paradox of Internet-Based Virtual Firms

A large number of de novo Internet-based firms have adopted a unique organizational form, a variant of the virtual-firm model, to manage the dynamic nature of their environment in the short term. Harrigan (2001) describes this variant of a virtual-firm arrangement as a transitory business arrangement en route to a new strategic posture and new industry cluster structure. An Internet-based virtual firm—in contrast to a traditional virtual firm that subcontracts most of its core activities—is essentially a hybrid form[5] of economic organization that also utilizes the market form of governance (Jonas, 1985; Bettis, Bradley, & Hamel, 1992). It is thus supported by both classical and neoclassical contract laws.[6] This paradoxical structural arrangement is facilitated by an equally paradoxical conduct wherein the Internet-based virtual firm combines strategic alliances with arm's-length contract manufacturing and spot-market transactions for outsourcing of both components and services.

According to the strategic behavior and social structural perspective, the phenomenon of the evolution of virtual firms can be explained as an organizational response to environmental uncertainty caused by various factors such as rapidly changing technological capabilities that are further accentuated by additional factors such as information asymmetry. Thus, action of market players under conditions of uncertainty and imperfect information is guided by the use of the network of interorganizational relationships. Firms aim at reducing uncertainty through embedded partnerships. The evolution of a virtual mode of governance[7] is accompanied by an increased ability of the focal firm to take risks and a decreased ability to settle conflicts and coordinate activities (Chesbrough & Teece, 1996). Long-term contracts with limited clauses[8]—characteristic of the hybrid form of governance—require special adaptive mechanisms to affect realignment and restore efficiency when exposed to unanticipated disturbance (Williamson, 1991). Given this backdrop, the widespread adoption of a variant of the virtual-firm model in the "Internet economy" presents an interesting paradox.

The Internet-based virtual firm—as distinct from a traditional virtual-firm model—is a logical arrangement that merits a distinct and discrete position between the market and the hybrid forms of governance because of a lack of satisfactory way of characterizing organizations in terms of continuous variation over a spectrum (Ward, 1967; Williamson, 1991). By retaining the control mechanisms within its boundary while moving out the activities and their coordination—thereby minimizing asset specificity—an Internet-based virtual firm gains the superior ability of the market form of governance to respond to uncertainty. At the same time, the Internet-based virtual firm does not shed its hybrid character. It moves the physical activities and their coordination outside the boundary of the firm by relying on a network of alternate or multiple vendors.

It forms opportunistic alliances with these vendors on a transaction-to-transaction basis by operating through the electronic markets, which embody the spirit of one-shot transaction, that is, auction. By virtue of its centrality in the value network, an Internet-based virtual firm is able to control (1) the customer touch points (ordering, service, and sometimes delivery), and/or (2) the information, knowledge, and relationships associated with the various activities. While the former enable it to be free to outsource everything else (the inner firm processes), the latter enable it to maintain control of analytical, relationship-building, and partner-management skills (Bovet & Martha, 2000).

An Internet-based virtual firm outsources most of the activities that comprise its value chain while still maintaining overall control (Hagel & Singer, 1999). Characterized by minimal physical asset ownership and hence reduced mobility barriers, an Internet-based virtual firm tends to collaborate freely with any firm in any way by using any kind of business arrangement that may be expedient for the case at hand (Harrigan, 2001). It acts as an effective systems integrator and seeks ways to control an industry's value network by placing itself centrally (Rayport & Sviokla, 1995; Harrigan, 2001). An Internet-based virtual firm enjoys opportunistic freedom in the web of relationships and flexibility of temporary and nonbinding alliances (Ahuja & Carley, 1999), uses loosely coupled transactions (Granovetter, 1985), and establishes performance-based relationships with value-net partners (Bovet & Martha, 2000) in order to implement its strategy effectively.

An Internet-based virtual firm outsources activities both to drive value and to lower costs (Harrigan, 2001). It captures demand in real time and transmits the same digitally to other participants in the value net (Slywotzky & Morrison, 2000). It derives economies of scale, scope, experience, and vertical integration by establishing strong linkages with firms in its value network (Barua et al., 2000). The competitive advantage of this approach lies in forging advantaged relationships with trading partners, knowing and fulfilling customer needs, anticipating future requirements, using online customer knowledge to create new products and services, designing pricing and promotion schemes that match customers' willingness to pay, and building network-based alliances and partnerships (Barua et al., 2000).

A necessary condition for the evolution of virtual mode of governance is that the focal firm be embedded in a network of interorganizational relationships (Ahuja & Carley, 1999). An Internet-based virtual firm is embedded in a network of opportunistic alliances and is thus a paradox, because by indulging in opportunistic alliances—to harness the power of market forces to develop, manufacture, market, distribute, and support its products—it erodes its value as a collaborator. Although neoclassical economics highlights the possibility of instrumental rationality being subordinated to embedded action, this opportunistic conduct of an Internet-based virtual firm contradicts not only the theory of economic organizations (Williamson, 1991) but also the strategic behavior (Harrigan, 1985; Teece, 1986) and social structural perspectives (Walker et al., 1997; Gulati & Gargiulo, 1999).

The virtual-firm model lends itself to an interesting metamorphosis in the Internet economy due to the propensity of Internet-based virtual firms to form short-term opportunistic alliances along with long-term strategic alliances. The conduct of Internet-based virtual firms is paradoxical from the strategic behavior perspective, which posits that interorganizational ties are characterized by bilateral dependency that results in some form of enduring commitment between the partners. It is also paradoxical according to the social structural perspective, which posits that a network emerges out of an accumulation of interfirm alliances by helping the embedded firms decide with whom to form new alliances. Internet-based virtual firms have demonstrated superior ability to generate wealth by adopting this paradoxical structure and conduct. In the next section, we seek to explain the strategy that underlies this paradoxical structure and conduct.

E-Space Opportunism

The short-term behavior of Internet-based virtual firms can be summarized as dynamically traversing the imagined continuum[9] between markets and hierarchies, albeit nearer the market end of the continuum (Figure 17.1). The exact position of an Internet-based firm on the continuum can be specified as a function of the opportunism that it is willing to embrace in the e-space. We consider opportunism to be an optimal firm strategy wherein—contrary to the assertions of comparative economic organization or transaction cost

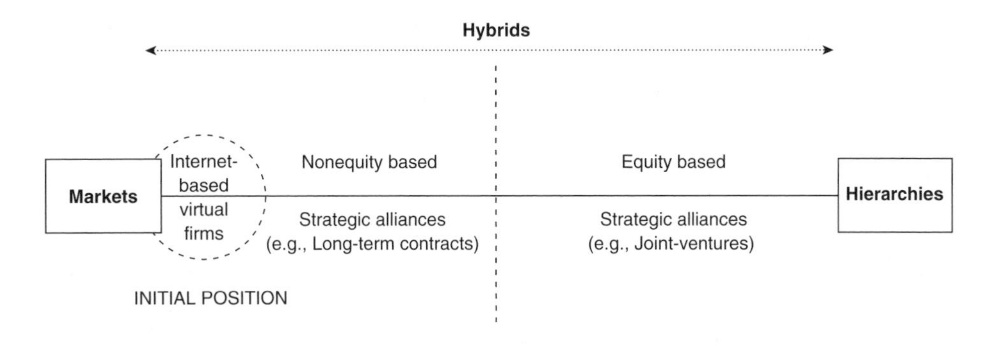

Figure 17.1 An Internet-Based Virtual Firm

economics—firms can act as needed to carry out the same types of transactions under different organizational modes depending upon the stage of the firm's life cycle or that of its industry. Thus, de novo firms in nascent industries transact in a highly virtual and collaborative manner to survive the initial ferment.

Comparative economic organization, or transaction cost economics, involves comparative analysis of transaction costs between predominantly three modes of organizing—markets, hybrids, and hierarchies (Williamson, 1991). The most important assumption underlying the principal assertion in this stream of thought is that an actor can calculate transaction costs under each type of governance and compare them. Under a dynamic information-intensive environment, characterized by uncertainty of myriad nature—namely, technological, demand, and policy—firms cannot compare the transaction costs due to lack of complete information.

Technological complexity affects the choice of governance of a de novo entrant in a nascent industry in two ways. First, the focal firm may not be in a position to compare the actual cost of transaction under different modes of organizing and hence may be unable to arrive at a conclusion regarding which mode to choose because of a lack of knowledge concerning costs—both within and outside the organization—due to the newness of the industry. Second, even if the focal organization does learn the cost of transactions after a certain period, the complexity of the technological environment renders it obsolete, as costs keep changing with time.

Tautological as it may initially seem,[10] the conceptualization of opportunism as an explanatory construct underlying the opportunistic behavior of Internet-based firms does indeed serve its purpose of explaining the superior performance of such Internet-based firms. A more detailed exposition on the nature and/or various types of opportunism as a firm strategy would merely deflect the focus of this chapter away from alliances. Hence, it suffices to argue that an Internet-based firm's willingness to embrace opportunism in the e-space determines the virtuality of its organizational structure, the asset intensity of its activities, and the level of digitization of its business processes.

Among the universe of Internet-based firms, the most opportunistic ones would prefer to carry out their entire gamut of transactions through the market, which is practically infeasible. They therefore adopt a mix of transactions: market, short-term opportunistic alliances, and longer-lived strategic alliances based on technologies or other standardization attributes. The ability of firms to adopt a mix of transactions can be attributed to the extent or level of digitization across the business components of a firm's business model, strategies, and processes. Transition from managing physical activities to managing information, that is, vertical to virtual governance, involves establishment of linkages with other firms to manage the focal firm's physical activities by outsourcing those functions. Internet-based firms do this by using spot-market transactions or entering into alliances—short-term opportunistic alliances (involving more commitment than spot-market transactions) or strategic alliances (involving high levels of commitment).

The choice of the level of digitization of firm processes corresponds to the propensity of firms to embrace opportunism in the e-space. Digitization of firm processes determines the success of a firm in terms of the network structure developed by it. A higher level of digitization of firm processes enhances a firm's attractiveness as a potential partner because it increases the scope of activities that can be outsourced by the firm. Further, the fact that the Internet deals with creation, storage, processing, dissemination, and sharing of information and knowledge indicates a higher viability of Internet-based firms offering intangible products and services as compared with firms that sell tangible products over the Internet (e.g., Choi et al., 1997). This suggests that firms' choice of organizing mode depends in part on the nature of products or services offered via the Internet, for reasons developed below.

Physical proximity to buyers becomes irrelevant for goods that can be produced anywhere and delivered over the Internet. On the other hand, the e-retailer still needs to dispatch tangible products physically, as opposed to digital products, which are deliverable online. Firms are motivated to establish a Web-based presence as a surrogate for physical distribution channels due to its cost advantage vis-à-vis the latter; the Web-based presence is also more suitable for selling digital products. Firms that sell products or services in digital format (e.g., information-intensive products over the Internet) digitize particular firm processes to do so. That is, the extent of digitized infrastructure required is higher in the case of digital products or services than for physical products or services. It would be clearer to consider the sum total of firm processes to be equal in both types of products or services. Now, firms that serve digital products or services are a couple of levels higher on the digital value chain than firms that serve physical products over the Internet. Thus, firms that deal with tangible products will feel less motivated to adopt virtual organizational structure. Hence, the tangibility of the products offered by the focal firm determines the extent to which it will digitize its business processes.

An Internet-based firm's increased willingness to embrace opportunism in the e-space translates into a decreasing level of asset intensity of activities carried on within the firm boundary. In a dynamically evolving environment such as the Internet economy, firms do not resort to accumulating assets by integration—in accordance with the theories of vertical integration, which attribute the motive of integration as arising from an inability to write comprehensive contracts (see Williamson, 1975, 1985), at least during the initial stages of the evolution of an industry cluster. A firm would not wish to tie itself down to investments that lose their significance due to the changing requirements of its technological environment. Such a firm continuously develops new relationships to access resources in order to manage the risks due to technological uncertainty in a rapidly evolving market, the frequency of which reduces as the industry matures and dominant designs emerge (e.g., Tushman & Murmann, 1998).

Opportunistic Alliances

De novo entrants in nascent industries hesitate to develop committed long-term relationships for accessing critical resources. This is because the critical asset or resource position required for success is subject to constant and rapid transformation and reconfiguration due to the complexity of the technological environment. For example, in cases where various firms enter into an agreement to supply different components of a complex technological system,[11] some component suppliers may go out of business as particular components are replaced rapidly by more efficient components or even rendered redundant by change in architecture of the system itself (see Henderson & Clark, 1990).

Moreover, information asymmetries, such as in reference to costs, cannot be surmounted by designing a comprehensive contract. The outsourcing problem in the Internet economy is hence one of ex post adaptations rather than ex ante screening (Bajari & Tadelis, 2001) because of the flux in the market for components that are sought by Internet-based firms. This affects one of the major reasons underlying firms' formation of strategic alliances: access to complementary assets. When the critical asset configuration keeps on changing, so does a focal firm's requirement for complementary assets. By embodying opportunism in its choice of partners, an Internet-based virtual firm does away with any kind of relationship-specific investment and commitment—essential characteristics of long-lived interfirm alliances.

The extent of digitization of firm processes affects the ability of business firms to transfer and replicate critical organizational capabilities to new markets or to suit rapidly changing environmental conditions. In dynamic information-intensive environments, it becomes imperative that firms are able to replicate and transfer these organizational capabilities that enable firms to create, transfer, assemble, integrate, and exploit difficult-to-imitate assets, of which knowledge assets are the key. Digitization of firm processes affects all the distinct organizational processes of coordination and integration, learning, reconfiguration, and transformation. This enables the focal firm to move the coordination outside the boundary of the firm while still maintaining control. Hence, a firm with a higher level of digitization finds it easier to routinize the process of forming interfirm linkages, as the requirements for these are less for it than for a firm with a lower level of digitized processes. Similarly, firms that carry out fewer activities within their boundaries and possess lower levels of assets as compared to traditional firms will find it easier to routinize the process of forming interfirm linkages. This in turn results in their higher propensity to form short-term opportunistic alliances to gain access to whatever resources are required for the operation of the firm processes.

Developing and Leveraging Collaborative Capability

It is possible to view collaborative capability as a learned organizational skill; the more frequently practiced, the easier it is to accomplish (Powell et al., 1996). The ability of firms to build network-based, short-term, opportunistic alliances at a rapid pace depends on two factors: first, the extent to which the firms in question have routinized the process of forming interfirm linkages, that is, whether there exists a template for deciding on the formation of interfirm alliances; second, the ease of replication and transfer of these routines to new contexts, that is, whether the template allows adequately for deviations in settings or contextual conditions. We therefore define the ability of a firm to routinize the replication of routine(s) for forming interfirm linkages as collaborative capability. The extent of routinization and the replicability of these routines are driven by exogenous interdependencies and are facilitated by information on the availability, competencies, and reliability of prospective partners internalized by the focal firm's network (Gulati & Gargiulo, 1999).

But as the particular industry segment matures, the behavior of Internet-based firms operating in that particular segment converges with that explained in the literature on evolution of industries, product markets, and organizations (e.g., Winter, 1987; Klepper, 1996; Hannan & Freeman, 1977, 1989; Amburgey, Kelly, & Barnett, 1993; Tushman & Anderson, 1986). Firms begin to understand their context-specific transaction costs better as the frequency of the initial bursts of innovation decreases over time. They come to terms with the complexity of their technological environment and are in a better position to commit to asset-intensive relations over a longer period. Hence, after an initial period of exhibited high opportunism, Internet-based virtual firms slowly settle into long-term strategic alliances with their partners. The proportion of short-term opportunistic alliances by virtual firms declines over time, with a corresponding increase in the proportion of long-term strategic alliances.

Managing the Demand Environment

Demand-side externalities influence the market outcome in industries based on systemic technologies. Such industries are often subject to market failure, that is, the market may tip in favor of a particular firm (or technological standard) due to the presence of inertia in customers' purchases (Katz & Shapiro, 1985; Arthur, 1989; Besen & Farrell, 1994). In such industries, market power—defined as a dominant firm's ability to set prices at levels that drive out marginal competitors—often accrues due more to firms' demand-side competences than to supply-side competences.

Network effects exacerbate consumer inertia; that is, once a firm establishes a substantial lead in its installed base, it is difficult for transactional relationships to be displaced by a superior alternative until, say, the next major technological disruption. Where network externalities are strong, start-up firms race to establish a large installed base, as in the example of the free e-mail or instant-messaging services offered by various Internet-based firms during their early days (e.g., Besen & Farrell, 1994). For instance, AOL accumulated substantial losses to build its brand and infrastructure by continually buying market share to develop a larger installed base than competitors such as Microsoft, AT&T, and others. AOL retained these customers through a range of free services, thus exploiting systemic switching cost barriers for as long as possible.

Demand-Side Externalities and Market Outcome

The role of demand-side externalities is critical in determining the success of firms competing in industries based on systemic technologies. These include such industries as railroads, airlines, and telecommunications. In these industries, a large number of economic objects—generic technologies, products (or services), firms, or even technological systems—compete for adoption by consumers, but the market outcome may not always favor the best (and sometimes not even the earliest) entrant (e.g., Arthur, 1989; Shapiro & Varian, 1999; Katz & Shapiro, 1985, 1986a, 1986b,1992, 1994).

In these markets, where one *virtual* network can dramatically increase its value by interconnecting with other *virtual* networks, firms compete by expanding the size of their virtual networks. A firm with a small initial advantage in a network market may be able to parlay its small initial advantage into a larger and lasting one, eventually influencing the demand-side outcome favorably through economies of scale by forming alliances astutely.

The short-term opportunistic alliances formed by Internet-based firms are akin to quasi-structures that link *virtual* networks (or installed base) of complementary components, with each component offered by a different firm. The theoretical rationale explaining this behavior is that such associations foster adoptions of a particular mix of components as a system, thereby indirectly benefiting individual firms that supply the components. Hence, the competitive advantage of individual component suppliers arises from their ability to influence market outcome by exploiting indirect network effects (at the system level) to their advantage. In markets subject to indirect network effects, start-up firms endeavor to join existing networks of complementary components (e.g., Katz & Shapiro, 1986b).

Forming Systems and Consumer Adoption

During the race for consumer adoptions within industries based on systemic technologies, the effect of forming systems further exacerbates transactional inertia. Briefly, if the demand for a combination of products is higher than the sum of the individual products, with the mix of such products constituting a forming system, that combination of complementary components (both products and services) that become an interoperable system creates customer switching cost barriers (Katz & Shapiro, 1994). For instance, the simple transaction of enabling a consumer to purchase a book from an Internet-based retailer involves the coordination of a large number of complementary activities performed by different firms. The credit card company coordinates with the retailer to offer its service for the transaction (while another company validates the authenticity of the payment process) every time a transaction takes place. Each of these companies provides a single and complementary service that together constitutes a system for providing valued retailing services to the customer.

Benefits accrue to network participants indirectly through consumers' adoption decisions; their impact influences the future variety, availability, and prices of components used in forming systems. Cooperation is vital in this context, because ownership of entire forming systems by single firms is unlikely in embryonic industry settings where market outcome uncertainties are so high. No single firm would have all the internal capabilities necessary for success (Powell et al., 1996), and no investors would underwrite such high risks. The presence of strong partners legitimizes the system and enhances its development.

Complementarity, Compatibility, and Alliance Formation

Forming systems indicate the group of tangible products or services that need to be used together to generate consumer value, whereas virtual networks refer to the combined installed base of the group of firms supplying the potential components that comprise forming systems (Katz & Shapiro, 1986a, 1986b). The virtual network is tied together by means of alliances, and start-up Internet-based firms exploit the network of alliances to gain access to the interconnecting, virtual networks of partner firms. They do so opportunistically, forming as many alliances with as many partners as possible to increase the size and scope of their individual virtual networks and avoid excess opportunity costs due to idle capacity.

Two critical considerations that guide formation of Internet alliances are *compatibility* (whether products offered by sponsoring firms are useable together) and *complementarity* (whether add-on products increase a network's utility for consumers). A typical component firm can expand the size of its own virtual network by linking it with that of firms offering complementary components only if the components are compatible. Compatibility enhances adoption because it increases legitimacy; consumers are not afraid that the new system they select will end up a loser, forcing them to reinvest in an alternative system, and the benefits of compatibility are augmented in markets where network externalities are substantial.

Within systems of compatible components, there are greater opportunities to take advantage of economies of scale, learning effects, and technological spillovers in the development and production of specific components if many complements are available to increase usage. Compatibility between different systems leads to a greater choice for the consumers by allowing them to mix and match the complementary components that constitute the systems (Matutes & Regibeau, 1988). Complementary component suppliers can work together—as would an Internet-based florist, a greetings card company, and a gift retailer to create a service for the romance market—to increase sales volumes for the whole team.

Conclusion

This chapter contributes to the argument that firms in the new economy have broadened the scope of alliances to include such objectives as building organizational legitimacy and propagating technological standards, among many more that await scholarly exploration. This occurs as firms in the new economy are increasingly competing to appropriate the increasing returns to their demand-side investments. The increasing importance of demand-side competition, especially in the context of industries based on systemic technology, necessitates a fresh analytical approach to explaining various novel organizational structures.

We highlight the inability of arguments in strategy such as the dynamic capabilities perspective and/or the social structural perspective to explain the paradoxical behavior of Internet-based firms during the early stages of industry evolution. Incorporation of Internet technologies into organizational routines has indubitably transformed and significantly broadened the strategic options of Internet-based firms. In the Internet economy, a strategy of structural opportunism not only results in the firms choosing their level of virtuality but also, paradoxically, enables them to develop evolving collaborative capabilities.

Collaborative capabilities enable Internet-based firms not only to survive in the short term but also to generate superior performance in the long term. While the survival of de novo entrants can be hypothesized to be a function of their ability to position themselves appropriately in a network of short-term opportunistic alliances, their ability to generate wealth can be hypothesized to be an ability to convert their short-term opportunistic alliances into long-term strategic alliances. The reduction in environmental uncertainty that occurs along the evolutionary path of an industry corresponds to the emergence of a more definite industry structure. This includes crystallization of basic demand-and-supply conditions such as price elasticity, market segments, industry cost structure, production function, and so on. The members of a network of short-term opportunistic alliances seek to convert it into a network of long-term strategic alliances with the reduction in environmental uncertainty.

The theoretical arguments in this chapter concerning the strategy and conduct of de novo entrants await empirical verification, specifically in the case of new entrants into the Internet economy. Patterns like the phenomenon of promiscuity are generalizable in the context of those high-technology industries whose conception was influenced predominantly more by de novo than by de alio entrants. Among such industries that come to mind, computer software, biotechnology, and others may exhibit similar structural patterns.

Notes

1. For instance, Bresnahan, Gambardella, and Saxenian (2001) conceptualize the distinction as follows: "Old economy is a shorthand for a number of concepts: organizational and firm building activities, investment in general and industry specific human capital, larger companies and related economies of scale at level of the firms, lengthy periods of investment in capability before their exploitation. New economy means instead entrepreneurship, economies of scale at the level of regions or industries rather than firms, external effects, etc."

2. A value net or a value network is a network of alternative partners with each activity of the value chain being carried out by different partner firms, rather than by a single firm as in the case of a value chain. An increasing number of Internet-based firms have relinquished ownership of most value-chain activities—to suppliers and contract manufacturers—to do business in the most productive and efficient manner (Bovet & Martha, 2000). They rely on real-time information and customer knowledge to leverage Internet-based partnerships.

3. For instance, digitization of customer interface would be effective if the Internet retailing firm also digitizes the process of payment, which requires it to develop electronic linkages with, say, a bank. The digitization of the customer interface would not be effective if the Internet retailer were to accept only orders online and the payment offline.

4. The dynamic capabilities perspective views the asset structure of a firm as comprising its current specific endowments of technology, specialized plant and equipment; intellectual property, knowledge assets and assets complementary to them; reputational and relational assets, customer base, and its external relations with suppliers and complementors (Teece, Pisano, & Shuen, 1997).

5. The literature of transaction cost economics classifies organizations into three generic forms of governance—markets, hybrids, and hierarchies (Williamson, 1991).

6. Classical contract law applies to the ideal transaction in law and economics in which there exists no bilateral dependency (e.g., spot-market transactions), whereas neoclassical contract law applies to transactions in which there exists substantial bilateral dependency (e.g., contract manufacturing) between the autonomous parties entering into contract (Williamson, 1991).

7. Virtual governance entails all activities being performed outside the boundary of the firm, in contrast to vertical governance, which entails almost all activities being performed within the boundaries of the firm.

8. That is, incomplete contracts.

9. Williamson (1991) describes the entire spectrum of governance choice as discrete structural alternatives and not as a continuum.

10. The argument is not actually tautological because we do not use opportunism to represent both cause and effect. Opportunism is used as an explanatory construct that underlies firms' opportunistic alliances, thereby leading to superior performance.

11. For instance, a personal computer is an embodiment of a technological system rather than a single technology. The various components based on different technologies include microprocessors, based on semiconductor technology, the operating system, based on software technology, and so on.

References

Ahuja, G. (2000). Collaboration networks, structural holes and innovation: A longitudinal study. *Administrative Science Quarterly, 45*(3), 425–455.

Ahuja, M. K., & Carley, K. M. (1999). Network structure in virtual organizations. *Organization Science, 10*(6), 741–757.

Amburgey, T. L., Kelly, D., & Barnett, W. P. (1993). Resetting the clock: The dynamics of organizational change and failure. *Administrative Science Quarterly, 38*(1), 51–73.

Arthur, W. B. (1989). Competing technologies, increasing returns, and lock-in by historical events. *Economic Journal, 99,* 116–131.

Ashby, W. R. (1956). *An introduction to cybernetics.* London: Chapman and Hall.

Bajari, P., & Tadelis, S. (2001). Incentives versus transaction costs: A theory of procurement contract. *Rand Journal of Economics, 32*(3), 387–407.

Balkin, D. B., Markman, G. D., & Gomez-Mejia, L. (2000). Is CEO pay in high technology firms related to innovation? *Academy of Management Journal, 43,* 1118–1129.

Barua, A., Pennell, J., Shutter, J., & Whinston, A. B. (2000). *Measuring the Internet economy: An exploratory study.* Working Paper, Center for Research in Electronic Commerce.

Besen, S. M., & Farrell, J. (1994). Choosing how to compete: Strategies and tactics in standardization. *Journal of Economic Perspectives, 8,* 117–131.

Bettis, R., Bradley, S., & Hamel, G. (1992). Outsourcing and industrial decline. *Academy of Management Executive, 6,* 7–21.

Bovet, D., & Martha, J. (2000). *Value nets: Breaking the supply chain to unlock hidden profits.* New York: John Wiley.

Bower, J. L., & Christensen, C. M. (1995). Disruptive technologies: Catching the wave. *Harvard Business Review, 73*(1), 43–53.

Bresnahan, T., Gambardella, A., & Saxenian, A. (2001). Old economy inputs for new economy outputs: Cluster formation in the new silicon valleys. *Industrial and Corporate Change, 10*(4), 835–860.

Caton, H. (1985). The preindustrial economics of Adam Smith. *Journal of Economic History, 45*(4), 833–853.

Chesbrough, H. W., & Teece, D. J. (1996, January/February). When is virtual virtuous? Organizing for innovation. *Harvard Business Review,* 65–74.

Choi, S. Y., Stahl, D., & Whinston, A. (1997). *The economics of electronic commerce.* Indianapolis, IN: Macmillan Technical.

Christensen, C. M. (1997). *The innovator's dilemma: When new technologies cause great firms to fail.* Boston: Harvard Business School Press.

Christensen, C. M., and Bower, J. L. (1996). Customer power, strategic investment, and the failure of leading firms. *Strategic Management Journal,* 17 (3): 197–218.

Coase, R. (1937). The nature of the firm. *Economica, 4,* 386–405.

Cohen, W. M., & Levinthal, D. L. (1990). Absorptive capacity: A new perspective on learning and innovation. *Administrative Science Quarterly, 35,* 128–152.

Dess, G. G., & Beard, D. W. (1984). Dimensions of organizational task environments. *Administrative Science Quarterly, 29,* 52–73.

Dill, W. R. (1958). Environment as an influence on managerial autonomy. *Administrative Science Quarterly, 2,* 409–443.

Duncan, R. B. (1972). Characteristics of organizational environments and perceived environmental uncertainty. *Administrative Science Quarterly, 17*(3), 313–327.

Emery, F. E., & Trist, E. L. (1965). The causal texture of organizational environments. *Human Relations, 18,* 21–32.

Galbraith, J. (1973). *Designing complex organizations.* Reading, MA: Addison-Wesley.

Granovetter, M. (1985). Economic action and social structure: A theory of embeddedness. *American Journal of Sociology, 91,* 481–510.

Granovetter, M. (1992). Problems of explanation in economic sociology. In N. Nohria & R. Eccles (Eds.), *Networks and organizations: Structure, form and action.* Boston: Harvard Business School Press.

Gulati, R. (1995a). Familiarity breeds trust? The implications of repeated ties on contractual choice in alliances. *Academy of Management Journal, 38,* 85–112.

Gulati, R. (1995b). Social structure and alliance formation pattern: A longitudinal analysis. *Administrative Science Quarterly, 40,* 619–652.

Gulati, R., & Gargiulo, M. (1999). Where do interorganizational networks come from? *American Journal of Sociology, 104*(5), 1439–1493.

Hagel, J., III, & Singer, M. (1999, March/April). Unbundling the corporation. *Harvard Business Review,* 133–141.

Han, S. (1994). Mimetic isomorphism and its effects on the audit service market. *Social Forces, 73,* 637–663.

Hannan, M. T., & Freeman, J. (1977). The population ecology of organizations. *American Journal of Sociology, 82,* 929–964.

Hannan, M. T., & Freeman, J. (1989). *Organizational ecology.* Cambridge, MA: Harvard University Press.

Harrigan, K. R. (1985). *Strategies for joint ventures.* Lexington, MA: Lexington Books.

Harrigan, K. R. (1986). Matching vertical integration strategies to competitive conditions. *Strategic Management Journal, 7*(6), 535–555.

Harrigan, K. R. (1988). Joint ventures and competitive strategy. *Strategic Management Journal, 9*(3), 141–158.

Harrigan, K. R. (2001). Strategic flexibility in the old and new economies. In M. A. Hitt, R. E. Freeman, & J. S. Harrison (Eds.), *Handbook of strategic management.* New York: Basil Blackwell.

Henderson, R. M., & Clark, K. B. (1990). Architectural innovation: The reconfiguration of existing product technologies and the failure of established firms. *Administrative Science Quarterly, 35*(1), 9–30.

Jonas, N. (1985, March 3). The hollow corporation. *Business Week,* 56–58.

Jurkovich, R. (1974). A core typology of organizational environments. *Administrative Science Quarterly, 19*(3), 380–394.

Katz, D., & Kahn, R. L. (1966). *The social psychology of organizations.* New York: Wiley.

Katz, M., & Shapiro, C. (1985). Network externalities, competition and compatibility. *American Economic Review, 75*(3), 424–440.

Katz, M., & Shapiro, C. (1986a). Technology adoption in the presence of network externalities. *Journal of Political Economy, 94,* 822–841.

Katz, M., & Shapiro, C. (1986b). Product compatibility choice in a market with technological progress. *Oxford Economic Papers, 38,* 146–165.

Katz, M., & Shapiro, C. (1992). Product introduction with network externalities. *Journal of Industrial Economics, 40*(1), 55–84.

Katz, M., & Shapiro, C. (1994). Systems competition and network effects. *Journal of Economic Perspectives, 8*(2), 93–115.

Klepper, S. (1996). Entry, exit, growth and innovation over the product life cycle. *American Economic Review, 86*(3), 562–583.

Kogut, B., Shan, W., & Walker, G. (1992). Competitive cooperation in biotechnology: Learning through networks? In N. Nohria & R. Eccles (Eds.), *Networks and organizations: Structure, form, and action.* Boston: Harvard Business School Press.

Levinthal, D. A. (1997). Adaptation on rugged landscapes. *Management Science, 43*(7), 934–950.

Matutes, C., & Regibeau, P. (1988). Mix and match: Product compatibility without network externalities. *Rand Journal of Economics, 19*(2), 219–234.

Meyer, J. W., and Scott, W. R. (1983). *Organizational environments: Ritual and rationality.* Beverly Hills, CA: Sage.

Mizruchi, M. S., & Stearns, L. B. (1988). A longitudinal study of the formation of interlocking directorates. *Administrative Science Quarterly, 33,* 194–210.

Nelson, R. R. (1991). Why do firms differ, and how does it matter? [special issue]. *Strategic Management Journal, 12,* 61–74.

Nelson, R. R., & Winter, S. G. (1982). *An evolutionary theory of economic change.* Cambridge, MA: Harvard University Press.

Palmer, D., Friedland, R., & Singh, J. V. (1986). The ties that bind: Organizational and class bases of stability in a corporate interlock network. *American Sociological Review, 51*(6), 781–796.

Podolny, J. M. (1993). A status-based model of market competition. *American Journal of Sociology, 98*(4), 829–872.

Powell, W. W., Koput, K. W., & Smith-Doerr, L. (1996). Interorganizational collaboration and the locus of innovation: Networks of learning in biotechnology. *Administrative Science Quarterly, 41*(1), 116–145.

Rayport, J. F., & Sviokla, J. J. (1995, November/December). Exploiting the virtual value chain. *Harvard Business Review,* 75–85.

Schumpeter, J. (1934). *The theory of economic development.* Cambridge, MA: Harvard University Press.

Schumpeter, J. (1942). *Capitalism, socialism & democracy.* New York: Harper & Brothers.

Shan, W., Walker, G., & Kogut, B. (1994). Interfirm cooperation and startup innovation in the biotechnology industry. *Strategic Management Journal, 15*(5), 387–394.

Shapiro, C., & Varian, H. (1999). *Information rules: A strategic guide to the network economy.* Boston: Harvard Business School Press.

Singh, K. (1997). The impact of technological complexity and inter-firm cooperation on business survival. *Academy of Management Journal, 40*(2), 339–367.

Singh, K., & Mitchell, W. (1996). Precarious collaboration: Business survival after partners shut down or form new partnerships [special issue]. *Strategic Management Journal, 17,* 99–115.

Slywotzky, A. J., & Morrison, D. J. (2000). *How digital is your business?* New York: Random House.

Teece, D. J. (1986). Profiting from technological innovation: Implications for integration, collaboration, licensing and public policy. *Research Policy, 15,* 785–805.

Teece, D., Pisano, G., & Shuen, A. (1997). Dynamic capabilities and strategic management. *Strategic Management Journal, 18*(7), 509–533.

Terreberry, S. (1968). The evolution of organizational environments. *Administrative Science Quarterly, 12*(4), 590–613.

Thompson, J. D. (1967). *Organizations in action: Social science bases of administrative theory.* New York: McGraw-Hill.

Thompson, J. D., & McEwen, W. J. (1958). Organizational goals and environment: Goal setting as an interaction process. *American Sociological Review, 23,* 23–31.

Tushman, M. L., & Anderson, P. (1986). Technological discontinuities and organizational environments. *Administrative Science Quarterly, 31*(3), 439–465.

Tushman, M., & Murmann, J. P. (1998). Dominant designs, technology cycles, and organizational outcomes. *Research in Organizational Behavior, 20,* 231–266.

Useem, M. (1984). *The inner circle.* New York: Oxford University Press.

Uzzi, B. (1996). The sources and consequences of embeddedness for the economic performance of organizations: The network effect. *American Sociological Review, 61*(4), 674–698.

Walker, G., Kogut, B., & Shan, W. (1997). Social capital, structural holes, and the formation of an industry network. *Organization Science, 8*(2), 109–125.

Ward, B. N. (1967). *The socialist economy: A study of organizational alternatives.* New York: Random House.

Wernerfelt, B. (1984). A resource based view of the firm. *Strategic Management Journal, 5*(2), 171–180.

Williamson, O. E. (1975). *Markets and hierarchies.* New York: Free Press.

Williamson, O. E. (1985). *The economic institutions of capitalism.* New York: Free Press.

Williamson, O. E. (1991). Comparative economic organization: The analysis of discrete structural alternatives. *Administrative Science Quarterly, 36*(2), 269–296.

Williamson, O. E. (1999). Strategy research: Governance and competence perspectives. *Strategic Management Journal, 20*(12), 1087–1108.

Winter, S. G. (1987). Knowledge and competence as strategic assets. In D. J. Teece (Ed.), *The competitive challenge* (pp. 159–184). Cambridge, MA: Ballinger.

18

Entrepreneurial Alliances and Networks

R. Duane Ireland

Michael A. Hitt

Justin W. Webb

Increasing amounts of research at the interface of entrepreneurship and strategy is being completed (Hitt, Ireland, Camp, & Sexton, 2001; Meyer, Neck, & Meeks, 2002, Michael, Storey, & Thomas, 2002). Yet debate continues regarding the degree to which the entrepreneurship and strategic management disciplines differ in their focus (Meyer et al., 2002). Nonetheless, efforts to integrate the two literatures' insights is widely seen as crucial to a firm's ability to create and, it is hoped, sustain competitive advantages that are important for creating value over time (Hitt, Ireland, Camp, & Sexton, 2002). Thus, firms integrate entrepreneurship and strategic management actions in order to create and sustain value (Hitt et al., 2001; Ireland, Hitt, & Sirmon, 2003; Sirmon, Hitt, & Ireland, in press). From the perspective of strategic entrepreneurship, entrepreneurship is viewed as opportunity-seeking behavior, whereas strategic management entails advantage-seeking behavior (Hitt et al., 2002; Ireland, Hitt, Camp, & Sexton, 2001). As advantage-seeking behavior, strategic management encompasses the actions the firm takes to manage its resources to create rare, valuable, nonsubstitutable, and inimitable capabilities that are leveraged to achieve competitive advantages to create value (Barney, 1991; Porter, 1980; Sirmon et al., in press).

As opportunity-seeking behavior, entrepreneurship encompasses actions taken with the intent of "organizational creation, renewal, or innovation that occur within or outside an existing organization" (Sharma & Chrisman, 1999, 17). Exploration is the core of opportunity-seeking behavior and entails the organizational-learning processes of seeking and generating new knowledge to fill voids within a knowledge structure. In contrast, exploitation concerns the leveraging of novel, innovative combinations of this knowledge and other firm resources to take advantage of market opportunities (Kazanjian, Drazin, & Glynn, 2002). Exploration enables a firm to identify and investigate multiple opportunities in the external environment, thereby creating flexibility for dealing with environmental uncertainty and the future competitive landscape. The actual value the firm can create through its exploration activities is uncertain (Covin, Ireland, & Kuratko, 2004; Ireland & Webb, in press). Indeed, the full value of exploration commonly materializes over the long term. In contrast, the advantage-seeking behaviors of exploitation supply the firm with a known, current stream of value through the leveraging of current resources to exploit existing market opportunities.

Continued firm success is a function of symbiotically balancing exploration and exploitation activities (March, 1991). Exploration and exploitation activities require allocations from the firm's set of resources (financial, human, and social capital). Success is achieved when the firm develops an appropriate balance between exploration and exploitation. Achieving such a balance requires careful attention to the allocation of resources between the two types of processes (McGrath & MacMillan, 2000; Rothaermel & Deeds, 2004). Successfully managing resource allocations between exploration and exploitation is difficult, however, in that exploration demands the pursuit of unique knowledge, whereas exploitation mandates a focus on current knowledge. However, resources must be drawn from the same set of financial, human, and social capital to support simultaneously exploring for new opportunities while exploiting current capabilities to create maximum value (March, 1991). These conditions highlight the need for a strategic approach to entrepreneurship in order to balance the allocation of firm resources to support simultaneously the short-term objective of exploitation behaviors and the long-term intentions of exploration.

In this chapter, we discuss entrepreneurial alliances as a means by which a firm can manage its resources using a strategic approach to entrepreneurship. An entrepreneurial alliance is a collaborative arrangement the firm undertakes for an entrepreneurial purpose (i.e., to identify and/ or exploit opportunities) (Reuer, 2004). Often, the intent of these entrepreneurial alliances is to improve the firm's competitive position and performance by sharing resources with partnering firms (Ireland, Hitt, & Vaidyanath, 2002). This intent heightens the importance of managing the alliances. Herein, we analyze the use and management of a portfolio of entrepreneurial alliances as a means by which the firm can successfully balance its exploration and exploitation behaviors.

Entrepreneurial alliances enable firms to bundle and leverage internal resources with resources external to the firm that cannot be efficiently acquired (Das & Teng, 2000), perhaps because of high transaction costs. Among a firm's motivations for entering an entrepreneurial alliance is its desire to identify and explore new opportunities or to exploit existing resources in pursuit of a current opportunity (Koza & Lewin, 1998; Rothaermel & Deeds, 2004). Both exploration and exploitation alliances offer firms an additional option for organizational learning. Exploration alliances enable firms to cope with environmental uncertainty by reducing the risks and costs associated with exploration (Ireland et al., 2002). Through an alliance, the firm can accelerate the development of new capabilities as a means of coping with environmental uncertainty (Lane & Lubatkin, 1998). The firm can also use exploration alliances to integrate its diverse knowledge stocks with knowledge owned by partnering firms in order to develop organizational innovations (Nonaka, 1994). Exploitation alliances can be viewed as the union of complementary assets (Teece, 1986), thereby assisting the creation of a foreign sales base (Leiblein & Reuer, 2004), the creation or development of social legitimacy, and the expansion of manufacturing, distribution, and marketing resources (Alvarez & Barney, 2001). Despite serving as an important source of social capital for the firm, the high proportion of failed alliances suggests the need to improve our understanding of managing alliances (Parise & Henderson, 2001; Parkhe, 1993).

In the following sections, we identify characteristics inherently unique to exploration and exploitation alliances. These unique characteristics mandate that the alliance types be managed

Table 18.1 Guidelines for managing individual alliances

	Idiosyncratic Characteristics of Managerial Emphasis		
	Trust vs. Power	*Equity vs. Non-equity Control*	*Knowledge Diversity vs. Complementarity*
Exploration Alliances	Manage with a greater emphasis on trust	Emphasize the utilization of equity alliances	Emphasize knowledge diversity in partners
Exploitation Alliances	Manage with a greater emphasis on power	Emphasize the utilization of non-equity alliances	Emphasize complementary knowledge in partners
	Financial Flexibility		Strategic Flexibility

differently. Our arguments focus on single alliance relationships, providing an initial step to enhancing our understanding of how to manage a portfolio of alliances (Parise & Casher, 2003). We then examine the management of a portfolio of alliances, taking into consideration external environmental factors, industry and competitive characteristics, and issues that may arise in alliance relationships originating from a firm's existing or intended alliance relationships. Understanding factors external to the firm, such as those we examine, is critical to the firm's efforts to construct an alliance portfolio that is appropriately balanced between exploration and exploitation alliances to develop and, it is hoped, sustain competitive advantages.

Exploration and Exploitation Alliances: Idiosyncratic Characteristics Requiring Unique Management

Exploration and exploitation alliances are often created with the intent of leveraging shared resources to support both opportunity-seeking and advantage-seeking behaviors (Koza & Lewin, 1998). Exploration alliances are formed to discover new opportunities; in contrast, exploitation alliances involve maximizing returns on an investment by leveraging shared, complementary assets and resources (Koza & Lewin, 1998; Rothaermel & Deeds, 2004). Exploration and exploitation alliances differ in the contextual reasoning behind their formation as well as their intended purposes and outcomes. Although objective performance measures can be used to assess and monitor the performance of exploitation alliances, the ability to measure the performance of exploration alliances is impeded by their long-term, causally ambiguous benefits, implying the need for process and behavioral controls (Koza & Lewin, 2000).

In the following sections, we describe the differential management of exploration and exploitation alliances. We present guidelines for managing the two alliance types in Table 18.1. To construct Table 18.1, we relied on the research literature to identify dimensions that enable a firm to sustain simultaneously the financial and strategic flexibility needed to achieve the desired balance between exploration and exploitation. It is also important to note that financial capital, human capital, and social capital are the firm's primary resources for sustaining the balance between exploration and exploitation that is at the heart of strategic entrepreneurship (Ireland et al., 2003).

As shown in the table, trust should be the foundation or dominant logic for managing exploration alliances, whereas differential power relationships between partners should constitute the dominant logic for managing exploitation alliances. Trust and power—or any of the other comparative dimensions in Table 18.1—do not exist in isolation, and no relationships are based exclusively on a single dimension. Indeed, to different degrees, trust and power dynamics affect the management of both types of alliances. However, trust is relatively more critical to the management of exploration alliances, whereas differential power relationships are relatively more critical to managing exploitation alliances. Similarly, equity partnerships and knowledge diversity are more important for exploration alliances, whereas nonequity relationships and knowledge complementarity are more important in exploitation alliances.

We also suggest in Table 18.1 that firms seek to enhance their financial flexibility when managing alliances to develop a balance between exploitation and exploration alliances. Degrees of financial freedom increase when exploration alliances are managed primarily through trust, whereas the same outcome is achieved by emphasizing power to manage exploitation alliances. Moreover, equity alliances tend to increase financial flexibility when firms use exploration alliances, and an emphasis on nonequity alliances creates the path to greater financial flexibility in the instance of exploitation alliances.

As shown in Table 18.1, strategic flexibility is as important to the balance between exploitation and exploration alliances as is financial flexibility. Indeed, the ability to identify and exploit entrepreneurial opportunities is essential to strategic flexibility. A firm's knowledge structure can facilitate these activities. Increasing the diversity of a firm's knowledge inventory can enhance its capacity to identify entrepreneurial opportunities, whereas an emphasis on complementary knowledge stocks contributes to the effectiveness of an exploitation alliance.

Trust Versus Power

A number of scholars have argued that trust is critical to generating positive performance in alliances (Currall & Inkpen, 2002; Garcia-Canal, Duarte, Criado, & Llaneza, 2002; Inkpen, 2000; Koka & Prescott, 2002; Parkhe, 1993; Sarkar, Echambadi, Cavusgil, & Aulakh, 2001; Volery & Mensik, 1998). In an alliance context, trust is a decision to rely on a partner, based on positive expectations of and confidence in the partner to act in accordance with the agreement, under a condition of relational risk that the partner may not act as expected and desired (Currall & Inkpen, 2002). Relational risk is concerned with unanticipated, negative variations in cooperative relationships, such as opportunistic behaviors (Das & Teng, 1998a). Although control mechanisms (e.g., formal contracts, formal evaluation of alliance performance) can eliminate some of the uncertainties associated with relational risk, a minimum level of trust is required for any alliance to be successful (Garcia-Canal et al., 2002).

Trust facilitates an alliance's relational activities in several ways. Firms can overcome relational risk by using control mechanisms such as tighter integration, shared equity ownership, and limiting a partner's exposure to patented technologies (Das & Teng, 1998a). However, because of transaction costs, these mechanisms can be expensive to maintain. On a relative-cost basis, trust can result in a more efficient management of alliances (Dwyer, Schurr, & Oh, 1987; Dyer & Singh, 1998). Trust can also facilitate the exchange of knowledge within an alliance, because the partners may not feel the need to protect themselves from opportunistic behavior (Inkpen, 2000; Ring & Van de Ven, 1992; Uzzi, 1997). Trust enriches the cooperating firms' opportunities, access to resources, and flexibility (Uzzi, 1997). In relationships lacking a minimum level of trust, knowledge exchanges are impeded by partners' fears and unwillingness to share valuable information, leading to the exchange of information lower in accuracy, comprehensiveness, and timeliness (Inkpen, 2000; Zand, 1972).

In addition to its benefits, trust also has disadvantages for managing at least some types of alliances. For example, although trust helps partners absorb some or much uncertainty and risk in present contexts, it simultaneously produces future risk, because the firm must assume the nature of its partner's future behavior (Bachmann, 2001). A second disadvantage of using trust for managing relationships is the fact that trust is not an immediate outcome of forming an alliance. Rather, trust develops through repeated, consistently positive, reciprocal exchanges between two firms over an extended period of time (Dyer & Singh, 1998; Garcia-Canal et al., 2002). Firms involved in alliances, however, may not have the resources to sustain those alliances until trust is fully developed. Also, the alliance's intended purpose may decrease in value because of environmental changes while trust is evolving between the partners. These conditions have the potential to reduce the value created by an alliance. Finally, trust can be disturbed by other factors emerging in a firm's external environment. For example, the adoption of technology advancements can change a partner's expectations, thereby disturbing the level of trust (Hart & Saunders, 1997). Often, a lengthy period of time is required to regain trust that has been lost, perhaps longer than the time required to build the trust initially.

Power is a second factor affecting relationships in organizational alliances (Child & Faulkner, 1998). Although to a certain extent trust is a precursor to all successful alliances, a power relationship between partners may sometimes play a greater role than trust in determining an alliance's success (Bachmann, 2001; Cox, 2001a). Power has the ability to "influence the selection of actions in the face of other possibilities" (Lane & Bachmann, 1997; Luhmann, 1979, 112). Power stems from a number of sources, including a firm's economic base, resource or knowledge base differentials with a partner, and legitimacy (Thorelli, 1986).

To manage effectively a relationship with power, a decision-making unit must possess the capability to mobilize sanctions. However, there is a difference between coercive and noncoercive power when exercising sanctions (Lane & Bachmann, 1997; Rokkan & Haugland, 2002). Using coercive power, for example, as when opportunistic behavior is displayed, usually implies a breakdown in the alliance relationship, and relational exchange is impeded (Rokkan & Haugland, 2002). On the other hand, noncoercive power is an effective substitute for trust, stemming from the ability and willingness of a firm to withhold resources valuable to an alliance (Lane & Bachmann, 1997).

When the exercise of power is pertinent, a persuasive, noncoercive approach, compared to a coercive approach, is more effective in achieving objectives and maintaining favorable relations (Hart & Saunders, 1997). The power asymmetry does not necessarily imply asymmetry in the overall interests of alliance partners or in the commitments of the partners to mutually achieve an intended purpose (Rokkan & Haugland, 2002). Rather, power asymmetry exists when one partner's potential contributions (in terms of one or more dimensions) exceed the potential contributions of the other partner. Superior experience and more expansive knowledge sets are examples of sources of value creation that one firm may have in greater amounts compared to its partner.

Asymmetrical power relationships result in somewhat explicit expectations from each partner regarding its contributions to an alliance. Because the expectations associated with asymmetrical relationships are well known, the relational risks of and disruptions created by opportunistic behavior or some other unforeseen breakdown may be reduced (Bachmann, 2001). Overembeddedness, created by the use of trust in an alliance network, increases the efficiency of transactions within the network. However, disruptions involving one actor in the network, possibly because of the exit of the actor from the network or the rationalization of the market by external forces, can destabilize the entire network, subsequently leading to the failure of a previously effective alliance (Uzzi, 1997).

In addition, whereas trust evolves in relationships over an extended period of time, power asymmetry often is formally established at the time of alliance formation, thereby endowing the alliance with the foundation to quickly function in ways that allow the alliance to operate and move toward achieving its objectives. This type of power relationship can also be more effective than a trust approach in dealing with external environment transitions and facilitating levels of innovation within the alliance (Cox, 2001b; Hart & Saunders, 1997).

Nevertheless, risks are also present in alliances managed primarily on the basis of asymmetrical power-based relationships. The most common risk is for the more powerful firm to act opportunistically. For example, when technology is a firm's only valuable investment in an alliance, a partner can terminate or minimize its own investments in the relationship after gaining access to the firm's technological knowledge (Alvarez & Barney, 2001; Khanna, Gulati, & Nohria, 1998). A second risk exists because of the weaker firm's ability to learn from the relationship. If the weaker firm is able to capture knowledge from its cooperative relationship, it could increase its own bargaining power and demand additional reciprocal investments from the partner to maintain the current relationship (Hamel, 1991).

Exploration alliances are often more open-ended arrangements formed to enhance the individual firm's organizational-learning capabilities in uncertain, risky environments (Koza & Lewin, 2000). These alliances are initiated with the intent of identifying and exploring new market opportunities. The success of exploration alliances depends on the individual firms' willingness to integrate and share respective knowledge bases. Because trust facilitates the exchange of tacit knowledge, higher levels of cooperation, and greater flexibility in exploring opportunities, we offer the following proposition:

> P1: Trust is a more effective basis for managing exploration alliances than are asymmetrical power relationships.

Exploitation alliances are characterized by the combination of resource and knowledge complementarities to take advantage of market opportunities (Koza & Lewin, 2000). Integrating tacit knowledge and developing close interfirm cooperation are less important in exploitation alliances than in exploration alliances. However, the ability to organize and move quickly to exploit market opportunities as early as possible is critical. Therefore, the following proposition is offered:

> P2: Power is a more effective basis for managing exploitation alliances than is trust.

It should be noted that the partners in an alliance can have different motives. For example, one partner may enter an alliance with the purpose of exploiting its current knowledge and capabilities, whereas the other partner could enter the alliance to obtain new and tacit knowledge. Such is often the case in alliances between a firm based in a developed market and a local firm based in the emerging market the developed firm desires to enter (Hitt, Dacin, Levitas, Arregle, & Borza, 2000). In such cases, management of the alliances is more complex and challenging.

Alternatively, Hitt, Li, and Worthington (2004) argue that many developed-market firms entering emerging markets also need to learn tacit knowledge in order to be successful in these markets. For example, they must learn about the culture and the informal institutional arrangements that operate in the country. Thus, if they enter an emerging market and form alliances with only the purpose of exploiting their current knowledge, they may be unsuccessful. Additionally, with this purpose, the developed-market partner may try to use asymmetrical power to manage the alliances, making it more difficult for it to gain access to and learn the tacit knowledge needed to be successful in the market. Such alliances likely require the development of trust. The developed-market partner also needs to share the technological and managerial knowledge desired by the partner for the partner to help it learn the culture and informal institutional norms and rules. Therefore, partners must find a balance in the approaches used to manage an alliance when they have different goals (exploitation versus exploration).

Equity Versus Nonequity Arrangements

Controls operate in parallel to trust and power in generating cooperation in an alliance (Das & Teng, 1998b). Even when the functional motivation for forming an alliance is clear and well intended, creating inadequate control and coordination mechanisms can negatively affect the alliance's performance (Pangarkar & Klein, 2001; Reddy, Osborn, & Hennart, 2002).

The proportion of equity partners share influences the extent to which the hierarchical structure established within an alliance—control and coordination mechanisms—models arrangements in stand-alone organizations (Gulati & Singh, 1998). At one end of the continuum are joint ventures in which partners share equity equally in a new entity. This new entity generally has its own hierarchical structure independent from parent firms. Equity alliances often involve considerable costs and time to negotiate and organize the arrangements as well as potentially significant exit costs (Gulati, 1995a). Although a joint venture equity arrangement requires substantial relation-specific investments in establishing control mechanisms (Colombo, 2003; Das & Teng, 1996), it creates "a mutual hostage in the form of shared equity that helps align the interests of all the partners, inasmuch as each partner is concerned about the value of its equity in the alliance" (Gulati & Singh, 1998, 791). Forming an entirely new hierarchical structure reduces the likelihood of opportunistic behavior. Within the alliance, an independent hierarchical structure guides actions with clearly defined rules and responsibilities (Das & Teng, 1996; Gulati & Singh, 1998). Because the hierarchical structure is independent from the parent firms' structures, there is also less opportunity for parties external to the alliance to affect it through opportunistic behavior (Das & Teng, 1996).

These arguments suggest that firms pursuing joint ventures or other equity arrangements with proportionally large amounts of shared equity (e.g., equity alliances) accept higher coordination costs to minimize potentially high appropriation costs (Gulati & Singh, 1998; Hennart, 1991; Reddy et al., 2002). In exploration alliances, partner firms integrate their knowledge structures to identify and explore market opportunities successfully. More intimate experiences lead to higher performance stemming from organizational learning (Inkpen, 1998; Luo & Peng, 1999; Nonaka, 1994; Zahra, Ireland, & Hitt, 2000). However, without sufficient control mechanisms within these alliances, there is an increased potential for tacit knowledge spillover to the partnering yet potentially competing firms.

In addition, exploration alliances are usually formed in uncertain, dynamic environments. Because of the uncertainty involved and the ambiguity of future market trends, the alliance requires flexibility in exploring multiple, diverse opportunities. Because of the independence of joint ventures from parent firms, this alliance form has greater flexibility to identify areas to prospect for opportunities while engaging in exploration activities (Birnberg, 1998; Das & Teng, 1996; Pangarkar & Klein, 2001). Collectively, research suggests the following proposition:

> P3: Joint ventures and equity arrangements are a more desirable form of a cooperative arrangement than are nonequity arrangements when forming exploration alliances.

In contrast to equity alliances, nonequity alliances do not involve equity transfers or the creation of new, independent entities (Das & Teng, 1996). Rather, nonequity alliances are contractual arrangements lacking specific, independent controls beyond what is specified in the original contract. Therefore, the level of commitment compared to that in equity alliances is limited, because the partners do not share jointly in the alliance's success or failure (Das & Teng, 1996). The advantages of nonequity alliances lie in their comparatively low costs associated with control and coordination mechanisms and the possibility for dissolving the relationship easily and inexpensively should it be necessary to do so (Das & Teng, 1996; Gulati & Singh, 1998). In alliances characterized by less integration of partners' knowledge and resource structures, as in nonequity alliances, appropriation concerns are lower because the necessary linkages required for knowledge transfer are minimal (Gulati & Singh, 1998). In addition, because firms in nonequity alliances operate primarily independently, these relationships can be organized more quickly, enabling firms to cooperate flexibly to exploit market opportunities (Gulati, 1995a; Reddy et al., 2002).

Exploitation alliances are formed as two firms combine complementary resources to take advantage of market opportunities. Being a fast mover can be a source of competitive advantage (Lee, Smith, Grimm, & Schomburg, 2000). Thus, if an alliance is necessary to exploit a new opportunity, it must be formed quickly to gain competitive benefits. In addition, close interfirm cooperation is ordinarily not required in exploitation alliances, meaning that the threat of tacit knowledge spillovers and the need for control and coordination mechanisms are reduced. The evidence suggests the following proposition:

> Proposition 4: Nonequity arrangements are a more desirable form of a cooperative arrangement than are joint ventures and other equity arrangements for exploitation alliances.

Diversity Versus Complementarity of Knowledge

As we describe above, exploration and exploitation alliances are used to pursue different outcomes/objectives. These differences suggest the need for firms to seek partners with knowledge bases that increase the resource effectiveness or resource efficiency of their own knowledge structures. Resource effectiveness refers to the ability of the firm to "do the right things" (Ireland & Webb, in press; Webb & Ireland, 2004). It is achieved by focusing resources on the exploration of multiple market opportunities, consequently placing the firm in an advantageous position to exploit new opportunities once they have been identified (Ireland & Webb, in press). In contrast, resource efficiency denotes the ability of the firm to "do things right" and is realized by managing resources in a way that minimizes related transaction costs (Ireland & Webb, in press; Webb & Ireland, 2004).

Resource effectiveness improves when firms enhance their exploration skills. Identifying new prospective opportunities is dependent on the firm's bisociative skills—its ability to integrate two or more previously unrelated matrices of knowledge (Koestler, 1964; Smith & Di Gregorio, 2002). Firms possessing knowledge stocks of greater depth and breadth are better positioned to combine and examine unrelated matrices of knowledge effectively to explore for new opportunities (Cohen & Levinthal, 1990; Smith & Di Gregorio, 2002). This evidence suggests the following proposition:

> P5: Exploration alliances should be formed with partners that expand the diversity of a firm's current knowledge stocks, thereby increasing the firm's resource effectiveness.

Of course, a certain amount of knowledge complementarity must exist between partners in exploration alliances. Distinct from the *combination* of similar resources in an alliance that produces economies of scale or increased market power, the *integration* of complementary resources between partnering firms facilitates the development of valuable, inimitable capabilities that can serve as a source of competitive advantage (Harrison, Hitt, Hoskisson, & Ireland, 1991, 2001). To fully integrate and utilize a certain diversity of knowledge in a bisociative process, the firm must first possess a complementary variety of knowledge internally (Cohen &

Levinthal, 1990; Nonaka, 1994). When a firm lacks the capacity or quality of knowledge stocks necessary for absorbing knowledge gained from exploration alliances, it is inefficiently investing valuable financial and human capital in an entrepreneurial activity (Cohen & Levinthal, 1990). Although resource complementarity plays an important role in exploration alliances, its importance is greater in exploitation alliances for achieving resource efficiency.

Firms must concentrate on the management of resources to increase resource efficiency. Resource management involves structuring the resource portfolio, bundling resources to create capabilities, and leveraging the capabilities to create value (Sirmon et al., in press; Sirmon & Hitt, 2003). Structuring the resource portfolio entails decisions and actions taken to acquire, accumulate, and divest resources. Resource bundling involves integrating resources to develop capabilities. Leveraging capabilities is concerned with the market-oriented strategies used to create value by coordinating, mobilizing, and deploying resources and capabilities in chosen competitive arenas. Thus, resource management encompasses three value-creating activities undertaken to exploit market opportunities (Sirmon et al., in press).

Entrepreneurial alliances in which firms gain access to their partner's resources enrich their resource portfolios. Alliances also offer firms additional, potentially more efficient use of valuable resources for the alliance management process, thereby increasing the value of the firm's entrepreneurial activities. For example, to increase the resource efficiency of its exploitation activities, a firm can seek alliance partners with resources complementary to its own. More specifically, after identifying a potential market opportunity, a firm must structure its resource portfolio to exploit it. During this step, the firm should identify potential alliance partners that can fulfill its additional unmet resource acquisition and accumulation needs. Following the structuring of the resource portfolio, the alliance partners can then cooperate to enhance the bundling and leveraging of the shared resources, thereby jointly exploiting the market opportunity more efficiently than could be done by either alone.

The resource management process is critical to exploiting recognized market opportunities. Therefore, it is important that firms be able to integrate resources quickly and efficiently. Diverse knowledge and resource stocks may be too complex to integrate easily or quickly, even when partner firms possess the absorptive capacities and managerial capabilities needed to accomplish this task. Resource similarities between partner firms can potentially facilitate certain dimensions of the resource management process; however, the bundling of similar resources rarely evolves into sources of sustainable competitive advantage, because competitor firms can usually identify the causal attributes for the alliance's competitiveness (Harrison et al., 2001). Conversely, the bundling of complementary resources can be achieved quickly when the absorptive capacity is sufficient and managers in the alliance well understand the specific complementarities, enabling partner firms to take advantage of new opportunities. Furthermore, the bundling of resource complementarities can lead to causally ambiguous sources of competitive advantage (Harrison et al., 2001). This evidence leads to the following proposition:

P6: Exploitation alliances should be formed with partners that possess complementary resource stocks, thereby increasing the firm's resource efficiency.

Certain resource similarities can facilitate exploitation alliances. In alliances that involve firms with similar resources, less time is wasted in learning new skills, allowing the cooperating firms to quickly manage resources for exploiting opportunities (Harrison et al., 2001; Madhok, 1997). Furthermore, the combination of similar resources in exploitation alliances can produce economies of scale, economies of scope, and increased market power, which, although more imitable, can still provide sources of temporary

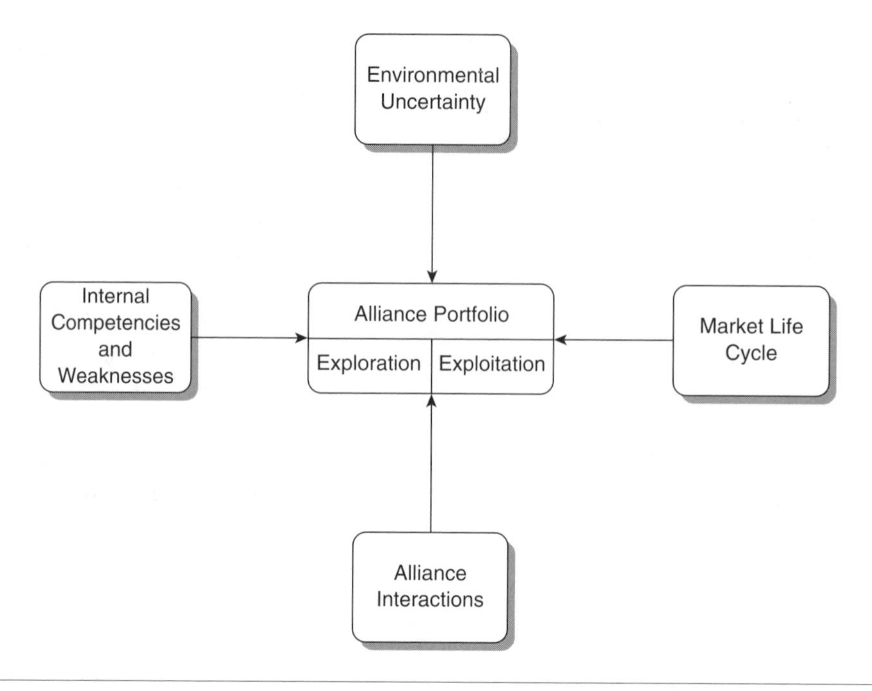

Figure 18.1 Factors Influencing the Management of an Alliance Portfolio

competitive advantage (Harrison et al., 2001; Harrison et al., 1991).

Alliance Portfolio Management: Balancing Exploration and Exploitation

Studying individual alliances between firms is important to identify the unique managerial approaches to each. However, this method overlooks synergistic effects among a firm's multiple alliances. Indeed, carefully examining the alliances with which a firm is involved is a critical part of an effective alliance management process (George, Zahra, Wheatley, & Khan, 2001). In addition to the potential synergy among a firm's alliances, several other factors also affect the number and type of alliances a firm should form when they are being used to achieve an appropriate balance between the firm's exploration and exploitation activities. The firm's competencies and weaknesses, the type of market cycle within which a firm competes, and uncertainty in a firm's external environment are important contextual variables. Unfortunately, firms often fail to consider the potential or actual contextual factors affecting their alliances, resulting in a situation in which the "alliance portfolio grows into a random mix of ventures assembled over the years by various units" (Bamford & Ernst, 2002, 37).

We show the four important contextual factors mentioned above in Figure 18.1. With a focus on their importance as part of the firm's alliance portfolio management process, we discuss these factors in the materials below. Of course, other contextual factors (e.g., actions taken by competitors to strengthen their alliance networks) could affect a firm's alliance portfolio management process. However, the firm-specific (i.e., a firm's competencies and weaknesses), industry-specific (i.e., the market cycle), and external environment–specific (i.e., degree of environmental uncertainty) factors included in Figure 18.1 are the most critical for developing a valuable network of alliances to balance exploration and exploitation activities.

Internal Competencies and Weaknesses

In general, smaller entrepreneurial firms are more resource-*effective* in their efforts to identify opportunities but are simultaneously less resource-*efficient* in developing the competitive advantages needed to exploit the opportunities, compared to larger firms (Ireland et al., 2003). Small firms are more resource-effective because they are not hindered by large firms' hierarchical and structural impediments. In contrast, the relative resource inefficiency of small entrepreneurial organizations stems from a lack of resources, skills, and experience (Calof, 1993; Freeman, Carroll, & Hannan, 1983; Hannan & Freeman, 1984; Levinthal & Fichman, 1988; Stinchcombe, 1965). This type of inefficiency suggests that small firms should focus efforts on overcoming their entrepreneurial weaknesses. Exploitation alliances with larger, more experienced firms can help entrepreneurial firms access the skills needed to improve the efficiency in using their resources. Over time and through experience, large firms develop routines enabling them to coordinate resource and capability bundles efficiently (Alvarez & Barney, 2002; Sirmon et al., in press). This experiential knowledge and the greater resource stocks owned by the large firm, integrated with the small firm's tacit knowledge of potential market opportunities, has the potential to benefit both firms in their exploitation activities. These arguments suggest the following proposition:

> P7: Small, entrepreneurial firms seek to partner with companies to enhance their resource efficiency skills and help them achieve an appropriate balance between resource effectiveness and resource efficiency.

In comparison, although large, established firms possess experiential knowledge, resources, and routinized capabilities and consequently are more capable of forming competitive advantages to exploit known opportunities (Ireland et al., 2003), certain inherent characteristics of their resource stocks undermine their ability to identify valuable market opportunities. Large firms' structures, strategies, and routines facilitate advantage-seeking behaviors but may counteract forces to innovate (Burgelman, 1983; Dougherty & Hardy, 1996; Hannan & Freeman, 1984). For example, in many cases, reward systems in large, established organizations have evolved to a point of benefiting individuals who concentrate on short-term responsibilities while punishing individuals attempting to enhance innovation as a source of the firm's long-term competitiveness (Dougherty & Hardy, 1996). Likewise, organizational routines limit communication between various functional units, undermining the ability of different business units to share their knowledge resources, which are vital to innovation efforts (Dougherty, 1990). Large firms also suffer from strategic transparency. Because of their resource endowments, large firms usually focus on extending their current strategies in known domains. This focus is transparent to competitors, which increases the imitability of the firm's strategies (Mosakowski, 2002).

Forming exploration alliances with smaller, entrepreneurial firms can increase large firms' resource effectiveness. A decision to participate in several exploration alliances can channel knowledge of new market opportunities to the large firm, offsetting the large firm's structural constraints. In addition, because such exploration alliances offer large firms potential access to diverse resource stocks embedded in the small partner firms, the identification of radically innovative opportunities can diminish the transparency of the large firm's strategy. Therefore, we would expect large firms to participate in a proportionately larger number of exploration alliances than exploitation alliances to increase their resource effectiveness.

However, given our previous discussions of managing alliances, the different purposes of the large and small firms in the alliances could make them more difficult to manage. For example, should these alliances be managed through trust or asymmetric power? The small firm is likely to prefer trust, as the power differential will not favor their position. What form should these alliances take (equity versus nonequity)? These questions are important but challenging to answer because of the different goals held by the alliance partners. Through negotiations and compromises, partners derive answers to these questions. In general, the partner with the most significant stake in an alliance more strongly influences both the form and management of an alliance.

Alliance Interactions

In cases where firms have an alliance portfolio, interactions between the individual alliances often occur. Sometimes these interactions create synergy (George et al., 2001; Parise & Casher, 2003), whereas at other times they constrain the firm's scope of alliance opportunities (Ahuja, 2000; Portes & Sensenbrenner, 1993). Furthermore, certain relational characteristics of existing alliances may induce the firm to seek additional or specific types of alliances (Uzzi & Gillespie, 1999). A firm must be cognizant of these symbiotic relationships among its alliances and understand the effect of each relationship on the alliance portfolio's total value. Understanding the alliance portfolio's total value contributes positively to balancing the firm's entrepreneurial activities in terms of exploration and exploitation.

Several synergistic effects may occur within a firm's portfolio of alliances. For example, successful exploration alliances can provide partners with patentable innovations. Sequentially, these innovations attract potential partners seeking to exploit jointly the new patents or to explore for new, related market opportunities. These transactions form a cycle that creates greater network centrality, better access to strategic resources, and increased power for an alliance's founding partners (Smith-Doerr, Owen-Smith, Koput, & Powell, 1999; Tsai, 2001). Synergy can also be created when several of a firm's partners belong to the same external collaborative network, possibly increasing their willingness to share tacit market knowledge with the focal firm (Parise & Casher, 2003). In addition, because opportunistic behavior is easier to identify in networks of shared alliances, each partner is motivated to act in ways that support the good of the alliance. Such behaviors increase the likelihood that all partners will cooperate to pursue mutual benefits (Gulati, 1995b).

Alliance portfolios can also mitigate the risk associated with individual alliances (George et al., 2001; Parise & Casher, 2003). As with financial portfolios, a firm can compensate for uncertain ventures by engaging in ventures with more certain outcomes (thereby reducing its overall risk). Finally, the experiential knowledge gained from managing previous alliances contributes positively to the management of present and future alliances (Inkpen, 2000; Parise & Casher, 2003; Walker, Kogut, & Shan, 1997). Synergies among both exploration and exploitation alliances act to increase the firm's resource efficiency beyond that gained from participating in individual collaborative arrangements. Although some individual alliance relationships do not increase a firm's resource efficiency or resource effectiveness, their participation in a portfolio of alliances may contribute to synergies that benefit the firm's set of alliances (Parise & Casher, 2003).

Yet, although firms often seek to maximize synergies across their multiple alliances, they should simultaneously aim to minimize the alliance interactions that constrain their strategic flexibility and organizational learning. An example of a constraining exploitation alliance is when a firm partners with a market leader that demands exclusivity. Although this may temporarily be favorable to the focal firm, if a competitor of the market leader introduces a superior product to the market, the firm will be unable to cooperate with the new competitor, causing it to miss a potentially valuable opportunity (Parise & Casher, 2003). As a second example, in exploration alliances with partners engaged in multimarket competition outside the shared network, a firm may fail to gain benefits equal to its own investments because of its partners' concerns for knowledge spillovers (Inkpen, 1998; Parise & Casher, 2003). In these instances, the firm should decide if exploration alliances are beneficial to the total value of its alliance portfolio or if one or more alliances should be terminated because of appropriation risks.

Knowledge-based trust, or trust gained from knowledge of a partner firm's past behaviors, is a potentially important relational characteristic because it increases the efficiency of relationships by reducing the need for control mechanisms that often have high transaction costs (Kern, 2000). However, knowledge-based trust can encourage firms to focus primarily on the more efficient relationships, eventually causing them to reduce their search for additional external partnerships (Uzzi, 1997). In other words, it can lead to a form of path dependence. Although greatly benefiting the resource efficiency of the cooperative arrangements, knowledge-based trust and the resulting path dependence can produce relational inertia and resource ineffectiveness (Gargiulo & Benassi, 1999; Kern, 2000). If a firm discontinues knowledge search in exchange for resource efficiencies, the balance between exploration and exploitation is disrupted and the once-valuable exploration alliances contribute less to the firm's resource effectiveness. Therefore, a firm may be more resource-effective by forming both arm's-length and embedded exploration alliances (Uzzi & Gillespie, 1999). By constantly turning over a number of its exploration alliances, a firm benefits from recurring channels of diverse, current knowledge (Uzzi & Gillespie, 1999), which can then be shared among its other embedded cooperative arrangements in other bisociative activities (Koka & Prescott, 2002). These arguments suggest the following proposition.

P8: Firms can avoid disrupting the balance in exploration and exploitation alliances partly by continuously reviewing their exploration alliances and balancing the number of arm's-length and embedded exploration alliances.

Market Life Cycle

Resources and conditions unique to certain markets can sustain a firm's competitive advantage longer than in other markets (Williams, 1992). Markets characterized by factors such as patents and sole geographic access to valuable resources tend to be populated by firms capable of developing sustainable competitive advantages. Markets with these characteristics are slow-cycle markets, ones in which firms derive at least relatively sustainable competitive advantages from their unique access to or possession of certain value-creating resources (Williams, 1992). Firms able to successfully explore different market opportunities, identifying and gaining early access to the valuable proprietary resources, are able to exploit the advantage for extended periods of time until competitors discover product substitutes or until the source of the competitive advantage is exhausted (Williams, 1992). Therefore, the source of sustainable competitive advantage is primarily linked to the firm's resource effectiveness, whereas the firm's resource efficiency is important—although a competitive advantage can rarely be built on it—in creating additional value during the firm's exploitation activities. Because of this, the following proposition is offered:

P9: Successful firms in slow-cycle markets usually pursue a greater number of exploration alliances than exploitation alliances.

Fast-cycle markets involve competitive advantages garnered by valuable resources not easily shielded from imitation and therefore lack sustainability (Williams, 1992). Here, competitive advantages are sustained by the firm's ability to move consistently early in each new cycle (Lee et al., 2000). First-mover advantages, for example, are based on a firm's ability to be a technology leader and capture a large market share while simultaneously constructing high switching costs before competitors can enter the industry

(Lieberman & Montgomery, 1988). However, certain characteristics, such as the ability to reduce technological uncertainty or incumbent inertia, enable second-movers sometimes to gain a competitive advantage over first-movers. Nevertheless, early movers usually gain a competitive advantage over late movers (Lee et al., 2000; Lieberman & Montgomery, 1988, 1998). The firm needs to own or have access to knowledge gained in exploration alliances to exploit opportunities effectively. However, in fast-cycle markets, it is imperative that firms have the skills required to mobilize quickly to exploit new opportunities. This necessity suggests the value of exploitation alliances for firms competing in fast-cycle markets. These arguments suggest the following proposition:

> P10: In fast-cycle markets, successful firms pursue a larger number of exploitation alliances than exploration alliances to sustain competitive advantage.

Standard-cycle markets are the median of slow-cycle and fast-cycle markets. Competitive advantages in these markets are based on the firm's ability to develop innovative products and processes. Relying primarily on economies of scale in standard-cycle markets in which large volumes of goods are produced, firms can partially shield their competitive advantages (Williams, 1992). These arguments suggest the following proposition:

> P11: To be successful in a standard-cycle market, a firm needs to build an alliance portfolio that is virtually evenly balanced with exploration and exploitation alliances.

Environmental Uncertainty

Understanding the effects of environmental uncertainty is critical for developing effective entrepreneurial strategies (Covin & Slevin, 1989; Lee et al., 2000). Environmental uncertainty stems from a number of factors, including regulatory changes, political transitions, changing trends in technology, and emerging, rapidly changing market conditions. Increased strategic flexibility, which is a product of the firm's knowledge stocks and financial capital (Cheng & Kesner, 1997; Hitt & Reed, 2000; Ireland & Webb, in press), enables the firm to cope successfully with environmental uncertainty (Shimizu & Hitt, 2004, 2005). By creating an additional path for organizational learning to occur, exploration alliances are particularly effective in increasing a firm's strategic flexibility. In addition, by sharing the resource requirements to explore opportunities in uncertain environments, alliance partners also share the associated risks and financial costs (Inkpen, 2000). Thus, the following proposition is offered:

> P12: In competitive contexts characterized by high levels of uncertainty and complexity, firms pursue a greater number of exploration alliances than exploitation alliances to maintain more strategic flexibility.

On the other hand, lower levels of environmental uncertainty moderate the need for the firm to engage in significant amounts of exploration. Rather, the ability of the firm to exploit more commonly recognized opportunities efficiently is of greater importance. Therefore, firms' alliance portfolios are likely to contain a greater proportion of exploitation alliances than exploration alliances in environments with lower uncertainty.

Evolving the Alliance Portfolio

Over time, firms experience changes in their industry's life cycle as well as in the general external environment. In addition, different internal competencies and weaknesses surface, affecting the firm's ability to explore for new opportunities while exploiting existing competitive advantages. Changes to these factors or conditions affect the balance required in the firm's portfolio of alliances. After transforming the portfolio, the firm must further analyze its new set of alliance interactions.

To this point, our focus has been on how a firm should structure and manage its alliance portfolio in order to balance its exploration and exploitation activities. Our final focus is the termination of alliances. Ending relationships and established linkages has been found to increase the strategic flexibility of the firm and may allow it to overcome inertial forces (Shimizu & Hitt, 2004). Therefore, terminating an alliance may be as important to the overall value of a firm's alliance portfolio as is creating a new alliance.

Commonly, alliances are terminated for one of three reasons. First, some alliances are terminated because their objective has been accomplished. In these instances, the partners may form another alliance either at the point of termination or at some time in the future. A second reason for terminating alliances is that the partners mutually agree that the alliance is not achieving its objectives and hence the cooperative relationship should be dissolved. Finally, some alliances end with hostile feelings between the partners. In these cases, the ending can result from a misunderstanding about the alliance's objectives and about what each partner is expected to contribute to the alliance (Child & Faulkner, 1998).

Too often, firms delay terminating nonperforming alliances. A number of reasons explain this behavior, including the difficulty and cost of creating alliances, difficulty in measuring alliance performance, and opposing, involved constituencies (Inkpen & Ross, 2001). It is somewhat easier to determine a termination point for an exploitation alliance, in that the business opportunity is usually exhausted at the end of the industry life cycle (Koza & Lewin, 2000). On the other hand, exploration alliances are usually more ambiguous but should be terminated when the underlying business model is no longer economically viable (Koza & Lewin, 2000).

Complicating the termination decision, though, is the possibility that a single poorly performing alliance can contribute synergistic benefits to the alliance portfolio that offset its individual costs (Bamford & Ernst, 2002; Parise & Casher, 2003). Therefore, a firm should establish control mechanisms upon the formation of individual alliances that facilitate possible termination but that also consider each alliance's contribution to the total alliance portfolio in addition to individual performance (Inkpen & Ross, 2001). These mechanisms take the form of process or behavioral controls in exploration alliances and financial or operational controls in exploitation alliances (Koza & Lewin, 2000). Firms should be proactive in enforcing these controls to curtail opportunistic behaviors, escalation of commitment, and passive partners (Inkpen & Ross, 2001).

Conclusion

Strategic entrepreneurship is concerned with integrating entrepreneurial (i.e., opportunity-seeking) and strategic (i.e., advantage-seeking) behaviors to design and implement entrepreneurial strategies that lead to wealth creation (Hitt et al., 2002). Exploration and exploitation are the two main phases of entrepreneurship that require strategic actions to use the firm's resources effectively and efficiently. One of the ways firms can effectively balance the use of their resources is by managing an alliance portfolio consisting of entrepreneurial-oriented exploration and exploitation alliances. Because each alliance type has different purposes, the approach used to manage an alliance should be unique to the outcomes desired from the alliance.

However, a number of factors external to each individual alliance, including the parent firm's own competencies and weaknesses, interactions with other alliances, the type of market in which the cooperating firms compete, and environmental uncertainty, increase the complexity of the alliance management process. Nonetheless, firms able to manage alliances successfully to create both resource effectiveness and resource efficiency increase the probability of successfully achieving competitive advantages and thereby creating value for owners.

References

Ahuja, G. (2000). The duality of collaboration: Inducements and opportunities in the formation of interfirm linkages. *Strategic Management Journal, 21,* 317–343.

Alvarez, S. A., & Barney, J. B. (2001). How entrepreneurial firms can benefit from alliances with large partners. *Academy of Management Executive, 15,* 139–148.

Alvarez, S. A., & Barney, J. B. (2002). Resource-based theory and the entrepreneurial firm. In M. A. Hitt, R. D. Ireland, S. M. Camp, & D. L. Sexton (Eds.), *Strategic entrepreneurship: Creating a new mindset* (pp. 89–105). Oxford: Blackwell.

Bachmann, R. (2001). Trust, power, and control in trans-organizational relations. *Organization Studies, 22,* 337–365.

Bamford, J., & Ernst, D. (2002). Managing an alliance portfolio. *McKinsey Quarterly, 3,* 29–39.

Barney, J. B. (1991). Firm resources and sustained competitive advantage. *Journal of Management, 17,* 99–120.

Birnberg, J. G. (1998). Control in interfirm co-operative relationships. *Journal of Management Studies, 35,* 421–428.

Burgelman, R. (1983). Corporate entrepreneurship and strategic management: Insights from a process study. *Management Science, 29,* 1349–1363.

Calof, J. G. (1993). The impact of size on internationalization. *Journal of Small Business Management, 3*(4), 60–69.

Chandler, G. N. (1993). Reward perceptions and the performance of emerging technology dependent and non-technology dependent manufacturing firms. *Journal of High Technology Management Research, 4*(1), 63–76.

Chandler, G. N., Keller, C., & Lyon, D. W. (2000). Unraveling the determinants and consequences of an innovative-supportive organizational culture. *Entrepreneurship Theory and Practice, 25*(1), 59–76.

Cheng, J. L. C., & Kesner, I. F. (1997). Organizational slack and response to environmental shifts: The impact of resource allocation patterns. *Journal of Management, 23,* 1–18.

Child, J., & Faulkner, D. (1998). *Strategies for cooperation: Managing alliances, networks and joint ventures.* New York: Oxford University Press.

Cohen, W. M., & Levinthal, D. A. 1990. Absorptive capacity: A new perspective on learning and innovation. *Administrative Science Quarterly, 35,* 128–152.

Colombo, M. G. (2003). Alliance form: A test of the contractual and competence perspectives. *Strategic Management Journal, 24,* 1209–1229.

Covin, J. G., Ireland, R. D., & Kuratko, D. F. (2004). *The exploration and exploitation functions of corporate venturing.* Working Paper, Indiana University.

Covin, J. G., & Slevin, D. P. (1989). The strategic management of small firms in hostile and benign environments. *Strategic Management Journal, 10,* 75–87.

Cox, A. (2001a). The power perspective in procurement and supply management. *Journal of Supply Chain Management, 37,* 4–7.

Cox, A. (2001b). Managing with power: Strategies for improving value appropriation from supply relationships. *Journal of Supply Chain Management, 37,* 42–47.

Currall, S. C., & Inkpen, A. C. (2002). A multilevel approach to trust in joint ventures. *Journal of International Business Studies, 33,* 479–495.

Das, T. K., & Teng, B. (1996). Risk types and inter-firm alliance structures. *Journal of Management Studies, 33,* 827–843.

Das, T. K., & Teng, B. (1998a). Resource and risk management in the strategic alliance making process. *Journal of Management, 24,* 21–42.

Das, T. K., & Teng, B. (1998b). Between trust and control: Developing confidence in partner cooperation in alliances. *Academy of Management Review, 23,* 491–512.

Das, T. K., & Teng, B. (2000). A resource-based theory of strategic alliances. *Journal of Management, 26,* 31–61.

Dougherty, D. (1990). Understanding new markets for new products. *Strategic Management Journal, 11,* 59–78.

Dougherty, D., & Hardy, C. (1996). Sustained product innovation in large, mature organizations: Overcoming innovation-to-organization problems. *Academy of Management Journal, 39,* 1120–1153.

Dwyer, R. F., Schurr, P. H., & Oh, S. (1987). Developing buyer-seller relationships. *Journal of Marketing, 51,* 11–27.

Dyer, J. H., & Singh, H. (1998). The relational view: Cooperative strategy and sources of interorganizational competitive advantage. *Academy of Management Review, 23,* 660–679.

Freeman, J., Carroll, G. R., & Hannan, M. T. (1983). The liability of newness: Age dependence in organizational death rates. *American Sociological Review, 48,* 692–710.

Garcia-Canal, E., Duarte, C. L., Criado, J. R., & Llaneza, A. V. (2002). Time compression diseconomies in accelerated global alliances. *Management Decision, 40,* 745–754.

Gargiulo, M., & Benassi, M. (1999). The dark side of social capital. In R. Th. A. J. Leenders & S. M. Gabbay (Eds.), *Corporate social capital and liability* (pp. 298–321). Boston: Kluwer Academic.

George, G., Zahra, S. A., Wheatley, K. K., & Khan, R. (2001). The effects of alliance portfolio characteristics and absorptive capacity on performance: A study of biotechnology firms. *Journal of High Technology Management Research, 12,* 205–226.

Gulati, R. (1995a). Does familiarity breed trust? The implications of repeated ties for contractual choice in alliances. *Academy of Management Journal, 38,* 85–112.

Gulati, R. (1995b). Social structure and alliance formation patterns: A longitudinal analysis. *Administrative Science Quarterly, 40,* 619–652.

Gulati, R., & Singh, H. (1998). The architecture of cooperation: Managing coordination costs and appropriation concerns in strategic alliances. *Administrative Science Quarterly, 43,* 781–814.

Hamel, G. (1991). Competition for competence and inter-partner learning within international global alliances. *Strategic Management Journal, 12,* 83–103.

Hannan, M. T., & Freeman, J. (1984). Structural inertia and organizational change. *American Sociological Review, 49,* 149–164.

Harrison, J. S., Hitt, M. A., Hoskisson, R. E., & Ireland, R. D. (1991). Synergies and post-acquisition performance: Differences versus similarities in resource allocations. *Journal of Management, 17,* 173–190.

Harrison, J. S., Hitt, M. A., Hoskisson, R. E., & Ireland, R. D. (2001). Resource complementarity in business combinations: Extending the logic to organizational alliances. *Journal of Management, 27,* 679–690.

Hart, P., & Saunders, C. (1997). Power and trust: Critical factors in the adoption and use of electronic data interchange. *Organization Science, 8,* 23–42.

Hennart, J. F. (1991). The transactions cost theory of joint ventures: An empirical study of Japanese subsidiaries in the USA. *Management Science, 37,* 483–497.

Hitt, M. A., Dacin, M. T., Levitas, E., Arregle, J. L., & Borza, B. (2000). Partner selection in emerging and developed market contexts: Resource-based and organizational learning perspectives. *Academy of Management Journal, 43,* 449–467.

Hitt, M. A., Ireland, R. D., Camp, S. M., & Sexton, D. L. (2001). Strategic entrepreneurship: Entrepreneurial strategies for wealth creation [guest editors' introduction to the special issue]. *Strategic Management Journal, 22,* 479–491.

Hitt, M. A., Ireland, R. D., Camp, S. M., & Sexton, D. L. (2002). Strategic entrepreneurship: Integrating entrepreneurial and strategic management perspectives. In M. A. Hitt, R. D. Ireland, S. M. Camp, & D. L. Sexton (Eds.), *Strategic entrepreneurship: Creating a new mindset* (pp. 1–16). Oxford: Blackwell.

Hitt, M. A., Li, H., & Worthington, W. (2004, June). *Emerging markets as a source of learning: Managing knowledge flows between emerging market firms and foreign partners.* Paper presented at the International Association for Chinese Management Research, Beijing.

Hitt, M. A., & Reed, T. (2000). Entrepreneurship in the new competitive landscape. In G. D. Meyer, & K. Heppard (Eds.), *Entrepreneurship as strategy: Competing on the entrepreneurial edge* (pp. 23–48). Thousand Oaks, CA: Sage.

Inkpen, A. C. (1998). Learning and knowledge acquisition through international strategic alliances. *Academy of Management Executive, 12,* 69–80.

Inkpen, A. C. (2000). Learning through joint ventures: A framework of knowledge acquisitions. *Journal of Management Studies, 37,* 1019–1043.

Inkpen, A. C., & Ross, J. (2001). Why do some strategic alliances persist beyond their useful life? *California Management Review, 44,* 132–148.

Ireland, R. D., Hitt, M. A., Camp, S. M., & Sexton, D. L. (2001). Integrating entrepreneurship and strategic management action to create firm wealth. *Academy of Management Executive, 15*(1), 49–63.

Ireland, R. D., Hitt, M. A., & Sirmon, D. G. (2003). A model of strategic entrepreneurship: The construct and its dimensions. *Journal of Management, 29,* 1–26.

Ireland, R. D., Hitt, M. A., & Vaidyanath, D. (2002). Alliance management as a source of competitive advantage. *Journal of Management, 28,* 413–446.

Ireland, R. D., & Webb, J. W. (in press). International entrepreneurship in emerging economies: A resource-based perspective. In A. Cooper, S. Alvarez, A. Carrera, L. Mesquita, & R. Vassolo (Eds.), *Entrepreneurship and innovation in emerging economies.* Oxford: Blackwell.

Kazanjian, R. K., Drazin, R., & Glynn, M. A. (2002). Implementing strategies for corporate entrepreneurship: A knowledge-based perspective. In M. A. Hitt, R. D. Ireland, S. M. Camp, & D. L. Sexton (Eds.), *Strategic entrepreneurship: Creating a new mindset* (pp. 173–199). Oxford: Blackwell.

Kern, H. (2000). Lack of trust, surfeit of trust: Some causes of the innovation crisis in German industry. In C. Lane & R. Bachmann (Eds.), *Trust within and between organizations: Conceptual issues and empirical applications* (pp. 203–213). New York: Oxford University Press.

Khanna, T., Gulati, R., & Nohria, N. (1998). The dynamics of learning alliances: Competition, cooperation, and relative scope. *Strategic Management Journal, 19,* 193–210.

Koestler, A. (1964). *The act of creation.* New York: Dell.

Koka, B. R., & Prescott, J. E. (2002). Strategic alliances as social capital: A multidimensional view. *Strategic Management Journal, 23,* 795–816.

Koza, M. P., & Lewin, A. Y. (1998). The co-evolution of strategic alliances. *Organization Science, 9,* 255–264.

Koza, M., & Lewin, A. (2000). Managing partnerships and strategic alliances: Raising the odds of success. *European Management Journal, 18,* 146–151.

Lane, C., & Bachmann, R. (1997). Co-operation in inter-firm relations in Britain and Germany: The role of social institutions. *British Journal of Sociology, 48,* 1997.

Lane, P. J., & Lubatkin, M. (1998). Relative absorptive capacity and interorganizational learning. *Strategic Management Journal, 19,* 461–477.

Lee, H., Smith, K. G., Grimm, C. M., & Schomburg, A. (2000). Timing, order, and durability of new product advantages with imitation. *Strategic Management Journal, 21,* 23–30.

Leiblein, M. J., & Reuer, J. J. (2004). Building a foreign sales base: The roles of capabilities and alliances for entrepreneurial firms. *Journal of Business Venturing, 19,* 285–307.

Levinthal, D. A., & Fichman, D. (1988). Dynamics of interorganizational attachments: Auditor-client relationships. *Administrative Science Quarterly, 33,* 345–369.

Levinthal, D. A., & March, J. G. (1993). The myopia of learning. *Strategic Management Journal, 14,* 95–112.

Lieberman, M. B., & Montgomery, D. B. (1988). First-mover advantages. *Strategic Management Journal, 9,* 41–58.

Lieberman, M. B., & Montgomery, D. B. (1998). First-mover (dis)advantages: Retrospective and link with the resource-based view. *Strategic Management Journal, 19,* 1111–1125.

Luhmann, N. (1979). *Trust and power.* Chichester, UK: Wiley.

Luo, Y., & Peng, M. W. (1999). Learning to compete in a transition economy: Experience, environment, and performance. *Journal of International Business Studies, 30,* 269–296.

Madhok, A. (1997). Cost, value and foreign market entry mode: The transaction and the firm. *Strategic Management Journal, 18,* 39–61.

March, J. G. (1991). Exploration and exploitation in organizational learning. *Organization Science, 2,* 71–87.

McGrath, R. G., & MacMillan, I. (2000). *The entrepreneurial mindset.* Boston: Harvard Business School Press.

Meyer, G. D., Neck, H. M., & Meeks, M. D. (2002). The entrepreneurship-strategic management interface. In M. A. Hitt, R. D. Ireland, S. M. Camp, & D. L. Sexton (Eds.), *Strategic entrepreneurship: Creating a new mindset* (pp. 19–44). Oxford: Blackwell.

Michael, S., Storey, D., & Thomas, H. (2002). Discovery and coordination in strategic management and entrepreneurship. In M. A. Hitt, R. D. Ireland, S. M. Camp, & D. L. Sexton (Eds.), *Strategic entrepreneurship: Creating a new mindset* (pp. 45–65). Oxford: Blackwell.

Mosakowski, E. (2002). Overcoming resource disadvantages in entrepreneurial firms: When less is more. In M. A. Hitt, R. D. Ireland, S. M. Camp, & D. L. Sexton (Eds.), *Strategic entrepreneurship: Creating a new mindset* (pp. 106–126). Oxford: Blackwell.

Nonaka, I. (1994). A dynamic theory of organizational knowledge creation. *Organization Science, 5,* 14–37.

Pangarkar, N., & Klein, S. (2001). The impacts of alliance purpose and partner similarity on alliance governance. *British Journal of Management, 12,* 341–353.

Parise, S., & Casher, A. (2003). Alliance portfolios: Designing and managing your network of business-partner relationships. *Academy of Management Executive, 17,* 25–39.

Parise, S., & Henderson, J. C. (2001). Knowledge resource exchange in strategic alliances. *IBM Systems Journal, 40,* 908–924.

Parkhe, A. (1993). Strategic alliance structuring: A game theoretic and transaction cost examination of interfirm cooperation. *Academy of Management Journal, 36,* 794–829.

Porter, M. E. 1980. *Competitive strategy.* New York: Free Press.

Portes, A., & Sensenbrenner, J. (1993). Embeddedness and immigration: Notes on the social determinants of economic action. *American Journal of Sociology, 98,* 1320–1350.

Reddy, S. B., Osborn, R. N., & Hennart, J. F. (2002). The prevalence of equity and non-equity cross-border linkages: Japanese investments and alliances in the United States. *Organization Studies, 23,* 759–780.

Reuer, J. J. (2004). Entrepreneurial alliances. In M. A. Hitt & R. D. Ireland (Eds.), *The Blackwell encyclopedia on management: Entrepreneurship* (pp. 64–66). Oxford: Blackwell.

Ring, P. S., & Van de Ven, A. H. (1992). Structuring cooperative relationships between organizations. *Strategic Management Journal, 13,* 483–498.

Rokkan, A. I., & Haugland, S. A. (2002). Developing relational exchange: Effectiveness and power. *European Journal of Marketing, 36,* 211–230.

Rothaermel, F. T., & Deeds, D. L. (2004). Exploration and exploitation alliances in biotechnology: A system of new product development. *Strategic Management Journal, 25,* 201–221.

Sarkar, M. B., Echambadi, R., Cavusgil, S. T., & Aulakh, P. S. (2001). The influence of complementarity, compatibility, and relationship capital on alliance performance. *Academy of Marketing Science, 29,* 358–373.

Sharma, P., & Chrisman, J. J. (1999). Toward a reconciliation of the definitional issues in the field of corporate entrepreneurship. *Entrepreneurship Theory and Practice, 23*(3), 11–27.

Shimizu, K., & Hitt, M. A. (2004). Strategic flexibility: Organizational preparedness to reverse ineffective strategic decisions, *Academy of Management Executive, 18*(4), 44–59.

Shimizu, K., & Hitt, M. A. (2005). What constrains or facilitates the divestiture of formerly acquired firms? The effects of organizational inertia. *Journal of Management, 31,* 50–72.

Sirmon, D. G., & Hitt, M. A. (2003). Managing resources: Linking unique resources, management, and wealth creation in family firms. *Entrepreneurship Theory and Practice, 27*(4), 339–358.

Sirmon, D. G., Hitt, M. A., & Ireland, R. D. (in press). Managing firm resources in dynamic environments to create value: Looking inside the black box. *Academy of Management Review.*

Smith, K. G., & Di Gregorio, D. (2002). Bisociation, discovery, and the role of entrepreneurial action. In M. A. Hitt, R. D. Ireland, S. M. Camp, & D. L. Sexton (Eds.), *Strategic entrepreneurship: Creating a new mindset* (pp. 129–150). Oxford: Blackwell.

Smith-Doerr, L., Owen-Smith, J., Koput, K. W., & Powell, W. W. (1999). Networks and knowledge production: Collaboration and patenting in biotechnology. In R. Th. A. J. Leenders & S. M. Gabbay (Eds.), *Corporate social capital and liability* (pp. 390–408). Boston: Kluwer Academic.

Stinchcombe, A. L. (1965). Social structure and organizations. In J. G. March (Ed.), *Handbook of organizations* (pp. 142–193). Chicago: Rand-McNally.

Teece, D. J. (1986). Profiting from technological innovation: Implications for integration, collaboration, licensing and public policy. *Research Policy, 15,* 285–305.

Thorelli, H. B. (1986). Networks: Between markets and hierarchies. *Strategic Management Journal, 7,* 37–51.

Tsai, W. (2001). Knowledge transfer in intraorganizational networks: Effects of network position and absorptive capacity on business unit innovation and performance. *Academy of Management Journal, 44,* 996–1004.

Uzzi, B. (1997). Social structure and competition in interfirm networks: The paradox of embeddedness. *Administrative Science Quarterly, 42,* 35–67.

Uzzi, B., & Gillespie, J. J. (1999). Corporate social capital and the cost of financial capital: An embeddedness approach. In R. Th. A. J. Leenders & S. M. Gabbay (Eds.), *Corporate social capital and liability* (pp. 446–459). Boston: Kluwer Academic.

Volery, T., & Mensik, S. (1998). The role of trust in creating effective alliances: A managerial perspective. *Journal of Business Ethics, 17,* 987–994.

Walker, G., Kogut, B., & Shan, W. (1997). Social capital, structural holes and the formation of an industry network. *Organization Science, 8,* 109–125.

Webb, J. W., & Ireland, R. D. (2004). *Resource efficiency of start-up ventures: The link to effectiveness in terms of the creative destruction process.* Paper presented at the Babson/Kauffman Research Conference.

Williams, J. R. (1992). How sustainable is your competitive advantage? *California Management Review, 34*(3), 29–51.

Zahra, S. A., Ireland, R. D., & Hitt, M. A. (2000). International expansion by new venture firms: International diversity, mode of market entry, technological learning, and performance. *Academy of Management Journal, 43,* 925–950.

Zand, D. E. (1972). Trust and managerial problem solving. *Administrative Science Quarterly, 17,* 229–239.

19

Strange Bedfellows

Alliances Between Corporations and Nonprofits

Ted London

Dennis A. Rondinelli

Hugh O'Neill

Alliances between corporations have become relatively common during the past quarter century (Das & Teng, 2000a), but cross-sector alliances—collaborative relationships between organizations in different sectors, such as those between corporations and nonprofit organizations (NPOs)—are emerging as a new, different, and important form of partnership. In general, alliances provide firms with access to different sets of knowledge or core competencies from those existing within the organization (Das & Teng, 2000b). Firms facing growing pressures from customers, shareholders, and other external stakeholders to deal with social and environmental opportunities and issues often do not have internal capabilities to address these challenges effectively (Freeman, 1984; Hart & Milstein, 1999; Rondinelli & London, 2001). As a result, some firms are turning to alliances with cross-sector partners to gain access to new knowledge and to integrate a different set of skills or core competencies (Harrison, Hitt, Hoskisson, & Ireland, 2001; Prahalad & Hamel, 1990).

By partnering with corporations, NPOs are exploring new ways to achieve their social or environmental missions. With companies open to NPO suggestions for dealing with social and environmental challenges, collaboration may be a more effective way for nonprofit organizations to influence the private sector than through adversarial or legal actions. Environmental NPOs, for example, can work with companies to improve their corporate partners' internal processes and

AUTHORS' NOTE: The research for this article was funded in part by the Nonprofit Sector Research Fund of the Aspen Institute, Washington, DC. The conclusions and interpretations, however, are those of the authors.

products. By using a collaborative approach, these NPOs help avert negative environmental impacts before they occur instead of simply responding to the results. Additionally, by working with corporations, NPOs can obtain greater visibility for their programs, influence business leaders' thinking on societal issues, and highlight workable approaches for other companies in the same industry or in related industries (Rondinelli & London, 2003).

Both nonprofit organizations' and corporations' participation in cross-sector alliances, however, poses complex challenges in theory and practice. For example, NPOs have fundamentally different structures and values from corporations. Westley & Vredenburg (1991), for instance, note that corporations typically adopt a hierarchical structure for decision-making, whereas nonprofits frequently use more democratic approaches. Furthermore, corporations and NPOs have a history of being on different sides of an argument (Gray, 1985). Relations between these two types of organizations have been marked by mutual hostility and mistrust. What allows mistrustful organizations with such differences in structures and values and so few direct relational ties (Gulati, 1995a) to create the context (Westley & Vredenburg, 1991) and the trust (Das & Teng, 1998; Ring & Van de Ven, 1992) necessary to consider working cooperatively?

Once allied, cross-sector partners face unique challenges in successfully managing the alliance (London & Rondinelli, 2003; Rondinelli & London, 2003). As in any knowledge-sharing alliance, effective communication requires at least a moderate level of domain similarity (Lane & Lubatkin, 1998; Van de Ven & Walker, 1984). Given their disparate backgrounds, values, and expertise, effective knowledge exchange between cross-sector partners may be especially difficult. For example, although a corporate partner may view an alliance as an entrepreneurial opportunity for profit-making, this form of opportunistic behavior may be antithetical to the charter of the NPO partner. What knowledge-sharing strategies do managers in these cross-sector alliances use to successfully overcome low domain similarity (Van de Ven & Walker, 1984)?

These questions suggest that for cross-sector alliances, the internal and cross-organizational factors that contribute to alliance success are highly stressed and represent key issues of concern. Given the potential for mistrust and poor conditions for learning that cross-sector alliance partners face, skeptics might view their creation as the triumph of hope over common sense. Alternatively, these alliances may provide important clues about how disparate organizations create the conditions that overcome significant differences in thinking, trusting, and knowledge. The move from disparity to synthesis may be an important one in any effort at organizational learning and change.

In this chapter, we describe an emerging and relatively unique phenomenon—cross-sector collaborations between corporations and NPOs. We first briefly review the corporate alliance literature and highlight the particular problems faced by cross-sector alliances. We then suggest a framework to explain how the alliances deal with these problems. The framework draws on a model that describes two types of cross-sector alliances across three stages. We use extant literature to draw important distinctions across type and stage. We conclude by discussing the implications for theory and practice and suggesting possibilities for extensions and tests of the model. Although our interest here is in alliances between corporations and nonprofits, we believe the work has implications for all forms of cross-sector alliances (e.g., collaborations between nonprofits or corporations and governments), and for within-sector alliances that extend beyond normal focal networks (e.g., cross-cultural alliances) (Shaffer & Hillman, 2000).

Learning Alliances

Das and Teng (2000a, 77) define strategic alliances as "interfirm cooperative agreements aimed at pursuing mutual strategic objectives." An alliance can take a variety of forms, including equity joint ventures, nonequity collaborations, and licensing agreements (Inkpen, 2001), for a variety of purposes, including market entry, resource sharing, and learning. Our inquiry explores nonequity learning alliances between corporations and environmental NPOs.

Learning alliances—in which learning from the partner organization is a primary goal—are considered to be particularly difficult to manage. Hamel (1991) observes how these collaborative relationships can easily turn into a race to learn, with the loser landing in a much weaker position vis-à-vis its alliance partner. For cross-sector alliances, learning extends beyond appropriation of private learning benefits to the two partners. Here, the learning outcomes lead to problem solving that has both a private and a social component. These alliances, if successful, can lessen the social costs related to the tragedy of the commons and, as a result, lower systemwide transaction costs. Other scholars have concluded that alliances are simultaneously competitive and cooperative and that firms need to manage the level of transparency (Larsson, Bengtsson, Henriksson, & Sparks, 1998) and the balance between common and private benefits (Khanna, Gulati, & Nohria, 1998) in a cross-organizational learning process. Starting conditions (Lane & Lubatkin, 1998) and the evolutionary path (Kumar & Nti, 1998) of the alliance, as well as the development of the partners' strategies and competitive environments (Koza & Lewin, 1998), can also impact interorganizational outcomes in learning alliances. To date, however, there has been little consideration of how alliances can diffuse forms of socially valued learning.

Although firm-level strategic considerations (such as the need for learning) may drive the decision to consider an alliance with a particular partner, individual-level issues, such as cognitive sense-making (legitimacy) and interpersonal relationships (trust), play a key role in successfully concluding formal negotiations that result in a commitment to an alliance agreement. The individual-level issues may prove essential to the alliance's chances for start-up and ultimate success.

Ring and Van de Ven (1994), for example, describe the cognitive issues in successful alliance formation through two propositions. First, they propose that congruent sense-making increases the likelihood of concluding formal negotiations to engage in cooperative alliances. Second, they argue that congruent psychological contracts increase the likelihood of formal commitment to the alliance. In discussions of trust issues in alliance-building, Gulati (1995b) notes that the willingness of partners to enter into an alliance is negatively related to the belief that a chosen partner will act opportunistically. The belief that the partner will not act opportunistically is a form of trust that is facilitated by prior relationships between firms (a historical trail of relationships by which the partner's behavior can be predicted) and by independent ties to other organizations (a network of relationships through which a partner's opportunistic behavior can incur costs and/or reputation effects).

Van de Ven and Walker (1984) suggest that some level of domain similarity, defined as the degree to which organizations have the same clients and personnel skills and offer the same services, is also necessary to promote alliance success after the initiation of collaborative activities. Domain similarity impacts congruent sense-making and a sense of trust. International ventures, for example, may suffer low levels of congruent sense-making due to dissimilarity in partners' organizational domains. As such, these ventures may be more prone to failure. From a knowledge-sharing perspective, Cohen and Levinthal (1990) use the similar concept of "absorptive capacity" to explain a firm's readiness to learn (that is, to absorb new knowledge). As Lane and Lubatkin (1998) show in a study of research and development alliances, similarity in partners' knowledge bases and dominant logics increases the probability of cross-organizational learning in alliances.

Cross-Sector Alliances: Challenging Requirements

The literature is not optimistic about the prospects of corporate-NPO alliances, as the precursors of success—transparency, absorptive capacity, congruent sense-making, trust, domain consensus—will be sorely lacking. For example, with respect to congruent sense-making, Ring and Van de Ven (1994) describe issue-framing as one of the bases of commonality in decision making. Partners who frame issues in a similar manner will be more successful than partners with divergent frames. Consider an alliance between a corporation and an environmental NPO.[1] For most environmental issues, the levels of prealliance common framing between a corporation and its NPO partner are likely to be low. Many NPO leaders feel that what is good for business is bad for the environment, and corporate executives often believe that what is good for the environment is bad for business. These differences are deeply rooted in individual cognitions and assumptions about the nature of organizations and social behavior. Cross-sector alliances, then, may require substantive changes in the way members in each organization think about not only the partner but themselves.

Similarly, trust may be lacking. Although trust may evolve after initial alliance success (Koza & Lewin, 1998), some trust appears necessary before potential partners commit themselves to joint activity. Yet corporations and nonprofits have a history of being on different sides of an argument. For example, antiglobalization demonstrations in Seattle, Davos, Prague, and Washington, D.C., highlight major differences in NPO and corporate perspectives on a number of issues. Given their conflicting views on many important and emotion-laden issues (such as globalization and the environment), corporations and NPOs have developed a history of mutual distrust that has often resulted in adversarial confrontation (Gray, 1985).

Finally, NPO and corporate domains are more dissimilar than similar. In seeking partners, organizations frequently rely on existing social resources (Eisenhardt & Schoonhoven, 1996), repeated ties (Gulati, 1995a), and access to network resources (Gulati, 1999) to achieve internal legitimacy and to establish trust. However, a corporation's existing social or network resources (Gulati, 1995b) may not always provide relevant information about or access to appropriate partners for cross-sector alliances.

NPOs and corporations, then, face conditions characterized by incongruent sense-making, low trust, and domain dissimilarity. In this situation, relational risks and the potential for opportunism by both partners—for example, the public disclosure of sensitive corporate documents and practices by NPOs or the unauthorized use of an NPO's reputational assets by corporations—lead to concerns within each partner organization about the legitimacy of cooperative action (Das & Teng, 1996; Hill, 1990). Without prior relationships or high levels of trust, members of an alliance in general might rely on the "shadow of the future" to build contracts that provide for protection against opportunism (Dyer, 1997). The contract holds parties accountable for malfeasance and often implies the potential for valuable future interactions that would be abandoned if the alliance fails (Hill, 1990; Macaulay, 1963). This shadow of the future, however, may not offer as much protection for cross-sector alliances as it does for collaborations between corporations for two reasons.

First, any attempt to build trust or contracts in cross-sector alliances will prove a more difficult challenge than those faced by traditional alliances. It is commonly accepted that alliances across national cultures require unique adjustments to accommodate differences in cultural assumptions concerning trust (Parke, 1991). Simon and Lane (2004) argue that organizational culture differences are more disruptive than national differences and professional culture differences are the most disruptive. Cross-sectional alliances may not face differences of national culture, but they invariably involve major differences in organizational culture and professional culture.

Second, the specific nature of malfeasance may be less predictable in cross-sector alliances, and as such, an a priori allocation of remedies is not possible. In fact, the main issue may not be concern about opportunism but concern about the basic identity of the organization itself. Theft of bounded amounts of opportunity should be less threatening than the theft of identity. To complicate matters, the nature of identity is so different across the partners in this form of alliance that common ex ante remedies may not be possible.

The challenges continue even if a cross-sector alliance bridges the initial formation difficulties. Domain dissimilarity is likely to yield low levels of absorptive capacity for both partners. As a result, once joined in common efforts, these partners must find ways to exchange and share knowledge across organizations under conditions that may not favor easy information transfer. Larsson et al. (1998) use the terms *receptivity* and *transparency* to point out that a firm's learning and sharing capabilities have both motivational and ability components. Due to the low level of partner domain similarity (Van de Ven & Walker, 1984), both the motivation and ability for knowledge-sharing between alliance partners may be diminished (Lane & Lubatkin, 1998). The need for individual managers to learn the new repertoires of decision making and analysis necessary for successful collaboration imposes significant costs and challenges. At the individual level, corporate decision makers must learn how to understand and frame environmental issues in a manner that permits effective response. At the organizational level, the firm needs to build the conditions to facilitate cross-organizational learning in situations where both motivation and ability may be low. Given the dissimilarity in domains, the nature of the learning may be asymmetric across the partners, causing concerns about distributive equity.

In sum, compared with corporate collaborations, the individual- and organizational-level factors that contribute to cross-sector alliance success are more stressed, creating major issues of concern. Interest in and commitment to the idea of pursuing an interdependent relationship are likely to be low for both partners (Gulati & Singh, 1998). Simply put, cross-sector alliances face difficult conditions from the outset. Yet corporations do engage in these difficult alliances (Stafford, Polonsky, & Hartman, 2000; Westley & Vredenburg, 1991). The issues concerning the justification, formation, and execution of cross-sector alliances to accommodate seemingly disparate entities exceed the reach of current theories concerning alliances. For example, current theory presumes there are substitutes available if trust is lacking, in the form of contracts or hostages. Similarly, current theory presumes some level of calculative trust is possible, based on the partner's ability to define expected gains. The substitutes for trust and the clarity of future gains do not exist for the cross-sector alliance. Therefore, we will develop a new framework for explaining these alliances between strange bedfellows and the conditions that might foster effective participation by each party.

A Framework: Type and Stage

In developing our framework for cross-sector alliances, we build on two key assumptions. First, alliances are formed for different reasons, as internal contexts and external pressures vary among firms (Pfeffer & Salancik, 1978; Westley & Vredenburg, 1991). Second, alliances pass through several stages (Van de Ven & Walker, 1984), and at each stage, different factors are crucial for continued progress (Das & Teng., 2000b; Ring & Van de Ven, 1994).

Cross-sector alliances form for different purposes. Miles and Cameron (1982), describing how firms respond to environmental pressures, argue that firms can use either a defensive or an offensive response. The form of the response varies, based on the decision maker's perception of the external and internal environment (Dutton & Jackson, 1987; Sharma & Vredenburg, 1998). There should be similar response profiles for corporations engaged in alliances with NPOs, based on higher or lower coercive pressures from the government or from stakeholders (Milstein, Hart, & York, 2002). We call one form of response reactive and the other form proactive.

We further discuss each type below and illustrate them by describing specific alliances.

Reactive alliances are formed in response to the threat of regulation from governmental authorities. In recent years, for example, industries involved with extraction or energy production have faced increasing pressure due to concerns about loss of unrecoverable physical assets or pollution. For example, managers in three corporations (MeadWestvaco, DuPont, and Shell) involved in natural resource extraction describe their alliances as a response to potential threats in their environment and discuss the alliances as a form of protection against isolation (London, Rondinelli, & O'Neill, 2004).

In contrast, where reactive alliances are threat-driven, proactive alliances are opportunity-driven. Firms engaged in proactive alliances also perceive pressure in the environment, but the pressure is less coercive and involves minimal risk of government regulation. The pressure may come from other stakeholders in the firm's environment, and proactive firms may perceive opportunity for effective (that is, rent-creating) strategic differentiation. This differentiation is possible only if the sources of the pressure are diffuse and relatively weak, as strong pressures would produce similar responses across firms. For example, retail companies (McDonald's, Wal-Mart) and consumer products firms (Nike) face public scrutiny but do not face the regulatory pressures seen in extractive industries. Consider the case of Starbucks, which is involved in a cross-section alliance with Conservative International to produce shade-grown coffee in Mexico. The coffee fields serve as a buffer for a conservation zone, and Starbucks sells the coffee under a specific brand name. This alliance offers the potential for creating environmental and social benefits and a differentiated brand for Starbucks (London & Rondinelli, 2003).

Similar to alliances between corporations, cross-sector alliances evolve through stages including rationale, formation, and performance (Das & Teng, 2000b). For this framework, we describe each stage as separate and sequential. Recursive iterations may be typical, as partners move through the stages at different rates, double back and forward through the process, and experience different interpretations of the transition points. However, for purposes of clarity and parsimony and with only limited loss in reality, the alliance development process can be presented in a linear fashion (Ring & Van de Ven, 1994).

The *rationale stage* occurs before the alliance is formed and involves the identification of potential valuable partner resources that cannot be obtained through the market or via merger or acquisition (Das & Teng, 2000b). To move past this stage, the organization must successfully address issues of internal legitimacy. In other words, for the alliance to proceed, internal decision makers must recognize that a potential partner has useful knowledge and must also value the opportunity to combine this external knowledge with the knowledge and resources currently residing within the firm. A crucial part of the *formation stage* entails establishing a cross-organizational relationship and structure that enhance the transfer of knowledge resources between the partner organizations. To pass through this stage, members from both organizations must trust their partner to share valuable knowledge within but not outside alliance boundaries. Although the issue of internal legitimacy within each partner remains important, the key success factor at the formation stage is likely to be the capability to build trust among the participants. If the partners are successful at establishing legitimacy and trust, the alliance can move into the *performance stage*, which includes sharing knowledge and implementing action plans. In the performance stage, as the cross-sector partners overcome the natural limitations in absorptive capacity, they can implement an effective knowledge-sharing strategy.

Table 19.1 presents the important issues at each stage. Just as structure follows strategy in corporate design, the form of these cross-sector alliances follows alliance type. As a result, the solutions to these issues at each stage differ for reactive and proactive alliances, respectively. In the following section, we describe how the two types of alliances vary in their solutions across the stages.

Table 19.1 Strange Bedfellows: The Stages and Issues

The Rationale Stage
How are issues framed?
How do partners link across domains?
The Formation Stage
How is trust formed?
How is information transferred?
The Performance Stage
What is the learning style?
How is information diffused?

The Rationale Stage

During the rationale stage, the incipient cross-sector alliances face two key processes. The first, issue-framing, combines the steps of recognizing that cross-sector partners may have resources valuable for addressing environmental opportunities and challenges and legitimizing the importance to these environmental issues within the organizations' decision-making group. The second process, domain linkage, involves the identification and selection of appropriate partners from the alternate domain, whereby corporations identify and select NPOs, or NPOs identify and select corporations. For the sake of simplicity, our discussion will illustrate each stage from the perspective of the corporations involved in these activities.

Issue-Framing. Corporations faced with environmental challenges can choose among ignoring signals in the environment, resisting signals in the environment, or responding to signals in the environment by engaging in activities such as cross-sector alliances. The response choice hinges on which options become legitimate in the view of the major stakeholders. Options include a rigid response (ignoring), an aggressive response (resistance), or an engaging response (opportunity-seeking). The exact response emerges based on the decision makers' abilities to make the response legitimate.

Legitimacy can emerge quickly or slowly. Quick legitimacy occurs if a powerful member of a dominant coalition champions the idea. In closely held firms, for example, successful CEOs may become champions of a particular issue (Rondinelli & Morrison, forthcoming). An issue's adoption by a dominant leader defines the issue as legitimate. Legitimacy can emerge more slowly in conditions where champions other than a dominant leader adopt issues or in conditions where there is conflict about the legitimacy of the issue. In these situations, the process and skill of issue selling become important (Dutton, Ashford, O'Neill, Hayes, & Wierba, 1997). An early champion may convince a dominant leader, who, in turn, influences opposing coalitions. Alternatively, champions may emerge within coalitions and work with their respective coalitions to convince others of the salience of the issue.

Reactive alliances occur in response to a threat—the threat of regulation. In threat conditions, an aggressive response, such as resistance, might frequently be expected. In addition, the threat provokes some form of in-group bonding, so the level of resistance is likely to be widespread. Therefore, legitimacy building requires either issue adoption by a very strong leader or lengthy processes of issue selling by champions within the organization. Proactive alliances present a different scenario. These alliances are opportunity-driven. Opportunities are less likely to evoke aversive or rigid responses. In addition, the interpretation of an issue as an opportunity implies some level of fit between the external issue and the skill or value set of the firm. As such, for proactive alliances, issue recognition and legitimacy can occur simultaneously.

Domain Linkage. In addition to recognizing an issue as legitimate, organizations need to link with potential partners. Corporations need to find NPOs, and NPOs need to find corporations, as potential alliance mates. Corporate alliances generally form between firms already involved in close networks. For cross-sector alliances, potential partners may not be in the firm's extant networking set, so some process of linking is necessary to find and engage partners.

The concepts of *repeated ties* and *structural holes* help provide a description of the patterns of linkage. *Repeated ties* represents a pattern of repeated interactions between two parties in which the repetition builds legitimacy and trust which, in turn, make future ties easier to form (Gulati, 1995a). Certain individuals within a firm, such as the alliance champion, may have had interactions with NPO colleagues (Rondinelli & London, 2001, 2002). Yet these relationships are at the individual and not the organizational level. Thus, at the rationale stage, a firm engaging in a cross-sector alliance for the first time lacks any organizational ties with potential partners, so repeated ties are not possible (Rondinelli & London, 2003). *Structural holes* is a description of a pattern in a network of relationships (Burt, 1992). If an organization has a connection with two different organizations, and the latter two have no connection with each other, there is a structural hole between the latter two that is "linked" by the first. The linkage through a structural hole can substitute for missing repeated ties, as the existing relationships between the first and the second and the first and the third parties might generalize to quick trust between the second and the third parties.

With respect to domain linkage, then, we suggest that linkage is quicker and easier if "linked" structural holes exist in the firm's networks. Put simply, the firm seeking to find NPO partners first searches its extant network for links across structural holes. If no connecting organization exists, then the firm must rely on building a pattern of repeated ties.

As with issue-framing, the patterns of linkage differ for reactive and proactive alliances. Proactive alliances pursue opportunities with requirements that match their set of skills and values. Those values can offer links to stakeholders in the environment who are connected to NPO networks, and these stakeholders, in turn, help with access across the structural hole to NPOs. As Gulati (1999, 399) notes, firms get information from "interfirm networks that channel valuable information." As an example, the apparel manufacturer Norm Thompson Outfitters leveraged an existing relationship to cross a structural hole and establish a collaborative partnership with the Alliance for Environmental Innovation, a nonprofit with expertise in reducing waste and encouraging recycling. The third party, Business for Social Responsibility, a membership organization that provides environmental and social information, tools, and advisory services, served as a conduit to connect the two organizations quickly (Rondinelli & London, 2001, 2003)

Reactive firms are less likely to have values and skills that are related to the regulatory challenges they are facing. In this environment, their networks do not provide similar access across existing structural holes, and these firms are forced to adopt the more difficult step of developing repeated ties without the reputation effects provided by an introduction from a link in the normal social network. The champions in these firms might provide access through interpersonal connections across organizations, but the move from interpersonal connections to organizational connections requires a cascading sequence of social connections across a wider set of individuals within the potential partners.

For instance, in 1996, an individual at MeadWestvaco, a global manufacturer of paper, paperboard, and packaging, worked with an employee at The Nature Conservancy (TNC) to develop recommendations for protecting particular species in some of MeadWestvaco's forestland. From that initial collaboration, MeadWestvaco began to talk to TNC, an environmental NPO, about the issue of ensuring the identification of all important areas and threatened species. This led to an agreement, signed in 1998, for TNC to survey Westvaco's land in West Virginia. This arrangement served as the model for a broader agreement, signed in 1999, to survey 1.3 million acres owned by Westvaco (Rondinelli & London, 2001, 2003). Although feasible, this process of cascading trust-building is longer-term, more difficult, and riskier than the process of generalizing trust across structural holes.

The Formation Stage

The differences between the proactive and reactive alliances at the rationale stage lead to differences in the emergent processes that occur through the formation stage. The differences are a function of the partners' perceived relational risks or the possibility that the partners in the alliance will not commit themselves fully to the joint effort (Das & Teng, 1996). This difference in the levels of prealliance trust leads to different forms of information-sharing between the partners.

Trust. Relationships follow different forms based on the levels of trust between the participants. In more traditional corporate alliances, for example, where risk of opportunism is high (and, therefore, trust is low), contracts serve as a means for anticipating and forestalling opportunistic behavior on the part of either partner. For learning alliances, though, it may be difficult to anticipate the form of opportunism. Therefore, firms might be hesitant to engage in contracting if they suspect opportunistic behavior by the partner. Under conditions of trust, the suspicion of opportunistic behavior would be lower, and firms are likely to make strong commitments to the alliance, where strong commitment includes contracts based on shared expectations of outcomes.

As might be expected, given the difference in the initial issue-framing in the two forms of alliance and the difference in the use of social networks to gain access to partners, the initial level of trust will vary across the two types of alliances. Proactive alliances start with a higher level of trust than reactive alliances. In turn, the different trust levels determine the sequence and type of information-sharing that will take place as the alliance forms.

Information Transfer. The rate and form of information-sharing and analysis will influence the speed and efficacy of problem solving, according to decision and planning theorists. Faster, better decisions occur with free discussion across multiple levels of the organization (Brown & Eisenhardt, 1997). The proactive alliance occurs in a context that favors this form of exchange, whereas the reactive alliance does not. Therefore, the sequence of information transfer will differ in the two forms of alliance.

In the proactive alliance, members in each partner perceive a match between the purpose of the alliance and the existing values of the organization. For example, in Norm Thompson Outfitters collaboration with the Alliance for Environmental Innovation, support for the alliance diffused quickly throughout both organizations. In proactive alliances, information is shared widely within and across the partners. As a result, learning can occur more effectively.

In contrast, the reactive alliance lacks the context for easy diffusion of information, as members of the organization may not accept the need for the alliance and/or the validity of the partner. As a result, the need for internal coalition-building is high in both partners. Although the level of information-sharing may be high between champions across the partners (as these champions built some trust during the linking stages), levels of intrafirm information sharing by the champion may be low, as firm members sense conflict between the historical values of the firm and the mission of the alliance. The need to build both intrafirm and interfirm trust will lead to a sequenced process of extension, as occurred in the alliance between MeadWestvaco and TNC, in which the twin steps of building intrafirm and interfirm trust are repeated across the differentiated units in each partner. The length of time required to complete this process depends on the internal reputation of the champions, the champions' ability to create support, and the patterns of organizational differentiation.

The process increases in difficulty for organizations with high levels of organizational differentiation, suggesting that small projects concentrated in one unit within the firm may provide the easiest path to generating the trust required to proceed with implementation. Indeed, the need to start small may be a requisite characteristic of reactive alliances. Given the difficulties of establishing trust across organizations that lack any prior network connections, success may require a number of restarts or experiments if initial partners do not work out.

The Performance Stage

The differences between the two alliance types at the performance stage follow directly from the differences in the precedent stages. The levels of trust and the patterns of information transfer create the conditions for differences in learning styles and variance in the extent of internal diffusion of learning.

Learning Styles. Successful execution of cross-sector alliances requires an effective knowledge-sharing strategy. Cross-organizational learning, however, requires some level of common experience (Cohen & Levinthal, 1990), a condition that is often weak or missing in alliances between profit-making and nonprofit organizations. Individual managers with disparate organizational backgrounds must have the motivation and the ability to share knowledge (Larsson et al., 1998), and the partners must find creative ways to overcome a lack of relative absorptive capacity (Lane & Lubatkin, 1998).

Proactive and reactive firms choose somewhat different learning strategies to overcome limitations in relative absorptive capacity. The conditions in proactive alliances favor knowledge absorption, whereas the conditions in proactive alliances favor knowledge leverage. Knowledge absorption occurs if, when two partners interact, one absorbs knowledge from the other so that, after the absorption, the partner can make decisions using that knowledge (Lane & Lubatkin, 1998). This strategy also enables the alliance partners to combine their expertise to create new knowledge and capabilities (Cohen & Levinthal, 1990). Knowledge leverage occurs if, when two partners interact, one partner uses its unique knowledge to inform the second partner about decision options and choices (Conner & Prahalad, 1996). Although the former strategy emphasizes acquiring and jointly developing knowledge, the latter is closer to a consulting relationship in which the firm uses but does not absorb the knowledge of its partner organization.

Knowledge absorption is dependent on high levels of interaction across firms and widely shared information. Given the relatively high levels of trust and legitimacy, this pattern can occur easily (and relatively quickly) in the proactive alliance. In the Norm Thompson Outfitters–Alliance for Environmental Innovation collaboration, for instance, the partners reciprocally shared knowledge and jointly worked on each step of the project. The greater overlap in skills and values in proactive cross-sector relationships also facilitates knowledge absorption, as there is a larger base of relative absorptive capacity.

In contrast, knowledge leverage can take place in relationships with lower levels of cross-organization interaction, trust, and legitimacy. For example, in MeadWestvaco's alliance with TNC, the knowledge-sharing was sequential and therefore did not require a full understanding or absorption. At each stage, one partner was primarily responsible for a specific aspect of the project, and the organizations transferred this responsibility between each other. By working relatively independently and proceeding in a serial fashion, partners in reactive alliances can use knowledge leverage as a learning strategy that overcomes limitations in trust, legitimacy, and domain similarity.

Internal Diffusion of Learning. The learning strategy impacts what the organization and its members learn. The systemwide diffusion of knowledge and insight that occurs with knowledge absorption creates conditions for exploration, or identifying new opportunities (March, 1991). By solving problems jointly, the partners may synergistically generate new knowledge. The more sequential sharing of information present in knowledge leveraging, alternatively, creates conditions more suited for effective exploitation. In a reactive cross-sector alliance, a corporation uses a nonprofit's expertise to enhance its existing capabilities. The changes created as a result of proactive alliances will, therefore, be more novel than those that occur in reactive alliances.

Strange Bedfellows: Implications for Theory and Practice

This framework describing the differences between proactive and reactive cross-sector alliances has implications for these specific forms of alliances as well as for more general forms of alliances. One implication of the framework of the model is that it provides a path to understanding why many specific alliance types might fail. For example, in the absence of a strong champion who provides a signal of legitimacy, the reactive alliance requires that champions who are not dominant leaders pay attention to the process of internal trust-building. The internal trust-building is a necessary step to creating the capability for cross-organizational transfer of knowledge.

Although reactive alliances may be more difficult because of the challenges of trust formation, the proactive firm is not without risk. The framework implies that the trust necessary at the formation stage is high (compared to reactive firms) because of the related network links that the corporation and its NPO partner share. If a proactive firm chooses a partner that lacks these related links, the problems of trust formation will be the same as those faced by the reactive firm. If the pattern of information transfer or the learning strategy remain unchanged, the alliance may fail, as partners on each side, lacking trust, may not share the information necessary for knowledge absorption.

Although we have focused our examples here on the issues present in the corporate partner, the results apply to the NPO partner as well. If an NPO's charter is to influence corporate performance, the NPO can choose between alliance and lobbying as a form of influence. Effective alliance-building requires an understanding of the different pressures that corporations face and an approach to domain linkage and information transfer that facilitates the corporation's effective response to the pressures and the alliance.

Cross-sector alliances provide an opportunity for understanding the early diffusion of radical ideas across organizational forms. This is an important form of organizational learning, in which learning might be directed from social agents outside the organization and by means other than self-regulation or government regulation. To the extent that self-regulation is self-serving and government regulation is expensive, cross-sector alliances may serve important social purposes.

Similarly, cross-sector alliances provide a venue through which to study the emergence of cooperation under conditions of distrust. Traditional theories of alliances, drawn generally from sociological and economic theories, emphasize trust or its substitutes as a necessary characteristic of alliances (Zaheer & Harris, 2005). Alliances, though, do start in the absence of trust. The stages prior to trust development or the identification of trust substitutes may be as important as later stages of the alliances. The study of alliances that take place in nontrusting contexts might further benefit from investigation in fields that deal with conflict, such as political science.

At the societal level, the engagement of NPOs in alliances with corporations provides a way of influencing corporate behavior and social innovation. These alliances might be encouraged through grants to NPOs or tax incentives to corporations. The use of alliances might be more effective than direct regulation, especially in those conditions requiring novel innovations. If sufficient resources could be provided to corporations or NPOs to generate the conditions for proactive alliances, competing alliances could create alternative solutions for the targeted social issue that seek to maximize both organizational and societal benefits. Across time, the competition among alternative solutions might lead to a set of best practices that could then diffuse across the organizational population.

Although the framework positions the two types of alliances as exclusive types, it is possible that successful reactive alliances can lead to conditions between the partners that change into proactive conditions. If this is the case, even in industries under the threat of regulation, a public policy encouraging cross-sector alliances could lead to effective learning if a sufficient number of alliance partners pass through the difficult early stages of legitimacy and trust-building.

Similarly, although we propose the framework based on alliances between organizations with different underlying purposes (profit-making corporations and nonprofit organizations), it is common that organizations with similar charters can also lack trust. Although the intended purpose of alliances between these types of organizations may be to form a proactive alliance, the low level of trust might cause the alliance to fail if its managers do not pay careful attention to building trust and to understanding the specific information-sharing sequences in the reactive alliance. For example, we are beginning to understand how corporations from differing national cultures create alliances that bridge their differences. We know very little, though, about how alliances extend across differences in organizational or professional cultures or across substantive diversity in political beliefs. For example, alliances between competitors in the same industry might have the properties of cross-sector alliances if competition has created different organizational cultures between the partners. Former competitors make strange bedfellows, too.

As Harrison et al. (2001) note, resource complementarity is often a necessary prerequisite to optimal value creation. The theory, though, presumes some similarity in assumptions between the partners concerning the nature of rents and value creation and the validity of the partners' claims on the rents. Alliances that bridge these differences, as cross-sector alliances do, are in essence transformational and worthy of specific study. Perhaps more important, cross-sector alliances can lead to significant changes in the pattern of resource consumption and sharing, providing important benefits to the common good.

Our framework is not meant to be exhaustive. There may be other types of alliances. Further, within each type, there may be recurrent patterns. We suspect, though, that for managers planning to engage in cross-sector alliances or researchers trying to understand the pattern of success in these alliances, the issues we cover here are important. Managers in corporations and NPOs can create the conditions that facilitate effective alliance-building to the benefit of each.

Note

1. Throughout, we use the example of alliances between corporations and environmental NPOs. These represent one of the more common forms of cross-sector collaboration. The points developed apply equally to other forms of cross-sector alliances, such as those between corporations and charitable groups or corporations and social-interest groups.

References

Brown, S. L., & Eisenhardt, K. M. (1997). The art of continuous change: Linking complexity theory and time-paced evolution in relentlessly shifting organizations. *Administrative Science Quarterly, 42,* 1–34.

Burt, R. S. (1992). The social structure of competition. In N. Nohria & R. G. Eccles (Eds.), *Networks and organizations: Structure, form, and action* (pp. 57–91). Boston: Harvard Business School Press.

Cohen, W. M., & Levinthal, D. A. (1990). Absorptive capacity: A new perspective on learning and innovation. *Administrative Science Quarterly, 35,* 128–152.

Conner, K. R., & Prahalad, C. K. (1996). A resource-based theory of the firm: Knowledge versus opportunism. *Organization Science, 7,* 477–501.

Das, T. K., & Teng, B. S. (1996). Risk types and interfirm alliance structures. *Journal of Management Studies, 33,* 827–843.

Das, T. K., & Teng, B. S. (1998). Between trust and control: Developing confidence in partner cooperation in alliances. *Academy of Management Review, 23,* 491–512.

Das, T. K., & Teng, B. S. (2000a). Instabilities of strategic alliances: An internal tensions perspective. *Organization Science, 11,* 77–101.

Das, T. K., & Teng, B. S. (2000b). A resource based theory of strategic alliances. *Journal of Management, 26,* 31–61.

Dutton, J. E., Ashford, S. J., O'Neill, R. M., Hayes, E., & Wierba, E. E. (1997). Reading the wind: How middle managers assess the context for selling issues to top managers. *Strategic Management Journal, 18*(5), 407–423.

Dutton, J. E., & Jackson, S. E. (1987). Categorizing strategic issues: Links to organizational action. *Academy of Management Journal, 12*(1), 76–90.

Dyer, J. H. (1997). Effective interfirm collaboration: How firms minimize transaction costs and maximize transaction value. *Strategic Management Journal, 18,* 535–556.

Eisenhardt, K. M., & Schoonhoven, C. B. (1996). Resource-based view of strategic alliance formation: Strategic and social effects in entrepreneurial firms. *Organization Science, 7,* 136–150.

Freeman, R. E. (1984). *Strategic management: A stakeholder approach.* Boston: Pitman.

Gray, B. (1985). Conditions facilitating interorganizational collaboration. *Human Relations, 38,* 911–936.

Gulati, R. (1995a). Does familiarity breed trust? The implications of repeated ties for contractual choice in alliances. *Academy of Management Journal, 38,* 85–112.

Gulati, R. (1995b). Social structure and alliance formation: A longitudinal analysis. *Administrative Science Quarterly, 40,* 619–652.

Gulati, R. (1999). Network location and learning: The influence of network resources and firm capabilities on alliance formation. *Strategic Management Journal, 20,* 397–420.

Gulati, R., & Singh, H. (1998). The architecture of cooperation: Managing coordination costs and appropriation concerns in strategic alliances. *Administrative Science Quarterly, 43,* 781–814.

Hamel, G. (1991). Competition for competence and inter-partner learning within international strategic alliances [special issue]. *Strategic Management Journal, 12,* 83–103.

Harrison, J. S., Hitt, M. A., Hoskisson, R. E., & Ireland, R. D. (2001). Resource complementarity in business combinations: Extending the logic to organizational alliances. *Journal of Management, 27,* 679–690.

Hart, S. L., & Milstein, M. B. (1999). Global sustainability and the creative destruction of industries. *Sloan Management Review, 41*(1), 23–33.

Hill, C. W. L. (1990). Cooperation, opportunism, and the invisible hand: Implications for transaction cost theory. *Academy of Management Review, 15,* 500–513.

Inkpen, A. C. (2001). Strategic alliances. In M. A. Hitt, R. E. Freeman, & J. S. Harrison (Eds.), *The Blackwell handbook of strategic management* (pp. 409–432). Oxford: Blackwell.

Khanna, T., Gulati, R., & Nohria, N. (1998). The dynamics of learning alliances: Competition, cooperation, and relative scope. *Strategic Management Journal, 19,* 193–210.

Koza, M. P., & Lewin, A. Y. (1998). The co-evolution of strategic alliances. *Organization Science, 9,* 1–10.

Kumar, R., & Nti, K. O. (1998). Differential learning and interaction in alliance dynamics: A process and outcome discrepancy model. *Organization Science, 9,* 356–367.

Lane, P. J., & Lubatkin, M. (1998). Relative absorptive capacity and interorganizational learning. *Strategic Management Journal, 19,* 461–477.

Larsson, R., Bengtsson, L., Henriksson, K., & Sparks, J. (1998). The interorganizational learning dilemma: Collective knowledge development in strategic alliances. *Organization Science, 9,* 285–305.

London, T., & Rondinelli, D. A. (2003). Partnerships for learning: Managing tensions in nonprofit organizations' alliances with corporations. *Stanford Social Innovation Review, 1*(3), 28–35.

London, T., Rondinelli, D. A., & O'Neill, H. M. (2004). Exploring uneasy learning alliances between corporations and non-profit organizations. In D. H. Nagao (Ed.), *Proceedings of the Sixty-Third Annual Meeting of the Academy of Management* (CD), ISSN 1543-8643.

Macaulay, S. (1963). Non-contractual relations in business: A preliminary study. *American Sociological Review, 28,* 55–67.

March, J. G. (1991). Exploration and exploitation in organizational learning. *Organization Science, 2*(1), 71–87.

Miles, R. H., & Cameron, K. S. (1982). *Coffin nails and corporate strategies.* Englewood Cliffs, NJ: Prentice Hall.

Milstein, M. B., Hart, S. L., & York, A. S. (2002). Coercion breeds variation: The differential impact of isomorphic pressures on environmental strategies. In A. J. Hoffman & M. J. Ventresca (Eds.), *Organization, policy, and the natural environment* (pp. 151–172). Palo Alto, CA: Stanford University Press.

Parkhe, A. (1991). Interfirm diversity, organizational learning, and longevity. *Journal of International Business Studies, 22*(4), 579–601.

Pfeffer, J., & Salancik, G. R. (1978). *The external control of organizations: A resource dependence perspective.* New York: Harper & Row.

Prahalad, C. K., & Hamel, G. (1990). The core competence of the corporation. *Harvard Business Review, 68*(3), 79–91.

Ring, P. S., & Van de Ven, A. H. (1992). Structuring cooperative relationships between organizations. *Strategic Management Journal, 13,* 483–498.

Ring, P. S., & Van de Ven, A. H. (1994). Developmental processes of cooperative interorganizational relationships. *Academy of Management Journal, 19,* 90–118.

Rondinelli, D. A., & London, T. (2001). *Partnering for sustainability: Managing nonprofit organization-corporate environmental partnerships.* Working Paper Series, Nonprofit Sector Research Fund, Aspen Institute, Washington, DC.

Rondinelli, D. A., & London, T. (2002). Stakeholder and corporate responsibilities in cross-sectoral environmental collaborations: Building value, legitimacy and trust. In J. Andriof, S. Waddock, B. Husted, & S. Rahman (Eds.), *Unfolding stakeholder thinking: Theory, responsibility and engagement* (pp. 201–215). Sheffield, UK: Greenleaf.

Rondinelli, D. A., & London, T. (2003). How corporations and environmental groups cooperate: Assessing cross-sector alliances and collaborations. *Academy of Management Executive, 17*(1), 61–76.

Rondinelli, D. A., & Morrison J. (2005). How a nonprofit corporation creates value for the private sector: Advanced Energy and Environments for Living program. *Corporate environmental strategy, 12,* 65–72.

Shaffer, B., & Hillman, A. J. (2000). The development of business-government strategies by diversified firms. *Strategic Management Journal, 21,* 175–190.

Sharma, S., & Vredenburg, H. (1998). Proactive corporate environmental strategy and the development of competitively valuable organizational capabilities. *Strategic Management Journal, 19,* 729–753.

Simon, D. G., & Lane, P. J. (2004). A model of cultural differences and international alliance formation. *Journal of International Business Studies, 35,* 306–319.

Stafford, E. R., Polonsky, M. J., & Hartman, C. L. (2000). Environmental NGO-business collaboration and strategic bridging: A case analysis of the Greenpeace-Foron alliance. *Business Strategy and the Environment, 9,* 122–135.

Van de Ven, A. H., & Walker, G. (1984). The dynamics of interorganizational coordination. *Administrative Science Quarterly, 29,* 598–561.

Westley, F., & Vredenburg, H. (1991). Strategic bridging: The collaboration between environmentalists and business in the marketing of green products. *Journal of Applied Behavioral Science, 27,* 65–90.

Zaheer, A. & Harris, J. (2005). Interorganizational trust. In O. Shenkar & J. Reuer (Eds.), *Handbook of Strategic Alliances.* London: Sage.

PART VI

Alliance Research Methodologies

20

Research Methods in Alliances

Arvind Parkhe

Organizational theorists have correctly argued that management lies at the intersection of a variety of disciplines, including economics, sociology, and psychology, and, therefore, the study of management of organizations is inherently complex. This complexity is compounded in the context of the management of business alliances. Alliances between microorganisms, between individuals, between groups, between nonprofit organizations, and between nation-states have long been studied in fields such as biology, interorganizational relations, political science, and game theory. Relatively new is the study of alliances between for-profit organizations in the literatures on strategic management, marketing, and international business. This literature has grown exponentially in recent years, reflecting the rapid growth in business alliances in recent years.

The purpose of this chapter is to assess the body of work on alliances. More specifically, I attempt to focus on select aspects of the alliance literature, including the research methods most commonly employed and the impact of such choices on the development of knowledge of alliances. At the core, the questions addressed in this chapter include the following: What do we know about alliances, what do we not know, and how do we fill the gaps in knowledge? The remainder of this chapter is organized as follows. First, I briefly review the central issues surrounding research methods and theory development in alliances. Next, I assess the tremendous progress made over the past decade in alliance research along with identifying the significant knowledge gaps that stubbornly persist. To what root causes can these gaps be traced? In turn, what fresh steps may be needed to accelerate rigorous theory development in alliances? These are among the issues I discuss, based upon an analysis of the extant alliance literature. I conclude with some observations about and recommendations for alliance research.

The Central Issues: A Review

In his classic book, *The Conduct of Inquiry,* Kaplan (1964) noted that there is no subject matter that in itself precludes exactness of treatment. But, he argued,

> the state of our knowledge and the techniques of observation and measurement available to us at any given time not only can but surely do impose such limits. Models are often improperly exact: they call for measures that we cannot in fact obtain, or that we would not know how to use if we did obtain them. (1964, 283)

Kaplan also observed a "mystique of quantity," which is "an exaggerated regard for the significance of measurement, just because it is quantitative, without regard either to what has been measured or to what can subsequently be done with the measure. Number is treated as having an intrinsic scientific value" (1964, 172).

These are important thoughts. Similar thoughts were echoed more recently in the context of the international management literature by Werner (2002). Werner suggested that because the field of international management is relatively young, more qualitative methodologies are necessary, because qualitative methodologies facilitate grounded theory-building. The central issues for the present chapter, then, are: Which aspects of alliances have researchers identified as theoretically salient? How much research attention has each aspect received? Are the treatments of theoretical salience and research attention consistent, and if not, why not?

These were among the issues I raised in an article in the *Academy of Management Review* in 1993 (Parkhe, 1993). Specifically, I argued that progress in the study of alliances has been mixed, dramatic advances notwithstanding. Although several theoretical dimensions have been emphasized in the literature, researchers have not addressed certain crucial questions at the heart of the alliance relationship, and hence, individually useful alliance studies have not coalesced into a collectively coherent body of work with an underlying theoretical structure. I proposed that this weakness in theory development stems from the convergence of "hard" methodological approaches with "soft" behavioral variables, such as trust, reciprocity, opportunism, and forbearance.

Fast-forwarding to 2004: in the ten-year period since the publication of the above-cited article (1994–2003), how much progress has been made? Along what paths has research in the field evolved? What are the remaining gaps in alliance knowledge today, and to what factors can these gaps be traced? After a review of the current alliance literature, I attempt to answer these questions. The next section begins with a description of the sampling technique for article selection and analytical technique for data extraction from each selected article.

Assessing the Progress and the Remaining Gaps, 1994–2003

A Note on Data and Methods

Three sample selection criteria were employed: (1) time period, (2) publication outlet, and (3) type of publication. The first criterion was an attempt to capture the recent rapid growth of the alliance literature and major trends of current and future relevance by selecting alliance-related articles published between 1994 and 2003. The second criterion implied that certain top-tier outlets were the most likely to represent cutting-edge thought in alliance research, and targeted those outlets: *Academy of Management Review, Academy of Management Journal, Organization Science, Journal of International Business Studies, Strategic Management Journal, and Administrative Science Quarterly.* The third criterion restricted the study to all research notes and full-length articles on interfirm cooperative relationships, but excluded nonoriginal work such as book reviews. Taken together, these three criteria generated a domain of inquiry that is relevant and significant and that meets the needs of this research particularly well.

Application of the three criteria using computerized search of the literature generated a sample of 129 articles. Of these, one was excluded from further analysis as it was primarily an editorial review piece introducing a special issue on alliances (Osborn & Hagedoorn, 1997).

The remaining 128 articles formed the database upon which this chapter is based. Consistent with the arguments in Parkhe (1993), I examined each article for the following factors:

1. Theoretical/conceptual or empirical?
2. For empirical papers, qualitative or quantitative methods, or both?
3. Primary theoretical focus (a) on "traditional" alliance research dimensions, or (b) on "soft" behavioral variables?
4. Traditional alliance research dimensions include (a) motives for alliance formation, (b) partner selection/characteristics, (c) control/conflict, and (d) alliance stability/performance
5. Behavioral variables posited to be at the heart of the cooperative relationship include (a) trust, (b) reciprocity, (c) opportunism, and (d) forbearance. The degree of importance accorded to one or more of the behavioral variables (trust, reciprocity, opportunism, and forbearance): 5 = extremely important, 1 = not at all important.

Findings

Twenty-five articles were theoretical/conceptual in nature, and the other 103 articles were empirical. It may be worth pausing to reflect on whether 19.5% (25 out of 128) of published work devoted to advancing theoretical/conceptual aspects of alliance research constitutes an appropriate amount at the current stage of theory development, or whether this amount may be "excessively high" or "excessively low." One view would be to suggest that regardless of the evolutionary stage of a particular topic, given the continuing pressures to publish empirical research imposed by the tenure/promotion/annual review procedures, 19.5% of theoretical/conceptual work may in fact be surprisingly high. But another view, one to which I subscribe, is to state that greater intellectual talent may be fruitfully directed at the present time to deepening our theoretical understanding of the alliance phenomenon. We need to put the horse before the cart and start asking the right questions before empirically trying to find the answers. To be sure, the research process is iterative, not either/or; empirical studies and theoretical/conceptual studies go hand in hand, each helping the other lift the level of understanding of the alliance phenomenon. Yet it is puzzling to find over four out of every five published papers testing existing theory rather than developing new theory to test.

Of the 103 empirical articles, an overwhelming majority (91) were quantitative. Only eight articles were qualitative, and a mere four combined qualitative and quantitative methodologies.

Quantitative studies, particularly those published in the six reputable journals chosen for the present chapter's data sample, tend to be methodologically impeccable. Yet rigor alone cannot substitute for fundamental limitations of a study. Quantitative studies are typically theory-testing (not theory-generating); adopt a deductive approach (not inductive approach); and use an objective/nomothetic/outsider perspective (not a subjective/idiographic/insider perspective). Each of these factors inherently limits the capacity to advance our understanding that can result from such work. The continuing dominance of quantitative methods in alliance research is depicted in Figure 20.1.

Prior to 1993, alliance research tended to be focused primarily on the "traditional" dimensions of alliance motives, partner selection/characteristics, control/conflict issues, and stability/performance of alliances. Parkhe (1993) urged the development of alliance theory centering

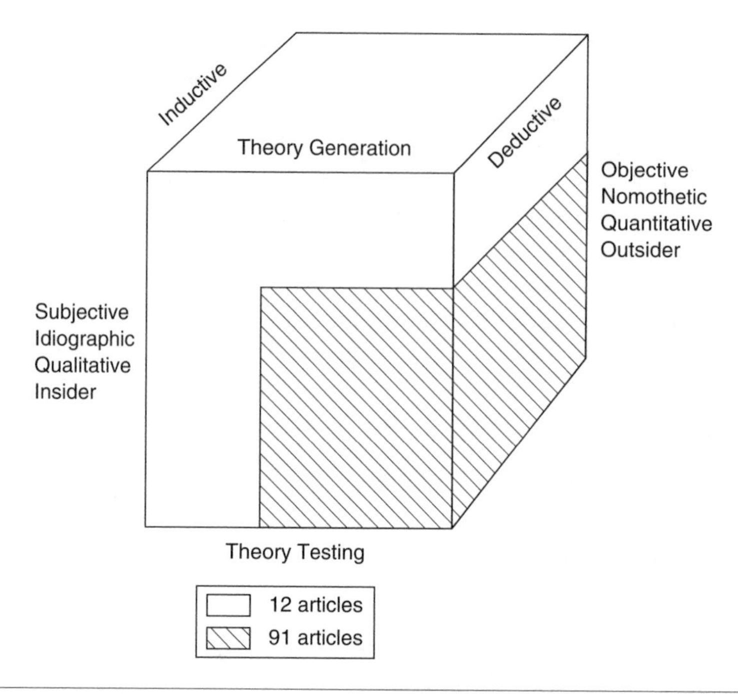

Figure 20.1 Continuing Dominance of Quantitative Methods in Alliance Research, 1994–2003

around the core concepts of trust, reciprocity, opportunism, and forbearance. Post-1993, how much of a shift in research foci has taken place, if any? Figure 20.2 shows the number of articles published during the 1994-to-2003 period, focusing on each of the traditional and behavioral variables.

It is evident from Figure 20.2 that 109 of the 128 articles examined here continue to focus on the traditional dimensions of alliance research, and only 19 articles focused on core behavioral variables. The question must again be posed: If, in fact, "soft" behavioral variables are at the heart of the cooperative relationship, is 14.8% (19 out of 109) an acceptable number that will take alliance theory development to the next level? Relatedly, is it possible to break out of current research emphases on traditional dimensions (Figure 20.2), so long as current research methods heavily tilt toward the quantitative approach (Figure 20.1)? Disappointingly, the answers to both questions would seem to be no. Research on alliances was—and a decade later continues to be—trapped in certain ways.

Drilling deeper, Figure 20.2 shows an interesting breakdown. Of the "traditional" alliance research dimensions, 31 articles focused primarily on alliance motives, 18 on partner selection/characteristics, 7 on control/conflict issues, and a full 53 articles examined stability/performance issues. Possible reasons for the dominance of stability/performance studies may be the notoriously high failure rates of alliances as well as the growing importance of alliances in companies' competitive strategies. And of the behavioral variables, trust dominated, with 12 articles focusing primarily or exclusively on it, followed by reciprocity (6), opportunism (1), and forbearance (0). The year-by-year publication summaries by each type of variable are presented in Table 20.1.

Finally, regardless of an article's primary theoretical focus (traditional or behavioral), all articles were rated according to the degree of importance accorded to one or more of the

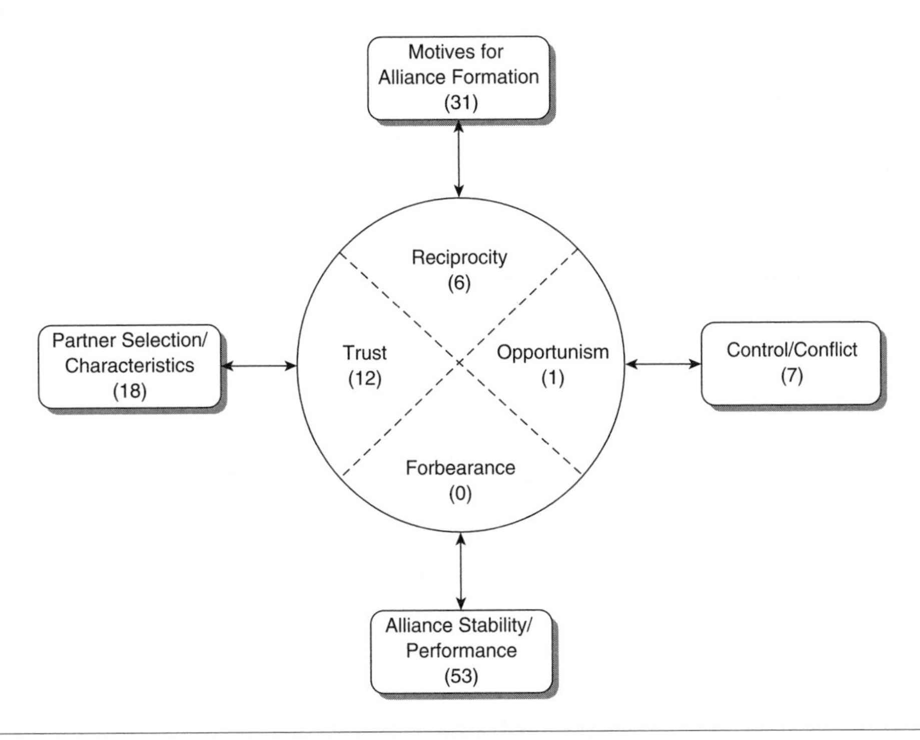

Figure 20.2 Major Dimensions of Alliance Research, 1994–2003

Note: Numbers represent the number of articles published focusing primarily on this research dimension

behavioral variables (trust, reciprocity, opportunism, and forbearance), with 5 signifying extremely important and 1, not at all important. The data showed 23 articles in category 5, 7 in category 4, 13 in category 3, 19 in category 2, and 66 in category 1. It would be tempting to suggest that the results should have been reversed, with 66 articles in category 5, 19 in category 4, and so on. Yet it is encouraging to note that the 23 category 5 articles exceed the number of articles (19) focusing explicitly on behavioral variables. In other words, even researchers focusing on "traditional" alliance dimensions may be starting to take into account the central role of behavioral variables in alliances and incorporating this role in their research.

Conclusions

> If investigators continue to be exact, to quantify, as they examine more complex aspects of organizations, they may tend to oversimplify. . . . exclusive reliance on statistical techniques may mean that we interpret the texture of organizations in a way similar to interpreting Shakespearean plays exclusively by word counts and ratios. The complex, intangible, emotional dimensions of organizations probably cannot be processed through the fine filter of linear statistics. Case studies and other high-variety techniques may be more appropriate for these dimensions. (Daft, 1980, 632)

Willful noncompliance with the letter and spirit of a cooperative agreement has often been cited as a source of instability in alliances (Das & Teng, 2002; Inkpen & Beamish, 1997). Such noncompliance (1) drives down alliance performance, (2) generates conflict, and calls into question (3) the selection of a partner and (4) the partner's motives for alliance formation. Put another way, these four "traditional" dimensions of alliance research

Table 20.1 Alliance Article Summaries by Year, 1994–2003

Primary Research Dimension	*1994*	*1995*	*1996*	*1997*	*1998*	*1999*	*2000*	*2001*	*2002*	*2003*	*Total*
Trust	—	4	2	1	1	—	3	—	1	—	12
Reciprocity	—	—	1	—	2	—	—	—	2	1	6
Opportunism	—	—	—	—	—	1	—	—	—	—	1
Forbearance	—	—	—	—	—	—	—	—	—	—	0
Subtotal	0	4	3	1	3	1	3	—	3	1	19
Motives	—	1	7	3	5	2	6	—	7	—	31
Partner	—	1	2	4	2	1	2	1	5	—	18
Control	1	—	—	2	3	—	—	1	—	—	7
Stability/ Performance	2	2	4	4	9	4	11	7	8	2	53
Subtotal	3	4	13	13	19	7	19	9	20	2	109
Total	3	8	16	14	22	8	22	9	23	3	128

(Figure 20.2) are closely linked to managerial behaviors. Yet it is surprising that willful noncompliance—labeled "defection" in game theory and "opportunism" in transaction cost economics—was the focus of only one article over the past ten-year period (Hennart & Roehl, 1999). Trust was the focus of twelve articles in the database, but it is important to recognize that trust and distrust and trust and opportunism do not share a direct, simple relationship. Violation of expected behaviors produces a sense of disruption of trust, of profound confusion, but not of distrust (Zucker, 1986). Distrust arises only when there is suspicion that expectations were violated intentionally and that such violations are likely to occur repeatedly (Parkhe, 1998).

This illustrative example points out how far we still have to go in grappling with fundamental notions in alliance research. It is to be hoped that a ten-year review of the alliance literature in 2014, covering the period 2004-to-2013, will reveal dramatic progress in systematically integrating behavioral variables with the traditional dimensions in alliance research. That said, it seems fair to note that some progress is evident along these lines, including the fact that more researchers appear to be explicitly incorporating behavioral variables into their work, whether or not behavioral variables form the central mission of their papers. This is encouraging. But much more work is needed, and in undertaking this work, alliance researchers need not reinvent the wheel. Branching out into other, related literatures (e.g., Rusbult & Van Lange, 2003; Sethi & Somanathan, 2003) that have explored similar issues may facilitate both theoretical and empirical work.

The question can appropriately be asked: Even if it is granted that behavioral variables are central to effective alliances, is it not possible to study such behavioral variables using qualitative methods, quantitative methods, or some combination? Clearly, the answer is yes. However, paper-and-pencil surveys, archival records, and mass databases tend to form the major data sources in empirical studies of alliances, and such sources are unlikely to deal adequately with the nuances, subtlety, and complexity of alliances. Sooner, rather than later, alliance researchers must accept that Shakespearean plays cannot be interpreted exclusively by word counts and ratios, and likewise, we have a rich story to tell, and greater use must be made of qualitative research methods in discovering and reporting this story (Figure 20.1).

Relatedly, although it is beyond the scope of the present chapter, we may note that further work is needed—and is occurring—into other important aspects of alliances, including learning, networks, and culture. Learning in an alliance and through an alliance, both legitimate and illicit, has surged as an area of research interest. Likewise, although dyadic alliances remain vitally important, multiparty networks have become the organizational structure of choice in many industries, including autos, biotechnology, airlines, and multimedia. Finally, with growing globalization, the role of organizational and societal culture (particularly as it relates to behavioral variables) has drawn increasing research attention in recent years. These are encouraging trends.

In conclusion, (1) behavioral variables are beginning to receive growing attention in alliance research; (2) however, a much greater focus on behavioral variables is needed if theoretical salience and research attention are to correspond more closely; (3) such a shift in focus will not be possible with the continuing methodological biases in favor of quantitative approaches; and (4) finally, there is a lack of an integrated systemic view that simultaneously takes into account the multiple processes involved in a collaborative relationship.

References

Ahuja, G. (2000). The duality of collaboration: Inducements and opportunities in the formation of interfirm linkages. *Strategic Management Journal, 21*(3), 317–344.

Ariño, A. (2003). Measures of strategic alliance performance: An analysis of construct validity. *Journal of International Business Studies, 34,* 66–79.

Ariño, A., & de la Torre, J. (1998). Learning from failure: Towards an evolutionary model of collaborative ventures. *Organization Science, 9*(3), 306–326.

Aulakh, P. S., Cavusgil, S. T., & Sarkar, M. B. (1998). Compensation in international licensing agreements. *Journal of International Business Studies, 29*(2), 409–420.

Aulakh, P. S., & Kotabe, M. (1996). Trust and performance in cross-border marketing partnerships: A behavioral approach [special issue]. *Journal of International Business Studies, 27*(5), 1005–1033.

Barkema, H. G., Shenkar, O., Vermeulen, F., & Bell, J. H. (1997). Working abroad, working with others: How firms learn to operate international joint ventures. *Academy of Management Journal, 40*(2), 426–443.

Barkema, H. G., & Vermeulen, F. (1997). What differences in the cultural backgrounds of partners are detrimental for international joint ventures? *Journal of International Business Studies, 28*(4), 845–865.

Baum, J. A. C., & Calabrese, T. (2000). Don't go it alone: Alliance network composition and startups' performance in Canadian biotechnology. *Strategic Management Journal, 21*(3), 267–295.

Bharat, A. N., & Khanna, T. (2000). Do firms learn to create value? The case of alliances. *Strategic Management Journal, 21*(3), 295–315.

Brouthers, K. D., & Bamossy, G. J. (1997). The role of key stakeholders in international joint venture negotiations: Case studies from Eastern Europe. *Journal of International Business Studies, 28*(2), 285–309.

Buckley, P. J., & Casson, M. (1996). An economic model of international joint venture strategy. *Journal of International Business Studies, 27*(5), 849–878.

Chi, T. (2000). Option to acquire or divest a joint venture. *Strategic Management Journal, 21*(6), 665–688.

Chi, T., & McGuire, D. J. (1996). Collaborative ventures and value of learning: Integrating the transaction cost and strategic option perspectives on the choice of markets entry modes. *Journal of International Business Studies, 27*(2), 285–308.

Cullen, J. B., & Johnson, J. L. (1995). Japanese and local partner commitment to IJVs: Psychological consequences of outcomes and investments in the IJV relationship. *Journal of International Business Studies, 26*(1), 91–114.

Currall, S. C., & Inkpen, A. C. (2002). A multilevel approach to trust in joint ventures. *Journal of International Business Studies*, 33(3), 479–496.

Daft, R. L. (1980). The evolution of organization analysis in *ASQ*, 1959–1979. *Administrative Science Quarterly, 25*, 623–636.

Danis, W. M., & Parkhe, A. (2002). Hungarian-Western partnerships: A grounded theoretical model of integration processes and outcomes. *Journal of International Business Studies, 33*(3), 423–456.

Das, T. K., & Teng, B. (1998). Between trust and control: Developing confidence in partner cooperation in alliances. *Academy of Management Review, 23*(3), 491–513.

Das, T. K., & Teng, B. (2002). Instabilities of strategic alliances: An internal tensions perspective. *Organization Science, 11*(1), 77–102.

Das, T. K., & Teng, B. (2002b). Alliance constellations: A social exchange perspective. *Academy of Management Review, 27*(3), 445–457.

Das, S. S., Sen, P. K., & Sengupta, S. (1998). Impact of strategic alliances on firm valuation. *Academy of Management Journal, 41*(1), 27–68.

Dickson, P. H., & Weaver, M. K. (1997). Environmental determinants and individual-level moderators of alliance use. *Academy of Management Journal, 40*(2), 404–426.

Doney, P. M., Cannon, J. P., & Mullen, M. R. (1998). Understanding the influence of national culture on the development of trust. *Academy of Management Review, 23*(3), 601–621.

Doz, Y. L. (1996). The evolution of cooperation in strategic alliances: Initial conditions or learning processes? *Strategic Management Journal, 17*(7), 55–84.

Dussauge, P., & Garrette, B. (1995). Determinants of success in international strategic alliances: Evidence from the global aerospace industry. *Journal of International Business Studies, 26*(3), 505–531.

Dussauge, P., & Garrette, B. (2000). Learning from competing partners: Outcomes and durations of scale and link alliances in Europe, North America and Asia. *Strategic Management Journal, 21*(2), 99–127.

Dyer, J. H. 2000, The determinants of trust in supplier-automaker Relationships in the U.S., Japan and Korea. *Journal of International Business Studies, 31*(2), 259–286.

Eisenhardt, K. M., & Schoonhoven, C. B. (1996). Resource-based view of strategic alliance formation: Strategic and social effects in entrepreneurial firms. *Organization Science, 7*(2), 136–151.

Elg, U. (2000). Firms' home-market relationships: Their role when selecting international alliance partners. *Journal of International Business Studies, 31*(1), 169–178.

Garcia-Pont, C., & Nohria, N. (2002). Local versus global mimetism: The dynamics of alliance formation in the automobile industry. *Strategic Management Journal, 23*(4), 307–322.

Griffith, D. A. (2000). Process standardization across intra- and inter-cultural relationships. *Journal of International Business Studies, 31*(2), 303–325.

Gulati, R. (1995a). Does familiarity breed trust? The implications of repeated ties for contractual choice in alliances. *Academy of Management Journal, 38*(1), 85–113.

Gulati, R. (1995b). Social structure and alliance formation patterns: A longitudinal analysis. *Administrative Science Quarterly, 40*(4), 619–653.

Gulati, R., & Singh, H. (1998). The architecture of cooperation: Managing coordination costs and appropriation concerns in strategic alliances. *Administrative Science Quarterly, 43*(4), 781–815.

Gulati, R., & Westphal, J. D. (1999). Cooperative or controlling? The effects of CEO-board relations and the content of interlocks on the formation of joint ventures. *Administrative Science Quarterly, 44*(3), 473–507.

Hagedoorn, J., & Narula, R. (1996). Choosing organizational modes of strategic technology partnering: International and sectoral differences. *Journal of International Business Studies, 27*(2), 265–285.

Hagedoorn, J., & Schakenraad, J. (1994). The effect of strategic technology alliances on company performance. *Strategic Management Journal, 15*(4), 291–310.

Haiyang L., & Kwaku A. (2002). The adoption of agency business activity, product innovation and performance in Chinese technology ventures. *Strategic Management Journal, 23*(6), 469–491.

Hennart, J., & Roehl, T. (1999). "Trojan horse" or "workhorse"? The evolution of U.S.-Japanese joint ventures in the United States. *Strategic Management Journal, 20*(1), 15–30.

Hennart, J., & Zeng, M. (2002). Cross-cultural differences and joint venture longevity. *Journal of International Business Studies, 33*(4), 699–717.

Hennart, J., Kim, D., & Zeng, M. (1998). The impact of joint venture status on the longevity of Japanese stakes in U.S. manufacturing affiliates. *Organization Science, 9*(3), 382–396.

Hill, R. C., & Hellriegel, D. (1994). Critical contingencies in joint venture management: Some lessons from managers. *Organization Science, 5*(4), 594–608.

Hitt, M. A., Dacin, M. T., Levitas, E., Arregle, J., & Borza, A. (2000). Partner selection in emerging and developed market contexts: Resource-based and organizational learning perspectives. *Academy of Management Journal, 43*(3), 449–468.

Inkpen, A. C., & Beamish, P. W. (1997). Knowledge bargaining power and the instability of international joint ventures. *Academy of Management Review, 22*(1), 177–201.

Inkpen, A. C., & Dinur, A. (1998). Knowledge management processes and international joint ventures. *Organization Science, 9*(4), 454–469.

Isobe, T., Makino, S., & Montgomery, D. B. (2000). Resource commitment, entry timing, and market performance of foreign direct investments in emerging economies: The case of Japanese international joint ventures in China. *Academy of Management Journal, 43*(3), 468–485.

Johnson, J. L., & Cullen, J. B. (1996). Setting the stage for trust and strategic integration in Japanese-U.S. cooperative alliances. *Journal of International Business Studies, 27*(5), 981–1005.

Jones, C., Hesterly, W. S., Fladmoe-Lindquist, K., & Borgatti, S. P. (1998). Professional service constellations: How strategies and capabilities influence collaborative stability and change. *Organization Science, 9*(3), 396–411.

Kale, P., & Singh, H. (2000). Learning and protection of proprietary assets in strategic alliances: Building relational capital. *Strategic Management Journal, 21*(3), 217–238.

Kale, P., Dyer, J. H., & Singh, H. (2002). Alliance capability, stock market response, and long term alliance success: The role of the alliance function. *Strategic Management Journal, 23*(8), 747–768.

Kaplan, A. (1964). *The conduct of inquiry: Methodology for behavioral science.* San Francisco: Chandler.

Khanna, T. (1998). The scope of alliances. *Organization Science, 9*(3), 340–356.

Khanna, T., Gulati, R., & Nohria, N. (1998). The dynamics of learning alliances: Competition, cooperation and relative scope. *Strategic Management Journal, 19*(3), 193–211.

Koka, B. R., & Prescott, J. E. (2002). Strategic alliances as social capital: A multidimensional view. *Strategic Management Journal, 23*(9), 795–817.

Kotabe, M., Martin, X., & Domoto, H. (2003). Gaining from vertical partnerships: Knowledge transfer, relationship duration and supplier performance improvement in the U.S. and Japanese automotive industries. *Strategic Management Journal, 24*(4), 293–317.

Koza, M. P., & Lewin, A. Y. (2002). The co-evolution of strategic alliances. *Organization Science,* 9(3), 255–265.

Kumar, R., & Nti, K. O. (1998). Differential learning and interaction in alliance dynamics. *Organization Science.* 9(3), 356–368.

Kumar, S., & Seth, A. (1998). The design of coordination and control mechanisms for managing joint venture-parent relationships. *Strategic Management Journal, 19*(6), 579–600.

Lampel, J., & Shamsie, J. (2000). Probing the unobtrusive link: Dominant logic and the design of joint ventures at General Electric. *Strategic Management Journal, 21*(5), 593–603.

Lane, P. J., Salk, J. E., & Lyles, M. A. (2001). Absorptive capacity, learning and performance in international joint ventures. *Strategic Management Journal, 22*(12), 1139–1162.

Lane, P. J., Salk, J. E., & Lubatkin, M. (1998). Relative absorptive capacity and interorganizational learning. *Strategic Management Journal, 19*(5), 461–478.

Larsson, R., Bengtsson, L., Henriksson, K., & Sparks, J. (1998). The interorganizational learning dilemma: Collective knowledge development in strategic alliances. *Organization Science,* 9(3), 285–316.

Lawrence, T., Hardy, C., & Phillips, N. (2002). Institutional effects of interorganizational collaboration: The emergence of proto-institutions. *Academy of Management Journal, 45*(1), 281–291.

Lee, C., & Beamish, P. W. (1995). The characteristics and performance of Korean joint ventures in LDCs. *Journal of International Business Studies, 26*(3), 637–655.

Li, J., Lam, K., & Oian, G. (2001). Does culture affect behavior and performance of firms? The case of joint ventures in China. *Journal of International Business Studies, 32*(1), 115–132.

Lin, X., & Germain, R. (1998). Sustaining satisfactory joint venture relationships: The role of conflict and resolution strategy. *Journal of International Business Studies, 29*(1), 179–197.

Lyles, M. A., & Salk, J. E. (1996). Knowledge acquisition from foreign parents in international joint ventures: An empirical examination in the Hungarian context. *Journal of International Business Studies, 27*(5), 877–904.

Luo, Y. (1997). Partner selection and venturing success: The case of joint ventures with firms in the People's Republic of China. *Organization Science,* 8(6), 648–663.

Luo, Y. (2001). Antecedents and consequences of personal attachment in cross-cultural cooperative ventures. *Administrative Science Quarterly, 46*(2), 177–202.

Luo, Y. (2002a). Contract, cooperation, and performance in international joint ventures. *Strategic Management Journal, 23*(10), 903–920.

Luo, Y. (2002b). Product diversification in international joint ventures: Performance implications in an emerging market. *Strategic Management Journal, 23*(1), 1–21.

Luo, Y. (2002c). Stimulating exchange in international joint ventures: An attachment-based view. *Journal of International Business Studies, 33*(1), 169–182.

Luo, Y., Shenkar, O., & Nyaw, M. (2001). A dual parent perspective on control and performance in international joint ventures: Lessons from a developing economy. *Journal of International Business Studies, 32*(1), 41–59.

Madhok, A. (1995). Revisiting multinational firms' tolerance for joint ventures: A trust-based approach. *Journal of International Business Studies, 26*(1), 117–138.

Madhok, A., & Tallman, S. B. (1998). Resources, transactions and rents: Managing value through interfirm collaborative relationships. *Organization Science,* 9(3), 326–340.

Makhija, M. V., & Ganesh, U. (1997). The relationship between control and partner learning-related joint ventures. *Organization Science,* 8(5), 508–528.

Makino, S., & Beamish, P. W. (1998). Performance and survival of joint ventures with non-conventional ownership structures. *Journal of International Business Studies, 29*(4), 797–819.

Makino, S., & Delios, A. (1996). Local knowledge transfer and performance implications for alliance formation in Asia. *Journal of International Business Studies, 27*(5), 905–928.

Merchant, H., & Schendel, D. (2000). How do international joint ventures create shareholder value? *Strategic Management Journal, 21*(7), 723–738.

Millington, A. I., & Bayliss, B. T. (1995). Transnational joint ventures between UK and EU manufacturing companies and the structure of competition. *Journal of International Business Studies, 26*(2), 239–255.

Mitchell, W., & Singh, K. (1996). Survival of businesses using collaborative relationships to commercialize complex goods. *Strategic Management Journal, 17*(3), 169–196.

Mjoen, H., & Tallman, S. (1997). Control and performance in international joint ventures. *Organization Science, 8*(3), 257–275.

Monge, P. R., Fulk, J., Kalman, M. E., Flanigan, A. J., Parnassa, C., & Rumsey, S. (1998). Production of collective action in alliance-based interorganizational communication and information systems. *Organization Science, 9*(3), 411–434.

Mowery, D., & Oxley, J. E. (1996). Strategic alliances and interfirm knowledge transfer. *Strategic Management Journal, 17,* 77–92.

Nooteboom, B., & Berger, H. (1997). Effects of trust and governance on relational risk. *Academy of Management Journal, 40*(2), 308–339.

Nordberg, M., & Campbell, A. J. (1996). Can market-based contracts substitute for alliances in high technology markets? *Journal of International Business Studies, 27*(5), 963–980.

Osborn, R. N., & Hagedoorn, J. (1997). The institutionalization and evolutionary dynamics of interorganizational alliances and networks. *Academy of Management Journal, 40*(2), 261–279.

Pan, Y. (1996). Influences on foreign equity ownership level in joint ventures in China. *Journal of International Business Studies, 27*(1), 1–27.

Pan, Y. (1997). The formation of Japanese and U.S. equity joint ventures in China. *Strategic Management Journal, 18*(3), 247–255.

Pan, Y. (2000). Joint venture formation of very large multinational firms. *Journal of International Business Studies, 31*(1), 179–190.

Pan, Y. (2002). Equity ownership in international joint ventures: The impact of source country factors. *Journal of International Business Studies, 33*(2), 375–385.

Pan, Y., & Tse, D. K. (1996). Cooperative strategies between foreign firms in an overseas country. *Journal of International Business Studies, 27*(5), 929–947.

Park, S. H., & Ungson, G. R. (1997). The effects of national culture, organizational complementarity, and economic motivation on joint venture dissolution. *Academy of Management Journal, 40*(2), 279–308.

Park, S. H., & Ungson, G. R. (2001). Interfirm rivalry and managerial complexity. *Organization Science, 12*(1), 37–54.

Park, S. H., Chen, R., & Gallagher, S. (2002). Firm resources as moderators of the relationship between market growth and strategic alliances in semiconductor start-ups. *Academy of Management Journal, 45*(3), 527–546.

Parkhe, A. (1993). "Messy" research, methodological predispositions, and theory development in international joint ventures. *Academy of Management Review, 18*, 227–268.

Parkhe, A. (1998). Understanding trust in international alliances. *Journal of World Business, 33*, 219–240.

Pothukuchi, V., Damanpour, F., Choi, J., Chao, C., & Park S. H. (2002). National and organizational culture differences and international joint venture performance. *Journal of International Business Studies, 33*(2), 243–266.

Rao, A., & Schmidt, S. M. (1998). A behavioral perspective on negotiating international alliances. *Journal of International Business Studies, 29*(4), 665–694.

Reuer, J. J. (2000). Parent firm performance across international joint venture life-cycle stages. *Journal of International Business Studies, 31*(1), 1–21.

Reuer, J. J. (2001). From hybrids to hierarchies: Shareholder wealth effects of joint venture partner buyouts. *Strategic Management Journal, 22*(1), 27–45.

Reuer, J. J., & Koza, M. P. (2000). Asymmetric information and joint venture performance: Theory and evidence for domestic and international joint ventures. *Strategic Management Journal, 21*(1), 81–89.

Reuer, J. J., & Miller, K. D. (1997). Agency costs and the performance implications of international joint venture internalization. *Strategic Management Journal, 18*(6), 425–439.

Reuer, J. J., Zollo, M., & Singh, H. (2002). Post-formation dynamics in strategic alliances. *Strategic Management Journal, 23*(2), 135–152.

Robins, J., Tallman, S., & Fladmoe-Lindquist, K. (2002). Autonomy and dependence of international cooperative ventures: An exploration of the strategic performance of U.S. ventures in Mexico. *Strategic Management Journal, 23*(10), 881–892.

Rothaermel, F. T.(2001). Incumbent's advantage through exploiting complementary assets via interfirm cooperation. *Strategic Management Journal, 22*(6/7), 687–700.

Rusbult, C. E., & Van Lange, P. A. M. (2003). Interdependence, interaction, and relationships. *Annual Review of Psychology, 54*, 351–375.

Sarkar, M. B., Echambadi, R. A. J., & Harrison, J. S. (2001). Alliance entrepreneurship and firm market performance. *Strategic Management Journal, 22*(6/7), 701–712.

Saxton, T. (1997). The effects of partner and relationship characteristics on alliance outcomes. *Academy of Management Journal, 40*(2), 443–462.

Sethi, R., & Somanathan, E. (2003). Understanding reciprocity. *Journal of Economic Behavior and Organization, 50*, 1–27.

Seungwha, C., & Singh, H. (2000). Complementarity, status similarity and social capital as drivers of alliance formation. *Strategic Management Journal, 21*(1), 1–23.

Shenkar, O., & Li, J. P. (1999). Knowledge search in international cooperative ventures. *Organization Science, 10*(2), 134–144.

Shrader, R. C. (2001). Collaboration and performance in foreign markets: The case of young high-technology manufacturing firms. *Academy of Management Journal, 44*(1), 45–61.

Silverman, B. S., & Baum, J. A. C. (2002). Alliance-based competitive dynamics. *Academy of Management Journal, 45*(4), 791–807.

Simonin, B. L. (1997). The importance of collaborative know-how: An empirical test of the learning organization. *Academy of Management Journal, 40*(5), 1150–1175.

Simonin, B. L. (1999a). Ambiguity and the process of knowledge transfer in strategic alliances. *Strategic Management Journal, 20*(7), 595–624.

Simonin, B. L. (1999b). Transfer of marketing know-how in international strategic alliances: An empirical investigation of the role and antecedents of knowledge ambiguity. *Journal of International Business Studies, 30*(3), 463–491.

Singh, K., & Mitchell, W. (1996). Precarious collaboration: Business survival after partners shut down or form new partnerships. *Strategic Management Journal, 17*(7), 99–116.

Spencer, J. W. (2000). Knowledge flows in the global innovation system: Do U.S. firms share more scientific knowledge than their Japanese rivals?

Journal of International Business Studies, 31(3), 521–531.

Steensma, H. K., & Corley, K. G. (2000). On the performance of technology-sourcing partnerships: The interaction between partner interdependence and technology attributes. *Academy of Management Journal, 43*(6), 1045–1068.

Steensma, H. K., & Lyles, M. A. (2000). Explaining IJV survival in a transitional economy through social exchange and knowledge-based perspectives. *Strategic Management Journal, 21*(8), 831–852.

Stuart, T. E. (2000). Interorganizational alliances and the performance of firms: A study of growth and innovation rates in a high-tech industry. *Strategic Management Journal, 21*(8), 791–812.

Stuart, T. E., Hoang, H., & Hybels, R. C. (1999). Interorganizational endorsements and the performance of entrepreneurial ventures. *Administrative Science Quarterly, 44*(2), 315–350.

Thompson, A. G. (1996). Compliance with agreements in cross-cultural transactions: Some analytical issues. *Journal of International Business Studies, 27*(2), 375–391.

Tsang, E. W. K. (2002). Acquiring knowledge by foreign partners from international joint ventures in a transition economy: Learning-by-doing and learning myopia. *Strategic Management Journal, 23*(9), 835–855.

Vanhaverbeke, W., Duysters, G., & Noorderhaven, N. (2002). External technology sourcing through alliances or acquisitions: An analysis of the application-specific integrated circuits industry. *Organization Science, 13*(6), 714–734.

Werner, S. (2002). Recent developments in international management research: A review of 20 top management journals. *Journal of Management, 28,* 277–305.

Wong, P. L., & Ellis, P. (2002). Social ties and partner identification in Sino-Hong Kong international joint ventures. *Journal of International Business Studies, 33*(2), 265–288.

Yan, A. (1998). Structural stability and reconfiguration of international joint ventures. *Journal of International Business Studies, 29*(4), 773–796.

Yan, A., & Gray, B. (1994). Bargaining power, management control and performance in United States–China joint ventures: A comparative case study. *Academy of Management Journal, 37*(6), 1478–1518.

Yan, A., & Ming, Z. (1999). International joint venture instability: A critique of previous research, a reconceptualization, and directions for future research. *Journal of International Business Studies, 30*(2), 395–413.

Young-Ybarra, C., & Wiersema, M. (1999). Strategic flexibility in information technology alliances: The influence of transaction cost economics and social exchange theory. *Organization Science, 10*(4), 439–460.

Zaheer, A., & Venkatraman, N. (1995). Relational governance as an interorganizational strategy: An empirical test of the role of trust in economic exchange. *Strategic Management Journal, 16*(5), 373–392.

Zeng, M., & Chen, X. (2003). Achieving cooperation in multiparty Alliance Research alliances: A social dilemma approach to partnership management. *Academy of Management Review, 28*(4), 587–606.

Zhang, Y., & Rajagopalan, N. (2002). Inter-partner credible threat in international joint ventures: An infinitely repeated Prisoner's Dilemma model. *Journal of International Business Studies, 33*(3), 457–479.

Zollo, M., Reuer, J. J., & Singh, H. (2002). Interorganizational routines and performance in strategic alliances. *Organization Science, 13*(6), 701–714.

Zucker, L. G. (1986). Production of trust. In B. Staw & L. L. Cummings (Eds.), *Research in organizational behavior* (Vol. 8, pp. 53–111), Greenwich, CT: JAI Press.

21

Research Outside the "Core"

Opportunities in Alternative Approaches and Methods for Studying Cooperative Alliances

Jane E. Salk

Davina Vora

Since the early 1980s, alliances have been a major focus of management studies. Despite the tremendous accumulation of empirical and conceptual studies, alliance research has tended to be limited in its theoretical and methodological scope. Although we believe that research to date has made important contributions to both theory and practice, we also agree with scholars who contend that these limitations preclude the development of a comprehensive theory of interfirm cooperation and learning that can account for processes underpinning cooperation and their outcomes (Doz, 1996; Salk & Simonin, 2003). This chapter seeks to redress these limitations by highlighting those areas of knowledge that are underdeveloped and suggesting how social identity, social capital, and social network theories and methodologies can be applied to the study of interfirm cooperation.

Definitions of "alliances" vary greatly (see Salk & Simonin, 2003, for a broader discussion). For this chapter, we define alliances as any goal-oriented contractual cooperation between two or more partner organizations, involving some asset-specific investment by one or more of the partners. Goals might often, though not necessarily or exclusively, be economic in nature. The breadth of this definition is intentional. Although this definition includes research and development alliances and joint development and equity joint ventures, which have been the object of most alliance research to date, it further encompasses joint action and cooperation between headquarters and subsidiaries of multinational corporations (MNCs), cooperation between firms and not-for-profit organizations, external sourcing, and codevelopment and subcontractor arrangements. Though these topics have been studied by individuals in such fields as technology management, sociology, and supply chain and information systems fields, they have to date largely fallen outside the phenomena spotlighted by alliances research.

Recent economic trends, such as rapid growth of outsourcing and virtual codevelopment in industries such as telecommunications and automobiles, force alliance research to draw on theory and methods that can account for arrangements where the boundaries within partners as well as the boundaries defining the cooperation itself are fuzzy. Complex matrices of reporting relations within firms and even within the purview of a specific interfirm cooperation (for example, a software development project jointly staffed by a North American and an Indian firm with subsidiaries and members from India and China involved), can make it difficult even for members involved in the project to define membership (Gibson & Cohen, 2003; Cramton & Hinds, forthcoming). Technological mediation of the cooperative interface between cooperating groups across organizational boundaries (via e-mail, teleconferencing, and other tools) is common. With these recent developments, how members constitute and use identities, roles, and relationships remains theoretically and empirically underdeveloped in the social sciences.

We begin by briefly reviewing the topics and methods that have dominated traditional alliances research. Because other chapters will concentrate upon mainstream trends in alliances theory and research, we try to focus on the lacunae and phenomena that to date have been relegated to the fringes of the literature by most researchers. After indicating the areas where greater effort is needed, we review the studies in the alliance and related literatures that have made preliminary attempts to address these gaps. Our review of the literature will suggest that social identity theory and social capital theory, accompanied by social network theory and methods, show particular promise for generating research that can complement the overwhelmingly structural and cross-sectional bias of "core" alliance research streams. We presume that many readers may be only minimally aware of research traditions in these areas. Hence, the chapter will outline their central assumptions and offer examples of studies using these approaches to address issues that fall within the purview of alliances and will then offer concrete methodological suggestions for how to apply them fruitfully in alliance research.

Review of Central Tendencies in Alliances

Though there is excellent research concerned with alliances dating back to the 1960s and 1970s (examples include Berg & Friedman, 1978; Bivens & Lovell, 1966; Pate, 1969), the study of alliances first came into its own in the 1980s. Important publications in the 1980s include Killing (1983), Harrigan (1986, 1988), and the volume edited by Contractor and Lorange (1988). Key research concerns in this period included the effects of constructs such as equity structures, relatedness of partner skills and goals (competitive or complementary), and the effect of the number of partners on international joint ventures (IJVs), with performance and survival of alliances as commonly used dependent variables. Toward the end of the 1980s into the beginning of the 1990s, the issues of learning in alliance contexts began to be explored—both in terms of how firms learn to be more effective in their partnering activities (Lyles, 1988; Parkhe, 1991) and in how learning by one or both partners affects joint venture stability (Hamel, Doz, & Prahalad, 1989; Hamel, 1991). Other, more strategic management–oriented streams of research came into their own during this period, including how webs of alliances can be used to identify strategic groups (Nohria & Garcia-Point, 1991).

An article by Hamel et al. (1989) foreshadowed a growing theme in looking at "learning races" in alliances during the 1990s (Gulati & Singh, 1998). These studies tended to assess partner learning indirectly by looking at the relative performance of the partners and the degree to which partners appeared to have expropriated or assimilated skills and knowledge that was originally part of the motivation for an alliance. However, these studies did not directly elucidate the processes involved. In the 1990s through the present, the effects of partner selection, mode of cooperation (equity IJV, licensing, etc.), and contractual arrangements have increasingly drawn upon transaction cost economics (Gulati & Singh, 1998; Mjoen & Tallman, 1997) for theoretical underpinnings, and these studies have typically used cross-sectional, secondary data sources.

A growing number of studies looking at learning in IJVs during this time began to assess structural prerequisites for learning and knowledge transfers, typically using proxies such as organizational reward and motivational methods, clear business goals and plans, and absorptive capacity and training (Lyles & Salk, 1996; Lane, Salk, & Lyles, 2001). Survey methods were used in this research that allowed for the benefits of studying large numbers of IJVs but had the disadvantage of having to assume that the structural variables were accurate proxies for capturing certain processes.

In terms of theory and methods, a *clear majority of studies have relied upon secondary data sources and quantitative cross-sectional data.* Longitudinal approaches remain rare, and the emphasis in these studies continues to be structural—hence this research still is close to the core of traditional research. Rarer yet are qualitative case studies. Moreover, as the following section reveals, such studies at the periphery are only marginally taken into account by "core" research, and the community of scholars at the periphery, tending to take cross-disciplinary approaches, has lacked the coordinated agendas found in mainstream alliance research.

Research and Theory Beyond the Core: Social and Relational Aspects of Alliances

Various streams of research cited above, as well as research showing that parental contributions of resources and support affect IJV survival (Steensma & Lyles, 2000), converge to suggest that managerial and social processes are critical for IJV effectiveness. However, research that tries to capture such processes directly remains limited. Given the wide citation of Parkhe (1993), who calls for "messy research," and Doz (1996), who calls for more process research on the evolutionary dynamics of cooperation, this continued and possibly widening gap is surprising at first blush.

Attention paid to processes and social aspects have so far mainly been in the areas of the bargaining power perspective (Yan & Gray, 1994; Inkpen & Beamish, 1997) and work on the role of trust (Inkpen & Currall, 1997). The bargaining power perspective focuses on the relative dependence of partners over time in an alliance. Learning as well as exogenous changes in the partner organizations and external environments can lead to a reassessment and change or termination of the relationship. Inkpen and Beamish (1997) used the example of an alliance that remained stable over time and linked its stability in the face of opportunities for expropriating skills to trust between the two parties. They asserted that trust is the lubricant that allows for effective cooperation to apply skills and knowledge, as well as to adjust the cooperative relationship over time as needed.

These and other authors beg the question of what should be understood by "process" in an alliance context (de Rond & Bouchikhi, 2004). Drawing upon prior work by Van de Ven and Poole (1995), de Rond and Bouchikhi identify four conceptualizations of process: life-cycle, teleology, evolutionary, and dialectical. Life-cycle conceptualizations seek to find and assess "linear, irreversible and predictable" progressions of events or states over time (de Rond & Bouchikhi, 2004). Teleological approaches are diverse but unified in their emphasis upon purposeful cooperation by entities toward desired end states, whereas evolutionary conceptualizations look at change and development in terms of "recurrent, cumulative, and problematic sequence(s) of variation, selection and retention events" (de Rond &

Bouchikhi, 2004: 60). The position of these authors is that the preponderance of alliance research tends to treat alliances and participating entities as relatively homogeneous (i.e., we can talk about a partner's rationale or level of trust as if it were a social fact). De Rond and Bouchikhi propose a dialectical point of view whereby heterogeneity and the social constriction of purpose become points of departure and process can be seen as the ongoing dialectic within and across areas of tension and contradiction. The lack of process-oriented research is also bemoaned as a barrier to advancement in organization studies more generally (see Aldrich, 2001).

DeRond and Bouchikhi (2004) and the more general overview of organization studies research trends given in Aldrich (2001) suggest why certain so-called "objective variables," such as survival, are popular. Their analyses moreover suggest why so little specific research on processes is done and why, when it is done, it tends to be quite formulaic and functionalist in its point of view. It further suggests why there is much apparent eclecticism in this area of inquiry. Gulati (1998) and others who take an evolutionary point of view sometimes draw on the legitimacy of the larger community of sociological ecology and social networks as a basis of legitimation. The lifecycle models often appeal to authors with a normative practitioner-oriented bent.

As to others among the relatively few published studies directly assessing processes within alliances and IJVs, one can say that a "preference" for case studies is shared, and sometimes a preference for qualitative fieldwork as well. Beyond that, process research can by no means be seen as a coherent and well-bounded community of knowledge.

Larson (1992) used case studies to look at exchange relationships between firms. Child and Markoczy (1993) used comparative case studies of Chinese and Hungarian IJVs to look at different perspectives that might explain managerial behavior in these IJVs: system of industrial governance, national culture, the nature of industrialization and resistance to change. The system of industrial governance, coupled with influences stemming from culture and industrialization, provided the best explanation of managerial behavior. Salk (1996) used comparative case studies to look at how perceptions of national cultural differences as a framing of daily reality were sometimes reframed abruptly over time as key events or exogenous threats confronted IJV teams. Salk and Brannen (2000) combined interviews, participant observation, and network approaches to examine the determinants of individual influence in a 50:50 German-Japanese joint venture top management team. In a grounded-theory approach with a multiple-case methodology, Danis and Parkhe (2002) examined the adoption of partners' values, practices, and systems in international cooperative ventures. They used semistructured interviews as well as archival data to identify constructs and processes that explained differences in integration among partners. Gulati (1998) advocated theorizing and testing alliances issues with the network perspective, which Ahuja (2000) used to test how collaboration networks in the chemicals industry can affect innovation.

These examples, as well as others cited earlier in this chapter, have established links to other literatures if not methods to legitimate their approaches and research agendas. These few examples illustrate that process studies, unlike mainstream alliance research, are highly eclectic and do not cohere as a community that has established norms for either the research questions or the methodologies to be employed. Indeed, many of these exceptions mentioned above draw upon approaches from outside the strategy and international management fields—from sociology, social psychology, and anthropology—for inspiration and legitimation. The lack of community can be an advantage in that it offers a lot of liberty. At the same time, we feel that the negative results of this "fringe" phenomenon is that there is more risk in trying to get such studies published in top journals; worse yet, the authors are often central neither to the alliance literature nor to the literature they attempt eclectically to borrow from. Hence, at the periphery of alliance research, although there is excellent work being done, there is a lack of the sorts of shared roots that allow for comparing and accumulating knowledge.

In the following sections, we take a closer look at theoretical framings and methods—some proximate and some less likely to be obvious to readers focused on mainstream alliance research. Our goal is to introduce these streams to those from alliance research who are relatively unfamiliar with them, offer a map to help understand and appreciate these streams on their own terms, as well as, we hope, to stimulate readers to use theoretically and methodologically well-informed approaches based on these to enrich alliances research.

Theoretical Framing and Methods for a More Social Process–Informed Research Agenda

Social Identity Research

Social identity theory (SIT) has a long history in experimental psychology dating back to the 1970s. SIT posits that individuals seek identification with in-groups to enhance self-esteem (Erez & Earley, 1993; Tajfel, 1974, 1978). Experiments based on SIT demonstrate that the structure of tasks and even random assignment of individuals into groups can create in-group/out-group discrimination and dynamics (e.g., Tajfel & Turner, 1986; Tajfel, Billig, Bundy, & Flament, 1971). For example, individuals who were divided into groups based on random coin tosses and who did not socially interact with their group members showed in-group favoritism in allocation of points that were worth money (Billig & Tajfel, 1973).

Despite the plethora of research on SIT in the field of social psychology, SIT interest in the management field as well as in nonexperiment-based testing of this theory is a more recent phenomenon. Much of the management literature using SIT has concentrated on organizational identification. Ashforth and Mael (1989) draw upon SIT to develop the concept of organizational identification. They suggest that strong identification with an organization is related to motivation, organizational citizenship behaviors, and, hence, performance. Empirical research using survey data suggests that organizational identification is associated with intention to stay in the organization (Abrams, Ando, & Hinkle, 1998; Wan-Huggins, Riordan, & Griffeth, 1998), participation in organizational functions (Mael & Ashforth, 1992), job involvement (Mael & Tetrick, 1992), and extra-role behavior (Tyler & Blader, 2001).

Cross-cultural researchers have also used SIT to explain phenomena. For example, Earley and Mosakowski (2000) apply insights from SIT to explain why multicultural groups can experience conflict and poor performance. They suggest that presence of strong subgroup identities increases conflict and hinders group performance. Consistent with research on faultlines (e.g., Lau & Murnighan, 1998), they find a curvilinear relationship between cultural diversity and team functioning, whereby moderately heterogeneous groups demonstrated more communication problems and relational conflict and lower levels of team identity and performance than highly homogeneous and heterogeneous groups. Thus, identification with one group (versus subgroups) seems to reduce relational conflict and improve performance. As Earley and Mosakowski (2000) point out, this finding has implications for IJVs, in which strong identification with a cultural subgroup (rather than the IJV as a whole) can create problems.

Strategic alliance research has occasionally used SIT as a basis for theory and empirical research. Li, Xin, and Pillutla (2002) suggest that SIT and organizational identification processes can help to explain why IJV teams often have difficulty working with one another. Based on theory and preliminary interviews with IJV managers, they propose that parent firms' relative status and power as well as IJV success impact top management team organizational identification with the IJV and parent firm(s). They suggest that strong parent identification may hinder IJV team functioning and IJV performance. Salk and Shenkar (2001) applied SIT, recoding interviews with members of a bicultural British-Italian joint venture team. The original field research was not designed to test this theory, but they nevertheless found a linkage over time between many aspects of the IJV environment and functioning and in-group/out-group categorizations based on the national cultures. They suggest that a nondeterministic (and punctuated equilibrium) view of development fits this case, whereas a deterministic life-cycle or evolutionary view shaped by actual cultural differences does not fit the data well.

SIT increasingly plays a role in studies of collaboration outside a traditional business alliance context. It has provided a theoretical and methodological basis for studies of nontraditional collaborations such as special forces (Elron, Shamir, & Ben-Ari, 1999). Very recently, its influence has begun to be felt in studies of virtual collaboration and teams (Espinosa, Cummings, Wilson, & Pearce, 2003; Gibson & Cohen, 2003; Cramton & Hinds, 2005; Gibson & Vermeulen, 2004). All of these studies are relevant for alliance research in the questions they pose as well as the methods they employ. However, further advances in this line of inquiry would entail specifically designing research to assess social identification patterns and measure organizational identification. We outline suggestions on how this can be accomplished later in this chapter.

Social Capital Research

Studying what patterns of social identification and organizational identification prevail in an alliance setting begins to illuminate why some alliances are dysfunctional whereas others manage to perform well. However, approaching this via SIT and organizational identification alone cannot illuminate why the human capital invested in an alliance does not result in its effective mobilization. The concept of social capital can shed light on this area. With its roots in sociology, social capital refers to "the aggregate of the actual or potential resources which are linked to possession of a durable network of more or less institutionalized relationships of mutual acquaintance or recognition" (Bourdieu, 1985, p. 248). Thus, social capital focuses on the resources that can be obtained through networks of relationships. In sociology, research on social capital has been applied to such topics as school attrition, children's intellectual development, and sources of employment (Portes, 1998).

Recently, social capital research has begun to receive more attention in the management literature. Consistent with the sociological perspective, social capital in a management context focuses upon the actual networks of relationships and their mobilization to obtain resources and knowledge vital to firms and alliances.

Nahapiet and Ghoshal (1998), moving the concept to the organizational level, suggest that organizations are capable of developing social capital, which facilitates the creation of new intellectual capital and gives firms competitive advantage. They propose three dimensions of social capital: structural embeddedness (network attributes), relational embeddedness (quality of relationships in the network), and a cognitive dimension (resources having shared systems of meaning among network nodes). Kostova and Roth (2003) posit that social capital is a fundamental factor in headquarters/subsidiary relationships. They argue that the varying characteristics of interdependence between headquarters and subsidiaries differentially affect the need for certain types of social capital. They also propose that boundary-spanners' networks and experience with interactions in the network affect the level of social capital of both the boundary-spanner and the organizational units. Chung, Singh, and Lee (2000) look at the effects of social capital and status similarity on the formation of alliances by investment banks. They conceive of social capital in terms of macroembeddedness—banks' direct and indirect collaborative experiences—finding that this plays an important positive role in alliance formation, but the effect is stronger for initial public offerings than for secondary offer deals. Other research on women and minorities in organizations suggests the link between social capital and social identification through findings that show differential patterns of network building and use for women and minorities as opposed to majority group members (Ibarra, 1993).

Kogut and Zander's (1993) research on knowledge, though not explicitly discussed as social capital, suggests that firms have knowledge embedded in their networks and that such knowledge has economic value. Almeida and Kogut (1999) look at patterns of employee movements across organizations in Silicon Valley to explain differential performance of firms. They find that interfirm mobility of engineers impacts local knowledge transfer. Their findings are consistent with a social capital argument that these individuals affect the performance of the firms they join via their social capital.

Virtual teams—teams whose members are geographically dispersed and that must rely to a large measure upon e-mail and other forms of mediated communication—increasingly reflect arrangements and dilemmas likely to be found in other alliance settings as well. Recent research on such teams highlights the importance of better understanding the effects over time of factors associated with social capital. In particular, these studies suggest that the nature of social networks and trust in such teams helps explain why the skills and resources of team members can be coordinated and channeled to foster high performance in some teams and not in others (Gibson & Cohen, 2003; Cramton & Hinds, 2005). For example, Aubert and Kelsey (2003) find that although initial trust levels do not significantly impact performance, final levels of trust between local and remote subteams are positively related to team performance. Thus, the relational aspect of social capital, which is related to trust (Tsai & Ghoshal, 1998), is key to virtual team performance.

The social network is also important for virtual teams' social capital. Maznevski and Chudoba (2000) allude to this in their case study of virtual teams. They note that communication frequency and form (e.g., face-to-face, e-mail messages) among virtual team members affect decision processes such that teams with little cohesion tend to have lower levels of communication and effectiveness. Thus, network characteristics can impact the ability of teams to access social capital in the form of expert knowledge resources.

As is clear from the discussion above, in the management literature, empirical studies have helped to further understanding and theory development about social capital theory. However, in the strategic management literature, the tendency has been to focus on the embeddedness of relationships at the organizational-unit level (e.g., Chung et al., 2000; Kostova & Roth, 2003). The relationships between this and social capital at other levels, such as interpersonal and intergroup relationships and trust, are often implied but not measured directly. The Almeida and Kogut (1999) study mentioned above is among the few exceptions in that it looks at employee movements to explain social capital formation and its effects on performance of firms. On the other hand, the literature on virtual teams (e.g., Maznevski & Chudoba, 2000) focuses on interpersonal and intergroup relational capital and its effects within teams, but this is not extended to macrolevels.

This brief review suggests that alliance research has opportunities to address an important gap: How do relational and structural embeddedness relate to one another over time and across levels to affect alliance formation, longevity, and performance? Similar to the case of SIT, it is essential to consider how to design and execute research to reap the potential benefits of studying alliances through this lens. The following discussion offers suggestions for research design and data collection.

Methodological Approaches to Incorporating SIT and Social Capital into Alliance Research

The review above suggests that advancing alliance research requires use of ethnographic and other qualitative methods coupled with survey methods as appropriate. Ethnographic and field research is vital in order to capture the meaning systems that members use to navigate in such complex social settings over time. An emphasis on SIT and social capital requires that research pays more attention to levels of analysis and the relationships across levels. In the following sections, we elaborate on key methodological alternatives and issues for research.

Methodological and Design Issues for Studying SIT

One major issue when using an SIT approach is salience of identities. According to SIT, individuals have multiple social identities, and different identities become salient in different contexts (Turner, 1982, 1984). Therefore, it is important to determine which identities are salient for participants. Further complicating matters, it cannot be presumed a priori whether cultural origins, organization, function, location, or other social categories capture the primary social identification of participants in an alliance. As Abrams (1999) notes, it is impossible to determine which category will become salient without extensive knowledge of the context. Hence, researchers would benefit from observing participants in different situations, conducting interviews, and possibly designing tests to determine which identities are particularly salient among alliance participants.

One possible test of existing identities could be adapted from Deaux, Reid, Mizrah, and Cotting (1999). They created a list of identities based on participants' responses regarding identities and used multidimensional scaling to cluster these identities for further analysis. Gibson and Zellmer-Bruhn (2001) studied understandings of the meaning of cooperation across cultures via metaphors. They combined an analysis of interview transcripts with a card-sort exercise in which informants were asked to sort words that interviews suggested were related to cooperation metaphors into similar piles. This revealed patterns of expectations about team roles, scope, membership, and objectives that were associated with embeddedness in different cultural identity contexts. Such an approach could potentially provide the basis for looking at how such expectations shape behavior and interaction processes in alliances.

It is also methodologically important to consider whether identification in alliances should be treated as an emergent aspect of alliances. Given that tenure in an organization has been shown to relate positively to identification with that organization (Mael & Ashforth, 1992; Wan-Huggins et al., 1998), respondents are likely to have different levels of identification with an alliance and participating parties depending on their tenure in the alliance and in the partnering organization(s). If so, one cannot simply aggregate individual responses, because this would not adequately capture the level of identification among individuals in the alliance. Hence, multilevel analyses such as hierarchical linear modeling could be beneficial by indicating both individual- and group-level effects of alliance identification. Moreover, levels of identification can vary across time for different participants, depending upon the division of labor, the business context of the partner organizations, performance, and perceived linkages between alliance activity and individual rewards.

The appropriate framing of populations and samples of respondents are also critical when using SIT in the study of alliances. Some studies (e.g., Salk & Shenkar, 2001) assert that the appropriate population to study the effects of SIT in alliances is the top management team. They reason that it is top management that instills and develops organizational culture (Schein, 1992). They further contend that the top management team is where social identification is the most problematic due to team members' prior and/

or ongoing relationships to parent organizations and because it is at this most visible level that the cultural and organizational backgrounds of members appointed to key posts can take on symbolic significance (e.g., media coverage on DaimlerChrysler).

Both idiographic and nomothetic approaches to SIT are possible. One can use fieldwork such as interviews to bring to the surface the range of relevant idiographic identity faultlines or boundaries. These might further be refined and their meaning better understood using the card-sorting technique described above (Gibson & Zellmer-Bruhn, 2001). In terms of nomothetic, or theoretically derived, identities, it might be appropriate to extend extant measures of identification to alliance contexts. The Mael and Ashforth (1992) items might be a sound point of departure for designing questionnaires regarding organizational identification, although there are a number of alternative organizational identification scales (e.g., Bergami & Bagozzi, 2000; Brown, Condor, Matthews, Wade, & Williams, 1986; Hinkle, Taylor, Fox-Cardamone, & Crook, 1989).

It is important to note, however, that despite the applicability of organizational identification to the study of strategic alliances, the organization might not be the appropriate or only social referent in a particular study. In some cases, it may be more appropriate, for example, to study identification with the team responsible for the alliance. Here, researchers may wish to use scales that were developed to tap identification with a group (e.g., Brown et al., 1986; Karasawa, 1991) or to adapt items of existing organizational identification scales so they refer to the group level rather than the organizational level.

Methodological and Design Issues for Studying Social Capital

Social capital theory is another useful approach to studying alliances. As noted earlier, most of this research utilizes social network analysis to study social capital. Drawing upon Nahapiet and Ghoshal's (1998) conceptualization of social capital, Tsai and Ghoshal (1998) use betweenness centrality to measure the structural dimension of social capital, and in-degree and out-degree centrality to measure the relational dimension. In contrast, Burt (1997a) measures social capital in terms of the network characteristics of size, density, and hierarchy. Similarly, Podolny and Baron (1997) study size, density, and duration of ties in a network. Walker, Kogut, and Shan (1997) measure social capital in terms of structural equivalence in interorganizational networks.

As is demonstrated by these few examples, there are many differing perspectives concerning which network attributes are the most important when studying social capital. Much of this decision may be based on whether the researcher tends to believe that social capital exists due to structural holes or due to network closure. The structural holes argument is that boundary-spanners of dense networks have more social capital than nodes in dense networks because they can exploit opportunities in these holes (Burt, 1992, 1997a, 1997b; Gargiulo & Benassi, 2000; Walker et al., 1997). The network closure argument is that dense, cohesive, closed networks are sources of social capital because individuals in such networks can internalize expectations that allow them to be more effective and to develop trust with others that allows them to access resources (Coleman, 1990; Gargiulo & Benassi, 2000; Podolny & Baron, 1997; Walker et al., 1997).

With regard to applying these two perspectives, if it is believed that network closure underlies social capital formation, Podolny and Baron's (1997) approach may be useful. If, on the other hand, the researcher believes that structural holes are primary for social capital, it may be useful to follow Burt's (1997a) approach. Finally, if the primary interest is examining how networks vary between the parties in the alliance, Walker et al.'s (1997) approach of utilizing structural equivalence may be relevant.

A critical issue with the study of social capital using network analysis is the method of determining who is in the network. Typically, in these studies a free recall approach (Wasserman & Faust, 1994) of name generation is used, whereby individuals state the names of people they are in contact with and then respond to questions about these relationships (e.g., Burt, 1997b). This method is useful when attempting to determine the size of a network or when the boundaries between networks are fuzzy or unclear. An alternative approach to obtaining network members is to have a roster approach where individuals within the network are known and hence selected a priori, and participants respond to questions about individuals listed on the roster (Wasserman & Faust, 1994). This method is appropriate when studying interactions within a network that has strict boundaries, such as alliance-team interactions, where all members of the network are known already and the researcher is not interested in individuals outside of the alliance team. However, if one shifts the focus to, for example, the relationship between learning flows in and across partners and social capital in alliances, establishing the appropriate team boundaries can be a difficult issue. Individuals and groups may contribute only small and variable amounts of time to work related to the alliance, and this participation can vary over time according to task requirements, environmental influences, and other contingencies (see Ariño & de la Torre, 1998; Doz, 1996; Kumar & Seth, 1998; Pearce, 1997).

Understanding the content of social capital in alliance settings can be important: different participants might infuse structural forms of social capital with different meanings. Burt, Hogarth, and Michaud (2000) found that although the forms of social capital were similar for French and American senior managers, the content of these networks were different in some cases. The duration of the oldest relationships varied in that friendship was the basis for social capital for the French, who tended to have long-standing personal relationships, whereas Americans tended to have long-standing work relationships, indicating that Americans had a more porous network where social capital was based on a network of colleagues. Given these results, it is possible that different types of networks (e.g., friendship, work, advice networks) may elicit different levels of social capital among international strategic alliance partners. This is an added complexity that researchers may wish to examine. Thus, future studies of international strategic alliances could benefit from examining the content and context of social capital in addition to its presence among all parties.

An Example of a Framework Employing Social Identity, Social Capital, and Networks

The review in this chapter suggests many paths that future research might take. We chose to develop and to elaborate on one model, summarized below in Figure 21.1. Figure 21.1 draws upon the theories reviewed and is elaborated to offer one potential basis for future empirical work. Exogenous to the model are the strategic rationales and expected contributions that influence incentives and interdependence of work flows at the individual and alliance levels. We posit that social identity faultlines (or their absence within the alliance interface) will initially depend primarily upon the incentive systems and interdependence of work flows, on the one hand, and the array of potential identities, on the other. Diversity in such areas as societal culture, national context, corporate culture, and management practices as well as relative status and power affects attraction and a sense of shared identity with others (e.g., Earley & Mosakowski, 2000; Li et al., 2002; Parkhe, 1991; Salk & Shenkar, 2001). Meanwhile, the identities that predominate at a given time are shaped by critical incidents and structural phenomena such as incentives and work flows (Salk & Shenkar, 2001).

Research we review above suggests that strong organizational identification with the alliance should be positively associated with performance (e.g., Earley & Mosakowski, 2000; Li et al., 2002).

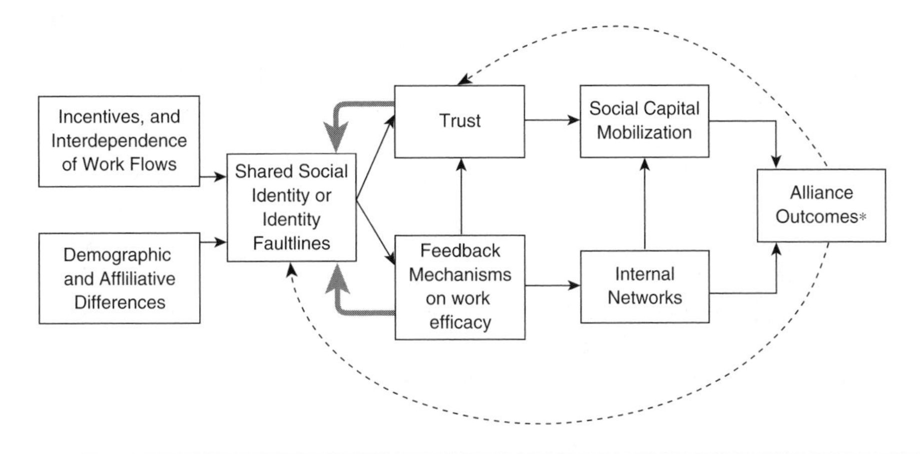

Figure 21.1 A Cross-Level Social Process Model of Alliances

*Alliance outcomes include: Performance, satisfaction of partner organizations, average level of satisfaction of

However, several processes influenced by social identification should more proximately influence various alliances outcomes, including performance. One of these is how trust develops and another is the degree to which there are feedback loops that make efficacy of work in the alliance apparent to participants. Shared social identity and faultlines have been suggested to affect trust. Pearce (1997) suggests that joint venture top management teams characterized by factions in which members identify more with subgroups than the team as a whole (i.e., where faultlines are present) tend to have low levels of trust. Similarly, those who identify strongly with a group such as an IJV, and therefore have a shared social identity, have greater trust in the group (Kramer, 1993; Li et al., 2002).

Furthermore, shared identity and faultlines can negatively affect work efficacy because the presence of faultlines or low levels of identification is associated with conflict and low levels of trust and cooperation (Kramer, 1993; Lau & Murnighan, 1998), which can negatively affect performance. Evidence of efficacy may feed back into social identities by further reinforcing the existing faultlines or by motivating alliance managers to change identifications or somehow reduce their salience to enhance group processes and outcomes. We further suggest that the degree of feedback concerning efficacy might affect trust at a given time: If there is much evidence of ineffectiveness or poor communication, this might initially have a negative effect on trust at the interpersonal, intergroup, and interorganizational levels.

Trust, in turn, is associated with the mobilization of social capital, which affects alliance outcomes. Lower levels of trust might be associated with lower levels of social capital mobilization. That is, members might be less willing to draw upon their external social resources to aid the alliance if trust is low. This can have negative effects on alliance outcomes, because social capital is positively related to performance, particularly in terms of interunit resource exchange and innovation (Tsai & Ghoshal, 1998).

Adding social networks to the picture, however, provides an interesting potential refinement to our understanding. The structures of the networks that begin to crystallize as the alliance begins its work and members begin seeing how their actions affect efficacy should influence social capital formation and its mobilization, which impact alliance outcomes. As Gulati (1998) and Kostova and Roth (2003) note, networks can affect the social capital of organizational and interorganizational units. Hence, when individuals feel invested in the alliance identity and in its fate, they are more likely to use their external ties to obtain resources, information, and political support for the alliance. They not only have access to social capital and mobilize it to enhance performance, but also are embedded in a network that enables them to have positive organizational outcomes. Gulati (1998), for example, suggests that alliances with embedded ties perform better and continue longer than those without such networks.

Finally, we propose a feedback loop from alliance performance to trust and shared social identity/faultlines. When an alliance performs poorly or members of the alliance are not satisfied with the partner, trust may be reduced, because they may believe the partner has not fulfilled its obligations. Ariño and de la Torre (1998) agree, stating that poor performance in alliances can lead to a poor relationship, whereas the fulfillment of expectations reinforces the quality of the relationship and interpartner trust. With regard to the feedback loop to social identity, Li et al. (2002) suggest that success of the IJV is positively related to identification with the joint venture. Broadened to alliances in general, we can expect performance outcomes to positively affect identification with an alliance. Negative outcomes might tend to weaken identification with an alliance if members have alternatives for constituting their social identities. However, when they are under common pressures or scrutiny by external entities, negative performance might reinforce their shared identity, even if that identity now becomes a negative one.

Conclusions

The example in the preceding section is only one of many ways that alliance researchers might draw upon theories and methods outlined in this chapter. In order to pursue the above or the wider array of potentially interesting questions that the SIT and social capital literatures suggest, qualitative research methods such as participant observation and interviews are needed to determine which identities are salient. Questionnaires can then help sort out the salience and relevance of these various identities. Network data would need to be collected within the formal boundary of the alliance. However, it would also be critical to tap the mobilization of external social capital by asking informants whom they communicate with outside the formal organization (especially in the parent organizations) for advice, resources, and support.

A social capital approach can shed light on alliances through the use of network analysis at the individual, group, and organizational levels to determine the structure and content of relationships between parties. Researchers can examine the levels of social capital in alliances through measuring centrality, density, and structural equivalence of the alliance networks within the boundaries of the interpersonal and intergroup collaborative interfaces as well as at the broader organizational levels. The morphology and contents of networks may well be interrelated over time, and their interactions with salient social identities might well mediate the effects of variables previously linked to alliance performance and longevity, such as role investment, skill complementarities, learning, and resource and knowledge mobilization. Further, qualitative data regarding attitudes towards others in the networks and the potential associations of salient identities and structural characteristics could be beneficial when determining the reasons for social capital formation and use and hence why certain resources may be more available in some strategic alliances versus others.

Although this chapter could not discuss every nontraditional method that can be employed to study strategic alliances, it spotlights two approaches that can open new avenues of understanding for alliance research and theory: social identity theory and social capital theory. These two theories are emerging in strategic alliance research and deserve more attention in the future. The key to their future potential to contribute to theory and practical knowledge hinges on developing and exploring cross-level and longitudinal approaches to studying their origins and effects on dependent variables such as alliance formation, longevity, and performance. Further, a combination of both qualitative and quantitative methods can and should be used when employing SIT and social capital theory in strategic alliance research.

References

Abrams, D. (1999). Social identity, social cognition, and the self: The flexibility and stability of self-categorization. In D. Abrams & M. Hogg (Eds.), *Social identity and social cognition* (pp. 197–229). Malden, MA: Blackwell.

Abrams, D., Ando, K., & Hinkle, S. (1998). Psychological attachment to the group: Cross-cultural differences in organizational identification and subjective norms as predictors of workers' turnover intentions. *Personality and Social Psychology Bulletin, 24,* 1027–1039.

Ahuja, G. (2000). Collaboration networks, structural holes, and innovation: A longitudinal study. *Administrative Science Quarterly, 45,* 425–455.

Aldrich, H. E. (2001). Who wants to be an evolutionary theorist? Remarks on the occasion of the year 2000 OMT distinguished scholarly career award presentation. *Journal of Management Inquiry, 10*(2), 115–127.

Almeida, P., & Kogut, B. (1999). Localization of knowledge and the mobility of engineers in regional networks. *Management Science, 45,* 905–917.

Ariño, A., & de la Torre, J. (1998). Learning from failure: Towards an evolutionary model of collaborative ventures. *Organization Science, 9,* 306–325.

Ashforth, B., & Mael, F. (1989). Social identity theory and the organization. *Academy of Management Review, 14,* 20–39.

Aubert, B., & Kelsey, B. (2003). Further understanding of trust and performance in virtual teams. *Small Group Research, 34,* 575–618.

Berg, S., & Friedman, P. (1978). Joint ventures in American industry: An overview. *Mergers and Acquisitions, 13,* 28–41.

Bergami, M., & Bagozzi, R. (2000). Self-categorization, affective commitment and group self-esteem as distinct aspects of social identity in the organization. *British Journal of Social Psychology, 39,* 555–577.

Billig, M., & Tajfel, H. (1973). Social categorization and similarity in intergroup behavior. *European Journal of Social Psychology, 3,* 27–52.

Bivens, D. K., & Lovell, E. B. (1966). *Joint ventures with foreign partners.* New York: The Conference Board.

Bourdieu, P. (1985). The forms of social capital. In J. Richardson (Ed.), *Handbook of theory and research for the sociology of education* (pp. 241–258). New York: Greenwood Press.

Brown, R., Condor, S., Matthews, A., Wade, G., & Williams, J. (1986). Explaining intergroup differentiation in an industrial organization. *Journal of Occupational Psychology, 59,* 273–286.

Burt, R. (1992). *Structural holes: The social structure of competition.* Cambridge, MA: Harvard University Press.

Burt, R. (1997a). The contingent value of social capital. *Administrative Science Quarterly, 42,* 339–365.

Burt, R. (1997b). A note on social capital and network content. *Social Networks, 19,* 355–373.

Burt, R., Hogarth, R., & Michaud, C. (2000). The social capital of French and American managers. *Organization Science, 11,* 123–147.

Child, J., & Markoczy, L. (1993). Host country managerial behavior and learning in Chinese and Hungarian joint ventures. *Journal of Management Studies, 30,* 611–631.

Chung, S., Singh, H., & Lee, K. (2000). Complementarity, status similarity and social capital as drivers of alliance formation. *Strategic Management Journal, 21*(1), 1–22.

Coleman, J. (1990). *Foundations of social capital.* Cambridge, MA: Belknap Press of Harvard University Press.

Contractor, F., & Lorange, P. (1988). *Cooperative strategies in international business.* Lexington, MA: Lexington Books.

Cramton, C. D., & Hinds, P. J. (2005). Subgroup dynamics in distributed teams: Ethnocentrism or cross-national learning. In B. Staw & R. Kramer (Eds.), *Research in organizational behavior.* Greenwich, CT: JAI Press.

Danis, W., & Parkhe, A. (2002). Hungarian-Western partnerships: A grounded theoretical model of integration processes and outcomes. *Journal of International Business Studies, 33,* 423–455.

Deaux, K., Reid, A., Mizrah, K., & Cotting, D. (1999). Connecting the person to the social: The functions of social identification. In T. Tyler, R. Kramer, & O. John (Eds.), *The psychology of the social self* (pp. 91–113). Mahwah, NJ: Lawrence Erlbaum.

De Rond, M. and Bouchikhi, H. (2004). On the dialectics of strategic alliances. *Organization Science, 15*(1), 56–69.

Doz, Y. (1996). The evolution of cooperation in strategic alliances: Initial conditions or learning processes? [special issue]. *Strategic Management Journal, 17,* 55–83.

Earley, P. C., & Mosakowski, E. (2000). Creating hybrid team cultures: An empirical test of transnational team functioning. *Academy of Management Journal, 43,* 26–49.

Elron, E., Shamir, B., & Ben-Ari, E. (1999). Why don't they fight each other? Cultural diversity and operational unity in multinational forces. *Armed Forces and Society, 26,* 73–98.

Erez, M., & Earley, P. C. (1993). *Culture, self identity, and work.* New York: Oxford University Press.

Espinosa, J. A., Cummings, J. N., Wilson, J. M., & Pearce, B. M. (2003). Team boundary issues across multiple global firms. *Journal of Management Information Systems, 19*(4), 157–190.

Gargiulo, M., & Benassi, M. (2000). Trapped in your own net? Network cohesion, structural holes, and the adaptation of social capital. *Organization Science, 11,* 183–196.

Gibson, C. B., & Cohen, S. G. (2003). *Virtual teams that work.* San Francisco: Jossey-Bass.

Gibson, C. B., & Vermeulen, F. (2004). A healthy divide: Subgroups as a stimulus for team learning behavior. *Administrative Science Quarterly, 48,* 202–239.

Gibson, C. B., & Zellmer-Bruhn, M. E. (2001). Metaphors and meaning: An intercultural analysis of the concept of teamwork. *Administrative Science Quarterly, 46,* 274–303.

Gulati, R. (1998). Alliances and networks. *Strategic Management Journal, 19,* 293–317.

Gulati, R., & Singh, H. (1998). The architecture of cooperation: Managing coordination costs and appropriation concerns in strategic alliances. *Administrative Science Quarterly, 43,* 781–814.

Hamel, G. (1991). Competition for competence and inter-partner learning within international strategic alliances [special issue]. *Strategic Management Journal, 12,* 83–103.

Hamel, G., Doz, Y., & Prahalad, C. (1989). Collaborate with your competitors, and win. *Harvard Business Review, 67,* 133–139.

Harrigan, K. (1986). *Managing for joint venture success.* Lexington, MA: Lexington Books.

Harrigan, K. (1988). Joint venture and competitive strategy. *Strategic Management Journal, 9,* 141–158.

Hinkle, S., Taylor, L., Fox-Cardamone, D., & Crook, K. (1989). Intragroup identification and intergroup differentiation: A multicomponent approach. *British Journal of Social Psychology, 28,* 305–317.

Ibarra, H. (1993). Network centrality, power, and innovation involvement: Determinants of technical and administrative roles. *Academy of Management Journal, 36,* 471–501.

Inkpen, A. C., & Beamish, P. W. (1997). Knowledge, bargaining power and international joint venture instability. *Academy of Management Review, 22*(1), 177–202.

Inkpen, A. C., & Currall, S. (1997). International joint venture trust: An empirical examination. In P. W. Beamish & P. J. Killing (Eds.), *Cooperative strategies: North American perspectives* (pp. 308–336). San Francisco: New Lexington Press.

Karasawa, M. (1991). Toward an assessment of social identity: The structure of group identification and its effect on in-group evaluations. *British Journal of Social Psychology, 30,* 293–307.

Killing, P. (1983). *Strategies for joint venture success.* New York: Praeger.

Kogut, B., & Zander, U. (1993). What firms do? Coordination, identity, and learning. *Organization Science, 7,* 502–518.

Kostova, T., & Roth, K. (2003). Social capital in multinational corporations and a micro-macro model of its formation. *Academy of Management Review, 28,* 297–317.

Kramer, R. (1993). Cooperation and organizational identification. In J. Murnighan (Ed.), *Social psychology in organizations: Advances in theory and research* (pp. 244–268). Englewood Cliffs, NJ: Prentice Hall.

Kumar, S., & Seth, A. (1998). The design of coordination and control mechanisms for managing joint venture-parent relationships. *Strategic Management Journal, 19,* 579–599.

Lane, P., Salk, J. E., & Lyles, M. A. (2001). Absorptive capacity, learning and performance in international joint ventures. *Strategic Management Journal, 22*(12), 1139–1162.

Larson, A. (1992). Network dyads in entrepreneurial settings: A study of the governance of exchange relationships. *Administrative Science Quarterly, 37*(1), 76–104.

Lau, D., & Murnighan, J. (1998). Demographic diversity and faultlines: The compositional dynamics of organizational groups. *Academy of Management Review, 23,* 325–340.

Li, J., Xin, K., & Pillutla, M. (2002). Multi-cultural leadership teams and organizational identification in international joint ventures. *International Journal of Human Resource Management, 13,* 320–337.

Lyles, M. (1988). Learning among joint venture sophisticated firms. *Management International Review, 28,* 85–98.

Lyles, M., & Salk, J. (1996). Knowledge acquisition from foreign parents in international joint venture: An empirical examination in the Hungarian context. *Journal of International Business Studies, 27,* 877–903.

Mael, F., & Ashforth, B. (1992). Alumni and their alma mater: A partial test of the reformulated model of organizational identification. *Journal of Organizational Behavior, 13,* 103–123.

Mael, F., & Tetrick, L. (1992). Identifying organizational identification. *Educational and Psychological Measurement, 52,* 813–824.

Maznevski, M., & Chudoba, K. (2000). Bridging space over time: Global virtual team dynamics and effectiveness. *Organization Science, 11,* 473–492.

Mjoen, H., & Tallman, S. (1997). Control and performance in international joint ventures. *Organization Science, 8*(3), 257–274.

Nahapiet, J., & Ghoshal, S. (1998). Social capital, intellectual capital, and the organizational advantage. *Academy of Management Review, 23,* 242–266.

Nohria, N., & Garcia-Point, C. (1991). Global strategic linkages and industry structure. *Strategic Management Journal, 12,* 105–124.

Parkhe, A. (1991). Interfirm diversity, organizational learning and longevity in global strategic alliances. *Journal of International Business Studies, 22,* 579–602.

Parkhe, A. (1993). "Messy" research, methodological predispositions, and theory development in international joint venture research. *Academy of Management Review, 18,* 227–268.

Pate, J. (1969). Joint venture activity, 1960–1968. *Economic Review* (pp. 16–23). Federal Reserve Bank of Cleveland.

Pearce, R. (1997). Toward understanding joint venture performance and survival: A bargaining and influence approach to transaction cost theory. *Academy of Management Review, 22,* 203–225.

Podolny, J., & Baron, J. (1997). Resources and relationships: Social networks and mobility in the workplace. *American Sociological Review, 62,* 673–693.

Portes, A. (1998). Social capital: Its origins and applications in modern society. *Annual Review of Sociology, 24,* 1–24.

Salk, J. E. (1996). Partners and other strangers: Cultural boundaries and cross-cultural encounters in international joint venture teams. *International Studies of Management and Organization, 26*(4), 48–72.

Salk, J. E., & Brannen, M. Y. (2000). National culture, networks, and individual influence in a multinational management team. *Academy of Management Journal, 43,* 191–202.

Salk, J. E., & Shenkar, O. (2001). Social identities in an international joint venture: An exploratory study. *Organization Science, 12*(2), 161–178.

Salk, J. E., & Simonin, B. (2003). Beyond alliances: Towards a meta-theory of collaborative learning. In M. Lyles & M. E. Smith (Eds.), *The Blackwell handbook of organizational learning and knowledge management* (pp. 235–277). Malden, MA: Blackwell.

Schein, E. (1992). *Organizational culture and leadership* (2nd ed.). San Francisco: Jossey-Bass.

Steensma, M., & Lyles, M. A. (2000). Explaining IJV survival in a transitional economy through social exchange and knowledge-based perspectives. *Strategic Management Journal, 21*(8), 831–851.

Tajfel, H. (1974). Social identity and intergroup behavior. *Social Science Information, 13,* 65–93.

Tajfel, H. (1978). Social categorization, social identity, and social comparison. In H. Tajfel (Ed.), *Differentiation between social groups: Studies in intergroup behavior. European monographs in social psychology* (Vol. 14, pp. 61–76). London: Academic Press.

Tajfel, H., Billig, M., Bundy, R., & Flament, C. (1971). Social categorization and intergroup behavior. *European Journal of Social Psychology,* 1(2), 149–178.

Tajfel, H., & Turner, J. (1986). The social identity theory of intergroup behavior. In S. Worchel &

W. G. Austin (Eds.), *Psychology of intergroup relations* (pp. 7–24). Chicago, IL: Nelson-Hall.

Tsai, W., & Ghoshal, S. (1998). Social capital and value creation: The role of intrafirm networks. *Academy of Management Journal, 41*, 464–476.

Turner, J. (1982).Towards a cognitive redefinition of the social group. In H. Tajfel (Ed.), *Social identity and intergroup relations,* (pp. 15–40). London, UK: Cambridge University Press.

Turner, J. (1984). Social identification and psychological group formation. In H. Tajfel (Ed.), *The social dimension: European developments in social psychology* (pp. 518–538). London: Cambridge University Press.

Tyler, T., & Blader, S. (2001). Identity and cooperative behavior in groups. *Group Processes and Intergroup Relations, 4*, 207–226.

Walker, G., Kogut, B., & Shan, W. (1997). Social capital, structural holes, and formation of an industry network. *Organization Science, 8*, 109–125.

Wan-Huggins, H., Riordan, C., & Griffeth, R. (1998). The development and longitudinal test of a model of organizational identification. *Journal of Applied Social Psychology, 28*, 724–749.

Wasserman, S., & Faust, K. (1994). *Social network analysis.* Cambridge, UK: Cambridge University Press.

Van de Ven, A., & Poole, M. (1995). Explaining development and change in organizations. *Academy of Management Review, 20*, 510–540.

Yan, A., & Gray, B. (1994). Bargaining power, management control and performance in United States-Chinese joint ventures: A comparative case study. *Academy of Management Journal, 33*, 1478–1517.

22

Modeling and Measuring the Performance of Alliances

Paul Olk

The proliferation of the use and study of strategic alliances has produced considerable knowledge about select alliance issues. Over the last few decades, advances have been made in understanding motives for using alliances, in anticipating challenges in negotiating an alliance, and in developing routines for how to manage alliances. So far, however, we have not attained the same level of insight about how to gauge performance. Nonetheless, assessing a strategic alliance has been found to be problematic both in practice and in research. For practice, many managers report low levels of confidence in the measures used for evaluation (e.g., Anderson Consulting, as cited in Kale, Dyer, & Singh, 2000; Bamford & Ernst, 2002). For research, one finds a variety of measures in use with limited discussion of their comparability.

This situation is in many ways not too surprising. Research on the more general question of how to evaluate organizational performance has also not achieved a consensus. Even currently popular multidimensional approaches suffer from questions about how to combine different types of measures. In part, the failure to find an ideal measure stems from the need for a measure to achieve sometimes competing goals, such as reflecting past performance while indicating future potential (Meyer, 2002). In addition, it may be difficult to derive a measure that is both valid and comparable. To create a measure (or set of measures) that validly reflects performance may require incorporating indicators that capture the subtleties of the organization's context. The more one develops such a measure, however, the less likely it is that it will apply to an organization

AUTHOR'S NOTE: Funding for this research was provided by the Alliance Edge, University of Queens, Kingston, Ontario, Canada. I am grateful to its sponsors, as well as to the director, Tina Dacin, and to the center's staff for the funding and the opportunity to present and discuss this research with them. I also appreciate the helpful comments from an anonymous reviewer and the editors of this volume, Jeff Reuer and Oded Shenkar. A preliminary version of this paper was presented at the Western Academy of Management Meetings, Palm Springs, CA, 2003.

in a different context. Alternatively, creating measures that usefully compare different organizations may result in not capturing any one organization's situation.

Assessing strategic alliance performance is arguably even more complicated, because an alliance is a hybrid structure. Although some alliances may have clear boundaries from the partnering companies, for others the separation may be less defined. For these latter arrangements, it may not be clear to an evaluator—particularly from outside the alliance—the degree to which the alliance creates value and transfers it to the partnering companies. For example, in trying to establish boundaries, an evaluator may consider an alliance as a stand-alone entity. Finding that the alliance has created significant value, the observer may conclude that it is performing well. However, if the partnering companies do not capture these benefits (Doz & Hamel, 1998), the companies may consider the alliance a poor performer. Alternatively, a terminated alliance may be considered a failure by some because it is no longer active. But at least one partner may consider it successful if the partner learned lessons from the alliance's experiences and transferred these throughout the company.

These challenges have likely slowed researchers' efforts to develop a comprehensive understanding of strategic alliance performance. This situation has not gone unnoticed. Several researchers have tried to make sense out of the breadth of performance measures by arguing that a measure's appropriateness varies by the context (Yan & Gray, 1995) or by the research question (e.g., Gulati & Zajac, 2000; Reuer & Koza, 2000a), or by developing conceptual frameworks that categorize different perspectives on performance (e.g., Gray, 2000; Olk, 2002). Although researchers have empirically assessed the comparability of select measures (e.g., Ariño, 2003; Geringer & Hebert, 1991; Glaister & Buckley, 1998; Hatfield, Pearce, Sleeth, & Pitts, 1998), there is no broad understanding of how the underlying constructs are related or whether they are substitutions for or even predictors of one another. Therefore, in this paper I take a more comprehensive effort by proposing a model of the relationships between and among these measures. I begin with an overview of three evaluation approaches found in the organizational performance literature and provide corollaries in the strategic alliance literature. I close this discussion by noting that although these approaches help to identify various types of measures, a challenge facing organizational performance research is in understanding the association among different performance indicators. In the following section, I develop such a model for strategic alliances. I conclude the paper by discussing implications of this model and suggestions for future research.

Different Approaches to Evaluating Alliance Performance

To begin to understand how to gauge strategic alliance performance, I first turn to models of organizational performance. Although the challenges of evaluating an organization have been discussed for many years (see, e.g., Cameron & Whetten, 1983; Campbell, 1977; Pennings & Goodman, 1977; Scott, 1992), the last decade has seen a rejuvenation in this research, leading to what appear to be three approaches: searching for an ideal measure, recognizing the need for multiple measures, and claiming that these efforts will likely not lead to an ideal solution. I briefly review each, describing its advantages and shortcomings, and provide parallels in strategic alliance research.

Single Measure

Studies in the first approach either explicitly advocate or implicitly assume a single measure of performance. The preferred measure is argued to provide greater reliability and validity than other measures. This has often been an accounting return (e.g., return on assets [ROA], return on equity) or stock market reaction to an announced event. Critiques of such measures have included concerns that accounting measures reflect past performance but do not provide information about future performance, and that the stock market reaction, although providing information about expected future performance, has not been linked to actual performance. Meyer and Gupta (1994) also note that single measures tend to become ineffective over time. Because the criteria are well known, companies manage toward them and attempt to ensure that performance is not too far below the average. Over time, this reduces the variance between the best and the worst performers and the ability of the measure to distinguish between good and poor performers. Recently, Meyer (2002) proposed an activity-based profitability analysis as a possible measure. Akin to activity-based cost accounting, this procedure breaks the organization down into discrete activities and examines the degree to which each activity enhances the company's profitability.

In alliance research, single measures have been used to calculate both alliance and company performance. At the alliance level, two common measures are whether the alliance continues to exist (i.e., termination) and restructuring or stability in alliance ownership levels. The measures have the advantages of being relatively easy and less expensive to collect than other measures. Objections to this method stem primarily from what the measures include and how to interpret them. Termination combines natural and untimely deaths and are either/or decisions; absent a termination, no information is gained (Gulati, 1998). Further, a measure of termination assumes that only the fittest alliance survives and that stability is in the partners' best interest, and tells us little about the reasons for terminating. That is, termination does not convey whether it was one partner's decision to withdraw or if both agreed, whether the partners' strategic interests changed, making the alliance no longer relevant although it performed well, or whether one partner decided to internalize the activities of the alliance and no longer wanted a separate entity (Reuer & Koza, 2000).

At the company level, there have been two general uses of single measures to evaluate performance. One employs the aforementioned stock market reaction, accounting and financial measures—such as net income, ROA, and market to book ratios and risk, among others—as well as perceptual measures of financial performance. These measures not only have the aforementioned advantages and disadvantages but include problems specific to alliances. For example, financial return measures from an alliance are not always publicly available, the financial benefits may not be the same for all partners, or they may reflect transfer pricing decisions about where to locate profits.

A second use consists of measures reflecting the company's dominant coalition interests. This commonly used effort emphasizes the strategic reasons for participation. Such studies have typically used one of three likely correlated measures: managers' general evaluation of alliance success, managers' satisfaction with alliance performance on a single or on related dimensions of performance, and combining several managers' evaluations of the alliance's performance compared to specific goals—such as objectives met, initial expectations, and learning—into a single measure. The primary concerns with this method center on criteria validity. One validity issue is that one partner's objectives may not necessarily reflect another's. A second is that a company's objectives may change over time, and collecting data at one time will not capture later, emergent objectives (Yan & Gray, 1995). Finally, these indicators do not permit an assessment against alternatives. The alliance may have met the goals identified by the dominant coalition, but this does not provide information about whether resources committed to the alliance could have been used more effectively elsewhere.

In summary, these single-item indicators are often relatively easy to collect, allow for comparison across a portfolio of alliances, and provide some information about alliance performance. However, they do not capture the additional information that some observers believe is needed to represent alliance performance fully. We turn to a discussion of this approach.

Multiple Measures

Many current evaluation discussions argue that a single measure cannot represent organizational performance. Rather, one must rely upon multiple measures that collectively make up performance. Although the notion has been discussed previously by organizational effectiveness scholars, more recently the Balanced Scorecard (BSC) has been advocated, using multiple measures. As described by Kaplan and Norton (e.g., 1992, 1993), performance is based upon four types of measures: financial, customer satisfaction, internal business processes, and innovation, learning, and growth. Central to their argument is that determining performance is not a choice between short- or long-term, subjective or objective, internal or external, or financial or nonfinancial measures. Rather, it consists of all of these. Also, the BSC is helpful in connecting the company's mission and strategy to specific objectives and measures (e.g., Kaplan & Norton, 1996). Important in implementing the BSC is that management must customize, based upon the company's context, the recommended 20 to 25 measures to indicate the four types listed above. Although the BSC has achieved widespread acceptance in practice, it has been criticized as requiring data that are difficult to collect and for uncertainty as to how to combine these data into an overall evaluation of performance (Meyer, 2002). For example, Ittner and Larcker (2003) reported that less than 30% of the companies they surveyed had developed a causal model of how subjective measures predicted objective measures. Further, over 70% of these companies did not consider the measures reliable or valid.

For alliances, multiple measures to estimate performance, although generally not as common as a single-measure approach, have been recommended (e.g., Yan & Gray, 1995). One example is Eli Lilly's use of a "spider web" (Futrell, Slugay, & Stephens, 2001). The company examines three alliance dimensions—strategic fit, operational fit, and cultural fit—which are represented by 14 specific performance dimensions. The performance of Eli Lilly is evaluated on these constructs, each measured through several items, by both Eli Lilly and partner managers. These are then presented in a "spider web" image, which allows one to see simultaneously the ratings by Eli Lilly and the partner as well as the consistency across the constructs. Likewise, Bamford and Ernst (2002) recommend that managers evaluate an alliance on four dimensions of fitness: financial, strategic, operational, and relationship. Finally, several academics have used multiple measures in assessing alliances (e.g., Harrigan, 1986; Lyles & Salk, 1997; Mjoen & Tallman, 1997; Steensma & Corley, 2000). In these efforts, researchers have combined different measures (e.g., financial, managerial satisfaction) to derive a composite score representing the alliance's or the company's performance. As this discussion indicates, alliance research has also not solved the issues of which specific performance measures to use and how these relate to one another, as well as the alliance-specific problem of the appropriate level of analysis (i.e., alliance, company, partner, or company and partner). Although this perspective shows promise, a number of implementation issues remain unsettled. Some of these are not new and, as the next section notes, may not be solved.

Never-Ending Process

A third outlook comes from a few articles that have examined why the multitude of research into organizational performance has not produced a definitive finding. This perspective claims not only that there is no single way to evaluate an organization but that the effort to find the ideal measure will not succeed. March and Sutton (1997) argue that the problem stems from competing interests of rigor and speculation.

To conduct careful research and produce substantiated findings about the causes of organizational effectiveness requires rigorous measures of predictors and performance. However, to explain how the findings might apply to situations beyond those studied requires speculation, which thereby reduces the level of rigor. These incompatible goals lead researchers to emphasize either rigor or speculation, making it difficult to develop general organizational effectiveness predictors.

Hirsch and Levin (1999) built upon this tension in describing the dialectic that developed in organizational effectiveness research. On one side are those who favor investigation of organizational effectiveness. These "umbrella advocates" encourage researchers to embark on studies of effectiveness and are more concerned that researchers are trying to assess performance than with finding the right measure. On the other side are those researchers, labeled "validity police," who recommend using reliable and valid measures. They argue that without developing such measures, the field will not be able to develop a coherent body of knowledge. Hirsch and Levin propose that the dialectic between these proponents keeps the debate from making any progress and that eventually researchers became tired of the topic and moved on to others.

Although there has not been a parallel case made for a lack of progress in strategic alliance performance, there have been attempts to calculate the validity and reliability of different measures. For example, Geringer and Hebert (1991) report agreement between managers at a company and its partner in their evaluation, as well as between subjective and objective indicators. These findings are revisited by Glaister and Buckley (1998), who show generally limited replication and that the organizing mode (i.e., equity or nonequity alliance) and national culture of the partnering companies affect the relationships. Likewise, Hatfield et al. (1998) reveal that alliance goal achievement, duration, and survival indicators are related but measure different phenomena. Ariño (2003) finds that outcome measures, such as goal fulfillment, are separate from process measures (e.g., satisfaction and net spillovers) and argues that both need to be incorporated into a definition of alliance performance. Finally, Olk and Ariño (2002) tested several assumptions common to alliance research. Among their findings are that satisfaction and termination are correlated only when one considers general satisfaction. But if one examines satisfaction in terms of achieving strategic goals (i.e., strategic satisfaction), it is not significantly associated with termination. They also find no support for convergence in how partners gauge performance.

Taken together, these various studies advocate the need for a better understanding of how to evaluate an alliance. Currently, managers and researchers of alliances are making decisions about alliances based upon faulty or incomplete information. Whether strategic alliance research avoids recreating the above dialectic depends, perhaps, on how successfully researchers and managers overcome some of the aforementioned implementation issues. Toward that goal and in an effort to provide an overall understanding of strategic alliance performance, this chapter draws from the measures identified in the above perspectives and proposes a model of how the various performance indicators might be connected to one another.

Model of Strategic Alliance Performance Measures

To develop this model, I began by reviewing over 120 articles on strategic alliances that appeared in the past twenty years in such journals as *Strategic Management Journal, Academy of Management Review, Organization Science, Administrative Science Quarterly, Journal of International Business Studies,* and *Organization Studies,* as well as several edited volumes. I first catalogued the various measures used. Table 22.1 provides a description of the various types and examples of specific indicators. I then incorporated empirically

Table 22.1 Types of Performance Measures

Performance Measures	*Representative Items*
Expectations at Formation	Stock market reaction to announcement Manager's initial high or low expectations
Process and Relational Measures	Degree of attaining milestone goals Level of conflict Degree of trust Presence of opportunistic behavior
Strategic Goal Fulfillment	Degree of attaining strategic goals Overall effectiveness of alliance Company patents Company level of learning from alliance Company survival
Strategic and Operational Satisfaction	Evaluation of overall satisfaction with alliance's operations Evaluation of overall satisfaction with alliance's strategic objective achievement.
Financial Outcomes	Return on investment Return on assets Net income Sales
Emergent Goals	Performance on new goals Performance on spillover goals
Stability	Contract restructuring Contract renegotiations Changes in membership
Duration	Age of alliance Tenure of company in the alliance
Termination	Dissolution of alliance Company withdrawal from alliance

validated relationships between different types of measures and drew an arrow between the appropriate measures. A solid line indicates empirical support for the relationship and a mixed dashed and dotted line indicates mixed support for a relationship (see Figure 22.1). Following this, I examined the literature for implicit relationships between measures. As noted above, several studies assumed a connection but did not test it. In a few places, I added arrows indicating relationships that have not been tested but in practice may be present. Both of these kinds of assumed relationships are indicated with a dashed line. Figure 22.1 presents the resulting model.

The model has three sections. Initial Indicators of Performance comprise the first section. These measures are future-oriented and are argued to indicate the potential of the alliance. The second consists of several Ongoing Indicators of Performance. These provide information on an existing

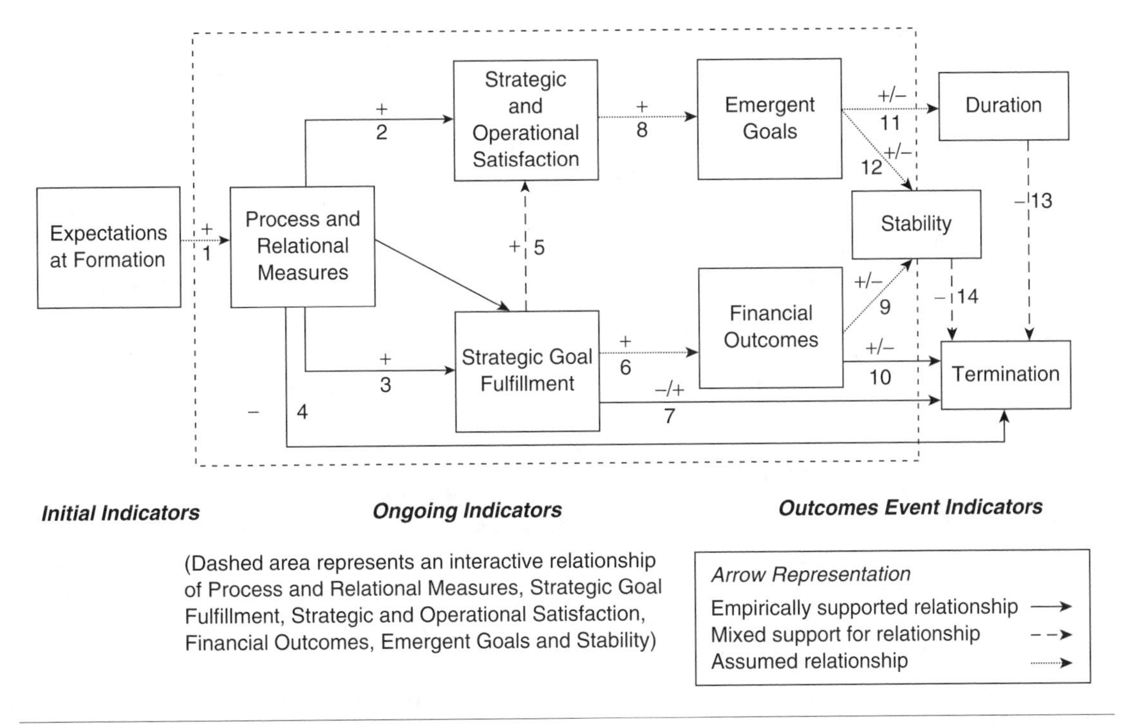

Figure 22.1 Model of the Relationships Among Strategic Alliance Performance Measures

alliance. Often, a researcher measuring ongoing performance will use multiple measures to specify performance, ones that require interviewing or surveying managers. An important quality of the indicators in this section is that they mutually influence one another. Although the model formally shows how initial measures (e.g., Process and Relational Measures) connect with subsequent ones (e.g., Strategic and Operational Satisfaction; Emergent Goals), as the alliance evolves, these "later" measures will in turn influence "earlier" ones. For example, performance in terms of developing Emergent Goals or of Financial Outcomes will affect subsequent Process and Relational Measures or Strategic and Operational Satisfaction. Because of the complexity in representing the various feedback processes with additional arrows, the model notes that the measures inside the dashed area are interactive. The third section consists of Outcome Event Indicators of performance. These measures reflect post hoc alliance performance.

Initial Indicators

Expectations at Formation. The model commences with performance expectations at the time of formation. Numerous researchers have used performance at the onset to indicate alliance effectiveness. For example, event history studies using stock market reaction to the announcement of an alliance argue that the capital asset pricing model (CAPM) provides reliable indication of the expected performance. Stock market reaction has been used to evaluate a variety of company actions—CEO succession, a merger or an acquisition—and it is a simple extension to expand it to the formation of an alliance (e.g., Anand & Khanna, 2000; Kale, Dyer, & Singh, 2002). As noted, this measure is relatively easy to collect and unambiguous about performance. An alternative initial measure has been to survey managers about the expected ease of achieving initial goals.

Ongoing Indicators

Process and Relational Measures. The second set of measures in the model consists of process and relational measures. These measures capture the nature of the interactions between the participants, and effectiveness is indicated by how well the alliance operates. Three subtypes of measures have been used to assess the process or the relationship. For some alliances, particularly those in early stages of development, the degree to which operational milestones are met serves as an indication of alliance progress (Bamford & Ernst, 2002). For more mature alliances, researchers have focused more on two other measures: the presence of opportunistic behavior or of partner conflict (e.g., Parkhe, 1993). These behaviors are believed to signal effectiveness because they represent both the degree to which partners have overcome competitive differences and the partners' ability to design and manage the collaborative effort (Cropper, 1996).

The model proposes a positive path between Expectations at Formation and the Process and Relational Measures (arrow 1). Although not tested empirically, it is anticipated that high expectations at the onset will enhance the relationship between the partners. Setting such expectations and getting commitment from top management to support the alliances have been argued to be critical for alliances (e.g., Merrifield, 2004). The high expectations will likely lead to more attention by the partners and may reduce initial levels of opportunistic behavior or partner conflict. Further, early indications of performance satisfaction set the tone for subsequent alliance development (Saxton, 1997). This "honeymoon" effect suggests that performance expectations at the time of formation will provide a good indication of the initial process and relational measures.

Strategic Goal Fulfillment. The next set of measures used to evaluate performance is the degree to which the alliance has achieved strategic goals. This represents perhaps the most common performance measures used by researchers collecting survey questionnaire data. The measures are typically derived by asking informants the extent to which the alliance has achieved specific goals that the company's management or alliance management has for the alliance. Notably, these goals may not be the same as the initial reasons for entering into the alliance. These indicators—often reflecting a variety of possible goals—have been either first weighted by the importance of the goal (e.g., Olk, 1997; Parkhe, 1993) or just summed up (e.g., Brockoff & Teichert, 1995; Lin & Germain, 1998, Yeheskel, Zeira, Shenkar, & Newburry , 2001). These also include company-level objective measures that researchers assume reflect company goals—for example, company patents (Hagedoorn & Duysters, 2002), learning, or company survival. The Strategic Goal Fulfillment measures are argued to provide reliable information on whether the alliance is helping the company achieve its overall strategy. As this summary suggests, researchers often have to make a decision about the appropriate level of analysis. There is no consensus as to whether one should examine the goals of the alliance, the goals for a specific company, or the joint goals for all of the companies engaged in the alliance.

In the model, it is anticipated that the Strategic Goal Fulfillment will be positively predicted by the Process and Relational Measures (arrow 3). That is, the better the Process and Relational Measures, the more likely a company will attain Strategic Goal Fulfillment. The clearest evidence for this can be found in Parkhe (1993), where he found lower levels of opportunistic behavior to be related to goal attainment. Likewise, numerous researchers investigating the importance of trust and of conflict avoidance have connected them to goal achievement (e.g., Whipple & Frankel, 2000).

Strategic and Operational Satisfaction. A third indicator is the extent to which managers report satisfaction with the alliance's performance. The measure is typically a one-scale item requesting an informant to determine the degree to which the company is satisfied with the performance of the alliance in general or in terms of achieving specific strategic goals. Support for this measure includes the claims that it is relatively easy for informants to provide—rather than detailed financial, accounting, or strategic goals data—and that it captures the overall evaluation managers use in making decisions about an alliance (e.g., Glaister & Buckley, 1999; Hebert & Beamish, 1997).[1] In addition, because it is a simple measure that incorporates the context, it provides for easy comparison across alliances.

The model proposes that two other performance measures will relate to Strategic and Operational Satisfaction. The first is Process and Relational Measures (arrow 2). Analogous to the argument for arrow 3, achieving milestones, creating trust, and the absence of conflict will each likely enhance the level of satisfaction with the alliance. Empirical evidence can be found in Doz, Olk, and Ring (2000), which shows each member company's commitment associated with managerial satisfaction. The second predictor is Strategic Goal Fulfillment (arrow 5). Implicit in many claims for using Strategic and Operational Satisfaction as a measure is that it stems in part from achieving goals for membership. Although several studies have found strong correlations between achieving strategic goals and satisfaction (e.g., Hatfield et al., 1998; Johnson, Cullen, & Sakano, 1995; Mjoen & Tallman, 1997), this relationship has not always been supported (e.g., Olk & Ariño, 2002).

Financial Outcomes. Financial Outcomes represent an application of traditional finance, accounting, or sales levels measures to alliances. Similar to evaluating performance for a standalone organization, these measures are believed to be reliable indicators of an alliance's value. These still suffer from the aforementioned lagging indicator problem, and an additional difficulty in using them in alliances is that this information is generally not reported in public filings or in annual reports. Researchers who use these measures often collect them via surveys or interviews. Despite these problems, these are fairly objective indicators and provide comparability across alliances. Examples of studies that have used this include Combs and Ketchen (1999) and Rowley, Behrens, and Krackhardt (2000).

Although not tested, it is assumed that Financial Outcomes measures are related to if not identical with measures of Strategic Goal Fulfillment (arrow 6). That is, either a company has engaged in the alliance for financial benefits (e.g., reduced costs) or, in achieving its strategic goals, the company will attain financial benefits.

Emergent Goals. During the life cycle of the alliance, the purpose of the alliance may evolve as the alliance achieves initial goals and managers decide to embark on new ones or as the initial goals become viewed as less relevant than newer ones. For example, SEMATECH, an early U.S. research and development consortium, initially focused on developing new production processes for the semiconductor companies that were the member companies (Browning, Beyer, & Shetler, 1995). After forming the consortium, the members realized that part of the challenge in enhancing their production processes was in obtaining better equipment. After some time, the members recognized that in order to improve their own performance, they needed to enhance the capabilities of their machine tool suppliers. This led member companies to refocus the goals of SEMATECH to include the viability of their suppliers. In collecting emergent goal data, some researchers have also measured "spillovers" to indicate benefits received that were not initially expected (e.g., Ariño, 2003; Parkhe, 1993). The argument for using emergent or spillover measures of performance is that because alliances are dynamic entities, using only initial goals will ignore possible benefits important to a company. Because these measures rarely appear in archival databases, researchers have generally relied upon interviews and survey questionnaires to collect these data.

Although not tested empirically, in the proposed model it is anticipated that Strategic and Operational Satisfaction will be positively related to measures of Emergent Goals (arrow 8). This relationship is likely to be affected by the impact of the Strategic Goal Fulfillment on Strategic and Operational Satisfaction (arrow 5). As an alliance achieves the strategic goals expected for it and as this leads to greater levels of satisfaction, the partners might begin to develop new goals for the alliance. The emergent goals may also stem from a failure to meet initial goals, and the inability to meet still-relevant goals may lead to company departure or alliance termination.

As noted, it is anticipated that these ongoing indicators of performance will have an interactive relationship. Although not all feedback loops have been considered in this description, these will be important to consider in empirical assessments. Performance on one ongoing measure will affect subsequent performance as evaluated by another ongoing indicator. For example, if new goals develop, measures of these new goals will likely relate to the Process and Relational Measures. New milestones will likely emerge, and the partners may need to adjust their behaviors to accommodate the new goals. For example, Ariño and de la Torre (1998) found that the new goals may provide an opportunity to deepen the bond between the two companies and to enhance their partnership. Similarly, Olk and Young (1997) provided evidence that meeting strategic goals affects a company's involvement in an alliance (i.e., Process and Relational Measures). As will be described in the following section, Stability has been used as both a process activity and an outcome event. In the former use (e.g., Yan & Zeng, 1999), stability discussions represent an effort to adjust the partnership. In this way, stability feeds back to such performance indicators as Process and Relational Measures, Strategic and Operational Satisfaction, and Emergent Goals. Others have used stability as an outcome. I note this dual interpretation in Figure 22.1 by drawing the ongoing indicator line through the middle of Stability.

Outcome Event Indicators

Stability. Stability represents any changes in the membership or in the contract between the partners. As noted, Stability has been used as an outcome variable (Blodgett, 1992; Young-Ybarra & Wiersema, 1999). Its importance stems from a perception that a lack of change reflects some degree of success in creating the arrangement (e.g., Steensma & Lyles, 2000) and in achieving symmetry in objectives (Marois & Abdessemed, 1996). Change is a signal that the partners have not been effective in establishing the relationship. For others (e.g., Ariño & de la Torre, 1998; Yan & Zeng, 1999), stability issues are part of the ongoing process. Stability provides the managers the opportunity to adjust the partnership. Regardless of the approach taken, Stability is generally a fairly objective measure to collect and is easy to compare across alliances. Depending upon the specific measure used, these data can either be from archival sources or collected via questionnaires or interviews.

The model proposes that measures of stability will be predicted by both Financial Outcomes (arrow 9) and Emergent Goals (arrow 12). Although not empirically verified, implicit in arguments for financial measures is that a company will not change its membership or renegotiate the contract with a partner if the alliance is achieving financial success. Only when the financial performance is poor will these changes take place. Although instability will not always indicate poor financial performance (Glaister & Buckley, 1999), good performance may have a stabilizing influence (Yan & Zeng, 1999). The presence of Emergent Goals can also be positively and negatively related to Stability. Although new goals may require renegotiating the contract, these goals may also enhance the long-term stability of the alliance by broadening the basis for collaboration (e.g., Ariño & de la Torre, 1998).

Duration. Another outcome measure is the Duration of the alliance or of a company's participation in the alliance. It indicates the alliance's length of operation or, in the case of three or more companies in an alliance, the tenure of an individual company. Similar to the arguments put forth for Stability, this measure is believed to reflect whether a company considers the alliance to be effective. In general, the relationship offered is that greater Duration reflects better performance. An exception to this is when the company takes a learning or an options approach (e.g., Hamel, 1991; Olk & Young, 1997). A company may have learned all it needs to know about a product or a market and, suggesting the alliance was a success, the company leaves and proceeds on its own. Likewise, a company pursuing several alliances may decide that although several are performing well, it is better to focus its efforts in one alliance; the shortened membership in the other alliances does not reflect poor performance, only that they were not as promising relative to another alliance. Duration measures are often collected from archival data sources (e.g., Barkema, Shenkar, Vermeulen, & Bell, 1997; Geringer & Hebert, 1991; Hennart, Kim, & Zeng, 1998).

The model proposes that measures of Emergent Goals both positively and negatively relate to Duration (arrow 11). As noted earlier, Emergent Goals may enhance the partnership and, besides leading to greater stability, may increase the Duration of the alliance. The new goals will prolong the reasons for continuing with the alliance. Alternatively, the presence of the new goals may lead to disruptions in the interactions between the partners. In addition, if new goals emerge, the partners may decide to terminate the existing alliance and create a new one that is better suited to attain the new goals.

Termination. The last type of measure in the model is Termination. It has been the focus of numerous studies, typically using archival databases that record when an alliance was terminated (e.g. Dussauge, Garrette, & Mitchell, 2000; Reddy, Osborn, & Hennart, 2002). Like Stability and Duration, the general assumption is that Termination represents failure. As described earlier, this measure is relatively easy to collect and the coding is fairly simple. However, as was also noted, the measure may not capture underlying reasons for Termination, may not capture whether just one or both partners were dissatisfied with the alliance, and provides information only at the end of the alliance's life.

The model proposes five different sets of measures related to Termination, because ending an alliance may be decided at several points in an alliance's development. The indicators proposed to be associated with termination are: Process and Relational Measures (arrow 4), Strategic Goal Fulfillment (arrow 7), Financial Outcomes (arrow 10), Duration (arrow 13) and Stability (arrow 14). Process and Relational Measures are expected to be negatively associated with Termination measures. When the alliance is performing well in terms of attaining milestones, developing trust, and avoiding opportunistic behavior and conflict, it is expected that the partners will not terminate (Doz, 1996). Strategic Goal Fulfillment and Financial Outcomes, alternatively, are each expected to have both a positive and a negative association with Termination. If an alliance is attaining its goal, whether strategic or financial, or has a strong likelihood of doing so in the future, companies may decide to remain in the alliance (e.g., Geringer & Hebert, 1991; Glaister & Buckley, 1998; Hatfield et al., 1998). Alternatively, if the goal is not renewable (e.g., develop a technical standard) or the financial potential is limited, there may be little reason to continue the alliance after attaining the goal, and it may be terminated. Finally, although Hatfield et al. (1998) find that Duration is negatively related to Termination, Ariño (2003) reports mixed support for a significant relationship of either Stability or Duration with Termination.

Discussion and Future Research

The intent of this chapter is to further our knowledge about the measurement of strategic alliance performance. To date, researchers, consultants, and practitioners have used a variety of effectiveness measures. Less attention has been devoted toward the causal associations among them. Therefore, I propose a model that draws from empirical research and from assumptions found in the literature to integrate nine commonly used performance indicators. What is clear from the discussion is that this model is an early step toward developing an integrated model of alliance performance measurement. The model can be improved by elaborating it, empirically testing the proposed relationships, and exploring the implications for theories about strategic alliances. I conclude the chapter by examining these issues in more depth.

The model draws upon a variety of different types of measures. One general difference is between objective and subjective measures. For example, arrow 1 connects Expectations at Formation with Process and Relational Measures. The former has been measured by stock market reactions to alliance announcements, whereas the latter has generally been measured via subjective estimators. Likewise, Strategic Goal Fulfillment is generally a subjective evaluation, whereas Financial Outcomes are typically more objective. The measures also differ in terms of single indicators or multiple measures of performance. Third, some measures can be collected from archival, secondary sources, whereas others require primary data.

Although this model connects these different measures, it ignores several other dimensions. Specifically, for simplicity reasons, the model does not explore how different contextual conditions might affect the relationships. One might see, for example, that for a set of alliances that vary in terms of age or technological or market uncertainty, so will the importance of Process and Relational Measures. The Process and Relational Measures connection to Strategic Goal Fulfillment (arrow 3) or to Termination (arrow 4) will also likely vary by such conditions. The model also does not attempt to account for the impact of industry or nationality. In slowly changing industries, however, measures of Duration may have a different relationship with Emergent Goals (arrow 11) than in fast-changing industries, where there may not be as much time for emergent goals to develop. Future research that can incorporate the influence of varying contextual conditions will enhance the model. In addition, the model does not account for corrective actions that managers can take when early performance measures reflect poor performance. Understanding how the type and timing of these actions affect the proposed relationships will further our understanding of alliance performance and management.

Another area for future research is to test the model. An assessment of the entire model may help account for inconsistent findings in the alliance literature. For example, Geringer and Hebert (1991) and Olk and Young (1997) each report a positive relationship between Strategic Goal Fulfillment and Stability, whereas Glaister and Buckley (1998) do not. Although there are differences among the studies' samples and measures, the difference may also be due to the unexamined influence of Financial Outcomes and Emergent Goals on Stability (i.e., arrows 9 and 12).

The challenges of providing a comprehensive test are considerable. As noted, the measures come from a variety of data sources and would require considerable effort to collect. Further, because the model attempts to capture changes in performance as the alliance evolves, longitudinal data are needed on each alliance. Testing this model will likely require causal modeling. This method is well suited for evaluating relationships among constructs, each with multiple indicators. Although some causal modeling approaches (e.g., Partial Least Squares [PLS]) do not require as large a number of samples as others (e.g., Lisrel), researchers will still have to collect data from more than one alliance. The magnitude of the data collection task means it is possible that future research will not assess the entire model but will end up focusing on a subset of the relationships.

For practice, testing this model will help managers understand when measures can be substituted for one another or, if a predictive link is shown, what actions can be taken to improve performance. As noted, choosing an appropriate performance measure depends in part on the need for validity and comparability. The more a measure captures the performance, as understood by managers familiar with the alliance, the more difficult it may be to compare the alliance's performance to other alliances. This may create a tension between managers involved in an alliance wanting to use context specific measures and those who are those less involved (e.g., more senior managers, external stakeholders) preferring measures that permit comparability. Showing how the different measures are connected should lead to a better understanding of whether the choice of performance measures will create significant differences in performance evaluation. Likewise, knowing the relationships among the measures will help managers understand the consequences of poor performance at an early stage. If there is a strong causal linkage between two indicators, managers will know that good performance on the first measure will likely mean good performance on the second. However, if the linkage is weak, even if performance on the first indicator is good, managers will know that additional efforts are needed to achieve good performance on the second.

Finally, this model has implications for theories of alliances. Studies that focus only on the commencement or termination of an alliance are probably missing important intermediary performance indicators. Until there is empirical support that initial indicators and event outcome indicators are related to such ongoing measures as strategic goal fulfillment or financial outcomes, using only the former measures may lead to a misrepresentation of alliance performance. Likewise, approaches that focus on goal attainment may not show whether these achievements are being measured by key stakeholders (e.g., investors), who may have to rely upon externally available measures (e.g., stability or termination) because they do not have access to the ongoing measures. As the model is tested and the relationships between and among the types of measures become better known, the consequences of researchers using different measures of alliance performance will become more evident. One possible outcome of this might be the development of a theory about strategic alliance performance. Just as researchers have developed an understanding of different types of alliance motives (Parkhe, 1993), formation processes (Doz et al., 2000), and control (Yan & Gray, 1994), we may begin to recognize different types of performance and when single, multiple, or a specific set of measures are appropriate.

There is much work that can be done on this topic—and, as the "never-ending process" perspective on organizational effectiveness argues, there may not be an end point. However, I believe that progress can be made by pursuing the above issues, and although all the answers may not be answered and new ones are likely to emerge, by developing a better understanding of how to measure performance we can improve our understanding of strategic alliances.

Note

1. Although some have argued that a measure of satisfaction also reflects managers' views of outcome events, such as termination (e.g., Hatfield et al., 1998), most research has used satisfaction to evaluate ongoing strategic alliances.

References

Anand, B., & Khanna, T. (2000). Do firms learn to create value? The case of alliances. *Strategic Management Journal, 21,* 295–316.

Anderson, E. (1990). Two firms, one frontier: On assessing joint venture performance. *Sloan Management Review, 31,* 19–30.

Ariño, A. (2003). Measures of collaborative venture performance: An analysis of construct validity. *Journal of International Business Studies, 34,* 66–79.

Ariño, A., & de la Torre, J. (1998). Learning from failure: Towards an evolutionary model of collaborative ventures. *Organization Science, 9,* 306–325.

Bamford, J., & Ernst, D. (2002). Managing an alliance portfolio. *McKinsey Quarterly, 3,* 29–39.

Barkema H. G., Shenkar, O., Vermeulen, F., & Bell, J. (1997). Working abroad, working with others: How firms learn to operate international joint ventures. *Academy of Management Journal, 40,* 426–442.

Blodgett, L. (1992). Factors in the instability of international joint ventures: An event history analysis. *Strategic Management Journal, 13,* 475–481.

Brockoff, K., & Teichert, T. (1995). Cooperative R&D and partners measures of success. *International Journal of Technology Management, 10,* 111–123.

Browning, L., Beyer, J., & Shetler, J. (1995). Building cooperation in a competitive industry: SEMATECH and the semiconductor industry. *Academy of Management Journal, 38,* 113–151.

Cameron, K., & Whetten, D. (1983). Organizational effectiveness: One model or several? In K. Cameron & D. Whetten (Eds.), *Organizational effectiveness: A comparison of multiple models* (pp. 1–24). San Diego, CA: Academic Press.

Campbell, J. (1977). On the nature of organizational effectiveness. In P. Goodman & J. Pennings (Eds.), *New perspectives on organizational effectiveness* (pp. 13–55). San Francisco: Jossey-Bass.

Combs, J., & Ketchen, D. (1999). Explaining interfirm cooperation and performance: Toward a reconciliation of predictions from the resource-based view and organizational economics. *Strategic Management Journal, 20,* 867–888.

Cropper, S. (1996). Collaboration in practice: Key issues. In C. Huxham (Ed.), *Creating collaborative advantage* (pp. 80–100). London: Sage.

Doz, Y. (1996). The evolution of cooperation in strategic alliances: Initial conditions or learning processes? *Strategic Management Journal, 17,* 55–84.

Doz, Y., & Hamel, G. (1998). *Alliance advantage: The art of creating value through partnering.* Boston: Harvard Business School Press.

Doz, Y., Olk, P., & Ring, P. S. (2000). Formation of research and development consortia. Which path to take? Where does it lead? *Strategic Management Journal, 20,* 239–266.

Dussauge, P., Garrette, B., & Mitchell, W. (2000). Learning from competing partners: Outcomes and durations of scale and link alliances in Europe, North America, and Asia. *Strategic Management Journal, 21,* 99–126.

Futrell, D., Slugay, M., & Stephens, C. (2001). Becoming a premier partner: Measuring, managing, changing partnering capabilities at Eli Lilly and Company. *Journal of Commercial Biotechnology, 8,* 5–13.

Geringer, J. M., & Hebert, L. (1991). Measuring performance of international joint ventures. *Journal of International Business Studies, 22,* 249–263.

Glaister, K. W., & Buckley, P. J. (1998). Measures of performance in UK international alliances. *Organization Studies, 19,* 89–118.

Glaister, K. W., & Buckley, P. J. (1999). Performance relationships in UK international alliances. *Management International Review, 39,* 123–147.

Gray, B. (2000). Assessing inter-organizational collaboration: Multiple conceptions and multiple methods. In D. Faulkner & M. de Rond (Eds.), *Cooperative strategies: Economic business and organizational issues* (pp. 243–260). Oxford, UK: Oxford University Press.

Gulati, R. (1998). Alliances and networks. *Strategic Management Journal, 19,* 293–317.

Gulati, R., & Zajac, E. (2000). Reflections on the study of strategic alliances. In D. Faulkner & M. de Rond (Eds.), *Cooperative strategies: Economic business and organizational issues* (pp. 365–374). Oxford: Oxford University Press.

Hagedoorn, J., & Duysters, G. (2002). Learning in dynamic inter-firm networks: The efficacy in multiple contacts. *Organization Studies, 23,* 525–548.

Hamel, G. (1991). Competition for competence and inter-partner learning within international strategic alliances. *Strategic Management Journal, 12,* 83–103.

Harrigan, K. (1986). *Managing for joint venture success.* Lexington, MA: Lexington Books.

Hatfield, L., Pearce J. A., Sleeth, R., & Pitts, M. (1998). Toward validation of partner goal achievement as a measure of joint venture performance. *Journal of Managerial Issues, 10,* 355–372.

Hebert, L., & Beamish, P. (1997). Characteristics of Canada-based international joint ventures. In P. W. Beamish & J. P. Killing (Eds.), *Cooperative strategies: North American perspectives* (pp. 403–427). San Francisco: New Lexington Press.

Hennart, J.-F., Kim, D., & Zeng, M. (1998). The impact of joint venture status on the longevity of Japanese stakes in U.S. manufacturing affiliates. *Organization Science, 9,* 382–395.

Hirsch, P., & Levin, D. (1999). Umbrella advocates versus validity police: A life-cycle model. *Organization Science, 10,* 199–212.

Inkpen, A., & Currall, A. (1997). International joint venture trust: An empirical examination. In P. W. Beamish & J. P. Killing (Eds.), *Cooperative strategies: North American perspectives* (pp. 337–369). San Francisco: New Lexington Press.

Inkpen, A., & Ross, G. (2001). Why do some strategic alliances persist beyond their useful life? *California Management Review, 44,* 132–148.

Ittner, C., & Larcker, D. (2003). Coming up short on nonfinancial performance measurement. *Harvard Business Review, 81,* 88–95.

Johnson, J., Cullen, J., & Sakano, T. (1995). Japanese and local partner commitment to IJVs: Psychological consequences of outcomes and investments in the IJV relationship. *Journal of International Business Studies, 26,* 91–115.

Kale, P., Dyer, J., & Singh, H. (2000). How to make strategic alliances work. *Sloan Management Review, 42*(3), 37–43.

Kale, P., Dyer, J., & Singh, H. (2002). Alliance capability, stock market response, and long term alliance success. *Strategic Management Journal, 23,* 747–767.

Kaplan, R., & Norton, D. (1992, January/February). The balance scorecard—measures that drive performance. *Harvard Business Review, 70,* 71–79.

Kaplan, R., & Norton, D. (1993, September/October). Putting the balanced scorecard to work. *Harvard Business Review, 71,* 134–143.

Kaplan, R., & Norton, D. (1996). *The balanced scorecard.* Boston: Harvard Business School Press.

Koza, M., & Lewin, A. (1998). The co-evolution of strategic alliances. *Organization Science, 9,* 255–264.

Lin, X., & Germain, R. (1998). Sustaining satisfactory joint venture relationships: The role of conflict resolution strategy. *Journal of International Business Studies, 29,* 179–196.

Lyles, M., & Salk, J. (1997). Knowledge acquisition from foreign parents in international joint ventures: An empirical examination in the Hungarian context. In P. W. Beamish & J. P. Killing (Eds.), *Cooperative strategies: European perspectives* (pp. 325–355). San Francisco: New Lexington Press.

March, J., & Sutton, R. (1997). Organizational performance as a dependent measure. *Organization Science, 8,* 698–710.

Marois, B., & Abdessemed, T. (1996). Cross-border alliances in the French banking sector. *International Studies of Management and Organization, 26,* 35–58.

Merrifield, D. B. (2004). "Gales of creative destruction" call for limited partnerships. *Research Technology Management, 47*(2), 9–12.

Meyer, M. (2002). *Rethinking performance measurement: Beyond the balanced scorecard.* Cambridge, UK: Cambridge University Press.

Meyer, M., & Gupta, V. (1994). The performance paradox. *Research in Organizational Behavior, 16,* 307–367.

Mjoen, H., & Tallman, S. (1997). Control and performance in international joint ventures. *Organization Science, 8,* 257–274.

Olk, P. (1997). The effect of partner differences on the performance of R&D consortia. In P. W. Beamish & J. P. Killing (Eds.), *Cooperative strategies: North American perspectives* (pp. 133–159). San Francisco: New Lexington Press.

Olk, P. (2002). Evaluating strategic alliance performance. In F. Contractor & P. Lorange (Eds.), *Cooperative strategies and alliances* (pp. 119–143). London: Elsevier Press.

Olk, P., & Ariño, A. (2002). *Testing assumptions about evaluating strategic alliance performance.* Academy of Management Meetings, Denver, CO.

Olk, P., & Young, C. (1997). Why members stay or leave an R&D consortium: Performance and conditions of membership as determinants of continuity. *Strategic Management Journal, 18,* 855–877.

Parkhe, A. (1993). Strategic alliance structuring: A game theoretic and transaction cost examination of interfirm cooperation. *Academy of Management Journal, 36,* 794–829.

Parkhe, A. (1998). Building trust in international alliances. *Journal of World Business, 33,* 417–437.

Pennings, H., & Goodman, P. (1977). Toward a workable framework. In P. Goodman & J. Pennings (Eds.), *New perspectives on organizational effectiveness* (pp. 63–95). San Francisco: Jossey-Bass.

Reddy, S., Osborn, R., & Hennart, J. F. (2002). The prevalence of equity and non-equity cross-border linkages: Japanese investments and alliances in the United States. *Organization Studies, 23,* 759–780.

Reuer, J. (2001). From hybrids to hierarchies: Shareholder wealth effects of joint venture partner buyouts. *Strategic Management Journal, 22,* 27–44.

Reuer, J., & Ariño, A. (2002). Contractual renegotiations in strategic alliances. *Journal of Management, 28,* 47–68.

Reuer, J., & Koza, M. (2000). International joint venture instability and corporate strategy. In D. Faulkner & M. de Rond (Eds.), *Cooperative strategies: Economic business and organizational issues* (pp. 261–280). Oxford: Oxford University Press.

Rowley, T., Behrens, D., & Krackhardt, D. (2000). Redundant governance structures: An analysis of structural and relational embeddedness in the steel and semiconductor industries. *Strategic Management Journal, 21,* 369–386.

Saxton, T. (1997). The effects of partner and relationship characteristics on alliance outcomes. *Academy of Management Journal, 40,* 443–462.

Scott, W. R. (1992). *Organizations: Rational, natural and open systems* (3rd ed.). Englewood Cliffs, NJ: Prentice Hall.

Steensma, K., & Corley, K. (2000). On the performance of technology-sourcing partnerships: The interaction between partner interdependence and technology attributes. *Academy of Management Journal, 43,* 1045–1067.

Steensma, K., & Lyles, M. (2000). Explaining IJV survival in a transitional economy through social exchange and knowledge-based perspectives. *Strategic Management Journal, 21,* 831–852.

Whipple, J., & Frankel, R. (2000). Strategic alliance success factors. *Journal of Supply Chain Management: A Global Review of Purchasing & Supply, 36*(3), 21–28.

Yan, A., & Gray, B. (1994). Bargaining power management control and performance in United States–China joint ventures: A comparative case study. *Academy of Management Journal, 37,* 1478–1517.

Yan, A., & Gray, B. (1995). Reconceptualizing the determinants and measurement of joint venture performance. *Advances in Global High-Technology Management, 5B,* 87–113.

Yan, A., & Zeng, M. (1999). International joint venture instability: A critique of previous research, a reconceptualization, and directions for future research. *Journal of International Business Studies, 30,* 397–414.

Yeheskel, O., Zeira, Y., Shenkar, O., & Newburry, W. (2001). Parent company dissimilarity and equity joint venture effectiveness. *Journal of International Management, 7,* 81–104.

Young-Ybarra, C., & Wiersema, M. (1999). Strategic flexibility in information technology alliances: The influence of transaction cost economics and social exchange theory. *Organization Science, 10,* 439–459.

23

The Legitimacy of Messiness

Interdisciplinary Research, Systems of Innovation, and Strategic Alliances

Mark de Rond

Sonja Marjanovic

> *When I examined myself and my methods of thought, I came to the conclusion that the gift of fantasy has meant more to me than my talent for absorbing positive knowledge.*
>
> —A. Einstein

Social and natural scientists alike increasingly look to interdisciplinary research design as a means of understanding complexity. But interdisciplinary research has yet to make its presence properly felt in alliance studies. Given the comparatively arbitrary and fluid boundaries of management research, it is curious that so few truly interdisciplinary studies of alliances exist.

This chapter is a response to the apparent paucity. After all, disciplines are not usually mutually exclusive. Metaphorically, disciplines may be likened to languages, in which certain ideas are more easily conveyed in one rather than another. Indeed, cross-pollination between languages is common, whereby expressions from one are adopted by others. Good examples of this are the German "angst," the Latin "a priori," and the French "laissez-faire." To paraphrase Sachs, the existence of English does not refute, replace, or supersede German, Latin, or French. Each language preserves a unique sensitivity. There are

AUTHOR'S NOTE: The authors are listed in alphabetical order. Each has contributed equally to the development of this chapter. They gratefully acknowledge helpful comments on an earlier draft by Oded Shenkar, Jochen Runde, Nelson Phillips, and Ilian Iliev.

things you can say in one that you cannot translate, without loss, into others. That is why we are enlarged by their multiplicity and would be impoverished if one disappeared (Sachs, 2000, 155). By the same token, certain features of strategic alliances are best expressed through specific disciplinary lenses. Bringing diverse disciplinary perspectives to bear on the same phenomenon may allow us to harness their unique sensitivities and produce more holistic accounts.

This chapter attempts to make the case for an interdisciplinary approach to alliance research and also to provide some practical ways forward. Following a brief introduction, the chapter is structured in three sections. Section 1 aims to explain *what* interdisciplinary research entails, *why* it can be useful, and *where* its potential advantages over single-discipline approaches lie. Section 2 then addresses *how* interdisciplinarity can be internalized in a future strategic alliance research agenda and suggests the systems of innovation (SI) approach as a useful theoretical and conceptual framework to guide such studies. This allows us to revisit four enduring themes in alliance research (alliance formation, evolution, management, and performance) and enables us to discuss the importance of interdisciplinarity in addressing key questions within these themes (Section 3). Despite our emphasis on the promise of interdisciplinary research, we try to be candid about its drawbacks and explore ways in which some of these can be accounted for in research design.

Introduction

To observe that strategic alliances have proliferated is not particularly novel. Evidence to support such statements is abundant. In the United States alone, companies announced nearly one new alliance for every hour of every day during the heady years of 1996 to 2000 (a figure that has dipped only slightly since then). Yet the reported failure rates of alliances remain high—at least 50% according to some authors (Harrigan, 1985; Auster, 1987; Kogut, 1988; Inkpen & Beamish, 1997; Dyer, Kale, & Singh, 2004). Management consultancies, market research institutions, and the popular business press estimate it to be anywhere from 50% to 70%. How, then, can we explain a growing recourse to strategic alliances when the chances of failing are statistically as high as, if not higher than, those of succeeding?

To some extent, the difficulty is one of definition. After all, failure is not easily defined in the context of alliances. For instance, when BP "farms out" the drilling of a prospective well to a partner, and this well subsequently turns out to be dry, has the joint exploration project failed or succeeded? On the one hand, it has clearly failed to identify a new source of oil. But on the other hand, by outsourcing the drilling, BP is able to minimize its financial exposure, which, under the circumstances, proves to be a prudent decision. Had the well turned out to have been full of untapped oil, BP would have been better off had it pursued its exploration without a second party. Obviously, the reverse scenario is true for the partner firm.

Or one might consider Glaxo Smith Kline's "real options" strategy, whereby, on a regular basis, it chooses to invest in a handful of alliances with biomedical drug discovery companies. Even if only one out of five such collaborations produces a drug candidate, the potential rewards easily justify the portfolio investment. A failure rate of 50% in this context would seem rather favorable. Likewise, one can easily think of scenarios in which alliances fail to meet any of their original objectives yet succeed in generating spin-off benefits for one or both partners. Or perhaps organizations are simply no better at innovating in-house and, faced with empty pipelines, are looking to alliances with start-up companies for windows on new technologies? Short of measuring failure as an irrecoverable financial or reputation cost to all relevant stakeholders, the difficulties of defining failure in the context of strategic alliances are clear. Arguably, the same is true of success.

Even so, the performance issue weighs heavily on the "priority agenda" of strategic alliance research and practice. As academics, we are expected to try to provide clarity in definition, to afford insight into the sorts of circumstances or choices that appear to be correlated with success, and, on this basis, to develop an agenda for research and practice. Moreover, this need for greater understanding is true not just of performance but also of other alliance issues such as formation and design, governance, management, dynamics, and evolution. Interorganizational alliances are inherently complex, possibly even more than other forms of organizations, given that they are likely to combine diverse agendas, accountabilities, cultures (corporate, national, academic), systems and processes, structures, stakeholder interests, and disciplinary backgrounds.

It is in confronting the multifaceted and complex nature of alliances that interdisciplinary research may prove beneficial. Although a single discipline may emphasize particular features of alliance life, interdisciplinarity allows us to bring together the diverse perspectives of individual disciplines. This multiplicity is also likely to impact on the way we interpret and negotiate research outputs. For example, one discipline may address the issue of alliance governance modalities from the perspective of cost minimization (e.g., some streams of economics). Another may emphasize power structures (e.g., some streams of sociology or politics). A third may focus on social networks and consider issues of interpersonal trust to mitigate appropriation concerns (e.g., sociology). A fourth may be concerned with issues of equity and fairness (e.g., ethics). To quote the philosopher William James,

> The obvious outcome of our total experience is that the world can be handled according to many systems of ideas, and is so handled by different men, and will each time give some characteristic kind of profit, for which he cares, to the handler, while at the same time some other kind of profit has to be omitted or postponed. (James, 1923, 120)

Yet ideally, we would incorporate each of these perspectives, allowing us to appreciate the trade-offs of different governance types more fully.

Alliance multidimensionality and multiplicity are likely to be particularly evident in the case of collaborations that span cultural, industrial, national, or disciplinary precincts. This is also true of policy-oriented research collaborations, given their systemwide impact. In fact, the potential of interdisciplinarity in alliance research becomes evident when surveying the diversity of theoretical interests that characterize the field. Yet despite this diversity, with few exceptions, the theories are typically employed in isolation, and it can be difficult to reconcile their contributions. Thus, we find interorganizational relationships studied from transaction cost theory (e.g., Hennert, 1988, 1991; Parkhe, 1993; Pisano, 1990), resource-based theory (e.g., Namgyoo, Mezias, & Song, 2004; Perks, 2004), game theory (e.g., Brandenburger & Nalebuff, 1996), relational contract theory (Kern & Willcocks, 2000), institutional theory (e.g., Lawrence, Hardy, & Phillips, 2002; Hitt, Ahlstrom, Dacin, Levitas, & Svobodina, 2004), social network theory (e.g., Powell & Brantley, 1992; Gulati, 1995), and learning (e.g., Hamel, 1991; Inkpen, 1995) perspectives.

Similarly, interorganizational relationships are frequently approached from individual disciplines, such as economics (e.g., Buckley & Casson, 1988; Williamson, 1991; Dunning, 1993), corporate strategy (e.g., Geringer & Hebert, 1989; Hamel, Doz, & Prahalad, 1989; Shan & Hamilton, 1991), sociology (e.g., March & Olsen, 1976; Shaan & Beamish, 1988; Galaskiewicz, 1985; Larson, 1992; Wasserman & Galaskiewicz, 1994), and politics (e.g., Mowery, 1989). Rarely are multiple disciplines combined in the same research agenda (cf. Osborn & Hagedoorn, 1997).

There may be several reasons for the prevalence of single-discipline approaches. Whether justified or not, interdisciplinary research may be considered too difficult to publish in leading journals. To some extent this may be a function of the excessive specialization of journals or the difficulty of finding suitable reviewers for papers that introduce literatures and methodologies that are less familiar. Predictably, given the need to publish—and to publish in leading journals—this is not usually a recommended strategy for tenure-track faculty (therein lies the irony of writing this chapter). Yet at the same time one hears repeated calls for interdisciplinary research efforts, not just within the academy (e.g., Van Maanen, 1995; Van de Ven, 1997) but increasingly by grant-awarding research councils. A straightforward Google search reveals the extent of interdisciplinary activity today—across the sciences, humanities, and social sciences—with a plethora of research and policy-oriented centers dedicated to this premise and to the promise held by it. Interdisciplinarity can be integral to the object of study as much as it can be applied to understanding this object through research. Our concern in this chapter is primarily with the latter.

And yet interdisciplinary research is anything but straightforward. The nature of the research may call for a review of multiple and unfamiliar literatures. It may also require the simultaneous application of different conceptual frameworks and methodologies, the philosophical premises of which can be at variance. Reconciling these differences is an important academic challenge and clearly worthwhile if it allows us to intensify our grasp of strategic alliances. Such reconciliation allows us to allude to the importance of selection when it comes to choosing which disciplines to draw on for intellectual guidance, given potentially incommensurable epistemological or ontological assumptions. It also highlights the importance of clarifying these assumptions at the onset of research design.

With this in view, we seek to make the case for interdisciplinary approaches to strategic alliance research. This chapter is structured in three sections:

- Section 1: *What is interdisciplinary research, and why engage in it?* We define interdisciplinary research in terms of what it is and is not. We discuss how interdisciplinary research differs from single-discipline approaches. One distinguishing feature is its consistency with epistemological and methodological pluralism. We define pluralism and proceed to outline the epistemological requirements for a framework to guide the interdisciplinary study of alliances. We also discuss the need for interdisciplinary research and what appears to be a renewed interest in interdisciplinary scholarship, based on its perceived advantages over single-discipline approaches. We highlight the relevance of interdisciplinarity insofar as it helps us to revisit key themes in the alliance literature.

- Section 2: *The relevance of a "systems of innovation" approach to interdisciplinary alliance research.* Seeking to move beyond a philosophical discussion of interdisciplinarity, we propose the SI approach as one example of a theoretical framework that seems well suited to the interdisciplinary study of strategic alliances. We outline the SI approach and discuss how it can usefully guide alliance research. As the proof of the pudding is in the eating, we explain how an SI framework can help "unpack" strategic alliances conceptually and provide several illustrations, focusing particularly on the specific example of "multiple-world" health research collaborations between developed and developing countries.

- Section 3: *Revisiting key themes in strategic alliance research.* Finally, we revisit four popular themes in alliance research: (1) alliance formation, (2) dynamics and evolution, (3) management and governance, and (4) performance. We identify a series of research questions that may benefit particularly well from an interdisciplinary approach. In short, we hope to show how an interdisciplinary agenda generally and an SI approach in particular can help open up fresh avenues for research within these themes.

We conclude the chapter by acknowledging some of the persistent challenges of interdisciplinarity and emphasize the potential of an integrative and pluralist SI framework to address them.

We leave the reader with thoughts on issues that may become part of a future research agenda.

Although we advocate interdisciplinary research, we have no intention of dictating which disciplines should be included in a future research agenda. Selection will depend on the nature of the question under consideration and, to some extent, on the degree of comfort felt by researchers from various disciplines. However, it is likely that disciplines such as strategy, economics, the organization sciences, studies of innovation, sociology or social theory, and also political science and ethics (especially in the cases of international and public/private-sector collaborations) will feature in an interdisciplinary alliance study. Although sparse, the existing literature contains some examples of such interdisciplinary approaches, including Sydow and Windeler (1998), Shenkar and Yan (2002), and de Rond (2003).

What Is Interdisciplinary Research, and Why Engage in It?

Understanding Interdisciplinarity

Interdisciplinary research design aims to allow diverse academic trajectories to inform multiple features and dimensions of a subject of interest. It intentionally brings contributions from several disciplines to bear on a specific problem or to address a specific topic. Such problems or topics are likely to revolve around attempts to better understand a complex social phenomenon or certain aspects thereof.

Before embarking on a justification for interdisciplinary research, it may be useful to differentiate interdisciplinary from single-discipline research. This is by no means easy to do. Even if the idea of disciplines is intuitively well understood (as suggested by the casual manner in which we refer to disciplines in academic circles), it is the sort of concept that eludes demarcation. What are disciplines, really? How are they different from fields of study? How do disciplines relate to theories? The relations and boundaries between disciplines and theories, between disciplines and fields of study, and even between different disciplines can seem vague.

Theories, for example, may originate within one discipline but can easily be applied in others. Such is the case with, for example, the resource-based view (with its origins in the work of the economists David Ricardo and Edith Penrose), game theory (with its origins in the mathematical economics of Von Neumann and Morgenstern, and Nash), and the "garbage can" model of organizational choice (which originated within the organizational sciences with Cohen, March, & Olsen [1972], and has been applied more widely). Theory can also serve different functions in research. For example, those following a Popperian tradition may adopt a research design focused on theory falsification, whereas interpretivists will tend to place greater emphasis on theory as a "sensitizing device" (Klein & Myers, 1999, 75). Moreover, the academic literature points to the variety embedded even within each individual discipline, including the use of different methodologies, units of analysis, and ontological assumptions. Hence, even the broadest disciplinary classifications (e.g., economics, organization science, history, literature) risk homogenizing what is intrinsically diverse.

Despite these difficulties, it might be useful to try to provide a general characterization of disciplines along three attributes: (1) their general focus on a particular object, theme, or method of analysis, (2) their provision of a sense of identity and community, and (3) their commitment to a "dominant" epistemology. These three features are inevitably very general and also subject to changing as disciplines evolve, but they are helpful in differentiating single-discipline from interdisciplinary approaches to research.

Disciplines and Interdisciplinarity: Their Focus of Interest

First, disciplines tend to gravitate around an object of interest. So, for example, astronomers are generally concerned with solar systems.

Epidemiologists study the distribution and determinants of diseases. Biochemists study the chemical reactions and interactions that exist within living organisms, whereas embryologists study their formation and early development. Economists are, broadly speaking, interested in the ways by which wealth is created, distributed, and consumed. Psychologists study the mental and behavioral characteristics of individuals, whereas sociologists focus on the structure and emergence of collective behavior. Although interdisciplinary studies likewise tend to focus on a specific object of interest, they do so by deliberately highlighting its different features, acknowledging its multidimensionality, multiplicity, and complexity up front.

Disciplines and Interdisciplinarity: A Sense of Identity and Community

Second, disciplines provide a sense of identity and belonging. Schoenberger's contribution is insightful:

> Disciplinary culture is . . . inextricably tied up with questions of identity—of who we understand *ourselves* to be in the world and what we do there. This is, in a way, automatically a product of the epistemological and ontological content of disciplinary culture. . . . [Consequently], our sense of self is assuredly at stake in conflicts within and between disciplinary cultures. (Schoenberger, 2001, 370)

Indeed, if identity is such an important feature of the disciplines within which we write and teach, that would help explain any discomfort felt by those working across different branches of knowledge. After all, it may be difficult to define one's intended audience (which would normally be the community of one's core discipline) and which of one's peers are best able to referee, use, and cite one's work. Research is a social enterprise that generally entails the iteration of writing and presenting. Unless one allows the same material to be critiqued by different specialist audiences (e.g., sociologists and complexity theorists when applying complexity theory to the study of organizations), interdisciplinary work can lead to a self-conscious rather than self-confident existence. Exposing one's research to a different audience can be an unsettling experience for fear of the research being weighed and found wanting. Of course, interdisciplinarity may also breed its own sense of identity and community. But by definition, any such community would need to be open-minded, tolerant of diversity, and democratic.

Disciplines and Interdisciplinarity: Epistemological Commitments

Third, disciplines may be characterized by a prevailing commitment to a particular epistemology. Even if there exist different "churches" of philosophical orientation within disciplines,[1] some are likely to be seen as dominant and more mainstream at any one point in time. This "mainstream" philosophical orientation can in some ways be likened to Kuhn's notion of paradigms, or "accepted" models for conducting research and criteria for choosing research problems (Kuhn, 1970, 37). As Kuhn explains, "Men whose research is based on shared paradigms are committed to the same rules and standards for scientific practice. That commitment and the apparent consensus it produces are prerequisites for normal science, i.e., for the genesis and continuation of a particular research tradition" (Kuhn, 1970, 11).

Schoenberger's clarification is also illuminating:

> Disciplines are bound up with *epistemological commitments*. In order to do the work of the discipline at all, we have to internalize a set of practices and understandings about how valid knowledge is created. This commitment may and ought to be provisional. We accept these practices and understandings *as if* they were true in order to do work. In principle, we are still

> free to assess the original commitments themselves from time to time; but it is hard to avoid the dilemma of accepting these practices and understandings as if they were true in order to test *whether* they are true—in order to assess the epistemological commitment in the first place. In other words, the epistemology under examination is itself the reference point for making epistemological judgments. It has become *our* world. (Schoenberger, 2001, 367; emphasis added)

Epistemological commitments entail specific (though perhaps implicitly held) assumptions on the nature, sources, justification, and scope of knowledge and the means by which it is (or may be) created. Yet these assumptions can vary across theories as well as within disciplines. Although scholars working within the same discipline may clearly employ a variety of models and methodologies in creating a picture of "their" world, there is likely to be a majority view on how this should be done. For instance, the positivism that seems to have dominated neoclassical economics (Lawson, 1997) may be incompatible with, say, the interpretivist orientation of critical management theory. Those who see reality as directly observable and objective might consider experimentation (e.g., using a hypothetico-deductive approach) as the primary means of acquiring knowledge, whereas those who hold to some form of social constructivism (which has its roots in idealism) are more comfortable with induction (e.g., through case study research) as a means to theory development.

Moreover, positivism is likely to promote a "value-free" position to research (Klein & Myers, 1999, 75). Interpretivism, by contrast, emphasizes the inevitability of our own historicity in research (Klein & Myers, 1999). These epistemological commitments can get in the way of our observations as much as they help structure them. In a real sense, they yield expectations about what there is to be discovered. And, as Osborn and Hagedoorn (1997, 274) point out, many of the basic assumptions of single-discipline approaches "appear too limiting when applied to the study of alliance and networks" in that they cannot easily cope with their complexity and multifacetedness.

It is not our intention here to provide a review of the different philosophical positions that exist within the social sciences. Whereas some disciplines appear dominated by a paradigm—or a particular set of scientific and metaphysical beliefs that govern a field of research (as appears to be the case with neoclassical economics and positivism)—it is by no means true that every neoclassical economist is also a logical positivist. If anything, this alludes to the difficulty of demarcating disciplines along philosophical grounds or indeed any other grounds. Here also the boundaries appear fuzzy at best.

Accordingly, to work across disciplines may force us to try to reconcile different epistemological commitments, and to do so explicitly. As Klein and Myers recommend:

> The researcher should make the historical intellectual basis of the research (i.e., its fundamental philosophical assumptions) as transparent as possible to the reader, and to himself or herself. . . . At minimum, the researcher should . . . relate the particular strengths and weaknesses of the preferred philosophical direction to the purpose of the work. (Klein & Myers, 1999, 74)

This by no means suggests attempting to reconcile fundamentally conflicting philosophical foundations. Rather, it points to the need to develop a new epistemological foundation on which to build an interdisciplinary research project, one that is "diversity-friendly." For interdisciplinary research, a way forward would be the adoption of epistemological pluralism, or the emphasis on diversity and multiplicity rather than on homogeneity and unity. This seems at odds with conventional ways of "doing" research, suggest Glynn, Bar, and Dacin: "On balance, organizational theorists have tended to emphasize the unifying principles that lend cohesion, focus, legitimacy, and identity; the result has been to problematize (or often overlook) the variety embedded in plurality" (Glynn, Bar, & Dacin, 2000, 726).

Indeed, if organizational life is as varied and pluralistic as suggested by Glynn, Bar, and Dacin, how much more likely is this to be true of interorganizational relationships? Does not this, then, also invite us to relax any assumptions we might have entertained on the homogeny and regularity of organizational life generally and that of alliances in particular? Such *monist* commitments are, in many ways, part and parcel of Western intellectual tradition. They are rooted in three relatively persistent but rarely questioned beliefs on the nature of knowledge: first, that to every genuine question there is but one answer; second, that these answers can be discovered through the application of reason; and third, that together these answers must be compatible in amounting to a coherent, general, and universal body of theory (cf. Berlin, 1999). Monism is the belief in a logically and harmoniously connected structure of laws and generalizations receptive to demonstration or verification through reasoning. For all we know, this may well be true of the natural world in general. But how about the social world? How easily does human agency lend itself to abstraction and generalization? What empirical proof do we have that these are ordinarily the properties of strategic alliances or even those of single organizations? Is this no more than a metaphysical attitude?

Clearly, interdisciplinary research arises out of the conviction that the social world is invariably more complex than can be accounted for by a single theory or within a single discipline. Behind the variety and chaos of common experience, there need not be a single, objective universe of facts and values.

Pluralism, as the logical alternative to monism, entails the belief not just in the multiplicity and diversity of the values and beliefs, views and ways of different cultures, societies, and social groups, but in the possibility of their incommensurability. Whereas some order and homogeneity may exist in organizational life, this cannot be taken for granted. Pluralism aims to see the general in the particular but also the particular in the general. A pluralist epistemology helps account for variety, irregularity, and the potentially dialectical nature of social organization—that is, the possibility of equally legitimate values, ideals, and purposes coexisting. Its corollary is methodological pluralism, including the use of differing explanations and multiple conceptual schemes to account for the varieties of human experience.

In this context, what interdisciplinarity calls for is not just the bundling of multiple theories but the pursuit of a new class of theory: theoretical approaches that are rooted in pluralism and thus are able to account for diversity and idiosyncrasy, inconsistency and internal tension, yet also for the possibility of some order and regularity. Expectations of diversity and complexity become points of departure in research design.

Accordingly, interdisciplinary research may be best served by theories *of* variety rather than theoretical variety per se (de Rond, 2002). This is particularly relevant in the context of strategic alliances. As Osborn and Hagedoorn (1997, 262) point out: "[the field of interorganizational alliances], a chaotic research field, replete with multiple theories, research designs, and units of analysis, is ripe for an era of integrative theoretical development." And this requires interdisciplinarity in the development and adoption of theoretical and conceptual frameworks that embrace, facilitate, and legitimate variety.

But why this interest in interdisciplinary research? And what promise does it hold for the study of interorganizational relationships?

Interdisciplinarity and Its Potential Benefits Over Single-Discipline Approaches

The renewed commitment to working across disciplines ("renewed" as, after all, in the past scholars were often polymaths) may be due partly to a discontent with the limitations of single-discipline approaches. The philosophical foundations, limited variety in method, and limited scope for abstraction processes in a single-discipline approach may be too narrow for the aims of addressing key strategic alliance research challenges (cf. Osborn & Hagedoorn, 1997; Klein & Myers, 1999). Interdisciplinary research, on the other hand, may help expose as well as circumvent some of the analytical shortcomings that relying on a single discipline can lead to. It does so by allowing different disciplines to guide the gathering of multiple observations on the same object of study, to address different levels of analysis, and to contribute diverse methods for collecting and examining data, based on their respective strengths and interests.

For instance, in the case of alliance performance, economists may often be concerned with measuring profitability, with identifying structural arrangements that can ensure economic gain, and with the quantification and measurement of performance. Sociology, by comparison, may place greater emphasis on understanding how performance is interpreted differently across diverse stakeholder groups, what roles reputation or legitimacy gains play in its social construction, and how such gains can be captured and measured. This is not to say that economists dismiss those features emphasized by sociologists (e.g., trust, social capital, or culture). Nor do sociologists dismiss economic gain. But each is likely to assess their impact on performance in different ways.

Once we acknowledge that strategic alliances are no less colored by human agency than are the organizations that comprise them, then understanding alliance complexity requires us to address alliances at the dimensions of individuals and stakeholder groups as much as at the level of the entire alliance entity. Even in those alliances characterized by all the quintessentially "objective" physical sciences, it is still the individuals who help write the plots of the stories (de Rond, 2003). Moreover, individuals are not just products of history but also its producers; the activity of an individual is influenced by the history of an alliance, as much as the results of an individual's activity influence the alliance's "future history" (Klein & Myers, 1999, 74).

In addition, to understand better the complexity of a social phenomenon requires us (beyond gathering data on multiple and diverse features) to revisit the way we make sense of this data. In this context, interdisciplinary research approaches are likely to foster a process of iteration and negotiation between making observations and abstracting inferences from data. This (partially) stems from the variety of perspectives that drawing on different disciplines exposes. In other words, closure in making inferences from empirical evidence is likely to be achieved through a process of negotiating research outputs by those contributing specific disciplinary backgrounds. This may lead to more robust explanations of social phenomena—explanations that are better informed, more comprehensive, and more "democratic." It may also lead us to expand, reinterpret, and reprioritize research.

Indeed, one aim of this chapter is to revisit some of the more popular questions in alliance research to see how these could be expanded, reinterpreted, or reprioritized in an interdisciplinary agenda. Those studying strategic alliances are typically faced with a nexus of diverse but interrelated challenges. Key themes in what has rapidly emerged as a popular subfield of strategy and the organization sciences include, (1) alliance formation and design, (2) alliance processes, their dynamics, and their evolution, (3) alliance management and governance, and (4) alliance performance. Whereas the key questions that characterize each of these themes may be of interest to researchers across disciplines, their treatments are likely to differ depending on the disciplinary agendas that are brought to bear on them. In this context, interdisciplinarity is likely to expand the nature of our questions and the scope of potential answers.

In summary, the advantages of interdisciplinary research approaches over those of single

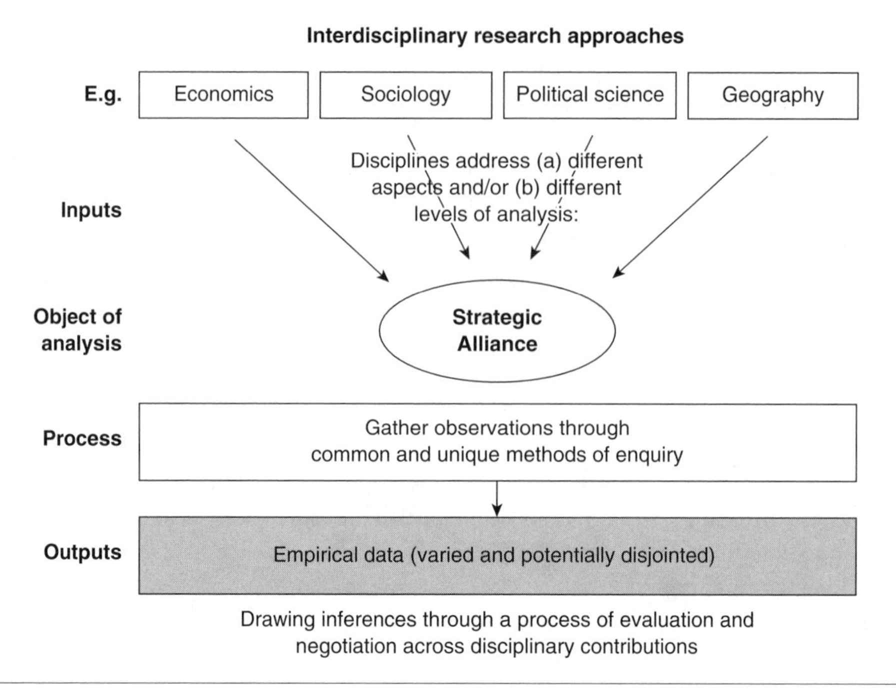

Figure 23.1 Conceptual View of the Interdisciplinary Research Process

disciplines reside at two levels (see Figure 23.1). First, they exist at the level of *inputs* into a research study. Interdisciplinarity deliberately highlights the diverse, multifaceted, and complex nature of social phenomena up front, brings different disciplines together to inform research design, and allows us to gather data on a broad range of features. Second, interdisciplinary research aims to leverage disciplinary contributions at the level of research *outputs*. The multiplicity of gathered empirical information is likely to impact on the way we draw inferences from data (what it signifies and implies) and to inspire a process of negotiating research outputs across disciplines. This may foster more comprehensive explanations of strategic alliances than can be provided through the lens of a single discipline.

In an effort to move beyond a conceptual discussion of interdisciplinarity, we now turn to outlining a pluralist framework that can guide interdisciplinary alliance research and that can emphasize the informative and abstractive potential of interdisciplinarity in practice. We suggest the *systems of innovation* approach as one way forward, albeit not the only way. We will attempt to show that the SI approach is well suited to the analysis of strategic alliances specifically (and that it is an attractive approach for interdisciplinary research more generally). Given its multidisciplinary nature, it helps avoid piecemeal data gathering, analysis, and interpretation that can result from the simple bundling of insights from different disciplines. The SI approach provides an epistemological orientation that is holistic yet tolerant of diversity and sufficiently focused to inform research design. It affords a clarity not easily achieved by the mere concurrent application of different theories.

In discussing the SI approach, we occasionally refer to the specific example of multiple-world (i.e., North-South) health research collaborations and to two disciplines that address these collaborations explicitly: global health and development studies. Multiple-world alliances are increasingly common and particularly interesting for interdisciplinary research because of the nexus of diverse political, commercial, legal, cultural, ethical, and developmental priorities, agendas, issues, conventions, and customs they bring into play. The discussion of the SI approach in Section 3 allows us subsequently to revisit some key themes in alliance research and the nature of questions that arise within these themes in light of an interdisciplinary perspective.

The Systems of Innovation Approach and Its Relevance to Interdisciplinary Alliance Research

In what follows, we outline the SI approach and its suitability for interdisciplinary alliance studies. We attempt to show that the SI approach supports studies of innovation in a manner that is compatible with the theoretical support needs of interdisciplinary alliance studies. We then address how interdisciplinary alliance research design can harness the potential benefits of the SI approach. We aim to do so by moving beyond a discussion of theory to conceptually "unpacking" alliances for empirical research purposes.

The SI approach should be well suited to interdisciplinary alliance research. After all, its principal interest, namely innovation, is integral to many alliance activities (if only to foster organizational process innovation). Also, any innovative activity almost always entails some form of cooperation. We discuss the relevance of the SI approach to alliance studies in more detail below.

The Origins of a Systems of Innovation Approach

The SI approach refers not to a single theory but, rather, to an open-ended and epistemologically pluralist theoretical approach that allows for different disciplines, conceptual devices, and methodologies to inform empirical research. Despite the fact that the SI approach has been put to use in disciplines as varied as biology, economics, engineering, politics, strategy, psychology, health, and development studies, its predominant aim remains that of supporting studies of innovation, broadly defined.

The SI approach evolved in response to critiques of neoclassical perspectives on innovation and is generally seen to have its strongest origins in evolutionary economics and capabilities theory (see Lundvall, 1992; Lall, 1996, 2000; Kim & Nelson, 2000; Iliev, 2004). But neither was it developed to support innovative activity in any one industry sector or discipline, nor were theories and literatures that inform it developed specifically for this purpose.

Surprisingly, very little of the SI literature addresses the SI approach (or its theoretical roots) in the context of systems theory (see Huber, 1984; Mitchell, 1992). Yet systems theory and the SI approach share many of the same research concerns. Von Bertalanffy, founder of systems theory, argued that certain general ideas can be applied across a broad spectrum of disciplines (von Bertalanffy, 1968). Disappointed with the increasing compartmentalization of the sciences in the post-World War II period, he recognized the multidisciplinary approach offered by systems theory and its relevance to the humanities as well as sciences (Irving, 1999). "Systems theory is concerned with problems of relationships, of structures, and of interdependence, rather than with the constant attributes of objects" (Katz & Kahn, 1966, cited in Hong, Al-Khatib, Magagna, McLoughlin, & Coe, 1998, 1).

The SI approach employs the notion of a system in its loosest and broadest possible sense, being most compatible with *open* systems perspectives in systems theory. Von Bertalanffy viewed human organizations and societies as open systems (von Bertalanffy, 1968; Boulding, 1968; Scott, 2002) as they "consist of component sub systems that are interrelated and interdependent, and connected by feedback links to their environment (Irving, 1999, 1).[2] In contrast, closed systems are those that exist and function with minimal or no interaction with the surrounding environment (Irving, 1999, 2).

In many ways, the SI approach is still comparatively new and some distance short of being considered a unified body of theory. This can be exemplified in the different degrees of emphasis that SI theorists place on specific and diverse features of innovation systems. These include *institutional* (Freeman, Nelson, Soete, Silverberg & Dosi, 1988; Nelson, 1993), *network* (Freeman et al., 1988; Nelson, 1993; Lundvall, 1992), *mediation* (Gristock, 2001), *relational* (Lundvall, 1988, 1992), and *knowledge and learning* dimensions (Patel & Pavitt, 1994). Consistent with the contributions of previous innovation theorists and building predominantly on Edquist's view (Edquist, 2004), we define an SI as a system of directly involved organizations, institutions, and agents and as indirectly influencing socioeconomic, cultural, and political environmental regimes (components), which interact through formal and informal relations, and manifest activities (functions) that form the structural and functional SI network (cf. Edquist, 2004, xx).

The SI approach has most commonly been used to understand how interactions between institutions and firms impact on innovation activity in a system. As such, it has been informed predominantly by mesolevel theories of technological change, path dependency, and cluster theory (cf. Edquist & McKelvey, 2000). Two alternative views of institutions are generally adopted for this purpose. Institutions are defined either more narrowly as formal state organizations, industrial structures, or industrial policies, or more broadly to include issues such as culture, norms, or informal regulations (Iliev, 2004) However, the SI approach is equally compatible with more microlevel, agent-centered perspectives, including those focused on trust and legitimacy, as developed in the interorganizational relations (IOR) literature.

Not only does the SI approach embrace the existence of a plurality of functional entities in innovation system structures, but it is both a process-friendly approach (see Nelson, 1993; Kim & Nelson, 2000) and consistent with methodological pluralism[3] (Iliev, 2004). The lack of an a priori commitment to a single methodological agenda stems from its focus on the object of analysis (i.e., innovative activity) rather than on method (Iliev, 2004) and from a belief that no single approach, theory, or discipline can capture the complexity of innovation processes nor their variations and diversity in different contexts. Instead, the SI approach shares features of several commonly used theoretical approaches in alliance research, such as the resource-based view, path dependency, organizational evolution, organizational learning, social network theory, and related literatures within the IOR field that address issues of trust, legitimacy, process, and internal tensions. These approaches may differ in scope and focus, yet they are surprisingly well attuned and can be seen to share a common pluralist orientation. We briefly elaborate on this below.

How Does the Systems of Innovation Approach View Innovation?

Innovation is a complex and multifaceted phenomenon that spans disciplinary fields and industry sectors. SI scholars typically assume that innovation is nonprescriptive, occurring at multiple levels within and between organizations. This is not least because the general socioeconomic gains of innovation are typically manifested through the pursuit of multiple (and sometimes competing) goals. These may be commercial-, academic-, political-, altruistic-, or development-related. Understanding the diffusion and impact of innovation requires a historical perspective, given that innovation may have multiple applications, some of which become evident only with the passing of time. Moreover, uses of innovation can be highly context-dependent.

Global health and development studies—as fields of research that seem particularly germane to multiple-world alliances—illustrate this well.

These fields have long viewed innovation as key to health advancements and socioeconomic sustainability in developing regions. Yet they suggest that innovation need not necessarily lead to radically new products or processes but rather to new applications and often modifications to existing innovations so as to meet local needs (cf. Kim & Nelson, 2000, 131; Nelson & Rosenberg, 1993; Gerstenfeld & Wortzel, 1977). As Ernst, Ganiastos, and Mytelka point out, "innovation is the process by which firms master and implement the design and production of goods and services new to them, irrespective of whether they are new or not to competitors" (cited in Velho, 2002, 42).

The consequences of innovation are also diverse, multiple, and occasionally unintended. In the case of multiple-world collaborations, global health and development studies show that systems of innovation can create problems and constrain progress as much as they fuel development and provide solutions to pressing developmental concerns (Velho, 2002; United Nations Development Programme, 2001). This "tension" is particularly clear when one looks at innovation from a multidisciplinary perspective. For example, such issues as genetically modified organisms in sustainable agriculture, the use of infectious agents as biological weapons, or the inequity gap in access to the innovative technologies and products that exists across world regions aptly illustrate the complexity and role of social construction in interpreting innovation system performance as well as the multidimensionality and nonlinearity of SI outputs.

How Is the Systems of Innovation Approach Suited to Interdisciplinary Alliance Research?

The epistemological assumptions of the SI approach are pluralist yet integrative. In other words, although the SI perspective emphasizes heterogeneity and multiplicity (within and across innovation system structures and functions), it is keen to explore how the many different elements of an innovation system interact. Together with its philosophical orientation, the SI approach's core features point well to the approach's suitability and relevance to *interdisciplinary* research on *alliances.*

The manner by which the SI approach addresses the diversity and complexity of innovation processes and outcomes is compatible with the manner in which strategic alliance diversity and complexity have been conceptualized in the literature. Innovation systems and strategic alliances alike are often characterized by a fair amount of social complexity, nonlinearity, interdependency, and a tendency toward instability. Besides, strategic alliances are often created for the purposes of innovation, even if only for "organizational (process) innovation" (i.e., nontechnological innovations such as managerial and organizational improvements, e.g., Garvin, 1993; cf. Kim & Nelson, 2000). Both alliances and innovation systems can be conceptualized as configurations of functional components (e.g., participating organizations and stakeholder groups, institutions and agents), relationships, and activities that interact in an open-ended, dynamic fashion. Both are also essentially network-embedded phenomena, in which social ties and learning play an important role (Hamel, 1991; Inkpen, 1995; Teece, Pisano, & Shuen, 1997; Kogut, 1988; Osborn & Hagedoorn, 1997; Kim & Nelson, 2000, 22). Thus, the SI approach appears useful in informing the design of strategic alliance research. This is particularly true for those alliances in which some form of innovation or knowledge transfer is expected as a corollary of collaborating.

Integral to this approach is an ability to capture and analyze important characteristics of alliances that are not easily captured by any single discipline or theory. In particular, the SI approach draws our attention to several features of alliance life:

1. alliances are multidimensional, open systems comprising both functional and structural cooperative networks,

2. alliance life entails a process subject to idiosyncrasy and rapid change,

3. alliances evolve, sometimes in unpredictable ways, are context-dependent, and their performance is subject to social construction,

We elaborate on each of these below.

Alliances Are Multidimensional, Open Systems and Entail Both Structural and Functional Cooperative Networks

The SI approach sees innovation systems as multidimensional and open systems (Edquist & McKelvey, 2000), and innovation processes as a collaborative and network-dependent activity. This allows us to account for both directly participating components in innovation processes (i.e., specific organizations, institutions, and relations) and, indirectly, regimes in which innovative activities are embedded and subject to, for example, social, economic, and political factors (Edquist, 2004).

The channels and networks through which this information circulates are embedded in a social, political, and cultural background; they are strongly guided and constrained by the institutional framework. The SI approach studies innovating firms in the context of external institutions, government policies, competitors, suppliers, customers, value systems, and social and cultural practices that affect their operation (Organisation for Economic Co-operation and Development, 1997, 18).

This open-endedness implies that innovation system performance is contingent on a complex and diverse range of inputs. The resource-based view informs the SI approach well in this regard. It helps explain performance differences between innovation systems as a function of differing abilities of organizations, institutions, and agents to ensure access to superior resources and capabilities. Aside from any physical assets, these include absorptive capacity (Cohen & Levinthal, 1990) and organizational routines (Nelson & Winter, 1982). As Scott proposes in relation to open systems: "all systems are characterized by an assemblage or combination of parts whose relations make them interdependent but they also suggest the bases for the differences among them" (cited in Hong et al., 1998, 2) and "the parts of systems are more complex and variable when systems move from mechanical through organic to social systems" (Hong et al., 1998, 2).

Awareness of this resource pool and means of access is typically relationship-dependent—that is, one "traces" resources and negotiates access to them by leveraging the social capital of various stakeholders. Thus, the SI approach views innovation as a network-dependent process, in which "interaction is the critical element" (Tidd, Bessant, & Pavitt, 1997, 29). Networks influence innovation at a number of levels and to varying degrees, from the intraorganizational level to the interrelational networks between different institutions, organizations, and agents, and across sectoral, regional, national, and international boundaries. As such, the SI approach is commensurate with social network approaches to empirical research. These networks consist of a distinct, enduring, and "structured" set of actors that cooperate on the basis of open-ended contracts so as to help them adapt to environmental contingencies and to coordinate and safeguard exchanges. They do so mostly based on socially rather than legally binding contracts (Jones, Hesterly, & Borgatti, 1997).

Alliance Life Entails a Process Subject to Idiosyncrasy and Rapid Change

The SI approach allows one to study not just the structural but also the process-related aspects of innovation systems. It does so not least by drawing on evolutionary, path dependency, and capability theories to capture and comprehend the components and functions of an innovation system, and through a theoretical compatibility with network perspectives. The SI approach emphasizes that innovation occurs in environments of uncertainty, places learning squarely at center stage, and allows for diversity of agent behavior, belief, and experience (cf. Fagerberg et al., 2004).

Within the SI context, learning processes become central in enabling organizations and agents to adapt efficiently to rapidly changing and uncertain innovation environments. The SI perspective thus shares some of the advantages of organizational learning approaches. Organizational learning addresses the complexity and multidimensionality of learning, the range of capabilities needed to acquire, disseminate, and retain new and competitive knowledge, and the evolutionary processes entailed in their development (cf. Child & Faulkner, 1998; Lall, 1996; Kim & Nelson, 2000). It views knowledge as essentially socially constructed, complex, and often tacitly held. It also examines the roles of repeated interactions, mediation and cooperation networks, experimentation, and monitoring, as well as issues of trust, legitimacy, incentives, and authority in learning processes.

Alliances Evolve, Sometimes in Unpredictable Ways, Are Context-Dependent, and Their Performance Is Subject to Social Construction

The SI approach treats innovation as a socially constructed activity and accounts for interdependencies and nonlinearity in the evolution of innovation. It entails both economic and sociological perspectives and sees economic actions as being influenced by the social context in which they are embedded. It acknowledges that social contexts can differ even between structurally similar institutional, organizational, and agent arrangements, and that this may lead to different outcomes from cooperative activities in innovation.

The SI approach to innovation places emphasis on "the interplay between institutions, looking at interactive processes in the creation of knowledge and in the diffusion and application of knowledge. It has led to a better appreciation of the importance of conditions" (Organisation for Economic Co-operation and Development, 1997, 18).

The SI approach emphasizes the role of institutions but accounts for interdependencies and nonlinearity in the ways that institutions are formed and reproduced. In an SI context, institutions that govern innovative activities are not always consciously built and are often inherited. They result from routine agent behavior as well as the unintended consequences of the activities of human agency (Nelson & Rosenberg, 1993). Their reproduction is a function of variant agent behavior as informed by social structure. Such views on institutions facilitate us to consider the role of sociology in accounting for the impact of knowledge, trust, learning, and interpersonal communication within and on innovation.

Although the SI approach can account for some social order, structure, and regularity in alliances, it does so without imposing these a priori. It seeks to understand rather than to prescribe generic models for system structure and function and acknowledges the diverse ways in which resources, capabilities, relations, and interactions are internalized and influence a system. It does not assume that whatever happens to alliances is either functional or dysfunctional (de Rond & Bouchikhi, 2004, 67). It is mostly concerned with "seeking meaning in context" (Klein & Myers, 1999, 74) or the pursuit of an inquiry without being absorbed by the compulsion either to generate elegant miniature universes or to produce a managerial agenda.

As Weick explains,

> Open systems are thought of as having both maintenance sub systems and adaptive mechanisms. . . . Successful systems are able to deal with the paradox of stability and instability. . . . Organizations operate in terms of positive and negative feedback interactions. . . . The implicit recognition of the non-linear relationships that exist within systems can cause autonomous change between stable/unstable depending upon the dominant form of feedback. (Weick, cited in Irving, 1999, 2)

Finally, the SI approach's pluralist orientation meets the requirements of an epistemology that can address the diversity of issues involved in interdisciplinary research. It is not overly deterministic or normative; it takes into account contextual differences; it helps account for the structural properties of social systems and the role of agency (in accounting for strategic choice); it is process-friendly in viewing innovation as potentially driven by a combination of teleological, evolutionary, and dialectical engines (Van de Ven & Poole, 1995); and it allows performance to be broadly interpreted against objectives that are themselves subject to ongoing processes of reassessment and renegotiation.

Unpacking an Alliance for Interdisciplinary Research Purposes

One of the first and most important challenges for designing interdisciplinary research studies (regardless of the key questions of interest in the study) lies in understanding what the object of study—in this case, strategic alliances—truly entails at as many dimensions as possible, but also in as focused a manner as possible. We propose the SI approach as a pluralist theoretical and conceptual framework that can aid us in gaining such insights. But realizing goals for breadth, depth, and focus (and managing the tensions between these objectives) is contingent on the ability of research design to facilitate the SI approach's application in a clear, focused, and sufficiently structured manner.

So how can one design an interdisciplinary project within the SI context? Specifically, what are the implications of the SI approach for conceptualizing the dynamics of strategic alliances with various different stakeholders? And what are the implications of an SI-based conceptualization for their analysis? The following is one suggestion.

The 3R Concept

So as to provide structure and conceptual clarity, a strategic alliance can be "unpacked" as an ongoing process of reconfiguration between three basic components: a nexus of *regimes,* a set of *relationships,* and *reasons* for existence (see Figure 23.2). Each of the interrelated examination levels (regime, relationship, and reason for existence) can be examined and described in terms of "SI-like" components and functions: in terms of institutions, organizations, and agents and the activities and interactions that propagate them in variable and nonlinear ways (see Figure 23.2).

A nexus of environmental *regimes* (socioeconomic, cultural and community, political and legal, physical and intellectual regimes)[4] helps frame and initiate specific *relationships* in a collaboration stakeholder network. It also helps agents to access the range of resources and capabilities needed for the alliance to fulfill its *reasons for existence.* At the same time, alliance goals, purposes, objectives, and desired outputs—which are integral in its *reasons for existence*—will impact the types of *relationships* that surface in the alliance network at any point in time (e.g., which particular stakeholder groups' activities and behavior are most important to acquire specific endowments). It will also impact the nature of features in environmental *regimes* that surface as functionally significant in impacting these relationships.

Moreover, the interplay of regimes, relationships, and reasons is likely to give rise to "internal tensions" (cf. Das & Teng, 2000; de Rond & Bouchikhi, 2004). These tensions include those between cooperation and competition, trust and vigilance, collectivism and individualism, flexibility and rigidity, replication and innovation, and exploration and exploitation, among others. The nature and scope of these tensions will vary across different alliances and even within an alliance over time, but are likely strongly to influence their evolutionary dynamics and potential (depending not least on how these tensions are managed). Understanding the interplay of these three components is important to understanding the nature, performance, and evolution of strategic alliances.

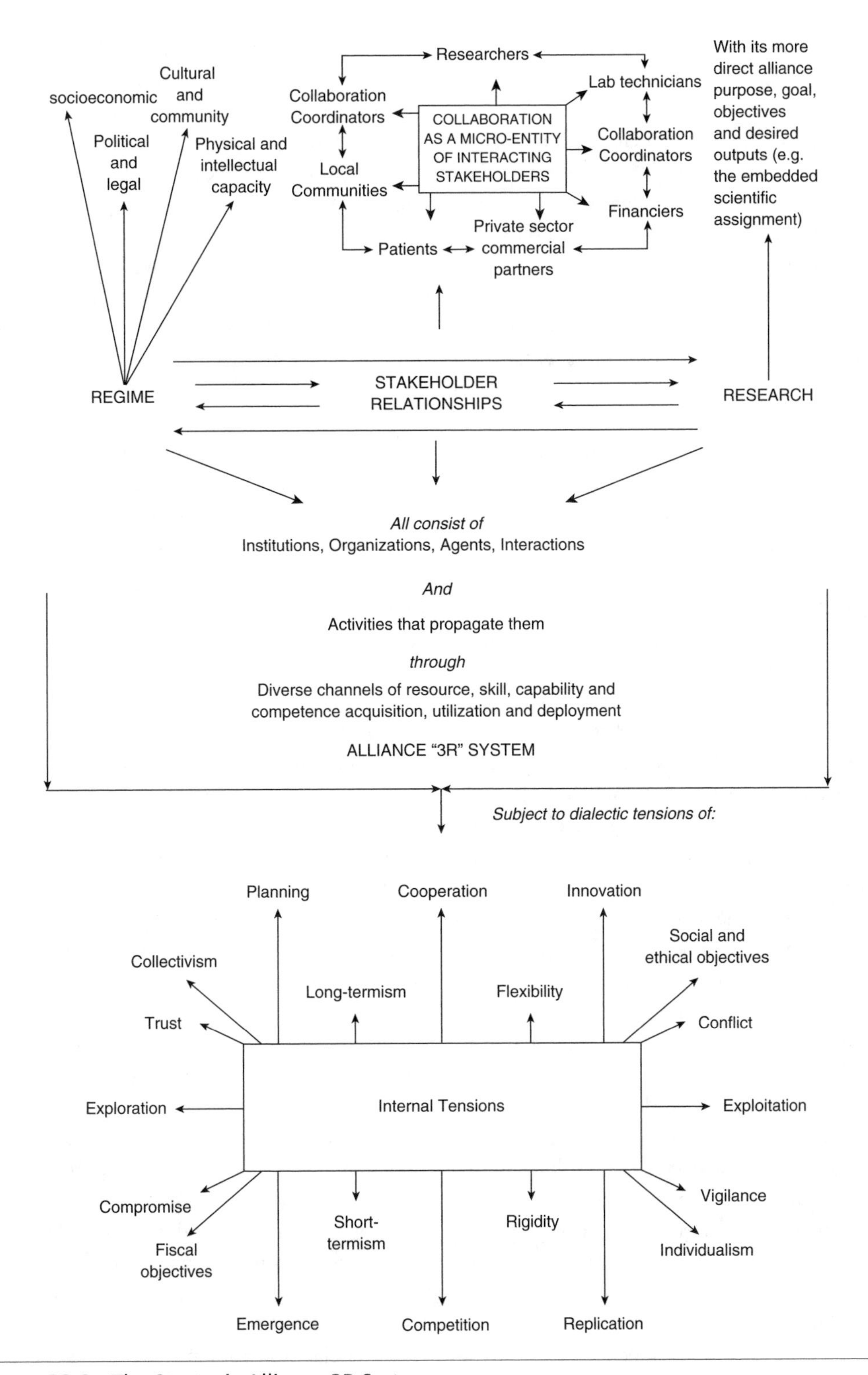

Figure 23.2 The Strategic Alliance 3R System

How Does This 3R Conceptualization Inform Alliance Research?

This "unpacking" may help capture various dimensions of an alliance in a relatively focused manner. For instance, the *regime* component may be particularly useful in understanding the open-system nature of alliances, their context dependence, and their proclivity to change. It can also emphasize the way in which environments precondition the goals and motivations entailed in alliance formation and how they impact on resource and capability acquisition, the related diversity of partner inputs and their implications on alliance ownership, and control and governance structures. Examining regimes through an interdisciplinary lens helps contribute toward understanding how environmental conditions (e.g., social or political environment uncertainties) impact on efforts to achieve stability or to manage instability in alliances.

Interdisciplinary accounts that focus on *relationships* may be particularly helpful in understanding the dynamics of learning and cooperation in alliances and the impact of diversity and unpredictability of institutional, organizational, and agent behavior on alliance stability, evolution, and performance. A focus on the relationship component across disciplines may also allow us to attain a richer account of the diverse nexus of relationship types that need to be established so as to realize alliance objectives and the implications of these relationship needs on the spatial organization of alliance activity (i.e., to what extent an alliance can function as a "virtual network" and to what extent it requires physical concentration in a specific area to engage in and meet specific relationship requirements). Spatial organization will affect alliance management and governance forms, and the virtues and benefits of different degrees of spatiality depend at least partly on the nature of relationships, communications, and interactions that are needed between alliance members.

Focusing on *reasons* may be helpful in allowing different disciplines to contribute insights into the diversity of goals, motivations, and purposes that drive cooperative activity and to highlight the degree to which these are socially constructed. Approaching the reasons for existence component from an interdisciplinary angle may help us understand to what level goals are common and united in an "alliance community" and to what extent they are (possibly more saliently) diverse and divergent between distinct stakeholder groups or organizations and agents from different environments, sectors, and disciplines. Such insights into the goals, objectives, and motivations behind alliance emergence are likely to influence the manner in which we capture and understand issues of alliance evolution and stability. Examining reasons from an interdisciplinary standpoint may also help us to understand better the internal tensions that may exist within alliances, especially those resulting from power imbalances or conflicting values.

Finally, subsequently examining the interactions between the three Rs (i.e., examining the alliance system in its entirety) should prove useful in understanding alliance multidimensionality, heterogeneity, and nonlinearity, the interdependencies of issues entailed in their formation, evolution, management, and governance, and the degree to which performance is socially constructed. It facilitates the "movement of understanding from the whole to the part and back to the whole" (Gadamer, 1976, cited in Klein & Myers, 1999, 71), repeated until conflicting interpretations can be reconciled (Klein & Myers, 1999, 73).

In sum, this SI-informed 3R conceptualization may enable us to design interdisciplinary studies of alliances in a manner that tries to make sense of their diversity and messiness. As such, it could serve as a useful analytical tool for interdisciplinary research efforts and help us to identify and tackle the key challenges and questions these social phenomena face and pose to researchers, through an awareness of alliance multidimensionality and complexity.

Revisiting Key Themes in Alliance Research

As suggested in the introduction to this chapter, we now turn to four recurring and well-researched themes in alliance research: (1) alliance formation, (2) evolution, (3) management and governance, and (4) performance. Although we expect an interdisciplinary approach to provide a richer response to the key research questions within each theme, it might be useful also to see whether such an approach impacts on the nature of the questions we might ask in examining these key themes.

We hope to provide some novel research questions within each theme, based on a wider reading of the literature and the deliberate embracing of a pluralist epistemology. We then turn to discuss and elaborate on the ability of an integrative and pluralist SI-based interdisciplinary approach to tackle those questions we see as particularly important in recurring research themes.

Key Themes in Alliance Research and the Benefits of Interdisciplinarity and a Systems of Innovation Lens in Addressing Them

Key Questions in Alliance Research

Each of the four key themes in alliance research is characterized by a substantial and growing literature. Although we make no claim to revolutionizing this literature, we think it worthwhile to review and revisit these themes in light of an interdisciplinary perspective and the contributions of an integrative SI-based theoretical lens. How, if at all, might such a perspective change the nature of our research questions and the ways by which we address them? How can it change the analytical angles we adopt in tackling key areas of concern in alliance formation and design, evolution, management and governance, and performance? We highlight below some of the questions that may be important in an interdisciplinary alliance research agenda.

- Alliance formation and design:
  - To what extent do traditional economic arguments based on financial and technological imperatives drive alliance formation, as opposed to potentially more salient features, such as political incentives, individual reputational gain aspirations, or altruistic motives? And how do these subsequently influence its evolution and performance?
  - To what extent are the broader goals of the alliance as a whole and the distinct goals, motivations, and objectives of individual stakeholder groups, organizations, and agents (often more salient) common from the onset? How and why do these change over time?
  - To what extent is partner selection contingent on leveraging existing social networks and reputation, as opposed to accessing needed resources and capabilities? How do institutions impact on the types of partners that can be selected?
  - What is the impact of different spatial organizations of collaborations (e.g., a "virtual partner network" organization versus alliance activity concentration in the boundaries of a specific geographical area) on the evolution and dynamics, management, governance, and control of alliances?

- Alliance dynamics and evolution:
  - How important is stability for the success of an alliance? What does stability mean (e.g., how is it "measured")?
  - Where does alliance instability stem from? How do factors such as differences in goals, motivations, and incentives between distinct stakeholder

groups, as well as individual traits, environmental uncertainty, dialectic tensions, and their management, affect stability?
  - Are there virtues to instability? If so, what are they? What competencies need to be established to harness the potential virtues of instability? How can instability best be managed?
  - How do alliances evolve over time? How does partner participation evolve? How do initial conditions change (e.g., objectives, absorptive capacity, skills pool, external conditions) over the life of an alliance?

- Alliance management and governance:
  - What are the benefits and limitations of hierarchical versus participatory alliance governance and management structures on the control and coordination of alliance activities? How does the adoption of a long-term or short-term perspective on an alliance affect the evaluation of the benefits and trade-offs of the two?
  - To what extent do transaction costs, interdependence, and power asymmetries influence alliance governance structures? What is the effect of social networks (which can mitigate appropriation concerns) on governance models?
  - How do resource and capability splits affect the distribution of ownership, decision-making power, control, responsibility, and accountability in alliances? How can the importance of contributions from different stakeholder groups and agents from different disciplines be accounted for and incorporated into the design of effective but "fair" alliance governance and management structures? How can fiscal and in-kind contributions be weighted?
  - How important are trust, a sense of equity and fairness, and the personal leadership traits of individuals to the manageability of alliances?

- Alliance performance
  - How should success and failure be defined in the context of strategic alliances?
  - Why do problematic alliances sometimes survive?
  - Why are successful alliances sometimes prematurely dismantled?
  - Given that alliance objectives are multifaceted, how does one value the relative importance of meeting distinct objectives? What are the "hidden costs" of achieving a specific performance outcome?
  - How does one measure performance? What are the implications of the "quantification criteria" on the multidimensionality and multidisciplinarity of the notion of performance?

We briefly illustrate the potential of interdisciplinarity below with examples (two of which relate to the particular case of multiple-world biomedical collaborations).

Example 1. First, from the perspective of more traditional disciplinary lenses, reasons for alliance formation are likely to place emphasis on direct economic incentives—to minimize transaction costs, to support competitive (re)positioning, to increase market power, or to facilitate organizational learning as a source of competitive advantage. Although such economic benefits may be a necessary condition, they are unlikely to furnish comprehensive explanations for alliance formation. Motives, which are not directly and explicitly economic, may include personal reputational gain, political incentives, altruism, or the quest for legitimacy and can significantly influence issues such as partner selection and governance structure.

Less traditional disciplines, such as global health and development studies, are likely to emphasize these "noneconomic" incentives well, given their awareness of the altruistic, political, diplomatic and relational, academic, and reputational justifications for alliances Although these may also be accounted for by more traditional approaches to alliance research (including economics), they are less likely to receive the same degree of emphasis. In this context, interdisciplinarity may better enable us, as researchers, to "read the social world behind the words of the actors, a social world that is characterized by power structures, vested interests, and limited resources to meet the goals of various actors who construct and enact this social world" (Klein & Myers, 1999, 78, in relation to the principle of suspicion in interpretivism).

Example 2. Second, understanding "spatiality" of organization is another issue that benefits from interdisciplinarity. Participants in an alliance from different disciplines may require different levels of actual concentration in a specific geographical area. For example, in the case of a multiple-world biomedical alliance (e.g., an AIDS drug trial), social science researchers working on patient mobilization will benefit from being immersed in a community so as to attain consent, acceptance, and trust. They are likely to benefit from locality and concentration rather than a widely dispersed form of organization. However, scientists engaged in laboratory-based "bench science" may be able to function perfectly well in a distributed, or "virtual," organization, having specimen samples sent to them and data communicated via the Web.

Example 3. Strategic alliances aim to align the interests of a diverse group of stakeholders. To understand performance requires us to appreciate the distinct disciplinary interests, goals, and accountabilities these stakeholders bring to bear on performance assessment processes. The criteria that drive these processes are often context-dependent and socially constructed. To refer to our example of multiple-world alliances, whereas a "North-North" alliance focused on the development of an innovative tuberculosis drug may be concerned primarily with criteria of ease of use and length of treatment, a "North-South" alliance for the development of an innovative tuberculosis drug may be concerned instead with the modification of an existing therapeutic so that it can be produced more cheaply.

"Softer" and indirect performance assessment criteria can also be important in the context of strategic alliances, and especially those with long time frames and a diverse group of stakeholders. Stakeholders bring different disciplines into play but often also different commercial, regional, and national interests. These interests can vary significantly and thus impose quite different criteria on the ongoing measurement of performance. And these criteria are not always explicit or straightforward. Consequently, this heterogeneity of interests can generate "tensions" inside the interorganizational relationship—a dialectic that is not easily addressed through the application of any single disciplinary or theoretical approaches. For example, collaborations in global health may emerge for a variety of reasons, including academic, political, and commercial interests or mere altruism. A malaria drug development alliance may be formed with the intention of addressing a significant health burden, to advance scientific knowledge on the infectious disease, as a symbol of good diplomacy between countries, or to produce a commercializable product.

Particularly in collaborations that involve governments, regional development agencies, academic institutions, or pharmaceuticals, "success" may mean something different for each of these stakeholders. Whereas a heightened overall awareness of the disease (its prevention and treatment) may suffice for governments, this is unlikely to be good enough for stakeholders with clear commercial or political interests.

Example 4. Much of alliance literature has focused on issues of alliance *stability* and on understanding the structures and functions that ensure stability. Yet we argue that alliances are complex, often unstable and unpredictable, and subject to internal tensions. Dialectical tensions vary in nature, scope, and intensity across alliances and even within them. This variance is likely to depend on the type of alliance, its place in the life cycle, the structural organization of an alliance (size, spatial organization, mode of ownership and control), and environmental regime features, as well as on the management and governance practices and related skills and abilities proactively to identify potential tensions before they emerge or to manage tensions and trade-offs once they emerge.

Is there any virtue to these internal tensions despite the discomfort they might bring to those involved? After all, cannot competition weed out inefficiencies even in cooperative environments? Trust is vitally important, but can it not be dangerous in the absence of vigilance? Autonomy is valuable in the context of scientific research collaborations, but can it not be inefficient in the absence of planning and design? Enduring alliances are likely to be those that have "survived," having changed, adapted, evolved, and continuously responded to destabilizing forces. Yet comparatively little research seems to have investigated the causes and consequences of their dialectical nature.

Understanding instability is likely to benefit from an interdisciplinary SI perspective. To illustrate:

- The degree to which individual and collective interests are common or divergent in alliances is likely to impact on alliance stability. Understanding this dynamic may call on us to revisit the reasons behind alliance formation and to examine how formal institutional, organizational, and network structures and less formal and perhaps more salient and idiosyncratic aspects of alliance arrangements (e.g., distinct norms and cultures and heterogeneous agent traits and behaviors) impact on the manifestation of individual and collective interests and motivations.
- Understanding instability may also ask us to examine carefully how the core participants in an alliance (organizations and agents) interact with institutional and environmental regime factors. This task includes elucidating the impact of both formal state and market institutions and informal institutions (culture, norms) on the emergence and management of tensions in alliances. The SI approach may prove particularly useful in helping us understand the nature of internal tensions that affect alliance stability (e.g., trust versus vigilance, flexibility versus rigidity, planning abilities versus emergence) in terms of the socioeconomic, political, and cultural features of institutions and environmental regimes within which alliance activities are embedded.

Conclusion

The potential of interdisciplinary research approaches to sensitize us to the complexity, multiplicity, and multidimensionality of social phenomena is relatively easy to appreciate. However, putting interdisciplinarity to use in research is a rather more difficult challenge. This chapter seeks to make a case for interdisciplinary research and to provide some novel insights as well as practical suggestions as to why and how it can be advantageous to understanding strategic alliances. To this extent, we seek to outline the chief motivations for interdisciplinarity. Central to our argument is the claim that interdisciplinary research may be best served by epistemological and methodological pluralism. We suggest that what interdisciplinarity needs is not the bundling of variant theoretical perspectives but the pursuit of integrative approaches that embrace variety and take multiplicity and heterogeneity to be empirical facts of the social world of organizations. We propose the "systems of innovation" perspective as one such approach for supporting interdisciplinary research on strategic alliances, given its open-ended, holistic, and pluralist treatment of collaborative activities in innovation processes. We briefly outline the SI approach, show how it shares the features of several commonly used perspectives in alliance research, and elaborate on its methodological implications. We then propose the 3R visualization as an analytical tool in designing and implementing interdisciplinary alliance research. Clearly, the potential of such visualization would benefit from future empirical studies, which could examine its analytical and abstractive capabilities.

Despite its merits, however, an interdisciplinary approach entails risks. First, embracing interdisciplinarity in research is challenging precisely because alliance complexity may impel us to study isolated variables rather than systems of interrelationships between clusters of variables. This complexity presents researchers with tough conceptual and methodological barriers (Parkhe, 1993). As Parkhe explains, "the response has been one of ignoring away the messy concepts and the soft issues, of studying outcomes, but not the processes" (Parkhe, 1993, 246).

Moreover, as Parkhe points out, the convergence of hard methodological approaches with soft behavioral variables has made it difficult to coalesce individually useful international joint venture studies "into a coherent body of work with a consistent underlying theoretical structure" (Parkhe, 1993, 227).

Second, we argue that an interdisciplinary approach to empirical research in alliances is desirable but calls for epistemological and methodological pluralism. Any attempt at "bundling" different disciplinary approaches (each with their own epistemological commitments) may be at risk of being criticized for combining incommensurable assumptions.

Third, efforts to adopt interdisciplinarity in strategic alliance research need to be framed around an awareness of the trade-off between ensuring breadth in the scope of analysis versus achieving sharpness in focus for accuracy and parsimony (Bacharach, 1989; Parkhe, 1993). Despite its promises, interdisciplinary research can make it difficult to maintain focus, particularly in analysis. Given a spectrum of lenses, one inevitably faces a trade-off between breadth and focus. It is not always easy to know when to stop pursuing one interpretation and commit to another, nor to know how to impose limits in the selection of disciplines, literatures, and theories. This is a particularly acute concern, as their relative merits cannot easily be gauged. Consequently, research design is likely to be emergent, even if this is counterintuitive to the traditional virtues of careful planning and controlling to warrant integrity.

In addition, it may be useful to consider when interdisciplinary research is most useful. Should interdisciplinarity be embraced from the onset, that is, in the early stage of research design? Or is it more appropriate to adopt interdisciplinarity in later stages of research, once individual disciplines have had time to inform a project? Or do they need to be conducted concurrently? These are all issues that require further research.

The SI approach as a conceptual framework is conducive to addressing some of these risks. As we hope this chapter illustrates, it can provide a relatively focused way of visualizing complex interorganizational relationships. The nonprescriptive and open-ended nature of the SI approach allows one to consider the relative messiness, diversity, and complexity of strategic alliances while still being able to account for some order and regularity. It does so by seeking to understand rather than prescribing universal models for system structure and function, by seeking to see the general in the particular and the particular in the general, and by acknowledging "a diversity of ways" by which resources, capabilities, relations, skills, competencies, and interactions are internalized and influence alliance activities. It achieves this by placing institutions, organizations, and agents in specific social, economic, political, legal, cultural, and ethical contexts, allowing one to examine them through different disciplinary or theoretical lenses.

Finally, themes in strategic alliance research are clearly relevant to both academics and practitioners. Although we acknowledge that the primary audience for this chapter is the former, we also believe that it is important for scholars to be aware of an underlying need to span the divide between the worlds of theory and practice, translating some of our ideas into managerial applications. An inherent openness to interdisciplinarity is essential for bridging this chasm. After all, theory and practice may themselves at times be viewed as distinct "disciplines." Translating theory to practice also requires us, as academics, to be open-minded, to think laterally, and to avoid the trap of disciplinary confinement in the design and conduct of research.

In the interest of generating novel insight, it may be worthwhile to consider the role of imagination on alliance theorizing. As Locke, Golden-Biddle, & Feldman explain,

> Musement—the setting of the mind free to wander from one thing to another—was one of philosopher Charles S. Pierce's favourite words. He used it to depict matters of possible significance (including hunches, images, etc.) that were generated in moments of intense inquisitive reflection when the mind could be freed up such that play will be converted into scientific study. For Pierce, musing was central to abductive inference, the first phase in the enquiry process and a form of reasoning distinct from both abduction and deduction. (Locke et al., 2004, 1)

We end with a poignant observation by Osborn and Hagedoorn, one that lends itself rather well to musing:

> A very prominent and retiring scholar suggested that new theory is best conceived by a few scholars via thoughtful discussion over fine wine in front of a roaring fire. In that context, a key to intellectual progress is to capture a sustaining of the intellect for inquiry. A second approach is to seek a collective focus among a group of interconnected scholars from different disciplines, paying attention to major social issues. (Osborn & Hagedoorn, 1997, 275)

We hope this chapter stimulates both approaches.

Notes

1. At any point in the history of a field, there are likely to be groups of academics who challenge and question the "leading," or most popular, philosophical assumptions of a particular time. But there is also likely to be a dominant view and a general prevailing epistemological commitment.

2. Open systems can be defined as a system of interdependent activities. Scott describes how "the parts of systems join and leave or engage in ongoing exchanges with the organization depending on the bargains they can strike. Some of these activities are tightly connected; others are loosely coupled." That is, all of the parts must be continuously motivated to produce and reproduce in a system. Scott also emphasizes that "systems are interdependent activities linking shifting coalitions of participants; the systems are embedded in—dependent on continuing exchanges with and constituted by—the environments in which they operate" (Scott, 2000). The salient characteristic of an open system is a self-maintenance based on a process of resources from the environment and interaction with the environment. Katz and Kahn summarize the essential characteristics of an open system as follows: "The open-system approach begins by identifying and mapping the repeated cycles of inputs, transformation, output and renewed inputs which comprise the organizational patterns. Organizations as a special class of open systems have properties of their own, but they share other properties in common with all open systems. These include the importation of energy from the environment, the through-put or transformation of the imported energy into some product form . . . the exporting of that product into the environment, and the re-energizing of the system from sources in the environment. The study of systems is by definition concerned with change" (cf. Hong et al., 1998, 2).

3. Hence, we find the SI approach being applied to studies that use diverse methodologies: case studies (in Cassiolato, Lastres, & Maciel, 2003), econometric analysis of panel data for industry and countries (Breschi & Malerba, 1997; Fagerberg, 1995), as well as analyses based on secondary literature (Bartholomew, 1997; cf. Iliev, 2004).

4. Physical resources and scientific research and innovation capacity (physical and intellectual resources). It is also important to note that these regimes are interrelated.

References

Auster, E. (1987). International corporate linkages: Dynamic forms in changing environments. *Columbia Journal of World Business, 22*(2), 3–7.

Bacharach, S. B. (1989). Organizational theories: Some criteria for evaluation. *Academy of Management Review, 14,* 496–515.

Bartholomew, S. (1997). National systems of biotechnology innovation: Complex interdependence in the global system. *Journal of International Business Studies, 28*(2), 241–267.

Berlin, I. (1999). *The hedgehog and the fox: An essay on Tolstoy's view of history.* London: Orion.

Boulding, K. E. (1956). General systems theory—The skeleton of science. *Management Science, 2*(3).

Boulding, K. (1968). General systems 1: General system theory, the skeleton of a science. In Walter Buckley (Ed.), *Modern systems research for the behavioral scientist* (pp. 11–17). Chicago: Aldine.

Brandenburger, A., & Nalebuff, B. (1996). *Co-opetition.* New York: Doubleday.

Breschi, S., & Malerba, F. (1997). Sectoral innovation systems: Technological regimes, Schumpeterian dynamics and spatial boundaries. In Edquist, C. (Ed.), *Systems of innovation: Technologies, institutions and organizations.* London: Pinter.

Buckley, P. J., & Casson, M. (1988). A theory of cooperation in international business. In F. J. Contractor & P. Lorange (Eds.), *Cooperative strategies in international business* (pp. 31–54). Lexington, MA: Lexington Books.

Caccomo, J. L. (1998). System of innovation approach [review]. *Economics of Innovation & New Technology, 7*(3), 245–270.

Cassiolato, J. E., Lastres, H., & Maciel, M. L. (2003). *Systems of innovation and development: Evidence from Brazil.* London: Edward Elgar.

Child, J., & Faulkner, D. O. (1998). Strategies of cooperation: Managing alliances, networks and joint ventures. In S. Clegg & G. Palmer (Eds.), *Producing management knowledge* (pp. 46–68). Sage: London.

Cohen, W., & Levinthal, D. A. (1990). Absorptive capability: A new perspective on learning and innovation. *Administrative Science Quarterly, 35*(1), 128–152.

Cohen, M. D., March, J. G., & Olsen, J. P. (1972). A garbage can model of organizational choice. *Administrative Science Quarterly, 17,* 1–25.

D'Aunno, T. A., & Zuckerman, H. S. (1987). A life cycle model of organizational federations: The case of hospitals. *Academy of Management Review, 12*(3), 534–545.

Das, T. K., and Teng, B. S. (2000). Instabilities of strategic alliances: An internal tensions perspective. *Organization Science, 11*(1), 77–102.

de Rond, M. (2002). Reviewer 198, the hedgehog and the fox: Next generation theories in strategy. *Journal of Management Inquiry, 11*(1), 36–46.

de Rond, M. (2003). *Strategic alliances as social facts: Business, biotechnology and intellectual history* Cambridge, UK: Cambridge University Press.

de Rond, M., & Bouchikhi, H. (2004). On the dialectics of strategic alliances. *Organization Science, 15*(1), 56–69.

Doz, Y. L. (1996). The evolution of cooperation in strategic alliances: Initial conditions or learning processes. *Strategic Management Journal, 17,* 55–83.

Dunning, J. H. (1993). *Multinational enterprises and the global economy.* Wokingham, UK: Addison-Wesley.

Dyer, J. H., Kale, P., & Singh, H. (2004). When to ally & when to acquire. *Harvard Business Review, 82*(7/8), 108–115.

Edquist, C. (2004). Systems of innovation: Perspectives and challenges. In J. Fagerberg, D. C. Mowery, & R. R Nelson (Eds.), *The Oxford handbook of innovation* (pp. 181–209). Oxford, UK: Oxford University Press.

Edquist, C., & McKelvey, M. (Eds.). (2000). *Systems of innovation: Growth, competitiveness and employment.* Cheltenham, UK: Edward Elgar.

Ernst, D. (2002). Global production networks and the changing geography of innovation systems. Implications for developing countries. *Economics of Innovation & New Technology, 11*(6), 497–524.

Fagerberg, J. (1995). Catching up and falling behind in economic development: Convergence or divergence? The impact of technology on "why growth rates differ." *Journal of Evolutionary Economics, 5*(3), 269–285.

Fagerberg, J., Mowery, D. C., & Nelson, R. (Eds.). (2004). *The Oxford handbook of innovation.* Oxford: Oxford University Press.

Freeman, C., Nelson, R., Soete, L., Silverberg, G. & Dosi, G. (1988). *Technical change and economic theory.* London: Francis Pinter.

Gadamer, H. G. (1976). The historicity of understanding. In P. Connerton (Ed.), *Critical sociology, selected readings* (pp. 117–133). Harmondsworth, UK: Penguin.

Galaskiewicz, J. (1985). Interorganizational relations. *Annual Review of Sociology, 11,* 281–304.

Garvin, D. A. (1993, July/August). Building a learning organization. *Harvard Business Review,* 78–92.

Geringer, J. M., & Hebert, L. (1989). Control and performance of international joint ventures. *Journal of International Business Studies, 20,* 235–254.

Gerstenfeld, A., & Wortzel, L. H. (1977, Fall). Strategies for innovation in developing countries. *Sloan Management Review,* 57–68.

Glynn, M. A., Barr, P. S., & Dacin, M. T. (2000). Pluralism and the problem of variety. *Academy of Management Review, 25*(4), 726–734.

Gristock, J. (2001) *Organisational virtuality in the UK publishing industry: A study of a system of innovation as a system of mediation.* Doctoral thesis, SPRU Science and Technology Policy Research, University of Sussex, Brighton, UK.

Gulati, R. (1995). Social structure and alliance formation patterns: A longitudinal analysis. *Administrative Science Quarterly, 40,* 619–652.

Gulati, R. (1998). Alliances and networks. *Strategic Management Journal, 19*(4), 293–317.

Hamel, G. (1991). Competition for competence and interpartner learning within international strategic alliances. *Strategic Management Journal, 12,* 83–103.

Hamel, G., Doz, Y. L., & Prahalad, C. K. (1989). Collaborate with your competitors and win. *Harvard Business Review, 67*(1), 133–139.

Harrigan, K. R. (1985). *Strategies for joint venture success.* Lexington, MA: Lexington Books.

Hennert, J. F. (1988). A transaction cost theory of equity joint ventures. *Strategic Management Journal, 9,* 361–374.

Hennert, J. F. (1991). The transaction cost theory of joint ventures. *Management Science, 37,* 483–497.

Hitt, M. A., Ahlstrom, D., Dacin, M. T., Levitas, E., & Svobodina, L. (2004). The institutional effects on strategic alliance partner selection in transition economies: China vs. Russia. *Organization Science, 15*(2), 173–185.

Hong, N., Al-Khatib, W., Magagna, B., McLoughlin, A., & Coe, B. (1998). *Systems theory.* Retrieved March 27, 2005, from http://www.ed.psu.edu/insys/ESD/systems/ theory/SYSTHEO2.htm.

Huber, G. P. (1984). The nature and design of post-industrial organizations. *Management Science, 30*(8), 928–952.

Iliev, I. (2004, May 16). *The methodological assumptions of the systems of innovations approach and its compatibility with critical realism.* Paper presented at Cambridge Realist Workshop, CRASSH, Cambridge University, UK.

Inkpen, A. C. (1995). *The management of international joint ventures: An organizational learning perspective.* London: Routledge.

Inkpen, A. C., & Beamish, P. W. (1997). Knowledge, bargaining power, and the instability of international joint ventures. *Academy of Management Review, 22*(1), 177–202.

Irving, A (1999). *Systems theory.* Retrieved March 27, 2005, from http://www.globalresearchbusiness.com/methods/stheory.php.

James, W. (1923). *The varieties of religious experience.* New York: Longmans, Green. (Original work published 1902).

Johnson, B., Edquist, C., & Lundvall, B.-A. (2003, November 3–6). Economic development and the national system of innovation approach. Paper presented at the First Globelics Conference, Rio de Janeiro. Retrieved March 27, 2005, from http://www.ie.ufrj.br/globelics/Slides/Johnson%20Edquist%20Lundvall%20slides.pdf.

Jones, C., Hesterly, W. S., & Borgatti, S. P. (1997). A general theory of network governance: Exchange conditions and social mechanism. *Academy of Management Review, 22*(4), 911–945.

Katz, D., & Kahn, R. L. (1966). *The social psychology of organizations.* New York: Wiley.

Keller, W. W., & Pauly, L. W. (2000). Crisis and adaptation in East Asian innovation systems: The case of the semiconductor industry in Taiwan and South Korea. *Business & Politics, 2*(3), 326–351.

Kern, T., & Willcocks, L. P. (2000). Cooperative relationship strategy in global information technology outsourcing: The case of Xerox Corporation. In D. O. Faulkner & M. de Rond (Eds.), *Cooperative strategy: Economic, business, and organizational issues* (pp. 211–242). Oxford, UK: Oxford University Press.

Kim, L. H., & Nelson, R. R. (Eds.). (2000). *Technology, learning and innovation: experiences of newly industrializing economies.* New York: Cambridge University Press.

Klein, H. K., & Myers, M. D. (1999). A set of principles for conducting and evaluating interpretive field studies in information systems (N1). *MIS Quarterly, 23*(1), 67–95.

Kogut, B. (1988) A study of the life cycle of joint ventures. In F. Contractor & P. Lorange (Eds.), *Cooperative strategies in international business* (Vol. 6, pp. 169–185). Lexington, MA: Lexington Books.

Kuhn, T. S. (1970) *The structure of scientific revolutions.* Chicago: University of Chicago Press. (Original work published 1962).

Lall, S. (1996). *Learning from the Asian tigers: Studies in technology and industrial policy.* London: Macmillan.

Lall, S. (2000). Technological change and industrialisation in the Asian newly industrialising economies: Achievements and challenges. In L. H. Kim & R. R. Nelson (Eds.), *Technology, learning and innovation: Experiences of newly industrializing economies* (pp. 13–69). Cambridge, UK: Cambridge University Press.

Larson, A. (1992). Network dyads in entrepreneurial settings: A study of the governance of exchange relationships. *Administrative Science Quarterly, 37,* 76–104.

Lawrence, T. B., Hardy, C., & Phillips, N. (2002). Institutional effects of interorganizational collaboration: The emergence of proto-institutions. *Academy of Management Journal, 45*(1), 281–290.

Lawson, T. (1997). *Economics and reality.* London: Routledge.

Locke, K., Golden-Biddle, K., & Feldman, M. S. (2004). Imaginative theorizing in interpretive organisational research. *Academy of Management Proceedings,* B1–B6.

Lundvall, B. A. (1988). Innovation as an interactive process: From user-producer interaction to the national system of innovation. In G. Dosi, C. Freeman, R. Nelson, G. Silverberg, & L. Soete, (Eds.), *Technical change and economic theory.* London: Frances.

Lundvall, B. A. (1992). Introduction. In B.-A. Lundvall (Ed.), *National systems of innovation—Towards a theory of innovation and interactive learning* (pp. 1–19). London: Pinter.

March, J., & Olsen, J. (1976). *Ambiguity and choice in organisations.* Bergen, Norway: Universitetsforlaget.

Mowery, D. C. (1989). **Collaborative ventures between U.S. and foreign manufacturing firms**. *Research Policy, 18*(1), 19–32.

Mitchell, K. D. (1992). VI. Theory in practice: Systems theory as an explanatory device: The case of institutional reform. *Praxiologies & the Philosophy of Economics–Praxiology,* 689–700.

Murray, E. A., Jr., & Mahon, J. F. (1993). Strategic alliances: Gateway to the new Europe? *Long Range Planning, 26*(4), 102–111.

Mytelka, L. K. (2000). Local systems of innovation in a globalized world economy. *Industry & Innovation, 7*(1), 15–33.

Mytelka, L. K. (2004). Clustering, long distance partnerships and the SME: A study of the French biotechnology sector. *International Journal of Technology Management, 27*(8), 791–809.

Nelson, R. (1993). *National innovation systems: A comparative analysis.* New York, Oxford University Press.

Nelson, R., & Nelson, K. (2002). Technology, institutions and innovation systems. *Research Policy, 31*(2), 265–269.

Nelson, R., & Rosenberg, N. (1993). Technical innovations and national systems. In R. R. Nelson (Ed.). *National innovation systems: A comparative analysis* (pp. 46–87). New York, Oxford University Press.

Nelson, R., & Winter, S. (1982). *An evolutionary theory of economic change.* Cambridge, MA: Harvard University Press.

Nonaka, I., & Takeuchi, H. (1995). *The knowledge-creating economy.* Oxford, UK: Oxford University Press.

Organisation for Economic Co-operation and Development. (1997). *The measurement of scientific and technological activities: Proposed guidelines for collecting and interpreting technological innovation data* (Oslo Manual). European Commission, Eurostat.

Namgyoo, P., Mezias, K., & Song, J. M. (2004). A resource-based view of strategic alliances and firm value in the electronic marketplace. *Journal of Management, 30*(1), 7–27.

Osborn, R. N., & Hagedoorn, J. (1997). The institutionalisation and evolutionary dynamics of interorganisational alliances and networks. *Academy of Management Journal, 40*(2), 261–278.

Park, N. K., Mezias, J. M., & Song, J. (2004). A resource-based view of strategic alliances and firm value in the electronic marketplace. *Journal of Management, 30*(1), 7–27.

Parkhe, A. (1993). "Messy" research, methodological predispositions and theory development in international joint ventures. *Academy of Management Review, 18*(2), 227–268.

Patel, P., & Pavitt, K. (1994). Uneven (and divergent) technological accumulation among advanced countries: Evidence and a framework of explanation. *Industrial and Corporate Change, 3*(3), 759–788.

Perks, H. (2004). Exploring processes of resource exchange and co-creation in strategic partnering for new product development. *International Journal of Innovation Management, 8*(1), 37–61.

Pisano, G. P. (1990). The R&D boundaries of the firm: An empirical analysis. *Administrative Science Quarterly, 35,* 153–176.

Powell, W. W., & Brantley, P. (1992). Competitive cooperation in biotechnology: Learning through networks? In N. Nohria & R. G. Eccles (Eds.), *Networks and organizations: Structure, form, and action* (pp. 366–394). Boston: Harvard Business School Press.

Powell, W. W., Koput, K. W., & Smith-Doerr, L. (1996). Interorganisational collaboration and the locus of innovation: Networks of learning in biotechnology. *Administrative Science Quarterly, 41,* 116–145.

Sacks, J. (2003). *Celebrating life.* London: Continuum.

Salk, J., & Shenkar, O. (2001). Social identities in an international joint venture: An exploratory case study. *Organization Science, 12*(2), 161–178.

Schoenberger, E. (2001). Interdisciplinarity and social power. *Progress in Human Geography, 25*(3) 365–382.

Scott, W. R. (2002). *Organizations: Rational, natural, and open systems* (5th ed.). Englewood Cliffs, NJ: Prentice Hall.

Shaan, J. L., & Beamish, P. (1988). Joint venture general managers in LDCs. In F. J. Contractor & P. Lorange (Eds.), *Cooperative strategies in international business* (pp. 279–299). Lexington, MA: Lexington Books.

Shan, W., & Hamilton, W. (1991). Country-specific advantage and international cooperation. *Strategic Management Journal, 12,* 419–432.

Shenkar, O., & Yan, A. (2002). Failure as a consequence of partner politics: Learning from the life and death of an international cooperative venture. *Human Relations, 55*(5), 565–601.

Sydow J., & Windeler A. (1998). Organizing and evaluating interfirm networks: A structurationist perspective on network processes and effectiveness. *Organization Science, 9*(3), 265–284.

Teece, D., & Pisano, G. (1994). Dynamic capabilities of firms. *Industrial and Corporate Change, 3,* 537–556.

Teece, D. J., Pisano, G., & Shuen, A. (1997). Dynamic capabilities and strategic management. *Strategic Management Journal, 18*(7), 509–533.

Tidd, J., Bessant, J., & Pavitt, K. (1997). *Managing innovation: Integrating technological, market and organisational change.* Chichester, UK: Wiley.

United Nations Development Programme. (2001). *Making new technologies work for human development.* New York: Oxford University Press.

Van de Ven, A. H. (1997, August 11). *The buzzing, blooming, confusing world of organization and management theory: A view from Lake Wobegon University.* Distinguished Scholar Lecture to the Organization and Management Theory Division of the Academy of Management, Boston.

Van de Ven, A. H., & Poole, M. S. (1995). Explaining development and change in organisations. *Academy of Management Review, 20*(3), 510–540.

Van Maanen, J. (1995). Fear and loathing in organization studies. *Organization Science, 6,* 687–69.

Velho, L. (2002). North-South collaboration and systems of innovation. In H. Oopschoor & J. Bouma (Eds.), *North-South research cooperation* (pp. 25–51). Proceedings of the Royal Netherlands Academy of Arts and Sciences International Conference 2001. Amsterdam: Royal Netherlands Academy of Arts and Sciences.

von Bertalanffy, L. (1968). *General systems theory.* New York: Braziller.

von Neumann, J. (1958). *The computer and the brain* (pp. 6–7). New Haven, CT: Yale.

Wasserman, S., & Galaskiewicz, J. (1994). *Advances in social network analysis.* Thousand Oaks, CA: Sage.

Williamson, O. E. (1991). Comparative economic organisation: The analysis of discrete structural alternatives. *Administrative Science Quarterly, 36,* 269–296.

Name Index

Subject Index

About the Editors

Oded Shenkar is Ford Motor Company Chair in Global Business Management and Professor of Management and Human Resources at the Fisher College of Business, the Ohio State University; and has taught in China, Japan, Israel, and the United Kingdom. He holds B.A. and M.Sc.soc. degrees in East Asian Studies and Sociology from the Hebrew University of Jerusalem and M.Phil. and Ph.D. degrees from Columbia University. In addition to strategic alliances, his main areas of interest are Chinese business, cross-border investment and the impact of culture on international business. He has published numerous articles in the *Academy of Management Review*, the *Academy of Management Journal, Human Relations*, the *Journal of International Business Studies, Management Science, Organization Science, Organization Studies*, and the *Journal of Applied Psychology*, among others, and is a member of the editorial board of the *Academy of Management Executive, Human Relations*, the *International Journal of Cross-Cultural Management*, the *Journal of International Business Studies, Management International Review*, and *Organization Studies*. His prior books include *Organization and Management in China 1979–1990* (M. E. Sharpe), *International Business in China* (Routledge, with L. Kelley), *Global Perspectives on Human Resource Management* (Prentice-Hall), *The Handbook of International Management Research* (Blackwell, 1st ed.; University of Michigan Press, 2nd ed., both with B. J. Punnett), *International Business* (Wiley, with Y. Luo), and *The Chinese Century* (Wharton). Professor Shenkar serves as an advisor to multinational firms and government and international agencies. He is a Fellow of the Academy of International Business and a member of the Conference Board Council of Integration Executives.

Jeffrey J. Reuer is an Associate Professor at the Kenan-Flagler Business School at the University of North Carolina. Prior to joining UNC, he served on the faculties of INSEAD, the European Institute of Business Administration in Fontainebleau, France, and the Fisher College of Business at Ohio State University. He received his Ph.D. in strategic management from Purdue University. His research is in the area of corporate strategy and his current work uses information economics and real options theory to examine the structuring and implications of corporate investments such as alliances and acquisitions. Current projects are on the contractual design of alliances and acquisitions, the roles initial public offerings play in corporate development processes, and firm outcomes associated with corporate investments in real options. His research has appeared in a number of academic journals, including the *Strategic Management Journal*, the *Academy of Management Journal, Organization Science*, the *Journal of Economic Behavior and Organization, Research Policy*, the *Journal of International Business Studies*, and the *Journal of Management.* Some of the results of his work have also been profiled in a number of practice-oriented articles in outlets such as the *Harvard Business Review, Sloan Management Review*, the *Financial Times, Long Range Planning*, and the *Academy of Management Executive.* He serves on the boards of the *Strategic Management Journal, Strategic Organization*, the *Journal of International Business Studies*, the *Journal of Management*, the *Journal of Management Studies*, and the *European Management Journal.*

About the Contributors

Jaideep (Jay) Anand is Associate Professor of Corporate Strategy and International Business at the Fisher College of Business, Ohio State University. Previously, Jay taught at the University of Michigan, the Ivey Business School in Canada, and the Wharton School, University of Pennsylvania. He is also a research fellow and faculty associate at the William Davidson Institute for the study of emerging economies at the University of Michigan. He earned a B.Tech. (Mechanical Engineering) from the Indian Institute of Technology, New Delhi, India, and master's and Ph.D. degrees from the Wharton School. His research interests include mergers and acquisitions, joint ventures and strategic alliances, corporate growth, and international strategies. His research has been published in the *Strategic Management Journal, Organization Science,* and the *Journal of International Business Studies,* among other journals.

Africa Ariño is Associate Professor of General Management at IESE Business School, University of Navarra. She received her Ph.D. from the Anderson School at UCLA. She serves as Associate Director for Faculty and as Academic Director of the Anselmo Rubiralta Globalization and Strategy Research Center at IESE. Her research interests include process issues in international strategic alliances, evolutionary aspects of the interpartner relationship, understanding alliance contractual features, and measuring alliance performance. Her research has been published in the *Academy of Management Executive,* the *California Management Review,* the *Journal of International Business Studies,* the *Journal of Management,* and *Organization Science,* among other outlets. She teaches a course on Managing Strategic Alliances.

Mark Casson is Professor of Economics and Director of the Centre for Institutional Performance at the University of Reading. His research interests include the economic theory of the multinational enterprise, the theory of entrepreneurship, business history, and transport history. He is the author of several books on international business, including *The Future of the Multinational Enterprise* (with Peter J. Buckley) and *The Economics of International Business.* He is a Fellow of the Academy of International Business and Visiting Professor at the University of Leeds and at Queen Mary College, University of London.

Tailan Chi is an Associate Professor at the School of Business, University of Kansas. He holds a Ph.D. in Business Administration from the University of Washington. His research focuses on choice of foreign-market entry modes, organizational structures of multinational corporations, and market valuation of firms' intangible assets.

He examines these phenomena from the perspectives of the new institutional economics, the resource-based view, and option theory, and uses both mathematical modeling and large-sample statistical methods in his work. He has published in journals such as the *Journal of International Business Studies, Management Science,* and the *Strategic Management Journal.* He has taught a variety of International Business and Strategy courses at the undergraduate, M.B.A., and doctoral levels. His main teaching interests at the M.B.A. and undergraduate levels include the global regime of international business, international business strategies, and doing business in China.

Mark de Rond is University Lecturer in Strategy at the Judge Institute of Management, University of Cambridge. He completed his D.Phil. in Management Studies (Strategy and Organization) at Oxford University. Mark's principal research interests are threefold: (1) strategic alliances (specifically research collaborations in the life sciences), (2) innovation in the context of distributed work, and (3) causation in strategy (specifically the relation of chance, choice, and inevitability, the nature of causal explanation, and the structure of serendipity). He has published two books on alliances and several articles in such journals as *Organization Science* and the *Journal of Management Inquiry.*

Andrew Delios (Ph.D., Richard Ivey School of Business) is Associate Professor and Head of the Department of Business Policy, NUS Business School, National University of Singapore. He is the author or coauthor of more than 50 published journal articles, case studies, and book chapters. His articles have appeared in journals such as the *Academy of Management Journal,* the *Administrative Science Quarterly,* the *Strategic Management Journal, Strategic Organization,* and the *Journal of International Business Studies.* He has authored five books, including *International Business: An Asia-Pacific Perspective* (Pearson) and *Strategy for Success in Asia* (Wiley). He has written case studies and conducted research on companies involved in Canada, China, India, Italy, Hong Kong, Japan, Singapore, and Vietnam. His research looks at foreign investment issues in emerging economies, particularly by Japanese multinationals, and the governance, strategy, and performance of China's listed companies.

Ben Gomes-Casseres specializes in alliance strategy; he has researched this topic for 20 years, taught it to M.B.A.s and executives, and consulted with major companies in the United States and abroad. A Professor at Brandeis University's International Business School, he previously served for a decade on the faculty of the Harvard Business School. He is author of *The Alliance Revolution: The New Shape of Business Rivalry* (Harvard University Press, 1996) and coauthor of *Mastering Alliance Strategy: A Comprehensive Guide to Design, Management, and Organization* (Jossey-Bass/Wiley, 2003). Ben's work has also appeared in the *Journal of Financial Economics,* the *Journal of International Business Studies,* the *Harvard Business Review,* the *Financial Times,* and elsewhere. He is a frequent speaker at major conferences and a consultant and executive trainer to Fortune 100 companies in high-technology industries, manufacturing, and services. He holds an M.P.A. from Princeton and a D.B.A. from Harvard. His expertise and writings are available at http://www.alliancestrategy.com.

Siegfried Gudergan is an Associate Professor within the Faculty of Business and the Deputy Director of ICAN Research—a Research Centre on Innovative Collaborations, Alliances & Networks, both within the University of Technology, Sydney. He holds a Ph.D. in Management from the Australian Graduate School of Management that was awarded by both the University of Sydney and University of New South Wales. He is an appointed member of the Strategic Management Society's Interest Group on Knowledge & Innovation and is affiliated with the Association of Strategic Alliance Professionals. His research has a focus on alliance governance and alliances' strategic performance, organizational learning, and innovation effects.

Kathryn Rudie Harrigan is the Henry Kravis Professor of Business Leadership at Columbia University. She has been a Columbia Business School professor since 1981. She holds a B.A. from Macalester College (1973), an M.B.A. from the University of Texas at Austin (1976), and a D.B.A. from Harvard Business School (1979). Her research interests include diversification, turnaround strategies, make-or-buy strategy, global strategies, strategic alliances, internal venturing, industry restructuring, mature (and declining) businesses, industry and competitor analysis, and strategic planning. She has written six books and numerous scholarly articles on these topics.

Jared Harris is a doctoral candidate in Strategic Management and Organization at the University of Minnesota's Carlson School of Management. His research interests include the long-term impact of ethical management processes on performance outcomes, the impact of ethical considerations on strategy formulation, interorganizational trust, and transparency. Jared was awarded a 2003 Booz Allen Hamilton/ Strategic Management Society Ph.D. Fellowship for his empirical research exploring the behavioral and agency forces that encourage financial misrepresentation.

Michael A. Hitt is a Distinguished Professor and holds the Joe B. Foster Chair in Business Leadership and the C. W. and Dorothy Conn Chair in New Ventures at Texas A&M University. He received his Ph.D. from the University of Colorado. He is the former President of the Academy of Management and the current President Elect of the Strategic Management Society. He is also the former Editor of the *Academy of Management Journal* and is a Fellow in the Academy of Management. He has coauthored numerous books and articles in such journals as the *Academy of Management Journal*, the *Academy of Management Review*, the *Strategic Management Journal*, *Organization Science*, and the *Journal of Management*, among others. His current research interests include international strategy, managing resources to create value, corporate governance, and strategic entrepreneurship.

R. Duane Ireland is a Professor of Management and holds the Foreman R. and Ruby S. Bennett Chair in Business Administration at the Mays Business School, Texas A&M University. Currently, he is an Associate Editor for the *Academy of Management Journal*. He is a former Associate Editor of the *Academy of Management Executive* and a former Consulting Editor for *Entrepreneurship Theory and Practice*. He has coauthored a number of books and articles. His work has been published in journals such as the *Academy of Management Journal*, the *Academy of Management*

Review, the *Academy of Management Executive*, the *Administrative Science Quarterly*, the *Strategic Management Journal*, and the *Journal of Management*, among others. His current research interests include alliances, strategic entrepreneurship, corporate entrepreneurship, and the management of organizational resources.

Prashant Kale is an Assistant Professor of Corporate Strategy and International Business at the Ross School of Business at the University of Michigan. His research examines questions such as how firms build an "alliance capability" to manage their alliance portfolio, the dynamics of alliance management and evolution in emerging business environments, and what factors firms should consider when choosing between alliances and acquisitions as alternative modes of achieving growth and competitive advantage. Prashant's work has been published in leading journals such as the *Strategic Management Journal*, the *Harvard Business Review*, the *California Management Review*, the *Sloan Management Review*, and others, and he has also received awards from the Academy of Management and the Strategic Management Society. He is a Faculty Associate of the William Davidson Institute, University of Michigan, and a Fellow of the Mack Center for Technology and Innovation at the Wharton School.

Kwok Leung (Ph.D. in Social and Organizational Psychology, University of Illinois, Urbana-Champaign) is Professor of Management at City University of Hong Kong. His research areas include justice and conflict, international business, and cross-cultural psychology. He is currently a Departmental Editor of the *Journal of International Business Studies*. He is on the editorial board of several journals, including the *Journal of Applied Psychology*, *Applied Psychology: An International Review*, the *Journal of Cross-Cultural Psychology*, the *Asian Journal of Social Psychology*, and *Organizational Research Methods*. He is the Chair-Elect of the Research Methods Division of the Academy of Management and a past President of the Asian Association of Social Psychology.

Ted London is on the faculty at the University of North Carolina's Kenan-Flagler Business School. In July 2005, he will move to the University of Michigan, where, in addition to teaching at the Ross School of Business, he will lead a new research initiative on base of the pyramid markets at the William Davidson Institute. His research focuses on strategic growth and change, including capability development for emerging markets and cross-sector alliances. He has won awards for his research, teaching, and case writing. Prior to pursuing a Ph.D., he worked for more than 10 years in senior management positions in the private and nonprofit sectors in Asia, Africa, and the United States.

Yadong Luo (Ph.D., Temple University) is Professor of Management and the Emery Findlay Distinguished Chair at the School of Business Administration, University of Miami. His research interests include global corporate strategy, foreign direct investment, international joint ventures, multinational corporations in emerging markets, and management in transition economies.

Marjorie Lyles is Professor of International Strategic Management at Indiana University Kelley School of Business and the American United Life Chair. She addresses organizational learning, international strategies, management of technology, and alliance management, particularly in emerging economies. She has more than 100 publications in such journals as the *Administrative Science Quarterly,* the *Academy of Management Review,* the *Strategic Management Journal,* the *Academy of Management Journal,* the *Journal of Management,* the *Journal of Management Studies,* and the *Journal of International Business Studies.* She is completing a National Science Foundation grant on Knowledge Development in Alliances under Conditions of Novelty in the pharmaceutical industry.

Lalit Manral is a Ph.D. candidate in Strategy at the Columbia Business School. His research in strategic management of firms borrows from evolutionary economics and industrial organization to explore the logic of economic selection of business firms in diverse industrial contexts related to systemic technologies. His research contributes towards developing the macrofoundations of evolutionary economics theory and furthering its contribution to organizational strategy. His doctoral dissertation examines the evolution of industrial market structure in response to endogenous processes triggered by firm investment strategies. It addresses a fundamental yet largely unaddressed issue in strategy: How do the continuously evolving markets guide firm (investment) strategy and how does firm (investment) strategy influence the origin and evolution of markets? His favored empirical research settings include the telecommunications services and equipment industry and the information technology services and equipment industry.

Sonja Marjanovic is a Wellcome Trust Ph.D. Scholar at the Judge Institute of Management Studies, Cambridge University. She holds an M.Phil. in Management Strategy and Marketing) from Cambridge University and a B.Sc. (honors) in Molecular Genetics from Wits University in South Africa. Her principal research interests include innovation in global health initiatives (especially through international alliances), interdisciplinary research methods, and science-industry commercialization. She has lectured on the Cambridge-Massachusetts Institute of Technology Institute Bioscience Enterprise M.Phil. course and is the joint Chief Executive Officer and Cofounder of a rapidly growing infectious disease diagnostics company (DiagnovIS). She has published her recent research in *Nature Drug Discovery* and was recently selected as Europe's Top Young Innovator in global technology by *Red Herring* magazine.

Michael J. Mol is a Research Fellow at the London Business School and a lecturer at the University of Reading, both in the United Kingdom. His main research is in the areas of sourcing strategy, in particular the causes and performance consequences of outsourcing and sourcing alliances, and management innovation, especially how the creation of management innovations can be a source of competitive advantage. He has recently authored or coauthored articles for, among others, the *Journal of International Management,* the *Journal of Purchasing and Supply Management,* and *Strategic Organization* and for a forthcoming book (*Global Supply Chain Management,* Edward Elgar). He is the director of Reading's ICA program. He holds a Ph.D. (2001) from the Rotterdam School of Management, Erasmus University Rotterdam. He can be reached at mmol@london.edu and through http://www. michaelmol.com.

Piero Morosini is an Adjunct Professor of Strategy and Leadership at the European School of Management and Technology, Berlin, and the founding president of PAYA Sàrl, Lausanne, a leadership institute that helps organizations build a strong "common glue" for successful performance across cultural and organizational boundaries. He is also an Affiliate Partner at the Executive Learning Partnership, Brussels. His professional background includes previous experiences as a full-time Professor at the International Institute for Management Development, Lausanne, a Strategy Consultant at Accenture in Milan and at McKinsey & Company in Madrid and London, and a Financial Executive at JP Morgan and at Robert Fleming in Milan. He attended graduate studies at the Wharton School, University of Pennsylvania, Philadelphia (1986–1988), where he obtained a Ph.D. in Management, an M.A. in Decision Sciences, and an M.B.A.

Paul Olk is an Associate Professor of Management at the Daniels College of Business, University of Denver. His current research interests focus on evaluating the performance of a strategic alliance as well as on the formation and management of high-technology entrepreneurial alliances. Paul's publications have appeared in several books and journals, including *Organization Science,* the *Strategic Management Journal,* and the *Journal of Personality and Social Psychology.* He currently serves as a Board Member of the Technology and Innovation Management Division of the Academy of Management and on the editorial review boards of *Organization Science, Group and Organization Management, IEEE Transactions on Engineering Management,* and the *Journal of Management Inquiry.* He received his Ph.D. from the Wharton School of Business at the University of Pennsylvania. Previously he was on the faculty of the University of California, Irvine.

Hugh O'Neill is Professor of Strategic Management, O'Herron Scholar, and Associate Dean of the M.B.A. Program for Executives at Kenan-Flagler. He has an M.S. degree from the Polytechnic Institute of New York and a Ph.D. from the University of Massachusetts. His research and practice focus on how organizations and individuals reform and reshape strategies.

Arvind Parkhe (Ph.D., Temple University) is Professor and Cochran Senior Research Fellow at Temple University, Philadelphia, where he is also the Chair of the M.B.A. Program. After earning an undergraduate degree in chemical engineering in India, he held corporate management positions with a German company in the United States and Germany. His research examines the evolution of organizational forms, management of loosely coupled innovation networks, robust structuring of strategic alliances, and research methods for studying trust, opportunism, and other "soft" phenomena in interfirm cooperative agreements. He recently served as guest editor at the *Academy of Management Review* for a special issue on "Building Effective Networks."

Anu Phene is Assistant Professor of Strategy at the David Eccles School of Business at the University of Utah. She received her Ph.D. in International Management from the University of Texas at Dallas. Prior to her Ph.D., she worked for several years in the Treasury Division of American Express Bank. Her research focuses on firm strategy in a multinational context, evolution of firms and subsidiaries, firm innovation, high-technology industries, and knowledge dissemination and geographic boundaries. Her work has been published in the *Strategic Management*

Journal and the *Journal of International Business Studies.* She teaches courses on Strategic Management and International Business.

Dennis A. Rondinelli is Glaxo Distinguished International Professor of Management at the University of North Carolina's Kenan-Flagler Business School. Prior to joining UNC, he was principal research scientist and senior policy analyst in the Office of International Programs at the Research Triangle Institute and Professor at the Maxwell School of Citizenship and Public Affairs at Syracuse University, and held faculty positions at the Graduate School of Management at Vanderbilt University and at the University of Wisconsin, Milwaukee. Dr. Rondinelli has been a consultant to the U.S. State Department's Agency for International Development, the World Bank, and several United Nations specialized agencies. He has authored or edited 18 books and published more than 250 articles in scholarly and professional journals and as book chapters.

Jane E. Salk (Ph.D., Massachusetts Institute of Technology) is Associate Professor of Organizations, Strategy, and International Management at the University of Texas at Dallas. She has also been a faculty member at Essec in France, Carnegie Mellon University, and the Fuqua School of Business, Duke University. Her research concerns how working cultures develop in international joint venture and other multinational teams and interorganizational learning in alliance contexts. She has over 30 publications, including articles in the *Academy of Management Journal,* the *Journal of International Business Studies, Organization Science,* and the *Strategic Management Journal.* She also is an associate of the Trias Network, a training and organizational development institute in Zurich.

Randall S. Schuler is a Professor of Strategic International Human Resource Management at Rutgers University and a Research Professor at the Graduate School of Business Administration in Zurich. His research interests are global and international human resource management, strategic human resource management, the human resource management function in organizations, and the interface of business strategy and human resource management tasks. He has written extensively in academic and professional journals and has just published a book with Dennis Briscoe entitled *International Human Resource Management* (2nd ed.). His other interests are the management of international joint ventures and alliances and knowledge transfer. His most recent book in this area is with Susan E. Jackson and Yadong Luo, titled *Managing Human Resources in Cross-Border Alliances.*

Anju Seth is a Professor of Strategic Management at the University of Illinois at Urbana-Champaign and is Coordinator of the Strategic Management area. Her research on value creation via corporate strategy examines acquisitions, restructuring, corporate governance, joint ventures, and globalization. Her research interests also include the philosophy of science in the strategic management field. Her research has been published in the *Strategic Management Journal,* the *Journal of International Business Studies,* the *Review of Economics and Statistics, Managerial and Decision Economics,* the *Journal of Management Studies,* the *California Management Review,* the *Journal of Applied Corporate Finance,* and others and has been presented at many meetings of the Academy of Management and the Strategic Management Society.

Steve Tallman is the David Eccles Professor of Management at the David Eccles School of Business of the University of Utah. He received his Ph.D. in Management from UCLA. He is the chairman of the Department of Management at the University of Utah. His research has focused on issues of global strategy and multinational firms, international alliances and joint ventures, and the role of regional industry clusters as they affect knowledge development and exchange. His work has been published in the *Academy of Management Review,* the *Academy of Management Journal,* the *Strategic Management Journal,* and the *Journal of International Business Studies.* He teaches courses on International Strategy and Merger and Alliance Strategies.

Ibraiz R. Tarique (Ph.D., Rutgers University, Human Resource Management) is an Assistant Professor at the Lubin School of Business at Pace University, New York City Campus. His research interests include international human resource management, with a focus on training and development of global assignees, strategic management of human resource in cross-border alliances, and global leadership development. He has presented numerous papers at the Annual Academy of Management Meetings, and his academic publications include several book chapters as well as articles in the *International Journal of Human Resource Management.* He teaches Strategic Human Resource Management, International Human Resource Management, Developing Human Capital, Training and Development, and Organizational Behavior.

Davina Vora (Ph.D., University of South Carolina) is Assistant Professor of Organizations, Strategy, and International Management at the University of Texas at Dallas. Her research interests encompass international management and organizational behavior and include forms of psychological attachment such as organizational identification in multinational contexts, international diversity issues, cross-cultural management, and subsidiary–multinational corporation relationships.

Gordon Walker is Professor and Chairman of the Strategy and Entrepreneurship Group at the Edwin L. Cox School of Business at Southern Methodist University. He received his B.A. from Yale University and an M.B.A. and Ph.D. from the Wharton School, University of Pennsylvania. Dr. Walker has previously taught at the Sloan School, Massachusetts Institute of Technology; the Wharton School, University of Pennsylvania; and Yale University. He is the author of numerous articles as well as a book, *Modern Competitive Strategy,* and is on the editorial boards of the *Administrative Science Quarterly, Organization Science,* and *Strategic Organization.*

Justin W. Webb is currently a Ph.D. candidate in the Mays Business School at Texas A&M University. Strategic management and entrepreneurship are his areas of interests in the Ph.D. program. He has published several chapters in scholarly books. His research interests include strategic entrepreneurship, managing resources, and sustaining organizational value.

Steven White is Assistant Professor of Asian Business and Comparative Management at INSEAD, the European Institute of Business Administration. He holds a

Ph.D. in Management from the Massachusetts Institute of Technology/ Sloan and an M.A. in Japanese Studies from the International University of Japan. His research focuses on the social dynamics of interorganizational relationships and system change, and much of his empirical work is based in China. He has published in the *Academy of Management Journal, Organization Studies,* the *Journal of Management Studies,* the *Asia Pacific Journal of Management, Research Policy,* the *International Journal of Technology Management,* and *Technovation,* and his books include *Biotechnology Japan* and a coedited volume, *Handbook of Asian Management.*

Akbar (Aks) Zaheer (azaheer@csom.umn.edu; Ph.D., Massachusetts Institute of Technology) is Curtis L. Carlson Professor of Strategic Management and Organization and Director of the Strategic Management Research Center at the Carlson School of Management, University of Minnesota. He has an M.B.A. from the Indian Institute of Management, Ahmedabad, India. Since joining the faculty at the Carlson School in 1991, he has been researching a number of issues around trust in organizational contexts, strategic alliances, and mergers and acquisitions. He was Guest Editor of recent special issues of the *Strategic Management Journal* on "Strategic Networks" and of *Organization Science* on "Trust in an Organizational Context." He is currently working on a special issue for the *Academy of Management Review* on "Repairing Relationships," due out in 2006. He serves on the Editorial Boards of the *Strategic Management Journal,* the *Academy of Management Review,* and *Organization Science.*

Maurizio Zollo is Associate Professor of Strategy at INSEAD, the European Institute of Business Administration, and is currently Visiting Professor of Management at the Wharton School of the University of Pennsylvania. He holds a Ph.D. in Management from Wharton. His work is concerned with researching and teaching the management of corporate development processes, from strategy implementation (acquisitions and strategic alliances) to organizational learning and social responsibility issues. The academic output of his work is published in the *Academy of Management Journal,* the *Strategic Management Journal, Organization Science,* and *Research Policy.* He is a former member of the Executive Committee of the Business Policy and Strategy division of the Academy of Management and a past winner of its Outstanding Dissertation Award. He is currently serving on the Management Committee of the European Academy of Business in Society, associate editor of *Industrial and Corporate Change,* and on the Review Boards of *Organization Science,* the *European Management Journal* and the *Journal of Management and Governance.*